D1329951

LEO BAECK INSTITUTE YEAR BOOK

2004

Aby Warburg, founder and first director of the Kulturwissenschaftliche Bibliothek Warburg

By courtesy of the Warburg Institute, London

LEO BAECK INSTITUTE

YEAR BOOK
2004

XLIX

BERGHAHN BOOKS • OXFORD
PUBLISHED FOR THE INSTITUTE
LONDON • JERUSALEM • NEW YORK

Editorial office: Leo Baeck Institute
4 Devonshire Street, London W1W 5LB
www.leobaeck.co.uk

THE LEO BAECK INSTITUTE
was founded in 1955 for the study of the history and culture of German-speaking Central European Jewry

The Institute is named in honour of the man who was the last representative figure of German Jewry in Germany during the Nazi period

LEO BAECK INSTITUTE

JERUSALEM: 33 Bustanai Street
LONDON: 4 Devonshire Street
NEW YORK: 15 West 16th Street

Published by Berghahn Books
www.berghahnbooks.com
ISBN 1 84545 070 1

Contents

ILLUSTRATIONS

Preface

The contributions in the 2004 edition of the *Leo Baeck Institute Year Book* reflect the deep interest and changing perspectives contemporary scholars bring to the past of German-speaking Jewry, including the very recent past.

The lead article, Andreas Kossert's *Endlösung on the 'Amber Shore'*, is a graphic account, based on documents in the Soviet Archives, showing how even as the war was lost and the Red Army was overrunning East Prussia, SS fanaticism and brutality did not lessen. In this period, the SS perpetrated the worst massacre of Jews to occur in East Prussia. However, the importance of this contribution does not only lie in the reconstruction of a largely neglected late-Second World War Nazi massacre; it also demonstrates how selective historical memory can be. The largely successful evacuation of German refugees by the German navy is a well-known episode, the sinking of the *Wilhelm Gustloff* by a Soviet submarine with the loss of 5,000 lives having been the subject of books and films. The fate of the Jews in this region, however, was a repressed chapter in German history.

There is a link between Andreas Kossert's article and that of Christian Wiese on the ambivalent relationship between Hans Jonas and Gershom Scholem as they tried to grapple with the Nazi years and the Holocaust. Their Zionist commitment, the ethical challenges of their time, attitudes to Jewish integration in Germany and their disillusionment with the integration process, as well as their commitment to Jewish religious history, are some of the important topics Wiese addresses in his documentary account. Their correspondence and Christian Wiese's interpretation throw new light on two eminent German-Jewish intellectuals.

As Jörg Hackeschmidt indicates, Norbert Elias is generally recognised as 'one of the most important cultural and social theories of the twentieth century'; scholars have examined his work from many perspectives. What is new in Hackeschmidt's essay is its examination of Elias's close connection with the early history of German Zionism—more particularly, his intense activity within the *Blau-Weiß* Zionist youth organisation, which Elias joined in 1913.

In Hamburg in the first decades of the last century, Aby Warburg was developing what now is commonly referred to as cultural history or interdisciplinary cultural studies. With the financial help of his banker brothers he established the celebrated and unique Kulturwissenschaftliche Bibliothek Warburg. As Dorothea McEwan reminds us in her article, it was Fritz Saxl—'Acting Director' of the library when Warburg was absent from 1920 to 1924, and the far more practical of the two figures—who "shaped the work in the library and moved it in a direction extending beyond its status as a collection of books and photographs purchased by its owner". Belatedly, McEwan's discussion does justice to Fritz Saxl's essential contribution to a seminal cultural enterprise.

In his article on Sigmund Freud, Robert Wistrich considers the nature of a sense of identification with Judaism maintained by the founder of psychoanalysis despite his view of religious rituals as empty and meaningless. In Freud's self analysis, we are reminded, he attributes such antipathy to a 'father-complex'. Robert Wistrich also provides us with an account of Freud's equivocal feelings towards the Jews from Eastern Europe living in Germany, his bitter reaction to the antisemitism he encountered, and his sense, tied to this, that the Jewish effort to assimilate into general German society was ultimately futile.

The six articles on Jewish remigration and concluding comment published in this *Year Book* have their origin in a June 2004 conference at the University of Haifa on 'Migration and Remigration: Jews in Germany after 1945', which the LBI London organised jointly with the Bucerius Institute for Research of Contemporary German History and Society at the University of Haifa in June 2004. We thank its director, Yfaat Weiss, for helping us with publishing the conference papers as well as the DIE ZEIT Foundation for their generous financial support.

In this section's opening article, Marita Krauss offers an overview of the history of the approximately 30,000 Jews who returned to Germany after the Holocaust: who were the returnees and why did they return? Both in West Germany and in Israel, remigration was perceived as a highly symbolical phenomenon; its political implications are examined in Meron Mendel's essay, while that of Tobias Winstel centres on the interaction of the material and non-material dimensions of the process of West Germany's *Wiedergutmachung*, its coming to terms with both the past in general and the specific reality of remigration.

Three additional articles add an intellectual-historical dimension to the political, economic and social issues discussed in this part of the *Year Book*. Arnd Bauerkämper considers the question of how three eminent scholars, Hans Rothfels, Ernst Fraenkel and Hans Rosenberg, transferred political values from their experience of exile in Western democracies to postwar Germany. Lars Rensmann compares the different ways in which Theodor W. Adorno and Hannah Arendt came to terms in their lives and writings with their experiences in Germany in the late 1940s and 1950s. As Gabriel Motzkin observes in his comment on the articles in this section, returned emigrants are never greeted with open arms.

There are, of course, exceptions to this rule, and in his contribution Nicolas Berg considers one of them: the conservative German historian Hans Rothfels. From a Jewish background in Wilhelminian Germany but himself a convert to Protestantism at the age of nineteen, Rothfels was embraced by non-Jewish German historians and this, Berg argues, played an important role in transforming Germany's "general apologetic reflexes" after 1945 into "an academic discipline". This article thus addresses key issues present in an ongoing, heated debate on postwar and contemporary German historiography, and on the general relation of postwar German intellectual life to the Nazi past.

In the final article of this *Year Book*, Moshe Pelli brings us back to the period of the first Jewish "enlightened ones"—the *maskilim*—in Germany. As Pelli shows, the early nineteenth century dispute among the *maskilim* whether the goals of the Jewish Enlightenment could best be served by continuing to publish works in pure German, or whether Yiddish should rather be used to reach the Jewish masses, was encapsulated in one particular work by Tuvyah Feder: a "dialogue of the dead" defending the use of German while attacking another *maskil*, Mendel Lefin, for his embrace of Yiddish.

One of the most valued features of the *Year Book* is the annual bibliography expertly compiled by Barbara Suchy and Annette Pringle. With interest in German-Jewish history continuing to grow, it has become increasingly difficult to compile a bibliography that remains within reasonable bounds. We are thus particularly fortunate in being able to rely on the good judgement of our two bibliographers of long experience. The bibliography has become an indispensable tool for scholars and we are grateful to the Friends of Bat Hanadiv Foundation, the Sheldon and Suzanne Nash Fund, and the Robert Bosch Stiftung for funding its publication.

This *Year Book* includes a new feature: a section devoted to abstracts of doctoral theses related to German-Jewish history. We hope this will prove to be a useful tool for research. All abstracts of foreign-language theses will be translated into English, and we will incorporate information concerning archival material used in the thesis whenever possible.

Our annual thanks to the *Bundesministerium des Innern* and the *Ständige Konferenz der Kultusminister der Länder der Bundesrepublik Deutschland* should not be read as routine. Through the decades, their support—which has remained unwavering in years of austerity—has been something of which all those who value the work of the Leo Baeck Institute are gratefully aware.

A publication whose submitted articles are not always in English makes particularly heavy demands on its editorial staff. In addition, Joel Golb and Gabriele Rahaman, our manuscript editors, are committed to presenting our authors with challenging queries and suggestions aimed at clarifying and shaping an argument's underlying meaning. Although their own intellectual input is not directly apparent in our contributions, as editors it gives us pleasure to receive many appreciative thanks in this respect from our contributors.

Once again we especially thank our Advisory Board members, together with numerous external referees, for reading and commenting on submitted manuscripts. Their input is essential, and their willingness to devote time to assessing manuscripts enhances the academic standing of the *Year Book*.

Our publishers, Berghahn Books, have once again proceeded in a very timely manner to produce an unusually complex volume, with its articles, bibliography and indexes. We wish to thank them for this—and for carrying out this work with an efficiency blended with good humour.

John Grenville *Raphael Gross*

It is our sad duty to announce the death of a long-standing contributor to the *Year Book* and a member of the Board of the Leo Baeck Institute, London. Dr. Albert H. Friedlander OBE died on 8 July 2004 in London. Born in Berlin in 1927, he became Rabbi of Westminster Synagogue, Vice-President of the World Union of Progressive Judaism and Dean of the Leo Baeck College in London. As a scholar he became well known for both his biographical and editorial work on Leo Baeck and for many other contributions to Jewish learning.

The End of the War and the Holocaust

"Endlösung *on the 'Amber Shore'*": *The Massacre in January 1945 on the Baltic Seashore— A Repressed Chapter of East Prussian History*

BY ANDREAS KOSSERT

For many Germans East Prussia has served as a myth, a product of collective memory. This has been especially true since 1945, when this isolated eastern province was lost to Germany. The fondly preserved image has been of a land of forests and lakes—the material of a rural idyll seen through the distorting lens of nostalgia and loss. In West Germany during the Cold War, the only trauma acknowledged for the region was the German population's mass exodus at the end of the Second World War. There has been far less willingness to acknowledge the fact that large portions—although as will be indicated certainly not the entirety—of that population, part of the Nazi Reich, had demonstrated full solidarity with the Nazi state.

Despite this broad repression of historical reality, a massacre of Jews in January 1945 on the Baltic seashore of the Samland close to Königsberg generated a great deal of public interest several years ago.[1] This was a belated response to the publication in 1994 of a memoir covering the war years by Martin Bergau, a former Hitler Youth member from the small town of Palmnicken—where the massacre was to reach its tragic climax—who had witnessed the crime at the age of sixteen.[2] Shortly after the massacre he had been taken prisoner by the Soviets; after his release he had not been allowed to return to his home in East Prussia. Until Bergau's account finally broke down the wall of silence, the region's expellees had defined themselves exclusively as victims. Until the 1990s, very little was known of Nazi rule in the eastern provinces in general—Pomerania, East and West Prussia, and Silesia—whereas due to many excellent studies the situation was very different for regions that became part of the Federal Republic after the war.

[1]See Michael Wines, 'Russians Awaken to a Forgotten SS Atrocity', in *The New York Times*, 31 January 2000, pp. 1 and 4; Reinhard Henkys, 'Endlösung am Bernsteinstrand. Das größte NS-Massaker in Ostpreußen fand noch Ende Januar 1945 statt', in *Die Zeit*, no. 45, 2 November 2000, p. 94.

[2]See Martin Bergau, *Der Junge von der Bernsteinküste. Erlebte Zeitgeschichte 1938–1945*, Heidelberg 1994. I would like to thank Martin Bergau for his assistance and his commitment to establishing a lasting memory of the massacre, as well as for entrusting me with his unpublished manuscript *Endlösung am Bernsteinstrand oder Dann fiel das Grauen über uns*, which includes numerous previously unpublished documents.

This article is intended as a reconstruction of the Samland massacre, based on the available historical sources, with a focus on the last days of the German province of East Prussia in early 1945.[3] Around 7,000 people, mostly Jewish women, died on a death march through the province that ended in mass murder on a Baltic beach. Many German civilians, who shortly afterwards fled their homeland before the arrival of the Soviet army, helped the SS. This recent chapter of German history provides a markedly different perspective on the former eastern regions from the one cherished for many decades after the war. As there are no known relevant documentary sources from the last phase of the war in East Prussia, the sources used are the testimonies provided during court hearings held in the public prosecutors' office in Ludwigsburg during the 1960s. 108 personal accounts of the Samland massacre were collected during these legal proceedings, including those from some of the few survivors living in Israel. This material has permitted a vivid reconstruction of the events.

* * *

East Prussia was the eastern province of Prussia and also of the German Reich. Its capital was Königsberg, home of Immanuel Kant and the most celebrated intellectual centre of the Baltic Sea area. Already by the end of the nineteenth century, the unique Baltic seashore and both the Frische Nehrung and Kurische Nehrung, with their dune landscape were drawing visitors from all over Europe. The Samland region was a special tourist attraction because of the famous baths at Cranz, Neukuhren, Rauschen and Brüsterort.

[3]Despite the journalistic attention the massacre would eventually receive, a full historical description of the events and their context has until now not been published. This lacuna was already noted by the Israeli historian Shmuel Krakowski around the same time as the appearance of Bergau's account, and Krakowski, who has published crucial relevant documents from various Soviet archives, has thus far been the only professional historian to address the events—or at least to do so in an accurate manner. See Shmuel Krakowski, 'Massacre of Jewish Prisoners on the Samland Peninsula. Documents, Introduction', in *Yad Vashem Studies*, vol. 24 (1994), pp. 349–387; here pp. 350 and 351. The events are first mentioned in *idem*, 'The Death Marches in the Period of the Evacuation of the Camps', in Yisrael Gutman and Avital Saf (eds.), *The Nazi Concentration Camps. Proceedings of the Fourth Yad Vashem International Historical Conference – January 1980*, Jerusalem 1980, pp. 480–482. Both the refugee organisation of former Königsbergers and the writer Reinhard Henkys are notable exceptions to this pattern of denial and repression: the former published the latter's reports on the massacre in its newsletter and took up the issue itself in several articles, directly appealing to eye witnesses to speak up about what they had seen. See Reinhard Henkys, 'Endlösung'; *idem*, 'Verdrängen, Vergessen, Verschweigen' in *Gegen Vergessen—Für Demokratie*, no. 26 (September 2000), pp. 16–18; *idem*, 'Wieder eine jüdische Gemeinde in Königsberg', in *Königsberger Bürgerbrief*, no. 52 (1999), p. 75, and readers' responses to these appeals , *ibid.* (excerpts from the responses are located in Bergau, *Endlösung*); Reinhard Henkys, 'Geschehen—1945 an der Ostsee', in *Königsberger Bürgerbrief*, no. 54 (2000), pp. 80–81. One Polish monograph has focused more on the death march to Pomerania from the main camp of the Stutthof concentration camp complex: Janina Grabowska, *Marsz śmierci. Ewakuacja piesza więźniów KL Stutthof i jego podobozów. 25 stycznia—3 maja 1945*, Gdańsk 1992. For an inaccurate brief account cf. Eberhard Jäckel, Peter Longerich and Julius H. Schoeps (eds.), *Enzyklopädie des Holocaust. Die Verfolgung und Ermordung der europäischen Juden*, 3 vols., Berlin 1993, vol. 3, p. 1114. Incorrect information is also noted in Martin Gilbert, *Atlas of the Holocaust*, 1st edn., New York 1988, London 1982, p. 217. See also Stefanie Schüler-Springorum, *Die jüdische Minderheit in Königsberg/Preußen, 1871–1945*, Göttingen 1996 (Schriftenreihe der Historischen Kommission bei der Bayerischen Akademie der Wissenschaften, 56), pp. 359–360. Schüler-Springorum bases her findings solely on survivors' reports in the Yad Vashem Archives, which have been partially published by Shmuel Krakowski.

Beach near Palmnicken and Sorgenau

The Samland, and Palmnicken in particular, was and still is the world's largest supplier of amber. The region's amber was used in the decoration of the famed Amber Room in St. Petersburg, and again in its reconstruction in 2003. As "Baltic gold", amber thus became the symbol of East Prussia. Palmnicken developed the world's only industrial surface mine for this precious commodity, exported throughout the world. After 1945, a Soviet amber collective took over production and Palmnicken was given the Russian name *Yantarny*—amber.

Until recently, Jewish life in East Prussia before and during Nazism was more or less passed over by historical scholarship;[4] at the same time, there has been little work done on the role played in the region by the Nazi Party, exceptions tending to emerge from the domain of ecclesiastical and regional history.[5] In fact, because of

[4]See Aloys Sommerfeld, *Juden im Ermland—Ihr Schicksal nach 1933*, Münster 1991 (Zeitschrift für die Geschichte und Altertumskunde Ermlands, Beiheft 10). For the modern history of the Königsberg Jews see Schüler-Springorum.

[5]See Reinhard Henkys, 'Noch wenig erforschte Zeitgeschichte: Ostpreußen zur Hitlerzeit', in *Gegen Vergessen*, no. 29 (2001), pp. 14–15; Gerhard Reifferscheid, *Das Bistum Ermland und das Dritte Reich*, Cologne–Vienna 1975 (Zeitschrift für die Geschichte und Altertumskunde Ermlands, Beiheft 1); Christian Tilitzki, *Alltag in Ostpreußen 1940–45. Die geheimen Lageberichte der Königsberger Justiz*, Leer 1991; Andreas Kossert, *Preußen, Deutsche oder Polen? Die Masuren im Spannungsfeld des ethnischen Nationalismus 1870–1956*, Wiesbaden 2001 (Deutsches Historisches Institut, Warschau. Quellen und Studien, vol. 12). For the conflict between church and state, see Hugo Linck, *Der Kirchenkampf in Ostpreußen 1933 bis 1945. Geschichte und Dokumentation*, Munich 1968; Manfred Koschorke (ed.), *Geschichte der Bekennenden Kirche in Ostpreußen 1933–1945. Allein das Wort hat's getan*, Göttingen 1976. There is an abundance of Polish research on National Socialism in East Prussia; the works of Bohdan Koziełło-Poklewski are especially noteworthy: *Narodowosocjalistyczna Partia Robotnicza w Prusach Wschodnich w latach 1921–1933*, Olsztyn 1995; *idem*, 'Przyczynki do działalnosci służby pracy w Prusach Wschodnich w latach 1931–1935', in *Komunikaty Mazursko-Warmińskie,* vols. 137–138, no. 4 (1977), pp. 391–402. One study has appeared in Polish on the East Prussian institution for the disabled in Kortau bei Allenstein: Stanisław Piechocki, *Czyściec zwany Kortau*, Olsztyn 1993.

overwhelming electoral successes in the region before 1933, Hitler incorporated the notion of his being the 'saviour of East Prussia' into his patriarchal image.[6] From 1928 onwards, Erich Koch, who later attained notoriety as the brutal *Reichskommissar* for the Ukraine, held East Prussia firmly in his grip as a Nazi party *Gauleiter*. According to a decree by Hitler issued on 8 October 1939, the northern Polish territory became a part of East Prussia; it was united with the administrative district of Ciechanów (Zichenau) on 26 October 1939. In addition, East Prussia acquired the Polish districts of Suwałki and Augustów, which enabled Erich Koch to expand the province by 12,000 square kilometres. These regions were home to 800,000 Poles, 80,000 Jews, and around 15,000 Germans. The crimes in the Ciechanów district have been investigated mainly by Polish historians; regrettably, the research has to a great extent been wanting.

A SUPPRESSED CHAPTER OF EAST PRUSSIAN HISTORY: CONCENTRATION CAMPS IN EAST PRUSSIA

Hardly anything is known about the East Prussian concentration camps. At the beginning of the Second World War, many prisoners of war and forced labourers from various European countries were sent to East Prussia. In addition to those workers assigned to agriculture, political prisoners – above all those from Poland – were sent to so-called labour-education camps. One of these was in Hohenbruch (Lauknen) in the district of Labiau in Großer Moosbruch, where mainly Polish political prisoners were used to drain the swampland.[7] In 1944, a punitive work camp for Polish prisoners was created close to the Palmnicken amber mines, the prisoners being employed in the surface mining of amber. Over the course of time, 'undesirable' German prisoners were transferred to Palmnicken from the courthouse prison in Königsberg.

In Soldau (Działdowo), which, as part of the Versailles Treaty, had been surrendered by Germany to Poland in January 1920 without a plebiscite, a camp to simultaneously serve transit, prison and concentration purposes was built in February 1940 on the site of former barracks. Pro-Polish Masurians, together with members of the Polish intelligentsia (particularly the Catholic clergy), Jews and the mentally ill from the East Prussian institutions at Allenburg, Kortau, Tapiau and Carlshof, were all imprisoned in Soldau. Between 21 May and 8 June 1940, 1,558 physically handicapped East Prussians and 300 mentally ill people deported from Poland were murdered in a mobile gas chamber at Soldau. All in all, around 200,000 people passed through the Soldau camp; at least 10,000 of these were murdered there,[8] but the only concentration

[6]On Hitler's success among the Masurians in the southern part of East Prussia see Andreas Kossert, *Preußen*, pp. 181–190.

[7]Concerning the forced labourers, especially in Hohenbruch, see Bohdan Koziełło-Poklewski, *Zagraniczni robotnicy przymusowi w Prusach Wschodnich w latach drugiej wojny światowej*, Warsaw 1977.

[8]For the crimes of euthanasia committed in Soldau, see the fragmentary remarks of Ernst Klee, *'Euthanasie' im NS-Staat*, 2nd edn., Frankfurt am Main 1983, pp. 190f.; Ewa Korc and Antoni Sołoma, 'Z badań nad hitlerowską eutanazją w Prusach Wschodnich', in *Acta Universitatis Wratislaviensis*, no. 923. *Studia nad Faszyzmen i Zbrodniami Hitlerowskiem*, vol. 12, Warsaw 1987, pp. 189–199. For a more detailed approach to the Soldau camp, see Janusz Gumkowski, 'Obóz hitlerowski w Działdowie', in *Biuletyn*

camp to gain international notoriety was the Stutthof camp, located in West Prussia east of Danzig.[9] In the second half of 1944, Paul-Werner Hoppe, its infamous commandant, gave carefully-prepared orders to kill Jewish prisoners by lethal injection, poison gas, or a bullet through the base of the skull.[10]

Less well known is the existence of several Stutthof sub-camps (*Aussenlager*), established in the summer of 1944. After the Baltic ghettos had been evacuated, particularly those in Riga and Kaunas (Kovno), the number of prisoners sent to Stutthof increased considerably; new accommodation needed to be found. Hence during the second half of 1944, *Aussenlager* were created in co-operation with the SS and the administrative departments, following a special directive from Hoppe and as agreed on with the SS.[11] The inmates of these East Prussian sub-camps were mainly from the ghettos in Kaunas and Riga, and had been transported to Königsberg by sea. Each commandant of the camps originally came from the SS troops of the Stutthof concentration camp. All in all, there were six camps in East Prussia, part of a network of around 30 Stutthof *Aussenlager*: Seerappen, Jesau (18 km south of Königsberg), Königsberg, Schippenbeil, Gerdauen and Heiligenbeil. Of these, almost all were used for slave labour to expand the airport; they were under the control of the *Luftwaffenbauamt* [airforce construction authority] *Königsberg Pr.* The camp at Königsberg was established in August 1944; its last commandant (from 4 October 1944), SS-*Oberscharführer* Fritz Weber, was responsible for the Palmnicken death march.[12] The camp was built at the site of the Steinfurt rail-coach factory, one of the most important East Prussian industrial concerns, located in Königsberg-Ratshof (near the *Nordbahnhof*). The Königsberg Jewish entrepreneur Fritz Radok had run the factory until the Nazis came to power.

Living conditions in the East Prussian *Aussenlager* were as inhumane as those in other Nazi concentration camps. There are testimonies from several former inmates. In 1963, Ester Frielman stated that towards the end of 1944 she was transferred from

---

Głównej Komisji Badania Zbrodni Hitlerowskich, vol. 10 (1958), pp. 57–88. On the camp structure, see Gabriele Lotfi, 'SS-Sonderlager im nationalsozialistischen Terrorsystem: Die Entstehung von Hinzert, Stutthof und Soldau', in Norbert Frei, Sybille Steinbacher and Bernd C. Wagner (eds.), *Ausbeutung, Vernichtung, Öffentlichkeit. Neue Studien zur nationalsozialistischen Lagerpolitik*, Munich 2000 (Institut für Zeitgeschichte. Darstellungen und Quellen zur Geschichte von Auschwitz, 4), pp. 209–229. One detailed German monograph on the city of Soldau does not mention the camp's existence, but simply bemoans the "unfortunate end … of the German city of Soldau" in 1945. See Fritz Gause, *Geschichte des Amtes und der Stadt Soldau*, Marburg 1959 (Wissenschaftliche Beiträge zur Geschichte und Landeskunde Ostmitteleuropas, 38, republished as Sonderschriften Verein für Familienforschung in Ost- und Westpreußen, 95, Hamburg 1998) p. 364.

[9]Marek Orski, 'Organisation und Ordnungsprinzipien des Lagers Stutthof', in Ulrich Herbert, Karin Orth and Christoph Dieckmann (eds.), *Die nationalsozialistischen Konzentrationslager—Entwicklung und Struktur*, vol. I, p. 285–308; Karin Orth, *Das System der nationalsozialistischen Konzentrationslager. Eine politische Organisationsgeschichte*, Hamburg 1999. See also the following memoirs: Renata Yesner, *Jeder Tag war Jom Kippur. Eine Kindheit im Ghetto und im KZ*, Frankfurt am Main 1995 (Wolfgang Benz (ed.), *Lebensbilder. Jüdische Erinnerungen und Zeugnisse*, vol. 12770, Die Zeit des Nationalsozialismus); Josef Katz, *Erinnerungen eines Überlebenden*, Kiel 1988 (Katz was working at the Schichau shipyard in Danzig which was also a Stutthof sub-camp).

[10]See Orth, *System*, p. 294.

[11]Danuta Drywa, *Zagłada Żydów w obozie koncentracyjnym Stutthof: wrzesień 1939–maj 1945*, Gdańsk, 2001, p.181.

[12]*ibid.*, p. 197.

the Belzec ghetto to the camps at Budzyn and Auschwitz, then to Stutthof, and finally to Steindorf, near the town of Heiligenbeil. In Stutthof and Steindorf, she witnessed the daily death of a great many people as the direct consequence of hunger, cold and physical abuse.[13]

There are highly contradictory statements on the number of Jewish inmates in the East Prussian camps. Shmuel Krakowski states that there were around 20,000, ninety per cent of whom were women from the Lodz ghetto, Hungary or Lithuania; the male inmates were mainly from the Baltic region.[14] Many of the prisoners were later transferred to different areas, or had already been killed by the time the last camp statistics were taken on 24 January 1945; the population of the East Prussian *Aussenlager* was then recorded as 4,685 (934 men and 3,751 women).[15]

EVACUATION OF THE EAST PRUSSIAN *AUSSENLAGER*: THE DEATH MARCH FROM KÖNIGSBERG TO THE SAMLAND

The Red Army began its offensive on 12 January 1945, attacking the German 5th Army from the rear. By 30 January, the Red Army, now not far from Palmnicken, were fighting units of the 28th Army Corps. Having established a bridgehead at Memel, they pushed on across the Kurische Nehrung into the Samland. Soviet units now completely surrounded the province of East Prussia.

On 26 January 1945, Soviet forces reached Neukuhren and became engaged in a ferocious battle with the German defences. On the afternoon of 29 January Soviet troops overcame Königsberg-Cranz and forged ahead into the western Samland. On Friday, 2 February they reached the Baltic Sea at the western shore of Groß Sorgenau south of Palmnicken and at Warnbicken and Georgenswalde in the north. As the result of heavy fighting on 3 and 4 February they were then pushed back by the *Wehrmacht*.[16] Terrified by the much-publicised brutality of the invading Soviet forces—Nazi propaganda had focused on the atrocities committed by invading

[13]Bundesarchiv-Außenstelle Ludwigsburg (henceforth BA Außenstelle LU), AR-Z 299/1959, Bl.944–. Untersuchungsstelle für N.S. Gewaltverbrechen beim Landesstab der Polizei Israel. Tel Aviv, 20 March 1964. Testimony: Ester Frielman (in Yiddish), Tel Aviv 30 December 1963. Zwischenbericht Nr. 3. Betr. Vernehmung von Zeugen im Vorermittlungsverfahren wegen der Ermordung von Juden in Palmnicken/Ostpreußen im Jahre 1945. Bezug: Schreiben der Zentralen Stelle der Landesjustizverwaltungen in Ludwigsburg vom 14. Nov. 1963 – 7 Ar-Z 299/59 [hereafter Zwischenbericht]. As a result of the aforementioned letter from the Zentrale Stelle der Landesjustizverwaltungen the following witnesses were also asked to give evidence in its offices:

(1) Frau Pola Zwardon, née Mondschein, born 26 June1909 in Lubaczow, resident of Ramat Itzchak, Israel.
(2) Frau Bluma Lonicki née Landgarten, born 30 December 1917 in Cracow, resident of Holon, Israel.
(3) Frau Ester Frielmann née Fischbein, born 11 June 1925 in Markoszow, resident of Petach Tiqva, Israel.
(4) Frau Dina Hertzberg née Blachmann, born 10 December 1926 in Lodz, resident of Ramat Gan, Israel.

[14]Krakowski, p. 349.

[15]Drywa, pp. 234–235.

[16]See Klaus von der Groeben, *Im Dienst für Staat und Gemeinschaft. Erinnerungen*, Kiel 1995, pp. 273–277.

Soviet soldiers in the East Prussian village of Nemmersdorf in October 1944—civilians fled their homes in panic.[17] *Gauleiter* Koch had long refused any form of orderly evacuation of East Prussian civilians, as this was considered "treason". But with the Red Army offensive of January 1945, those East Prussian civilians who could do so headed for the already overcrowded seaport of Pillau in the hope of being evacuated to the west across the Baltic Sea. For more than 5,000 refugees who left Gdingen (Gotenhafen) on the *Wilhelm Gustloff*, a steamer formerly assigned to the German Labour Front's elaborate *Kraft durch Freude* ("strength thorough joy") leisure-time programme, this escape route led directly to death. On the evening of 30 January 1945, just off the Pomeranian coast, a Soviet torpedo struck the *Gustloff*; in less than an hour, the icy sea had swallowed the ship. Remarkably, at exactly the same time, the inhabitants of Palmnicken were witnessing the last and largest SS massacre in East Prussia.

Many films and books have documented the *Gustloff*'s senseless fate and so have solidly anchored the refugees' deaths in the German psyche.[18] As already suggested, the massacre of several thousand Jewish women chased into the freezing Baltic Sea amidst salvos of machine-gun bullets has received substantially less attention. Although 108 witnesses were interrogated in Ludwigsburg during preliminary investigations in the early 1960s, those accused of the crime died before proceedings could begin in Lüneburg, and the case was eventually dropped. Yad Vashem has carefully preserved the statements of the few survivors, copies of the protocols made during the interrogations, and the reports written by Soviet military and secret services, who had investigated the events in April and May 1945. These Soviet documents, however, have never been made public.

* * *

When the Soviet offensive began, the SS had rapidly dismantled the Stutthof *Aussenlager*. In extremely chaotic circumstances, and at the very last minute—the Soviet troops were close behind—efforts were then made to remove all traces of the East Prussian concentration camps and their evacuation. The evacuation march of those Jews imprisoned in East Prussia thus needs to be seen in the context of the many death marches from Nazi concentration camps from January 1945 onwards. On 20 and 21 January 1945, the prisoners of the camps at Seerappen, Jesau, Heiligenbeil, Schippenbeil and Gerdauen were marched to Königsberg. Some were sent to the Steinfurt rail-coach factory and herded together with the prisoners already there; others were sent to the twine factory at Reichsstraße 1; and some to the barracks in Kalthof. Ester Frielman reported the following on the death march to Königsberg after the Heiligenbeil camp had been evacuated:

[17]For the Soviet attack on Nemmersdorf, see the study by Bernhard Fisch, *Nemmersdorf Oktober 1944. Was in Ostpreußen tatsächlich geschah*, Berlin 1997.

[18]This tragic incident has now achieved broader fame through Günter Grass's best-selling novel *Im Krebsgang*, Göttingen 2002; (English transl., *Crabwalk*, New York 2003). On the German response to this novel see Robert G. Moller, 'Sinking Ships, the Lost *Heimat* and Broken Taboos: Günter Grass and the Politics of Memory in Contemporary Germany', in *Contemporary European History*, vol. 12, no. 2 (2003), pp. 147–181.

> We were led into a big cellar, where we found many Jews who had already been herded together. We were in this cellar for about six days. Hans, the SS woman and the Ukrainian guards came daily, shot at us and killed many people this way. They also threw stones at us and injured many. The whole six days we did not get any food and many died of hunger. The living then ate the flesh of the dead. … [There had been] 10,000 women and 2,000 men.[19]

At the last roll call in the Königsberg *Sammellager*, Danuta Drywa mentions around 7,000;[20] and there were yet more camps not included in the statistics. In its final report, the public prosecutor's office in Ludwigsburg still assumed the Königsberg *Sammellager* had held around 6,500 people at the beginning of the death march to Palmnicken.[21]

On 26 January 1945, after several days in Königsberg, the Jews who had been herded together from across all of East Prussia began their march towards the Samland.[22] When the prisoners were led out of the Königsberg factory early that morning, there were no longer any overland routes to the Reich. Many of the prisoners were shot in the city of Königsberg, their corpses left on the streets. The prisoners whom the SS herded to Palmnicken went without food or warm clothes. They were marched there on byways across Metgethen, Drugehnen, Muhmehnen, Polemmen, Kirpehnen and Germau. Hundreds of East Prussians witnessed the events that unfolded as the prisoners marched to their deaths.[23] In a letter to Martin Bergau, one survivor of this death march, Maria Blitz (née Salz), recalled:

> We were wrapped in dirty, threadbare blankets and on our feet we wore crude wooden clogs, which made moving forward on the snow and ice—in addition to our constant mortal terror—pure torture. Our clothing consisted of rags and paper, which we had tied together with wires to protect ourselves from the cold. Anyone who could not go on or fell over was shot immediately or beaten with a rifle butt. My sister Gita could not go any further—she had violent diarrhoea and collapsed. We tried to get her back on her feet, but she asked us to leave her lying there, she wanted to go to her mother—whom we had already lost in Auschwitz. She was shot.[24]

Many of the inhabitants of Königsberg also remembered the march. Rose-Marie Blask witnessed it on a very dreary and cold afternoon:

> I was 14-years-old back then. … I saw a procession of people on the other side of General-Litzmann-Strasse [the former Fuchsberger Allee]. I stood near a tree, it was

[19]BA Außenstelle LU. AR-Z 299/1959, Bl.944–: Untersuchungsstelle für N.S. Gewaltverbrechen beim Landesstab der Polizei Israel. Tel Aviv, 20 March1964. Testimony: Ester Frielman (in Yiddish), Tel Aviv, 30 December 1963. Zwischenbericht.

[20]Drywa, p. 235.

[21]BA. Außenstelle LU. AR-Z 299/1959, Bl.944–: Abschlußbericht Staatsanwaltschaft Ludwigsburg. Ludwigsburg 27 May 1964.

[22]*ibid,* The public prosecutor's office proceeded on the assumption of a starting date of 23 January, which is, however, impossible, as final rolls were still being taken in each *Aussenlager*. Staatsanwaltschaft Lüneburg, 16 June 1967, Hoenisch, Staatsanwalt, Abschlußverfügung.

[23]See witness reports in Bergau, *Endlösung*

[24]*ibid.* p. 14. Maria Blitz only felt free to talk about her experiences following the appearance of the *New York Times* article by Michael Wines.

Maria Blitz (née Salz) in 1940, aged 22

By courtesy of Maria Blitz

> already getting dark, the air full of snow, and no one could see me. Then I saw in horror that the SS were driving a long procession of prisoners in front of them.
>
> Again and again, an SS man raised his arm and a person fell in the snow, though I could not hear a gunshot. I don't know how long I stood there, as if frozen. At any rate, I saw a lorry following on behind. The dead were lifted out of the snow and thrown into the back of the lorry.[25]

And Gert Herberg, *Luftwaffenhelfer* in the *Flak-Batterie* at Goldschmiede near Königsberg, saw "the long procession of wretched creatures, wrapped in rags, marching wearily towards the Samland. Every 20 or 30 metres, some of those who could not walk anymore and were falling exhausted into each other's arms were shot down with machine guns by the SS guards".[26]

The soldiers directing the march consisted of three SS-*Unterführer*, 22 members of the SS, as well as 120 to 150 members of the notorious *Organisation Todt*, which included Ukrainians, Belgians, Dutchmen, Lithuanians and Frenchmen. Fritz Weber, the SS-*Oberscharführer*, and Otto Knott, the SS-*Unterscharführer*, were the commanders-in-chief.[27]

[25]Reader's letter to the editorial office of the *Königsberger Bürgerbrief*, Dortmund, 27 March 2000, cited in Bergau, *Endlösung*.

[26]*ibid.*, p. 11.

[27]BA. Außenstelle LU. AR-Z 299/1959, Bl.944–: Angaben aus dem vorläufigen Abschlußbericht der Staatsanwaltschaft. Staatsanwaltschaft Lüneburg, 16 June1967. Hoenisch, Staatsanwalt, Abschlußverfügung.

It is highly likely that this death march was ordered by the commander of the Gestapo head office, an SS-*Sturmbannführer* only referred to as Gormig.[28] He had been informed by Gerhard Paul Rasch, head of the state amber works in Königsberg, that Palmnicken, with its amber surface mining and the Prussian Mining and Iron and Steel Works Association, Königsberg Division, would be the ultimate destination of the march. In his testimony to the court in Ludwigsburg in 1961, Rasch denied any role in the preparations for the massacre.[29] The public prosecutor's final report, however, concludes that Rasch had in fact given the state police the idea of using the Anna Grube, a disused mine shaft in the Palmnicken amber mines: Jewish prisoners were to be driven into the shaft and the entrance closed.[30] Drywa confirms that the decision by the *Gauleitung* to murder the Jews was made in agreement with Gerhard Rasch.[31] The plan was to seal the victims in the abandoned mine and Kurt Friedrichs, who was both the Palmnicken mayor and the regional Nazi Party group leader, was counted on to co-operate, as was the management of the regional amber mine. Neither quarters nor provisions had been provided for the prisoners—or, for that matter, for their murderers.[32]

THE ARRIVAL IN PALMNICKEN OF THE JEWISH PRISONERS

The distance from Königsberg to Palmnicken is approximately 50 kilometres. During the march, the guards shot around 2,000 to 2,500 prisoners who had collapsed from sheer exhaustion; they left the corpses on the side of the road. The *Begleitkommando* then went on its way, leaving an SS man nicknamed the *Genickschußkommissar* ("the shot-in-the-neck commissar") behind to murder any fleeing Jews.

Only 3,000 of the approximately 6,500 to 7,000 original prisoners arrived in Palmnicken, most probably on the night of 26–27 January 1945. Two hundred to three hundred corpses were found on the morning after their arrival, between Palmnicken and Sorgenau, a distance of about two kilometres.[33] The district's population awoke to gunfire—for weeks, the front had been approaching the Samland, and the inhabitants of Palmnicken were thus living in fear of the invading Soviet Army. Martin Bergau recalls that

[28]*ibid.*

[29]"I had already heard in Palmnicken of the rumour that I had caused the Jews to be brought to Palmnicken; only in Hamburg did I hear that I had also been informed of the reason and destination for this Jewish march." BA. Außenstelle LU. AR-Z 299/1959, Bd. II, Bl. 261–390: Palmnicken. Zentrale Stelle der Landesjustizverwaltungen. Testimony given in Hamburg, 20 June 1961 by Gerhard Paul Rasch, born 27 May 1905 in Rüdigsheim, now Hamburg.

[30]BA. Außenstelle LU. AR-Z 299/1959, Bl.944–: Abschlußbericht Staatsanwalt. Ludwigsburg, 27 May 1964.

[31]Drywa, p. 236.

[32]BA. Außenstelle LU. AR-Z 299/1959, vol. II, Bl. 261–390: Palmnicken. Zentrale Stelle der Landesjustizverwaltungen. Testimony given in Winsen, 23 June 1961 by Kurt Friedrichs, born 8 July 1883 in Königsberg.

[33]BA. Außenstelle LU. AR-Z 299/1959, Bl.944–: Angaben aus dem vorläufigen Abschlußbericht der Staatsanwaltschaft. Staatsanwaltschaft Lüneburg, 16 June1967. Hoenisch, Staatsanwalt, Abschlußverfügung

> One night, it must have been around three o'clock, I was torn from sleep by shots. My first thought was that the Russians had landed on the coast. … My father, who had also heard the shots, called after me to remain in the house. I saw a female figure trying to enter the garden gate. When she noticed me she turned immediately and staggered back into the street. Shots rang out, the woman collapsed. Still drowsy, I noticed an endless column of ragged figures in the dark, continually pushed forward by gunfire. I also noticed that again and again individuals were breaking away from the column and being shot down. But I also noticed that some were managing to escape.[34]

In circumstances marked by extreme chaos, the SS encountered an unanticipated obstacle on the procession's arrival at the amber mine in Palmnicken: awoken in the middle of the night, the mine-director, referred to by Bergau and in the testimony only as Landmann, refused to open any of the mine-shafts intended for the mass murder. After all, he argued, the mine was needed for the Palmnicken water supply.[35] Instead, he allowed the main gate be opened so that the exhausted and freezing victims could be housed in the mine's large workshop. The guards were permitted to sleep in the offices and corridors. The next morning, estate-manager Hans Feyerabend arrived; he was responsible for the three regions controlled by the amber mine—Dorbnicken, Palmnicken and Gross-Hubnicken. *Oberscharführer* Weber was now more or less forced to relinquish his command. Feyerabend's statement has been duly documented: as long as he was alive, the Jews would be fed and none killed; Palmnicken was not to become a second Katyn. He ordered straw, peas and bread and had cattle slaughtered. The factory canteen had to cook for the exhausted women.

Feyerabend was a highly respected man in the region. In the First World War he had been a reserve major; he was now commandant of the Palmnicken *Volkssturm*. He represented an insurmountable obstacle for the realisation of the planned murder, and it is very likely that mayor Friedrichs and *Oberscharführer* Weber engineered his removal:[36] Friedrichs had been a Nazi Party member and political leader since 1 February 1932. On 1 February 1936, he came to Palmnicken and assumed the full-time office of mayor, a position he would hold until mid-April 1945. Feyerabend seems to have received a threat from the *Sicherheitsdienst*, the intelligence branch of the SS in Königsberg. This was accompanied by an order to strengthen the *Wehrmacht*'s defences near Kumehnen with a hundred *Volkssturm* members.[37] On Tuesday, 30 January, these men marched out to join an army unit that had neither requested their support nor knew what to do with it. It appears that Feyerabend, who had entrusted the care of the Jewish refugees to his deputies, realised he had fallen into a trap with no way out. His comrades found him dead, his own gun in his mouth. It seems that there was no investigation as to whether he had committed

[34]Bergau, *Der Junge*, pp. 108–110.
[35]Bergau, *Endlösung*.
[36]Henkys, 'Endlösung'.
[37]See BA. Außenstelle LU. AR-Z 299/1959, vol. I, Bl. 1–260: Palmnicken. Zentrale Stelle. Testimony given in Düsseldorf, 24 January 1961. Record of proceedings of Rudolf Johann Folger. BA. Außenstelle LU. AR-Z 299/1959, vol. II, Bl. 261–390: Palmnicken. Zentrale Stelle der Landesjustizverwaltungen. Testimony given in Winsen, 23 June 1961 by Kurt Friedrichs.

suicide or had actually been murdered.[38] Danuta Drywa speaks of Feyerabend's murder on 30 January 1945.[39]

MASS MURDER ON THE BALTIC SEASHORE

On that Tuesday evening after the *Volkssturm* unit had left, Friedrichs sent for a dozen armed Hitler Youth members, welcomed them at the municipal office, gave them substantial amounts of liquor and then sent them down to the shore, together with three SS-men, to the disused Anna mine.[40] Martin Bergau was one of these Hitler Youth members. Friedrichs also prompted the same young men to ask civilians if they had seen fleeing Jews, as well as to search the woods for any in hiding. They could, he indicated, either shoot the victims immediately or hand them over to Friedrichs. Bergau recalls:

> When we left the municipal office with the SS-men, it was already quite dark. We walked in silence towards Franneks-Höh. When we reached the northern part of the town, we turned left and went down the path to the closed Anna mine. We reached the squalid buildings, situated at sea level. I noticed a group of around forty to fifty women and girls. They were captured Jews. A diffuse source of light sparsely illuminated what seemed a ghostly scene. The women had to line up in twos, and we were instructed by the SS-men to escort them. Around six to eight SS-men might have belonged to the command. I could not tell whether they were Germans or foreigners, as their commands were extremely terse. Once the line-up was complete, two women at a time were led around the side of the building by two SS-men. Shortly afterwards two pistol shots rang out. That was the sign for two more SS executioners to take the next two victims to the building, which was shrouded in twilight, and shots soon resounded there again. I had had to position myself pretty much at the end of the long line. A classmate stood right across from me with a cocked rifle, watching over the women on the other side. One woman turned to me and asked in good German if she could move two places forward; she wished to walk this last path with her daughter. In a voice nearly choked with tears, I granted this brave woman her request. … Then I accompanied a mother whom I will never forget to her daughter.[41]

Several former inhabitants of Palmnicken suspected of helping in the Jewish prisoners' murder were investigated in Ludwigsburg.[42] Kurt Friedrichs managed to escape over the Frische Nehrung to the West on 15 April; he was imprisoned by the British authorities in Neuengamme a month later, and released on 15 October 1947, after which he was granted a West German pension. His initial response to interrogation in Ludwigsburg in 1961 was as follows:

> One morning, it must have been towards the end of January 1945, the director of the amber mine, Assessor Landmann, called me and informed me that during the night a

[38]See *ibid.*

[39]Drywa, p. 238.

[40]Bergau, *Der Junge*, p 111; BA. Außenstelle LU. AR-Z 299/1959, Bl.944–: Abschlußbericht Staatsanwalt. Ludwigsburg, 27 May 1964.

[41]Bergau, *Der Junge*, pp. 111–114.

[42]BA. Außenstelle LU. AR-Z 299/1959, Bl.944–: Abschlußbericht Staatsanwalt. Ludwigsburg, 27 May 1964.

> column of several thousand Jewish prisoners had arrived in Palmnicken. … This took care of the matter for me. I did not concern myself any more with the prisoners, and I also did not hear anything more about them afterwards.

Upon being pressed by the prosecutor, he first indicated that "I personally cannot remember this incident. … I did not see any shootings, nor did I hear the shots. I also did not see any shot prisoners lying anywhere", before then confirming, when pressed again, that

> It is correct that Landmann called me and informed me that a column of several thousand Jews had come from Königsberg and had arrived in Palmnicken during the night. He was very angry and mentioned that Rasch was responsible. We discussed what should be done with the Jews. I decided to drive straightaway to the amber mine. On my way there I saw perhaps three corpses lying near the train station.

Finally, on being pressed even further, Friedrichs corrected his account as follows:

> It is correct that I knew that the Jews were originally supposed to be driven into the disused shaft of the Anna mine so that they could be eliminated [beseitigt] in this manner [auf diese Art und Weise]. Feyerabend objected strongly to this, so that initially the murder of the Jews could be prevented. … I simply continued to press for the Jews' removal.
>
> I also knew that this plan was not carried out only because Feyerabend used his authority to prevent it. Of course I was aware that the SS had not given up their plan to liquidate the Jews. After Feyerabend's death, when I went to the SS-leader and told him he should get rid of the Jews no matter how [auf irgendeine Art und Weise wegschaffen] and after he assured me it would be taken care of in the morning, I naturally was aware that this departure would be followed by liquidation. There was thus no need for the SS-leader and me to discuss the matter further.[43]

When on Wednesday 31 January 1945 a horse-drawn carriage with Hans Feyerabend's body arrived in the town, his staff was greatly discouraged, since the fate of the remaining 3,000 prisoners now lay in the hands of the SS.[44] For its part, the SS now opted for a different approach. On Wednesday evening the prisoners, under the pretence that they were being taken to safety from Pillau to Hamburg by ship, were led out of the factory's northern gate on the quickest route to the sea, from where they were forced to march south along the icy Baltic seashore. The seashore and the town thirty metres above were separated by a broad strip of park and woodland. Therefore only a few of the inhabitants of Palmnicken saw what happened that night. The SS machine gunners gathered together the widely dispersed column from the back, and, each time separating the last group from the rest, chased their victims onto the ice and into the water under machine gun fire.

In the darkness and haste, the SS could not murder all of the Jews systematically, in spite of their use of flares. Many Jews were initially only wounded, some not even hit. Some fainted and froze to death, or became trapped between ice floes and

[43]BA. Außenstelle LU. AR-Z 299/1959, vol. II, Bl. 261–390: Palmnicken. Zentrale Stelle der Landesjustizverwaltungen. Testimony given in Winsen, 23 June 1961 by Kurt Friedrichs.

[44]Bergau, *Endlösung*, for remaining testimony in this paragraph see Celina Manielewicz, YVA 03/1108.

drowned. Others died on the beach after days in agony. During the following days, many local people, among them Martin Bergau, saw corpses wash ashore along the west coast of the Samland.

Let us now look at two accounts of survivors of the massacre, and a corroborating account by a local resident, that have contributed to this historical reconstruction. The first account, centred on survival, was offered in Israel in 1961 by Zila Manielewicz, born in 1921 in Ozorkow :

> When we arrived on the shore, it was already darkest night. … Suddenly I was hit on my head with a rifle butt and I and I fell into a precipice. I gained consciousness in the water. At this time, dusk had already fallen. The shore was full of corpses and the SS men were still hovering over them. …. Towards morning the SS men disappeared. Around this time we became aware that about 200 of us were still alive. We got up and climbed onto the beach. The path we had taken that night was itself full of corpses and the seawater was red from the victims' blood. Together with two other Jewish women, I dragged myself to the closest German village; we entered the first house we reached. It turned out that the village of Sorgenau was close to Palmnicken. The house we entered belonged to a German family named Voss. … Voss came later and led us to the attic. During this time, the first units of the Russian military were approaching Palmnicken. After these units had been beaten back, Voss chased us from the attic and said that he did not intend to feed Jewish women. … After Voss left, another German came up to us; he turned out to be Albert Harder, and he told us he would hide us. First somebody hid us in some room and later in a storeroom over the chicken coop where we could only lie down. We hid in this room for about a week; later many German refugees from the Memel area arrived. Around that time Harder took us to his apartment, his wife drew us a bath and gave us new clothes. They burned our camp clothes themselves. From then on, we lived in the apartment of the Harders and remained there until liberation by the Red Army.[45]

The second account, centred on the mass execution itself, was offered in the same year, and also in Israel, by Pnina Kronisch, a Russian Jew born in 1927 in Belzec:

> Then they threw the murdered Jews into the water by kicking them. As the seacoast was covered with ice, the murderers pushed their victims into the icy water with their rifle butts. Since I was at the front of the column with my sister Sara, we were the last in line to be shot. I was also laid down on the seacoast together with my sister, though I was not killed by the shot that was aimed at me but only wounded in my left foot, and my face was soaked in the blood of the murdered Jews lying next to me. During this time my sister was killed. I did not wait until the Germans threw me into the sea—I threw myself in and remained lying next to the ice floe, which already was caught up in the water and hit by the waves. The Germans believed I was dead, and since I was alone, to my good luck, and last in line to be murdered, the Germans got into their sleds and drove off. Before dawn I scrambled out of the sea and hid in the coal store of a German farmer who did not live far from where these events occurred.[46]

[45]BA. Außenstelle LU. AR-Z 299/1959, Bd. III, Bl. 391–499: Palmnicken. Testimony: Zila [*sic*] Manielewicz, Jerusalem, 10 Oct. 1961 (in Polish).

[46]BA. Außenstelle LU. AR-Z 299/1959, Bd. III, Bl. 391–499: Palmnicken. Testimony: Pnina (Pola) Kronisch. Gerzlja, 4. Oct.1961 (in Russian). Pnina Kronisch had originally been imprisoned in the Bedzin concentration camp. She then spent periods in the camps at Wieliczka, Plaszów, Auschwitz and Stutthof before being finally sent to Heiligenbeil.

A thaw set in and the snow that had hidden the signs of murder soon melted; bloodstained puddles filled the ditches along the roads.[47] Confronted with the evidence of the atrocities, the psychological burden on the local population must have been intense. This is suggested by one former resident of Palmnicken, Helene Zimmer, in her account to the Ludwigsburg court:

> Then we went back to Palmnicken on foot, along the shore instead of along the completely congested road. It was a very painful march taking several hours. … Just before Palmnicken, actually between Nodems and Palmnicken, we suddenly saw countless corpses lying on the shore, and also heard desperate screams still coming from the water. As far as I could see, those lying on the shore were all dead, and every now and then we could hear desperate cries coming from the water. … The water along the shore was partly frozen and ice floes floated around, between them were the seriously wounded or dead people. Many of them were dressed in the same striped clothes. There were also many women among them. … I was so shaken at the sight that I covered my eyes with my hands. … We then quickly went on walking because we could not stand the sight.[48]

Some survivors managed to escape to the houses of neighbouring Germans. Doctors and nurses in the Palmnicken hospital offered protection to a severely wounded girl. Those who performed such actions were ordinary people—among them Loni and Albert Harder, a couple from Sorgenau who sheltered three Jewish women. A Dr. Schröder from Germau operated on Maria Blitz after her escape, removing her tattooed prisoner number.[49] Two Polish forced labourers—Stanislawa und Romualdo Zbierkowski—also helped save the surviving Jews.

In any event, only a tiny group of men and women survived the death march and subsequent massacre. It must be emphasized that this was improvised murder under chaotic circumstances; in a context of heavy military fighting, no records were kept, and most survivors had other concerns than offering detailed accounts of the events. For these reasons, we can only estimate the total number of those who survived as approximately fifteen of the original group of 7,000 individuals. The crime was reported to the Soviets when they captured Palmnicken ten weeks later. Krakowski mentions four statements from surviving Jewish women; these are stored in the Yad Vashem Archives. He had access to six other such statements, stored in the central archive of the Ministry of Defence of the Russian Federation in Podolsk near Moscow, where they have been off limits to researchers for decades.[50] Previous publications have not indicated that a German Jewish man was among the survivors, namely Walter Falkenstein, born 1899 in Hochneukirch, in the district of

[47]Bergau, *Der Junge*, pp.110.

[48]BA. Außenstelle LU. AR-Z 299/1959, vol. IV, Bl.500–748: Palmnicken. Landeskriminalamt Baden-Württemberg. Sonderkommission—Zentrale Stelle—Testimony given in Werdohl, 3 July 1962. Vernehmungsschrift. ("Having been summoned, the married housewife Helene Zimmer, born in Grossdirschkeim on 9 April 1902 and now living in Werdohl, Westphalia, appeared on 3 July 1962 in the offices of the police station Werdohl/Westphalia.").

[49]Bergau, *Endlösung.*

[50]Testimonies of Celina Manielewicz YVA 03/1108, Dina Hertzberg YVA 03/2279; Frida Kleinman YVA 03/2348; Yehezkel Vitkin YVA M-1/E-698/587. See also Krakowski, 'Massacre of Jewish Prisoners' pp. 363–366 (witness report of Dora Hauptman).

Grevenbroich, who had also endured the death march from Königsberg to Palmnicken, but had used the chaos in Palmnicken to escape from the mine workshop before the others were led to the sea. Falkenstein himself hid with German civilians until the Red Army's arrival.[51]

CONFRONTATIONS WITH SUFFERING: WOMEN FROM PALMNICKEN AND JEWISH MASS GRAVES

On 15 April 1945, the 32nd Division of the Red Army captured Palmnicken. On 17 April, an investigation began into the massacre, under the supervision of Major General Danilov. Contrary to fears widely held by the town's population, the victors did not seek revenge, even though the mutilated victims discovered in the many mass graves were classified as Soviet civilians. Instead, they tried to find those responsible for the atrocity—efforts that proved fruitless, since with the exception of a small number of Hitler Youth members, the perpetrators had fled after the Soviets' brief retreat from western Samland in February. At Pentecost, a sort of final rite took place, with around two hundred girls and women from Palmicken being forced to unearth 263 corpses with their bare hands. The bodies had been buried in a thirty metre long trench near the Anna mine—204 women and 59 men. Then German witnesses to the crimes were forced to explain in public and in front of the unearthed corpses when and how the Jews had been killed. In his account at Ludwigsburg, Rudolf Folger, whom the remaining inhabitants of Palmnicken elected mayor soon after the Soviets arrived, offered details furnishing a sense of the circumstances they now faced:

> After the bodies had been exhumed, they were laid out in an open area in two rows next to each other, and the women from Palmnicken, who had been assigned to dig them out, had to stand behind the corpses. The Russians had set up two machine guns and aimed them at the women. Afterwards a Russian major—a Jew—gave an address in German in which he expressed the view that the Russians could [but would not] now do the same thing to the women that had been done before to the Jews.[52]

* * *

If the results are weighed by the number of convicted persons, the investigation into the massacre by the public prosecutor's office in Ludwigsburg turned out largely to have been in vain. Although more than a hundred witnesses were heard, the guilt of

[51]BA. Außenstelle LU. AR-Z 299/1959, Bl.944–: Bericht, Hochneukirch, 4 February 1964. ("Having been summoned, the worker Walter Falkenstein, born 29 October 1899 in Hochneukirch, living in Hochneukirch, district Grevenbroich, appeared in the Hochneukirch police station.").

[52]BA. Außenstelle LU. AR-Z 299/1959, vol. I, Bl. 1–260: Palmnicken. Zentrale Stelle. Testimony given in Düsseldorf, 24 January 1961. Record of proceedings of Rudolf Johann Folger. See also the memoirs of Palmnicken's Protestant pastor, Johannes Jänicke, *Ich konnte dabeisein*, Berlin 1984. Jänicke served his flock until 1947; he was one of the few residents of the town to directly mention the massacre. Cited from Martin Bergau, *Endlösung*.

the individuals charges could not be legally proven. Presented with black and white photographs, the Israeli witnesses were asked to clearly identify SS members who had participated in the massacre. But in January 1945, after more than five years of Nazi brutality, much of this time spent in various camps and ghettos, how could the starved, half-frozen, and terrified Jewish women inscribe individual SS-men into their memories? Nevertheless, the leader of the death march and the main person accused of the crime, SS-*Oberscharführer* Fritz Weber, was incarcerated on 11 January 1965, pending trial, thanks to a committal order issued by a local court in Kiel. But on the night of 20–21 January 1965—precisely 20 years after the start of the death march—Weber committed suicide in his cell.[53] As indicated, Kurt Friedrichs was compelled to testify at Ludwigsburg; the teenage Hitler Youth members he had controlled and numbed with drink were imprisoned in Soviet detention camps, where several would succumb to starvation and typhoid fever.[54]

THE BELATED COMMEMORATION OF A REPRESSED CRIME

In 1945 Palmnicken became part of the Soviet Union; after the Soviet Union's collapse in 1992, it became part of the Russian Federation. As is well known, Königsberg was renamed Kaliningrad after the war. The fate then suffered by those Jews murdered in the city's environs has been described by Rabbi David Shvedik, a present-day resident of the city, as follows: "The victorious Soviet Union closed the book on Nazi atrocities once it seized Königsberg from the Germans at the end of World War II. Thousands of Germans were deported in rail cars to be replaced by Russian immigrants. Jewish Holocaust victims were reburied as 'Soviet heroes', stripped, here and elsewhere on Soviet soil, of religious identity".[55]

Accordingly, after the exhumation of the Jewish corpses, their reburial, and the Red Army's investigation, all memory of the massacre and the events surrounding it was officially and *de facto* erased.[56] The mass grave in the Anna mine disappeared into a sand dune. In the 1960s, the corpses would finally be unearthed—by amber excavators. The corpses were thought to be those of Soviet soldiers murdered by the Germans, and a memorial stone was duly erected, bearing the inscription 'Eternal Glory to the Heroes'. Until the collapse of the Soviet Union the *Komsomolzen* laid wreaths every year at the site and organised parades. Following the collapse—in 1994—it became possible for Martin Bergau to convince the regional authorities that the bodies lying at the site were in fact Jewish. In 1999, with the support of the

[53]BA. Außenstelle LU. AR-Z 299/1959, vol. VI, Bl. 944–: Oberstaatsanwaltschaft, Kiel, 22 January 1965.

[54]One such person eventually obliged to testify to the German authorities in 1962 was Horst Scharnowski. On 23 June 1945 he was arrested together with other teenage colleagues and taken to Königsberg, from where, in 1946, he was transferred to the Tapiau prison and then to an internment camp in Eylau, where he was tortured by the Soviet secret police. Charged with participating in the *Judenaktion* in Palmnicken, he was convicted *in camera* on 15 May 1948 by at a session of the military tribunal in Königsberg and sentenced to 25 years forced labour along with two other youths. He served his sentence in several camps in the Urals from 1948 until his release on 17 December 1953. See Bergau, *Endlösung*.

[55]Cited from Wines, p. 4.

[56]See Henkys, 'Endlösung'.

German Foreign Ministry, the *Volksbund Deutscher Kriegsgräberfürsorge* (German National Alliance for the Care and Preservation of War Graves) and the Russian organisation *Memorial*, the grounds were restored by young Germans and Russians. On 31 January 2000, the 55th anniversary of the massacre, the Jewish community of Königsberg/Kaliningrad consecrated a memorial stone for the victims in Russian and Hebrew. A monument made up of boulders was also set up close to the former Anna mine. Along the Samland's amber shore, the monument commemorates the largest Nazi massacre to have taken place in East Prussia.

THE PALMNICKEN MASSACRE: AN INITIAL ASSESSMENT

Soviet atrocities in East Prussia, the evacuation of German civilians and the sinking of the *Gustloff* have been the subject of many accounts whereas for a long time the death march from Königsberg to Palmnicken and the subsequent mass execution on the Baltic shore was allowed to pass into oblivion. This fact is closely tied to the German mythology of flight and expulsion, a mythology playing an important role in the German public's perception of Soviet Communism during the Cold War. The stark reality of a massacre of Jews in East Prussia did not correspond to the basic approach towards the "Eastern regions" encouraged in the postwar years of the German Federal Republic.

The reality of what transpired in the last days of German East Prussia is as complex as it is painful. It is clear, for a start, that military orders had by then become chaotic and the SS had begun to act independently. Its plans to murder the death march's survivors met with the resistance of at least one influential local representative, Hans Feyerabend, with his suicide—or his murder—itself testifying eloquently to a confused chain of command. In Feyerabend's fight with the SS, that organisation was to triumph. Towards the end of January 1945, a large percentage of East Prussia's civilian population had taken flight; at the time of the massacre, large parts of northern and southeastern East Prussia had been seized by the Soviets. The SS clearly imagined that icy temperatures, the ubiquitous roar of guns, and the presence on the roads of hundreds of thousands of civilians and soldiers would help cover up its crime. Nevertheless, as many testimonies confirm, at least hundreds of civilians observed the death march as it proceeded through the centre of Königsberg and across open country. In the small coastal town of Palmnicken, the arrival of several thousand Jewish prisoners led to direct, personal contact with the local population. Workers in the amber mine, regional officials, as well as many civilians witnessed the horrendous events that took place in the town; many participated in the events in one way or another. In the face of these atrocities, of piles of corpses on the streets and beaches, and with the mortal terror experienced by East Prussians in Nemmersdorf still fresh in communal memory, panic spread quickly. But despite such panic, some inhabitants of Palmnicken were willing to help the few Jews who had managed to survive the SS mass murder, some even hiding Jewish refugees for months. In this respect, the range of behaviour manifested by the residents of East Prussia did not differ from that evident in other segments of the German population. Perhaps more characteristic for the East Prussian and other refugees from

Germany's former eastern regions is the widespread vanishing, in the postwar period, of any strong sense of guilt for a broad complicity in Nazi crimes, and the replacement of any such self-reckoning with an increasing internalisation of the victim's role. This attitude no doubt reflected the experience of flight and expulsion, as well as bitterness at the loss of social status within the former Federal Republic.

The East Prussian death march and the massacre at Palmnicken represent the last chapter in the murder of European Jews. Whilst fires ravaged East Prussia and its inhabitants fled the Soviets for dear life, others who longed to be rescued by the Soviets died shortly before their army reached the amber shore.

Jewish Intellectuals

"For a Time I was Privileged to Enjoy his Friendship ...": The Ambivalent Relationship between Hans Jonas and Gershom Scholem

By Christian Wiese

In Germany at least, Hans Jonas is mainly known for his book on the dangers resulting from modern technological power, *The Imperative of Responsibility. In Search of an Ethics for the Technological Age*. An intellectual biography of Jonas remains a desideratum—such a study necessarily paying due attention to the Jewish elements in his life and thought. All told, the important ethical arguments Hans Jonas formulated in the areas of ecology and bioethics represent only one aspect of a career deeply rooted in the vicissitudes of the twentieth century. It is well known that along with Karl Löwith, Hannah Arendt and Emmanuel Levinas, Jonas was one of Martin Heidegger's foremost Jewish students during the Weimar Republic,[1] having written his famous work on *Gnosis und spätantiker Geist* under his supervision. It is also quite well-known that later, shocked by Heidegger's behaviour during the Nazi period and by what he perceived as the "philosophical catastrophe" this reflected,[2] Jonas distanced himself from Heidegger's ideas, abandoned his research on Gnosticism and proceeded to develop an anti-existentialist, anti-nihilist biology-centred philosophy that would become the basis of his approach to ethics. It is less known that Jonas was a convinced Zionist from his early youth onward—a position reflected in his leaving Germany immediately in 1933, moving in 1935 to Palestine where he joined a circle of German-Jewish intellectuals in Jerusalem and served in the British army between 1939 and 1945 for the sake of fighting Nazism. At the same time, throughout his adult life Jonas, always painfully aware of his mother's murder in Auschwitz, wrestled with the Holocaust's religious and philosophical implications for Judaism in general.

I would like to express my gratitude to Mrs. Lore Jonas for our conversations and for kindly sharing Gershom Scholem's letters to her husband with me. Furthermore I am indebted to Jeffrey Grossman from the University of Virginia, Charlottesville, who edited the first draft of this article, and to Joel Golb for his editing of my translation of the often quite complicated German sources and his remarkably thoughtful comments.

[1]See Richard Wolin, *Heidegger's Children. Hannah Arendt, Karl Löwith, Hans Jonas, and Herbert Marcuse*, Princeton, NJ 2001.

[2]Hans Jonas, *Erinnerungen*, ed. by Christian Wiese, Frankfurt am Main 2003, p. 299.

Gershom Scholem

Hans Jonas

By courtesy of Lore Jonas

Both Jonas's Zionism and his later speculations on what he referred to as "the concept of God after Auschwitz" deserve a more detailed analysis.[3] Jonas's recently published memoirs, a testimony to the German-Jewish experience before and during the Holocaust and a most interesting example of exile literature, are a key to understanding the connection of his biography in general, and his political convictions in particular, to his philosophical thinking. These memoirs reinforce a sense that although Jonas's rejection of efforts to define him as a Jewish philosopher were well grounded, it is also the case that the Jewish dimension of his work should not be underestimated.[4] Informed by this premise and based on previously unpublished material, the following discussion of Jonas's ambivalent friendship with Gershom Scholem is meant to form the basis for a clearer interpretation of Jonas's intellectual achievements.

I

Hans Jonas's relationship with Gershom Scholem was grounded in a set of common historical experiences that began in childhood and youth, over a period extending

[3]See Hans Jonas, 'The Concept of God after Auschwitz: A Jewish Voice', in *idem*, *Mortality and Morality: A Search for the Good after Auschwitz*, ed. by Lawrence Vogel, Evanston, IL 1996, pp. 131–143. On Jonas's Zionism, see Christian Wiese, 'Abschied vom deutschen Judentum. Zionismus und Kampf um die Würde im politischen Denken des frühen Hans Jonas', in *idem* and Eric Jacobson (eds.), *Weiterwohnlichkeit der Welt. Zur Aktualität von Hans Jonas*, Berlin 2003, pp. 15–33.

[4]For an initial exploration of this dimension see Christian Wiese, *Hans Jonas. Zusammen Philosoph und Jude*, Frankfurt am Main 2003.

from the First World War to the early Weimar Republic. It would be marked by shared ideological convictions and scholarly endeavours: a growing disillusionment with the prospects of Jewish integration into Germany which resulted in a Zionist commitment on the part of both Scholem and Jonas, as well as a strong interest by both in Jewish religious history. Jonas first encountered Scholem, albeit at a distance, in the early 1920s, during a turbulent meeting of the Zionist youth movement in Berlin, where Jonas was taking courses in philosophy and Jewish studies. Already then, Scholem perceived Jonas, in his later words, as a "tremendously stubborn, original personality deeply permeated by intellectual motivation."[5] Scholem emigrated to Jerusalem shortly after that meeting. Jonas had meanwhile completed several months of agricultural work with the *Hachshara* organisation—a Zionist organisation that provided agricultural training for young Jews willing to join the Yishuv—in order to prepare himself for immediate emigration to Palestine; but having decided that he was much more suited for intellectual than for agricultural work, he decided to finish his studies in Marburg. Written under Martin Heidegger's supervision, his doctoral thesis, *Der Begriff der Gnosis* (1930), was eventually published in 1934 under the title *Gnosis und spätantiker Geist* (a second volume followed in 1954).

In August 1933, recognising the political potential of antisemitism in Germany and the threat posed by the Nazis, Jonas left his home country for England, where he intended to prepare the publication of his book on Gnosticism. He contacted Scholem from London, asking him for a letter of recommendation in support of an application for a British fellowship. Scholem complied, and it seems from his recommendation that he appreciated Jonas's interpretation of Gnosticism—he praised Jonas as a gifted scholar, but not without taking note of Jonas's failure to have yet read his, Scholem's, work. This is the first manifestation of a lifelong bone of contention between the two scholars.[6]

After having finished his research in London's libraries, Jonas, who possessed an immigration certificate for Palestine, eventually left Europe, arriving in Jerusalem in April 1935, on the eve of Passover. He immediately joined the circle of German Jewish intellectuals at the Hebrew University, where its president Hugo S. Bergman offered to teach occasional courses in philosophy. Soon he and Scholem entered into a friendship, facilitated by regular Sabbath meetings of a small scholarly group he organised together with the orientalist Hans J. Polotsky and the philologist Hans Lewy. They called their circle "Pil", composed of their last names' Hebrew initials, and the first meeting seems to have taken place shortly after Jonas's arrival. Joining the circle that same year, Scholem promptly demanded that its name be changed; he suggested "Pilegesch"—the Hebrew word for a temple prostitute.[7] Other important scholars, including the physicist Shmuel Sambursky, gradually joined the "Pilegesch"

[5]Jonas, *Erinnerungen*, p. 97.

[6]The recommendation letter and the Jonas-Scholem correspondence is located in the papers of Gershom Scholem at the Jewish National and University Library in Jerusalem, JNUL 4⁰1599 (henceforth Scholem papers: unless otherwise indicated, all cited correspondence between Scholem and Jonas refers to that collection). The documents are published in Wiese, *Hans Jonas*, pp. 64–67.

[7]For the founding of the "Pilegesch" circle see Jonas, *Erinnerungen*, pp. 150–154.

circle, which met until the early 1940s. We have been left with a scattering of poems written by various members to describe each other—these suggest that the circle did not only discuss serious matters.[8] Correspondingly, the friendship between Jonas and Scholem was apparently founded not only on mutual respect, but also on a great deal of humour. Possessing some biographical interest, one example of such levity emerges from a matter that could not have been more sombre. In his memoirs Jonas recalls that in 1939, for the first time in his life, he made a bet on a historical question. When the "Pilegesch" circle turned to the question of whether England and France would keep their promise and defend Poland against a German attack, the general consensus—which included Scholem—was that they would certainly fail to do so.

> Then I made a bet with Scholem, who loved betting. As he loved sweets, too, he demanded a pound of marzipan or chocolate in case he won, while I would receive a roast duck prepared by Fanya Scholem, whom he had married in the meantime. … I had met her after moving to Jerusalem; she was still Fanya Freud then, and everybody told me she was a wonderful girl. She was not very attractive but she had a great personality and was a brilliant Hebraist. … People had different ideas about who would finally marry her, but in the end it was Scholem. At the time of our bet, they had already been married for a couple of years and Fanya was, as it were, part of the bet, because she would owe me a roast duck. It is well-known who won the bet: me – England did not fail. In the meantime I was serving in the army, and while on leave I was invited for dinner by the Scholems. However, I felt cheated of my prize since they had invited a number of other friends and my piece of the roast duck was not really very big.[9]

Scholem and Jonas agreed on most of the important political issues discussed in Palestine at the time. Both were members of the *Brith Shalom* movement, which supported the establishment of a bi-national (Jewish-Arab) state in Palestine. Jonas does appear to have been more concerned with the security of the *Yishuv,* since he soon became an active member of the Haganah. The two men agreed on the urgency of fighting against Nazi Germany. In September 1939, Jonas composed a passionately formulated text entitled 'Unsere Teilnahme an diesem Kriege' ('Our Participation in this War'); this was presented on 6 October 1939 in Gustav Krojanker's house in Jerusalem to a group of like-minded friends, including Gershom Scholem, Salli Hirsch, Benno Cohn, Alfred Berger, Georg Landauer, Max Kreutzberger and Robert Weltsch. In this text, Jonas called for the establishment of a Jewish army, and for all young Palestinian Jews to fight against the "principle of Nazism". This principle, he declared, was fundamentally opposed to Judaism, which

[8]See for example the poem written by Jonas and Polotsky entitled '25. August 1917–1937', Scholem papers, commemorating the day on which the German authorities classified Scholem as "permanently unfit for active duty; not to be examined further" (Gershom Scholem, *From Berlin to Jerusalem*, New York 1980, p. 104f.) in response to his feigned mental illness. The poem is published in Wiese, *Hans Jonas,* p. 68f.

[9]Jonas, *Erinnerungen*, pp. 164f. On Scholem's love of sweets see Jonas's poem of 5 December 1939, published *ibid.*, p. 165.

was an embodiment of humanism and the strongest ally of Western culture; if Jews did not fight the Germans and their "cult of power and contempt of humanity" German hatred would end in the annihilation of the Jewish people.[10]

Although Scholem expressed strong support for Jonas's position,[11] he did not draw identical personal conclusions. Jonas volunteered to join the British Army, postponing his academic goals in order to fight against the Nazis. On 7 September 1939 he wrote the following letter to the supreme command of the British forces in Palestine:

> In view of the fact that the British Empire is now engaged in a war against Nazi Germany which is bound to last—to quote the words of the Prime Minister—"till Hitlerism is destroyed", as a Palestinian and former German Jew I am eager to take up arms against the enemy of my people and not only to assist the British Forces in Palestine but to fight as a soldier on the Western front in Europe. I should be grateful to you if you would let me know where I am to enlist for military training.[12]

The same month Jonas became a member of the British army's First Palestine Anti-Aircraft Battery and, for several years, participated in defending Haifa's oil refineries against air strikes by Vichy troops from Lebanon and Syria; later he was stationed in Cyprus. In 1943 Jonas became a member of the newly established "Jewish Brigade Group" within the British Army. In this capacity, he participated in the campaign against Mussolini in Italy and, in 1945, march into Germany. There, in the country of his birth, upbringing, and humanistic education, he discovered that his mother had been murdered in Auschwitz.[13] Jonas's experiences in the Second World War and the direct impact upon him of the Nazi Holocaust were to serve as a powerful impetus to his thinking and a crucial biographical element within his ethics of responsibility—an element closely tied to his philosophy's Jewish dimension. In a letter to Scholem written from Germany, Jonas emphasised the importance he attached to his involvement in the war against Hitler: "Now that everything lies behind me and I'm looking back upon things, I am able to say, at full peace with myself, that I don't regret what I have done. If the same situation should occur again … I would do the same thing."[14]

The friendship between Hans Jonas and Gershom Scholem remained strong throughout the war. On 15 August 1940, in the course of an evening spent together in the Jerusalem house of the publisher Salman Schocken, Jonas presented a literary piece he had written and named '*Aus einem ungedruckten Fragment*

[10]For the complete text and a discussion of the impact of Jonas's wartime experience on his philosophy, see Wiese, *Hans Jonas*, pp. 34–61.

[11]See *idem*, '"Ein 'Bellum Judaicum' in des Wortes tiefster Bedeutung" – Hans Jonas' Kriegsaufruf 1939 im Kontext seiner Biographie und seines philosophischen Denkens', in *LBI-Almanach* 2001, Frankfurt am Main 2000, pp. 92–107, here pp. 96f.

[12]Papers of Hans Jonas, Philosophy Archives of the University of Konstanz (henceforth Jonas papers), HJ 13–40–37.

[13]See Jonas, *Erinnerungen*, pp. 208–214 and 215–222; Morris Beckman, *The Jewish Brigade. An Army with two Masters 1944–45*, Staplehurst 1988.

[14]Jonas to Scholem, 20 June 1945.

zum Zauberberg von Thomas Mann' ('From an Unpublished Fragment of Thomas Mann's *Magic Mountain*'). Imitating Mann's style and borrowing the main characters of his novel, Jonas here offered a portrait of Scholem, depicting the Jonas-Scholem friendship through a dialogue between the "stranger" (Scholem) and Settembrini (Jonas himself) observed by two witnesses, the cousins Hans Castorp and Joachim:

> When the two cousins came near the crossroads, they became aware of the noise from a seemingly very lively, if not to say heated, conversation that was growing louder and louder, a conversation in which the familiar, melodious voice of their friend Settembrini appeared to have a lot of trouble asserting itself against a reckless organ of thoroughly unhumanistic querulousness and torrent-like rhetorical rapidity and plenitude. And now Settembrini's voice was completely drowned, like an exhausted swimmer surrendering to the superior strength of the raging elements, his head remaining longer and longer under water. An already scarcely audible interjection by Settembrini, maybe only the attempt at one, had just been silenced by the stranger's strained, impatient cry: "Would you please let me finish speaking!" The stranger then promptly—if by no means smoothly but rather with drawn-out vowels and expletives like "thingamajig"—proceeded to exploit his thus-gained right of being the only speaker. No, this was not the kind of dialogue the old dialogic protagonists had so often engaged in up here with paedagogic intent before youths thirsty for knowledge. This certainly had nothing to do with the fierce, but elegant duel, characterised by unwritten rules, in which, with strenuous politeness or restrained malicious pleasure, one opponent would allow the other to finish speaking in order to then commence a sober counter-argument certain of being able to expect the same consideration as had the other man—in a word, it had nothing to do with the estimable convention of civilised conversation, the mother of freedom and progress according to Settembrini. "Over there my friend Settembrini's in trouble", Hans Castorp thought and quickened his pace in pleasurably tense excitement, while reminding Joachim, who was reluctantly keeping pace, how they had first encountered the small sharp-witted Naphta accompanied by Settembrini at almost this very spot. Presently they caught sight of both figures, and, coming nearer, Hans Castorp could satisfy his curiosity about the stranger. Did we say "stranger"? Indeed, a stranger appearance had hardly ever been seen here. Pacing up and down with long legs describing a slight outward movement, so that they endowed the entire figure with a kind of lurching quality; gesticulating with long arms and enormous hands, one hand playing its own game with an object that upon closer inspection turned out to be strips of paper alternately being rolled and unrolled with restless twisting movements; the upper body slightly bent forward, head jutting forth from the neck even more; with ears of dimensions not inferior to those of the other extremities—the figure of the stranger, although dressed in a lounge suit as is customary in the civilised Occident, had such a fantastical, we might even say fluttering, quality, probably because of his manifold rolling movements, that the friends would not have been surprised if at dusk he had unfolded blackish wings like a bat, flying away with swinging movements while darkness descended over the valley.
>
> But at first nothing of that sort happened, despite the contents of the stranger's talk being odd enough, appearing to move even more bizarre possibilities than these into the

> realm of the expectable and, so to speak, the self-evident. "It is well known", Hans Castorp heard him say just then, "it is well known that ghosts have no silhouette". At this point Settembrini managed, with fine-spun dignity, to observe that it was "well known" that reason knew nothing of ghosts, indeed did not wish to know anything of them, and happily had finally done away with this medieval superstition which had disgraced mankind for such a long time—at least, he added, for all those who took the progress and honour of humanity to heart. Disconcertingly, his opponent responded to these words, offered with noble warmth and as it were seeming to appeal to his better self and to evoke a common conviction placed higher than their different standpoints, with the single word "Backobst" ["dried fruit"], a word whose possible connection to the debated matter remained totally incomprehensible to the friends, but which in any case in some way, despite the irreproachable nature of the product of the fruit-processing industry that had been mentioned, was not perceived by Mr. Settembrini, rightly or wrongly, as a very flattering characterisation of his argument, this being revealed in a brief clouding of his otherwise pleasant face, indicating he had taken offence. However, he immediately overcame this trace of annoyance with striking elegance, setting about to introduce the gentlemen to each other, accentuating as pompously as possible—in the Italian manner—the status of those being introduced.[15]

Most immediately, this vignette reflects Jonas's *Bildung*, his deep roots—shared with the other German-Jewish intellectuals in Jerusalem and throughout the world—in German literature and culture. When it comes to his relationship with Scholem, the text offers good evidence of a forthright friendship in the Jerusalem years marked, of course, by humour and irony and involving the encounter of two strong characters—although, in Jonas's self-ironical portrait, a certain degree of domination on Scholem's part seems obvious.

Other, far more seriously oriented evidence of their friendship in fact suggests a profound emotional and intellectual relationship based on a common interest in Gnosticism and early Jewish Mysticism. Still, a close look at this evidence also points to a certain distance, perhaps reflected in the fact that Jonas and Scholem never address each other with the familiar *Du* but maintain the formal *Sie* throughout their correspondence. In 1942 Scholem presented Jonas with a copy of his recently published *Major Trends in Jewish Mysticism* and included the following handwritten dedication in German: "For my Gnostic colleague / as a warning accompaniment/ when he descends further / into the depths of the void/ a small treatise /about mysticism and dialectics/ dedicated in friendship / by the analytic and unanalysed author. – G. Scholem, Jerusalem, 8.3.1942." On 15 January 1943 while Jonas's unit was stationed near Haifa, Scholem sent him a second copy with another dedication and a poem containing a cautious confession with regard to the ambiguous effect on his personal thinking of his scholarly research on Jewish mysticism. With its expression of loneliness, alienation and indeed suffering in face of the strange religious worlds he was treating, this poem offered Jonas a rare glimpse into Scholem's normally hidden inner life:

[15]A copy of the text is located in the Scholem papers.

I threw myself into ancient books,
I was awestruck by their signs.
I spent too much time alone with them.
I could no longer leave them behind.

The glimmer of truth is ancient,
Yet disaster is unforeseen:
Generations are weakly linked,
And knowledge is not clean.

I have brought back the blurred face
Of the Fullness of time.
I was ready to leap into the abyss,
But was I really primed?

The ancestral symbols are here explained;
The Kabbalist was no dope,
But what transformed time proposes
Remains foreign, beyond our scope.

Time transformed casts us a fearsome glance,
For it is unwilling to turn back again.
Yet abandoned joys grow palpable
Once your Vision has dissolved in pain.

(To Hans Jonas, my Gnostic colleague, for him to heed when descending into the depths of nothingness and when ascending into the even more unknown, presented in friendship by Gerhard Scholem.)[16]

Jonas answered in a rather agitated letter of thanks dated 4 February 1943, sent from Haifa:

> Dear Scholem, how could I possibly thank you? I have never before been given such a present, and I will hardly find an appropriate expression for the emotion I feel whenever I read the generous and wonderful confession you have honoured me with. I am happy that you chose my copy for it, and even more so that I now seriously know what has so often preoccupied me and others as a question—partly out of "curiosity", partly as a pressing intellectual concern linked with the phenomenon "Scholem". From my personal viewpoint I could say: worried me. For you are certainly aware that your intellectual

[16]A copy of the two dedications is located in the Scholem papers. The English translation is taken from Gershom Scholem, *The Fullness of Time. Poems*, transl. by Richard Sieburth, introduced and annotated by Steven M. Wasserstrom, Jerusalem 2003, pp. 109–111. For an interpretation of Scholems poems, see Sigrid Weigel, 'Scholems Gedichte und seine Dichtungstheorie. Klage, Adressierung, Gabe und das Problem einer biblischen Sprache in unserer Zeit', in Stéphane Mosès and Sigrid Weigel (eds.), *Gershom Scholem. Literatur und Rhetorik*, Cologne 2000, pp. 16–47.

> existence as such, not only your research-life with its scholarly results, through which it manifests itself while at the same time barricading itself behind it, means a deep challenge for our time—the "transformed time"; a challenge that many would like to take up, if only it could be encountered in a straightforward (may I say: unambiguous), palpable manner, whether in a confessional form or one suitable for dialogue. That barricading of oneself within the object of research, legitimate as it is, (and binding, if not through its object, then in any case through the objectivity of cognition)—instructive and obstructive at once, both hint and masquerade (and to this extent something like a symbol-reality in the authentic sense)—renders it difficult even to simply ascertain the explicit *terms* [word in English in original] of the "grappling" with an issue. At least the direct sort [of grappling]: the indirect sort has to pursue the same "symbolical" path as your thesis (or challenge)—and this path of immanent self-declaration and hence of veiled speech and response is indeed taken by the rest of us as well, each in his own way and with his own (more modest) means, involuntarily or intentionally—each one of us does this in his specific field when confronting history by researching and interpreting it. But as you know, precisely in regard to yourself, the mystery of the relation between the scholar and his object, in your case a more *legitimate* interest, a sharper question, than in most other cases, has for a long time been a favourite object of partly humorous suppositions (with corresponding formulations), partly of serious questions and deep reflection: but all of these, I think, are in the end an expression of the same worry I mentioned above with respect to myself. All of this does not "entice" you out of your shell. Which understanding person would not wish to honour the self discipline, the restraint, of the scholar, and at the same time the discretion [*Verschwiegenheit*] indeed the aloofness of the person (*I* see your talkativeness in this light) and shrink from direct questions? But [our] need and waiting remain: and there are moments in the history of a mind [*Geschichte eines Geistes*] when, after all the insights [*Erkenntnisse*] one has received, one desires a confession [*Bekenntnis*] where at least a corner of the curtain might be lifted and the latent standpoint declared in a new, more immediate approximation, in the language of trust—for the sake of one's own soul and that of one's friends. Your dedicatory poem did this for me. You will forgive me if for the time being I postpone the only worthy answer to which it obligates my feeling – the *response* emerging from my centre.[17]

Unfortunately, as most of Scholem's letters to Jonas from this period are lost, we do not know whether he responded to this letter. Nor do we know whether there was, for instance, a subsequent deepening dialogue between Jonas and Scholem concerning the personal dimension of research on Jewish history and traditions, or if this letter marked a culmination of shared confidentiality. It seems, however, that the degree of frankness and emotional openness expressed in both Scholem's dedication and Jonas's letter of thanks is unique in the history of their friendship. Scholem's openness was much more veiled and "symbolic" in nature than was Jonas's—after all, he discusses his feelings through a dedicatory poem, while along with expressing thanks, Jonas speaks of his suffering because of Scholem's aloofness, his hiding of his real thoughts and feelings behind a scholarly mask.

[17] Jonas to Scholem, 4 February 1943.

At the same time the two texts illustrate what Jonas means when, in his recently published memoirs, he ponders the "unsolved enigma of Scholem": the question posed by all his Jerusalem friends, namely whether "Scholem himself had a relationship of faith with Judaism": "What did he believe? How much did he want to believe but could not believe? He has never expressed himself clearly with respect to this question."[18] Jonas's confusion with respect to Scholem's personal relation to Judaism and the Jewish religion, beyond his Zionism and his immersion in the history and literature of Jewish mysticism, corresponds precisely to Joseph Dan's observation that even in his autobiographical writings Scholem was most reluctant to display personal motivations and feelings.[19] What Jonas describes in his letter as Scholem's "secrecy"—at least partially abandoned in his poem, with its references to a personal religious search, a fascination with mystical texts and a concomitant disillusionment with and estrangement from mysticism—has itself been interpreted by later critics as revealing confusion with respect to the relation between religious traditions and secular modernity. What is clear is that Scholem's devotion to the study of Jewish mysticism was inspired by a rejection of assimilation and a correspondingly strong sense of the neglect suffered by the irrational, mystical currents within Jewish tradition. Scholem appears to have become increasingly intrigued by the subject of his research, although without having developed mystical inclinations of his own.[20]

In trying to come to grips with such a complex personal and intellectual position, scholars have tended to oscillate between the opinion that Scholem perceived the Kabbalah in a completely detached way, that is, as a strictly historical phenomenon, and the opinion voiced by Theodor W. Adorno, according to whom "the mystical spark [must have] ignited in [Scholem] himself",[21] and by Ernst Simon, according to whom Scholem's silence with regard to God implied a hidden confession of faith, a kind of "indirect communication".[22] Scholem would only directly address the implicit ambivalence of his own attitude in his later essays and interviews. In a biographical interview he gave in 1973–1974 to Muki Tsur, he described himself as a religious (as opposed to atheistic) anarchist[23] who did not believe in a Torah handed down to Moses on Mount Sinai. Scholem similarly distanced himself from atheism, indicating that he did not even consider himself a secularist: "My secularism fails right at the core, owing to the fact that I am a religious person, because I am sure of my belief in God. My secularism is not secular." Despite his strictly historical approach to Jewish mysticism, he said, he shared the fundamental feeling of the Kabbalists "that there is a mystery—a secret—in the world".[24]

[18]Jonas, *Erinnerungen*, p. 270.

[19]Joseph Dan, *Gershom Scholem and the Mystical Dimension of Jewish History*, New York–London 1987, pp. 5–16.

[20]For the development of Scholem's interpretation of Jewish Mysticism, see David Biale, *Kabbalah and Counterhistory*, Cambridge, MA–London 1979, especially pp. 113–128; and Eliezer Schweid, *Judaism and Mysticism According to Gershom Scholem. A Critical Analysis and Programmatic Discussion*, Atlanta GA 1985.

[21]Theodor W. Adorno, 'Gruß an Gershom G. Scholem. Zum 70. Geburtstag', in *Neue Zürcher Zeitung*, 2 December 1967.

[22]Ernst Simon, 'Über einige theologische Sätze von Gershom Scholem', in *Mitteilungsblatt des Irgun Olej Merkas Europa*, 8 December 1972, pp. 3–5, and 15 December 1972, pp. 4–6.

[23]'With Gershom Scholem: An Interview', in Gershom Scholem, *On Jews and Judaism in Crisis*, ed. by Werner J. Dannhauser, New York 1976, pp. 1–48, here p. 35.

[24]*ibid.*, pp. 46, 48.

Without of course being intended as such, the following statement by Scholem regarding the relationship between faith and scholarship in his research on mysticism sounds like a belated response to Jonas's own response to the poem Scholem had dedicated to him:

> The fact that I addressed myself to Kabbalah not merely as a chapter of history but from a dialectical distance—from [a point of] identification and distance at the same time—might stem from the fact that I had the feeling that Kabbalah had a living centre, that it expressed itself in a way appropriate to that generation, but that in another form it could perhaps have said something else in another generation. Something unknown of this sort must have motivated me beyond all the philological games and masquerades at which I excel. I can understand that something of this sort inspired my secularist listeners the way it inspired me.[25]

There is no evidence that Scholem ever formulated such a response, conceding "games and masquerades", in personal exchanges with Jonas. It is actually not at all clear whether Scholem and Jonas, after cautiously touching on religion, faith, doubt, secularism and modernity, ever continued a conversation on such topics, and indeed whether Jonas ever read Scholem's later texts. But Scholem's essay of 1974 entitled 'Reflections on Jewish Theology' does display a strikingly strong affinity with Jonas's theological thinking.[26] Despite occasionally different emphasis and although Scholem could rely on an incomparably greater degree of Jewish knowledge, both he and Jonas were concerned with the loss of tradition's authority, the relevance of Judaism in a secularised technological world, and the meaning of the Holocaust for Jewish thought. And Scholem and Jonas came to remarkably similar conclusions.

In the first place, both scholars felt a strong but sometimes ambiguous commitment to Judaism. Despite his strong sense of Jewish identity rooted in his Zionist convictions, Jonas did not want to be understood as a Jewish philosopher; rather, he explains in his memoirs that:

> From the moment I started to think independently, my relationship to Judaism was as ambiguous as probably the relation of any modern contemporary Jew to the Jewish heritage, at least if he does not simply abandon and forget it. I was deeply moved by the Bible, and at the same time I did not believe. I did not possess the belief in a personal God, the creator of Heaven and Earth, who had divided the Red Sea and thundered from Mount Sinai, but I thought that certain parts of the Bible contained something tremendously important for humanity to which I felt deeply committed. … How this attachment to Judaism is linked with my general world-view always remained somewhat unclear to me. … Again and again, I perceived something unique, enigmatic, mysterious and binding in Jewish history … something that was even deeper and more important than my Zionist belief. I could imagine rethinking my Zionism, but I find detaching myself from the *b'rith*, from the covenant between God and Israel, unimaginable—even if the notion of the divine partner in this covenant has remained completely inscrutable

[25] *ibid.*, p. 46 (translation modified).

[26] Gershom Scholem, 'Reflections on Jewish Theology' in *idem*, *On Jews and Judaism*, pp. 261–297; for a more detailed interpretation, see Wiese, *Hans Jonas*, pp. 154–166.

> to me. There is a mystery that binds us all together, beyond the time-bound, private, personal positions according to which we spiritually and consciously act.[27]

This passage has an obvious similarity to Scholem's statement "that there is a mystery – a secret – in the world"; it is perhaps Jonas's clearest and most personal description of his attitude towards Judaism. Beyond Jonas's ambiguity, it points to his sharing with Scholem of the *ambivalence* felt by many secular Jewish intellectuals regarding traditional Jewish rituals and patterns of faith: an ambivalence to which they sometimes responded by developing personal forms of Jewish identity and personal ideas of Jewish relevance. Jonas's motif of "mystery" extends beyond mere connotations of the "enigmatic", aiming at a transcendent dimension that demands reverence and responsibility. For his part, Scholem indicates in 'Reflections on Jewish Theology' that, although rejecting atheism, he does not belong to those fortunate people with a "positive theology of an inflexible Judaism";[28] he ponders over the tension existing in his view between secular modernity, with its philological and historical approach to Jewish history and literature, and the claim staked by Jewish tradition to an authority rooted in revelation, between scholarly research and the notion of the "Torah as the absolute word".[29]

From Scholem's perspective, traditional Jewish religion has lost its binding character; but he considers belief in God's existence to be unaffected by this loss of authority, since Judaism can "be regarded as entirely independent of Revelation"—for example in the acceptance of the idea of the creation of the world by God "out of nothing".[30] In modern times, he maintains, the affirmation of God's existence, and the religious and moral consequences of this, have often been translated into philosophical convictions. These possess "the value of provocations which may perhaps prove themselves indissoluble in the melting pot of modern nihilism and full of future possibilities".[31]

Scholem's observation would appear to correspond quite closely to Jonas's sense of a Jewish-Christian continuum within Western philosophy.[32] It also seems to share the hope embedded in Jonas's religious philosophy that despite secularism, the philosophical plausibility of central elements of the Jewish faith – especially the notion of the sanctity of life and the creation of man in the image of God—still have the power to oppose nihilistic world-views: to establish an ethic of responsibility in an age stamped, as a result of human technological power, by threats to earthly life itself.[33]

[27] Jonas, *Erinnerungen*, pp. 339–341.

[28] Gershom Scholem, 'Reflections on Jewish Theology', p. 261.

[29] *ibid.*, p. 271. It should be noted that such a tension is central to the history of the *Wissenschaft des Judentums* (its historical orientation and methods perceived as a threat by Jewish traditionalists), from which Scholem's own scholarly enterprise in part emerges.

[30] *ibid.*, pp. 276f.

[31] *ibid.*, p. 276.

[32] Hans Jonas, 'Jewish and Christian Elements in the Western Philosophical Tradition', in *Commentary*, vol. 44, no. 5 (1967), pp. 61–68.

[33] As an example of Jonas's effort to ground his ethics of responsibility in Jewish values, see *idem*, 'Contemporary Problems in Ethics from a Jewish Perspective', in *Central Conference of American Rabbis Journal* vol. 15, no. 1(1968), pp. 27–39.

In the second place, Jonas and Scholem share a critical approach to Jewish messianism. In his *Imperative of Responsibility* Jonas offers a strong critique of Ernst Bloch's utopian thinking, which he condemns as irresponsible: such thinking, he argues, involves a fantasy menacing an urgently needed politics of humility and technological self-restriction—hence potentially menacing human life itself.[34] Jonas entirely rejected messianism since he understood it as an attempt to escape a necessary acknowledgment of the ambiguity, fragility and radical mortality of human life.[35] Whenever Jonas links his own ethics to Jewish thinking, he thus draws not on concepts of messianism and redemption but on that of creation and the sanctity of life. In contrast, Gershom Scholem devoted much space and thought to the phenomenon of Jewish messianism, which he appreciated as an important, driving element within Jewish tradition;[36] at the same time, in the framework of that appreciation, he spelled out his sense of that messianism's political dangers in a now-famous passage:

> Little wonder that overtones of Messianism have accompanied the modern Jewish readiness for irrevocable action in the concrete realm, when it set out on the utopian return to Zion. This readiness no longer allows itself to be fed on hopes. Born out of the horror and destruction that was Jewish history in our own generation, it is bound to history itself and not to meta-history; it has not given itself up totally to Messianism. Whether or not Jewish history will be able to endure this entry into the concrete realm without perishing in the crisis of the Messianic claim, which has virtually been conjured up—that is the question which out of his great and dangerous past the Jew of this age poses to his present and to his future.[37]

Scholem also voiced a scepticism regarding secular, utopian, and apocalyptic forms of Jewish messianism in general, in a manner appearing to echo Jonas's own preoccupations:

> It is one of the peculiarities of the present age that the idea of Redemption, either in its pure form or in its secularised metamorphoses, has been maintained much more vigorously in the mind of wide circles than, for instance, the idea of Creation. The very people who talk most loudly about Redemption and its implication are often enough those who want to hear least of Creation. Yet no Jewish theology whatever can renounce the doctrine that the world is a creation—as a one-time event or as a continual always self-renewing process. ... The Jewish faith in God as Creator will maintain its place, beyond all images and myths, when it is a matter of choosing an alternative: the world as a Creation and the world as something that creates itself by chance.[38]

[34]Hans Jonas, *The Imperative of Responsibility. In Search of an Ethics for the Technological Age*, Chicago–London 1984, pp. 178–204; see Michael Löwy, 'Ernst Blochs "Prinzip Hoffnung" versus Hans Jonas' "Prinzip Verantwortung"', in Wiese and Jacobson (eds.), pp. 290–300.

[35]See for example Hans Jonas, 'The Burden and Blessing of Mortality', in *idem*, *Mortality and Morality*, pp. 87–98; and 'Immortality and the Modern Temper', *ibid.*, pp. 115–130.

[36]See, for example, several of the contributions in Gershom Scholem, *The Messianic Idea in Judaism and Other Essays On Jewish Spirituality*, New York 1971.

[37]*idem*, "Toward an Understanding of the Messianic Idea", *ibid.*, pp. 1–36, here p. 36.

[38]*idem*, 'Reflections on Jewish Theology', p. 277.

Jonas would certainly have endorsed Scholem's insistence that "God as Creator" is much more important than "God in his capacity as Revealer or Redeemer" and that it would be possible "to imagine a theology in which the only Revelation is the Creation itself".[39] Still, a certain difference with Jonas emerges when Scholem insists on the need, in response to the challenges of modern technology and modern nihilism, for a specifically religious ethics of creation. Jonas had argued similarly in lectures to Jewish audiences in the United States; but later, apparently from a sense that he had to convince a secular generation out of touch with religious thinking, he attempted to provide a universal philosophical foundation for his responsibility-centred ethics, omitting any reference to the concept of the "sanctity of life".[40]

Scholem's strong emphasis on the opposition between religious and secular ethics left little space for Jonas's effort to establish an ethical system based on an inner teleology of nature. Jonas, on the basis of a "philosophy of life", postulated a non-religious foundation for the "sanctity of life", claiming that humanity had to "learn fear and trembling again and, even without God, a respect for the sacred".[41] Without necessarily knowing this text, Scholem explicitly contradicted Jonas's conviction: "The secularizing talk of the 'sanctity of life' is a squaring of the circle. It smuggles an absolute value into a world which could never have formed it out of its own resources, a value pointing surreptitiously to a teleology of Creation which is, after all, disavowed by a purely naturalistic rationalistic view of the world."[42] In any potential dialogue held between Scholem and Jonas in heaven—despite Jonas's personal views concerning mortality— this issue would certainly play a paramount role. Philosophical differences between the two men notwithstanding, Jonas would certainly have agreed with Scholem's conviction that religion could play an important role in a "technological world" in which humanity often appeared "a helpless instrument of overpowering forces, and at the same time atomized and isolated, standing unprotected in the face of the loneliness and senselessness which oppress and suffocate him".[43] Confronted with what they perceived as a science-engendered loss of the sense of a magical cosmos and even of the value of human life, both Jonas and Scholem hoped to reinvigorate conceptual categories tied to reverence, sanctity and mystery: Jonas through his personal faith in a Creator who has relinquished his power (see below); Scholem through both the stress he laid on the basic sensibility of Jewish mysticism and his warning not to lose that sensibility.[44]

Finally, there are striking parallels between the theological concepts held by Jonas and Scholem. Both men felt deeply challenged, morally, intellectually, personally, by the Holocaust and were convinced that traditional Jewish theology did not provide any real response to what it signified. In 1984, two years after Scholem's death, Jonas

[39]*ibid.*, p. 279.

[40]Jonas, *Imperative of Responsibility*, pp. 22–25. For a discussion of the relation of secular and Jewish elements in Jonas's ethics, see Christian Wiese, '"Weltabenteuer Gottes" und Heiligkeit des Lebens', in Wiese and Jacobson (eds.), pp. 202–221.

[41]Hans Jonas, 'Mikroben, Gameten und Zygoten. Weiteres zur neuen Schöpferrolle des Menschen', in *idem*, *Technik, Medizin und Ethik. Zur Praxis des Prinzips Verantwortung*, Frankfurt am Main 1985, pp. 204–218, here p. 218.

[42]Scholem, 'Reflections on Jewish Theology', p. 290.

[43]*ibid.*, p. 291.

[44]See, for example, Scholem, 'With Gershom Scholem', p. 48.

delivered his famous lecture, 'The Concept of God after Auschwitz', dedicated to his murdered mother. The Holocaust, he maintained, had destroyed traditional theological concepts, in particular that of a powerful God acting in history. In place of such a historical agent, Jonas suggested the presence of a divine being who, for the sake of human freedom, had relinquished his power at some point in the evolutionary process: in other words, a powerless, suffering God who was himself at risk of experiencing the failure and destruction of his creation, completely incapable of intervening in human affairs, completely dependent on human responsibility. Now unmistakably, in his attempt to justify his views on the basis of Jewish tradition, Jonas was relying on Scholem's detailed, deeply influential description of Lurianic Kabbalah, and especially his analysis of the concept of *tzimtzum* at work in that mystic system.[45] But Jonas, making use of his own speculative, evolution-centred myth, radicalised the idea of God's self-limitation in the process of creation, divesting it of its messianic elements in order to accentuate the creator's utter powerlessness and humanity's radical responsibility for God's "world-adventure": the project of life created by a God endangered by his own creation.

From his deeply informed historical perspective, Scholem would probably have been highly critical of such a variation on Lurianic Kabbalah. In his 'Reflections on Jewish Theology', he did concede that "in the face of the concrete experience of the Hitler years—which affected our lives as Jews in such an overwhelming, unfathomable manner, and in one which basically is probably unthinkable as well", the "existential situation" facing Jews had completely changed, so that Jewish tradition could no longer simply be handed down without its reinterpretation.[46] In this context, Scholem cited the tradition of Lurianic Kabbalah—in order to emphasise that its world view had been completely destroyed by the Holocaust. In an implicit contrast to the philosophy espoused by Jonas, Scholem does *not* see the concept of *tzimtzum* as involving God turning away from affairs of the human world; rather, he sees it as articulating a hope in divine providence and for the world's permanent re-creation and renewal. As Scholem describes it, *tzimtzum* was not conceived as a single act at the start of creation, but as a perpetually self-creating process in which "again and again a stream streams into the void, a 'something' of God":

> This, to be sure, is the point at which the horrifying experience of God's absence in our world collides irreconcilably and catastrophically with the doctrine of Creation that renews itself. The radiation of which the mystics speak and which is to attest to the Revelation of God in Creation—that radiation is no longer perceivable by despair. The emptying of the world to a meaningless void not illuminated by any ray of meaning or direction is the experience of him whom I would call the pious atheist.[47]

[45]See *idem*, *Major Trends in Jewish Mysticism*, Jerusalem 1941, pp. 240–282. In 'The concept of God after Auschwitz', p. 142, Jonas explicitly refers to Lurianic Kabbalah: "The mighty undercurrent of the Kabbalah, which Gershom Scholem in our days has brought to light anew, knows about a divine fate bound up with the coming-to-be with a world. There we meet highly original, very unorthodox speculations in whose company mine would not appear so wayward after all. Thus, for example, my myth at bottom only pushes further the idea of the tzimtzum, that cosmogonic centerconcept of the Lurianic Kabbalah."

[46]Scholem, 'Reflections on Jewish Theology', p. 262.

[47]*ibid.*, p. 283.

Unlike Jonas, Scholem did not spurn the messianic side of Judaism. But like Jonas, he reacted to the radical challenge to Judaism posed by the Holocaust by emphasising the need to abandon any hope for messianic redemption in favour of a focus on the existential and ethical meaning of God's creation. One of Scholem's most notable poems, 'To Ingeborg Bachmann. After her visit to the ghetto of Rome', written on 4 February 1967, underscored his sense that the Nazi genocide meant such a drastic break. In this poem, Scholem was responding to an essay by Bachmann from 1955 ('What I Saw and Heard in Rome') in which she inscribed a trace of hope into an imagined scene from Rome's old Jewish ghetto, which she had visited as a tourist: "It is not yet the evening of all days, but on the Day of Atonement everyone is pardoned in advance for an entire year." Reading this passage twelve years later, Scholem interpreted it as addressing a problematic messianic expectation refuted by Auschwitz's civilisational break; he responded to that message with an expression of sadness about the shattering of any hope for redemption:

In the ghetto you saw what few can see
and what memory too easily mislays:
That nothing that happens is entirely fulfilled,
that evening has not yet fallen on all the days.

It is the oldest of those ancient tidings
which we read in the prophet's words.
We Jews have always remembered this news,
though the price we paid has been absurd.

We have existed in the rifts of history,
taking shelter in what is never quite closed.
The final day was the focus of those visions
from which in exile we drew our hopes.

For all days have an evening in the end.
Yet there was a promise of exemption:
The final evening, soothing us, consoling us,
ingathering all the rays of redemption.

So the spirit of Utopia spoke to us,
Where consolation darkly joins with fear.
But instead we fell into melancholy,
finding solace only in our tears.

Zion's messengers speak to us of elation,
but we can never quite return back home.
Though we were once filled with anticipation,
this call to homecoming cannot be restored.

The message that called us home
reached the ghetto far too late,
The hour of redemption is over,
the final day's decline – too plain.[48]

In its suggestion that the catastrophe of Auschwitz confronts Judaism and the Jewish people with a powerful moral-historical breach, this poetic expression of post-messianic "melancholy" and disillusionment appears to endow Jonas's insistent rejection of Jewish messianism with a much deeper resonance—one implicit if not explicit in Jonas's own writings. We cannot know how Scholem might have reacted to Jonas's concept of divine powerlessness. It seems clear enough in any event that had Jonas and Scholem ever confronted the concept in a personal dialogue, the theological and existential religious and philosophical impact of the Holocaust would have figured as a prominent theme. Unfortunately, all the pertinent documentation we have suggests a growing personal alienation between Jonas and Scholem—an alienation rendering highly unlikely any involved discussion of this or other crucial issues of the day.

II

It appears, then, that the cautious openness emerging in Jonas's and Scholem's initial encounter in Jerusalem—an openness finding its expression in their early personal correspondence—was not maintained after the dissolution of the "Pilegesch" circle in the 1940s and Jonas's emigration to Canada after the Second World War. Rather, unpublished sources suggest the development of a sharp conflict that would overshadow the relationship between these two scholars in an enduring way. What now remained was ambiguity: continued mutual affection expressed as a peculiar mixture of kindness, irony and permanent controversy.[49] But even this distanced form of friendship would eventually be burdened by increasing dissonance, partly resulting from different temperaments, partly from diverging experiences in Israel and in Canada, and later on to an ever-greater degree, from openly expressed disagreement regarding the correct interpretation of religious history.

At the start, however, the main issue separating Jonas and Scholem was how to define loyalty to Zionism and to the recently established Jewish state. Jonas had returned to Palestine in November 1945 after a long period of military service and after having spent long depressing months in Germany as part of the British occupation forces. For two years he lived in the Arab village of Issawyje near Jerusalem, offering a few lecture courses at the Hebrew University and teaching history and philosophy at the English Council of Higher Studies. Since there was no permanent position open at the Hebrew University, Jonas began to consider other

[48]Scholem, *The Fullness of Time*, pp. 122–125. See the interpretation of this and Bachmann's poem in Sigrid Weigel, *Ingeborg Bachmann. Hinterlassenschaften unter Wahrung des Briefgeheimnisses*, Vienna 1999, pp. 5–15.

[49]Jonas, *Erinnerungen*, pp. 268f.

alternatives. Upon being drafted for military service at the very start of the Israeli-Arab war of 1948, aged 45, having already spent five years fighting in the war against Germany, he decided to accept a grant from the Lady Davis Foundation to teach at McGill University. He arrived with his family in Montreal in August 1949, moved on to Ottawa in 1951, and in 1955 was offered a chair in philosophy at the New School for Social Research in New York.

It would have been clear to Jonas that his decision to opt for Diaspora security over Zionist ideals would not find the approval of most of his Jerusalem friends, including Gershom Scholem, and that the Hebrew University would interpret his decision as a betrayal by an old Zionist.[50] Jonas's farewell to both those ideals and his dream of teaching at the Hebrew University had not been an easy one; it had come as a complete surprise to Scholem. In his first several letters from Canada, Jonas had expressed his homesickness for Jerusalem and had asked about his prospects of being offered a chair at the university.[51] Following the death of Julius Guttmann on 19 May 1950 and looking ahead to the retirement of Hugo Bergman in 1952, Scholem expressed a great deal of optimism regarding Jonas receiving a chair in the foreseeable future.[52] In December 1950 he encouraged Jonas to "assiduously continue" his research in Canada, "in order to prepare yourself in this way for the Jerusalem career that awaits you." Scholem proffered the advice to "do something for your Hebrew heart, so that you don't forget your Tora, which you will then need to convey in melodious Hebrew to men and maidens—for the latter are flooding our lecture-halls at present". He also informed Jonas that the third individual to hold a chair in philosophy, Leon Roth, would soon "retire to private life in England" and that Nathan Rotenstreich would presumably take the position. If three professorships in philosophy were to be retained, two additional chairs would be open in 1952, "and you are one of the two gentlemen who will be under consideration".[53]

In 1951 Scholem informed Jonas that although Jerusalem colleagues doubted he really wanted to return, he, Scholem, had defended him as a faithful Zionist and suggested in his official capacity that the university offer him a professorship.[54] On 17 May 1951 he was able to inform Jonas that the philosophy department had officially decided to appoint him, adding "I congratulate you and wish that our friendly relations may continue."[55] A short time later, Jonas received a letter from

[50]For the strongly Zionist character of the Hebrew University at that time, see David N. Myers, *Re-Inventing the Jewish Past. The European Jewish Intellectuals' Zionist Return to History*, New York 1995.

[51]Jonas to Scholem, 24 April 1950 and 28 July 1950 (in this letter Jonas writes: "I would like to make completely clear that my aim is Jerusalem, not Ottawa.").

[52]Scholem to Jonas, 22 May 1950 (private possession of Lore Jonas). Scholem continues: "Since to my bitter disappointment Leo Strauss has declined to come back at all (he would have had the choice between two or three professorships)—in Chicago we received an entirely different impression of his positive readiness to come over—we now have to look around elsewhere. ... In any case the whole question of the new appointments in philosophy is open, and I do not need to tell you that your name is not in the least danger of being forgotten in these discussions."

[53]Scholem to Jonas, 10 December 1950 (private possession of Lore Jonas). Scholem thus advised Jonas "urgently" "to keep himself free if at all possible and take on no duties" for autumn 1952, "without clarifying with us beforehand if the matter is certain".

[54]Jonas, *Erinnerungen*, p. 265.

[55]Scholem to Jonas, 17 May 1951 (private possession of Lore Jonas).

Hugo Bergman offering him a professorship in philosophy. In his memoirs, Jonas indicates that the offer sparked an "inner struggle" and that he finally turned it down for a combination of "reasonable and egoistic but morally appropriate" reasons: he wanted his two young children to grow up in security and not endure either "a Spartan life of privation" or death in one of the wars he was sure would follow ("and this," Jonas adds, "after having experienced the death of my brother-in-law in one of them"); having finally succeeded in finding an academic position, he was now in a position to write and teach freed from "public affairs or crises"—and unburdened by "the spectre of Hebrew", a language he felt he had never fully mastered; finally, he simply could not bear the thought of one more "new beginning".[56] In a rather long letter written (despite his own self-doubts in this respect) in Hebrew to Moshe Schwabe, the Hebrew University's rector, confirming the difficulty of his decision and expressing deep regret and the hope for some sort of continued relation with the university, Jonas indicated that the personal price for this chair and a life in Jerusalem would be too high for his family.[57] A copy of the letter—which Jonas later characterised as "clumsy" and "undiplomatic" in its directness[58]—was forwarded to Scholem.

As his correspondence with Jonas indicates, Scholem was shocked and deeply hurt by his decision and reacted harshly, accusing Jonas of having betrayed Zionism, as well as of abandoning his solidarity with both Israel and the Hebrew University. Jonas anticipates Scholem's reaction in a letter dated 10 October 1951:

> Dear Scholem, I had meant to write to you for a long time and the fact that I postponed it again and again has to do with the content of this letter. As long as my painful deliberations hadn't led to a conclusion, I did not feel strong enough for an epistolary encounter with you, the main supporter of my appointment. That I finally decided the way I did at least ends the situation of uncertainty, and while it probably first leaves me open to the entire strength of your displeasure, deeply involved as you are, it nonetheless allows *me*, in awareness of my good reasons, to have a normal relationship with you again. As I already wrote to Bergman, I hope that despite all the disappointment I had to inflict on them, my friends treat me justly, although I disappointed them. In your letter—by now half a year old—you expressed your conviction that in view of my past, I would be prepared to share the life of the people there on the same conditions. This may be the case for me personally – although I'm honest enough to add: only to a certain degree, when one is to decide in favour of the situation from the outside and one is not already in it; but in my case, as you know the terms of the calculation have changed considerably over the past years due to the emergence of new factors. When I observe daily what it takes to raise children, and what stress it already places on Lore [Jonas's wife], who is not all that strong, in normal and smoothly functioning circumstances, then I don't dare imagine how the current conditions [in Israel] will have to affect *all* involved in the long run. This applies among other things to my opportunities for creative work, which I need to jealously protect after having sacrificed 10 of the best years of my life. This is only one side of the responsibility that I have to consider: I'm no longer travelling through life with

[56]Jonas, *Erinnerungen*, p. 265f.
[57]Jonas to Moshe Schwabe, the rector of Hebrew University, 3 October 1951.
[58]Jonas, *Erinnerungen*, p. 266.

the light luggage of earlier years. Material arrives by every letter, every report, from over there. [It has reached] the point where there's nothing more to deliberate over, or, rather, where I mustn't deliberate any further, for the sake of those directly affected by the decision. This is linked with my deepest sympathy for those who don't have any choice and who will have to endure all of that. To refuse to accept such an appointment cuts into one's soul: never has a "no" been more difficult for me—especially with regard to yourself, if I leave aside my own attachment to the matter, since you intervened on my behalf in a very personal way, and because you represent the absolute criterion valid beyond all [economic] deliberations. … Believe me, we have kept in touch with things over the last few months and are quite well informed. In the end the correct decision was clear—which doesn't mean it was easy—but we needed the *cumulative evidence* [words in English in original] emerging over the last weeks. May I assume that our friendship will not be affected by these developments?[59]

Unfortunately, the friendship was indeed affected, as is apparent in subsequent letters. In a letter dated 18 October 1951, apparently written before having received Jonas's letter, Scholem expressed his disappointment while still addressing Jonas's decision in a relatively conciliatory tone:

Dear Jonas, I wrote to you during the summer, when your appointment here became an issue, but I didn't receive any answer. I thus had to confine myself to waiting. … Yesterday, however, I received a copy of your letter to the rector in which you reject the offer of an appointment, arguing that you cannot expect your family to switch from normal living conditions to the anomalous ones prevailing here. … In the most painful way, your letter has surprised and affected all of us actively involved in bringing you back to Israel, i. e. mainly Bergman, Buber and myself. It was not the response that we had expected from you. …. It is not my task to offer any comments on a decision you have made after such serious deliberations. … You are not the first and will not be the last person to reject our offers in these times of crisis. … It is clear that in future years the university will need to depend entirely on itself and its own academic trainees. Our dreams will not evaporate because of this. Each individual who no longer comes here is of course, from his point of view, completely right, and I'm the last who would deny this. … I'm sending you and your wife my best wishes for the New Year and for your – henceforth – American future. Your old friend Gerhard Scholem.[60]

[59]Jonas to Scholem, 10 October 1951 (original in German). In an earlier letter Scholem had offered Jonas advice for survival in Israel: "Since nothing can be purchased one cannot live off one's salary but in case you do need somewhat more you can earn it through courses and lectures. You will after all want to share the life of the others around you who also manage to exist. The main thing is: bring everything you would need for your household, and I mean everything, and buy it [in advance]. … Hence refrigerator, washing machine, … all sorts of items from cooking pots … etc. to a *colour ribbon* for your typewriter, thread, needles and even nails. *At present* you would not find *any* of this here. Toiletries for all of you, for the children whatever you might be able to get hold of, even additional shoe-soles. … Let me finish with the remark that in fact none of us has come here in order to live especially easily, and as you have shown over many years, you are indeed one of us 'old ones'. (Scholem to Jonas, 17 May 1951, private possession of Lore Jonas.)

[60]Jonas papers, HJ 5–5–43 (original in German).

Although some bitterness does manage to seep through, this letter refrains from polemics and accusations; it was, however, followed by a much harsher letter, in which Scholem speaks of "disloyalty" and emphasises Jonas's ingratitude. Its gist is conveyed in the following passage:

> What particularly hurts me in this matter is that following the first chance ever of a permanent academic post at the university opening up for you, we offered you this position, and you nevertheless complain to others about the allegedly bad behaviour of the university as an additional reason for your behaviour. When I recently read this again in a letter from George Lichtheim, I did not trust my ears. No one can judge better than Bergman and myself if the university, within the limits of its capacity, has ever acted towards you in a way justifying such remarks, and I am thus very upset that you harbour such thoughts. It is not only that we did everything to prepare your candidacy, starting a long time ago; in the end it is also true that the fact you are now in Canada is a result of Ernst Simon's approach to Leo Strauss [Strauss had recommended Jonas to the Lady Davis Foundation for a grant] and of our intervention with the army. I cannot simply toss that aside. It is regrettable enough that you did not believe yourself able or obliged to seize the chance to return to Israel, and you offered both me and the university entirely different reasons for this. We truly did not need to embitter our lives further with additional alleged complaints far removed from the matter at hand.[61]

Jonas responded in a letter dated 6 February 1952:

> Dear Scholem! I'm astonished and dismayed by your letter, and I hasten to correct the misunderstandings. The reasons why I don't want to return *now* are those reasons, and exclusively those reasons, I mentioned in my letters, and at least Buber (in New York) was understanding and objective enough to accept them as my good right without moralising. … My reasons are of a temporary nature and I made clear that my decision—as far as my own intentions are concerned—is so as well, hoping (not very confidently but honestly) that the university might treat it as such and not as final, i.e. without necessarily prejudging the entire future. That is mainly and first of all a matter of attitude beyond foreseeable practical possibilities. I can't expect, for example, that in several years time, when my children are a little older, there will be another vacant position, and I will have to risk confronting the opposite situation but I may wish and hope that in such a case the university might still be interested in me—and therefore I may also wish, putting aside my relationship with my friends, that nobody [at the University] should react with annoyance to my behaviour. … To do anything more than touch on such hopes and prospects for the future would have been unsuitable at the moment of declining the offer, in view of the fact, which I am very aware of, that with even such a temporary "no" I have given up all claims. (Buber in any event discussed future possibilities with me in a very concrete manner). But what was there to read in my letter to the rector, not through hints but *expressis verbis*, was the direct contents of and only opinion expressed in my decision itself: namely that it relates only to present circumstances there in the land and here in my

[61]Scholem to Jonas, 2(?) January 1952 (date unreadable), private possession of Lore Jonas (original in German).

family, and directly to the date fixed by the university. … The real weight of your comments is directed at my purported "complaints". May I confirm that this complex matter, apparently conveyed to you imprecisely based on my *off the record* [words in English in original] remarks, has never played a role in how I have proceeded, either as a reason, or (even) as a (supplementary) justification, or as a positive factor in any way? If I brought up the past, this was done in order to state—in anticipation of the possibility that there might be something like a "trial" against me—that there is nothing in the past that binds me directly to the university, or in relation to it [*sic*], in an obligatory way, taking the decision out of my hands. It establishes the absence of a motive and not a motive. As far as the matter itself is concerned this is just an establishment of facts, not a complaint—but before I briefly go into the former I want to at least indicate that the above-mentioned anticipation was only too justified, as shown by the echoes emanating from Jerusalem, e.g. the admonitory and moralising tone of the letter that [the secretary] Posnansky wrote in the rector's name, a document you can look up in the *files* [word in English in original]. Buber, to whom I gave it to read, was outraged, and, going beyond that, termed it "untrue" or rather: the claim I was "the first who refused to return" was only true precisely in terms of the fact that I only named my real reasons in my justification [*daß ich eben allein meine wirklichen Gründe in meiner Begründung genannt habe*] and scorned their masking. But apparently one would have preferred something more melodious, or, as someone quite naïve—reporting the general displeasure people felt against me—expressed it: surely you could have come up with a more comprehensive justification! Our mutual source of information, George Lichtheim, summarised the reaction in Jerusalem (apparently it is that of our common friends after all) roughly as follows: my exaggerated esteem for the Canadian fleshpots is resented. I have to take on this *odium*, painful as it is, when it comes from friends whom I would have liked to have counted on to understand the less material motive, that someone past the middle of life, the first half of which was not used too well, wants to have a few years to work in good conditions, i.e. without the external losses through wear and tear to which my energy for work (as self-knowledge unfortunately tells me) would fall victim only too soon. But while I neither can nor wish to defend myself against the fleshpots-reproach, I can certainly discredit that of disloyalty from the start, and that is what the purported motive of resentment is really about, a resentment that does not exist. I have not lodged any complaint and have not spoken of "bad behaviour" by the university against me, but simply raised the objective fact that my 14 years in Jerusalem were spent outside and not inside the university's gates—and I am fully aware of the reasons for this. The validity of these reasons does not negate the fact, and the fact—itself no object of reproach—eliminates certain charges that could otherwise be levelled against me and lie heavily in the air. This concerns my relation to the institution, not to individual members. I regret that you believe you need to remind me of what I owe to several persons, since even without such a reminder I don't forget what you and Fanya, Ernst Simon and Toni [Ernst Simon's wife] have done for me—but I don't quite see what this has to do with my relation to the university: why it turns me into a debtor, probably even taking in my entire Canadian existence? (I would rather have been spared the invocation of your "intervention with the army"). Let me assure you that I am not ungrateful to you and others and that on the other hand I do not wish to draw up an account of mutual debt: I here simply want a *clean sheet* [words in English in original]—

> no recriminations from *either* side—in the hope that at some point something positive will be written on it. In this sense I am, with kindest regards to you and Fanya, your old friend Hans Jonas.[62]

The "complaints" Jonas refers to in his own quotation marks refer to the fact that Jonas had fruitlessly waited for many years for a Hebrew University position. In a letter to his friend Scholem on 15 October 1968, the historian George Lichtheim speculated that the real reason for this had been Jonas's ambivalent relationship with the Jewish faith. On 21 October 1968 Scholem responded as follows:

> Your assertion that Hans Jonas received no appointment in Jerusalem for 15 years because—as I am supposed to have told him then—"there is no room for atheists at the university" is total nonsense. And indeed in every respect. When the chance for a chair in Jewish philosophy came about after '33 (which I was originally meant to take up myself and from which I then voluntarily withdrew in the spring of '33—although the appointment had already been confirmed by a senate resolution—in order to make way for a German Jew), I spoke up emphatically for Leo Strauss—well-known to me as an atheist—to be appointed should Julius Guttmann not be able to come. In what serious context I would have uttered a sentence like the one you have put in my mouth, especially directed at a person I in no way considered an atheist (and as you yourself say, justly), is a complete mystery to me. The truth is, easily demonstrated as well, that at the University of Jerusalem, as a result of decisive opposition by Leon Roth, who had declared two professorships in philosophy to be too many already, a third chair could not be created for many years. Jonas was given whatever substitute appointments were possible, and the first additional professorship (as *associate professor* [words in English in original]) that was created, and this by request of a commission I myself was a part of, had been [sic] offered Hans Jonas (and not [the intellectual historian Nathan] Rotenstreich). The first door that opened in this field was opened for Jonas. That, and nothing else, is the recorded truth. That Jonas had already left Palestine by then, shortly after the end of the 1948 war, has nothing to do with either his atheism or other sinister machinations [*sinistre Machenschaften*]. Many of us regretted that he had not already been offered the position he deserved at an earlier point, just as they also regretted that Jonas then declined the professorship offered to him, in an incomprehensible manner. This has nothing to do with the theme of atheism and clerical rule in Israel.[63]

That there nevertheless might be a grain of truth in Lichtheim's speculation, even if it was much exaggerated, is suggested by one passage in Jonas's memoirs. In a conversation with Scholem held after the end of the Second World War, he recalls, Scholem had both maintained that an atheist should not teach at the Hebrew University and informed him that his research on Gnosticism was "too strongly inspired by Christianity"; he had also asked Jonas point blank if he believed in God. As Jonas views things in his memoirs, this was "somehow an inappropriate question

[62]Jonas to Scholem, 6 February 1952 (original in German).

[63]Gershom Scholem, *Briefe*, vol. 2 (1948–1970), ed. by Thomas Sparr, Munich 1995, pp. 216–217. Lichtheim's letter is not included in the English-language edition of Scholem's correspondence.

to be posed by one scholar to another", a "foolish question", one of Scholem's usual *faux pas*: "Scholem", Jonas recalls, "had a great talent for *faux pas*. He was able to say and do the most impossible things. And if later somebody made him explain himself, he either denied it with an '*ach*, I never said that' or claimed: 'that was simply meant as a joke'. I remember that I somehow got out of the question—I only remember it because I found it extremely inappropriate, but I don't remember my answer, which was probably very lame."[64]

It is important to note that although there was an element of bitterness in it, the dispute that broke out between Jonas and Scholem after Jonas's emigration had nothing to do with disagreement concerning Zionism, Israel or political practice; rather, it centred on a personal decision about whether to live in Israel or the Diaspora. That Jonas chose the latter option did not necessarily result from a revision of his Zionist principles, even if he seems to have developed a certain scepticism when it came to prevailing circumstances in Israel. The degree to which he in fact continued to identify himself with the Zionist cause is revealed in his response to the intense and famous controversy sparked by publication of Hannah Arendt's *Eichmann in Jerusalem*.[65] Arendt had been one of Jonas's most important intellectual friends since their time together under Heidegger in Marburg in the early 1920s. It is well known that one personal aspect of the controversy was a complete and permanent break between Arendt and Scholem. The accompanying bitter correspondence between these two prominent German Jews eventually prompted Jonas to take sides with Scholem—and to question the basis of his lifelong friendship with Arendt.[66]

From the very beginning of that friendship, Jonas had felt that Arendt, despite her conscious Jewish identity, did not know too much about Judaism; he came to understand her as a basically apolitical person who had been forced to deal with politics by the events of the Nazi era.[67] For a time Arendt, reflecting the influence of the Zionist activist and theorist Kurt Blumenfeld, adopted a Zionist perspective and was active in the Youth Aliyah movement; but she never really agreed with Jonas's political opinions and later, in view of the conflict between Jews and Arabs in Palestine, dissociated herself from Zionism.[68] Although Jonas was "shocked" by this development, he did not mention it when he encountered her in New York in the 1950s "because I had left the Jewish state myself and could not possibly argue as a spokesman for Zionism".[69]

A decade later, the basic differences between Jonas and Arendt concerning both Zionism and the Holocaust, now aggravated by the most passionate controversy

[64]Jonas, *Erinnerungen*, p. 270.

[65]On the controversy see Larry May and Jerome Kohn (eds.), *Hannah Arendt. Twenty Years Later*, Cambridge, MA–London 1997; Gary Smith (ed.), *Hannah Arendt Revisited: "Eichmann in Jerusalem" und die Folgen*, Frankfurt am Main 2000; Steven E. Aschheim (ed.), *Hannah Arendt in Jerusalem*, Berkeley–Los Angeles–London 2001.

[66]Jonas, *Erinnerungen*, pp. 110–116.

[67]*ibid*, p. 124.

[68]See Hannah Arendt, 'Zionism Reconsidered', in *Menorah-Journal*, vol. 33, no. 2 (1945), pp 162–196; Richard J. Bernstein, 'Hannah Arendt's Zionism?' in Aschheim (ed.), pp. 194–202; Moshe Zimmermann, 'Hannah Arendt. The Early Post-Zionism', *ibid.*, pp. 181–193.

[69]Jonas, *Erinnerungen*, pp. 289f.

among Jewish intellectuals about the Holocaust in the postwar period, nearly destroyed their friendship.[70] Jonas recalls his response to Arendt's basic arguments at one point in his memoirs:

> She was not aware that [a sense of the threat posed by antisemitism in the Diaspora] runs like a line straight through the Jewish historical consciousness. Rather, she tried to convince herself and others that the concept of antisemitism, as something like a natural element of Jewish existence, simply represents a Zionist invention and obsession. Well and good: I was shocked by such ignorance about Judaism, but above all by the way she gave us, especially the Zionists but also the Jews in general, a share of the blame for the Holocaust, instead of describing the enforced participation in one's own annihilation as a tragic, horrible fact. Hannah did not describe this like Primo Levi, who had been there himself, but made herself into a judge over the behaviour of people in this terrible situation—she was extremely sure of herself in this regard and hinted, without saying it explicitly, that she would have behaved entirely differently if she had been there. I was less and less able to forgive her for this, especially since she also advocated the thesis of the "banality of evil", as if Eichmann had basically been an innocent man who did not really know what he was doing, but simply faithfully fulfilled what he was commissioned to do. She said nothing at all about his own fanaticism, rather falling for his self-description. … Hannah here drew a horribly distorted picture of both Jews and Nazis.[71]

One letter from Jonas to Arendt sheds additional light on the crisis between them, while directly addressing the affinity between Jonas's and Scholem's response to the Eichmann debate.[72] Jonas wrote this letter in order to prepare the ground for a personal conversation in which he would persuade Arendt to alter her assessment of Zionism, in particular. Its harsh tone—indeed, the hurt and anger that sometimes comes through—is a sign of the crucial nature of the core issues at stake, in the aftermath of the Holocaust and the establishment of the Jewish state. It shows how profoundly Jonas was affected by the wider debate about these events, and about German Jewish history in general, a debate in which Arendt's work had taken on a pivotal role; at the same time it illustrates how passionately he desired to rescue a precious and threatened friendship. The letter opens as follows:

> Dear Hannah, writing this letter goes against all logic and reason. When the time seemed right, I failed to do so; now that it is over, I am doing so. When I read, with horror, the third article [in the *New Yorker* magazine] of "Eichmann in Jerusalem", I meant to implore you by telegraph to at least abstain from a German version. (There, in 1945, it already seemed to me that the excuse "at night all cats are grey" was the slyest of excuses). But then, in mind of the lesson I increasingly learned over the years that you are not open to reason, do not like listening to anyone and always simply want to be in the right, I said to myself: there is no point. But maybe this omission was wrong. Then, observing the expected storm of criticism and outrage over several months—a storm in which, to the

[70]See *ibid.*, pp. 286–294 and Wiese, *Hans Jonas*, pp. 95–114.

[71]Jonas, *Erinnerungen*, pp. 291–292.

[72]The complete letter was first published and interpreted in Wiese, *Hans Jonas*, pp. 100–109.

sorrow of the friends of truth, intellectual inferiority sometimes led to disadvantage for the better cause, but in which the embarrassing nature of your responses, to the grief of the friends of Hannah, more than made up for this and unswervingly continued to weave the rope with which you are hanging yourself without letting anybody prevent you from doing so—my sense of futility grew stronger, and this to the extent that a material issue had become a personal matter, so that the neglected (now obsolete) public duty had become a private one which I had to shirk if I wanted our friendship to survive and again could not shirk if it were to survive. What finally prompted me to nevertheless attempt the hopeless—and precisely at the moment that the hopelessness was finally demonstrated—was your published correspondence with Scholem. When I read it—rather late—I was appalled to the core of my heart and said to myself: she is lost. If even the voice of a friend does not reach her any more, if the personal legitimacy acquired over decades, the competence based on a lifetime, the proven independence of a powerful and moral mind is not able to at least make her reflect, stop for a moment and look into herself—if the answer is the foolish one that it is not his voice but that of fabricated public opinion, the base answer that the Zionist's eye is blind to the truth, the hopelessly vain answer that your thinking only stems from yourself (as if it were an achievement to learn nothing from others' insights)—then you have to be given up as lost. This dismaying self-exposure, conforming so little with your intelligence that it makes one want to believe in a malicious fake, this clueless parading of what always posed a danger to you but has now become, according to your own self-representation, a deadly weakness, had to arouse the fear and pity of your friends and the *Schadenfreude* of your enemies – however not of your worst enemy, which is to say yourself.

And if logic were the decisive criterion, this would have had to suppress my last impulse to come to your help against yourself. For why should I succeed in achieving what Scholem failed at and against which you had shown yourself to be so horridly armed?[73] Namely, to make you listen? And how should I, who did not wait for only six weeks like Scholem but for ten months [to respond], be protected against the accusation of having meanwhile become a victim of public opinion? But the paradox is that precisely the hopelessness makes the effort unavoidable, for in the case of a life-long friend, moreover one with a noble nature which one is aware of precisely as a friend, one cannot say: she is lost, without having tried everything. Hence I mean to take on the thankless task, although I fear I know your refutations in advance, of demonstrating with one or two examples what is wrong and reprehensible in what you say. I am concerned with revealing the method, not with the correction of facts, which many others have undertaken in a competently and valid manner. And when it comes to contents I choose relatively harmless examples relating to living persons that can be dealt with rather dispassionately, since the unforgivable sins against the dead would conjure up words that once expressed could perhaps prove really deadly for our friendship.[74]

[73]See the exchange between Arendt and Scholem over the Eichmann book in Gershom Scholem, *A Life in Letters, 1914–1982*, ed. and transl. by Anthony David Skinner, Cambridge, MA–London 2002, pp. 384–400.

[74]Hans Jonas to Hannah Arendt, n.d. [1963]. Papers of Hannah Arendt, general Correspondence, 1938–1976, Hans Jonas, Hannah Arendt Papers, Manuscript Division, Library of Congress, Washington, DC (original in German).

This introduction is followed by an extended discussion of Arendt's—now well-known—allegations against Robert Weltsch, the editor of the main Zionist newspaper in Germany before the Nazi rise to power, the *Jüdische Rundschau.* According to Arendt, in his famous article of 1933, 'Tragt ihn mit Stolz, den gelben Fleck' ('Wear it with pride, the yellow patch') Weltsch had signalled German Zionist agreement with Nazi policies of legal disenfranchisement and persecution of the German Jews.[75] This thesis and its broader implications seemed to Jonas, unsurprisingly enough, to constitute a historical judgement as malicious as it was misleading—one judgment among others that, as the above excerpt suggests, called their very friendship into question. Arendt's reaction to the letter was so hostile that Jonas came to feel, like Scholem, that there was no basis for renewed dialogue.[76] In the end, the dispute—so deeply grounded as it was in the individual emotions and experiences of these two strong German-Jewish figures—led to nothing more than a year's silence between them. Their reconciliation was based on a tacit agreement to never raise the painful issues that were at stake.[77]

There was no obvious disagreement between Scholem and Jonas regarding Arendt's basic position. After having read Jonas's letter to Arendt, Scholem commented in a letter to Jonas written on 4 October 1964 that "Unfortunately, imploring H[annah] does not reach her any more".[78] Later on, Scholem would express some implicit criticism of Jonas's willingness to make peace with Arendt. In this respect, he seems to have sensed a certain inclination to repression on Jonas's part, based on an urge for harmony. In 1976, following Hannah Arendt's death the previous year, Scholem mentioned to Günther Anders that during a meeting in New York, Jonas once quoted Arendt to him to the effect that "the fact that Jews persecute Jews is demonstrated by the story of Jesus, then by Spinoza's story and eventually, in our century, by my own story".[79] After Jonas, in a letter to Anders, vehemently denied having reported such words, attributing Scholem's claim to his "strange ways of mythmaking",[80] Scholem insisted at some length (and at times in a quasi-legalistic tone) that he distinctly remembered the conversation, summing up his argument with the remark that "I don't know whether after your reconciliation with Hannah Arendt you dismissed this conversation from your consciousness or whether I, who

[75]See Hannah Arendt, *Eichmann in Jerusalem: A Report on the Banality of Evil*, New York 1994 (revised and expanded edition [1965] of first edition published in 1963), pp. 59f.; Robert Weltsch, *Tragt ihn mit Stolz, den gelben Fleck. Eine Aufsatzreihe der "Jüdischen Rundschau" zur Lage der deutschen Juden*, Nördlingen 1988, pp. 24–29. For Weltsch, see Herbert A. Strauss, 'Zum zeitgeschichtlichen Hintergrund zionistischer Kulturkritik. Scholem, Weltsch und die "Jüdische Rundschau"', in Peter Freimark and Alice Jankowsky (eds.), *Juden in Deutschland. Emanzipation, Integration, Verfolgung und Vernichtung*, Hamburg 1991, pp. 375–389.

[76]For one interpretation of the rift between Arendt und Scholem, see Stéphane Mosès, 'Das Recht zu urteilen: Hannah Arendt, Gershom Scholem und der Eichmann-Prozeß', in Smith (ed.), pp. 78–92.

[77]Jonas, *Erinnerungen*, p. 293.

[78]Gershom Scholem to Hans Jonas, 4 October 1964, Jonas papers, HJ 3-22-8.

[79]See Hans Jonas to Gerschom Scholem, 17 May 1976, in Gershom Scholem, *Briefe*, vol. 3 (1971–1982), ed. by Itta Shedletzky, Munich 1999, p. 374 (Jonas here cites Anders's description of his conversation with Scholem).

[80]Hans Jonas to Günther Anders, 17 May 1976, *ibid.*, p. 374.

was so deeply affected by this statement that I immediately reported it here [in Jerusalem], might have had hallucinations. I am as sure about my certainty as you are about yours. There is nothing further to say".[81]

In his rather convoluted response, its underlying tone reflecting grief for his recently deceased friend, Jonas implicitly conceded Scholem's point:

> I have not entirely succeeded [in overcoming the "internal difficulties" caused by the "discrepancy" with Scholem]. But I have in any case come to the conclusion that I can only insist on my lack of recollection and not on refuting your own. The latter is a *positivum*, and as such enjoys a natural advantage over a sheer *negativum*. It would be different if I could counter your report with a report of that erstwhile conversation that deviates from it; in that case it would be an issue of recollection versus recollection and their relative credibility, an issue that, to be sure, given the mutually granted integrity of the persons concerned plus fallibility of memory, could not be decided but would at least allow for honest objections. But I in fact do not have such a recollection and am enough of a philosopher to know that not remembering something cannot compete with remembering something. Thus reason, although not feeling, forces me to concede that a lively memory like yours must "have something to it". My only remaining criterion for doubting that it was exactly as you remember is: what the object of recollection, the Hannah Arendt I know so well, can be thought of as having done or not done. But it is clear to me that with respect to you this doubt must remain ineffectual since you do not share this criterion; indeed that you can hold its power responsible for precisely my lack of recollection. In actuality, after having conceded the superiority of recollection per se over the lack of it, and despite all doubts regarding the reliability of your memory, I must try to supply myself with an explanation of the complete lack of even a deviating variant in my memory. It might therefore be possible that the resumption of the friendship after an interruption of one year with the strictly upheld resolution to never again bring up the Eichmann-matter in our conversations eventually "deleted" the statement (whatever its character) that I am supposed to have conveyed to you. This is by no means convincing to me, since I have a vivid memory of other things from the quarrel preceding the rift. But with or without the help of psychology, I have to leave it at the fact that I have forgotten something and you remember something, and that I have nothing with which to counter the reliability of your memory … other than my—in any case unbroken—feeling of inner, character-centred disbelief (although the devil knows the pigheadedness was extreme). So, I feel relieved that I'm finally rid of this. What I had to say is hardly likely to shake your faith in your memory. Nevertheless you might possibly let the pronouncement of the deceased, now no longer confirmed by the one and only source, die the death of silence. In any case, I am certain that with your integrity, even if you do not wish to refrain from handing it down further, you will add that the evidence for it is uncertain. I'm sorry, dear Herr Scholem, that this issue, emotionally charged as it is by grief about the death of a precious friendship, has come between us. May it not continue to divide us. I will add that regarding the matter that really counts, the "Eichmann Affair", my opinion, as you know, never differed from yours (a letter to Hannah that I also

[81]Gershom Scholem to Hans Jonas, 24 May 1976, *ibid*, p. 136.

sent you *à propos* her response to you made my standpoint clear) and did not change because of the personal reconciliation. May I wish you a happy New Year in the spirit of peace? With amicable regards now as before, your Hans Jonas.[82]

III

Alongside the conflict resulting from Jonas's decisions to remain in Canada and then move to the USA—decisions Scholem would reproach him for over the decades, sometimes only half seriously[83]—and alongside disagreements sparked by their different temperaments, new controversial issues emerged linked to a different development of research interests. Scholem's view of Jonas's approach to Gnosticism as "too strongly inspired by Christianity" appears to have been an early expression of a latent scholarly disagreement. Crystallising only gradually, this disagreement, ironically, burdened the friendship between Jonas and Scholem at a time when Jonas already had for the most part left research on Gnosticism behind for the sake of his new ethical philosophy.

After 1945, the insights Jonas drew from his now-sporadic work on Gnosticism were mainly used for a critique of Heidegger, whose activities during the Nazi era he viewed as reflecting an ethical irresponsibility tied to existential nihilism. Based on the categories of Heidegger's *Being and Time*, Jonas's *Gnosis und spätantiker Geist* had focussed on describing the nihilism inherent in Gnostic mythology and identifying the unifying categories behind its disparate forms of ideological expression. In contrast, Jonas's later reflections on Gnosticism were meant to expose the Gnostic-nihilistic character of existential philosophy, mainly in its Heideggerian version.[84] In line with what has been indicated above, Jonas's broader purpose was to refute a "gnostically" dualistic interpretation of the relation between human beings and nature, and instead to argue for the essential rootedness of humanity in a meaningful natural world—the basis of his mature ethical position.[85] Although Jonas continued to be invited to conferences in his capacity as author of *Gnosis und spätantiker Geist*, he only superficially kept up with developments in the field, openly admitting that as far as new sources and their religious-historical interpretation were concerned, developments were rapidly surpassing him.[86]

Scholem, on the other hand, continued to deal intensively with Gnosticism, any discussion about the phenomenon between him and Jonas thus being complicated by

[82]Hans Jonas to Gershom Scholem, 23 September 1976, *ibid*, pp. 374–475. In a letter dated 5 October 1976 Scholem answered in a conciliatory tone (*ibid.*, pp. 375–376).

[83]Hans Jonas, *Erinnerungen*, pp. 268f.

[84]Hans Jonas, 'Gnosticism and Modern Nihilism', in *Social Research* 19 (1952), pp. 430–452. For a detailed analysis of Jonas's relationship to Heidegger, see Vittorio Hösle, 'Hans Jonas' Stellung in der Geschichte der deutschen Philosophie', in Wiese and Jacobson (eds.), pp. 34–52; and see Jonas, *Erinnerungen*, 108–128 and 299–309.

[85]Hans Jonas, *The Phenomenon of Life. Toward a Philosophical Biology*, New York 1966; see Reinhard Löw, 'Zur Wiederbegründung der organischen Naturphilosophie durch Hans Jonas', in Dietrich Böhler (ed.), *Ethik für die Zukunft. Im Diskurs mit Hans Jonas*, Munich 1994, pp. 68–79.

[86]See Christian Wiese, 'Revolte wider die Weltflucht', in Hans Jonas, *Gnosis. Die Botschaft des fremden Gottes*, Frankfurt am Main 1999, pp. 401–429.

the fact they were not arguing on the same level of expertise. When Jonas published a shortened and popularised English version of his German work in 1958, Scholem complained about his own work not having been considered, which in his reply Jonas apologetically acknowledged was the case. (Jonas blamed the lacuna on his lack of Hebrew, to which Scholem replied by referring him to *Major Trends in Jewish Mysticism.*)[87] The two scholars developed sharply different views regarding one question in particular—that of the relationship between Gnosticism and Judaism. This had not only been a fundamental question posed by (Christian) historians of religion, but, since the nineteenth century, by (Jewish) historians of Judaism as well, who either postulated a Gnostic influence on rabbinical sources (this was, for instance, the position of Heinrich Graetz) or a Jewish influence on Gnosticism.[88] Nevertheless, under the influence of the emerging "History of Religions School" within German Protestant theology, the focus on investigating Gnosticism's origins had here begun to shift from Judaism to Zoroastrianism, a so-called orientalising approach that had a deep impact on Jonas's own interpretation.[89]

For Jonas, Judaism and Gnosticism were dialectically intertwined in a manner shaped, however, by a fundamental opposition. Although he did not deny that Gnosticism had used Jewish themes and elements, even acknowledging a link between Gnosticism and a certain form of heterodox, occult Judaism, he strongly emphasised an anti-Jewish impulse he saw at work in what he defined as a vehement Gnostic antinomianism as well as in Gnosticism's identification of Yaldabaoth, the demiurge it despised, with the God of the Hebrew Bible. Radical adversity towards Jews and Judaism, Jonas maintained, was an essential characteristic of the Gnostic rebellion against the notion of a good world created in the image of God; Gnosticism was bound to discover its natural counterpart in the anti-dualism of Jewish monotheism.[90] In the 1930s Jonas still thought that he shared this view with Scholem, who in a conversation with him in Jerusalem had characterised Gnosticism as the most important conceptual framework within a "metaphysical antisemitism" not aimed at the Jewish people but at the Jewish God.[91] Some contemporary research on Gnosticism still shares such an assessment. Micha Brumlik, for example, himself speaks of Gnosticism as always having perceived Judaism as its worst enemy because of its belief in a rational creator, concluding that "historically it is no coincidence … that anti-Judaism and antisemitism live on Gnostic thoughts". But Brumlik adds a qualification that contradicts Jonas in a basic way: Gnostic anti-Judaism does not affect the fact that "Gnosticism most probably emerged from the lap of Jewish sects and that Gnostic tendencies won considerable influence within

[87]Scholem to Jonas, 1 November 1958, Jonas papers, HJ 7–13b–1; Jonas to Scholem, 17 November 1958; Scholem to Jonas, 23 November 1958.

[88]For a general overview of the debate on this question until the present see Nathaniel Deutsch, *The Gnostic Imagination, Gnosticism, Mandaeism and Merkabah-Mysticism*, Leiden 1995, pp. 1–18; Josef Dan, 'Jewish Gnosticism?', in *Jewish Studies Quarterly*, vol. 2, no. 4 (1995), pp. 309–328.

[89]See Carsten Colpe, *Die religionsgeschichtliche Schule. Darstellung und Kritik ihres Bildes vom gnostischen Erlösermythos*, Göttingen 1961.

[90]Hans Jonas, *Gnosis und spätantiker Geist*, vol. 1, Göttingen 1988, pp. 228f., and vol. 2, Göttingen 1993, pp. 340–42.

[91]*ibid*, vol. 2, p. 354.

Judaism, especially in Kabbalah and Hasidism."[92] And Brumlik's opinion reflects new tendencies in research on Gnosticism and Jewish mystical, esoteric traditions, from antiquity to medieval Kabbalah and early modern times—tendencies underscoring the Jewish ties with Gnostic thinking.

Already in 1945, in *Major Trends in Jewish Mysticism*, Gershom Scholem had attempted to redefine the borderlines between Gnosticism and Judaism. According to Scholem, Jewish mysticism in antiquity had clear Gnostic features. He described Gnosticism as a reaction against rabbinic Judaism, later even as an inner-Jewish development inspired by apocalyptic writings. While his concept of a Jewish Gnosticism did not postulate any immediate historical link between ancient Jewish mysticism and the Gnostic movement of the second and third centuries AD, it did postulate the existence of a Jewish religious-mystical movement phenomenologically related to Gnosticism; this movement, Scholem suggested, had emerged from ancient Jewish religious ideas and symbols that eventually came to serve as material for non-Jewish Gnosticism as well. However, Scholem emphasised certain fundamental differences between Gnosticism and Judaism, based on the fact that systems of belief such as *Merkabah* mysticism followed orthodox Judaism in strictly preserving monotheism, in contrast to the dualism of Gnostic mythology. One of Scholem's pioneering achievements was his exploration of the impact of Gnostic or gnosticising thinking on medieval Kabbalah—from the *Sefer Bahir* to the *Zohar* to sixteenth-century Lurianic Kabbalah.[93] Hans Jonas, on the other hand, urged Scholem to use the concept of Gnosticism much more cautiously in relation to Jewish mysticism of late antiquity, even if he differentiated his own position, later conceding the possibility of Jewish "forerunners" and of an emergence of Gnosticism "from the margins" of Judaism.[94] In other words, Jonas himself began to perceive Gnosticism as a phenomenon near to and challenged by Jewish themes and ways of thinking.

A major confrontation between Scholem and Jonas was catalysed by Jonas's publication in 1965 of an article combining detailed criticism of a one-sided derivation of Gnosticism from Judaism, as proposed in the works of Gilles Quispel, with a gentle polemic against Scholem's concept of a Jewish gnosis: using such a concept to designate orthodox-monotheistic Jewish mysticism, he argued, was likely to smooth out the radical difference between Judaism and Gnosticism, whose decisive characteristic still was a heretical dualism between the true God of Light and the fallen God of the realm of darkness.[95] In a lengthy letter Scholem

[92]Micha Brumlik, *Die Gnostiker. Der Traum von der Selbsterlösung des Menschen*, Frankfurt am Main 1992, p. 20.

[93]Scholem, *Major Trends in Jewish Mysticism*, pp. 39–78; *idem*, *Jewish Gnosticism, Merkabah Mysticism, and Talmudic Tradition*, New York 1960. For the influence of Gnostic mythological elements in the Kabbalah and a critical assessment of Scholem's approach, see Moshe Idel, *Kabbalah. New Perspectives*, New Haven 1988 and *idem*, 'Subversive Catalysts. Gnosticism and Messianism in Gershom Scholem's View of Jewish Mysticism', in David N. Myers and David Ruderman (eds.), *The Jewish Past Revisited. Reflections on Modern Jewish Historians*, New Haven–London 1998, pp. 39–76.

[94]Jonas, *Gnosis und spätantiker Geist*, vol. 2, pp. 352–354. For common and differing views in Jonas's and Scholem's interpretation of Gnosticism, see Elisabeth Hamacher, *Gershom Scholem und die Allgemeine Religionsgeschichte*, Berlin–New York 1999, pp. 184–195.

[95]Hans Jonas, 'Response to G. Quispel's 'Gnosticism and the New Testament': 1. The Hymn of the Pearl. 2. Jewish Origins of Gnosticism?' in J. Philip Hyatt (ed.), *The Bible in Modern Scholarship*, Nashville, TN 1965, pp. 279–293, esp. pp. 287–289.

reproached Jonas for treating him "with poisonous scorn" without ever really having read his works, sarcastically observing that as a philosopher he should be able to understand his, Scholem's, "dialectical" approach. After rebutting Jonas's ideas and offering a summary of his own, Scholem commented that "If this, dear Jonas, provokes merriment on your side, I can only wish you good luck".[96] In his response, Jonas once again backed down. "Dear Scholem", he wrote, "I owe you a confession of bad behaviour and a request for forgiveness, which I can only hope you will grant for the sake of our friendship, even if I cannot come up with anything that justifies the request." In the face of Scholem's reaction, he had realised that he "had indeed not been fair"—that, annoyed by Quispel, he had succumbed to "inappropriate polemical rhetoric", and that he had to reconsider some of his arguments. Referring, somewhat ironically, to Scholem's anger, he appealed for a shift "from *midat-ha-din* (right) to *midat-ha-rachamim* (mercy) and evoked their "old friendship"—which, of course, was meant seriously. After additional apologising, Jonas added that: "admittedly, I do not read everything you write … but I do read everything of yours that comes into my hands, and each time with the admiration and instruction that all *Scholemiana* has always elicited in me".[97]

Although ending with Jonas's complete surrender, this intellectual skirmish had a late reverberation in Scholem's decision not to show up at a large conference on Gnosticism held at Yale University in 1978—a conference in which he was scheduled to participate with Jonas in a panel discussion. When Jonas expressed his "bitter personal disappointment", stressing that the main reason for his own participation had been the presence of Scholem,[98] Scholem replied as follows:

> The main reason for my declining to come to Yale was the completely impossible timing. … It is the case that one or another consideration was also in play, connected with entirely different ideas we apparently have concerning the concept of 'gnosis' about which you have surely carried on often enough. What, in fact, should be the outcome of such a conversation, in which we are at cross purposes? Your definition of Gnosticism is not mine, and to make this an object of discussion would be completely pointless. For me gnosis is a constantly self-repeating structure within religious thinking, for you it is a unique historical-philosophical phenomenon. … You have written the book on Gnosticism that absolutely needed to be written, and we all, including myself, owe you a great deal of thanks for that. Historical research, however, as far as I am in a position to understand it, has developed in completely different directions, and I have read your two or three attempts to take this into account with great respect, and even more reservations. To discuss this publicly with you would mean my devoting months of work to the problem, and due to my work-situation and agenda I have no foreseeable time for that. … I hope both of us will be granted a few more years of good work. This is my deepest wish for both of us. With affectionate regards, your Gershom Scholem.[99]

[96]Scholem to Jonas, 23 March 1966, Jonas Papers, HJ 5–5–43.
[97]Jonas to Scholem, 19 May 1966.
[98]Jonas to Scholem, 14 September 1977, in Gershom Scholem, *Briefe*, vol. 3, pp. 392–393.
[99]Scholem to Jonas, 14 November 1977, *ibid.*, p. 160.

These words quite candidly expressed what until then had only been intimated—that although Scholem considered Jonas's early work on Gnosticism to be a fascinating philosophical interpretation, he also considered it outdated from a historical-philological perspective. Despite his own historical distinctions, Jonas had always been more interested in philosophically reconstructing the Gnostic world view, in order to demonstrate the unity of an apparently diverse phenomenon; recent work by scholars such as Michael Williams has pointed to such unity as, indeed, a construction offering few satisfactory answers to specific religious-historical questions.[100]

On a personal level, Scholem's letter underscores the manifest alienation, as well as a certain asymmetry, that had emerged and deepened between Jonas and Scholem since Jonas had left Israel. While Jonas apparently deeply admired Scholem's scholarly achievements, there are no extant documents indicating whether or not Scholem appreciated the philosophical work Jonas produced after leaving Gnosticism behind. Unfortunately, the religious, political and ethical dialogue initiated during the time they shared in Jerusalem found no continuation. Thus the two scholars seem to have failed to fully appreciate each other, their common interests and perspectives. Still, despite all the tensions overshadowing their friendship, an underlying mutual affection and esteem (however grudgingly it was sometimes expressed on Scholem's part), grounded to some degree in common political and ideological convictions, appear to have survived. Two additional letters illuminate Jonas's experience of this ambivalent friendship that lasted nearly half a century. On the occasion of Scholem's eightieth birthday in 1978 Jonas wrote:

> Dear Mr. Scholem! … According to everything I am told, you are unchanged, the same person you always were, and my main wish is that this may continue for many years to come. The other wish arises from the first one: that you may continue to let us share the results of your strength. You certainly do not have to add anything to your fame, because your worldwide importance, as far as a living thinker can enjoy it, is indisputable, but the world still has more to expect from you, and your well-being means the fulfilment of this expectation. … I certainly know that you were often dissatisfied with me and are perhaps so permanently. As for myself, allow me to confess that I consider myself happy to have once been part of your inner circle and that you were and have remained an important figure in my life. I combine my tribute with the warmest wishes for the life and work still to come. Your Hans Jonas.[101]

In February 1982, Jonas sent Fanya Scholem a letter of condolence following Gershom Scholem's death. It contains what must be some of the most memorable words that have been written on the Jerusalem scholar:

> Dear Fanya, the news about Gershom's death fills me with sadness for the loss we all have suffered—and you in particular. For me personally, the no-longer-being of this most

[100]See Michael A. Williams, *Rethinking "Gnosticism": An Argument for Dismantling a Dubious Category*, Princeton, NJ 1996.

[101]Jonas to Scholem, 23 January 1978, Scholem papers (original in German).

unique spirit, whom I was privileged to meet and for a time draw close to, means a gaping hole in what I see as my own world, which I shared with him despite the emerging personal distance. Memories stretching back over fifty years are now reviving. His image is ineradicable, intensive [*intensiv*], unique, not conceivable as separate from the span of this entire century, or from my own life, and comparable with no other figure. For me, he was the essence of Jerusalem: the thoughts, the moods, the gestures, the din of passionate discussions, the electric high tension of each exchange, the lightning-quick statements and rebuttals, the inexhaustible originality, the tireless curiosity, the ever-fresh interest, the pugnaciousness paired with generous recognition of the other, assured in both [his] self-confidence and generous benevolence, displaying wit in seriousness and seriousness in wit, humour amidst a passion for knowing and naming; and in all this the palpably dark, uncanny, agitated depths behind the blinding brightness of the intellect—in this way he dominated our unforgettable circle, "Pilegesch"; he was the focal point, wherever *he* was, was the centre, the moving force, the generator always recharging itself to produce rebounding energy, what Goethe called an *Urphänomen.* I do not need to mention his monumental body of work, which will guarantee him the immortality in posterity that mortals may be granted and I have nothing to add concerning the extraordinary recognition already bestowed on him by his contemporaries. For a time I was privileged to enjoy his friendship and would like to believe that even from a distance he preserved a certain affection for me. Mine for him remained constant through all the ups and downs of our relationship. His passing is the end of an epoch—and here I am thinking not only of his epoch, dear Fanya, but of yours as well. I can still see his courtship of you, and the stormy days before your marriage when you came to me with Hans Lewy. And then the many years when "Scholem" always meant: Gerhard + Fanya. Having as strong a personality as his own, you were never stifled by his might and could be his companion for an entire lifetime with your own elemental riches. I salute you in this sad moment and wish you continued strength of soul as you face life without him, now and in the future. Please accept this expression of my sympathy and confidence. From your and Gershom's old friend, Hans Jonas.[102]

[102]Scholem, *A Life in Letters*, pp. 494–495 (retranslated version).

The Torch Bearer: Norbert Elias as a Young Zionist

BY JÖRG HACKESCHMIDT

I

Norbert Elias was one of the most important cultural and social theorists of the twentieth century. He never thought of himself as simply a sociologist; rather his aim was always an interdisciplinary synthesis. For this reason, he referred to himself as a *"Menschenwissenschatftler"*—a scientific analyst of human beings. His major work, *Über den Prozeß der Zivilisation*, was published in 1939;[1] however, the theory of process sociology developed in this work only began to exert its strong influence in the 1970s. Since then, the number of scholars inspired by Elias's writings has steadily risen. Initially, the focus of interest was on analysing his work and adopting his methodology. In more recent years, historians have also explored the sources of his scholarly biography, and have begun to reconstruct the formative phase of his intellectual development, as well as to analyse his specific conceptual style and the ties to other thinkers of his epoch. This historicisation of Norbert Elias's career has resulted in some remarkable findings with regards to both the genesis of his sociological works and his biographical interconnections with other social and cultural theorists (for example Erich Fromm and Leo Strauss). Beyond his work's socio-cultural significance, Elias is presently regarded as one of the intellectual fathers of historical anthropology; his influence on the history of mentalities is also recognised. The purpose of this essay is to show that he was also involved in a rather surprising way in the history of Zionism.

* * *

In 1925 Norbert Elias left his hometown of Breslau for the University of Heidelberg where Alfred Weber took him on as a *Habilitation* candidate in the department of sociology. In most discussions of Elias, this date is still viewed as marking the start of his academic career. Meanwhile it has nonetheless become clear that the earlier Breslau years left more of a mark on Elias than was long assumed. For as the Swiss philosopher Peter-Ulrich Merz-Benz has noted, Elias created the "basic forms of some of his most fundamental concepts" during this earlier period, as well as the foundation for rendering "history—including the process of civilisation—

This essay was translated from the German by Deborah Cohen.

[1]Norbert Elias, *Über den Prozeß der Zivilisation. Soziogenetische und psychogenetische Untersuchungen.* 2 vols., Basel 1939; *idem, Selected Writings*, ed. by Stephen Mennell and Johan Goudsblom, Chicago–London 1998.

understandable to himself".[2] In Breslau Elias had been a doctoral student under Richard Hönigswald, one of the most pre-eminent philosophers of his day. He attended Hönigswald's seminars over many years, immersing himself in the history of philosophy and the classics of Greek philosophy, along with—and this would prove important for the theoretical approach to be taken by the future sociologist—the reception of Greek thought during the Italian Renaissance. Elias was above all interested in the methods used and intellectual capacities shown by the Renaissance pioneers in establishing, by way of a large group of students and admirers, academic traditions that unleashed great powers of social transformation. But there is another reason why Elias's Breslau years were of decisive importance: in this period, Elias was one of the leading intellectual lights of the largest Zionist youth organisation in Germany, *Blau-Weiß* ("Blue-White"),[3] which understood itself as the spearhead of a Jewish renaissance. In both *Blau-Weiß* and Germany's main Zionist organisation, the *Zionistische Vereinigung für Deutschland* (ZVfD), a generational conflict was unfolding that was closely bound up with Norbert Elias's intellectual development. In essence, this conflict had to do with how the idea of a Jewish renaissance was to be understood concretely. It was clear to all those involved that the conflict was central to the basic orientation of the Jewish national movement: at stake was the question of the cultural-historical foundations of a Jewish nation-state. Was Israel to become a modern, secular nation-state with a bourgeois face? Or should a Jewish state be built on the fundament of a newly interpreted, ideologically charged Jewishness oscillating between fidelity to the *Torah* and a socialist view of humanity? This, of course, is a question that remains unresolved today.

Norbert Elias was not highly impressed by the biographical works written about him. Moreover, his responses to questions about himself reveal a certain reluctance to furnish information about the intellectually formative Breslau years following the First World War.[4] He himself explained this reluctance as a repressive reaction to terrible experiences during that war, including time spent as an ambulance driver in a convalescent unit: a connection that does not seem convincing on logical grounds. It thus appears quite likely that Elias simply wished to leave this very decisive phase

[2]Peter-Ulrich Merz-Benz, 'Verstrickt in Geschichte. Norbert Elias in seiner Breslauer Zeit', in Karl-Siegbert Rehberg (ed.), *Norbert Elias und die Menschenwissenschaften. Studien zur Entstehung und Wirkungsgeschichte seines Werkes*, Frankfurt am Main 1996, pp. 40–57.

[3]For a general orientation on this topic, see Jörg Hackeschmidt, 'Jüdische Jugendbewegung', in *Religion in Geschichte und Gegenwart*, 4th edn., Tübingen 2001, col. 666f.

[4]Hermann Korte, 'Norbert Elias in Breslau. Ein biographisches Fragment', in *Zeitschrift für Soziologie*, vol. 20, no. 1 (1991), pp. 3–11; see also Norbert Elias, *Norbert Elias über sich selbst*, Frankfurt am Main 1990, including 'A. J. Heerma van Voss und A. van Stolk: Biographisches Interview mit Norbert Elias', pp. 7–105 and Norbert Elias 'Notizen zum Lebenslauf', pp. 107–197. See also the following recent discussions of Norbert Elias: Hermann Korte, *Über Norbert Elias. Das Werden eines Menschenwissenschaftlers*, Frankfurt am Main 1988; Reinhard Blomert, *Intellektuelle im Aufbruch. Karl Mannheim, Alfred Weber, Norbert Elias und die Heidelberger Sozialwissenschaften der Zwischenkriegszeit*, Munich–Vienna 1999; Annette Treibel, Helmut Kuzmics and Reinhard Blomert (eds.), *Zivilisationstheorie in der Bilanz. Beiträge zum 100. Geburtstag von Norbert Elias*, Opladen 2000; Robert van Krieken, *Norbert Elias-Key Sociologist*, London 1998; Stephen Mennell and Eric Dunning (eds.), *Norbert Elias*, London 2003. Two excellent research tools are the newsletter *Figurations*, published online by the Norbert Elias Foundation at www.norberteliasfoundation.nl; and the HyperEliasWorldCatalogue, published online by the University of Linz at www.kuwi.uni-linz.ac.at/hyperelias/z-elias.

of his life shrouded in darkness.[5] However much one must respect such a desire on the part of an autonomous subject, it has not made things easy for those interested in the origins of Elias's ideas.

The same desire, now manifest as a blurring of facts, seems to inform Elias's denial of having had any points of contact with Zionism.[6] For among the papers left behind by Martin Bandmann (1900–1986),[7] one of the national leaders of *Blau-Weiß* and later to become a doctor, were sections of a correspondence between him and other leaders of the organisation, including three long-unknown letters from the pen of his friend Norbert Elias.[8] Furthermore, it turned out that as a young student, Bandmann had kept a detailed and conscientious diary, and this has proven to be a first-class historical source: both for evaluating many substantive—at times vehement—debates within German Zionism in the post-First World War period and for gaining some informed understanding of the development of Elias's way of thinking, as unfolding in the framework of these debates.[9] In this regard, it is striking that the same scholarly instruments developed by the sociologist of culture Norbert Elias are now making it possible to explore the system of interconnections in which he himself was decisively involved—and which he tried his best to shield from the prying eyes of intellectual historians and biographers.

It thus becomes clear that the central motifs shaping Elias's mature thinking—his reflections on social formations, the historical position of the individual, and the impact of ideologies on group behaviour—are often tied to his experiences in *Blau-Weiß* and the ZVfD. Put pointedly, the Zionist youth organisation and its Zionist milieu constituted the social and political microcosm from which many of Elias's central ideas emerged. In any event, certain passages from Elias's writings can be read as either the scholarly echo of personal experiences or as the development of themes already discussed within *Blau-Weiß*. This is the case with early works such as *Kitschstil und Kitschzeitalter* (1935), in which Goethe and Mozart are represented as "societal bearers of good taste",[10] as well as with his compilation of works about Germany and the Germans, published as *Studien über die Deutschen* (1989), in which Elias considers the phenomenon of West-German terrorism in terms of generational

[5]No doubt for the sake of underlining his rejection of academic philosophy for historically oriented sociology, Elias was—exceptionally—willing to discuss the Breslau period in response to questions about his relationship with Richard Hönigswald. See Reinhard Blomert, *Intellektuelle im Aufbruch. Karl Mannheim, Alfred Weber, Norbert Elias und die Heidelberger Sozialwissenschaften der Zwischenkriegszeit*, Munich–Vienna 1999, pp. 226–232; as well as Elias, *Über sich selbst*, pp. 120–121; regarding Elias's relationship to Zionism cf. Blomert, *Intellektuelle im Aufbruch*, p. 430, note 7.

[6]See Korte, 'Norbert Elias in Breslau', p. 5.

[7]Bandmann's papers are located in the Central Zionist Archives (CZA), Jerusalem, under the archive number A 365.

[8]For a first discussion of the two most lengthy of these three letters, see Jörg Hackeschmidt, '"Die Kulturkraft des Kreises". Norbert Elias als Vordenker der zionistischen Jugendbewegung. Zwei unbekannte Briefe aus den Jahren 1920 und 1921' in *Berliner Journal für Soziologie*, vol. 7, no. 2 (1997), pp. 147–168. The third letter (Norbert Elias to Martin Bandmann, 14 June 1920) is also reprinted without commentary in *idem, Von Kurt Blumenfeld zu Norbert Elias. Die Erfindung einer jüdischen Nation*, Hamburg 1997, pp. 327–332. The original may be found in CZA, A 365/62.

[9]For a fuller treatment of this subject see Jörg Hackeschmidt, *Von Kurt Blumenfeld zu Norbert Elias.*.

[10]Norbert Elias, 'Kitschstil und Kitschzeitalter', in Klaus Mann (ed.) *Die Sammlung. Literarische Monatsschrift unter dem Patronat von André Gide, Aldous Huxley, Heinrich Mann*, vol. 5, no. 11 (1935), pp. 252–263.

conflict. Elias's concern with the problem of "insiders" and "outsiders" can also be traced back to his Zionist phase, when he was able to intimately observe how majority opinions are formed and politically realised in societal groups.[11] Within the bourgeois *Blau-Weiß*, Elias was a member of the mainstream, an "insider". But the tone of the broader German Zionist community was not only set by followers of Martin Buber and by young ideologues such as Gershom Scholem, but also by Eastern European Zionists in circles close to Poland's David Gruen (later David Ben-Gurion), who fervently desired to endow the nascent Jewish collective in Palestine with a socialist character, and who, in Danzig in 1924, actively prevented an agreement between the leading West-European youth organisation, the *Blau-Weiß*, and the largest East European Youth Movement, the *Hashomer Hazair*, for plainly ideological reasons.[12] In the light of this context, Elias and his friends were certainly "outsiders".

That the *Blau-Weiß* youth organisation played a role in the intellectual development of Norbert Elias has already been suggested by Hermann Korte.[13] But Korte's supposition that Elias joined the organisation as a reaction to his experiences as a soldier is mistaken: he had already joined in 1913.[14] This fact is crucial for appreciating the organisation's role as a forum for many of the ambitious young people among whom Elias more or less underwent his entire intellectual socialisation. and to whose cultural-political agenda he would make a decisive contribution. Elias unintentionally suggested as much in a comment corresponding to the source findings like a puzzle piece: some members of the group of "brilliant fellow pupils" at the liberal *Johannes-Gymnasium* to whom he refers, with whom he had already formed a circle while at the *Gymnasium*, would enter the Breslau leadership circle of *Blau-Weiß*; and inversely, this common intellectual background was reflected in the regular attendance at Richard Hönigswald's lectures by Bandmann, Elias and other leaders of the group.[15]

In a "biographical interview' conducted with Elias by A. J. Heerma van Voss and A. van Stolk, Elias refers directly to only one of his friends from that era, Franz Meyer.[16] Apparently, the incorrect spelling in this interview of Meyer's surname as "Maier" has contributed to this student of Ernst Cassirer, Zionist, and future

[11]Norbert Elias, *Studien über die Deutschen. Machtkämpfe und Habitusentwicklung im 19. und 20. Jahrhundert*, ed. by Michael Schröter, Frankfurt am Main 1989; Norbert Elias and John L. Scotson, *Etablierte und Außenseiter*, Frankfurt am Main 1993.

[12]Cf., for example, Michael Bar-Zohar, *Ben Gurion. A Biography*, London 1978, pp. 101–104. Beginning in 1924, the middle-class *Blau-Weiß* organisation tried to establish a co-operative named *Blau-Weiß Werkstätten* in Palestine; regarding the conflict between *Blau-Weiß* and the strictly socialist *Histradut* led by Ben Gurion cf. Hackeschmidt, *Von Kurt Blumenfeld zu Norbert Elias*, pp. 255–259.

[13]See Korte, *Über Norbert Elias*, pp. 78–87.

[14]See Jörg Hackeschmidt, 'Norbert Elias – Zionist and "Bündisch Activist"', in *Figurations. Newsletter of the Norbert Elias Foundation*, no. 3 (1995), p.4–5. The brief travelogue 'Die dreitägige Riesengebirgsfahrt'is reprinted in Norbert Elias, *Gesammelte Schriften*, vol. 1 (*Frühschriften*), Frankfurt am Main 2002, pp. 7-8.

[15]On the importance of this philosopher for both *Blau-Weiß* and Norbert Elias, see Hackeschmidt, *Von Kurt Blumenfeld zu Norbert Elias*, pp. 138ff. Hönigswald's advanced seminars were extremely influential; they were of course not only attended by the young Zionists around Elias and Bandmann, Hans-Georg Gadamer himself being one of the visitors. Gadamer was a contemporary of Bandmann, receiving his doctorate under Hönigswald in the same year that Elias submitted his thesis *Idee und Individuum. Eine kritische Untersuchung zum Begriff der Geschichte*. It remains unclear how well Gadamer and Elias knew each other.

[16]'Biographisches Interview', in Elias, *Über sich selbst*, p. 36.

member of the Leo Baeck Institute advisory board not being linked until recently[17] with Elias. Meyer, who died in 1972—that is, before Elias had become famous—was himself regarded as brilliant. When Elias recalled the "friendly rivalry" at work within the circle of philosophically-oriented pupils, he was referring in part to Meyer.[18] In his curriculum vitae that appears on the last page of his doctoral thesis, *Zur systematischen Stellung der Descartes'schen Irrtumstheorie* (Breslau 1920), Meyer thanks the same teachers—Dr. Krüger and Dr. Julius Stenzel whom Norbert Elias would describe sixty years later as having been particularly important.[19] Until 1923, when the life paths of the two began increasingly to diverge, Meyer was always a step ahead of Elias. He had been active in *Blau-Weiß* from the beginning and had probably introduced Elias and others to the group. Since 1917 he had been the driving force behind the efforts of a generation of German Zionists inspired by Germany's youth movement to intellectualise its German Zionist variant. In 1918–1919 *Blau-Weiß* freed itself from the reform-paedagogical influence of older students and was re-founded as an autonomous organisation.[20] In 1916 Franz Meyer began to study philosophy under Ernst Cassirer and Ernst Troeltsch in Berlin and under Heinrich Rickert in Heidelberg. His thesis supervisor nonetheless remained Richard Hönigswald in Breslau, under whom he received his doctorate. Bandmann's diary reveals that numerous friends from *Blau-Weiß* were present at his oral examination.[21] Why Meyer chose the Cassirer critic Hönigswald as his thesis advisor is unclear. In any event, the sources from those years suggest that Cassirer's influence on Meyer—and through him, on the leadership circle of *Blau-Weiß* in general—was as great as that of Hönigswald.

In the developing cultural-philosophical work of Ernst Cassirer, a student of Hermann Cohen, the Renaissance occupied a key position—an interest shared by Elias and his friends in *Blau-Weiß*. The age of the Renaissance, Cassirer argued in his 1916 book *Freiheit and Form. Studien zur deutschen Geistesgeschichte*, showed the peoples of Europe the way towards a common, free, worldly ideal of education and personal formation. This development bound the great nations of Europe together, Germany here being no exception. With this argument, Cassirer positioned himself against a contemporary intellectual tendency to speak of a national—and indeed ethnic-*völkisch—Sonderweg*, a special path within German scholarship and German culture.[22] What is interesting is that the circle around Franz Meyer and Norbert Elias applied essential points of criticism from Cassirer's book to the inner-Jewish discussion of the nature and core of a distinctly Jewish national culture—thereby likewise positioning themselves against the trend.

17Cf. Hackeschmidt, 'Kulturkraft des Kreises', p. 149.

18Meyer retained a life-long interest in philosophy and as late as 1969 published an insightful monograph entitled *Ernst Cassirer*. It was published in the Schriftenreihe der Niedersächsischen Landeszentrale für politische Bildung, Hanover.

19Elias, 'Notizen', in *idem, Über sich selbst*, p. 110f.

20See Hackeschmidt, *Von Kurt Blumenfeld zu Norbert Elias*, p. 115ff.

21It was, and often still is, the custom at many universities in Germany and elsewhere for oral examinations of doctoral candidates to be accessible to the general public.

22See the important study by Ulrich Sieg, *Jüdische Intellektuelle im Ersten Weltkrieg. Kriegserfahrungen, weltanschauliche Debatte und kulturelle Neuentwürfe*, Berlin 2001, esp. pp. 267f.

Grounds for bringing Cassirer into their debates about Jewish identity and Zionist educational work certainly existed: especially in *Blau-Weiß* the tradition had established itself to invest heroic tales and myths of ancient Israel with ideological import in the group's work with children and young people, such material thus being used as a counterfoil to the Nordic-Germanic ideology of German nationalists and antisemites, focussed as it often was on heroic deeds. The saga of the Maccabees here ranked particularly highly, cultural-historical events being rapidly reinterpreted to distinguish warlike, heroic Judaism from the degenerated ancestors of early Christianity, with whose cultural and value system true Zionists had nothing in common.[23]

A good example of this Maccabee-focussed national and cultural self-reinforcement is the essay "Mattathias, der jüdische Held", appearing in the *Blau-Weiß-Blätter* in December 1917 to mark the advent of Chanukah. Its author was Ferdinand Ostertag, a bookseller from Glogau, one of the reform-minded and pedagogically inspired leaders of the pre-war *Blau-Weiß*.[24] In Ostertag's contribution, the murder by the Hasmonite patriarch Mattathias of an apostate Jew about to comply with the Syrian king Antiochus IV's demand to offer sacrifice to Zeus is celebrated as an intuitively heroic act—as the "original source of Jewish humanity" (*Urquell jüdischen Menschentums*), and as an "expression of the Jewish essence" (*Ausdruck jüdischen Wesens*) and of the "Jewish soul" (*jüdische Seele*). In the spring of 1918, Franz Meyer—himself engaged in Zionist youth work—was the first to publicly oppose "pedagogical reevaluations" (*pädagogische Umwertungen*) such as those made by Ostertag. Even the slogan *Mensch werden und es jüdisch werden* ("Become a person and do so in a Jewish way"), often cited in the Zionist literature of the time, was nonsense, he observed; it should have read *Jude werden und es menschlich werden* ("Become a Jew and do so in a human way"). And referring to Sigmund Freud's work on the affinity between myth and wish-dreams, he reminded his readers of a basic methodological problem, one of the main problems of both the Jewish renaissance and the Jewish search for identity. The contemplation of history, Meyer argued, derived "the values it emphasises first and foremost from us and from our ideal of personality". "The question 'What was the Jewish hero like? Come, let's strive to emulate him' is thus wrong in principle. The hero is not actually a given quantity [...] but rather an ideal figure we shape in the course of history." What Jewish nationalist youth culture badly needed was "a just and rational education towards reason and justice". The upshot of Meyer's essay encapsulated the credo of the group surrounding Elias, Meyer, Bandmann and the young elite of *Blau-Weiß*, who saw the building blocks for a new Jewish national culture above all in themselves. One needed only to convince Jewish youth "a bit more than has been the case thus far that goodness, benevolence and restraint are the human virtues forming the basis of a community. If Jewish youth

[23]See Hackeschmidt, *Von Kurt Blumenfeld zu Norbert Elias*, pp. 107–114.

[24]See *Blau-Weiß-Blätter*, vol. 5, no. 4 (December 1917), pp. 123–127. In the following pages, references will be made to the *Blau-Weiß-Blätter*, the *Blau-Weiß-Führerzeitung*, and the *Breslauer Heft* of the *Blau-Weiß-Blätter, Führerzeitung.* The reader's attention is drawn to the fact that the *Blätter* and *Führerzeitung* were distinct publications, appearing with some interruptions due to war, economic crises and so forth and co-existing in a state of some ideological tension. The *Breslauer Heft* was one of a series of "thematic pamphlets" for the (slightly renamed) *Führerzeitung*, meant to be published by various larger *Blau-Weiß* associations such as that based in Breslau; these were only published sporadically.

only knew this, they would search for their own heroes, and these would be Jewish heroes—perhaps not from the past, but from the future."[25]

Meyer again expressed this position—which may well have been inspired by Cassirer—in Siegfried Bernfeld's *Jerubbaal*, a journal that saw itself as a platform for all the Jewish youth organisations in Germany. In its conception, *Jerubbaal* drew on the tradition of the legendary youth-journal *Der Anfang*, which Bernfeld had been in overall charge of before the Great War together with Walter Benjamin, Hans and Peter Kollwitz (the sons of the artist Käthe Kollwitz), Georges Barbizon and Martin Gumpert. In his new essay, entitled 'Zur Problemlage der national-jüdischen Jugendbewegung', Meyer stressed his conviction that Zionism was ultimately an "educational task": "The task at hand is to make this youth doubt all givens, question everything handed down to them, train their powers of distinction as finely as possible, sharpen their intelligence." Meyer here also once more underlined that the Jewish people and their cultural development were by no means to be viewed as separate from the cultural development of Europe—a conclusion whose resemblance to Cassirer's introduction to *Geist und Form* is unlikely to have been coincidental.[26]

In this simultaneously Zionist and humanist-universalist framework, Meyer stressed that

> Emancipation was more than an outer liberation of the Jews. It signified a complete upheaval in the spiritual foundations of the Jewish cultural community as well; with it, the Jewish Middle Ages came to an end. What had shaken the European cultural realm three hundred years earlier now took place within the "last enclave of the Middle Ages in modern Europe". In place of fixed social and spiritual cohesion … came the freedom of Renaissance man.[27]

In Franz Meyer's opinion the most important goal of Zionist educational work was thus inducing Jewish youth "to reflect about themselves". And in expressing this view he got to the heart of the work of *Blau-Weiß* over the coming years.

II

Franz Meyer's critique of an ethos of Jewish heroism and his insistence that the cultural traditions of the Occident were essential to the proper formation of the emerging Zionist generation can be understood as the catalyst for founding *Blau-Weiß* as a self-contained, independent youth organisation and for undertaking its

[25]Franz Meyer in *Blau-Weiß-Führerzeitung*, vol. 1, no. 4 (March 1918), pp. 73–75. The article does not have a title but rather is preceded by what is indicated to be a Goethe quotation, meant to be understood as an ironic commentary on the idealism of the youth movement, centred around the idea of the heroic deed: "How can one know oneself? Never by thinking, always by doing. Try to do your duty, and you'll know right away what you amount to. And what is your duty? Whatever the day calls for."

[26]Franz Meyer, 'Zur Problemlage der national-jüdischen Jugendbewegung' in *Jerubbaal*, vol. 1 (1918/1919), pp. 254–256.

[27]*ibid.*

impressive educational work. The perspective formulated by the group in discussions held between 1917 and 1919 is a key to understanding its dissatisfaction in the 1920s with the approach being taken by most older German Zionists to creating a new Jewish identity. The intellectual leaders of *Blau-Weiß* continued to reject a superficial reception of Jewish myths and Old Testament heroic sagas and the fashionable forms of expression of the "Jewish renaissance" à la Martin Buber: a movement meant to self-referentially bolster one's own national identity. Furthermore, they did so with good reason and with good arguments, developed with reference to the works of their academic teachers Cassirer and Hönigswald. In their view, the invention of a new Jewish tradition based on a romantic transfiguration of Old Testament heroic figures—or of East European Jews regulating their lives according to Talmudic law—could not serve as the basis for a genuine national renaissance. *Blau-Weiß* was driven by a contrasting vision: using their circle as a basis for setting in motion a cultural movement that would exert an effect on the Jewish people's modernisation and re-nationalisation similar to that exerted by the leading minds of the Italian Renaissance within their city-states.

In hoping that the "cultural strength of the circle"[28] might lay the educational foundations for a new national society, *Blau-Weiß* was trying to realise Ernst Cassirer's cultural-philosophical ideas; or as Cassirer's biographer Heinz Paetzold put it with reference to Cassirer's own fascination for the Renaissance and the Enlightenment, to enable "an abstract idea" to become "a political 'act' or even a new 'social reality'".[29] For Norbert Elias and his friends, a work such as Cassirer's *Philosophy of Symbolic Forms*, with its analysis of cultural self-consciousness and its forms of expression, fell on fertile soil: ultimately, the dispute about the "proper", forward-looking forms of cultural expression for a "Jewish renaissance" centred around the same set of entities to which Cassirer attributed so much power in forming consciousness and creating identity.

In the years 1919 and 1920, through the influence of Elias, Meyer, Bandmann and others, *Blau-Weiß* became an ambitious project of self-formation. The youth-organisation worked to develop its members' analytical skills and intellectual horizons, as well as to cultivate the intellectual aptitude of its younger members. The "form" it chose for itself was of an avant-garde community within the autonomous youth movement. *Blau-Weiß* did not wish to be a simple debating club, and it rejected the bourgeois forms of sociability its members' parents had practised. Its goal (classical in nature but often embraced by social groups experiencing upheaval) was the development of character and the transmission of values: a process deemed crucial for any community to deal with its environment and flourish.[30]

[28]See letter from Norbert Elias to Martin Bandmann, 14 June 1920, reprinted in Hackeschmidt, *Von Kurt Blumenfeld zu Norbert Elias*, pp. 327–342 as well as in *idem*, 'Kulturkraft des Kreises. pp. 147–168 (with commentary); CZA, A 365/62.

[29]See Heinz Paetzold, *Ernst Cassirer. Von Marburg nach New York. Ein philosophische Biographie*, Darmstadt 1995, p. 221.

[30]See Aleida Assmann, *Arbeit am nationalen Gedächtnis. Eine kurze Geschichte der deutschen Bildungsidee*, Frankfurt am Main 1993, p. 19f.

* * *

Although Richard Hönigswald did not provide as much cultural-philosophical armour as Ernst Cassirer, his scholarly interests were also highly compatible with the basic interests of *Blau-Weiß*. Hönigswald was already working on his project of clarifying the "preconditions for pedagogical action",[31] in other words, to subject educational processes to systematic philosophical clarification, itself bound up with the *creation* of what was conceived of as culture. Accordingly, in his seminars Hönigswald addressed the question of what education was, how it functioned and the criteria for deciding which of a culture's values were to be transmitted.

One of his chief focal points was, as already mentioned, the Italian Renaissance which he approached—both in his influential works and in his teaching—in terms of the standard model of the élite of the Italian city-states embracing the long-faded values and substantive knowledge of the ancient world.[32] Hönigswald declared personalities to be the real bearers of culture—and this was music to the ears of the circle around Norbert Elias and Martin Bandmann. For these ambitious young Zionists, fascinated by the Italian Renaissance, aspired to be, precisely, bearers of a new Jewish national culture. While hoping to emigrate together in the near future to Palestine and viewing themselves as, in Norbert Elias's words to Martin Bandmann in 1920, the "germ … of the future tradition and custom and culture" of a new Jewish nation, they were also aware that what they wished to initiate involved a long-term cultural process.[33]

Evidence of the strong generational self-image of *Blau-Weiß* can be found in various sources. This self-image contributed to the group's at times painful conflicts with the previous generation of Zionists led by Kurt Blumenfeld (1885–1963) and Felix Rosenblüth (1887– 1978): individuals who had founded *Blau-Weiß* before the First World War as a youth organisation guided by reform-pedagogical principles and now resented the ethos of *bündisch* autonomy that the organisation had begun embracing.[34] The feeling of being a "generational unit" with a distinctive style corresponded to the goal of establishing an authentic Jewish and Zionist renaissance—one based on the transmission of cultural values along the lines that Hönigswald had established. For Elias, the Greek phrase "handing on the torch (of knowledge)" thus took on centrality, eloquently conveying the basic ethos of *Blau-Weiß*.[35] Elias also lays stress on this ethos in his 1920 letter to Bandmann: "A people [*ein Volk*] must grow elsewhere for

[31]Richard Hönigswald, *Über die Grundlagen der Pädagogik. Ein Beitrag zur Frage des pädagogischen Universitäts-Unterrichts*, 2nd edn., Breslau 1927, (1st edn. 1918), p. 16.

[32]Among the texts reflecting Richard Hönigswald's approach see his 'Giordano Bruno' in *Große Denker*, Leipzig 1912; *Philosophische Motive im neuzeitlichen Humanismus*, Breslau 1918; *Die Geschichte der Philosophie von der Renaissance bis Kant*, Berlin 1923.

[33]Elias to Bandmann, 14 June 1920.

[34]See Martin Bandmann, 'Die Generationen' in *Jüdische Rundschau*, no. 21 (13 March 1923), p. 124; see also Hackeschmidt, *Von Kurt Blumenfeld zu Norbert Elias*, pp. 221ff.

[35]Elias included the phrase in his article 'Vom Sehen in der Natur', *Blau-Weiß-Blätter, Führerzeitung* ("Breslauer Heft"), vol. 2, nos. 8–10 (May-July 1921), pp. 133–144. In his 'Adorno-Rede. Respekt und Kritik' in Norbert Elias and Wolf Lepenies, *Zwei Reden anläßlich der Verleihung des Theodor W. Adorno-Preises 1977*, Frankfurt am Main 1977, pp. 35–68, esp. p. 67, Elias also makes use of the metaphor to describe the inter-generational transmission of knowledge in the study of human culture; cited in Korte, *Über Norbert Elias*, p. 86.

generation upon generation until its culture acquires security and direction and unity of form throughout its whole life." Similar sentiments can be found in many other statements of the *Blau-Weiß* group.[36]

In time, Norbert Elias established himself within *Blau-Weiß* as an intellectual trailblazer—but one who was sometimes difficult and moody. On 5 March 1920 Bandmann observed that:

> Norbert is indeed proving to be an *outside man* [original term in English]. He hasn't the least ability to empathise with people, has no understanding of 'interpersonal' matters, although he presumptively claims to; he ... remains dogmatic and precious. What he wants and does is in itself excellent, but he wants and does nothing simply as a matter of course and with the confidence-inspiring self-confidence of a person who is or (in the Kantian sense) should be someone, but rather does everything in a pointed, over-precise and nervous manner.[37]

The interest of this not necessarily authoritative *ad hominem* comment lies mainly in its context: a meeting between several *Blau-Weiß* members and the *Blau-Weiß* girls' association, which had existed independently of the boys' group since 1918. The possibility of introducing joint leadership meetings had been discussed in this venue. Whereas Bandmann favoured entering into a co-operative relationship with the girls' organisation while still remaining formally independent, Norbert Elias, as a committed proponent of an ideal of the *Männerbund* (i.e. of manly camaraderie), favoured a strict division between the two organisations.

The fact that Norbert Elias was homosexual was tolerated without any hint of resentment in the *Blau-Weiß-Bund*, which understood itself as a men's organisation. That Elias, with his occasionally apodictic and overly intellectual manner, was sublimating an "inhibited Eros" to the point of "petrifaction", as Bandmann noted at one point in his diary, would also have been clear to his other friends.[38] Despite his sometimes truly eccentric character and his occasionally non-committal manner, his friends valued him—and not only for his analytic talents and depth of intellect.

III

Elias's involvement in *Blau-Weiß* became intermittent over the course of the year 1923. He had finished his thesis nearly a year previously, and Germany was in the midst of a serious economic crisis. At this time Elias was himself undergoing a personal crisis. In contrast to many of his friends, he had not found any satisfying professional perspectives. His thesis was lying on Hönigswald's desk, the latter having refused to accept certain passages, with the consequence that Elias was not allowed to proceed to the oral examination for two years.[39] Apart from such difficulties, Elias

[36]Cf. letter from Martin Bandmann to Benno Cohn, 9 May 1921, CZA A 365/31 and *idem*, 'Die Generationen'.

[37]Bandmann diaries, CZA A 365/1.

[38]Bandmann diaries, CZA A 3365/10, 25 August 1923.

[39]See Blomert, *Intellektuelle im Aufbruch*, pp. 230f.; Blomert (*ibid.*, pp. 228f.) indicates that Hönigswald resented Elias's deep interest in Ernst Cassirer's philosophy.

had come to realise that he was not really suited for pedagogically oriented youth-work such as that carried out by Franz Meyer; under pressure from the group's younger members, he was thus obliged to stand down as leader of *Blau-Weiß*'s Breslau section.[40] Bandmann described Elias in this situation as a "tragic case"—that of an individual possessing "the greatest longing for the irrational who yet remains entirely stuck in his intellect; he wants to be a leader and nevertheless possesses nothing of the strength to truly form people".[41]

But despite all the difficulties besetting a loner who was not at one with himself and who had not yet found a real life-plan, until the start of 1923 Elias remained part of the leadership of the *Blau-Weiß-Bund,* as one of its most active programme-developers, now engaging himself, at the age of twenty-six in the so-called *Blau-Weiß-Älterenbund* or Older Members' Organisation.

In this period, until the end of 1922, Elias was also active as an organisational spokesman. In the run-up to the national convention of *Blau-Weiß* in Hausen in August 1921, for which the *Breslauer Heft* of the *Blau-Weiß-Führerzeitung* served as a preparatory forum, Bandmann wrote to unnamed *Blau-Weiß*-friends of his in Heidelberg that only "Norbert [is] in a position to say with the necessary clarity what needs to be said," even if some tact would be required to win the other organisations over to the programme of self-improvement worked out in Breslau.[42] At the leadership conference held in advance of the national congress, the circle of Breslauers around Bandmann and Elias came in closer contact, apparently for the first time, with the heads of the Frankfurt *Blau-Weiß*. The latter, however, were working on a competing concept of a "Jewish renaissance" that would only take clear shape in 1922. Bandmann's diary merely records that at the conference, Erich Fromm, one of the spokesmen of the Frankfurt group, accused the controversial and charismatic national leader of *Blau-Weiß,* Walter Moses, of a "lack of moral feeling". From this encounter, Bandmann nevertheless derived a very positive first impression of Fromm.[43]

* * *

Elias's engagement was most manifest in the period following the national congress, held at Schloß Prunn in Altmühltal in the summer of 1922. There, *Blau-Weiß* had decided to become the avant-garde of German Zionism and to organise itself as a "Zionist order", with Walter Moses representing the organisation.[44] Opponents of

[40]See Bandmann diaries, CZA A 365/8, 16 and 24 January, 4 February 1923.

[41]Bandmann diaries, CZA A 365/8, 5 February 1923.

[42]Martin Bandmann to unnamed friends, n.d. (May 1921?), CZA A 365/31.

[43]Bandmann diaries, CZA A 365/4, 6 and 7 August 1921. The national convention ended with a performance by the Breslau section, led by Norbert Elias, of Shakespeare's *A Midsummer Night's Dream*; *ibid.*

[44]For a more detailed discussion of this and the following information, see Hackeschmidt, *Von Kurt Blumenfeld zu Norbert Elias*, pp. 179ff. An eleven-page letter from Walter Moses to Martin Bandmann, dated 15 August 1922 (CZA A365/32), explains how the reorganisation was to proceed. Moses's idea was to move *en bloc* to Palestine as a small "colony" in two or three years, the cultural and educational work of the *Blau-Weiss* serving as an intellectual foundation for this project. As Moses (correctly) foresaw strong resistance from the ZVfD, he wished to have a new journal founded in which all spokesmen for *Blau-Weiss* could explain this "programme of action" and make it concrete. The authors Moses

such a *bündisch* development among Zionist youth had responded by, among other things, accusing *Blau-Weiß* of being orientated towards Italian fascism.[45] For this reason, future development of the Zionist youth movement topped the agenda at the delegates' conference of the ZVfD, held in Kassel at the beginning of September 1922, with Elias, like Bandmann and colleagues from all over the *Reich*, arriving to defend *Blau-Weiß* against the Zionist establishment.[46] Bandmann indicates in his diary that Elias tossed a few heated words into the debate, directed at, among others, Viktor Arlosoroff, the young leader of the socialist *Hapoel Hazair*, and his followers.[47] That Norbert Elias's contribution to the debate at the Zionist congress in Kassel has only now come to light must at least partly be due to the fact that only excerpts from the stenographic record were reprinted in the *Jüdische Rundschau.* Furthermore, the heated debate surrounding *Blau-Weiß* was reported in only a very general—and

---

specifically names here are Martin Bandmann, Georg Strauss, Benno Cohn—and Norbert Elias, who was also meant to become the *Gauführer* of Lower Saxony's *Blau-Weiß*. This was confirmed a month later at a meeting of the organisation's national executive in Berlin (cf. transcript of this meeting, 15 September 1922, signed by Georg Strauss, CZA A365/32). On the figure of Walter Moses see Martin Bandmann's illuminating obituary, 'Walter Moses zum Gedächtnis' in Irgun Olej Merkas Europa, *Mitteilungsblatt*, no. 16 (22 April 1955), p. 4. The best insight into Walter Moses's Zionist vision is offered by his essay 'Zur nationalen Kolonisation', in *Blau-Weiß-Blätter*, new series, vol. 2, no. 1 (September 1925), pp. 15–21. Retrospectively his ideas for the economic development of a future Jewish state can be regarded as groundbreaking.

45 Despite all the problematic aspects of Walter Moses's character, manifest in his role as *Blau-Weiss-Führer* citing "fascist" elements in the organisation amounted to a planned effort at undermining its work with children and young people, and indeed at making its continued activities, and those of Moses himself, impossible within the Jewish community, Cf. the article on *Blau-Weiß* in *Jüdische Rundschau*, vol. 28, no. 14 (16 February 1923), p. 78.

46 Cf. Bandmann's diary entry of 5 September 1922: "Thinking all the time of the delegates' meeting (*Delegiertentag*) in Kassel. Sunday: Youth Day (*Jugendtag*). Everything is geared up for the decisive battle. Walter is expected to opt for an avoidance manoeuvre and not show up. That would be the nicest argument for all the opponents and doubters. The target is Walter himself anyway. The *Blau-Weiß* is supposed to have been 'seduced' by him." (CZA A 365/5.) On 6 September, four days before the start of the delegates' meeting, Bandmann received a telegram from Georg Strauss in Berlin with the request to take as many group leaders as possible with him from Breslau to Kassel.

47 Elias and his fellow *Blau-Weiß* members were indignant about the actions of some members of the strictly socialist *Hapoel Hazair*, skilfully brought in against *Blau-Weiß*, as "chief witnesses for the prosecution", by the organisers of the congress. Among these individuals were Arlosoroff and Leo Kaufman, both former members of *Blau-Weiß* who had been living in Palestine for only a few years. Arlosoroff was said to have accused the organisation of a "lack of connection to the [Jewish] Palestinian workers" and Kaufmann spoke of its members "being estranged from the people and the workers"; cf. reports in the *Jüdische Rundschau*, nos. 76/77 (29 September 1922), pp. 517f. and Bandmann's diary of that period (CZA A 365/5). The remarks by Arlosoroff in particular show that socialist groups within the Zionist organisation in Palestine were not interested in working with *Blau-Weiß* or with a co-operative led by it, unless members were willing to put themselves under *Hapoel Hazair* command. In this context, see esp. the retrospective article by-lined "Kaufmann" (Kadmann), 'Von den Anfängen der Chaluz-Bewegung in Deutschland' in *Jüdische Rundschau,* 28 September 1934, reprinted in Eli Rothschild (ed.), *Meilensteine. Vom Wege des Kartells Jüdischer Verbindungen (K.J.V) in der Zionistischen Bewegung. Eine Sammelschrift*, Tel Aviv 1972, pp. 68–72. Kaufmann stresses that the German *Chaluzim* only became "part of the great workers' movement of Palestine" after the "reality of Palestine"—i.e. the *Histradut*—"had broken *Blau-Weiß*" (p. 72), a sideswipe clearly referring to the fact that the "*Blau-Weiß* workshops" in Palestine, which had been involved in the construction of the Hebrew University, were boycotted by *Histradut* strikes in order to bankrupt them. For a more detailed discussion, see Hackeschmidt, *Von Kurt Blumenfeld zu Norbert Elias*, esp. pp. 228f. and 256–259.

ideologically toned-down—way. Understandably the ZVfD wanted to avoid leaving a fractured impression on the public.

Blau-Weiß refused to back down on programmatic issues—not even under massive pressure from the broader Zionist organisation. However, a sustained disagreement did arise between the Frankfurt *Blau-Weiß*, centred around Erich Fromm and Ernst (Akiba) Simon, and the spokesmen of the new course, to whom Norbert Elias belonged. This quarrel, which revolved around basic questions of Jewish identity, had strong political implications, as the majority of *Blau-Weiß* was bourgeois in background and anti-socialist in orientation, while the Frankfurt group around Fromm and Simon saw the future of the Jewish nation as resting in an alliance between neo-orthodox Judaism and a kind of mystical socialism. This ideological battle was pursued in the columns of the *Jüdische Rundschau*, where the group around Erich Fromm, Ernst Simon and Leo Löwenthal, who had seceded from *Blau-Weiß*, also presented their notions of how a Jewish identity was to be worked out.[48] For their neo-orthodox circle, there was only one path to *Eretz Yisrael*: "The recognition of the nature and singularity [*Eigenart*] of the Jewish people." It was assimilated Jewish nationalism that had "destroyed the basis for any national life—against its own will".[49]

The arguments of Fromm, Simon and Löwenthal underscore a view of the spiritual foundations of a future Israel very different from that of the Breslau circle around Bandmann and Elias. But between the lines, one can also discern a competition between two groups of younger Jewish intellectuals about the proper understanding of Jewish identity as well as about the process of forming a new Jewish culture and civilisation. In contrast to the transfigured neo-religious view of the Frankfurters, the Breslau *Blau-Weiß* group around Elias and Bandmann clung to the ideal of the Enlightenment—albeit the Enlightenment with a Nietzschean and vitalistic twist (see below)—wishing to see its achievements integrated into Zionism. And as far as the methods to be used in the search for Jewish self-identity were concerned, they spoke in one voice with the neo-Kantian Paul Natorp, who had been one of Ernst Cassirer's teachers. Natorp had stated: "Forward movement and method are everything; to use the Latin word: Process."[50] With their neo-Kantian backgrounds, the members of the Breslau group would have been well aware that Natorp was here playing on the close affinity between the Greek word *méthodos*, signifying a systematic course, and the Latin word *procedo*, meaning to move forward or develop.

At this point, the resonance of these debates within the thinking of the mature Norbert Elias, author of *Über den Prozeß der Zivilisation*, seems apparent. How deep the

[48]'Ein prinzipielles Wort zur Erziehungsfrage', in *Jüdische Rundschau*, nos. 103/104 (29 December 1922), pp. 675f. In view of this, it is possible to read the "autobiographical conversation" between Leo Löwenthal and Helmut Dubiel in a different light. See Leo Löwenthal, *Mitmachen wollte ich nie. Ein autobiographisches Gespräch mit Helmut Dubiel*, Frankfurt am Main 1980.

[49]*ibid.*

[50]Paul Natorp, *Die logischen Grundlagen der exakten Wissenschaften*, Leipzig and Berlin 1910, p. 14, cited in Ulrich Sieg, *Aufstieg und Niedergang des Marburger Neukantianismus. Die Geschichte einer philosophischen Schulgemeinschaft*, Würzburg 1994, p. 272. This is also the essence of Norbert Elias's argument in his essay 'Vom Sehen in der Natur'; see Blomert, *Intellektuelle im Aufbruch*, p. 224.

divide was that opened up as a result of this conflict within *Blau-Weiß* between two world-views can only be guessed at. One might interpret the divide as re-emerging later on in Frankfurt, when Elias, now working as an assistant to Karl Mannheim, once again found himself competing against the ideological axioms of the Institute for Social Research, with which Löwenthal and Fromm were associated. In any event, in July 1924, over a year after the conflict with the Frankfurt circle, Franz Meyer informed Bandmann that "the Heidelbergers have now gone psychoanalytic". Bandmann's sarcastic comment in his diary is as follows: "How quickly all that pompous ruckus died down".[51] The neo-orthodox fashion for Buber, he was suggesting, had given way to the new, contemporary fashion for Freud.

IV

In contrast to the Frankfurt circle, the Breslau group would cling to their ideals, their model remaining the Italian Renaissance, their goal the self-reflective, self-educating personality. The whole*Blau-Weiß* movement under the influence of the Breslau group ideas insisted upon a vision of generational process, each generation taking up the civilising project, developing it further, passing it on to the next generation, all the while—as they had learned from Hönigswald and the art historian Wilhelm Pinder[52]—retaining the right to develop its own "generational style". If their ideals were historical ones, the educational model they favoured was forward-looking: what they and other Zionists wanted to create and promote was a Jewish national culture. A nation *is* what it wants *to be*. This was ultimately a far more reflective stance than that of the followers of Martin Buber, who wished to regrasp the thread of Jewish culture through a romanticised and socialistically refashioned reinterpretation of Old Testament heroes and prophets. The Breslau group rejected the transfiguration of the "spirit of Massada" as the "Zionism of redemption".

In their efforts to become the avant-garde of Zionism, the *Blau-Weiß* members nurtured what Helmut Lethen has described as a a "cult of distance [*Sachlichkeit*]", thereby gaining more leeway within the ideologically crusty Zionist movement, and indeed within German society in general in the socially and politically difficult years after the First World War.[53] Against the background of the connections, elaborated by Lethen, between social disintegration, the self-dramatisation of a young generation of intellectuals, and a new set of behavioural teachings in the 1920s and 1930s, *Blau-Weiß* appears to constitute a more or less typical agent for "behavioural

[51]Bandmann diaries, CZA A 365/11, 5 July 1924.

[52]The influential art critic W. Pinder must have been an inspiring academic teacher, as one can gather from Bandmann's diaries. A critical evaluation of his academic work, from which Karl Mannheim, Norbert Elias and many others profited, would certainly be a useful undertaking. See Horst Bredekamp's brief tribute to Pinder '"Kunsthistoriker Hitlers"? Zum fünfzigsten Todestag Wilhelm Pinders. Sympathie für die klassische Moderne', in *Der Tagesspiegel*, 13 May 1997, p. 29.

[53]See Helmut Lethen, 'Norbert Elias' Konstruktion der "satisfaktionsfähigen Gesellschaft. Die Wandlungen des "verbürgerlichten Kriegerethos" und das Ideal des Lebens in der Distanz', in Reinhard Blomert, Hans Ulrich Eßlinger, Norbert Giovannini (eds.), *Heidelberger Sozial- und Staatswissenschaften: das Institut für Sozial- und Staatswissenschaften zwischen 1918 und 1958*, Marburg 1997, pp. 291–309, esp. p. 294f.

teachings on functionality".[54] These new teachings, which created distance and promised clear insights into deeper social-political interconnections and cultural-historical mechanisms, served the majority of the young *Blau-Weiß* leaders in the early 1920s as a protective mechanism and as new style of thinking—as a means of securing their status and as an intellectual basis of their Zionist vision. These young Zionists discovered an ideal of self-empowerment rooted in classical concept of life as art, as articulated among classical authors such as Aristotle, Epictetus and Seneca whom the Breslau *Blau-Weiß* branch encountered for example in Hönigswald's seminars, and as found in some of Nietzsche's writings—that author being revered not only by the circle around Elias and Bandmann.[55] Regarded from this angle, the ideological conflict between Bandmann and Elias's group, on the one hand, and the followers of a socialistically refashioned, scripturally fundamentalist understanding of Jewish identity, on the other, appears in a new light. For it was not merely a conflict over one's own self-understanding, one's own Jewish identity, but went deeper and was more fundamental. It was an *ethical* dispute. In the understanding of Elias and his friends, ethics could no longer be regarded as a tradition-derived substance to be simply handed down in turn, but rather was primarily grounded in the position of the individual, in his or her *ethos*.[56]

It is interesting that these new "Zionist behavioural teachings" exercised strong powers of attraction for the young Jewish intellectuals of the generation born around 1900. The future philosopher Leo Strauss, for example, considered the possibility, after receiving his doctorate in 1922, of joining the Breslau *Blau-Weiß* group in order to work together with Bandmann, Elias and others on common Zionist projects.[57]

The interpretation of the above-cited newly discovered sources, revealing new aspects of Norbert Elias's life until 1925, will no doubt produce various interesting conclusions regarding the genesis of his thinking. One significant finding has already emerged: the centrepiece of his sociology, his figurational model, as well as his scholarly credo of "handing on the torch", can be traced back surprisingly clearly to his days in *Blau-Weiß*. Without his contact with others in this group who possessed extraordinary intellectual abilities, without having had the chance to elaborate a Zionist-oriented vision in a particularly intense social and intellectual atmosphere over many years, the future cultural sociologist and *Menschenwissenschaftler* Norbert

[54]See Helmut Lethen's path-breaking *Verhaltenslehren der Kälte. Lebensversuche zwischen den Kriegen*, Frankfurt am Main 1994, now translated as *Cool Conduct. The Culture of Distance in Weimar Germany*, Los Angeles 2002.

[55]See Wilhelm Schmid, 'Uns selbst gestalten – Philosophie der Lebenskunst bei Nietzsche', in *Nietzsche-Studien* 21 (1992). The Breslau *Blau-Weiß* members were also inspired by Georg Simmel, particularly by his attention to the relationship between life and form as well as to 'style of life'.

[56]See Wilhelm Schmid, *Philosophie der Lebenskunst. Eine Grundlegung*, Frankfurt am Main 1998, esp. pp. 27–94.

[57]See the Bandmann diaries CZA A 365/5, 7 September 1922. See also Hackeschmidt, *Von Kurt Blumenfeld zu Norbert Elias*, p. 222. In his review 'Verfolgung und die Kunst des Schreibens. Die Moderne ist antiker, als sie glaubt: Eine Renaissance von Leo Strauss?' in *Frankfurter Allgemeine Zeitung*, 3 December 1996, p. 21, Rüdiger Bubner concludes that "Strauss' conflict with Spinoza exists in the context of a Jewish attempt at self-understanding after the First World War". Further research on this topic could shed light on the inner-Zionist and inner-Jewish debates of that period, a subject thus far receiving little attention either within German historiography or outside it.

Elias is indeed hardly imaginable. And this fact may go far to explain why, after his entry into the world of academic sociology, Elias chose to keep his time as a pioneer and leader of the *Blau-Weiß* group a secret. When, after reading *Was ist Soziologie?* Martin Bandmann tracked down the friend of his youth in December 1972 and wrote to him from Israel, Elias revealed no gaps of memory in his response:

> I was happy to receive your letter. .... But this as well as my other books and essays swim against the tide, so to speak. ... I am therefore all the more pleased that you so clearly recognised the meaning of this little introduction. Perhaps something like a tradition of our Breslau circle does exist, even if I sometimes ask myself what it was that we actually did there. But in any event we never liked vague speaking. Speaking and thinking clearly was always our thing.[58]

The circle in which the seeds of *Über den Prozeß der Zivilisation* were sown, aimed precisely at a modern Jewish society of the future, was not only scattered to the four winds by the turmoil and terror of the 1930s and 1940s. With the exception of Norbert Elias, its leading members all entered professions in which the intellectual work of their student days could not be further developed in a scholarly framework. This marks a contrast to the Frankfurt *Blau-Weiß* group, distinguished by members such as Erich Fromm, Leo Löwenthal, Ernst Simon and Gerhard Scholem who went on to enjoy long and illustrious careers.[59] As his late, unexpected fame set in, it was thus possible for Elias to appear as an intellectual loner—as an individual who had managed to found an entire school against all odds. In Elias's own eyes fifty years later, those with a share in his early intellectual development would have been of little interest to anyone. Furthermore, the fact that the national *Blau-Weiß*—unlike its Zionist-socialist milieu—had experimented with a charismatic leadership model, and the fact that it had failed with its dubious leader, did not favour drawing attention to this formative but far from self-explanatory period of his life.

[58]Martin Bandmann to Norbert Elias, 28 December 1972; Norbert Elias to Martin Bandmann, 29 March 1973. Both letters are in the Norbert Elias papers, manuscript collection, general inventory nos. 1–55, box no. 32 (documents received), Deutsches Literaturarchiv, Marbach.

[59]Even today, the circle of young Jewish intellectuals around the so-called *Freie jüdische Lehrhaus* in Frankfurt during the 1920s, which more or less emerged from the circle of Rabbi Nehemia Anton Nobel, is still celebrated as part of an "intellectual dawn" (Wolfgang Schivelbusch, *Intellektuellendämmerung. Zur Lage der Frankfurter Intelligenz in den zwanziger Jahren*, Frankfurt am Main 1982). Had the individuals associated with the Breslau circle not become doctors, politicians, solicitors, mathematicians and journalists but rather prominent scholars like Löwenthal, Fromm, Scholem and Simon, Elias would most likely himself have gained timely renown as part of an exceptional circle of Weimar-period Jewish intellectuals.

"The Enemy of Hypothesis": Fritz Saxl as Acting Director of the Bibliothek Warburg

BY DOROTHEA MCEWAN

It is a great achievement for an individual to turn a private library into a centre of excellence appreciated by the wider community. It must rank as an outstanding achievement to effect the same task twice in very different situations and in two different countries. But Fritz Saxl accomplished this in addition to producing his own research and guiding the work of other scholars. Despite the fact that his managerial qualities were at times chaotic, in the years 1920 to 1924 a Hamburg scholar's private library indeed emerged as a centre for scholarship in institutional contact with Hamburg University and well known to a wider community of international scholars. And after some ten years, in December 1933, under the threat of the library's imminent destruction by the Nazis, he managed to transport it and its collection of photographs lock, stock and barrel to London, where he would negotiate its continued existence as a research institute: a process that culminated in forging enduring institutional links with the University of London in 1944.[1] These achievements were all the more remarkable in that neither Saxl nor his collaborators in the Warburg Library were trained librarians, their research interests rather coinciding with those of the library.

This article discusses Saxl's work as acting director of the library in Aby Warburg's absence from 1920 to 1924.[2] The main source for the following information is the correspondence collection in the archives of the Warburg Institute. More than one thousand letters covering a period of four and a half years furnish insight into the way Saxl both shaped the work in the library and moved it in a direction extending beyond its status as a collection of books and photographs purchased by its owner.

[1]Gertrud Bing, 'Fritz Saxl (1890–1948): A memoir', in D. J. Gordon, *Fritz Saxl. 1890–1948. A volume of Memorial Essays from his friends in England*, London and Edinburgh1957, pp. 1–46; Fritz Saxl, 'The History of Warburg's Library (1886–1944)', in E. H. Gombrich, *Aby Warburg. An Intellectual Biography*, Oxford 1970, pp. 325–338; Dorothea McEwan, 'A Tale of One Institute and Two Cities: The Warburg Institute', in Ian Wallace (ed.), *German-Speaking Exiles in Great Britain. The Yearbook of the Research Centre for German and Austrian Exile Studies*, vol. 1 (1999); Hans-Michael Schäfer, *Die Kulturwissenschaftliche Bibliothek Warburg*, Berlin 2003, (Berliner Arbeiten zur Bibliothekswissenschaft 11).

[2]For a discussion of the collaboration of Warburg and Saxl from 1920 to Warburg's death in 1929 see the forthcoming publication by Dorothea McEwan, *Wanderstrassen der Kultur. Die Aby Warburg—Fritz Saxl Korrespondenz von 1920 bis 1929*, Hamburg 2004.

Fritz Saxl, 1890–1948, librarian and second director of the Kulturwissenschaftliche Bibliothek Warburg in Hamburg and first director of The Warburg Institute in London.

All illustrations in this article by courtesy of The Warburg Institute, London.

The Warburg-Saxl collaboration had its beginnings before 1920. Warburg used his collection of books and photographs – his tools – to interpret the *Wanderstrassen der Kultur*,[3] the pathways of intellectual activity and in particular images as they metamorphosed over time—in this way investigating, among other topics, the cultural history of astrology. The link between the world of symbols and the world of images, between a mythical and a rational worldview,[4] was made visible in the iconography of planets, the topic that was the immediate point of contact between Warburg and Saxl. In 1910, when he was barely twenty years old, Saxl turned to Warburg while researching medieval astrological illustrations, in particular the contrast between the oriental belief in stars and the Christian understanding of wisdom.[5] At that time Warburg was researching the cycle of astrological frescoes in the Palazzo Schifanoja in Ferrara and was excited at the chance to cultivate "a fertile astrological cabbage

[3]'Wanderstrassen der Kultur' is a phrase used by Saxl in his article 'Das Nachleben der Antike. Zur Einführung in die Bibliothek Warburg', in *Hamburger Universitätszeitung*, 11/4. 1921, p. 245. Saxl also used 'Wanderstrassen der Tradition' in his article 'Die Kulturwissenschaftliche Bibliothek Warburg in Hamburg', in Ludolph Brauer *et al.* (eds.), *Forschungsinsistute: Ihre Geschichte, Organisation und Ziele,* Hamburg 1930, p. 355.

[4]'Microcosm and Memory', book review by Roger Hinks of Fritz Saxl's *Lectures*, in *The Times Literary Supplement*, 23 May 1958.

[5]Ernst H. Gombrich 'Introduction', in *A Heritage of Images. A selection of Lectures by Fritz Saxl*, Harmondsworth 1970, p. 10.

patch".[6] Saxl and Warburg must have instantly sensed each other's fascination for this field of research. Following Saxl's first visit to Warburg in March 1910, a correspondence began marked by deference on the part of Saxl and a paternal, *Doktorvater* attitude on the part of Warburg.

Warburg thus became a mentor to the eager young Viennese student. He paid for Saxl's travel to England in the autumn of 1911 for research in the Bodleian Library and put Saxl in touch with Carl Heinrich Becker, the editor of the journal *Der Islam*, where Saxl published his 'Beiträge zu einer Geschichte der Planetendarstellungen im Orient und Okzident' in April 1912.[7] Likewise, after Saxl graduated from the University of Vienna in July 1912, Warburg contacted Franz Boll in Heidelberg, and Boll arranged a scholarship for him from the Academy of Sciences in Heidelberg to travel to Italy and work in the Vatican Library on medieval Latin astrological and mythological manuscripts.

It was an ideal collaboration: Warburg had the contacts and Saxl the "good nose"[8] for finds. Following Saxl's discovery in the Vatican Library of the Ms. Urb. Lat. 899, the description of the wedding at Pesaro of Costanzo Sforza and Camilla d'Aragona in 1475, embellished with illustrations of gods and astral divinities, Warburg observed in one letter that "Your discovery urb. 899 is simply splendid".[9] After the scholarship funds were exhausted, he offered Saxl more money from his regular annual library budget. From very early on in their collaboration Warburg used the term "work schedule", so as to make it clear to Saxl that there was work to do and they would do it together. Newly married and, as a Jew, without hope of employment as an art historian in one of the Imperial museum collections in the Austro-Hungarian civil service,[10] Saxl accepted the offer of a research assistantship to Warburg in January 1914.[11]

However, with the onset of the First World War, Saxl had to join the Austro-Hungarian army, spending the years from 1915 to 1918 on the Italian front. In his many letters and postcards from the front, he told Warburg of his ideas for the future—in particular building a bridge between astrology and Rembrandt's *oeuvre* and in general engaging in research that remained unaffected by the swings of politics. He expressed his hopes of returning to Hamburg and of working in the Warburg Library, or alternatively, of starting another Warburg Library in Vienna.[12]

Although Warburg had told Saxl not to worry about the future, Warburg himself was thinking about the future of his life's work, the library. In a diary entry of 12 February 1917[13] he recorded a conversation he had had with his son Max Adolf, who was then fifteen years of age, in the course of which he stressed that he spoke as a

[6]Universitätsbibliothek Heidelberg (UH), Heid.Hs. 2109, Aby Warburg to Franz Boll, 11 November 1910.
[7]*Der Islam. Eine Zeitschrift für Geschichte und Kultur des islamischen Orients*, vol. 3, Straßburg 1912, pp. 151–177.
[8]UH, Heid.Hs. 2109, Aby Warburg to Franz Boll, 27 June 1913.
[9]WIA, GC and Copybook 4, p. 151, Aby Warburg to Fritz Saxl, 27 April 1913.
[10]See WIA, GC, Fritz Saxl to Aby Warburg, 11 August 1912.
[11]WIA, Copybook 5, p. 322, Aby Warburg to Fritz Saxl, 10 January 1914; GC, Aby Warburg to Fritz Saxl, 16 January 1914 and GC, Fritz Saxl to Aby Warburg, 17 January 1914.
[12]See Dorothea McEwan, *Das Ausreiten der Ecken*, Hamburg 1998, *passim*.
[13]WIA, III.10.7, p. 885; Tagebuch 1917.

Bildhistoriker, a historian of images, and not as a *Kunsthistoriker*, a historian of art. Should his heirs not want to preserve the library, Warburg informed his son, he did not want it to become public property. The war, he explained, had taught him that a public building would be much more vulnerable to aerial bombing than a private house.

Apart from this very practical consideration, what then would be the long-term future for a private library if the heirs did not wish to continue with it? In 1917 Warburg did not see a solution, but Saxl, cut off on the Austro-Italian front from his research tools in Hamburg, frequently referred in his letters to the desirability of transforming Warburg's library into a centre for scholarship. This was to become the third way: a privately owned and financed institution, but open to students and scholars free of charge, hence a valuable and practical resource precisely at the time when a university was being established in Hamburg.

The political collapse of Germany and Austria in 1918 proved too much for Warburg, whose health, never very good, now deteriorated. He spent the years leading up to August 1924 in sanatoriums, first shortly in Hamburg and Jena and then from 1921 onwards in Kreuzlingen, Switzerland. In October 1918, Warburg had entrusted Saxl and Wilhelm Printz in his last will with directing the library after his death.[14] In November 1919 Max Moritz Warburg took the practical step of offering Saxl the directorship, his main duty being to safeguard the library's continued existence.[15] The family knew that Aby Warburg thought highly of Saxl; at a time of political chaos and unemployment, Saxl, who had been on a short-term contract in the *Reichsbildungsamt*[16] in Vienna, jumped at the offer and accepted a financially secure position. At a time when public libraries did not have funds for basic maintenance, Saxl could continue to purchase both books and photographs from the funds available to Warburg's library. He set out to shape his work in the spirit of the conversation he had had with Aby Warburg in Florence in April 1914, that "only the institution of scholarships attached to the library would attract a succession of scholars from Germany and from abroad".[17]

Saxl started work as acting director in April 1920. He had to continue Warburg's tasks,[18] checking sales catalogues, buying books, continuing preparation of the library's alphabetical catalogue. In addition, he adopted a colour coding scheme as a finding aid, three bands of colour on every volume facilitating the search for books on the same topic.[19] Saxl now set about publicising the library as a research centre, writing articles on its research directions and the methods incorporated into its organisation; he also saw to the library being listed in official catalogues, book clubs,

[14]WIA, Copybook 6, pp. 392, 392, 394. Aby Warburg, Last Will, 19 October 1918.

[15]WIA, GC, Max Moritz Warburg to Fritz Saxl, 3 November 1919.

[16]The *Reichsbildungsamt*, an adult education facility, was organised by the army to keep returned soldiers in education.

[17]Fritz Saxl, 'The History of Warburg's Library (1886–1944)', in E. H.Gombrich, *Aby Warburg. An Intellectual Biography*, Oxford 1970, pp. 329–330.

[18]WIA, GC, Fritz Saxl to Franz Cumont, 14 September 1923. Saxl here indicates that research in the Warburg library has continued along the lines established by Cumont, building on Cumont's efforts to understand the religions and through this the culture of late antiquity.

[19]In one letter, Saxl indicates that a cupboard full of colour-coded books resembles a parrot; *ibid.*, Fritz Saxl to Aby Warburg, 23 September 1922.

and bibliographies. Finally, he initiated plans for a new building: a project made urgent as a result of an ever-increasing number of books crowding an albeit large, patrician private house, but not large enough to accommodate a sizeable and growing collection of books used by a steadily increasing number of readers. In July 1924, immediately before Warburg's return to Hamburg, Saxl referred to a tension between two needs: on the one hand, a need to shelve books according to the strict cataloguing system called 'Prussian Instructions' for libraries; on the other hand, a need to accommodate new categories of books. Warburg had shelved books treating similar topics alongside each other, the principle of "good neighbourliness" is still in use at the collection of the Warburg Institute to this day. But Saxl did not complain about this principle, rather about the fact that the system which should resemble a rank and file "tree nursery", resembled more a "thicket", in constant need of Warburg's pruning hand to balance unity and richness.[20]

In addition to such interrelated tasks Saxl turned his attention to finding new ways of forming ties with a widespread scholarly community. In May 1921 he sent a proposal to Max M. Warburg: he wanted to start evening lectures in the library, to be delivered by its users on topics related to their research. In this way the library could become a research venue for scholars in Hamburg and attract scholars from outside the city; the lectures would also provide a forum for publishing their work. He envisioned a format of twelve lectures per year, with their ensuing publication in an annual volume. Saxl, we learn from one letter, had contacted the philosopher Ernst Cassirer, the medievalist Richard Salomon, the orientalist Heinrich Junker (all professors at Hamburg University) and Karl Reinhardt (retired headmaster of the Goethe Gymnasium in Frankfurt am Main), all of whom thought highly of this project. The academic backing was thus in place; Saxl now only needed financial support to cover an anticipated annual budget of some 50,000 marks.[21] He began negotiations with two publishers in Berlin: Weidmann and the *Verein wissenschaftlicher Verleger*;[22] two in Leipzig: J. C. Hinrichs and B. G. Teubner; and the Oskar Beck publishing house in Munich.[23] In August 1921 in one of his regular letters to Warburg, Saxl summarised that both, a lecture and a publication programme, had achieved what Saxl had aimed for all along: "your library has become an academic institute with tangible results".[24]

Within two months Saxl had received positive replies from Karl Reinhardt, Ernst Cassirer, the orientalist Hellmut Ritter and Richard Salomon in regard to a lecture programme for 1921–1922. By mid-October 1921, he was circulating the lecture programme to editors of scholarly journals with an accompanying request to publicise the programme.[25] Saxl delivered the first lecture on 29 October 1921. It

[20]*ibid.*, Fritz Saxl to Aby Warburg, 26 July 1924.

[21]*ibid.*, Fritz Saxl to Max M. Warburg, 20 May 1921.

[22]*ibid.*, Fritz Saxl to Max M. Warburg, 6 June 1921.

[23]*ibid.*, M.M. Warburg & Co to Fritz Saxl, 30 November 1921.

[24]*ibid.*, Fritz Saxl to Aby Warburg, 8 August 1921. "Damit ist endlich das erreicht, was mir immer vorgeschwebt hat: Ihre Bibliothek ist vollkommen ein wissenschaftliches Institut geworden mit produktiven Ergebnissen."

[25]*ibid.*, Fritz Saxl to George Sarton, editor of *Isis* in Brussels, and to Johann Ilberg, editor of the *Neue Jahrbücher* in Leipzig, both 20 October 1921.

was a presentation of the aims of the library as an aid to academic research, that is, as a *Problembibliothek* providing tools for exploring the network of topics comprising the historical continuum of classical motifs and ideas.[26] Clara Hertz, the library's administrator, wrote to Wilhelm Printz that "no one but Saxl could have spoken so totally in accordance with Warburg".[27]

It is important to note that at this time to be offered a honorarium for a lecture, full reimbursement of expenses, and the lecture's assured publication was a rare opportunity (and one of the main motivations for Saxl's fund-raising activities).[28] From 1921 onwards, there was a flurry of letters inviting scholars to deliver the lectures; the letters cover practical matters and logistics: subject areas to be discussed, slides to be shown, finding the right titles, fixing or changing lecture dates, financial arrangements, hospitality to be provided by Mary Warburg in Hamburg, and so forth.[29]

Saxl sent detailed reports after the lectures to Warburg. After the Gustav Pauli lecture, which he described as brilliant in its details but weak on the whole, Saxl took the opportunity to spell out how he himself lectured: he demonstrated to students that images alone will not make them understand art. He instilled in them that it was necessary to use textual sources as well.[30] The initial "tangible result" of Saxl's efforts was the first volume of lectures, covering the years 1921–1922 and published by the B.G. Teubner publishing house the following year.[31] The volume contained articles by Fritz Saxl, Ernst Cassirer, Adolph Goldschmidt, Gustav Pauli, Eduard Wechßler, Hellmut Ritter and Heinrich Junker. Saxl also started a second series of monograph-length scholarly *Studies*, often the result of reworking and expanding lecture texts. The first volume of this series was published in 1922.[32]

The library came to serve as an example for other similar institutions. One letter, for example, refers to the information offered to Saxl by Wilhelm Waetzoldt, Aby

[26]F. Saxl, 'Die Bibliothek Warburg und ihr Ziel', in *Vorträge 1921–1922*, Leipzig and Berlin 1923 (Vorträge der Bibliothek Warburg, herausgegeben von Fritz Saxl), p. 9.

[27]WIA, GC, Clara Hertz to Wilhelm Printz, 4 November 1921.

[28]*ibid.*, Fritz Saxl to Paul Tillich, 22 June1921; Richard Salomon, 23 June1921; Julius von Schlosser, 12 July 1921.

[29]*ibid.*, Fritz Saxl to Richard Reitzenstein, 24 January 1922.

[30]*ibid.*, Fritz Saxl to Aby Warburg, 24 November 1922. Pauli lectured on 'Dürer, Italien und die Antike'. Gertrud Bing also sent a series of interesting reports on lectures to Warburg in 1923 and 1924. See *ibid.*, Gertrud Bing to Aby Warburg, 29 January 1923 (concerning Ernst Cassirer's 'Eidos und Eidolon. Das Problem des Schönen und der Kunst in Platons Dialogen'; published in *Vorträge 1922–23, 1. Teil*, Leipzig and Berlin, 1924, pp.1–27); 17 March 1923 (Alfred Doren's 'Fortuna im Mittelalter und in der Renaissance'; *ibid.*, pp. 71–144); 16 November 1923 (Richard Reitzenstein's 'Augustin als antiker und mittelalterlicher Mensch' in *Vorträge 1923–24*, Leipzig and Berlin 1926, pp. 28–65; 31 March 1924 (Hugo Gressmann's 'Die Umwandlung der orientalischen Religionen unter dem Einfluß hellenischen Geistes'; *ibid.*, pp. 170–195); 9 May and 21 May 1924 (Ulrich von Wilamowitz-Möllendorff's 'Zeus'; *ibid.*, pp. 1–16); December [no day] 1923 (on Fritz Saxl's lecturing technique in general).

[31]Fritz Saxl (ed.), *Vorträge 1921–22*, Leipzig and Berlin 1923.

[32]Ernst Cassirer, *Die Begriffsform im mythischen Denken*, Leipzig and Berlin 1922 (Fritz Saxl (ed.), Studien I). Nine volumes in the series of *Vorträge* and twenty-one in the series of *Studien* would appear before the library moved to London. In London, the first volume of the *Journal of the Warburg Institute*, more or less serving the same function as the *Vorträge*, appeared in 1937; from 1940–1941 until the present, this latter publication has been published as the *Journal of the Warburg and Courtauld Institutes*; sixty five volumes of the *Journal* have been published to date.

Warburg's first research assistant, since 1912 professor of art history at the University of Halle, from 1927 onwards director general of the State Museums in Berlin: the Zurich art historian Heinrich Bodmer wished to have a look at the library since he had established an endowment for a library at the University of Basel and wanted to see for himself how to set one up.[33] Likewise, in thanking Saxl for receipt of the lecture programme, Professor Wilhelm Cappelle of Hamburg University stressed that the Warburg Library stood out in the hard times that had now hit Germany,[34] while Dagobert Frey, an Austrian colleague of Saxl's who had delivered a lecture at the library in June 1923, was enthusiastic about its superb research facilities. Acknowledging Saxl's achievement in continuing publication when other journals had folded—his budget being tied to the U.S. dollar—Frey suggested a close collaboration between the Warburg Library and the Vienna School of Art History, which had developed its own methodology.[35] Saxl was being approached by family members or friends of deceased scholars who, in need of money, wished to sell whole libraries: the correspondence records this being the case for the libraries of Rudolf Pagenstecher and Franz Boll.[36] At the same time, Saxl was being mailed recommendations for scholars deemed worthy of lecturing at the library and was being approached by various individuals—graduates, scholars, and artists—wishing to discuss employment possibilities, for instance by the young historian Percy Ernst Schramm (member of a Hamburg senatorial family and, in fact, Warburg's personal friend).[37] Saxl's need to find highly capable collaborators is attested to in his indication that "the operations are expanding and my strength does not grow in proportion".[38]

A large part of Saxl's time was devoted to keeping up his correspondence with Aby Warburg. "Every nine days a letter was sent to Kreuzlingen", he stated in the library's annual report for 1922,[39] but in fact he wrote twice as many letters brimful with organisational matters, research findings, acquisition news and many more topics. On his side of the correspondence, Warburg revealed some impatience, making numerous requests regarding the shelf-location of newly purchased books, how the colour coding worked, and who was using the library.[40] Saxl meticulously addressed every item in every letter, whether the subject was trivial like ordering pencil leads in Vienna or ambitious projects such as Warburg's preparation of an enlarged version of his Luther book.[41] These letters may thus be viewed as

[33]WIA, GC, Wilhelm Waetzoldt to Fritz Saxl, 5 June 1921.

[34]*ibid.*, Wilhelm Cappelle to Fritz Saxl, 27 October 1923.

[35]*ibid.*, Dagobert Frey to Fritz Saxl, 29 June 1923; *ibid.*, Dagobert Frey to Fritz Saxl, 9 October 1923.

[36]*ibid.*, Fritz Saxl to the widow of the late Rudolf Pagenstecher, 8 April 1922; *ibid.*, extensive correspondence in 1924 between Fritz Saxl, Gustav Herbig, Emilie Boer, Jürgen Boll, and others.

[37]*ibid.*, Percy Ernst Schramm to Fritz Saxl, 22 April 1922 and Fritz Saxl to Percy Ernst Schramm, 1 May 1922.

[38]*ibid.*, Fritz Saxl to Aby Warburg, 23 March 1922. "Ich muss ja jetzt schauen, Mitarbeiter zu bekommen, da der Betrieb sich immer mehr ausdehnt und eigentlich meine Kraft nicht im gleichem Maasse [!] wächst."

[39]WIA, V.2.1.3.1.2.Jahresbericht, 1922, p. 2.

[40]WIA, GC, Wilhelm Printz to Aby Warburg, 16 March 1924.

[41]*ibid.*, Fritz Saxl to Aby Warburg, 12 January 1924. See Aby Warburg. *Heidnisch-antike Weissagung in Wort und Bild zu Luthers Zeiten*, Heidelberg 1920 (Sitzungsberichte der Heidelberger Akademie der Wissenschaften 26). In fact, it was published as a separate volume in May 1921 and re-published in Aby Warburg, *Gesammelte Schriften*, vol. II, Leipzig and Berlin 1932, pp. 487–558 and pp. 647–656.

Gertrud Bing, 1892–1964, librarian and third director of The Warburg Institute in London.

anticipating the *Bibliothekstagebuch* that from 1926 onwards contained nearly always daily entries by Warburg, Saxl and Gertrud Bing, offering information to each other on the day's comings and goings in the library and listing both Warburg's questions and Saxl's and Bing's answers.

Saxl also had to report to Max Moritz Warburg and the other Warburg brothers on developments in the library. And he had to deal with various matters other than business: in 1921, after the publication of the Luther book, he did a great deal to publicise it, arranging for its review in fifteen newspapers and journals;[42] in 1923 we find him offering birthday greetings to the University of Hamburg's chancellor, Werner von Melle, in a letter stressing the contribution of the library to the academic life of Hamburg.[43] In the midst of it all he submitted his publications and application forms to qualify for a teaching post in the University of Hamburg, the so-called *Habilitation*, and was duly awarded the degree in July 1922. He modestly declared in a letter to Warburg that this had been as a result of Saxl's post as acting director of Warburg's Library; he called the process a "farce".[44] On the same day he thanked

[42]See Dorothea McEwan 'Making a Reception. Fritz Saxl and Warburg's Book *Heidnisch-antike Weissagung in Wort und Bild zu Luthers Zeiten*', in Richard Woodfield (ed.), *Art history as cultural history. Warburg's projects*, Amsterdam 2000, pp. 93–120.

[43]WIA, GC, Fritz Saxl to Werner von Melle, 17 October 1923.

[44]*ibid.*, Fritz Saxl and Clara Hertz to Aby Warburg, 3 July 1922, Warburg/Saxl file. The topic of Saxl's *Habilitation* was his research into Jacopo Zucchi's cycle of frescoes, published as *Antike Götter in der Spätrenaissance. Ein Freskenzyklus und ein Discorso des Jacopo Zucchi*, Leipzig and Berlin 1927 (Studien der Bibliothek Warburg 8).

Richard Salomon for guiding him through the process, promising that he would not bring "shame" on the university—and offering to hold a seminar at the Warburg Library free of charge.[45] In addition to his work in Hamburg, Saxl spent several weeks each year with Aby Warburg in the Kreuzlingen sanatorium. This made it necessary to keep up a correspondence with the sanatorium's director, the now famous existential psychologist Ludwig Binswanger, as Saxl needed his permission to come to Kreuzlingen.[46] Warburg looked forward to Saxl's visits, urging him to stay as long as possible. Saxl worked unstintingly to help Warburg overcome his illness. The close collaboration of the two men resulted in two major achievements along with the Luther book: the publication in 1922 of Warburg's lecture—delivered to the Tenth International Congress of Art History in Rome in 1912—on the frescoes in the Palazzo Schifanoja in Ferrara,[47] and the important lecture Warburg delivered in the sanatorium Bellevue in Kreuzlingen in April 1923 on the Serpent Ritual of the Hopi people in Colorado.[48]

Among the reasons for giving a lecture in Kreuzlingen might have been the encouragement Ludwig Binswanger gave him to write his autobiography. Another reason might have been a lecture by Binswanger in November 1922 on "Phenomenology", which was meant to demonstrate that Binswanger had fully regained his intellectual powers after a long period of illness; possibly Warburg felt encouraged to do likewise. Warburg's trip to America in 1895–1896 had made a deep impression on the young man; to return to this experience from a distance of some thirty years was an exciting project. Saxl had slides prepared from the photographs that Warburg had taken in America; he reviewed the text with Warburg and supplied literature on the Hopi religious rituals as well as on the major topic of the lecture, the function of magic and fear. In general, Saxl served as Warburg's moral support throughout an extremely difficult time—a role leading to Saxl's cancellation of his own lecture course scheduled to be given at Hamburg University in the spring of 1923. The dean of the philosophy faculty, Conrad Borchling, responded to Saxl's apologies with generosity: it was important to the university, he indicated, that Saxl work with Warburg in Kreuzlingen so that one day Warburg might be well enough to return to Hamburg.[49]

On his return from the sanatorium to Hamburg on 13 August 1924, Warburg, who was ordinarily not lavish with praise, expressed strong appreciation in a letter to his brother of both Saxl's and Bing's running of the library in his absence: they truly had understood his intentions; he was assured that the library would remain an important institute beyond his death. Furthermore, he indicated, he was convinced that he had created something new and was only surprised that "this potentially

[45]*ibid.*, Fritz Saxl to Richard Salomon, 3 July 1922.

[46]For instance *ibid.*, Fritz Saxl to Ludwig Binswanger, 25 March 1922.

[47]'Italienische Kunst und internationale Astrologie im Palazzo Schifanoja zu Ferrara', in *Italia e l'Arte Straniera. Atti del X. Congresso internazionale di Storia dell'Arte,* Roma 1922, p. 179 and in Aby Warburg, *Die Erneuerung der heidnischen Antike. Gesammelte Schriften,* Leipzig and Berlin 1932, vol. II, pp. 459–481 and pp. 627–644.

[48]First published in English, 'A Lecture on Serpent Ritual', transl. by W.F. Mainland, *Journal of the Warburg Institute,* vol. 2, no. 4 (1938–1939), pp. 277–292.

[49]*ibid.*, Conrad Borchling to Fritz Saxl, 16 April 1923.

poisonous substance called money can produce so much intellectual work".[50] Six weeks later, Aby Warburg resumed work, bolstered by the conviction that "my ideas have created an organism which has its own energies for growth". He applied to the Warburg family for more funds – double the annual budget.[51]

Upon sending out copies of the *Vorträge* and *Studien*, Warburg noted that both publications were the fruit of the library's lecture programme, organised "thanks to the friendship, understanding and energetic support of my friend Fritz Saxl"[52]—and again, "thanks to Saxl's enthusiasm".[53] In the same vein, he wrote elsewhere that "the world of scholarship and I owe a great debt of gratitude" to "my friend and tireless helper Dr. Saxl … for creating and organising the *Vorträge* and *Studien* after having selflessly taken up the ideas of the Warburg Library".[54] And in a letter to the bookseller C.Boysen in Hamburg, complaining about the library's publications not being on sale in his shop, he specifically mentioned that Saxl and not Warburg should be credited with the two publication series.[55]

On 24 October1924, Aby Warburg attended a library lecture for the first time—Karl Reinhardt's lecture on Ovid's *Metamorphoses*. He addressed the participants in a short opening statement, thanking them for their loyalty to the library and singling out his wife, his brothers, his friend Heinrich Embden, the librarian Gertrud Bing, Clara Hertz, and Ernst Cassirer together with the "always reliable" Fritz Saxl.[56] In December of the same year, in a letter to the ethnologist Franz Boas, he explained that in his absence Saxl had organised the lectures, which had highlighted the library's central purpose: an exploration of the cultural-historical influence of classical antiquity. In this letter, Warburg described this influence as the phenomenological result of a psychological problem, researching the social function of the memory of images. Warburg here also identified Cassirer's work as a product of the library. And he conveyed his fear to Boas of a growing tendency among Germans to attribute spiritual qualities to race, contrasting such superstition with Warburg's sense of Germany's potential role as an intellectual wellspring.[57] That Warburg was himself one such wellspring was obvious to

[50]*ibid.*, Aby Warburg to Felix M. Warburg, 2 September 1924.

[51]*ibid.*, Aby Warburg to Max M. Warburg, 23 September 1924. "daß meine Ideen ein Organ geschaffen haben, das selbständige Wachstumsenergie besitzt".

[52]*ibid.*, Aby Warburg to Federico Hermanin, 1 October 1924; "dank der freundschaftlichen und verständnisvollen Energie meines Freundes Fritz Saxl".

[53]*ibid.*, Aby Warburg to Heinrich Brockhaus, 7 April 1925.

[54]*ibid.*, Aby Warburg to Dagobert Frey, 6 October 1924. "Mir liegt daran, meinen Freund und unermüdlichen Helfer Dr. Saxl, der durch seine selbstlose Aufnahme der Idee der K.B.W. [Kulturwissenschaftliche Bibliothek Warburg] als Schöpfer und Organisator der Vorträge und Studien die wissenschaftliche Welt und mich zu grossem Dank verpflichtet hat, nur zu unterstützen."

[55]*ibid.*, Aby Warburg to C. Boysen Buchhandlung, 23 February 1925.

[56]The statement was printed on a separate sheet, inserted in *Vorträge 1922–1923, I. Teil*, Leipzig 1924.

[57]WIA, GC, Aby Warburg to Franz Boas, 13 December 1924. "Im Grunde ist das Problem vom Einfluss der Antike nur der phänomenologische Niederschlag eines ganz innerlichen psychologischen Problems; es soll versucht werden, das individuelle Bildgedächtnis – Bild im allgemeinsten Sinne gemeint – als soziale Funktion bei der Umschaltung dynamischer Entladung und intentionaler Spannung am historischen Präparat zu begreifen." Warburg further uses the expression "ich glaube mich nicht zu irren, trotzdem meine Familie wirklich keinen Grund hat, besonders optimistisch zu sein, wenn ich geistige Morgenluft wittere". Scholars writing to Warburg also confirmed his sense of the lecture programme's importance; see, for example., *ibid.*, Paul Clemen to Aby Warburg, 7 December 1925.

Warburg Institute Archive, General Correspondence. Picture postcard dated 11 June 1924 by Warburg to Saxl; colourprint of Carl Spitzweg's *Der Bücherwurm;* on the verso side is a congratulatory poem by Warburg: *'Lob mir Bibliothecarium / auf Seelenleitersprossen / im engsten animarium / studiert er unverdrossen. / Viel Glück beim Gekraxel / mein lieber Fritz Saxl.'*[58]

Warburg Institute Archive, photographs Fritz Saxl. A drawing by Mary Warburg showing Fritz Saxl sitting on the library steps reading a book in the Kulturwissenschaftliche Bibliothek Warburg, Hamburg.

Saxl. In 1924, when asked by Alfred Doren whether any preparations were being made to celebrate the cultural historian's sixtieth birthday (in 1926), he replied that he hoped to publish the printed catalogue of Warburg's library, "which would present the best introduction to his field of activity".[59] The catalogue, however, would in fact not be published until long after Warburg's death—in the 1960s in London.[60]

[58]In his poem Aby Warburg congratulates Fritz Saxl and wishes him good luck with the library. In a play on words, combining the notion of the librarian as a 'leader of souls' (*Seelenleiter*) and of Saxl climbing the rungs of a ladder (*Leitersprossen*) leading to the books—the essence of the library (*animarium*)—he implies that it is the librarian's task to create a place for the human spirit.

[59]*ibid.*, Fritz Saxl to Alfred Doren, 11 June 1924.

[60]*Catalog of The Warburg Institute Library. University of London*, Boston, MA 1967, 13 vols.

In a letter to Percy Schramm written in 1924, Warburg defined the main purpose of the Warburg library as offering a basis for exploring the cross-fertilisation of art, religion and history. The publications of the library were, he suggested, the building blocks for such a project, Erwin Panofsky (then professor of art history at the University of Hamburg) its "foreman" and Fritz Saxl its "pathfinder".[61] Saxl's outstanding achievement regarding the Warburg Library's publications would even be registered in London, John Leofric Stocks noting in 1926 in the *Classical Review* that "The care with which the volumes have been produced and the illustrations selected deserves the highest praise."[62] In recognition of his contribution to the library's scholarship, Saxl was appointed to a professorship of art history by Hamburg University on 25 November 1926.[63]

The renowned classicist Eduard Norden was one of many scholars aware of how meticulously Saxl worked. He knew, for example, how desperate Saxl became when researchers such as Franz Kampers—himself supported by the Warburg Library—submitted and re-submitted their self-defined hypotheses as facts.[64] This was the context for Norden referring to Saxl as an "enemy of hypothesis", forced to explain to "*homo Campestris*" that his "meadows" were in fact large "swamps" and not fertile "agricultural land".[65] Nevertheless, despite Saxl's influence and reputation, after Aby Warburg's return to Hamburg his position at the library was certainly difficult. He now asked the editors of *Kürschners Deutscher Literatur-Kalender* to note that his title was Librarian, no longer director of the library.[66] It redounds to Saxl's honour that he did not leave, but stood by his life's work—what followed was a few years' hiatus before the library's famous, momentous escape to London. The escape would present Saxl with an entirely fresh set of problems: with Nazi appropriation growing steadily closer, the core of the library's collection of books and photographs would be packed up, then moved four times and housed in five different locations in Hamburg and England. And integrating the Institute into British academic life was a challenge in its own right—one in which Saxl would once more prove his mastery of solving complex tasks.[67]

[61]*ibid.*, Aby Warburg to Percy Ernst Schramm, 11 November 1924.

[62]John Leofric Stocks, 'The Warburg Library', in *The Classical Review*, vol. 40 (1926), p. 76.

[63]Hamburg State Archives, pp. 361–366, Hochschulwesen—Dozenten- und Personalakten, 1, p. 357, Bernhard Schädel, Dean of the University of Hamburg, to the Hamburg university authorities, 1 July 1926.

[64]WIA, GC, Fritz Saxl to Eduard Norden, 8 February 1924.

[65]*ibid.*, Eduard Norden to Fritz Saxl, 8 March 1924. See Franz Kampers, *Vom Werdegang der abendländischen Kaisermystik* (Gedruckt mit Unterstützung der Bibliothek Warburg/Hamburg), Leipzig 1924.

[66]WIA, GC, Fritz Saxl to *Kürschners Deutscher Literatur-Kalender*, 10 February 1925.

[67]Cf. Dorothea McEwan, *Die Wanderstrassen der Kultur. Die Aby Warburg—Fritz Saxl Korrespondenz von 1920 bis 1929*, Hamburg and Munich 2004, (in press).

The Last Testament of Sigmund Freud

BY ROBERT S. WISTRICH

On the occasion of his seventieth birthday in 1926, Sigmund Freud wrote to his friend and disciple Marie Bonaparte with a characteristic touch of irony:

> The Jewish societies in Vienna and the University of Jerusalem (of which I am a trustee), in short the Jews altogether, have celebrated me like a national hero, although my service to the Jewish cause is confined to the single point that I have never denied my Jewishness. The official world – the University [of Vienna], Academy, Medical Association – completely ignored the occasion. Rightly, I think; it was only honest, I could not have looked upon their congratulations and honours as sincere.[1]

In the same letter Freud singled out the celebration of the Jewish lodge "to which I have belonged for twenty years" and the speech in his honour made there by his private physician Professor Ludwig Braun (1867–1936), "which cast a spell over the whole audience, including my family". Braun, who joined the Viennese lodge of the B'nai B'rith in 1900 (three years after Freud) and had known the founder of psychoanalysis for nearly forty years, defined him in this celebratory speech as a *Ganzjude*.[2]

Freud's quality of wholeness, his ability to recognise the unity of nature and mind behind discordant surface phenomena, his independence from religious dogma or conventional taboos and especially his courage in opposing the rest of society, had stamped him as a genuine Jew. In his spiritual "optimism", tenacious persistence, dignity and composure in the face of social rejection he had exhibited precisely those traits which explained why Jews had always been in the forefront of the fight for freedom. These same characteristics, Professor Braun suggested, had naturally drawn Freud to B'nai B'rith and its humanitarian ideals. They had also been expressed in his brainchild, the new science of psychoanalysis, which Braun described as an "authentically Jewish conception of life" (*Lebensanschauung*), devoted to seeking the general laws of nature and fearlessly exploring the depths of the mind.[3]

Freud's own address to the B'nai B'rith on 6 May 1926, with its strong affirmation of his "Jewish nature", of the humanist goals of the Viennese lodge and its importance as a forum for independent-minded men of principle, amplified Braun's

This article is based on the Max Kochmann Memorial Lecture delivered by the author on 26 November 2003 at the Austrian Embassy in London. This event was organised jointly by the Leo Baeck Institute, the Wiener Library and the Centre for German Jewish Studies, University of Sussex.

[1]Sigmund Freud to Marie Bonaparte, 10 May 1926, in *Letters of Sigmund Freud*, ed. by Ernst L. Freud, New York 1961, p. 221 (henceforth, *Letters*).

[2]Ludwig Braun, 'Die Persönlichkeit Freuds und seine Bedeutung als Bruder', in *B'nai B'rith Mittheilungen für Österreich*, no. 26, (May 1926), pp. 118–131.

[3]*ibid.*, pp. 128 ff.

remarks and demonstrated his high regard for the fraternity. Beyond that, it also provided an important testimony to his personal development, beliefs, and the nature of his Jewish identification. Freud recalled that his attraction to the lodge crystallised in the years after 1895 when he had been like a virtual pariah in Vienna.

> On the one hand I had gained the first insight into the depth of human instinct, had seen many things which were sobering, at first even frightening; on the other hand the disclosure of my unpopular discoveries led to my losing most of my personal relationships at that time. I felt as though outlawed, shunned by all. This isolation aroused in me the longing for a circle of excellent men with high ideals who would accept me in friendship despite my temerity. Your lodge was described to me as the place where I could find such men.
>
> That you are Jews could only be welcome to me, for I was myself a Jew, and it has always appeared to me not only undignified, but outright foolish to deny it. What tied me to Jewry was – I have to admit it—not the faith, not even the national pride, for I was always an unbeliever, have been brought up without religion, but without respect for the so-called "ethical" demands of human civilization. Whenever I have experienced feelings of national exaltation, I have tried to suppress them as disastrous and unfair, frightened by the warning example of those nations among which we Jews live. But there remained enough to make the attraction of Jews and Judaism irresistible, many dark emotional powers [*dunkle Gefühlsmächte*] all the stronger the less they could be expressed in words, as well as the clear consciousness of an inner identity, the familiarity of the same psychological structure [*die Heimlichkeit der gleichen seelischen Konstruktion*].[4]

According to Freud, this "uncanny" primordial feeling of solidarity, with its particularist ethnic nexus and common psychic structure, had nothing to do with Jewish religious identity. Though he could not define it, these "dark emotional powers" were in fact profoundly rooted in the Galician Jewish background from which he originated and to which he was to remain attached all his life in a typically ambivalent fashion. His personality had indeed been formed in an East European Jewish home and then nurtured in the semi-proletarian Leopoldstadt district of Vienna to which Freud's parents had moved in 1859 from his birthplace in Freiberg, Moravia (now Příbor, Czech Republic).[5]

Freud's father Jakob, born in 1815 in the Galican *shtetl* of Tsymenitz, was originally an observant Jew, the son of a hasidic rabbi. Steeped in Jewish learning and rituals he had remained strictly orthodox until the age of twenty when he moved to Freiberg. Replying to a correspondent in 1930, Sigmund Freud observed in this connection:

> It may interest you to hear that my father did indeed come from a Chassidic background. He was forty-one when I was born and had been estranged from his native environment for almost twenty years. My education was so un-Jewish that today I cannot even read your dedication, which is evidently written in Hebrew. In later life I have often regretted this lack in my education (*dieses Stück in meiner Unbildung*).[6]

[4] *Letters*, pp. 366–367. For contrasting efforts to interpret the meaning of this "inner identity", see Yosef Hayim Yerushalmi, *Freud's Moses: Judaism Terminable and Interminable*, New Haven—London 1991 and Emmanuel Rice, *Freud and Moses. The Long Journey Home*, Albany 1990.

[5] Cf. *Letters*, pp. 407–408 for Freud's letter to the Mayor of P?íbor, dated 25 October 1931, where he describes himself as the "happy child from Freiberg, the first-born son of a youthful mother, the boy who received from this air, from this soil, the first indelible impressions".

[6] *Letters*, p. 395. See Abraham A. Roback, *Freudiana*, Cambridge, MA 1957. Roback was the recipient of this letter, dated 20 February, 1930. Yerushalmi, pp. 69–70 questions Freud's claim that his education was "so un-Jewish".

Jakob Freud at the age of seventy-five.

By courtesy of the Leo Baeck Institute, New York

Sigmund Freud

By courtesy of the Oesterreichische Nationalbibliothek, Bildarchiv, Vienna

This recollection is consistent with the fact that by the time the family had migrated to Vienna for economic reasons, Freud's father had already abandoned many of his earlier religious observances. But Jakob Freud still remained Jewish to the core in his appearance (he had a long beard and dignified countenance), his ability to recite the Passover service by heart, his diligent study of the Talmud, and his knowledge of Hebrew literature.[7]

On his son's thirty-fifth birthday, Jakob Freud proudly gave him the rebound copy of the Bible that Sigmund had read as a boy, with a special Hebrew dedication written in the spirit of Jewish religious tradition:

> To my Dear Son, Solomon [Freud's Hebrew name was Shlomo, in memory of his paternal grandfather.] It was in the seventh year of your life that the spirit of G-d began to stir you and spake to you [thus] "Go thou and pore over the book which I wrote, and there will burst open for thee springs of understanding, knowledge and reason. It is indeed the book of books. Sages have delved into it and legislators have derived [from it] knowledge and law." Thou hast seen the vision of the Almighty. Thou hast listened and ventured and achieved, soaring on the wings of the wind.[8]

The gift, a token of his father's "undying love", was clearly intended to impress upon Sigmund the continuing importance of the religious tradition in which he had been

[7]Judith Bernays Heller, 'Freud's Mother and Father', *Commentary* (May 1956), pp. 418–421; Ernest Jones, *The Life and Work of Sigmund Freud,* London—New York 1953, p. 19 and *The Life and Work of Sigmund Freud,* New York 1955, p. 409. A number of scholars have shown that Jakob Freud, despite his attraction to the Haskalah (Hebrew Enlightenment) remained a devoted student of the Talmud into his old age. See David Stern, 'The Ego and the Yid', in *The New Republic*, 21 September 1992, pp. 43–49.

[8]Roback, p. 92. See Yerushalmi, pp. 71–74. The elaborate and lengthy inscription was composed by Jakob Freud in the ornate style known as *melitsah*, consisting of arcane allusions and quotations from the Bible. It shows Jakob's virtuoso command of Jewish sources and his Hebrew knowledge. Both Yerushalmi and Rice argue that it expressed the father's desire that Sigmund renew ties to the Jewish tradition he had abandoned.

raised. Yet Jakob Freud must surely have been aware that in his son's eyes the religious rituals of Judaism had long seemed to be empty and meaningless. Indeed the vehemence of Sigmund Freud's antipathy to Judaism as a religion was almost certainly connected with a symbolic rejection of the father who could no longer properly observe the traditional Jewish way of life or transmit it to him fully intact. Like so many other Jewish fathers of this transitional generation, the textile merchant Jakob Freud had only brought fragments of the living tradition to Vienna from his ghetto community in the countryside. This residual loyalty to Judaism was insufficient for the following generation, forced to live between two worlds and two cultures. For these socially and spiritually uprooted young Viennese Jews, an inherently ambiguous situation produced a sense of inner conflict and of engaging in imposture, as well as despair—the kind of localised neuroses out of which Sigmund Freud was eventually to construct his universalist psychoanalytic typology. In this sense, the Oedipus complex can indeed be seen—in Marthe Robert's terms—as a portrait writ large of the primordial "murdered father", Jakob Freud.[9]

Sigmund Freud's father-complex, of which he only became fully aware during his self-analysis following Jakob's death on 23 October 1896, was closely linked to an early childhood experience that involved antisemitism. During one of their strolls together in Vienna when Sigmund was eleven or twelve years old, Jakob Freud had recounted an incident that had occurred many years earlier during his own youth in Freiberg. A local Gentile had come up to him, knocked his *Streimel* (fur hat) into the mud and ordered him off the pavement. Instead of resisting this assault, Jakob Freud had calmly picked up his cap in the roadway. For Jakob the point of the anecdote was to illustrate how much the condition of Jews had improved since the 1830s. However, this "unheroic" conduct by his father deeply shocked young Sigmund Freud and left an indelible impression on him. In the *Interpretation of Dreams* he would recall that "I contrasted this situation, which did not please me, with another, more in harmony with my sentiments—the scene in which Hannibal's father, Hamilcar Barca, made his son swear before the household altar to take vengeance on the Romans. Ever since then Hannibal has had a place in my fantasies."[10]

In the first edition of the *Interpretation* (1900), Freud had mistakenly given the name "Hasdrubal" (Hannibal's brother) in this passage instead of the Carthaginian general's real father Hamilcar Barca. In the *Psychopathology of Everyday Life* he subsequently explained that he had been unable to forgive the lack of courage his own father displayed towards "the enemies of our people". It was this stinging memory of paternal cowardice that caused Sigmund's "astonishing" error with regard to Hasdrubal.[11]

[9]Marthe Robert, *D'Oedipe à Moïse: Freud et la conscience juive,* Paris 1974, p. 24. However, following Jakob's death, in a letter of 2 November 1896, Sigmund wrote: "I valued him highly and understood him very well indeed, and with his peculiar mixture of deep wisdom and imaginative lightheartedness he meant a great deal in my life." In Sigmund Freud, *The Origins of Psychoanalysis: Letters to Wilhelm Fliess. Drafts and Notes, 1887–1902*, transl. by Eric Mosbacher and James Strachey, New York 1977, pp. 170–171.

[10]*The Interpretation of Dreams*, in *Standard Edition of the Complete Psychological Works of Sigmund Freud*, transl. and ed. by James Strachey, 24 vols., London 1953–1974 (henceforth *S.E.*), vol. 4, pp. 196ff.

[11]S. Freud, *Zur Psychopathologie des Alltagslebens,* Frankfurt am Main 1976, p. 174.

Sigmund Freud is unlikely to have felt a similar sense of shame with regard to his mother, a prime source of his unshakeable courage and self-confidence. This youthful and dominant woman, née Amalia Nathanson (1835–1930), who came originally from Brody in northeast Galicia, had arrived in Vienna when she was still a child (she actually witnessed the 1848 Revolution). According to the recollections of her grandson, Martin Freud, she was a typical Polish Jewess—"impatient, self-willed, sharp-witted and highly intelligent". The centre of the family, full of tender concern and devotion towards her eldest son, Amalia Freud still retained the language, manners and beliefs of her native environment. She belonged to a "peculiar race" distinct not only from the Gentiles,

> but absolutely different from Jews who had lived in the West for some generations. … These Galician Jews had little grace and no manners: and their women were certainly not what we should call "ladies". They were highly emotional and easily carried away by their feelings. … These [women] were not easy to live with and grandmother [Amalia], a true representative of her race, was no exception. She had great vitality and much impatience.[12]

Towards the *Ostjuden* from whom he sprang, Freud retained a degree of ambivalent affection. For years he collected Galician Jewish anecdotes and jokes, some of which he used in his book *Der Witz und seine Beziehung zum Unbewussten* (1905) and which he regarded as being "of deep significance". Mostly these jokes evoked the aversion of Galician Jews to baths, the wiles of Jewish marriage brokers, the impudence of *schnorrers* and the superstitions of "wonder rabbis". Freud himself noted the prevalence of self-criticism in these jests, which "have grown up on the soil of Jewish popular life". Unlike jokes told about Jews by foreigners, which rarely rose above the level of brutal derision, the anecdotes created by Jews themselves were based on a knowledge of "their real faults as well as the connection between them and their good qualities". Whether cynical, merely sceptical, tendentious or absurd, this humour realistically reflected (according to Freud) the "manifold and hopeless miseries of the Jews", the ambiguous relationship between rich and poor, the "democratic mode of thinking of Jews" and their ability to laugh at their own characteristics.[13]

Nevertheless Freud's response to this East European Jewish heritage during his late adolescence was marked by considerable equivocation, as his letters to Eduard Silberstein, a close Romanian friend, make plain. He was steadily moving away from the traditional customs, rituals, and pieties of his home environment. Not only did he proudly proclaim himself "godless", refusing to observe the Jewish festivals which his father still held sacred, but in letters to friends he indulged in open mockery of Jewish ritual observances. Reminders of his own provincial background and ties with unassimilated *Ostjuden* from Eastern Europe began to grate on his nerves. An encounter with just such a family on the return trip from Freiberg, Moravia to

[12]Quoted in John Murray Cuddihy, *The Ordeal of Civility: Freud, Marx, Levi-Strauss, and the Jewish Struggle with Modernity*, New York 1988, pp. 504–505. Amalia Freud appears to have remained religiously observant throughout her life and to have kept a kosher home. She most probably used her native Galician Yiddish when speaking to Sigmund and her other children.

[13]Sigmund Freud, *Jokes and their Relation to the Unconscious*, transl. by James Strachey, London 1978, p. 157.

Vienna in September 1872 prompted him to make some scathing remarks in a letter to his friend Emil Fluss:

> Now this Jew talked the same way as I had heard thousands of others talk before, even in Freiberg. His face seemed familiar – he was typical. So was the boy with whom he discussed religion. He was cut from the cloth from which fate makes swindlers when the time is ripe: cunning, mendacious, kept by his adoring relatives in the belief that he is a great talent, but unprincipled and without character. I have enough of this rabble.[14]

The transparent desire to dissociate himself from such mercantile and provincial Jewish characteristics coincided with Freud's growing desire to identify with liberal German *Kultur.* By the time he entered medical school in Vienna, Freud already regarded Jewish religious traditions as anachronistic. He looked to German-Austrian democratic ideals as the basis for social integration, progress and assimilation. This led to a desire to sever his connections with the *Ostjuden*, the "alien race" that had become a prime target of German national antisemitism.[15]

During the period of his university studies Freud felt increasingly torn between the contradictory pressures of assimilation into German culture, social radicalism, and rising antisemitism. From 1873 to 1878 he was an active member of the *Leseverein der deutschen Studenten Wiens*, a radical student society committed to the German national cause. Already an enthusiastic Darwinist and materialist, Freud was increasingly attracted to scientific positivism and anticlerical liberalism. This tendency drew him towards the North German physicalist school of Helmholtz, its foremost representative in Vienna being another Protestant German—his greatly admired teacher Ernst Brücke. At this time he also began to study the German materialist philosopher Ludwig Feuerbach, whose psychology of religion had a considerable influence on his radical views.[16]

Like other members of the *Leseverein*, Freud reacted to the financial scandals that helped discredit Austro-liberalism in the eyes of the younger generation, but he was already losing interest in politics—after 1875 he was far more concerned with philosophical and religious radicalism than with social democracy or German nationalism. His idols were the great medical teachers at the University of Vienna like Brücke, in whose laboratory he learned the art of detailed scientific observation; the brilliant psychiatrist from Dresden, Theodor Meynert, who specialised in the anatomy of the brain; and another North German, Richard Krafft-Ebing, author of *Psychopathia sexualis: Eine klinisch-forensische Studie* (1886).[17] The inspirational example

[14]Quoted in Dennis B. Klein, *Jewish Origins of the Psychoanalytic Movement*, Chicago—London 1985, p. 46.

[15]*ibid.*, pp. 46ff.

[16]Peter Gay, *A Godless Jew. Freud, Atheism and the Making of Psychoanalysis*, New Haven 1987, pp. 53–56. In 1875, while a student at the University of Vienna, he wrote to a friend that "Among all philosophers, I worship and admire this man [Feuerbach] the most." Thirty years earlier Feuerbach had exercised a similarly hypnotic effect on the young Karl Marx.

[17]See Peter Gay, *Freud, Jews and Other Germans*, Oxford 1978, pp. 34–35; Gay points out that medical Vienna in the late nineteenth century was "a microcosm of German scientific talent"; and that Freud lived and worked within a "larger German culture", regarding himself as culturally German rather than Austrian, *ibid.*, p. 90. See also William M. Johnston, *The Austrian Mind: An Intellectual and Social History, 1848–1938*, Berkeley and Los Angeles 1983, pp. 229–233. Much would seem to indicate that Freud was actually far more of an Austrian than Peter Gay's interpretation suggests.

of these great scientists from Protestant Germany helped to counteract the bitter disappointment Freud had felt at encountering rampant antisemitism in the student body on entering Vienna University in 1873.[18]

In his *Autobiographical Study*, Freud openly confronted the issue:

> Above all, I found that I was expected to feel myself inferior and an alien because I was a Jew. I refused absolutely to do the first of these things. I have never been able to see why I should feel ashamed of my descent or, as people were beginning to say, of my race. I put up, without much regret, with my non-acceptance into the community; for it seemed to me that in spite of this exclusion an active-fellow worker could not fail to find some nook or cranny in the framework of humanity. These first impressions at the University, however, had one consequence which was afterwards to prove important; for at an early age I was made familiar with the fate of being in the Opposition and of being put under the ban of the "compact majority". The foundations were thus laid for a certain degree of independence of judgment.[19]

Freud's sense of shock was understandable after having grown up in the tolerant, optimistic atmosphere of the 1860s and early 1870s, when integration and social acceptance still seemed relatively open to Jews.

By the early 1890s it had become clear to Freud that his earlier efforts at assimilation were futile. Like Herzl and Schnitzler he had come to recognise that his ethnic origins made him part of a distinct minority group which shared a common fate in an increasingly hostile world. The militantly Catholic Vienna of Karl Lueger's electoral triumphs virtually obliged Freud to see himself as a member of a targeted group of potential victims. Whether he liked it or not he could not escape being branded as a Jew in a community where antisemitism had become a rampant social disease rather than a mere individual idiosyncrasy. In Peter Gay's words "it pervaded and poisoned student organizations, university politics, social relationships, medical opinions".[20] This everyday reality provided the sobering backdrop to his scientific work. Living in a "laboratory for every known species of antisemitism", it became a matter of defiance and personal honour for Freud to affirm his Jewish origins or at least not to deny them.

After 1895, the year of the intellectual breakthrough that produced the new "science" of psychoanalysis, Freud himself gradually became a target for antisemites. Was he not the epitome of the "godless Jew", a subverter *par excellence* of religion, morals and the family, the destroyer of human illusions? "Be assured", he wrote in the summer of 1908 to his disciple, Karl Abraham, "if my name were Oberhuber, my innovations would have encountered far less resistance, despite everything."[21] Despite his bitterness, Freud accepted this sense of exclusion and

[18]Sigmund Freud, *An Autobiographical Study*, transl. by James Strachey, London 1936, p. 15. On Freud's encounters with antisemitism, see Klein, pp. 48–54 and Robert S. Wistrich, 'The Jewish Identity of Sigmund Freud', in *The Jewish Quarterly*, vol. 34, no. 3 (1987), pp. 47–52.

[19]Freud, *An Autobiographical Study*, pp. 14–15. See also the helpful essay on Freud's psychosocial identity in Peter Loewenberg, *Fantasy and Reality in History*, New York—Oxford 1995, pp. 33–45.

[20]Gay, *Freud, Jews and Other Germans*, p. 26.

[21]Letter of 23 July, 1908 in *Sigmund Freud—Karl Abraham, Briefe*, 1907–1926, ed. by Hilda C. Abraham and Ernst L. Freud, Zurich 1965, p. 57.

social marginality as constituting a major source of his own creative originality. It was no accident he wrote, that "the first advocate of psycho-analysis was a Jew", for to "profess belief in this new theory called for a certain degree of readiness to accept a position of solitary opposition with which no one is more familiar than a Jew".[22] Freud believed that this deeply rooted feeling of apartness from the Gentile majority made him and other secular Jews much less conformist. They were relatively uncluttered by vestiges of worn-out dogma and superstition or by the crushing burden of theological "delusions" bequeathed by Christian civilisation. This was the meaning of Freud's remark that only an absolutely irreligious Jew could have invented psychoanalysis.[23]

Ever since the mid 1890s, although he was distinctly alienated from traditional Judaism, Freud had come to identify with the culturalist interpretation of the ancestral faith promoted by the B'nai B'rith Lodge. Through the brotherhood he could articulate a congenial sense of ethical purpose and humanistic ideals, combining a secular Jewish identity with Enlightenment universalism.[24] This was the background to Freud's special attraction to Moses as a lawgiver, liberator of the Israelites and Hebrew prophet, which began to crystallise at the end of the nineteenth century. Already in his dreams of Rome in 1897, there were hidden but nonetheless unmistakeable references to himself as Moses seeing the "promised land" from a distance.[25] On 17 January 1909, he wrote to Carl Gustav Jung, then still his designated successor: "We are certainly getting ahead. If I am Moses, then you are Joshua and will take possession of the promised land of psychiatry, which I shall only be able to glimpse from afar."[26]

In December 1913, shortly after Jung's defection from the movement, Freud wrote his essay "The Moses of Michelangelo", which he was initially most reluctant to publish. When he eventually did issue the work, he insisted on anonymity, as if he feared it was too personal and revealing.[27] Already during his first visit to Rome in 1901 Freud had paid daily visits to the church in which the famous statue of

[22]Freud, 'The Resistances to Psycho-Analysis" (1925) in *S.E.*, vol. 19, p. 222.

[23]*Psycho-Analysis and Faith: The Letters of Sigmund Freud and Oskar Pfister*, transl. by Eric Mosbacher, London—New York 1963, p. 63. At the same time, Freud was acutely aware of what he believed to constitute racial difference and developed a strong feeling of solidarity with the Jewish *Volk*. For the ways in which this affected his scientific work, see Sander L. Gilman, 'Freud, Race and Gender', in *Psychoanalysis in its Cultural Context*, Austrian Studies III, edited by Edward Timms and Ritchie Robertson, Edinburgh 1992, pp. 20–38.

[24]Klein, pp. 69–102. See also Robert S. Wistrich, *The Jews of Vienna in the Age of Franz Joseph*, Oxford 1989, pp. 564–566.

[25]Klein, pp. 94–95. See also Martin S. Bergmann, 'Moses and the Evolution of Freud's Jewish Identity', in *The Israel Annals of Psychiatry and Related Sciences*, 4, (March 1976), pp. 3–26. It is quite possible that the figure of Moses had haunted Freud since childhood, as he would claim in 1935. See Peter Gay, *Freud. A Life for our Time*, London 1988, p. 605.

[26]*The Freud/Jung Letters. The Correspondence between Sigmund Freud and C.G. Jung*, ed. by William McGuire, Princeton 1974, pp. 196–197.

[27]*S.E.*, vol. 13, p. 233. See also Ernst Simon, 'Sigmund Freud, the Jew', in *Leo Baeck Institute Year Book*, vol. 2 (1957), pp. 302–305. In 1913 Freud could readily have identified with Moses as the embattled, patriarchal leader of a movement threatened by backsliding, rebellious sons. This reflected his own situation as head of the highly fractious psychoanalytical movement.

'Moses' by Michelangelo. Tomb of Julius II, S. Pietro in Vincoli, Rome.

Michelangelo was located. For three weeks in September 1913 he stood once more in front of the sculpture, studying, measuring and sketching it. What struck Freud most forcefully was the freedom with which Michelangelo had recast the character of the Hebrew prophet, placing "a different Moses on the tomb of the Pope, one superior to the historical or traditional Moses". The great Renaissance sculptor had modified the theme of the broken tablets: he did not let Moses break them in his wrath but "makes him calm that wrath, or at any rate prevent it from becoming an act". In this way, Michelangelo had given a new, more human dimension to Moses; so that the giant frame "becomes only a concrete expression of the highest mental achievement that is possible in a man, that of struggling successfully against an inward passion for the sake of a cause to which he has devoted himself".[28]

Freud's Moses, it should be noted, is far removed from any "Zionist" or Jewish national identification.[29] Though it may seem surprising in retrospect, Freud never met the *fin-de-siècle* "Moses", Theodor Herzl, though he lived in the same street in Vienna for several years. Yet we know that he esteemed "the poet and the fighter for the human rights of my people", to quote from his complementary letter of

[28]*S. E.*, vol. 13, p. 233 and Rice, pp. 126–127.

[29]For Freud's ambivalence about nationalism in general and the Zionist movement in particular, see Wistrich, *The Jews of Vienna*, pp. 574–582.

September 1902 to Herzl, accompanying a review copy of *The Interpretation of Dreams*.[30] A few years before, in 1898, Freud had seen Herzl's play *Das neue Ghetto* in Vienna and felt deeply troubled by its evocation of the "Jewish question" and his own inability to guarantee a secure homeland to his children.[31]

Herzl's "Mosaic" solution of a physical Exodus from Europe to the Land of Zion did not appeal to Freud on a personal level.[32] He remained cautious with regard to political Zionism, at times sympathetic, at times equivocal or even sharply critical. Theodor Herzl belonged in his eyes to a special group of practitioners of the politics of fantasy, commanding the world "while they themselves remain on the other side of the psychic mirror".[33] The Zionist leader's concept of redemption through political action ran contrary to Freud's scepticism about collective solutions, his commitment to the scientific analysis of dreams rather than their implementation, his fascination with the demythification of the unconscious and opposition to messianic ideals. In all those respects Freud was closer to the playwright Arthur Schnitzler than to Herzl.

Nevertheless Freud's ambivalence about Jewish nationalism did not preclude his confessing to Karl Abraham in December 1917 that "the only thing that [currently] gives me any pleasure is the capture of Jerusalem and the British experiment with the chosen people".[34] Nor did his underlying doubts prevent him from writing to Professor Friedrich Thieberger in 1926 that "Towards Zionism I have only sympathy, but I make no judgement on it, on its chances of success and on the possible dangers to it".[35] For Freud, this critical sympathy was part of his irrepressible sense of ethnic solidarity with other Jews, even if the link could not be expressed in clear words or given a "scientific" justification.

The Arab riots in Palestine in 1929 exposed some of Freud's deeper misgivings concerning the Zionist enterprise. The incidents at the Wailing Wall in Jerusalem in particular highlighted his anxieties about the *political* side of Zionism and his visceral revulsion against any form of religious fanaticism. Writing to the *Keren Hayesod* in Vienna in 1930, he revealed an attitude to Jewish nationalism that was nuanced but distinctly guarded about the future:

> Whoever wants to influence the masses must give them something rousing and inflammatory and my sober judgement of Zionism does not permit this. I certainly sympathise with its goals, am proud of our University in Jerusalem and am delighted with our settlements' prosperity. But on the other hand, I do not think that Palestine could ever become a Jewish State, nor that the Christian and Islamic worlds would ever be prepared to have their holy places under Jewish control. It would have seemed more sensible to me

[30]Freud to Herzl, 28 September 1902. Central Zionist Archives, Jerusalem.

[31]*S. E.*, vol. 5, p. 441.

[32]Peter Loewenberg, in 'A Hidden Zionist Theme in Freud's My Son, The Myops Dream', in *Journal of the History of Ideas*, vol. 31, no. 1 (1970) p. 132, suggests that unconsciously, Freud may have envied Herzl for the realisation of the repressed political ambitions of his own adolescence.

[33]William J. McGrath, *Freud's Discovery of Psychoanalysis: The Politics of Hysteria*, Ithica 1986, pp. 314–316.

[34]*A Psycho-Analytic Dialogue: The Letters of Sigmund Freud and Karl Abraham 1907/1926*, ed. by Hilda C. Abraham and Ernst L. Freud, transl. by Bernard Marsh and Hilda C. Abraham, London—New York 1965, p. 264.

[35]Quoted in Simon, p. 275.

> to establish a Jewish homeland on less historically burdened land. But I know that such a rational standpoint would never have gained the enthusiasm of the masses.[36]

Freud chose to blame the 1929 pogrom on "the unrealistic fanaticism of our people"—a fanaticism that had awakened Arab distrust. He also warned against efforts to inculcate "unjustified hope" in Jewish hearts and deplored the national-religious cult of sacred stones. "I have no sympathy at all", he told Dr. Chaim Koffler, "for the misdirected piety which transforms a piece of Herod's wall into a national relic, thereby challenging the feelings of the natives".[37]

Freud's interest in Palestine continued to be riddled with ambiguity. This was apparent in his special introduction to the Hebrew edition of *Totem and Taboo*, written in Vienna in December 1930. In his preface, Freud surprisingly claims complete ignorance of Hebrew (which he certainly studied to some degree in his youth) and insisted that he was "completely estranged from the religion of his fathers" as well as any nationalist ideals; at the same time he pronounced himself a Jew "in his essential nature with no desire to alter that nature".[38] He emphasised that despite having abandoned the national and religious characteristics of Judaism, "a very great deal of Jewishness" remained in his personality. Though adopting "no Jewish standpoint" and making no exceptions "in favour of Jewry", he concluded the preface by expressing the hope that "unprejudiced science cannot remain a stranger to the spirit of the new [Palestinian] Jewry".[39]

In the 1930s, though his interest in Zionism seemed to recede, the legend of Moses increasingly began to haunt and torment the powerful imagination of Sigmund Freud. But the analysis that emerged from his pen was not at all about the historical Moses of Judaism. Instead, Freud sketched a highly speculative portrait of a Moses who had been born as an Egyptian nobleman and whose presumed *murder*, by his "adopted" people, the Jews, had created Hebrew monotheism through a complex detour. In Freud's final version, as laid out in *Moses and Monotheism* (published in his London exile in 1939), "it was one man, the man Moses, who created the Jews". They were his "chosen people", their tenacity, obstinacy and intellectuality were shaped by his character and will.

The seeds of Hebraic monotheism were, however, not Jewish. They had been sown by a revolutionary, iconoclastic Egyptian Pharaoh of the 18th dynasty, Akhenaton, of whom Moses was a loyal disciple.[40] After the collapse of Akhenaton's "monotheistic revolution" from above, Moses had chosen the Hebrew slaves in Egypt to be the inheritors of his high-minded teachings. According to Freud (following a theory put forward by the German biblical scholar Eduard Sellin in 1922), the Hebrews had initially betrayed the hopes of Moses by killing him before

[36]Freud to Dr. Chaim Koffler, Keren Hayesod, Vienna, 26 February 1930, Schwadron Collection, Jewish National and University Library, Jerusalem.

[37]*ibid.*

[38]Quoted in Rice, p. 130.

[39]See Sigmund Freud, *Totem and Taboo,* trans. James Strachey (London 1960), p. XI. This preface was written by Freud in Vienna in December 1930.

[40]For a brilliant analysis of the Egyptian background and its implications, see Jan Assmann, *Moses the Egyptian. The Memory of Egypt in Western Monotheism*, Cambridge, MA 1997.

entering the Promised Land. To relieve their guilt they not only exalted his memory but eventually developed a sublime conception of God constructed in his image. However, such a transformation did not come about instantly. For many generations, the tribalistic Hebrews behaved like pagans worshipping Yahweh, "a coarse, narrow-minded local god, violent and bloodthirsty".[41] But as a result of the universalist ethical teachings of the Hebrew prophets, the memory and the message of Moses began to resurface and be accepted as the religion of the Jews. For Freud this fact demonstrated "a peculiar psychical aptitude in the masses who had become the Jewish people".[42] Unlike the ancient Egyptians, the descendants of slaves were willing to assume the exacting burdens of monotheism "in return for the reward of being the chosen people".

The founder of psychoanalysis hypothesised that the exalted moral consciousness Moses had imprinted "for all time" upon his "chosen people" was the source of such lasting "Jewish" character-traits as the commitment to rationality, legalism, austerity, tenacity and the will to separateness. Moses had thereby given a permanent anchorage to the self-esteem of the Jewish people. But his doctrine of chosenness also provided the deepest root of "much of the hostility it has experienced and still experiences".[43] In a letter to Arnold Zweig on 30 September 1934 Freud asserted that explaining the enigma of antisemitism was in fact his prime motivation in writing *Moses and Monotheism*: "Faced with the renewed persecutions, one asks oneself again how the Jew came to be what he is and why he has drawn upon himself this undying hatred. I soon found the formula: Moses created the Jew."[44]

Freud undoubtedly identified with the figure of Moses, yet the narrative in his book suggests both deep hostility to the "father-religion" of Judaism and the wish to reappropriate its message on his own, secular terms. A similar ambivalence emerges in his attitude towards Christianity which he acerbically described as "a cultural regression as compared with the older, Jewish [religion]", "as regularly happens when a new mass of people, of a lower level, break their way in or are given admission".[45] Freud emphasised that Christianity was not strictly monotheist. It had borrowed "numerous symbolic rituals from surrounding peoples", re-established the "great mother-goddess" and permitted "the entry of superstitions, magical and mystical elements" that would inhibit intellectual development for two thousand years. In a sarcastic gloss on European "Christian" antisemitism, Freud added the following: "We must not forget that all those peoples who excel today in their hatred of Jews became Christians only in late historic times, often driven to it by bloody conversion. It might be said that they are all "misbaptised." Hence for Freud, under a thin veneer of Christianity they had remained what their ancestors were—worshippers of a "barbarous polytheism".[46]

[41]*S.E.*, vol. 23, p. 50.
[42]*ibid.*, p. 111.
[43]*ibid*, p. 106. Freud made it clear that the "jealousy of the people which declared itself the first-born favourite child of God the Father" was one of the key factors in the genesis of antisemitism.
[44]Sigmund Freud and Arnold Zweig, *Briefwechsel*, ed. by Ernst L. Freud, Frankfurt am Main 1968, p. 102.
[45]*S. E.*, vol. 23, p. 88.
[46]*ibid.*, p. 91.

Unfortunately, Freud did not develop this interesting insight into antisemitism as an "anti-Christian" eruption of barbaric instincts by poorly baptised Gentiles. Instead in *Moses and Monotheism* he suggests that if only the Jews had confessed to their supposed "guilt" in killing the Primal Father—the Egyptian Moses—they might have been spared the Gentile-Christian accusation of having murdered God.[47] Yet Freud himself observes that both the murder of Moses and the crucifixion of Jesus were "providential" occurrences in so far as they changed the course of Western civilisation. A Father religion was replaced by a Son religion. But in both cases it was the guilt arising from a "primal murder" that supposedly laid the foundations of human morality.[48] This was hardly a theory that could endear Freud to religious Jews or believing Christians, as he understood perfectly well. His long-standing antipathy to religion was a matter of record, undoubtedly exacerbated by his view of the Catholic Church as a major bastion of antisemitism and clerical reaction in Austria. In opposition to the counter-Reformation, counter-Enlightenment and counter-revolutionary forces symbolised by papal Rome, Freud's *Moses and Monotheism* highlights and praises Jewish spirituality. The Jews' attainment of their spiritual heights was predicated on a renunciation of instincts, a cultivation of intellectual prowess, and manly self-control—all of these achievements embodied by Moses. This founder of civilisation had taken the greatest feats of the "Egyptian Enlightenment" under Akhenaton and bequeathed them to the Jews—a legacy that involved a sharp rejection of idolatry, image-making and magic, in turn encouraging a cult of reason, justice and truth as well as a radical commitment to moral rectitude. In this manner, Freud's approach to Moses was very much in the tradition of German Enlightenment discourse from Lessing to Kant and Schiller.

As has already been suggested, what prompted Freud to write *Moses and Monotheism* in the first place was the rising tide of Nazi antisemitism in the 1930s. Though he could see the catastrophe approaching, his focus was not at all on the motives of the oppressors and perpetrators but rather on how the Jews came to attract this undying hatred.[49] According to Freud's thinking, its ultimate source lay in ancient Egypt, as a backlash against a strict monotheism that the Jews themselves had initially repudiated. Subsequently, however the Jewish people did become identified with the historical outcome of abstract monotheism—a heightening of conscience, ethical purity and the rule of law. The atheist Freud sincerely believed it was precisely such traits that made Jewish survival possible.[50]

[47]*ibid.*, p. 136. See the discussion in Rice, p. 160 ff. of Freud's views concerning the psychodynamic origins of Christianity and the direct link he created between the "murder" of Moses and the crucifixion of Jesus.

[48]See Carl E. Schorske, *Thinking with History. Explorations in the Passage to Modernity*, Princeton 1998, p. 207. Schorske appears fanciful in arguing that Freud wished to give the Jews a basis for abandoning their exclusivist self-definition, preventing them "from realizing, as Christians do, their own universality." "The essential prerequisite for Freud," he indicates, "was that Jews recognise (as Christians supposedly do) their own patricidal crime and assume its guilt as participants in the brotherhood of man".

[49]Cf. Assmann, p. 6. See also Richard J. Bernstein, *Freud and the Legacy of Moses*, Cambridge 1998, for a close textual analysis of *Moses and Monotheism*.

[50]*S.E.*, vol. 23, p. 123.

The victory of the Mosaic religion in antiquity was seen by Freud as part of the gradual ascent of mankind towards greater rationality.[51] Though Judaism, like other religions, resembled a traumatic "neurosis", it was more advanced than others in its emphasis on reason, truth and abstract thought. Hence, it was more adapted to the "scientific age" and to psychoanalysis itself. At the same time, Freud realised that his views on Moses as an Egyptian would hurt Jewish religious sensitivities as well as robbing his co-religionists of their most famous son at a moment of acute danger. His book came out at a time when Nazi violence was beginning to threaten not only the survival of the Jewish people but the foundations of civilisation.[52] However, as he told an English correspondent in 1938, he had spent his whole life "standing up for what I have considered to be the scientific truth, even when it was uncomfortable and unpleasant for my fellow men. I cannot end up with an act of disavowal."[53]

Freud was not only concerned about offending Jews. He was much more worried by the likely disapproval of the Catholic authorities in Austria. In particular, he was alarmed by the political influence of Father Wilhelm Schmidt, a distinguished anthropologist and professor at the University of Vienna. Schmidt was a prolific author, a forceful personality and an aggressive antisemite who had sharply attacked Freud's *Totem and Taboo* for claiming that religion originates with totemism.[54] Freud, who had been a militant anticlerical throughout his adult life, had no illusions about the hostility of the Catholic Church to psychoanalysis. He wished to provide neither the "clerico-fascist" Austrian state nor church with any pretext for closing down the institutional basis of psychoanalysis in Vienna. His extreme prudence when it came to publishing *Moses and Monotheism* was directly due to such concerns. As Freud sardonically noted, the Roman Catholic Church had long been a relentless enemy of free thought and scientific advances; indeed, "violent methods of repression" were, as he delicately phrased it, by no means "alien to the Church".[55]

But crucially, he also felt strongly that nothing should be done to truly endanger what he referred to as the church's "protection" of the state. Paradoxically, as he wrote in February 1938 (a month before the *Anschluss*) while still in Vienna, it was the same reactionary Catholic Church "which puts up a powerful defence against the spread of this [totalitarian] danger to civilization".[56] Freud had no doubt that new

[51] *ibid.*, vol. 21, p. 53. In *The Future of an Illusion*, London 1928, Freud displayed a qualified optimism about the eventual triumph of reason: "The voice of the intellect is a soft one, but it does not rest till it has gained a hearing. Finally, after a countless succession of rebuffs, it succeeds." p. 53.

[52] Bernstein, p. 138.

[53] *Letters*, p. 453 (31 October, 1938).

[54] See Freud to Arnold Zweig in Eduard Fr. Elaine and William Robson-Scott (eds.), *The Letters of Sigmund Freud and Arnold Zweig*, New York 1970, pp. 91–92; a letter of 9 September 1934 describes Father Schmidt as an "inimical priest", "a confidant of the Pope and a student of comparative religion who abhorred psychoanalysis and would surely use any pretext to ban it in Vienna". Freud's preoccupation with avoiding a "state prohibition of analysis" by the ruling Catholic regime was repeated in a letter of 6 January 1935 to Lou Andreas-Salomé. In the same letter he informed her that the Moses story "has pursued me throughout the whole of my life." See Bernstein, p. 25. See also Ritchie Robertson, 'Freud's Testament: 'Moses and Monotheism'', in Edward Timms and Naomi Segal (eds.). *Freud in Exile. Psychoanalysis and its Vicissitudes*, New Haven 1988, p. 88.

[55] *S. E.*, vol. 23, p. 55. See Carl E. Schorske, 'Politics and Patricide in Freud's "Interpretation of Dreams"', in *American Historical Review*, vol. 78, no. 2 (1973), pp. 328–347.

[56] *S. E*, vol. 23, p. 55.

enemies like Fascism, Nazism and Communism were "more dangerous" than the old ones (like Catholicism) "with whom we have already learnt to come to terms".[57] In his preparatory note to Part I of *Moses and Monotheism* he added a cryptic comment on the regressive alliance of progress and barbarism in the contemporary world. There was, for example, the "most cruel coercion" in the Soviet Union that had robbed over a hundred million Russians "of any possibilities of freedom of thought". Freud also noted the growing violence in fascist Italy, and in the case of the German people what he called "a relapse into almost prehistoric barbarism".[58]

This was the new international context in which Freud had come to regard Austrian Catholicism as the last bulwark against German Nazism and as by far the lesser of two evils. In the summer of 1934 the founder of psychoanalysis noted in a family letter that if the swastika were ever to triumph in Austria "we shall have to leave". Austro-fascism, he added, while certainly unpleasant, was not a lethal danger—hence the willingness "to take it in our stride up to a certain point; it can hardly treat us as badly as its German cousin".[59] In February 1938, Freud wrote again to his son, Ernst, expressing the flimsy hope that Austria would not end up like Nazi Germany since "the Catholic Church is very strong and will offer strong resistance".[60] Even more pathetically, in a letter to Marie Bonaparte of 23 February 1938 he speculated about whether it might not be possible "to find safety in the shelter of the Catholic Church".[61] Unmistakably, he was clutching at reeds. Whether or not Freud believed in his own fantasies, the answer came swiftly in March 1938. The Austrian prelates, keepers of the Catholic conscience, did little or nothing to rally whatever forces of sanity still remained in the bosom of the church or in Austria itself. Cardinal Theodor Innitzer set the tone with his declaration of Austrian episcopal support for the Hitler regime; many priests chose to celebrate the Führer's achievements from the pulpits, promising to cooperate enthusiastically with the new Nazi order. Hitler's triumphant entry into Vienna was symbolically greeted with the ringing of church bells.[62]

[57]*ibid.* Freud realised that Catholicism could only regard psychoanalysis with suspicion, since it "reduces religion to a neurosis of humanity and explains its enormous power in the same way as a neurotic compulsion in our individual patients." In his letter of 6 January 1935 to Lou Andreas-Salomé he had explained that this compulsive strength of religion derived from "the return of the repressed"—the reawakening of memories derived from "very ancient, forgotten, highly emotional episodes of human history".

[58]*S.E.*, vol. 23, pp. 54–55 ('Moses, His People and Monotheist Religion', written in Vienna before March 1938).

[59]*Letters*, p. 420.

[60]Gay, *Freud. A Life*, pp. 617–618.

[61]*ibid.*, p. 618. In a letter to Max Eitingon of 6 February 1938, Freud wrote: "Our brave and in its way decent government is now more energetic than hitherto in keeping the Nazis at bay, although in view of the latest events in Germany no one can be sure what is going to happen."

[62]*ibid.*, p. 619. It should be noted that Hitler and the SS did see the Roman Catholic church as a major ideological opponent in Austria. On 8 October 1938 members of the Hitler Youth even stormed Innitzer's palace in response to an anti-Nazi demonstration by young Catholics. Cf. Evan Bukey, *Hitler's Austria. Popular Sentiment in the Nazi Era, 1938–1945,* Chapel Hill—London 2000, pp. 93–111. Burr emphasises the intense anti-Jewish sentiment within the Catholic Church and its compromises with the Nazis.

In writing his *Moses* book, Freud was painfully aware of the ominous threat represented by German Nazism to the future of the Jewish people. Throughout the text there are references to antisemitism and a number of fragmentary attempts to find an explanation. At one point Freud sensibly observes that a "phenomenon of such intensity and permanence as the people's hatred of the Jews must of course have more than one ground".[63] He was manifestly keen to distinguish between the superficial and the deeper causes. Jews were consistently reproached, for example, for being "aliens" even though they had often arrived in their host countries long before the "natives"; they were victimised as a small and exposed minority because "the communal feeling of groups requires, in order to complete it, hostility towards some extraneous minority".[64] Freud regarded these xenophobic aspects of anti-Jewishness as surface phenomena. He had no doubt that Jewish "difference" was deliberately exaggerated by the antisemites. Contrary to their racial myths, the Jews were "not Asiatics of a foreign race" but "remnants of the Mediterranean peoples and heirs of the Mediterranean civilization". A degree of distinctiveness—especially from the Nordic peoples—did indeed exist but this was due to "the narcissism of minor differences" that invariably exacerbated the intolerance of certain nations. Another facet of antisemitism—a facet Freud regarded as a reflection of reality itself—was focused on the ability of the Jews to survive the cruellest persecution. Despite being victimised, they were able to hold their own in commerce and still make "valuable contributions to every form of cultural activity".[65]

However, for Freud the deeper motivations for Judeophobia were of a different order altogether. They were "rooted in the remotest past ages", in "the unconscious of the peoples" and especially in envy at Jews having being elected as God's chosen people.[66] The belief that Jews were indeed a chosen people had made them proud and confident; this had been the pattern of Jewish behaviour from Hellenistic times to the modern age. No less striking was the fact that "host" nations reacted to Jewish chosenness "as though they too believed in the superiority which the people of Israel claimed for themselves".[67] The self-esteem of the Jews and their superiority complex were not in themselves unique. But these characteristics had been given a special religious anchorage by Moses—the founder of Judaic monotheism had imprinted this trait, "significant for all time", upon the Jewish people. Hence Freud's "blasphemous" conclusion that one man, Moses, had in effect "created the Jews" in his own image: "It is to him that this people owes its tenacity of life but also much of the hostility it has experienced and still experiences."[68] In other words, Moses was also responsible for antisemitism.

[63] *S. E.*, vol. 23, p. 90.

[64] *ibid.*

[65] *ibid.*, p. 91. In the same context Freud emphasised the vitality of the Jews, their "unexampled capacity for resistance" in the face of misfortune and ill-treatment; their high self-esteem, sense of superiority and "peculiar confidence in life"—"a kind of optimism" that "pious people would call … trust in God"; *ibid.*, p. 105.

[66] *ibid.*, p. 106.

[67] Freud thought that Jew-hatred was rooted in pagan Antiquity; it had been exacerbated by Christianity because the Jews "did not recognise the redeemer". But at its heart was sheer envy of the kind exhibited in the Biblical story of Joseph and his brothers.

[68] *S. E.*, vol. 2, p. 106.

In *Moses and Monotheism* Freud has moved a considerable distance from his earlier reluctance to deal seriously with Judeophobia. In 1927 he had written somewhat ill-temperedly to Arnold Zweig that "with regard to antisemitism I do not really want to search for explanations; I feel a very strong inclination to surrender to my affects in this matter and find myself confirmed in my wholly non-scientific belief that mankind on the average is a wretched lot [*elendes Gesindel*]".[69] But the massive assault on the Jews and also on psychoanalysis as a "Jewish science" brought a change in Freud's attitude. He now understood that the lives of his own family members were directly threatened, as was the future of the Jews and of civilisation itself. His letters of the late 1930s contain many traces of this well-grounded anxiety. On 28 May 1933 he wrote to Oskar Pfister from Vienna that his horizon "has become darkly clouded by events in Germany. Three members of my family, with their families, two sons and a son-in-law are looking for a new country and still have not found one. Switzerland is not among the hospitable countries. My judgement of human nature, above all the Christian-Aryan variety, has had little reason to change." On 12 November 1938, immediately after the "*Kristallnacht*" pogrom, he wrote from London to Marie Bonaparte concerning the plight of four of his five sisters, unable to leave Austria in time. They would in fact be deported and killed by the Nazis.[70] And in a letter to an English magazine written on 16 November 1938 Freud described with restrained but unmistakeable anguish how he had to leave Vienna after 78 years of assiduous work; how the psychoanalytic society had been dissolved, its institutions destroyed, its printing press taken over; how his books had been reduced to pulp and his children expelled from their professions. He was deeply pained to learn that even in England—a country for which he had immense admiration since his youth—antisemitism was growing.[71] This letter was written about five months after he had gratefully acknowledged the very friendly reception which he received in "lovely, free, magnanimous England".[72]

Moses and Monotheism was Freud's only text essaying a psychoanalysis of antisemitism. Among his hypotheses, circumcision was defined as a custom reinforcing Jewish separateness and making "a disagreeable, uncanny impression". Freud viewed the custom as having evoked the dread of castration and revived a gladly forgotten portion of the primeval past.[73] More significantly, he sought to link German Nazism to the ineradicable *ressentiment* of pagan barbarians "against the new religion [Christianity] which was imposed upon them". Their rage was projected and displaced onto the Jewish roots of the Christian religion – a shift of responsibility made easier by the fact that the Gospels were "set among Jews" and dealt almost exclusively with them. Hence, Freud's intriguing conclusion that Jew-hatred "is at bottom a hatred of Christians". There should be no surprise, he added, that "in the German National-Socialist revolution this intimate relation between the

[69]Freud to Zweig, *Briefwechsel mit Arnold Zweig*, Frankfurt 1968, p. 14 (letter of 2 December 1927).
[70]*Letters*, pp. 417–418.
[71]*S.E.*, vol. 23, p. 301 ("Antisemitism in England" [1938]—a letter from Freud written in English to the editor of *Time and Tide*).
[72]*ibid.*, p. 57.
[73]*ibid.*, p. 91.

two monotheist religions finds such a clear expression in the hostile treatment of both of them".[74] While important, Freud's insight was misleading if it implied any equivalence in the scale or quality of the persecution of Jews and Christians. There was no real comparison between the intensity of Nazism's Christophobia and the nature of its onslaught against the Jews. Freud was nonetheless correct in pointing out that while drawing heavily on the Christian legacy of anti-Judaism, Nazism lashed out with unconcealed fury against the entire Judeo-Christian corpus of ethical demands.

In general, Freud's last work revealed an acute understanding of this "return of the repressed", illuminating some of the hidden paths through which civilisation's archaic elements retain their psychic grip over millions of people. *Moses and Monotheism* first appeared in print in 1939 as the darkest chapter in all of Jewish history was beginning to unfold. Unfortunately, Freud had failed to develop any specific psychology of antisemitism or a practical politics of Jewish survival that could be of real help in this tremendous crisis.[75] He had remained too much of an Austrian *Grenzjude* to consider engaging in any effective political activity. Hitler's genocidal antisemitism could only confirm his worst misgivings about the fragility of civilisation and the bestiality that lurked beneath its thin veneer. Yet Freud's last testament, despite the stoic pessimism underlying its creator's philosophy of life, is in its way a moving tribute to the resilient spirit of the Jewish people and its capacity to prevail over the horrors of history.

[74] *ibid.*, p. 92.

[75] In the 1940s some of Freud's followers did make progress in analysing antisemitism. For a useful survey of psychoanalytic attempts to understand Fascism and antisemitism in this period, see David James Fisher, 'Vers une compréhension psychoanalytique du fascisme et de l'antisémitisme: perceptions des années 1940', in *Revue Internationale Historique Psychanalytique,* (1992), pp. 221–241.

Remigration

*Jewish Remigration: An Overview of an Emerging Discipline**

BY MARITA KRAUSS

Compared to emigration, remigration was not a mass phenomenon. Approximately 500,000 people emigrated from Europe's German-speaking regions after 1933.[1] Of those fleeing political persecution, about half would return, including some 4,000 Social Democrats, around 3,000 Communists and a handful of representatives of conservative parties.[2] Of those persecuted on "racial" grounds, only four to five percent returned: 12,000 to 15,000 of these were Jewish by faith and registered with the reorganising Jewish community.[3] Those returnees who had been persecuted as Jews but who do not fit into one of these categories are more difficult to quantify. A very rough estimate would place the total number of returnees at around 30,000.[4]

Who were these returnees? What kind of person returned, despite the experiences of expulsion and exile, to the land of his or her childhood, which had simultaneously become a land of murderers? As a rule of thumb, one can say that since politically engaged emigrants—with or without a Jewish background—wanted to participate in the reconstruction of Germany from within, the more politically motivated the emigration, the greater was the desire to return. But there were also those who had professional or financial reasons for returning—whether it was a desire to return to the German language on the part of writers, journalists or theatre people, the reacquisition of stolen property among business people, or lost pension claims among former civil servants. Far greater, if also more difficult to estimate, is the percentage

*The essays in this section were originally presented as papers at the conference "Migration and Remigration: Jews in Germany after 1945" held on 1–2 June 2003 at the University of Haifa which was sponsored by the DIE ZEIT Foundation and jointly organised by Raphael Gross and Yfaat Weiss for the Leo Baeck Institute London and the Bucerius Institute for Research of German Contemporary History and Society at the University of Haifa.

[1]See Herbert A. Strauss and Werner Röder (eds.), *International Biographical Dictionary of Central European Emigrés 1933–1945,* 3 vols., Munich–New York–London–Paris 1980–1983, vols. 2,1 and 2,2, *passim*; Claus-Dieter Krohn *et al.* (eds.), *Handbuch der deutschsprachigen Emigration 1933–1945*, Darmstadt 1998, *passim.*

[2]See Claus-Dieter Krohn, 'Einleitung' in *idem* and Patrik von zur Mühlen (eds.), *Rückkehr und Aufbau nach 1945: deutsche Remigranten im öffentlichen Leben Nachkriegsdeutschlands*, Marburg 1997, p. 9; Michael Scholz, 'Sowjetische Besatzungszone', in Krohn *et al* (eds.), pp. 1180–1188.

[3]See Michael Brenner, *Nach dem Holocaust. Juden in Deutschland seit 1945*, Munich 1995; Christiane Hoss, 'Kein sorgenfreies Leben. Erfahrungen mit dem neuen Deutschland', in *Leben im Wartesaal. Exil in Shanghai 1938–1947*, Berlin 1997, pp. 100ff.; Harry Maor, *Über den Wiederaufbau der jüdischen Gemeinden in Deutschland seit 1945*, Mainz 1961; Karola Fings, 'Rückkehr als Politikum–Remigration aus Israel', in Wolfgang Blaschke, Karola Fings and Cordula Lissner (eds.), *Unter Vorbehalt. Rückkehr aus der Emigration nach 1945*, Cologne 1997, pp. 22–32.

[4]See Marita Krauss, *Heimkehr in ein fremdes Land. Geschichte der Remigration nach 1945*, Munich 2001, p. 9f.

of those who never completely returned but nevertheless, through journalistic work, participation in a solicitor's practice, as guest professors or travelling lecturers, became active in Germany once again. These 'sojourners', that is temporary returnees, contributed significantly to the impact of those who had been exiled on postwar West German society without being returned emigrants in the strict sense of the word. Yet another circle consisted of those emigrants who did not themselves return but whose works were received in Germany over the years. As a "remigration of ideas", this knowledge transmitted through exile became very important in many areas, and thus has to be discussed under the rubrics of "internationalisation" and "modernisation".[5]

The past decades have seen a substantial body of research dedicated to post-1933 exile and emigration from Germany and Austria. Starting with literary history, this research then moved to politics and other areas of public life,[6] before proceeding to an extensive investigation of scientists and scholars in exile.[7] For some years, the focus has been on the question of remigration.[8] Alongside reminiscences and autobiographical accounts assembled from interviews,[9] biographies have been published of returned politicians such as Willy Brandt, as well as Communists, Social Democrats, and groups of exiles with political influence.[10] At the same time, regional

[5]See Mitchell Ash, 'Emigration und Wissenschaftswandel als Folgen der nationalsozialistischen Wissenschaftspolitik', in Doris Kaufmann (ed.), *Die Geschichte der Kaiser-Wilhelm-Gesellschaft im Nationalsozialismus. Bestandsaufnahme und Perspektiven der Forschung*, 2 vols., Göttingen 2000, vol. 2, pp. 610–631.

[6]For a good overview see the articles in Krohn *et al.* (eds.).

[7]Examples of such exilees may be found in Mitchell G. Ash and Alfons Söllner (eds.), *Forced Migration and Scientific Change. Emigré German-Speaking Scientists and Scholars after 1933*, Cambridge 1996; Klaus Fischer, *Changing Landscapes of Nuclear Physics: A Scientometric Study of the Social and Cognitive Position of German-Speaking Emigrants Within the Nuclear Physics Community 1921–1947*, Berlin 1993; Marianne Hassler and Jürgen Wertheimer (eds.), *Der Exodus aus Nazideutschland und die Folgen. Jüdische Wissenschaftler im Exil*, Tübingen 1997; Claus-Dieter Krohn, *Wissenschaft im Exil: deutsche Sozial- und Wirtschaftswissenschaftler in den USA und die New School for Social Research*, Frankfurt am Main–New York 1987; Horst Möller, *Exodus der Kultur. Schriftsteller, Wissenschaftler und Künstler in der Emigration nach 1933*, Munich 1984; Sven Papcke, *Deutsche Soziologie im Exil. Gegenwartsdiagnose und Epochenkritik 1933–1945*, Frankfurt am Main–New York 1993; Friedrich Stadler (ed.), *Vertriebene Vernunft. Emigration und Exil österreichischer Wissenschaft*, 2 vols., Vienna–Munich 1988; Alfons Söllner, *Deutsche Politikwissenschaftler in der Emigration. Studien zu ihrer Akkulturation und Wirkungsgeschichte, samt einer Bibliographie*, Opladen 1996; Herbert A. Strauss *et al.* (eds.), *Die Emigration der Wissenschaften nach 1933. Disziplingeschichtliche Studien*, Munich–London–New York–Paris 1991.

[8]Arbeitskreis selbständiger Kulturinstitute (eds.), *Rückkehr in die Fremde? Remigranten und Rundfunk in Deutschland 1945–1955*, Berlin 2000; Blaschke *et al.* (eds.); *Exil und Remigration. Jahrbuch Exilforschung* 9, Munich 1991; Krauss, *Heimkehr*, pp. 179–190; Claus Dieter Krohn and Martin Schumacher (eds.), *Exil und Neuordnung. Beiträge zur verfassungspolitischen Neuordnung in Deutschland nach 1945*, Düsseldorf 2000; Krohn and von zur Mühlen (eds.); Claus-Dieter Krohn and Axel Schildt (eds.), *Zwischen den Stühlen? Remigranten und Remigration in der deutschen Medienöffentlichkeit der Nachkriegszeit*, Hamburg 2002.

[9]For example Martina Kliner-Fruck, *"Es ging ja ums Überleben". Jüdische Frauen zwischen Nazi-Deutschland, Emigration nach Palästina und ihrer Rückkehr*, Frankfurt am Main–New York 1995; Franz J. Jürgens, *"Wir waren ja eigentlich Deutsche". Juden berichten von Emigration und Rückkehr*, Berlin 1997.

[10]For example Peter Merseburger, *Willy Brandt 1913–1992. Visionär und Realist*, Stuttgart and Munich 2002; Gregor Schöllgen, *Willy Brandt. Die Biographie*, Berlin and Munich 2001; Carola Stern, *Willy Brandt*, Reinbek b. Hamburg 1988; Julia Angster, *Konsenskapitalismus und Sozialdemokratie. Die Westernisierung von SPD und DGB 1940 bis 1965*, Munich 2003; Peter Erler, 'Heeresschau und Einsatzplanung', in Klaus Schroeder (ed.), *Geschichte der Transformation des SED-Staates. Beiträge und Analysen*, Berlin 1994, pp. 52–70; Jan Foitzik, 'Die Rückkehr aus dem Exil und das politisch-kulturelle Umfeld der Reintegration sozialdemokratischer Remigranten in Westdeutschland', in Wolfgang Briegel and Wolfgang Frühwald (eds.), *Die Erfahrung der Fremde*, Weinheim 1988, pp. 255–270; Karin Hartewig, *Zurückgekehrt. Die Geschichte der jüdischen Kommunisten in der DDR*, Cologne 2000; Mario Keßler, *Die SED und die Juden – zwischen*

studies have begun to appear—for instance on Cologne, Munich, Hamburg and Berlin[11]—together with studies of individual artists, literary figures, and scientists, as well as of groups of returnees engaged in such activities.[12] A repeated focal point of such research has been the influence of returned emigrants on West Germany's political culture—on its democratisation and westernisation.[13]

If one chooses to concentrate on Jewish returnees, it is important to clarify one point at the outset: after 1945 people who were self-avowedly of Jewish identity or faith returned to Germany, as well as those who had been persecuted as Jews but who nevertheless did not feel any strong sense of identification with Judaism or Jewry. Both groups need to be considered if one wants to avoid unduly narrowing the question of Jewish remigration.[14] What the two groups shared was a deeply disturbing knowledge of the war that had been started by the Germans and of the German "final solution", which had fundamentally affected all people of Jewish origin. Yet many of them continued as before to define themselves not primarily as Jewish but in terms of their political affiliation, "I am not a Jew; I am a Socialist." declared the Hamburg returnee politician Peter Blachstein in annoyance at being invited to an event "as a Jew".[15] For a long time after the war, most such returnees were obliged to continue bearing the same pejorative label that had been applied to them by the Nazis. Indeed, even the most dedicated Communists of Jewish origin could not help being affected by antisemitism—as the example of the Stalinist spheres of influence in the early 1950s shows.[16]

Due to the complexity of the emotions and perspectives at play here, it would appear appropriate to take account of the self-identity of the individuals under scrutiny here, distinguishing when necessary between people defining themselves in a central way as Jewish and the greater number of those who were of Jewish origin. And there are people who identify themselves openly and even primarily as Jewish

---

Repression und Toleranz. Politische Entwicklungen bis 1967, Berlin 1995; Hartmut Mehringer, 'Impulse sozialdemokratischer Emigranten auf die Modernisierung der SPD', in Krohn and von zur Mühlen (eds.), pp. 91–110; Gerhard Paul, '"Herr K. ist nur Politiker und als solcher aus Amerika zurückgekommen." Die gelungene Remigration des Rudolf Katz', in *idem* and Miriam Gillis-Carlebach (eds.), *Menora und Hakenkreuz. Zur Geschichte der Juden in Schleswig-Holstein, Lübeck, Altona: 1918–1998*, Neumünster 1998.

[11]For Cologne: Blaschke *et al.* (eds.); for Hamburg: Marita Krauss, 'Die Region als erste Wirkungsstätte von Remigranten', in Krohn and von zur Mühlen (eds.), pp. 29–40.

[12]See Andreas Schätzke, *Rückkehr aus dem Exil. Bildende Künstler und Architekten in der SBZ und frühen DDR*, Berlin 1999.

[13]See Axel Schildt, 'Reise zurück in die Zukunft. Beiträge von intellektuellen USA-Remigranten zur atlantischen Allianz, zum westdeutschen Amerikabild und zur "Amerikanisierung" in den fünfziger Jahren', in *Exilforschung*, vol. 9 (1991), pp. 25–45; Alfons Söllner, 'Normative Verwestlichung. Der Einfluß der Remigranten auf die politische Kultur der frühen Bundesrepublik', in Heinz Bude and Bernd Greiner (eds.), *Westbindungen: Amerika in der Bundesrepublik*, Hamburg 1999, pp. 72–92. Research in this field by Arnd Bauerkämper (Potsdam), Martin Kirsch (Berlin), and Lothar Mertens (Bochum) is also in progress.

[14]See Marita Krauss, 'Exil, Neuordnung und Erneuerung Deutschlands: Jüdische Remigranten im politischen Leben Nachkriegsdeutschlands', in Hans Erler, Arnold Paucker, and Ernst Ludwig Ehrlich (eds.), *Jüdischer Widerstand gegen den Nationalsozialismus*, Frankfurt am Main–New York 2003, pp. 388–406.

[15]Cited in Hellmut Kalbitzer, *Widerstehen oder Mitmachen. Eigensinnige Ansichten und sehr persönliche Erinnerungen*, Hamburg 1987, p. 112.

[16]See Hartewig, pp. 315–429.

but who have no faith whatsoever. Their identity is based on what amounts to a sense of ethnic, national, or cultural affiliation. While such affiliation was felt more strongly in Eastern Europe than in Germany, nonetheless many German and Austrian Jews did feel it as well.

For many Jewish victims of the Nazis from Germany, it seemed at first inconceivable to return to a country in which their friends and families had been persecuted and murdered, from which they themselves had been expelled, and where they had been stripped of their worldly belongings. Thus remigration was a heavily taboo-laden subject. This was particularly the case for remigration from Palestine/Israel.[17] Of those Jews who survived the Holocaust in Europe, many would leave Germany in the years after the war. Their number vastly exceeded that of the Jewish returnees.[18] Among the Jews who had fled from Germany, thoughts of returning were usually met with sharp disapproval; often it was the women who rejected any possibility of doing so.[19] The process of remigration was psychologically a very complicated one accompanied by extremely ambivalent thoughts and feelings, the mere idea of returning forcing a painful engagement with one's own experiences in Nazi Germany and with German crimes. This engagement was exceedingly painful, in that it also encompassed grieving for the dead and grieving for one's own shattered and subsequently barely pieced-together life.

For most returnees of Jewish origin or identity, the return involved confronting a profound, often irresolvable conflict between Jewishness and Germanness, or at least between a knowledge of Germany's terrible recent reality and a love of one's native language, culture, and surroundings. Having returned to Germany in 1950, Max Fürst expressed this conflict with startling ambivalence in one particular passage:

> I cannot really write anything about my being Jewish [*Judentum*], and just as little about my being German [*Deutschtum*]: I do not possess either of them, but rather they possess me. One is born into them, has endured a certain upbringing, and then, without having to do much about it, one is identified with them. Above all the Jewishness is very clingy; it sticks like pitch [*Pech,* this German term also signifying bad luck], and it takes a lot of effort to get rid of it. Many have tried and failed.[20]

Through the experiences of exclusion, persecution and emigration many returnees of Jewish origin who had had little or no consciousness of Jewish identity were forced into a stronger awareness of it. Many had much cause to reflect on their individual relationship to "German" and "Jewish" identities.

To study the history of Jewish remigration it is necessary to grasp the complexity of such feelings. What was at stake was one's former homeland, its loss and possible reappropriation, and with this a search for lost identities and new orientations. Trust in this homeland had for the most part been lost, but not the basic human desire for a better future. In this light, it seems that one basic thing was required if persons of

[17]See Fings, pp. 22–32.
[18]See Foitzik, pp. 255f.; Fings, pp. 24f.
[19]See, for example, Ron Chernow, *Die Warburgs. Odyssee einer Familie*, Berlin 1994, pp. 707–709.
[20]Cited in Hans-Jürgen Schultz (ed.), *Mein Judentum*, 2nd edn., Munich 1987, pp. 176–185.

Jewish origin were to contemplate a return to Germany: a sense that Enlightenment ideals had a future in Germany even when these ideals had been betrayed there in the most radical way possible.

COUNTRIES OF EXILE

The more inhospitable or hostile a country of refuge, the greater the desire of Jews who had fled Germany to return. Countries where such hostility was prevalent included Turkey and China (Shanghai); a number of other Asian countries as well as some in South America also fit into this category.[21] In England and the United States emigrants fared better—a fact producing an extensive "secondary migration" to the latter country after 1945.[22] Yet those who were unable to obtain any other visa, who were expelled from their host country or simply wanted to escape from an oppressive situation often ended up on board of one of the ships that collected Germans of all persuasions and provenances in order to bring them back to Germany.[23]

The situation of those Jews returning to Germany from Palestine/Israel was somewhat special. Naturally enough, there were few committed Zionists among them—many of these individuals had simply not fared well in the incipient Jewish state, which thus had not come to be considered a second homeland.[24] For many of these returnees, leaving Palestine for Germany meant also taking leave of Judaism. The decision to return to Germany has to a considerable extent been a taboo topic in Israel since the state's inception: a taboo that has contributed to the topic's neglect in scholarly discourse.[25] Some returnees attributed their decision to health factors; others to the difficult living conditions—the climate, unemployment, the housing shortage. Financial considerations were certainly in the foreground. A fair percentage initially returned for business reasons or to deal with questions of compensation but ended up staying in Germany permanently.

In Israel, returning to the land of the murderers was tantamount to an act of treason, or at least judged egoistic and lacking in solidarity.[26] In the 1950s, when the first German compensation payments and resettlement allowances made it easier to return there from Israel, doing so was regarded as a threat to the young state, with remigration being publicly branded as a form of "bounty hunting".

The return proceeded despite such condemnation. In 1956, at the request of the *Zentralrat der Juden in Deutschland*, the West German government began to issue emergency payments, termed *Soforthilfe*, of 6,000 marks to every returnee who had

[21]For the countries of exile see Krohn *et al.* (eds.), pp. 129–466.

[22]One example of this is the experience of Michael Blumenthal (now director of Berlin's Jewish Museum) who emigrated to the United States from Shanghai in 1947. See Strauss and Röder (eds.), vol. I, p. 73.

[23]Hence the ship *General Sturgess* brought 106 emigrants back from Shanghai in 1950; see Blaschke *et al.* (eds.), p.2.

[24]See Fings, pp. 22–32; Krauss, *Heimkehr*, pp. 125–136.

[25]Such neglect is manifest, for example, in Ludger Heid, 'Palästina/Israel', in Krohn *et al.* (eds.), pp. 349–358. On returnees from Israel, see the article by Meron Mendel in this issue of the *LBI Year Book*.

[26]See Fings, 27f.

emigrated between 1933 and 1945 and returned after 1 May 1945. This measure was taken because the tiny local Jewish communities that had managed to re-establish themselves in post-war Germany were not in a position to finance the resettlement of impoverished co-religionists.

This triggered a wave of remigration, other factors contributing to the process being the high rates of Israeli taxation on the slowly arriving compensation payments and Germany's "economic miracle" which was just getting started. Thus in his study of fifty Jewish communities in Germany between 1955 and 1959, Harry Maor speaks of 5,580 returnees, of whom sixty-three percent had come from Israel.[27] But the figure may well be a substantial underestimate. Karola Fings estimates that, in order to avoid being asked how they could reconcile their abandonment of the Jewish state with their consciences, around half of those returning from Israel made no contact with the Jewish community.[28] Quite a few children born in Israel who accompanied their parents to Germany would later return to their birthplace.

CITIES OF RETURN

Most of the Jewish returnees headed for the large German cities. By 1952 the Berlin Jewish community had registered 650 returned emigrants, the community of Hamburg 114 and that of Cologne 210. In the cases of Hamburg and Berlin, returnees made up eleven percent of the community's membership; in Cologne the figure was nearly thirty percent.[29] Far fewer Jews returned to southern than to northern Germany, the percentages there being correspondingly lower.[30] An exception was Saarbrücken, where returned emigrants made up eighty-eight per cent of the Jewish population, as a relatively large number had managed to survive in nearby France.

A close look at remigration to West German cities allows us to draw further conclusions about that remigration: it reveals the framework for returning laid down by the occupying powers and the particular local conditions. Some of the salient questions in such a microanalysis are: were local conditions in these cities in the period following 1945 favourable or unfavourable for remigration? Can this be traced back to the attitudes of the occupying Allied forces, to the local élites or to economic or mental structures? Could the returnees bring their experiences in exile to bear on their new situation, or did they suffer a social decline after their return—or even emigrate for a second time? Were the returnees integrated because of or despite the fact that they had this status? The initial studies of Cologne, Munich and Hamburg testify to the profitability of this approach.[31] Such an approach makes it possible to consider the ordinary returnees, not just the intellectual, political, and economic élite among them, with a special focus on their social networks and paths of migration.

[27]Maor, pp. 45f.
[28]See Fings, pp. 24f.
[29]See Maor, pp. 43–46.
[30]See Brenner p. 89.
[31]Krauss, 'Die Region'; Blaschke *et al.* (eds.).

THE IDENTITY AND CIRCUMSTANCES OF THE RETURNEES

In spite of all internal and external difficulties, a certain number of Jewish returnees to the German Federal Republic helped shape the new state's political and intellectual life.[32] Among the figures who need to be cited in any cursory overview are Hans Habe, who first as an American press officer and later as an influential German journalist and writer both critically commented on and furthered the evolution of postwar journalism in West Germany; Habe's colleagues Hans Wallenberg and Ernest Cramer;[33] Herbert Weichmann, who eventually became mayor of Hamburg; Josef Neuberger and Rudolf Katz, future Ministers of Justice in Nordrhein-Westfalen and in Schleswig-Holstein respectively; Ludwig Rosenberg, later to become chairman of the *Deutsche(r) Gewerkschaftsbund*; the political scientists Richard Loewenthal and Ernst Fraenkel as well as the philosophers and sociologists Max Horkheimer and Theodor W. Adorno. If one wishes to study the effects of remigration on the transfer of knowledge and the reception of ideas, research into remigration is virtually the study of an élite. While some members of this élite have received a great deal of attention, research into its broad spectrum—the impact it had on postwar Germany and the postwar world—is still in its initial stages.

Relatively few of those Jews returning from exile became leading representatives of the Jewish community in the postwar years.[34] Two of the exceptions were Hendrik van Dam, who would become general secretary of the *Zentralrat der Juden in Deutschland*, and Karl Marx, who together with his wife Lilly was to leave a decisive mark on the Jewish press in Germany through his *Allgemeine Wochenzeitung der Juden in Deutschland*. In Würzburg, David Schuster, a returnee from Israel, became chairman of the city's Jewish communal organisation and eventually president of the Bavarian *Landesverband der Israelitischen Kultusgemeinde*. A few of the younger returnees achieved important positions in the 1960s and 1970s, for instance Hans Lamm, who became Honorary President of the Jewish Community in Munich, as well as Arno Hamburger, who had served in Palestine's Jewish Brigade during the war, and later obtained the same position as Lamm in Nuremberg's *Israelitische Kultusgemeinde*. Scholarly research on Jews who engaged in political work on behalf of other Jews in Germany after 1945 did not look at these individuals from the perspective of remigration.[35]

At first the reception conditions facing most Jewish returnees were generally poor. In western Germany the returnees were often initially made into objects of rejection and projection. For many—perhaps the great majority—of ordinary Germans the emigrants, whether returned or not, remained outside the German *Volksgemeinschaft*; they had not shared in "German greatness" and now did not share in German guilt.[36]

[32]See Krauss, *Heimkehr*, pp. 94–110.

[33]See Marita Krauss, 'Hans Habe, Ernst Friedlaender, Hermann Budzislawski – drei Zonen, drei Städte, drei Schicksale', in Krohn and Schildt (eds.), pp. 245–266.

[34]See Brenner, p. 90.

[35]*ibid.*, pp. 87–91.

[36]See Marita Krauss, 'Projektion statt Erinnerung. Der Umgang mit Emigranten und die deutsche Gesellschaft nach 1945', in *Exil*, vol. 18, no. 1 (1998), pp. 5–16; Jost Hermand and Wigand Lange (eds.), *Wollt ihr Thomas Mann wiederhaben? Deutschland und die Emigranten*, Hamburg 1999.

Additionally, people feared their revenge. Repeatedly, secret and devious enemies were being invoked who could be held to blame for the world's negative attitude towards Germany; and who could be better suited for this role than the returnees, who themselves had so many good reasons to hate. In a reversal of the reality of victimisation, the returned German Jews were now held to account for the Germans' own suffering during the Allied bombing campaigns.[37] The emigrants, it was alleged, had drawn the better cards when, as Frank Thieß explained in his response to Thomas Mann during the "great controversy" (an exchange of letters between some writers in exile, especially Thomas Mann, and other writers who had stayed on in Germany opting for "inner emigration"), "they observed the German tragedy from the boxes and orchestra seats of foreign countries" [*von den Logen und Parterreplätzen des Auslandes*].[38]

In any event—as the psychoanalysts Leon and Rebeka Grinberg have indicated in their study of migration and exile[39]—emigrants are in general easy objects of resentment and anger. Like all emigrants, Jews who returned to Germany thus had to adapt, and do so under the most difficult emotional circumstances. On the whole, only those who were stoic enough to steadily shunt aside considerable mistrust and hostility managed to eventually gain a foothold in postwar Germany. On the one hand, antisemitism continued to exist after the war, even when such feelings were seldom openly and crudely formulated. But they formed a basis for rejecting the returned emigrants, standing as they did on the side of the victors.[40] On the other hand, Konrad Adenauer clearly recognised the significance of restitution for Nazi crimes as the entrance ticket to an alliance with the West.[41] West Germany thus created a legal framework for such restitution in the 1950s.

There were also a few timid appeals for Jewish emigrants to return. The most important such appeal was issued in the name of the first and only conference of presidents of the German *Länder* in 1947.[42] Among the din caused by the partition of the two Germanys, this appeal remained a mere footnote. Similar isolated appeals extended to former members of the Social Democratic or the Communist Party. Scholars and artists could not, however, conceal the fact that most former refugees waited in vain for Germany to need them again. Hence in the late 1950s, the vandalising of the Cologne synagogue (1959) increased the fear of antisemitic attacks among Jewish returnees and also more or less brought emigration from Israel to an abrupt end. At the start of the 1960s, only about 250 Jews were arriving in the Federal Republic per year.[43]

[37]Krauss, 'Projektion'; *idem*, *Heimkehr*, pp. 50–61.

[38]Johannes Franz Gottlieb Grosser (ed.), *Die große Kontroverse. Ein Briefwechsel um Deutschland*, Hamburg 1963, p. 22.

[39]Leon Grinberg and Rebeka Grinberg (eds.), *Zur Psychoanalyse der Migration und des Exils*, Munich 1991.

[40]Brenner, pp. 78–87; Krauss, *Heimkehr*, p.125–136.

[41]See Ludolf Herbst, 'Einleitung', in *idem* and Constantin Goschler (eds.), *Wiedergutmachung in der Bundesrepublik Deutschland*, Munich 1989, p. 18.

[42]See Krauss, *Heimkehr*, pp. 75,78.

[43]See Fings, p. 24.

RETURNEES IN EASTERN GERMANY AND THE GDR

Thus far this overview has focussed on the situation of Jewish returnees in western Germany and the Federal Republic; it is now appropriate to summarise the circumstances in the eastern, Soviet-occupied part of Germany well. At the end of the war, the Soviet Union assembled a group of about 250 German Communists who had survived both the Nazi and the Soviet purges of the 1930s and 1940s. These were then set up as the top political leadership in East Germany; for decades they would determine the fate of the German Democratic Republic.[44] This Soviet-appointed élite included a certain number of Jewish returnees. Alexander Abusch, Albert Norden and Gerhart Eisler, who had survived as emigrants in western countries and later became SED officials, also came from Jewish families. Other prominent Jewish returnees to East Germany included the writers Arnold Zweig, Anna Seghers, and Stefan Heym as well as the literary historians Hans Meyer and Alfred Kantorowicz. But in the 1950s, the persecution of substantial numbers of persons who had survived the Nazi period in Western countries (both Communists of various backgrounds and Jews who were not party members) would produce a *caesura*, many members of East Germany's Jewish communities then fleeing to the West.[45] During this period, objections of leading East German officials against compensation payments to Jews were often expressed in a way once again displaying the old unhappy alliance of anti-capitalism and antisemitism—for instance in the remark that one should not squander "the wealth of the German socialist people on foreign capitalists".[46] The non-Jewish Hermann Matern, who had fought for the cause of compensation, fell victim to a campaign ending with his being stripped of his positions and sent to prison.[47] And within the East German definitional category of "victims of fascism" itself, there were initially two sub-categories, the "fighters" and the "victims", Jewish victims thus counting for less than the Communist "fighters" from the start.[48] In this manner, the new German state that defined itself in terms of antifascism instituted antisemitism into its policies in a quasi-official manner.

REMIGRATION AND THE OCCUPYING POWERS

However limited, the presence of various occupying forces in both east and west played a certain role in the return of a Jewish élite to German soil. Both during the war and in the subsequent occupation, the American armed forces were unique in their extensive use of emigrants, mostly as translators, journalists, and cultural officers.[49] In this respect, the press-team surrounding Hans Habe, which included

[44]See Erler, pp. 52–70.
[45]See Jeffrey Herf, *Zweierlei Erinnerung. Die NS-Vergangenheit im geteilten Deutschland*, Berlin 1998, pp. 130–193; Hartewig, pp. 347–357.
[46]Herf, p. 111.
[47]Hartewig, pp. 347–357.
[48]Herf, p. 100.
[49]See Krauss, *Heimkehr*, pp. 62–72.

Stefan Heym and Klaus Mann, is especially noteworthy.[50] A number of officers of German-Jewish origin, responsible for theatre and music, were very helpful in restarting cultural life in German cities. For the most part, they quickly allied themselves with German artists against both German and American bureaucrats.[51] In addition, many Jewish GIs had previously suffered from the "emigration-syndrome" of exclusion and persecution; the future filmmaker Georg Stefan Troller reports at length in his memoirs about this.[52] Nevertheless, even among the Americans the proportion of German-speaking emigrants was extremely small—and of these only a small fraction remained behind after the withdrawal of the occupying troops from Germany, the majority in the service of the Americans. Hardly any renounced their American citizenship.[53] Since it had become clear to the occupiers that the local population placed no value on the return of emigrants, the Americans and the British in particular placed greater emphasis on re-educating the potentially democratic forces inside the country and outside in the prisoner of war camps. Emigrants were not placed in leadership positions in the U.S. army; they were allowed to travel to Germany at the specific request of the local population, which they had to depend on for advancement to leading cultural or political positions. The situation was of course different in eastern Germany due to the Soviet appointments referred to above.

EMIGRATION AND REMIGRATION AS COLLECTIVE BIOGRAPHY

The exodus of Jews from Nazi Germany and its neighbouring states was in its basic structure a family exodus. The experience of the extensive German-Jewish Feuchtwanger family reveals the extent and the definitiveness of the Jewish family exodus. A family tree drawn up in 1952 traces 1,400 descendants of the Fürth silverware merchant Seligmann Feuchtwanger (1786–1852).[54] In the early 1930s most of the approximately nine hundred family members, including the author Lion Feuchtwanger, lived in Germany; in 1952, when there were one thousand family members, six still lived there, the family having been dispersed over twenty countries, with nearly half its members in Israel. Eighty of them had been murdered by the Nazis. The compiler of the Feuchtwanger family chronicle suspects that the family's high degree of Jewish and Zionist awareness contributed to the survival of so many members, most having left Germany in time.[55]

The example of the Feuchtwanger family demonstrates the advantages of a collective biographical approach, one focussing on the fate of families, when

[50]Jessica C.E. Gienow-Hecht, *Transmission Impossible: American Journalism as Cultural Diplomacy in Postwar Germany, 1945–1955*, Baton Rouge 1999.

[51]Marita Krauss, *Nachkriegskultur in München. Münchner städtische Kulturpolitik 1945–1954*, Munich 1985.

[52]See the memoirs of film-maker Georg Stefan Troller (once himself such a soldier), *Selbstbeschreibung*, 2nd edn., Hamburg 1988, p. 189.

[53]Krauss, *Heimkehr*, pp.62–72; *idem*, 'Eroberer oder Rückkehrer? Deutsche Emigranten in der amerikanischen Armee', in *Exil*, vol. 13 (1993), p. 77f.

[54]See Olympia-Martin Feuchtwanger (ed.), *The Feuchtwanger Family. The Descendants of Seligmann Feuchtwanger*, Tel Aviv 1975.

[55]*ibid.*, p. 130.

studying Jewish emigration and remigration. Through this approach, which should be accompanied, it must be emphasised, by mindfulness to the individual features and personal frames of reference of the Jewish emigrants, the extent and nature of their Diaspora becomes evident, as well as the details of their "secondary migration" to other countries after 1945 and the return of some to the country of their birth. Although a few German-Jewish emigrant families such as the Warburgs, the Oppenheimers and the Rothschilds have been studied in considerable detail, there is still a great deal of space for research in this field on both an élite and an "ordinary" level.[56]

BORDER CROSSINGS

Studying Jewish remigration to Germany cannot be based on rough figures alone. Such figures need to be embedded in a wider context: that of the internal processes associated with migration. A very useful way of entering this context would seem to be through the notion of borders or frontiers—analysing various autobiographical accounts of crossing borders into or out of exile,[57] with the aim of isolating the deeper social-historical and psychological structures at work in this process.

A basic border that had to be crossed on the road into exile was one's previous life, with the prospect of childhood memories and friends gradually receding into oblivion. Such separations were often traumatic and usually irreversible. For the writer Stefan Heym, the border's threat condensed into the word "avalanche"—into the idea of snow "pressing heavily on the slope high above him, ready to break free at any moment and, rushing downward, to bury him under its weight". He was in a through coach on a winter's night, bypassing Germany in a wide arc, travelling from Prague via Paris to a ship meant to take him to America, when the train stopped on an open stretch of track. A rumour started that the train had to be diverted through Germany because of an avalanche threat. He was gripped by sheer terror:

> He forces open the window, but outside are only shadows, formless, and sparks flying skywards, and the locomotive's puffing. … Finally the train rolls forward and takes up its journey, slowly, as if the locomotive first had to feel its way, then gradually faster, and yet faster ever-deeper into the darkness; and then there is the border, but the official who slides open the compartment-door wears a Swiss uniform and has only a fleeting interest in the pale young man in the corner and in his passport with the American student-visa.[58]

[56]See Chernow; Frederic Morton, *Die Rothschilds. Ein Portrait der Dynastie*, Munich 1998; Michael Stürmer, Gabriele Teichmann and Wilhelm Treue (eds.), *Wägen und Wagen. Sal. Oppenheim jr. & Cie. Geschichte einer Bank und einer Familie*, Munich 1989.

[57]Grinberg and Grinberg (eds.), pp. 205–222; Mechthild Zeul, 'Rückreise in die Vergangenheit. Zur Psychoanalyse spanischer Arbeitsmigrantinnen', in Helga Haase (ed.), *Ethnopsychoanalyse*, Stuttgart 1996, pp. 219–255; Krauss, *Heimkehr*, pp.19–29; *idem* and Herbert Will, 'Innensichten. Grenzüberschreitungen bei Emigranten der NS-Zeit in interdisziplinärer Annäherung', in Hans Hecker *et al.* (eds.): *Grenzen. Gesellschaftliche Konstitutionen und Transfigurationen*, Düsseldorf 2003.

[58]Stefan Heym, *Nachruf*, Berlin 1990, p. 120f.

Years later his memory would deny him the word "avalanche", the terror of the experience having penetrated so deeply. The train-trip through darkness corresponds to an ever-deeper penetration into his own anxiety, similar to a nightmare's dynamic.

The philosopher Ludwig Marcuse, who returned to Germany for the first time in 1949, describes the experience as it were "in reverse"—which is to say in terms of his return:

> When I reached the border, I was overwhelmed—by what, I cannot express in a word. Between thirty-three and forty-five I thought it perfectly possible that one day I might visit Alaska or eastern Russia or China's interior … but Germany? I had made it an absolute taboo, so greatly did it frighten me; it seemed more dangerous to me to be there than to expose myself to deadly frost, lions or cannibals. During those thirteen years I was often visited by the same, very unsensational dream: I wander again and again through German streets, alongside SS and SA men bearing all the insignia of the Third Reich. Nothing happens, no one pays the slightest attention to me—and I am plagued, unbearably, by the vexing question: Why have I come back? Where can I still find a way out? … This accounts for the powerful sensation I experienced at the frontier; it was neither pleasurable nor painful. It bowled me over. Hatred, happiness, melancholy only came later, in very civil doses.[59]

For other refugees as well, re-crossing the frontier to Germany reactivated trauma and emotional fragmentation, kindled fears of and longing for a re-encounter with an unrepeatable chapter of one's own life—with the unburied ghosts of the past. At times, the trauma of having been an outcast would be alleviated through encounters with ordinary Germans: there they were, once again as at the time of their own departure, the former neighbours, the dialect-speaking maids and innkeepers and porters. [60] One tended to cling to such people as the "godparents" of one's new start in Germany and with the Germans.

Carl Zuckmayer and Georg Stefan Troller have reflected with particular clarity on the problem of returning to Germany after the war. They see this process as involving a quest for a lost childhood—as an attempt to reverse the migratory process of one's own life. Georg Stefan Troller wrote as follows:

> Emigrants are specialists in homesickness. But what is a homeland, anyway, or a fatherland? In any event, a place in which one has usually suffered the gravest loss of reality. Perhaps it is impossible to explain the magic of one's *Heimat*, because it is one with the indefinable magic of childhood. In the love of one's *Heimat*, one loves oneself retrospectively. For this reason the loss of one's *Heimat* leads to the loss of a good portion of healthy self-love, unconditional self-acceptance.[61]

Along with announcing the start of a quest for a fragment of lived life, the re-crossing of the German frontier offered the possibility of reintegrating segments of

[59]Ludwig Marcuse, *Mein 20. Jahrhundert*, Munich 1960, p. 359.

[60]See Marita Krauss, 'Grenze und Grenzwahrnehmung bei Emigranten der NS-Zeit', in Andreas Gestrich and Marita Krauss (eds.), *Migration und Grenze*, Stuttgart 1998, pp. 61–82.

[61]Troller, p. 233. See as well Carl Zuckmayer, *Als wär's ein Stück von mir. Horen der Freundschaft*, Stuttgart and Hamburg 1966, p. 519.

one's own personality that had become split off through pain. In this manner, the returnees faced both a crisis and an opportunity.[62]

* * *

A future history of Jewish remigration will need to approach the topic from multiple perspectives. Close scrutiny of the migration of the Jewish German-speaking intellectual élites and their ideas may underscore their role as forerunners of transnational hybrid cultures—as productive mediators of knowledge between many cultures.[63] At the same time, the investigation of the local postwar integrative environment may make visible the network composed of internal and external élites so central to successful remigration and resettlement. The investigation of Jewish families in the processes of emigration and return promises to unite quantifiable data with a qualitative research perspective. And investigating autobiographical documents with the aid of cultural hermeneutics offers the possibility of illuminating the psychological processes at work in both emigration and remigration. Reflecting such manifold viewpoints, Jewish remigration can and ought to become an exemplary field for interdisciplinary research.

62Marita Krauss, 'Heimat–Begriff und Erfahrung', in Hermann Haarmann (ed.), *Heimat, liebe Heimat. Exil und innere Emigration 1933–1945*, Berlin 2004.

63See Hartmut Kaelble, Martin Kirsch, and Alexander Schmidt-Gernig (eds.), *Transnationale Öffentlichkeiten und Identitäten im 20. Jahrhundert*, Frankfurt am Main 2000, esp. Martin Kirsch, 'Wissenschaftler im Ausland zwischen 1930 und 1960—Transferbedingungen und Identitätswandel einer erzwungenen Migration', *ibid.*, pp. 179–209.

The Policy for the Past in West Germany and Israel: The Case of Jewish Remigration

BY MERON MENDEL

I

On 10 September 1952 in Luxemburg's city hall, the West German chancellor, Konrad Adenauer, and the Israeli foreign minister, Moshe Sharett, met in order to sign a compensation agreement. In the agreement, Germany committed itself to pay compensation to the Jewish victims of the Nazi regime, to the Conference on Jewish Material Claims against Germany and to the State of Israel. It was an unusual ceremony: without speeches, without handshaking. One of the morning newspapers described the atmosphere in the signing hall as "ice-cold silence".[1]

This was the official onset of the special relations between the State of Israel and West Germany—relations that would only take diplomatic form in 1965. The agreement marked an important stage in German efforts to take responsibility for deeds of the recent past and signified international recognition of Israel as a moral representative of the Jewish victims.

Although it attracted less public interest and affected fewer people than the compensation agreement, the issue of Jewish remigration to Germany and the approach taken to the phenomenon by both Germany and Israel itself represents a chapter in the way the two countries confronted that past. Such remigration was a small-scale phenomenon. It began at the end of the war and reached its zenith during the 1950s, following the establishment of the Federal Republic and the passage of reparation laws in 1953 and 1956. A study from 1961 indicates that 9,000 Jews had returned to Germany by 1959 (less then four per cent of those who had fled before the war).[2] In the following years, the wave of remigration declined. According to several estimations the overall postwar remigration to Germany involved between 12,000 and 15,000 people.[3]

The allies were the first to develop a policy towards the returnees. The American, British and French authorities restricted the "right of return" to those whom they perceived as valuable, demanding that the returnees prove possession of initial

[1] *Süddeutsche Zeitung*, 11 September 1952, p. 1.

[2] Harry Maor, *Über den Wiederaufbau der jüdischen Gemeinden in Deutschland seit 1945*, Ph.D. thesis, Mainz 1961, p. 32.

[3] Erica Burgauer, *Jüdisches Leben in Deutschland (BRD und DDR) 1945—1990*, Ph.D. thesis, Zurich 1992, pp. 12–14; Marita Krauss, *Heimkehr in ein fremdes Land. Geschichte der Remigration nach 1945*, Munich 2001, pp. 9–10; Doris Kuschner, *Die jüdische Minderheit in der Bundesrepublik Deutschland. Eine Analyse*, Ph.D. thesis, Cologne 1977, pp. 233–234.

capital and a permanent job, along with a housing arrangement.[4] Only a few hundred persons were admitted to the Western zones under these restrictions. But with the founding of the Federal Republic under its Basic Law, the right of German Jews and other formerly persecuted individuals to regain their citizenship was established. Clause 116 paragraph 2 of the Basic Law is as follows:

> Former German citizens, who between 30 January 1933 and 8 May 1945 were deprived of their citizenship on political, racial, or religious grounds, and their descendants, are to have their citizenship restored on application. They are considered as never having been deprived of their citizenship, so long as they have established their domicile in Germany after 8 May 1945 and have not expressed a contrary intention.[5]

The clause does distinguish between those who have returned to Germany and those who have remained in the countries to which they emigrated. While the former have their citizenship restored automatically as persons who were "deemed never to have been deprived" of it, the latter must apply to the German authorities to become German citizens again.

During the 1950s the Bundestag passed two reparation laws (1953 and1956) and a restitution law (1957). These laws encouraged remigration by granting direct and indirect advantages to the returnees. Not only was it now considerably easier for those residing in Germany to have their confiscated property returned and gain compensation, but the returnees were also offered additional support from the government. The law of 1956 legislated for "urgent help" for the returnees—an unconditional grant of 6,000 German marks on arrival, a very significant sum of money in those days.[6]

Examination of Israeli policy reveals a different attitude. Perhaps not surprisingly, the Israeli authorities imposed all sorts of restrictions and obstacles intended to minimise the number of returnees. Every Israeli passport was stamped with the words "not valid for Germany";[7] and official declarations were printed in the press stating that Israeli citizens who applied for travel permits in order to settle permanently in Germany would not be allowed to re-enter Israel.[8]

Israel's diplomatic mission in Munich updated the Israeli authorities concerning potential returnees. For example, in response to a demand made in a letter to the *Frankfurter Neue Presse* by Max Binder, a Tel-Aviv resident, that the Bonn government call on Jews to return to Germany,[9] the Israeli consul in Munich, Eliahu Livneh, wrote to the Ministry of the Interior that "this is the nastiest publication I have ever read," instructing the ministry to "take care of this man in the proper way".[10]

[4]Ina S. Lorenz, *Gehen oder Bleiben. Neuanfang der Jüdischen Gemeinde in Hamburg nach 1945*, Hamburg 2002, p. 37.
[5]Karl-Heinz Seifert and Dieter Hömig, *Grundgesetz für die Bundesrepublik Deutschland: Taschenkommentar*, Baden-Baden 1995, p. 679.
[6]Maor, p. 31.
[7]Instructions from the Israeli Immigration Office to immigrant officers abroad and to regional offices, 22 December 1949, Israel State Archive, Jerusalem (henceforth ISA), 2413\2.
[8]The Israeli National Press Agency (henceforth NPA) (28 December 1949), ISA, 2413/2.
[9]Max Binder, 'Wiedergutmachung' (Leserbrief), in *Frankfurter Neue Presse*, 27 November 1951, p. 2.
[10]Eliahu Livneh to Jewish Agency's West Europe Department (henceforth WED), 11 December 1951, ISA 2527\12.

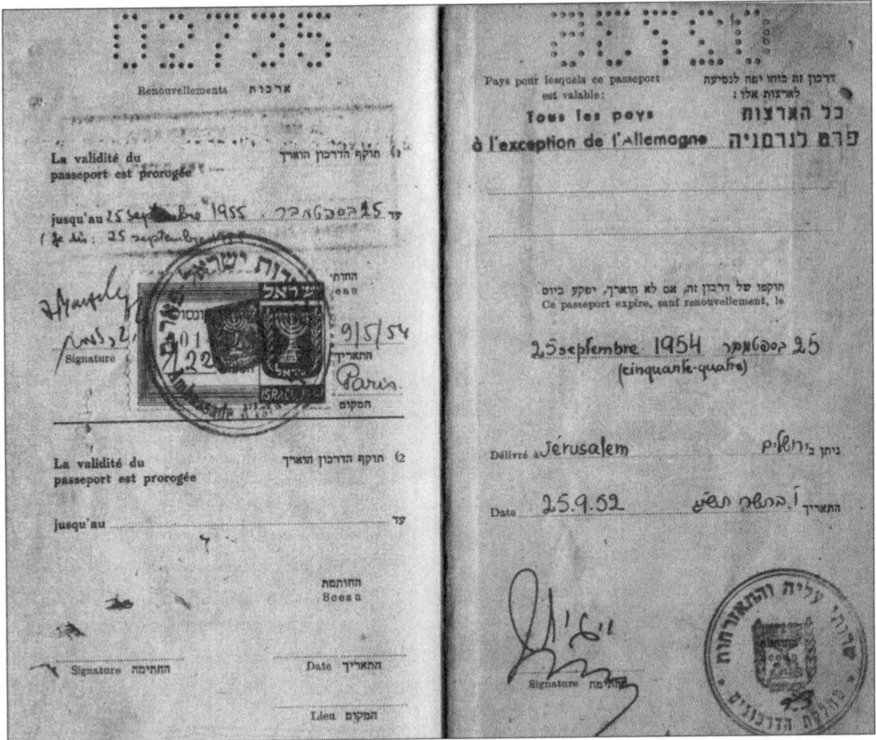

Israeli passport bearing the entry (in French and Hebrew) "valid for all countries with the exception of Germany".

In any event, the fact that both the German and Israeli authorities considered remigration something that had to be dealt with despite its small scale suggests that the significance of the phenomenon did not lie in its size. In both countries, Jewish return was perceived as a symbolic phenomenon with political and international implications. This article discusses the role which remigration played in the formation of the Israeli and postwar German collective memory. The section below focuses on West Germany, the two sections that follow on Israel and the perspective of the scattered Jewish communities in Germany, and a final main section on the viewpoint of the returnees themselves.

II

What Ralph Giordano has termed the "second guilt" involves the repression and denial of the "first guilt": the crimes committed under Hitler's regime.[11] At the core

[11]Ralph Giordano, *Die zweite Schuld oder von der Last Deutscher zu sein*, Zurich 1987, p. 11.

of this guilt lies what Giordano defines as a "big compromise with the perpetrators" (*der große Friede mit den Tätern*). This compromise was evident in the amnesty laws, as well as in the accompanying widespread social, political and economic re-integration of Nazi perpetrators into Federal Republic society during its first decade. In his book, Giordano points an accusatory finger not only at West Germany's politicians but also at the public which supported this process.[12]

Giordano's observations are backed up by a series of nationwide surveys conducted in West Germany during the fifties by the American High Commission for Germany. These revealed that every second German believed Nazism to be a good idea that was badly executed. Forty-one per cent of those polled perceived more good than evil in Nazi ideas. Only a minority (four per cent) believed that all Germans bore "a certain guilt for Germany's actions during the Third Reich".[13] Likewise, for every polled German who experienced guilt for crimes committed against the Jews more than four claimed that the Jews themselves were partly responsible for the Holocaust.[14]

The historian Norbert Frei has convincingly argued that in his policies regarding the past, Adenauer addressed such public sentiments through a process with three key elements: amnesty, integration, and disassociation with Nazism.[15] Behind this approach lay a conviction that in order to establish a functioning West German democracy, those who had gone astray had to be socially reintegrated. At the same time, however, Adenauer promoted a policy of appeasement vis-à-vis the Jewish people. The compensation agreement signed with Israel was one expression of this policy. Another expression was the series of three compensation laws passed by the Bundestag during the 1950s.

A small but prominent group within Germany's political and cultural élite believed that West Germany's policies towards the Jews would play a central role in the new country's integration into the Western world. As early as the summer of 1946, the German journalist Hans Habe, editor of the popular American-sponsored newspaper *Die neue Zeitung*, suggested steps to be carried out in order that Germany be accepted back into the "family of civilised nations":

> First of all: antisemitism must be institutionally banned in the new German constitution. … Secondly: the German Government, and not only that government, must attempt to summon back German Jews from emigration. … Thirdly: restitution for German Jews must become a German affair, not something for the Allies to take care of. … The world must feel it to be Germany's desire to make good for the injustices committed.[16]

[12]*ibid.*

[13]Anna and Richard Merritt, *Public Opinion in Semi-sovereign Germany: The HICOG Surveys 1949–1955*, Chicago 1980, p. 7.

[14]*ibid.*, p. 146.

[15]Norbert Frei, 'Das Problem der NS-Vergangenheit in der Ära Adenauer', in Heinrich Oberreuter and Jürgen Weber (eds.), *Freundliche Feinde? Die Alliierten und die Demokratiegründung in Deutschland*, Munich 1996, pp. 181–193. See also *idem*, *Adenauer's Germany and the Nazi Past: The Politics of Amnesty and Integration*, transl. by Joel Golb, New York 2002 (transl. of *Vergangenheitspolitik. Die Anfänge der Bundesrepublik und die NS-Vergangenheit*, Munich 1997).

[16]*Die neue Zeitung*, 16 August 1946, as quoted in Frank Stern, *The Whitewashing of the Yellow Badge*, Exeter 1992, pp. 266–267.

The first step in this direction was the complete rejection of all forms of antisemitism. The Jewish image in the postwar German media displayed a remarkable turnaround: the Jew as slanderously caricatured in *Der Stürmer* had now become an idealised, enlightened Jew along the lines of *Nathan der Weise*. Looking back on this public philosemitism, the historian Frank Stern observed that "Whatever was not compatible with this exaggerated image of the Jew, the Jewish special character and the Jewish contribution, was conveniently submerged in a kind of amnesia".[17] Yet a distinction was drawn, implicitly and explicitly, between German Jews, possessing noble qualities and rooted in the homeland, and Eastern European Jews—the displaced persons. Stern here observes that "DPs constituted the major object in the continuity of antisemitic stereotypes in the post-war years. They conformed with the traditional notion of the 'Eastern Jew', who remained the 'stranger', the 'foreigner' in public consciousness".[18]

This distinction was manifest in postwar West German immigration policy. While great efforts were made at the beginning of the 1950s to shut down the camps for displaced persons and force their inhabitants to leave the country,[19] German Jews were welcomed and perceived as potential contributors to the nation's reconstruction and Western integration. In 1949, Kurt Schumacher, the Social-Democratic leader, called upon German Jews to return in a speech in the Bundestag, observing that the German people would benefit from their intellectual and economic potential.[20] In his first visit abroad—in 1947 to London—Schumacher also expressed his surprise at the small number of returnees. His argument was that the returnees would help dismantle identification of Germany with the Third Reich: in order to prove the Nazis wrong, Jews had to return to Germany; otherwise antisemites throughout Europe would follow the example set by Nazi Germany in attempting to eradicate the Jews.[21] Theodor Heuss, the West German president, likewise told an American Jewish magazine that the Jews should return and not leave Germany isolated.[22]

As such statements by Schumacher and Heuss indicate, the Jewish return was not perceived among the West German political élite as a matter mainly affecting individuals, but rather as a symbolic phenomenon with political and international implications. During the late 1940s and the 1950s, the returnees turned into an unofficial barometer of antisemitism in Germany. Hence after several antisemitic incidents during 1957, a newspaper report commented:

> In 1950 there were 18,000 Jews in Germany. Today there are 45,000. Until 1 January 1957, around 3,000 Jewish families had returned; from this time on approximately 60 families have returned per week. … These facts seem to us to be a pleasing sign. They

[17] *ibid.*, p. xviii.
[18] *ibid*, p. 390.
[19] Protocol of a meeting in the German Foreign Ministry concerning displaced persons, 9 May 1955, ISA 2525\8.
[20] Jeffrey Herf, *Divided Memory: The Nazi Past in the Two Germanys*, London 1997, p. 273.
[21] Shlomo Shafir, *Yad Mushetet. Ha'socialdemokratim ha'germanim ve'yahasam la'yehudim ve'israel 1945–1967*, Tel Aviv 1986, p. 36.
[22] Hal Lehrman, 'The New Germany and her Remaining Jews', in *Commentary*, vol. 16, no. 6 (December 1953), pp. 513–524.

> show that despite the recent madness of isolated grave-desecrations, the Federal Republic is perceived as a solid, peaceful and tolerant country.[23]

Just four months after the end of the war, a newspaper report in the *Neue Zeit* defined the future role of the returnees as to affirm the blamelessness of the German people: the returnees would "recognise that civil courage, devoted loyalty and strong political resistance were not forgotten in Hitler's Germany"; they would discover that a good part of the people still held these positions, even though they had to disguise them because of the murderous terror.[24]

Still, however widespread, the approval of Jewish return was not always an indication that antisemitic views had disappeared. Behind several of the warm greetings one can find traces of the old ideas. In an article in honour of the novelist Alfred Döblin, who had converted to Christianity, the conservative *Rheinische Zeitung* commented on the "German and Jewish blood" flowing in the poet's "veins": "But he does not belong to the provocative Jewish circles held in contempt by noble Jews themselves and bearing the guilt, together with incompetent politicians, for the brown wave rolling over Germany in such a devastating manner."[25]

This article does not represent the common treatment of Jews in the press. A general taboo existed in postwar Germany against the use of terms such as "Jewish blood" and "German blood". Straightforward accusations that "the Jews" had played a role in the Nazi rise to power were uncommon. Still, one can here see the Jewish return emerging as a potential tool for those Germans still harbouring explicit antisemitic feelings.

The fact that antisemites still existed was rarely a subject of public discussion in postwar West Germany. The issue was still too recent and too sensitive. Fritz Kortner's 1949 film *Der Ruf* represented a courageous attempt (sponsored by the American authorities) to bring the issue into the open. Kortner had himself returned from exile in the United States two years earlier, and his script, in which an exiled German-Jewish professor in America is invited by his former university to take up his old position, is based on his personal experience. While the professor returns with high hopes, he soon finds out that much has remained the same, his colleagues and students still ostracising him because of his Jewishness. In the end he dies of a broken heart.

The film sparked a minor public controversy, some of the viewers utterly rejecting its message, claiming it to be both unrealistic and, in the words of Ursula Böttcher of the *Frankfurter Rundschau*, "almost anti-German".[26] Even the positive reviews tried to take the edge off the film's political critique: in the same newspaper, Norbert Schultze indicated that Kortner "has made his cautious declaration of love to all that is good in Germany", and suggested that the film's central contribution lay in

[23] *Echo der Zeit*, 23 June 1957, as quoted in Karola Fings, 'Rückkehr als Politikum – Remigration aus Israel', in Wolfgang Blaschke, Karola Fings and Cordula Lissner (eds.) *Unter Vorbehalt: Rückkehr aus der Emigration nach 1945*, Cologne 1997, p. 27.

[24] Anon., 'Wiedersehen mit der Heimat', in *Neue Zeit*, 7 September 1945, p. 1.

[25] Hermann Ulbrich-Hannibal, 'Willkommengruß für Alfred Döblin ', in *Rheinische Zeitung*, 31 August 1946, p. 3.

[26] *Frankfurter Rundschau*, 15 June 1949, p. 3.

promulgating the notion that the Germans are neither a "*Volk* of murderers nor heroes. There are good and bad people everywhere."[27] In *Die Zeit*, Jan Molitor took the stand that the occupying powers were contaminating the German film industry: the Americans "have for far too long a time encouraged films on contemporary circumstances [*Zeitfilme*] such as 'rubble-films' [*Trümmerfilme*]"[28]—themes that were meant only to be discussed in documentary films.[29]

The discussion surrounding Kortner's film demonstrates the basically one-dimensional character of the German media coverage. The returnees were presented as affirming the solidity, peacefulness, and tolerance of the new German democracy rather than as a group of individuals whose simple presence was a source of unease because of widespread, deeply-held antisemitic views and feelings. Having himself returned to Germany with his parents as a child, Peter Sichrovsky observes the same gap between reality and the German media's benign perspective enduring in the 1980s:

> German TV likes to show pictures of tearful older people returning from abroad to spend their last years in their old homeland. Again and again they say—and the audience eats it up—that they harbour no feelings of vengeance. But every time I see this sort of thing, I have the urge to shout out, "You out there, you don't have the faintest idea what these people [the returnees] say when they are among themselves!"[30]

III

In September 1949, Gershom Schocken, the chief editor and founder of the Israeli newspaper *Haaretz*, published an article entitled "We and the Germans", in which he expressed concern that the allies' efforts to integrate Germany into the civilised world would encourage Israelis to reside in Germany. He suggested three measures to prevent this from taking place: the Israeli state should forbid its citizens from holding permanent residence rights in Germany; a legal deadline should be passed after which every Jew who stayed in Germany would lose his right to immigrate to Israel; and a law was needed banning social contact with Germans, regardless of their past. These measures, Schocken believed, would have the benefit of both reducing the number of Jews in Germany and Austria and presenting to the world "a glorious demonstration of our feelings towards the German people. … We should not take part in the shame of the Jews in Germany", he indicated. "We are obliged to demonstrate in a clear political act that settling in Germany is not comparable to settling in any other Diaspora community and that one cannot simultaneously be a resident of Germany and enjoy Jewish national rights."[31] The decisions to add the

[27]Norbert Schultze, 'Fritz Kortners Wiederkehr', in *Frankfurter Rundschau*, 13 October 1949, p. 4.

[28]Jan Molitor, 'Glanz und Elend des deutschen Films', in *Die Zeit*, 21 April 1949, p. 9.

[29]*idem*, 'Glanz und Elend des deutschen Films', in *Die Zeit*, 5 May 1949, p. 9.

[30]Peter Sichrovsky, *Strangers in their Own Land: Young Jews in Germany and Austria Today*, transl. by Jean Steinberg, New York 1986, p. 7.

[31]Gershom Schocken, 'Anachnu vehagermanim' ('We and the Germans'), in *Haaretz*, 2 September 1949, p. 2.

stamp "not valid for Germany" to Israeli passports and to ban Israelis from permanent German residence were taken by the immigration ministry a few months after the article's publication.[32]

The public discussion over the possibility of Jewish return to Germany actually began during the war. *Haaretz* published several articles on this issue,[33] and even Ben Gurion estimated that "there are many Jews in our land who, if possible, will return to Germany after Germany rejects Hitler".[34] The question of such remigration was also discussed at the World Jewish Congress, the most prominent body in world Jewry. Already in 1944, before the war had ended, the Congress passed a resolution to the effect that it would be inappropriate for Jews to return to Germany or to apply for restoration of their citizenship there.[35] And an even firmer resolution was passed in 1948 under the pressure of Zionist organisations: no Jew was ever to acquire German nationality again.[36]

Before the establishment of the State of Israel, the *Haganah*—the paramilitary organisation of the pre-state Jewish community in Palestine (the *Yishuv*)—kept records of those individuals who had applied to the British authorities to enter Germany. It is nevertheless unclear if the *Haganah* initiated any action against the applicants.[37] Another quasi-official Jewish body that would deal with the returnees was the Jewish Agency, which established an office in Munich in 1945 to supervise the organisation of day-to-day life in the camps for displaced persons, the long-term goal being their emigration to Israel. And in July 1948, the State of Israel established a consulate in Munich. Although Israeli policy was for the state's representatives to avoid all contact with Germans, the very existence of such a diplomatic mission was highly unpopular among the Israeli public, whose criticism prompted the Israeli foreign minister, Moshe Sharett, to declare in 1952 that the consulate was soon to be shut down.[38] The Foreign Ministry carried out the closure in July 1953. This move in any event had more symbolic than practical significance—the "Israel Mission", which had settled in Cologne as part of the Luxemburg Agreement, continued to function as an unofficial consulate.

As suggested, the main objective of Jewish Agency representatives was eventually to "to bring the Jewish presence in Germany to an end".[39] When it came to this objective, no difference was made between Jewish displaced persons and Jews settled in German cities. After 1948, most of the former group emigrated to Israel and America, most of the latter preferring to stay put. In November 1949, the Jewish

[32]NPA, 28 Decenber 1949, ISA 2413/2.

[33]Robert Weltsch, 'Lavikuach Al Shiyva Le'germania' ('The Argument about Returning to Germany'), in *Haaretz*, 29 December 1939, p. 2.

[34]Labour party meeting, 19 March 1941, Labour Party Archive Tel-Aviv, 23\41, as quoted in Yoav Gelber, *Moledet Hadasha. Aliyat Oley Merkaz Eropa veklitatam 1933–1948*, Jerusalem 1990, p. 227.

[35]*Resolutions: War Emergency Conference Of The World Jewish Congress*, New York, 1944, p. 2, as quoted in Maor, p. 33.

[36]Monika Richarz, 'Jews in Today's Germanies', in *LBI Year Book*, vol. 30 (1985), p. 266.

[37]A list of applicants for emigration can be found in the Haganah-Archive Tel-Aviv, file 112/24. I wish to thank Adi Gordon for drawing my attention to this document.

[38]Protocol of the Israeli Foreign Relations and Security Commission, 7 January 1952, ISA 2457\12.

[39]Gerschon Avner, director of WED, to Eliahu Livneh, 1 November 1949, ISA 2457\12.

Agency published a manifesto to all the Jews in Germany, in which it declared that "Thousands of Jews are still living in Germany without any objective Jewish, Zionist, or human justification. The Jewish Agency and the public in Israel are deeply concerned about this since it carries severe danger: the danger of adjustment to the surroundings, the danger of national and moral degeneration." The manifesto ended with the following plea: "The gates of our homeland are open, the land cries out for you to come, to build it up and be built up by it. Come!!!"[40]

Despite all efforts to the contrary, the number of Jews in Germany (excluding those in the camps for displaced persons) rose steadily, due chiefly to immigration from Eastern Europe and the remigration of German Jews. The representatives of the Jewish Agency complained that this development made it impossible to demand emigration to Israel from those Jews currently living in Germany. The Agency's director, Amos Ravel, even defined this problem as the greatest obstacle to Israeli emigration efforts.[41]

The Israeli representatives blamed the absence of Jewish emigration from West Germany on the low moral standards of the Jews living there. Writing a few years after the Holocaust, some Israeli representatives did not hesitate to use antisemitic stereotypes. The head of the diplomatic mission, Eliahu Livneh, commented that:

> The Jewish community [in Germany] is far from having any moral standards. It is an element that thinks only in terms of money and profits and looks at Israel and Zionism with cynicism and indifference. Its private accounts are the only principle in its life. Its contributions to our project do not come from Zionist ideology but from the need to quiet its conscience. The usual propaganda is [consequently] not effective. We should admit our defeat in this regard.[42]

Some envoys also expressed the view that the returnees were both sabotaging the emigration efforts and, beyond that, diminishing the moral force Israel could exert in Germany. The first Israeli consul in Munich, Haim Yahil, reported that the returnees were slandering the Jewish state and causing a "decline in German confidence in the claim that the State of Israel, and only that state, represents the historical claims and destiny of the Jewish people".[43] (Other factors producing the same effect, according to Yahil, were Arabic propaganda, inner Jewish disagreements and Israel's unforgiving attitude towards Germany.) In another report Yahil offered a blunt warning about the returnees: "The danger is that an immoral, degenerate Jewish group will break Jewish solidarity and offer itself as a cheaper partner than the State of Israel and world Jewry."[44]

[40]Appendix to a letter from Baruch Yafe to Yitzhak Refael, 5 November 1949, Central Zionist Archives, Jerusalem (henceforth CZA) 6095/S6.
[41]Amos Ravel to the *Sochnut* board, 5 June 1950, CZA 6095\S6.
[42]Eliahu Livneh to the Israeli Immigration Office, 2 November 1949, ISA 2519/4. See also WED to Yissakhar Ben-Ya´akov (Jacobsohn), 10 July 1956, ISA 2520/3 and Livneh to WED, 14 October 1949, ISA 2519/4.
[43]Haim Yahil, 'Taskir al ha'yachasim beyn Germania ve'yehudeya' (A Report on Germany and its Jews), (12 May 1954), pp. 20–21, ISA 2413/2.
[44]Haim Yahil to WED, 11 October 1953, ISA 2520\3.

Livneh shared the same sentiment. After six months in Munich, he summarised the main aims of Israel's diplomatic mission as being to

> prevent the Jews in Germany from receiving political status here in the future. In this sense, we have a negative task, to inhibit the Jews in Germany from damaging our interests... If the question of restitution and reparation had not been on the political agenda, maybe it would have been possible for us to leave the Jews in Germany to their own devices. Since we cannot ignore the intention of the German government to "heal" its relationship with world Jewry through consolidation with local Jews, we need to have internal control over the Jews who live in Germany. ... Our aim should be to diminish German Jewry to the extent that it only remains a social problem, separate from the Jewish world and without any political power.[45]

It is thus apparent that Israeli policy was to enforce an informal boycott against the German-Jewish community; Israeli foreign representatives were instructed not to invite Jews from Germany to any official ceremony or event.[46] The policy reflected a fundamental Israeli anxiety: that the state might lose the right to represent the Holocaust victims. This was not simply a matter of reparations-linked economic calculation but involved sensitivity regarding the way in which the Jewish state itself viewed the Holocaust.

From its early days, the aspiration to create a homeland for persecuted Jews worldwide was a central element in the Zionist world-view. The main Zionist objection to Jewish assimilation was that antisemitism constituted an inherent element in European culture—an element that would persist even where Jews were fully emancipated. The fact that the Nazis emerged to power from within the Weimar Republic was used as a case in point. Another demonstration of the need for a Jewish homeland was that after the Nazi persecution many German Jews found themselves "standing before locked gates"—no other country wishing to absorb them.

In the early years of the state, this view was translated into a distinction between those who had taken control of their own destiny and immigrated to Palestine and those who had rejected the Zionist idea and as a result had fallen victim to Hitler. Moshe Zimmermann describes this schema as follows: "The history of the Holocaust, together with the history of the Diaspora, was the extreme opposite of the essence of Israel and its foundation-myth. There—like sheep to the slaughter; here—war heroes. There— *Luftmenschen*; here—productive Zionists."[47]

Simply through their presence, the returnees challenged the moral valuation implied by this distinction. Although, so to speak, they belonged to the side of the war heroes, they had chosen, by re-entering the Diaspora, to once again become *Luftmenschen*. The report delivered by David Zuriel (Weizman), an Israeli diplomat in Berlin, to Prime Minister Moshe Sharett demonstrates the role the returnees played in the Zionist view of the Diaspora:

[45] Eliahu Livneh to WED, 14 November 1949, ISA 2519\4.

[46] Eliahu Livneh to Israel's Propaganda Department, 10 September 1953, ISA , Foreign Ministry, 533\2.

[47] Moshe Zimmermann, 'Israels Umgang mit dem Holocaust', in Rolf Steininger (ed.), *Der Umgang mit dem Holocaust: Europa-USA-Israel,* (Schriften des Instituts für Zeitgeschichte der Universität Innsbruck und des Jüdischen Museums Hohenems 1), Vienna–Cologne–Weimar 1994, p. 391.

> [Berlin] is the coalescence of Diasporas in the Diaspora. Peoples' dust from the death camps, German Jews, who were saved on German soil … and returnees who returned in order to enjoy the "economic miracle" … many of them from Israel. As in a laboratory test tube the biological process of the Diaspora is reactivated even on this blood-soaked soil: an ideology that we believed to have expired … [to this ideology was] now added a new important and fundamental element: the establishment of the State of Israel. … It is a paradox: the state's existence gives them psychical relief and confidence … [on the other hand] they feel as if they have to slander the state in order to justify having left it. This phenomenon, I am afraid, will also keep us busy in the future and we need to form a calculated and cold-minded policy towards it.

Zuriel here observes the ingredients in his human test tube with curiosity, like a scientist in a laboratory. Although he does not criticise the objects of his curiosity—he even finds compassion for them—he is aware of the damage they pose to Israel. From this perspective, he suggests to Sharett that Israel change its hostile policy towards the returnees:

> To encounter the remigration phenomenon here [in Germany] is unavoidable … the existing [Israeli] regulations are more against the returnees than against remigration. I believe that we are increasing publicity for this disaster. The treatment of the returnees as traitors and enemies is missing the point and bringing about the opposite results … the returnee is a miserable Jew who—due to his own fault, to his Diaspora past, to others' fault, our fault—has experienced a disaster. Our approach should be that taken towards a disaster victim—human and Jewish solidarity. … This does not mean that we should not adopt a clear and even severe administrative approach. But we should not make the disaster larger, we should not destroy but build a bridge.[48]

Zuriel's report is unique in that it takes account of the problems faced by the returnees themselves. Other officials focused exclusively on the threat posed to Israel by remigration. Zuriel nevertheless shared the same basic assumption that remigration represented a national disaster—above all for Israel's intention to be the sole representative of Jewish claims.

IV

The Jews in Germany were not indifferent to the Zionist stance. Although only a minority saw itself as Zionist, many felt an emotional bond with Israel. Facing an uncertain future and in difficult economic circumstances, and with the German and Eastern European Jewish communities divided, they saw the connection with both Israel and world Jewry as vital. Following the announcement of the closure of its German offices at the end of 1949, the Jewish Agency received a letter from the Council of Jews in the British Zone, appealing for postponement of the decision: such closures would "create the impression among the local Jewish population that the *Yishuv* has made up its mind to abandon the Jews in Germany and deprive them of moral defence, despite [the population's] severe problems and tragic human

[48]David Zuriel to Moshe Sharett, 1 December 1954, ISA 2413/3.

destiny".[49] But the severe problems notwithstanding, the majority of the Jews in Germany did not emigrate to Israel. Instead, the leaders of the various Jewish communities simply attempted to reconcile their rejection of such emigration with a widespread desire to maintain ties to the Jewish State. In order to reduce Israeli criticism, the Jewish leadership in Germany tried to disassociate itself from returnees and potential returnees from Israel. In December 1953, the High Council for Jews in Germany (the *Zentralrat*) published this notice:

> In a declaration the directorate of the *Zentralrat* has emphatically warned against the return to—and even against passing through—[Germany] by persons who already lived [there] before the Second World War. In the opinion of the *Zentralrat*, the influx of Jews from Israel to Germany causes social, political and not least of all moral problems with far-reaching consequences. The directorate, the highest body of the *Zentralrat*, declared that it will in no way offer further support to emigrants and even to sojourners from Israel who belong to this group.[50]

The *Zentralrat*'s resolution expressed the objections to remigration from Israel in social, political and moral terms. On the social level, remigration did indeed place a burden on the community's shoulders. Research from 1961 reveals that almost half (44.3 per cent) of the returnees were over the age of fifty at the time of their remigration.[51] Most came without means and needed support from the community. Another reason for discomfort with the remigration was concern that a large-scale return would aggravate antisemitic tendencies. Although both these factors clearly played an important role in the *Zentralrat*'s resolution, one has to bear in mind that it was not addressed to all returnees but rather specifically to those coming from Israel.

The disapproval of the returnees from Israel is apparent in a letter by Jacob Persil, the president of Regensburg's Jewish community, informing Eliahu Livneh "with deep sorrow" in December 1949 that "several families from Israel have returned to Regensburg in the last few months" and asking for instructions on how to deal with this phenomenon.[52] The consul's response made clear that the Israeli state strongly objected to remigration: Livneh advised the Jewish community of Regensburg to inform the returnees that they should not expect any assistance, either from the community itself or from refugee relief organisations. The consul explained that such an attitude would encourage the returnees to leave Germany.[53]

Germany's Jewish community leadership was aware of the apparent contradiction between their opposition to emigration from Israel and their own residence in Germany. In 1950, one of the members of the Württemberg community assembly defended this position as follows:

[49]Telegram from the Jewish Council in the British Zone to the Jewish Agency (20 August 1950), ISA 533\13.

[50]'Zentralrat der Juden warnt vor Einwanderung', in *Münchner Merkur*, 15 December 1953, p. 2. see also: ISA 2527/13.

[51]Maor, p. 48.

[52]Jacob Persil to Eliahu Livneh, 19 December 1949, ISA 533\14. ("We would like to ask your advice as to how we should treat those people if they apply to us in order to settle their affairs.")

[53]Livneh to Persil, 4 January 1950, ISA 533\14.

> On this occasion it must be said that there is a difference between remigration from Israel on the one hand and remigration from all other countries on the other hand. What these other countries have in common with Germany (in comparison with Israel) is that for us they represent the *Galuth*. … But the case of Israel is something completely different: anyone who has made the decision [to choose Israel] has also decided to finally break with the *Galuth*. … It is entirely self-evident that this young state, which is our centre, will still have to go through many difficulties externally and internally. Those who go there should not expect better external conditions than what is perhaps possible here today. When they turn their back on Israel for this reason it is a serious and questionable matter; increasing the number of our members through this kind of remigration is the last thing we wish for.[54]

The first chairman of the *Zentralrat*, Hendrik George van Dam, was also troubled by remigration. In an interview with the newspaper *Das Parlament* he stated:

> I am indeed of the opinion that the Jewish communities in Germany certainly have their justification for existing. But they should grow slowly and organically—in other words from the inside out. I do not share the standpoint of many Jews in the world, who for a long time saw everyone who returned to Germany after the war as dishonourable. However, I must urgently warn against a rash, ill-considered return.[55]

Van Dam explained that since a return to Germany was burdened with psychological difficulties "no one should base his return solely on compensation payments", adding—in an obvious allusion to the returnees from Israel—"especially not those whose return is tied to abandoning ideals held for many years".[56] In an interview with S. Yardeni in the German-language Israeli newspaper *Yediot Hadashot*, van Dam was reported as having voiced far more emphatic opinions, to the effect that:

> There can be exceptions regarding remigration from Israel; but being exceptions they prove the rule. And the rule is: [Yardeni now cites van Dam directly] 'Just as Germany of the postwar period is generally speaking no country for immigration, it is also no country of remigration for Jews. Nobody has been waiting for them in today's Germany.' … [van Dam] explains that to him the returnees from Israel are basically just as alien when they present themselves in Germany as guardians of the holy grail, namely the Jewish state, as when, inversely, they unleash their resentment against the land that took them in and saved them in Hitler's time. Another group [van Dam adds] is that of "indirect emigrants" [*"indirekte Jordim"*], who allegedly have returned for a short time, but who prolong their stay again and again and frequently behave like "the purest of Israeli patriots" when their real motivation is abominable Mammon.[57]

Van Dam's position reflects the main motives in the *Zentralrat*'s policy regarding the returnee issue. In both his interviews, he emphasised the fact that Germany was not a land for immigration and that the postwar Jewish communities should grow slowly from the "inside out". His words appear to reveal apprehension at a rapid growth of the Jewish population that was liable to reinforce antisemitic sentiments among

[54]Assembly of the Württemberg Jewish community, 25 June 1950, as quoted in Maor, p. 36.
[55]*Das Parlament*, 18 December 1957, as quoted in Fings, pp. 29–30.
[56]*ibid.*
[57]S. Yardeni, 'Rückwanderung nach Deutschland', *Yediot Hadashot*, 29 May 1959, p. 3.

Germans; the sharpness of his remarks in the second interview may reflect a sense that by criticising the returnees he could demonstrate his loyalty to Israel.

Despite the general condemnation, no practical measures were taken by Germany's Jewish community against the returnees. The *Zentralrat* actually strongly supported the law of 1956 granting them emergency financial aid.[58] This decision underscores the dual direction of the Jewish leadership's policies: externally, towards Israel, they condemned the returnees, while internally, in their contacts with the German government, they supported a law that directly contributed to increasing the scale of remigration.

V

Thus far the issue of remigration has been considered from the perspectives of the German and Israeli states and the Jewish communities in Germany. The last part of this paper will examine the attitude of the returnees themselves, particularly those who returned from Israel. Standing at the centre of both Israeli and more general Jewish criticism, this last group represented a high proportion of the returnees: at the height of the remigration wave in the late 1950s, it constituted 63 per cent of total remigration.[59] The returnees' motives were highly individual: health problems, better occupation possibilities, homesickness, and so forth.[60]

Frequently, the decision to return was an outcome of circumstantial impulse, not the result of careful planning. In this respect, the Berlin businessman Karl Wolffsohn (1881–1957) serves as a typical example. Wolffsohn emigrated to Tel-Aviv in 1939 and returned to Germany in December 1949. There he wrote to a friend that he was waiting impatiently to return to Israel—"better yesterday than today".[61] Although the drawn-out legal procedures involved in the claims for his lost property led to Wolffsohn remaining in Germany until his death eight years later, he continued to regard himself as both an Israeli and a Zionist. In reply to a threat by the Israeli Ministry of the Interior to deprive him of his Israeli passport, he wrote to the Israeli immigration department that:

> I have a share in a firm in Tel Aviv, own land in Tel Aviv, and have other interests there, and anyway have ties to Israel because my children and grandchildren live there. … I myself have strong emotional ties to the country and thus the idea of returning [to Germany] has never occurred to me. … I naturally will fulfil my duty to our country, but one [*sic*] must have the possibility of doing without hindrance what I myself consider necessary to preserve my interests in Germany."[62]

[58]Krauss, pp. 127–128.

[59]Maor, p. 45.

[60]Ronald Webster, 'Jewish Returnees to West Germany after 1945: Why They Returned and How They Fared', *YIVO Annual* 21 (1992), p. 35.

[61]Karl Wolffsohn to Yissakhar Jacobsohn (Ben-Ya´akov), 17 March 1950, Institut für Zeitgeschichte, Munich, Karl Wolffsohn's personal estate (not classified).

[62]Karl Wolffsohn to the immigration department, Israeli Ministery of the Interior, 28 January 1955, *ibid.*

It is striking that in line with his view of his own position, every few months Wolffsohn applied to the Israeli authorities for permission to remain in Germany although as a German citizen doing so was completely unnecessary.

Wolffsohn's wife was the first family member to join him in Berlin, followed a few years later, in 1954, by his son and daughter-in-law, Max and Thea Wolffsohn, together with their son Michael. In contrast to Karl Wolffsohn, this younger generation felt fully comfortable in Germany and returned with the intention of settling there permanently.[63] In the words of Thea Wolffsohn's son Michael, born in Israel in 1947, returning there in 1967 to serve in the army, but now a history professor at the Armed Forces University in Munich: "My feeling was, the move to Israel was a kind of transplantation, Germany was my native soil, my nature—my nation."[64]

But such sentiments were far from universally held—many young Israelis accompanying their parents on their return to Germany experienced the move as a drastic identity conflict. In the 1960s, the sociologist Walter Oppenheimer conducted a comparative study of young people who grew up in Germany and counterparts who ended up there after a period of having been raised in Israel. Concerning the latter he observes that:

> In fact everything is extreme in this group, and the outer and inner contradictions are greatest of all here. Having grown up in Jewish freedom and ease, educated to feel national pride and Israeli self-confidence and to reject the Diaspora, Israeli children and young people now find themselves in the very country whose inhabitants had trampled on Jewish freedom and Jewish pride more than anyone previously. They were brought back against their will by their parents, who wanted to enjoy a small part of this country's prosperity. Feelings of humiliation, shame, inferiority and guilt are the outcome.[65]

Oppenheimer himself returned to Germany from Israel in 1955, continuing to travel between Germany and Israel until 1975, when he settled permanently in Frankfurt. His study thus appears to reflect his own inner conflict—for which, it seems, he found a resolution through adopting a Zionist stance. Along with defining return to Germany as a form of self-disgrace and arguing that it was driven primarily by economic motives, he recommends in his study's conclusion that all young Jews in Germany be sent to Israel for a year in order to allow them to experience "unfalsified, future-oriented Jewish life".[66]

Those who adopted such views naturally found it difficult to integrate into German society, and continued to live "double lives" following their resettlement. One expression of the difficulties returnees from Israel faced was the fact that many presented their return—to themselves, to their children, and to others around them—as merely temporary. Instead of joining local Jewish communities, some therefore chose to associate solely with their fellow returnees (while often shunning Gentile society altogether).[67]

[63]Author's interview with Thea Wolffsohn, Berlin, 9 April 2002.

[64]Michael Wolffsohn, 'Plea for an Inwardly-Directed German Nationalism', in Susan Stern (ed.), *Speaking Out: Jewish Voices from United Germany*, Berlin 1995, p. 128.

[65]Walter W. Jacob Oppenheimer, *Jüdische Jugend in Deutschland*, Munich 1967 , p. 81.

[66]*ibid*, pp. 169–170.

[67]Author's interview with Ani Buber, Frankfurt am Main (14 January 2002).

While such an attitude allowed remigrants from Israel to postpone a true confrontation with the question of how they could, in fact, remain in Germany, it also prolonged the process of absorption and increased inter-generational conflicts. In general, the returnees from Israel did not wish to challenge the prevailing consensus within Israeli society, understanding their return to Germany to be a private decision deriving from particular circumstances. Since they were not looking for confrontation with a society which had been their own for many years, they sometimes concealed their intention to return—even from family members. It is in any case clear that even after settling in Germany, most returnees continued to feel a close bond with the State of Israel, expressed among other ways through financial donations and activity in Zionist organisations; speaking Hebrew at home; subscribing to the *Jerusalem Post* and *Haaretz* and worrying mainly about political problems in Israel rather than Germany.[68] The choice of many returnees to retain their Israeli identity underlines the difficulty of formulating a German-Jewish identity in postwar Germany. These individuals were trying to bridge a chasm between two worlds—a chasm that in the 1950s was almost unbridgeable.

* * *

This article has focused on a social complex constituted by the states of West Germany and Israel, world Jewry, and the postwar Jewish community in Germany. At the centre of this complex is the small group of German Jews who decided to return to their former homeland. In the aftermath of the Holocaust, a symbolic act of this sort was self-evidently charged with emotional and political implications. In this light, the main question meant to be raised in these pages has not been whether Germany's Jews should have ever returned, but rather how compromise with Germany was defined—and who had the right to formulate it in the name of the Jewish people.

While the 1952 compensation agreement emphasised Israel's role as sole representative of the victims, remigration, in this author's view, has demonstrated that Israel possesses no monopoly over this claim. This would appear to be an important factor at work in the Israeli government's refusal to accept the German interpretation of return as an expression of forgiveness. The returnees were adversely affected by this refusal, since they were thus symbolically excluded from the Jewish collectivity. The response to remigration in Israeli and West German political culture reflects the first stage in the emergence of two separate conceptions or collective memories of the Holocaust—and two different understandings of its implications for each of these states.

[68]Author's interview with M. L and A. L, Wiesbaden (8 January 2002).

"Healed Biographies"?
Jewish Remigration and Indemnification for National Socialist Injustice

BY TOBIAS WINSTEL

PERSECUTION AND INDEMNIFICATION

The persecution of the Jews by Nazi Germany was a historical injustice. As banal as this statement may seem, it still requires some explanation. For the following reflections will not focus on the repeatedly debated question of whether the crimes of the Holocaust were unique and without historical parallel.[1] According to Elazar Barkan in his much-discussed study of the concept of international morality, historical injustice is a form of injustice that has itself come to an end but the consequences of which still affect its victims.[2] For the Jewish victims of the Nazis the deprivation of rights, theft of property, and physical violence suffered, together with the loss of close friends and relatives, of freedom and of the conditions and prospects for life itself certainly had long-lasting effects—often life-long. For many victims, especially in the case of German Jews, the rupture in their biography found particular expression in the fact that they were forced to flee their country as refugees in order to save their lives. But the involuntary sacrifice of an accustomed living situation did not end with the defeat of Nazism.

Rather, this experience of loss endured beyond 1945 and led in the case of some German emigrants to a postwar effort to recover their previous lives—or as John Torpey puts it in his "reflections on reparations": to "[make] whole what has been smashed".[3] The decision to return to Germany after the Nazi persecution—and perhaps even to remain there—was tied to the question of compensation, restitution, and "to repair the world".[4] It thus seems appropriate to study remigration in the context of both the material and non-material dimensions of West Germany's so-

This essay was translated from the German by Deborah Cohen.

[1]For a sample from this lively debate, see the anthology by Alan S. Rosenbaum, *Is the Holocaust Unique? Perspectives on Comparative Genocide*, Boulder 2001.

[2]Elazar Barkan, *The Guilt of Nations: Restitution and Negotiating Historical Injustices*, New York 2000, pp. XXXff.

[3]John Torpey, '"Making Whole What Has Been Smashed": Reflections on Reparations', in *The Journal of Modern History*, vol. 73, no. 2 (2001), pp. 333–362.

[4]See Stuart Eizenstat, *Imperfect Justice: Looted Assets, Slave Labor, and the Unfinished Business of World War II*, New York 2003, p. 355.

called *Wiedergutmachung*—its process of indemnification, or more literally, its effort to "make good" the past.[5]

The term *Wiedergutmachung* refers to the complete set of laws and international treaties governing the issuing of compensation for the damage caused by National Socialist acts of violence. Thus it also encompasses matters such as the repeal of discriminatory laws or—of particular relevance to the question of remigration—the re-naturalisation of Jews who emigrated from Germany.[6] However, the following reflections focus on the individual restitution and compensation payments introduced in West Germany after the end of the Second World War.[7] The intention in doing so is not to provide a general overview of such indemnification efforts, but rather to locate those emigrants who chose to return to West Germany within the field of entitled persons. One factor that makes them so interesting is that they were involved both passively, as applicants and claimants, and actively, for instance as lawyers, in the process of West German *Wiedergutmachung*.

The issue of indemnification inevitably begs the question of whether it is actually possible to make amends for millions of murders, to refund billions of dollars worth of stolen property. The answer is clearly no. To the survivors, nothing could ever compensate for the loss of the lives they had led before the advent of National Socialism – nothing could ever make up for the destruction wrought by Hitler and Nazism, for the persecution carried out by the various authorities including the police and the judiciary, for the betrayal at the hands of neighbours, for the various layers of devastation left by the Holocaust. Although this fact runs like a leitmotif through research into indemnification, it still needs some further clarification. In this context, a comment made in 1952 by Walter Schwarz, one of the most important figures in the history of West German indemnification, comes to mind. Even if "wieder gut machen" (that is literally "making good again") was an impossible task, he indicated, it could still "contribute to the efforts the survivors of this extermination all over the world will have to make to rebuild their shattered lives".[8]

Three categories have emerged in the attempt to find a model that can help measure this contribution: reconciliation, rehabilitation, and compensation.[9] They serve as a kind of idealised grid by means of which the case files relating to individual

[5]On the issues surrounding the concept of *Wiedergutmachung*, and on the various forms and historical developments of the process, see Hans Günter Hockerts, 'Wiedergutmachung in Deutschland. Eine historische Bilanz 1945–2000', in *Vierteljahrshefte für Zeitgeschichte*, vol. 49, no. 1 (2001), pp. 167–214.

[6]See Hans Georg Lehmann, 'Wiedereinbürgerung, Rehabilitation und Wiedergutmachung nach 1945. Zur Staatsangehörigkeit ausgebürgerter Emigranten und Remigranten', in *Exilforschung*, vol. 9 (1991), pp. 90–103.

[7]Intended merely as a social measure for the Communist Party faithful, the East German indemnification benefits for victims of the Nazi regime were so limited in scope that they are hardly worth mentioning in this context. See Constantin Goschler, 'Nicht bezahlt? Die Wiedergutmachung für Opfer der nationalsozialistischen Verfolgung in der SBZ/DDR', in Christoph Buchheim (ed.), *Wirtschaftliche Folgelasten des Krieges in der SBZ/DDR*, Baden-Baden 1995, pp. 169–191.

[8]Walter Schwarz, *Rückerstattung und Entschädigung. Eine Abgrenzung der Wiedergutmachungsformen*, Munich 1952, p. 1.

[9]For a more detailed treatment of the material in this article see Tobias Winstel, 'Über die Bedeutung der Wiedergutmachung im Leben der jüdischen NS-Verfolgten. Erfahrungsgeschichtliche Annäherungen', in Hans Günter Hockerts and Christiane Kuller (eds.), *Nach der Verfolgung. Wiedergutmachung nationalsozialistischen Unrechts in Deutschland?*, Göttingen 2003, pp. 199–227.

indemnification claims can be studied with a view to their content as *Erlebnisgeschichte*—history as it was personally experienced. Such a model can help shed light on the extent to which *Wiedergutmachung* directly affected the conditions and motivations leading Jewish emigrants to return to Germany.

In this light, the first part of the following discussion will concern the personally experienced history of those who returned to West Germany in the context of indemnification. Some attention will here be paid to the Jewish reparations lawyers, a group on which the breakdown of law in Nazi Germany certainly had a particularly drastic impact, and that then contributed in a major way to the reestablishment of the rule of law in West Germany.[10] The second section will focus on some possibilities for research on remigration emerging from work on *Wiedergutmachung*. It should be noted that these reflections make no claim to being conclusive but rather represent a report on a work-in-progress.[11]

JEWISH RETURNEES TO GERMANY AND THE EXPERIENCE OF *WIEDERGUTMACHUNG*

Jewish victims of Nazi persecution did not need to look for reasons to flee from Germany, emigration and exile being matters of compulsion. The question of returning to Germany was of course entirely different. Such a decision was in principle voluntary; one had to find good reasons and even excuses for returning to that "verfluchte Erde" ("accursed soil"). In contrast to politically motivated emigrants, who in their self-perception had only been temporarily exiled, Jews who fled because of being Jewish as a rule understood their flight as into permanent exile.[12] These different circumstances strongly affected the nature of remigration among the two groups and explains why the discussion about returning to Germany was conducted much more concretely and positively among political emigrants than among those who had been persecuted as Jews.[13]

Despite considerable reluctance, over time members of the latter group did begin returning to Germany, if from very different motives than the political refugees. (It is a little-known fact that the first group of emigrants to revisit Germany immediately after the war were not political exiles, but rather "ordinary" Jews who had fled for their lives, most of whom were now serving in the American occupation forces.) Naturally, few of the Jewish returnees intended to remain in Germany permanently, but a considerable

[10]See Cordula Lissner, '"In der Justiz lebe ich wie im Exil". Zur Rückkehr jüdischer Juristen und Juristinnen', in Anne Klein and Jürgen Wilhelm (eds.), *NS-Unrecht vor Kölner Gerichten nach 1945*, Cologne 2003, pp. 75–235.

[11]The framework for this article is an ongoing project, "Die Finanzverwaltung und die Verfolgung der Juden in Bayern" ("The Fiscal Administration and the Persecution of the Jews in Bavaria"), undertaken on behalf of the Bavarian Ministry of Finance, in collaboration with Professor Hans Günter Hockerts, Professor of Contemporary History at the Ludwig-Maximilians-Universität, Munich and the General Directorate of the Bavarian State Archives. The results of the study will be presented in 2004/2005. On this project see http://www.forschung.historicum.net/projekte/finanzverwaltung.html.

[12]Hans-Albert Walter, '"Als ich wiederkam, da kam ich nicht wieder" (A. Döblin). Vorläufige Bemerkungen zu Rückkehr und Reintegration von Exilierten 1945–1949', in Jörg Wollenberg (ed.), *Von der Hoffnung aller Deutschen. Wie die BRD entstand 1945 bis 1949*, Cologne 1991, pp. 172–194; here p. 172.

[13]Lehmann, p. 44.

number would find the very appraisal of their Nazi persecution, for example in the jurisdictional realm, to be a task tying them to Germany for a long time, quite often permanently. By the 1950s increasing numbers of Jewish emigrants were returning to Germany, many for financial reasons. As is well known, in the immediate postwar period the economic situation in Israel was bad: the 1948–1949 War of Independence and mass immigration into the new state lasting until around 1951 produced high rates of inflation and unemployment to which the government responded with rationing and cost-cutting measures.[14] Hence often economic considerations—especially the prospect of better professional opportunities—provided the initial impetus to return, while interest in social and financial benefits such as pensions, health and welfare services, and indemnification payments also played a role.[15]

Of course, restitution and compensation claims could also be pursued from abroad—provided, that is, one lived to the west of the Iron Curtain.[16] Naturally there were also survivors who wanted to have nothing more to do with Germany, a large number of whom correspondingly rejected any form of *Wiedergutmachung*. (Because of a lack of documentation, the precise size of the group of people that deliberately did not apply for compensation is difficult to determine.[17]) On the other hand, many found the restitution and compensation payments helpful for various reasons; their first contact with Germany after the war usually took the form of a trip to deal with indemnification matters. Malka Schmuckler, a native of Nuremberg, describes the personal significance of the indemnification process as follows: "The relationship to Germany re-entered my life a little bit for the first time when each of us received five thousand marks for our school education having been interrupted, both mine and my husband's. It wasn't a fortune, but for us young people it was still a considerable sum, and my husband said: 'Then let's go and check out Europe!'" Thus the two Israeli Jews visited Europe—although not Germany—on this first trip. They were only ready for that step two years later, and again indemnification claims played a role: "My father-in-law, who would have had to personally deal with his *Wiedergutmachung* in Germany, told us: 'Well, if you go there, I'll support you so you can stay there along with your family, and you deal with my *Wiedergutmachung*.'"[18] This led to the couple's fresh encounter with Germany—although they did not settle there permanently until 1967.

[14]The process of economic growth only began in the mid-1950s, one factor at work here being German reparations payments as provided for in the Luxemburg Treaty of 10 September 1952.

[15]Lehmann, p. 56f. In the face of the latent accusation—from both West German and Israeli society—that their indemnification payments were exorbitant, those affected generally continue to be reluctant to acknowledge economic motives for their remigration.

[16]On the exclusion of Eastern European victims of Nazism from indemnification benefits, see Ulrich Herbert, 'Nicht entschädigungsfähig? Die Wiedergutmachungsansprüche der Ausländer', in Ludolf Herbst and Constantin Goschler (eds.), *Wiedergutmachung in der Bundesrepublik Deutschland*, Munich 1989, pp. 273–302.

[17]There are some indicators in the literature; cf., for example, Walter Schwarz, *Späte Frucht. Bericht aus unsteten Jahren*, Hamburg 1981, p. 152 as well as Sigrid Weigel, 'Shylocks Wiederkehr. Die Verwandlung von Schuld in Schulden', in *Zeitschrift für deutsche Philologie*, vol. 114, no. 1 (1995), pp. 3–22; here p. 16.

[18]Cited from Franz J. Jürgens, *"Wir waren ja eigentlich Deutsche". Juden berichten von Emigration und Rückkehr*, Berlin 1997, p. 110; See also Malka Schmuckler, *Gast im eigenen Land. Emigration und Rückkehr einer deutschen Jüdin*, Ratingen 1997, pp. 117ff.

Encountering the Volksgenossen

This initial hesitation on the part of Jewish emigrants who would end up returning—in stages—to Germany was entirely typical. Most of them did not intend to resettle in Germany, and found themselves there in the early 1950s more by chance than through deliberate planning. Nevertheless the decision about whether one would return to Germany or not appears to follow no basic pattern; the question of how much property one had left behind there was often not the decisive one. Frequently, however, the occasion for a first return visit was the clarification of a restitution issue, particularly when the goal was compensation in kind. In such cases it was not always the actual material value of the real estate or other possessions that was primarily at stake. Rather the indemnification process also had the function of visibly rectifying acts of injustice before all those involved. In this light it is understandable that the father of David Schuster, for years the head of the Jewish community in Würzburg, would return to Franconia in the 1950s in order to resolve an issue of lost family property. For him, it was "a principle that none of those who acquired our property by violence should keep it."[19]

In retrospect and from today's interpretive vantage-point, this attitude seems self-evident; not so from the perspective of many of those obliged to pay compensation in the first postwar decade. As a result, not all indemnification proceedings went smoothly. Being dependent on a positive court decision, Jewish claimants not infrequently had to sacrifice a part of a legitimate claim if they wished to receive *Wiedergutmachung* in any form at all.

A particularly well-known case in point is that of the Rosenthal family of Jewish industrialists.[20] With the help of influential persons from politics and business circles, a network of former profiteers and "Aryanisers" managed to first drag out, then block, restitution to the family of its porcelain factory, and above all the return of a Rosenthal family member as head of the company. Philip Rosenthal, who had returned to Germany after the war in order to re-establish the family's control over the business, only succeeded with great effort in pushing through his claim; alongside a financial payout, part of the indemnification settlement involved contractual assurance of a seat on the board of directors, hence at least part of his father's former position in the company.

As a rule, Jewish returnees to West Germany were met with muted hostility, which was sometimes expressed quite openly in the indemnification proceedings.[21] A reconciliation between them and the German population on a broader societal level rarely occurred. To the contrary, the German "solidarity collective" often responded to the indemnification claims of the Jewish victims of Nazi antisemitism with overt

[19]Cited from Michael Brenner, *Nach dem Holocaust. Juden in Deutschland 1945–1950*, Munich 1995, p. 174.

[20]See Jürgen Lillteicher, 'Rechtsstaatlichkeit und Verfolgungserfahrung. "Arisierung" und fiskalische Ausplünderung vor Gericht', in Constantin Goschler and Jürgen Lillteicher (eds.): *"Arisierung" und Restitution. Die Rückerstattung jüdischen Eigentums in Deutschland und Österreich nach 1945 und 1989*, Göttingen 2002, pp. 127–159; here pp. 134–144.

[21]See Ronald Webster, 'Jüdische Rückkehrer in der BRD nach 1945: Ihre Motive, ihre Erfahrungen', in *Aschkenas*, vol. 5, no. 1 (1995), pp. 47–77; here pp. 62–74.

hostility,[22] particularly in regard to compensation cases (more on this below). For any sort of true reconciliation, compassion would have been needed on the part of the Germans—and this was generally reserved for "German victims"—that is, for refugees, war widows, the wounded, and so on. On the other hand, for the victims of the Germans even basic sympathy was in short supply,[23] the response of those Germans with a Nazi past obliged to relinquish property to Jews often being openly antisemitic.[24] As is well known, the transformation from *Volksgenosse* ("[German] *Volk*-comrade") to *Bundesbürger* ("citizen of the Federal Republic") was neither rapid nor smooth. Most saw the indemnification process as a "dictate of the occupying powers" to which they would only reluctantly submit.

As a result of such resistance as well as the generally "insensitive and bureaucratic nature" of the indemnification proceedings, it was often very difficult for Jewish returnees to "regain respect for their homeland".[25] During the proceedings, both the matter-of-fact and schematised work routines and the quite often narrow-minded interpretations of the law sometimes led to victims not being capable of seeing outstretched hands of reconciliation, but only opposition. Put somewhat differently, by and large an encounter within the framework of *Wiedergutmachung* only took place with a reversal of the persecution's basic roles: former perpetrators and profiteers were now defendants and liable parties; those who had been persecuted and dispossessed were now claimants. Consequently reconciliation on the path of *Wiedergutmachung* took place more on an abstract level with the West German state than on a concrete level with individual liable parties.

One could of course also cite cases in which those who were liable and those entitled to compensation reached an agreement. In their dealings with arbitration officials and in compensation offices, Jewish returnees would also encounter persons who clearly viewed them as victims of gross injustice. Furthermore, indemnification bolstered trust in the German legal system. This point will be taken up later in relation to Jewish lawyers; for now let it simply be noted that through the proceedings, both the claimants and their representatives became acquainted with a state that had admitted to state-planned and state-sanctioned crimes and had made it possible for claimants to take judicial action with regard to these crimes.

[22]See the well-known Allensbach survey, according to which 31% of those surveyed in 1949 disagreed with the statement that Germany had a duty to compensate German Jews who were still alive. Elisabeth Noelle and Erich Peter Neumann (eds.), *Jahrbuch der öffentlichen Meinung 1947–1955*, Allensbach 1955.

[23]See Peter Derleder, 'Die Wiedergutmachung. Rechtsanwendung an den Rändern der Unmenschlichkeit', in Rainer Eisfeld and Ingo Müller (eds.), *Gegen Barbarei. Essays M. W. Kempner zu Ehren*, Frankfurt am Main 1989, pp. 281–302; here p. 298.

[24]See Rainer Erb, 'Die Rückerstattung: ein Kristallisationspunkt für Antisemitismus', in: Werner Bergmann and Rainer Erb (eds.), *Antisemitismus in der politischen Kultur nach 1945*, Opladen 1990, pp. 238–252.

[25]Marita Krauss, '"Als Emigrant hat man Geduld gelernt" – Bürokratie und Remigration nach 1945', in *Exil*, vol. 17 (1997), pp. 89–105; here p. 101. Krauss focuses on the example of the Jewish lawyer Philipp Löwenfeld, whose negative experiences with his own compensation case caused him to state in resignation and bitterness: "'Nie wieder Deutschland'. Ich bin glücklich, daß es hierbei sein Bewenden hat." (*ibid.*)

The Transformation of Persecuted Individuals into Claimants

As reflected in the Rosenthal case, for many Jewish emigrants, especially those who had been industrialists, it was not only the material dimension of *Wiedergutmachung* that induced them to return to Germany but also its immaterial, symbolic dimension. During the years of persecution, not merely material valuables had been destroyed, but also, crucially, the life situation connected with it—to use Erving Goffman's phrase, the "identity equipment"[26] of the victims. It is thus not surprising that during compensation proceedings, the re-appropriation of houses, furnishings, and so forth was generally more important to Jews who had returned to Germany than compensatory payments. After years of powerlessness, the desire of these survivors to be reunited with tangible artefacts of their former lives, and thus to be able, at least fragmentarily, to piece their lives and identities together, was often very strong.[27] It is true that claims could also be pursued from abroad, but the rehabilitative character of the indemnification was often bound up with a return to one's earlier surroundings. The recovery of objects played as great a role within this process as the recuperation of a particular professional status. Hence stolen social prestige could *also* be regained through successful indemnification claims;[28] for professional status, wealth and property are "always also a biographical arrangement that in a very concrete sense reinforces and supports identity".[29]

This is particularly clear in the case of Jewish professors who fled for their lives and whose most important form of *Wiedergutmachung* was professional reinstatement.[30] The especially well-documented case of the eminent scholar of religion, Hans-Joachim Schoeps, will here represent a large group of similar cases.[31] In October 1933, after passing his examination to become a teacher of upper-level secondary education, Schoeps was barred from beginning his teacher training on racist grounds. Likewise, after first being informed by the *Reichsministerium für Wissenschaft, Erziehung und Volksbildung* (Reich Ministry for Education) that nothing stood in the way of his pursuing a *Habilitation* (postdoctoral thesis), this was ultimately also denied him. He then found work first in the private sector and later at a Jewish school, from which he was forced to resign in October 1938 on Gestapo orders. To avoid arrest he fled to

[26]Erving Goffman, *Asylums. Essays on the Situation of Mental Patients and Other Inmates*, New York 1961, p. 21.

[27]See Martin S. Bergmann and Milton E. Jucovy (eds.), *Generations of the Holocaust*, New York 1982, p. 59. On "repairing" identities in this context see Jael Geis, *Übrig sein – Leben "danach". Juden deutscher Herkunft in der britischen und amerikanischen Zone Deutschlands 1945–1949*, Berlin and Vienna 2000, p. 406.

[28]This observation applies more to older claimants at the time of their return. Young people were far less attracted by indemnification benefits since they had found it much easier to integrate socially and professionally into their countries of emigration.

[29]Harald Welzer, 'Vorhanden/Nicht-Vorhanden. Über die Latenz der Dinge', in Irmtrud Wojak, *"Arisierung" im Nationalsozialismus. Volksgemeinschaft, Raub und Gedächtnis*, Frankfurt am Main 2000, pp. 287–308; here p. 294.

[30]See for example Anikó Szabó, *Vertreibung – Rückkehr – Wiedergutmachung. Göttinger Hochschullehrer im Schatten des Nationalsozialismus*, Göttingen 2000. See also Lehmann, p. 59.

[31]Julius H. Schoeps, '"Nil inultum remanebit". Die Erlanger Universität und ihr Umgang mit dem deutsch-jüdischen Remigranten Hans-Joachim Schoeps (1909–1980)', in *Zeitschrift für Religions- und Geistesgeschichte*, vol. 52, no. 3 (2000), pp. 266–278.

Sweden. Eight years later, in October 1946, he returned to Germany and took his post-doctoral degree in February 1947 at the University of Marburg.

Schoeps's compensation claim was based on the fact that due to racist persecution, he had been prevented both from doing his teacher training and from being granted a lectureship or professorship on schedule. But financial indemnification was of far less importance to him than his appointment as Senior Lecturer, and then as Professor of Religion and the History of Ideas, at the University of Erlangen. The significance of this professional rehabilitation for Schoeps can only be measured if one is familiar with his strenuous protest at plans to either cancel his post—created for him personally in 1947 by the Minister of Culture, Alois Hundhammer, as an explicit part of Schoeps's *Wiedergutmachung*[32]—after his retirement, or else to redefine it. In letters to the ministry, Schoeps repeatedly emphasised that the chair had been created as an act of indemnification by the state of Bavaria, so its abolition would have to be understood as an abolition of that indemnification—a gesture that for him would "represent existential annihilation".[33] Some considerable bitterness can be read into Schoeps's conclusion: "Although my parents were murdered by the National Socialists in Auschwitz and Theresienstadt, I already returned to Germany in 1946, after seven years of enforced emigration—and I did so out of love for my fatherland [*aus Vaterlandsliebe*]."[34] It would have been better, he indicated, if he had remained abroad.

Less prominent claimants also experienced this sort of intense disappointment with *Wiedergutmachung*. In contrast to what counted for the legislators, what counted for them was not the law as it was written but as it was lived. The thoroughly complex juridical process of indemnification demanded that victims carve up their personal histories into various claims, in other words into the material constituents of damage. Hence for the claimants the compensation proceedings were often very taxing and frequently opened up new wounds instead of healing old ones.[35]

Yet even if the processing of indemnification claims went badly in individual cases, the rehabilitative dimension of *Wiedergutmachung* should not be underestimated. For a start, the claimants were only acknowledged as true *victims* within public perception as a result of this statutory indemnification.[36] Indemnification proceedings offered a platform for the victims to tell their stories—to receive a hearing.[37] In the postwar period in Germany, this was essentially the only public venue available for talking about the persecution and suffering one had experienced. In fact, in Israel and the United States as well as Germany "victimhood" was not a

[32]*ibid.*, p. 266.

[33]*ibid.*, p. 270.

[34]*ibid.*, p. 276.

[35]See W. Jacob, 'Zur Beurteilung der Zusammenhangfrage körperlicher und seelischer Verfolgungsschäden in der gutachterlichen Praxis des Entschädigungsverfahrens', in Hans-Joachim Herberg (ed.), *Die Beurteilung von Gesundheitsschäden nach Gefangenschaft und Verfolgung. Referate eines internationalen medizinisch-juristischen Symposions in Köln 1967*, Herford 1967, pp. 66–72.

[36]For an example of the increasing tendency of, above all, American researchers to focus on the question of such acknowledgment see Barkan, p. 323 and Torpey, pp. 333–362. Both authors use the term *Wiedergutmachung* not as a juridical category but as a cultural concept.

[37]See Martha Minow, *Between Vengeance and Forgiveness. Facing History after Genocide and Mass Violence*, Boston 1998, p. 93.

subject with which those who had been persecuted could generally count on public recognition in the 1950s and 1960s. William G. Niederland, a psychiatrist who wrote hundreds of reports for indemnification cases, thus observed that "it was not a specific monetary sum (often small enough) that counted most, but the acknowledgement of their suffering that it allowed for".[38]

At the same time, one particular aspect of *Wiedergutmachung* was of special importance to these victims: the fact that it offered visible proof of the restoration of law. Put pointedly: while persecution had stripped Jewish victims of their rights, indemnification offered legal restoration of these rights to Jewish claimants. They were now publicly acknowledged as legal subjects, visibly incorporated anew into a domain of civil rights. In short, they were once more full members of civil society.

Material Assistance

While many of those who had been persecuted found that this rehabilitative function of compensation and restitution made it psychologically possible to return to Germany, others had more concrete reasons for returning, such as reclaiming material and financial assets. It is by no means the case that following their flight from Germany, Jewish emigrants were able to rebuild a firm financial basis quickly and unproblematically. Often they had escaped with their lives and nothing else—no valuables and certainly no property. Even after the war only a relatively small minority was able to recover financially in a short time. Frequently, Jews who in Germany had been professionals or in business found it difficult to establish themselves in exile. Although it is the case that even an indemnification scheme as generous as the West German one could not "turn back the clock and let older businessmen take up again where they had left off in 1933 or 1939",[39] some former exiles could now use the monetary indemnification settlements, pensions and loans as the basis for starting anew professionally. Indemnification pensions were also paid out to those living in countries of emigration, thus helping Jewish families survive there. However in some of these countries, including Israel, such pensions were subject to very high taxes, while in Germany they were tax-exempt.[40] In addition, in the immediate postwar period, when no uniform federal indemnification programme as yet existed and compensation claims were assessed but not paid out, Jewish emigrants came to Germany to take advantage of emergency relief benefits. Furthermore, making a personal appearance at the compensation office often speeded up the proceedings considerably. Loans, welfare benefits and medical procedures covered by future *Wiedergutmachung* settlements motivated many Jewish emigrants to move back to Germany for good. Finally, with the economic condition

[38]William G. Niederland, *Folgen der Verfolgung. Das Überlebenden-Syndrom Seelenmord*, Frankfurt am Main 1980, p. 235.

[39]Hendrik George van Dam, 'Die Juden in Deutschland nach 1945', in Franz Böhm and Walter Dirks (eds.), *Judentum. Schicksal, Wesen und Gegenwart*, vol. 2, Wiesbaden 1965, pp. 888–916; here p. 908.

[40]See for example paragraphs 14/8 and 17/3 of the first German national Indemnification Law, the *Bundesergänzungsgesetz zur Entschädigung für Opfer der nationalsozialistischen Verfolgung* of 1953.

of the Jewish victims of the Nazis in the immediate postwar period being hardly better than their physical or mental condition, many ended up staying on in Germany —even if most had arrived with the aim of settling their indemnification affairs and paying only a brief visit to their old homeland.[41]

Unfortunately the claimants often had to endure long waiting periods for their indemnification payments, sometimes years or even decades. While compensation claims tended to be processed relatively promptly—above all under pressure from the occupying forces, who wanted property issues resolved as quickly as possible—the procedure of assessing the claims and paying-out of was often dragged out. But when money was indeed paid out it meant, as indicated, economic survival, basic financial security and a new professional beginning. Indemnification money had many possible uses, covering virtually every aspect of life: it financed apprenticeships, and it was used to purchase real estate for both residence and commercial use, as well as furnishings. Rather often, the possibility of such purchases played an important role in a decision to resettle in Germany by a German Jewish family that had managed to escape the Nazis.

With the amendment in 1956 of the West German Federal Indemnification Law, the question of remigration assistance took on more direct relevance for emigrants. This amendment provided for emergency assistance of 6,000 marks to Jewish returnees, which led to a sharp rise in their number. The indemnification files contain many cases of formerly persecuted individuals or their relatives who used this provision to come to Germany. Hence alongside the symbolic value inherent in indemnification discussed above, the importance of the material dimension of *Wiedergutmachung* should not be underestimated. Although indemnification legislation was not intended as a kind of welfare provision for those who had been persecuted but rather—based on civil law—as compensation for damages, it had the former effect as well. It contributed to economic survival after physical survival.

The Role of Returning Jewish Lawyers in the Indemnification Process

A number of Jewish lawyers helped the returnees in pursuit of their claims. Initially this fact may seem unsurprising; after all, they were often personally familiar with the kind of persecution their clients had endured, and they also had a personal motivation for turning to precisely this area of law. Nevertheless the question of why so many Jewish lawyers emigrated back to Germany and were then active in many restitution and compensation cases—as it happens not only on behalf of Jewish clients—still needs some explanation.

Jewish lawyers played an important role in the West German indemnification process from 1945 onwards. For example, Siegfried Neuland, Edward Kossoy and Uri Siegel, all living in Munich, were three of the most important lawyers in this

[41]On the material situation (food, clothing, housing, employment opportunities) of Jews in Germany after the war, see Geis, pp. 51–89.

field.[42] In addition, Robert Kempner, known above all as a prosecutor at the Nuremberg trials, was later active as a reparations lawyer in Frankfurt.[43] As a returnee, the Jewish Berlin lawyer Walter Schwarz became not only a central participant in the most important of the various reparations proceedings but also a leading advocate of West German *Wiedergutmachung* in the broader sense (see below). We should also take note of the many German-Jewish lawyers who travelled to Germany expressly to work for Jewish organisations in restitution and compensation cases.[44]

What were the factors leading Jewish jurists to return to live in a country where they had been victims of a total breakdown of German law a few years earlier? One factor has already been cited: regained trust in that law. As with other returning Jewish emigrants—and indeed in this case even more so—the lawyers saw *Wiedergutmachung* as a symbol of the reestablishment of law and civil peace. For even if belatedly, compensation and restitution annulled the *de facto* legitimation of the injustice committed against the victims. This motivation, to be sure, is exceedingly difficult to quantify. Another difficulty in weighing motivation results from the fact that quite a few of these lawyers had emigrated from Germany relatively early and thus had not experienced the persecution as directly or as physically as many of their clients had. In a sense, for them Germany's identity as a state under the rule of law may have been interrupted but had never really ceased to exist. This basically immeasurable factor made it easier for many to resume previous employment in a familiar setting.[45]

In addition, the professional prospects of emigrant Jewish jurists were better in Germany. Having been trained there, many felt out of place in the Anglo-Saxon legal systems—particularly the practising lawyers.[46] For their part, the German authorities signalled welcome and support to the Jewish lawyers through a provision in the compensation legislation ensuring readmission to the bar with few obstacles, and connected with this, an exemption, on grounds of previous persecution, from the residency requirement.[47] While professional success had eluded many jurists in their countries of emigration, it was generally less problematic to find clients in the framework of West German *Wiedergutmachung*, particularly in those German states

[42]The three had taken different routes: Neuland had stayed in Munich during the Nazi years and managed to survive; Kossoy had fled from Poland to Palestine, only coming to Germany in the early 1950s; Siegel, who came from a well-known Munich family of Jewish jurists, can be considered a prototypical returned remigrant. From 1934 onwards he lived in Palestine and worked there for the British administration before returning to Munich in 1953 as a lawyer. On Edward Kossoy see "Ein Pionier der Wiedergutmachung." (The author in conversation with Kossoy.) in *Aufbau*, vol. LXIX, no. 10 (2003), p. 12.

[43]See Robert M. W. Kempner (in collaboration with Jörg Friedrich), *Ankläger einer Epoche. Lebenserinnerungen*, Frankfurt am Main 1983.

[44]For example the numerous German-Jewish lawyers of the United Restitution Organisation (URO) or the Jewish Restitution Successor Organisation (JRSO). Among those worthy of mention in this context are Fritz Goldschmidt, Kurt May, Siegfried Ikenberg and Ernst Katzenstein; on this see Hans Günter Hockerts, 'Anwälte der Verfolgten. Die United Restitution Organization', in Herbst and Goschler (eds.), pp. 248–271, as well as Lissner, p. 86.

[45]These observations emerge from an interview by the author with the lawyer Uri Siegel in Munich on 9 April 2003.

[46]Lissner, p. 75.

[47]This is paragraph 67 of the Federal Restitution Law of 1956.

with large populations of displaced persons such as Bavaria and Hesse. And whereas for lawyers in Israel the number of solvent clients was small, in Germany—thanks to the irregular but nonetheless generalised practice of charging on a 'no win, no fee' basis—a certain financial profit was assured.[48] At the beginning very few jurists in Germany were willing to take on the new field of indemnification law, due to its complexity and difficulty and, above all, its seemingly short-lived nature. Hence compensation and restitution for Nazi injustice offered precisely the emigrant Jewish jurists a niche that they could fill in their old home-country.

One such emigrant was the lawyer Walter Schwarz, who, as a late-comer to the profession found it difficult to settle in Haifa; in Germany where, in his own words he would "never again have to scramble for clients",[49] he became one of the country's leading reparations lawyers and a prominent advocate of *Wiedergutmachung*.

In the 1920s Schwarz had worked in a law office that specialised in helping wounded veterans obtain benefits they were due. He had thus gained knowledge of legislation closely related to that governing reparations. Before the war he had also worked for the chairman of the Zionist Federation of Germany, Siegfried Moses, who in 1950 arranged for Schwarz to join the Munich office of the Jewish Agency for Palestine as a legal advisor on indemnification issues. Schwarz would be confronted repeatedly with the question of how he, a Jew, could live in Germany—particularly in view of the fact that his father had been murdered in Theresienstadt in 1942. Schwarz would dismiss the question by remarking that one should not lump all Germans together.

His role in the process of *Wiedergutmachung* helped him to cope successfully with a difficult balancing act: on the one hand he saw himself as a kind of "*Testamentsvollstrecker* [will-executor] of the Jewish people", but on the other he was neither able nor inclined to sever his deep inner connection to Germany. Since in the course of his work he encountered many Germans who displayed understanding and a willingness to compromise and cooperate, he did not feel he was living in "enemy territory". Schwarz considered his success rate in reparations cases of secondary importance; what really counted for him was dealing with a state and a society willing to confront this difficult problem at all. As one of the leading indemnification experts, he naturally saw the flaws in the process; taking advantage of his rhetorical gifts, he drew attention to every inconsistency, injustice, and scandal that he could uncover.[50] And yet, his deep belief in *Wiedergutmachung* was reflected in his enormous contribution to it. This belief is manifest in his autobiographical reflection that:

> I had never believed that some day indemnification would become my life's work. I do not regret it. *Wiedergutmachung*, that tough juridical field, that unjustly suppressed chapter of recent German history, will eventually be endowed with historical lustre. It already has curiosity value. Nothing similar has been achieved in humanity's early history or in our time.[51]

[48]Interview with Uri Siegel.

[49]Schwarz, *Späte Frucht*, p. 129.

[50]Summarised in Walter Schwarz, *In den Wind gesprochen? Glossen zur Wiedergutmachung des nationalsozialistischen Unrechts*, Munich 1969.

[51]Schwarz, *Späte Frucht*, p. 155 (excerpt translated from the German by T.W.). In his positive assessment Schwarz was not alone among Jewish restitution lawyers; cf. Kempner p. 380.

THE HISTORY OF *WIEDERGUTMACHUNG* AND RESEARCH ON REMIGRATION

As has been suggested, the individual and collective experience of *Wiedergutmachung* by Jewish emigrants who retuned to Germany were highly varied. Essentially each individual case can speak only for itself, while nonetheless referring to a wider context. It is clear that both the general process and effects of restitution and compensation had direct relevance for the lives of Jewish returnees. It should here be emphasised that, in contrast to the tendency thus far in research on remigration, the spotlight ought not be focused solely on prominent individuals but also on ordinary ones. To this extent, in scrutinising German-Jewish remigration from the perspective of experiential history, it seems important to take on the theme of indemnification. Three possibilities for doing so are briefly reviewed below.

A History of Encounters

The indemnification process can be approached not just as a history of laws and regulations but also as a history of encounters, and it is precisely at this point that it touches upon one of the central themes in the study of Jewish migration after 1945. It is well known that in postwar German society, the return from exile and emigration was sometimes treated as a taboo, sometimes as a public nuisance. A sense of guilt and shame played a role here, along with the "search for a whipping-boy, a fear of competition, an attempt to enhance one's own value by stigmatising others, and so on".[52] The famous German "inability to mourn" first discussed by Alexander and Margarete Mitscherlich "resulted not only in the wider public remaining uninformed about exile but also in returned emigrants frequently having the depressing feeling that they had not [in fact] returned home but rather to a foreign country".[53] While this was the case for returned emigrants in general, it was particularly the case for the Jews among them, perceived as "unpleasant witnesses to what had happened".[54]

The majority of former *Volksgenossen* closed themselves off to any feelings of sympathy for the emigrants, seeing themselves as having suffered enough themselves during the war[55] and thus meriting first consideration for compensation and primary attention when it came to past travails. In addition, many Germans enjoying appropriated property did not want to accept the fact of justified claims by those who once had no legal rights—claims intruding directly into their lives. In such cases they often responded "with vehement defensiveness, ignorance, demonstrative resentment, and an utter lack of understanding of the charges levelled against them. In their opinion they had in no way violated common business practices".[56] This phenomenon

[52]Sven Papcke, 'Exil und Remigration als öffentliches Ärgernis. Zur Soziologie eines Tabus', in *Exilforschung*, vol. 9, no. (1991), pp. 9–24; here p. 10f.
[53]Lehmann, p. 95f.
[54]Joachim Schlör, 'Exil und Rückkehr' in Heiner Lichtenstein and Otto R. Romberg (eds.), *Täter – Opfer – Folgen. Der Holocaust in Geschichte und Gegenwart*, Bonn 1997, pp. 154–169, here p. 156.
[55]Papcke, p. 19.
[56]Lillteicher, *Rechtsstaatlichkeit*, p. 124.

can be observed quite clearly in the records of the reparation proceedings—particularly in restitution cases, since these perhaps represented the only arena in which victims, former persecutors and profiteers confronted one another directly. The individual restitution files have proven to be a particularly good source. The limited scope of this article does not allow for a systematic evaluation from this perspective, which, however, could be quite valuable for future research on remigration.

Wiedergutmachung *and Its Influence on Displaced-Person Migration*

The indemnification files raise a basic question of definition. Remigrants are commonly understood to be former refugees or emigrants "who following the end of the Second World War returned to Germany of their own free will with the aim of resettling there on a permanent basis". Remigration "presumes that this voluntary return will lead to a reorientation of the geographical centre of their lives and is not intended to be merely temporary. Thus anyone who returned to Germany for military, professional or other extraneous reasons, i.e. in the service of one of the occupying powers … is not a 'remigrant' in the strict sense of the word."[57] This is not the place to debate the basic soundness of this definition; in the context of *Wiedergutmachung*, the definition's broadening appears advisable.

In this regard, one should not forget that the indemnification process also offered other victims of the Nazis, above all displaced persons, an opportunity to develop a new relationship with Germany. Mainly of Eastern-European origin, displaced persons arrived in Germany as a legacy of war. The compensation payments were meant to accelerate their return home, or else their emigration to a new country. On the whole this worked well; although in general the sums paid out were comparatively small, displaced persons—in contrast to most claimants—received these payments relatively quickly. Nevertheless, a certain percentage of displaced persons did choose to stay on in Germany. For one thing, some were not living in camps, but had already managed to make a new life for themselves in the country;[58] for another, many of those who did return to their Eastern European countries of origin could not endure the terrible conditions there and returned to Germany as quickly as they could in the early 1950s in the hope of gaining additional indemnification benefits and thus a minimum of financial security.

A subgroup of this latter group of returnees comprised displaced persons known as "illegals" who, to the astonishment of many, had returned to the camps (for the most part the camp at Föhrenwald). Many—around 3,500 persons—arrived directly from Israel, and the motives for doing so varied. In the words of one author, writing roughly a decade ago in these pages:

[57]Lehmann, p. 40f.

[58]In the autumn of 1947, for example, 367,173 displaced persons were living in Bavaria; 229,388 of these lived in camps and 137,785 in private accommodation. See inaugural speech of the Bavarian Minister President Hans Ehard on 24 October 1947, in: *Verhandlungen des Bayerischen Landtags*, second session 1947–1948, stenographic records, vol. 2, part 1, no. 28–56, pp. 82–95.

Some returnees found life in a pioneer country too difficult to master: or their personal difficulties were exacerbated by the fighting between Jews and Arabs in 1948 and after: or they returned because they feared that their often chronic medical problems could not be handled adequately in Israel. Others were lured by the expectation of an easier job market than that of Israel in the 1950s. Yet others viewed the German DP camp as a sort of "golden bridge", which would finally carry them across troubled bureaucratic waters to their most cherished destination: the United States. Finally the Adenauer-Ben-Gurion restitution negotiations of 1952 aroused hopes in some of personal compensation and they wished to be "on the spot" to arrange restitution for themselves.[59]

In this manner *Wiedergutmachung* created a new category of returned emigrant composed of persons who might be described as "survivor migrants"; these persons have received very little attention in exile and remigration research.[60]

Relativising the Caesura of 1945

One benefit of drawing on indemnification files as a historical resource still needs attention: as some of the documents date back to the onset of Nazi persecution, the information they provide allows one to explore questions pertaining to an individual's entire life history. Indeed, analysis of compensation case files provides the only means of reconstructing the story of who emigrated (and sometimes further migrated) where and when before returning to Germany after 1945. Hence a vast pool of almost entirely untapped sources is still awaiting discovery. The birth, marriage and death certificates, school-leaving certificates, work references, and certificates of inheritance, residency and identity in the case files provide a wealth of information about personal relationships before and after the persecution.[61]

Use of this archival material thus corresponds with a tendency in recent research to relativise (certainly not dismiss) the significance of the caesura of 1945. For the material appears to make it clear that for persecuted individuals—as opposed to perpetrators—events like being excluded from one's profession, having to flee, and even returning to Germany were more important than the formal end of military hostilities. Nevertheless in focussing on such experiences remigration research should not restrict itself to an élite group of persons, as has been the dominant trend.[62] With the help of this body of sources, it is now possible to begin reconstructing the history of the "remigration of ordinary people".

[59]Ronald Webster, 'American Relief and Jews in Germany, 1945–1960. Diverging Perspectives', in *LBI Year Book*, vol. 38 (1993), pp. 293–321; here p. 306.

[60]See Jacqueline Dewell Giere, *Wir sind unterwegs, aber nicht in der Wüste. Erziehung und Kultur in den jüdischen Displaced-Persons-Lagern der amerikanischen Zone im Nachkriegsdeutschland 1945–1949*, Frankfurt am Main 1993, esp. pp. 20–25 and pp. 440–452.

[61]Cf. Volker Eichler, 'Entschädigungsakten – Zeitgeschichtliche Bedeutung und Möglichkeiten der archivalischen Erschließung', in *Vom Findbuch zum Internet. Erschließung von Archivgut vor neuen Herausforderungen. Papers from the 68th-annual Conference of German Archivists (Deutsche Archivtage) from 23–26 September 1997 in Ulm*, Siegburg 1998, pp. 221–229; here pp. 226f.

[62]See for example Marita Krauss, *Heimkehr in ein fremdes Land. Geschichte der Remigration nach 1945*, Munich 2001, pp. 10f.

WIEDERGUTMACHUNG—A BRIDGE TO GERMANY?

The decision of Jews to return to Germany after 1945, and perhaps even to remain there, cannot be traced back to a single cause; the reasons were in fact many and varied. They ranged from the need to ensure economic survival, to difficulties adapting to a foreign culture, to the wish to complete professional training interrupted during the Nazi period, to the desire to contribute to Germany's denazification.[63] *Wiedergutmachung* could here serve as the condition, cause or even excuse for returning to a country whose core political programme just a few years earlier had consisted of the eradication of Jewish life in all its forms.[64]

As we have seen, in some cases the manner in which indemnification was implemented and the defensive attitude of the German population towards it were factors inhibiting a return to Germany. Remigration, of course, could not erase the trauma of persecution, expulsion and flight; thus for some, the decision to return was not free of severe reservations.[65] In this respect, the intent of this article has not been to write a "remigration" chapter in the success story of *Wiedergutmachung* but rather to add a new facet to the scholarly research on Jewish remigration to Germany after 1945.

The image of a bridge may here be useful: always keeping in mind that a rift existed, *Wiedergutmachung* forged such a bridge to the old, lost life. Over time, the bridge proved relatively solid and crossings that had first been very cautious became increasingly frequent. Purely material considerations such as restoring a livelihood played a role here as much as symbolic considerations. Correspondingly, as the prototype of what is now known as "reparatory justice",[66] the West German indemnification process had an impact on the claimants through the interplay of the three categories discussed above. This involved not only recovery of a previous set of circumstances, but above all the creation of something new.[67] *Wiedergutmachung* thus not only contributed to Jews coming to Germany after 1945 but also to their continued stay in the country. It also contributed to the partial fading of reservations felt by German Jews towards their homeland—towards the onset of a sort of "psychological remigration".

[63]Webster, 'Jüdische Rückkehrer', p. 60.

[64]It is worth noting that Hendrik van Dam, General Secretary of the *Zentralrat der Juden in Deutschland*, considered *Wiedergutmachung* "an important factor" in the remigration movement of Jews to Germany. See van Dam, p. 908.

[65]Krauss, 'Heimkehr', pp. 7f.

[66]Ruti G. Teitel, *Transitional Justice*, Oxford 2000, p. 119.

[67]See Constantin Goschler, 'Die Politik der Rückerstattung in Westdeutschland', in Goschler and Lillteicher, *"Arisierung"*, pp. 99–125; here p. 99.

Americanisation as Globalisation? Remigrés to West Germany after 1945 and Conceptions of Democracy: The Cases of Hans Rothfels, Ernst Fraenkel and Hans Rosenberg

By Arnd Bauerkämper

In recent historiography intellectual remigrés have often been considered intermediaries between different cultural traditions and representatives of an emerging global élite. More particularly, intellectuals who fled from Nazi Germany in the 1930s, took refuge in the United States and returned to West Germany after the collapse of the Third Reich, have been seen as bridging the gulf between the two sides of the Atlantic Ocean, sharing basic values like liberalism and commonly espousing political concepts like pluralist democracy. From this perspective, Jews who had been forced to leave Nazi Germany and then returned to Germany after the Second World War are considered indispensable transmitters of the political values needed for a viable democracy. The following consideration of the scholarship and political views of historians Hans Rothfels (1891–1976) and Hans Rosenberg (1904–1988) and political scientist Ernst Fraenkel (1898–1975) argues that although Jewish intellectual remigrés did indeed play a key role in transferring Western political values and models to West Germany, they did not become a global élite. For these refugee academics, and by inference many others like them, were torn between their German roots and their lasting experience of the United States. More crucially, although they transferred knowledge about the democracy established in the New World to West Germany, they firmly rejected a wholesale imitation of the American model.[1]

America was perceived as both a model and a threat in Germany throughout the twentieth century. It has thus been argued that the expectations and hopes as well as the anxieties and fears of various groups within German society have been projected onto the United States. However, the complex dynamics and modes of cross-cultural interaction between the two countries after 1945 have only begun to be examined in

[1]As examples of the conventional view of remigrés in recent historiography, see, for example, Marita Krauss, *Heimkehr in ein fremdes Land. Geschichte der Remigration nach 1945*, Munich 2001, p. 93; *idem*, 'Die Rückkehr einer vertriebenen Elite. Remigranten in Deutschland nach 1945', in Günther Schulz (ed.), *Vertriebene Eliten. Vertreibung und Verfolgung von Führungsschichten im 20. Jahrhundert*, Munich 2001, p. 112; Raimund Lammersdorf, 'Verwestlichung als Wandel der politischen Kultur', in Detlef Junker (ed.), *Die USA und Deutschland im Zeitalter des Kalten Krieges 1945–1990. Ein Handbuch, vol. 1: 1945–1968*, Stuttgart 2001, pp. 966–967, 969, 975.

recent scholarship. Research has rather tended to concentrate on the simple interchange of values and cultural goods, and because of the overwhelming influence of the United States, this process has largely been interpreted as "Americanisation". According to this paradigm, American political and social values were transferred to Europe, some of their elements being deliberately selected and adapted to European traditions. Accordingly, despite its political weakness as a defeated nation, postwar West Germany adaptability to indigenous traditions and demands by the general population shaped the reception and adoption of American socio-cultural transfer.[2]

In the 1950s and 1960s, remigré intellectuals certainly played a pivotal role in the gradual democratisation of the newly-established German Federal Republic. But because of both objective circumstances and personal inclination, these intellectuals accorded as much weight to Germany's deeply-embedded traditions and prevailing conditions as to the American values they had brought back with them; they were also very aware of traditional concerns about "Americanisation". Most German-Jewish remigrés thus flatly rejected the idea of a direct transfer of American political and cultural models to West Germany. On the one hand, with the prospects of American influence on the new state's political reorientation sparking strong resentments, traditional anti-democratic German values, particularly present among older Germans, could not be ignored.[3] On the other hand, some remigré intellectuals themselves continued to maintain conservative political views. They partially clung to preconceived notions of politics and traditional social values, only reluctantly and gradually modified during flight and exile. Other Jewish intellectuals like Hans Rosenberg were more outspoken in their criticism of German traditions which had at least facilitated the rise of Nazism in the Weimar Republic. This latter group significantly contributed to the concept of a German

[2]See, in particular, Philipp Gassert, 'Amerikanismus, Antiamerikanismus, Amerikanisierung. Neue Literatur zur Sozial-, Wirtschafts- und Kulturgeschichte des amerikanischen Einflusses in Deutschland und Europa', in *Archiv für Sozialgeschichte* 39 (1999), pp. 532, 541, 549, 553–554, 560; Alf Lüdtke, Inge Marßolek and Adelheid von Saldern, 'Amerikanisierung: Traum und Alptraum im Deutschland des 20. Jahrhunderts', in *idem* (eds.), *Amerikanisierung. Traum und Alptraum im Deutschland des 20. Jahrhunderts*, Stuttgart 1996, pp. 8, 15, 19–20; Heide Fehrenbach and Uta Poiger, 'Introduction. Americanization Reconsidered', in *idem* (eds.), *Transactions, Transgressions, Transformations: American Culture in Western Europe and Japan*, New York 2000, pp. XIII–XVI, XXXVI–XXVIII; Mary Nolan, 'America in the German Imagination', *ibid.*, pp. 5–6; *idem*, 'Americanization or Westernization?', German Historical Institute, Washington, Conference Papers on the Web (www.ghi-dc.org/conpotweb/westernpapers/nolan.pdf), pp. 1–9; Volker Berghahn, 'Conceptualizing the American Impact on Germany: West German Society and the Problem of Americanization', *ibid.*, (www.ghi-dc.org/conpotweb/westernpapers/berghahn.pdf), pp. 2f.; Kaspar Maase, '"Americanization", "Americanness" and "Americanisms": Time for a Change in Perspective?', *ibid.*, (www.ghi-dc.org/conpotweb/westernpapers/maase.pdf), pp 1–3.

[3]Mitchell G. Ash, 'Wissenschaft und Wissenschaftsaustausch', in Junker (ed.), pp. 638, 645; Willi Paul Adams, 'Amerikastudien in der Bundesrepublik', *ibid.*, pp. 451, 464; Anselm Doering-Manteuffel, *Wie westlich sind die Deutschen? Amerikanisierung und Westernisierung im 20. Jahrhundert*, Göttingen 1999, p. 63; *idem*, 'Transatlantic Exchange and Interaction – the Concept of Westernization', German Historical Institute, Washington (www.ghi-dc.org/conpotweb/westernpapers/doering.pdf), pp. 3–5, 8f. On the research agenda, see Christina von Hodenberg, 'Intellektuelle Aufbrüche und Generationen im Konflikt', in *Archiv für Sozialgeschichte* 41 (2001), p. 678.

"special path", the *Sonderweg* thesis, taken up by a new generation of German historians in the 1960s.[4]

Nevertheless, while they succeeded in achieving a rapprochement between American political notions and the guiding political-social values at work in the Federal Republic during the 1950s, traces of deeply-rooted traditions are still clearly discernible in the hybrid perspective emerging from the German-American encounter.

The purpose of this contribution is to shed some light on complex processes of American-West German transfer and accommodation without aiming at a full-scale investigation into the process's various stages. The response in the United States to Germany's appropriation of its democratic model will likewise not be discussed. Furthermore, important political contexts like the Cold War and the debate about the Nazi past can only be touched upon. And the theoretical foundations of the concepts advanced by Fraenkel, Rothfels and Rosenberg as well as their oeuvre itself will not be dealt with in detail. It is here worth stressing that the intent of their scholarship was not primarily political but rather as a contribution to academic debates.[5]

THE LONG LIFE OF THE AUTHORITARIAN STATE MODEL AND THE RELUCTANT APPROPRIATION OF AMERICAN DEMOCRACY: HANS ROTHFELS

Hans Rothfels was one of the most controversial German historians of the twentieth century. The son of a solicitor in Kassel, he was born into a Jewish family strongly integrated into German society. As his family had loosened its ties to traditional Jewish culture, Rothfels did not develop a strong identity as a Jew; eventually, he converted to Christianity, joining the German Protestant Church in 1910. Rothfels studied history at the universities of Freiburg, Munich, Berlin and Heidelberg. He soon became a disciple of the prominent and influential historians Friedrich Meinecke and Hermann Oncken. In November 1914, his military service in the Great War was abruptly

[4]For an overview, see Jürgen Kocka, 'German History before Hitler: The Debate about the German "Sonderweg"', in *Journal of Contemporary History*, vol. 23, no. 1 (1988), pp. 3–16. In retrospect: Jürgen Kocka, 'Nach dem Ende des Sonderwegs. Zur Tragfähigkeit eines Konzepts', in Arnd Bauerkämper, Martin Sabrow and Bernd Stöver (eds.), *Doppelte Zeitgeschichte. Deutsch-deutsche Beziehungen 1945–1990. Festschrift für Christoph Kleßmann*, Bonn 1998, pp. 364–375. On the revision of the concept, see Arnd Bauerkämper, 'Geschichtsschreibung als Projektion. Die Revision der "Whig Interpretation of History" und die Kritik am Paradigma vom "deutschen Sonderweg" seit den 1970er Jahren', in Stefan Berger, Peter Lambert and Peter Schumann (eds.), *Historikerdialoge. Geschichte, Mythos und Gedächtnis im deutsch-britischen kulturellen Austausch 1750–2000*, Göttingen 2003, pp. 383–438.

[5]Some of the ideas presented in this paper have been advanced in a previous study. See Arnd Bauerkämper, 'Remigranten als Akteure von Zivilgesellschaft und Demokratie. Historiker und Politikwissenschaftler in Westdeutschland nach 1945', in *idem* (ed.), *Die Praxis der Zivilgesellschaft. Akteure, Handeln und Strukturen im internationalen Vergleich*, Frankfurt am Main 2002, pp. 343–370. On the concepts of 'remigré' and 'sojourner', see Claus-Dieter Krohn, 'Einleitung: Remigranten in der westdeutschen Nachkriegsgesellschaft', in *idem* and Patrik von zur Mühlen (eds.), *Rückkehr und Aufbau nach 1945. Deutsche Remigranten im öffentlichen Leben Nachkriegsdeutschlands*, Marburg 1997, p. 8; Axel Schildt, 'Reise zurück aus der Zukunft. Beiträge von intellektuellen USA-Remigranten zur atlantischen Allianz, zum westdeutschen Amerikabild und zur "Amerikanisierung" in den fünfziger Jahren', in *Exilforschung* 9 (1991), p. 27.

terminated by an accident that necessitated the amputation of one of his legs. Rothfels was now free to begin work on his doctoral thesis, a study of the ideas of the military strategist Carl von Clausewitz. After receiving his doctorate in 1918, he worked as an archivist in Potsdam, while preparing a comprehensive documentation of Bismarck's social policy. He completed his *Habilitation* on Bismarck in 1923.

Rothfels was appointed professor of history at the University of Königsberg in 1926. Over the following years he would become a leading proponent of revision of the Versailles Treaty to rectify what many Germans resented as an unjust arrangement. In place of the treaty, he argued for the emergence of a new territorial order in East Central Europe under German predominance. His particular concern was the struggle over the Polish-German border. Despite his commitment to such territorial revisionism, his espousal of authoritarian political values and his early conversion, Rothfels was stigmatised on antisemitic grounds by the Nazis shortly after they gained power; he was deprived of his professorship in 1934. The following year, he submitted a request to continue his university teaching, and this was supported by conservative officials of the University of Königsberg—as well as by the leading Nazi functionary (and later Foreign Minister) Joachim von Ribbentrop. In the end, the request was categorically rejected, just as efforts to preserve his status as a citizen of the German Reich were stymied.[6]

With his hopes dashed that his conservative and nationalist stance would save him, Rothfels emigrated to Oxford in 1939. But after the defeat of France, he was interned on the Isle of Man as an "enemy alien". Demoralised by that experience and by poor employment opportunities in Britain, Rothfels now moved on to the United States, having secured a position as visiting professor at Brown University in late 1940.[7] Six years later, he was offered a professorship at the University of Chicago—already the intellectual home of a number of other conservative orientated German-Jewish intellectuals such as the political scientist Arnold Bergstraesser.[8]

[6]Hans Mommsen, 'Geschichtsschreibung und Humanität. Zum Gedenken an Hans Rothfels', in Wolfgang Benz and Hermann Graml (eds.), *Aspekte deutscher Außenpolitik im 20. Jahrhundert. Aufsätze Hans Rothfels zum Gedächtnis*, Stuttgart 1976, pp. 9–20; *idem*, 'Hans Rothfels', in Hans-Ulrich Wehler (ed.), *Deutsche Historiker*, vol. 9, Göttingen 1982, pp. 129–139; Karl-Heinz Roth, 'Hans Rothfels: Geschichtspolitische Doktrinen im Wandel der Zeiten. Weimar–NS-Diktatur–Bundesrepublik', in *Zeitschrift für Geschichtswissenschaft*, vol. 49, no. 12 (2001), pp. 1063–1068; *idem*, '"Richtung halten": Hans Rothfels und die neo-konservative Geschichtsschreibung diesseits und jenseits des Atlantik', in *Sozialgeschichte* vol. 18, no. 11 (2003), pp. 44–61. For a less critical view, see Werner Conze, 'Hans Rothfels', in *Historische Zeitschrift* 237 (1983), pp. 311–338; Wolfgang Neugebauer, 'Hans Rothfels (1891–1976) in seiner Zeit', in Dietrich Rauschning and Donata von Nerée (eds.), *Die Albertus-Universität zu Königsberg und ihre Professoren. Aus Anlaß der Gründung der Albertus-Universität vor 450 Jahren*, Berlin 1995, pp. 245–249; *idem*, 'Hans Rothfels' Weg zur vergleichenden Geschichte Ostmitteleuropas, besonders im Übergang von früher Neuzeit zur Moderne', in *Berliner Jahrbuch für osteuropäische Geschichte* 1996/1, pp. 333–378. On Rothfels and territorial revisionism, see Andreas Kossert, '"Grenzlandpolitik" und Ostforschung an der Peripherie des Reiches. Das ostpreußische Masuren 1919–1945', in *Vierteljahrshefte für Zeitgeschichte*, vol. 51, no. 2 (2003), pp. 132f., 144.

[7]Due to the rigid labour regulations, most German refugee academics in fact only lived or stayed in Britain temporarily before deciding to move on to the United States. See Alfons Söllner, 'On Transit to America – Political Scientists from Germany in Great Britain after 1933', in *idem*, *Deutsche Politikwissenschaftler in der Emigration. Studien zu ihrer Akkulturation und Wirkungsgeschichte. Mit einer Bibliographie*, Opladen 1996, pp. 85f., 89f., 93f.

[8]Roth, 'Rothfels', pp. 62–67.

When he visited Germany in 1949, Rothfels was warmly received by his former colleagues. His speech to the annual convention of German historians, the *Historikertag*, struck a strong chord among the assembled scholars, because Rothfels firmly rejected all theses of "collective guilt" on the part of the Germans, as well as the notion of a basic continuity in German history from Luther or Bismarck to Hitler. In contrast to such interpretations, he still extolled the Bismarckian state as the defining moment of German history, likewise maintaining his belief in the traditional paradigm of the sovereign German nation-state. Moreover, as early as 1946 Rothfels criticised the Potsdam Agreement and condemned the expulsion of ethnic Germans from the Reich's former eastern provinces. In his book *The German Opposition to Hitler*, published in 1948, Rothfels even asserted that Germany had been "an occupied country" after 1933. Obviously, he regarded his research on this conservative German opposition as a tool for Germany's moral and political rehabilitation.[9]

Hans Rothfels' apologeticist view that the Nazi seizure of power was the product of an upsurge of the 'masses' and a result of excessive democratisation also secured him considerable support in postwar Germany. Returning there in 1951 to take up a professorship at the University of Tübingen, he now became one of the most respected historians in the early Federal Republic. He inaugurated a comprehensive documentation of the expulsion of Germans from East Central and South Eastern Europe and played a leading role in the foundation of the *Institut für Zeitgeschichte* in Munich. In accordance with his predilection for closely linking historiography to the perceived needs of the present, Rothfels was instrumental in legitimising the new West German state as a bulwark against totalitarianism. Not least because of his anti-communist posture and his insistence on upholding the traditions of the German nation-state, Rothfels commanded considerable influence, both in academia and in politics. As the guiding force behind the study of contemporary history in Germany, Rothfels gained international prominence. He was awarded the German *Pour le Mérite* decoration in 1961.[10]

[9]Hans Rothfels, *The German Opposition to Hitler. An Appraisal*, Hinsdale, IL 1948, p. 16. See Nicolas Berg, *Der Holocaust und die westdeutschen Historiker*, Göttingen 2003, pp. 143–192, and the contribution by Nicolas Berg in this volume. On Rothfels' book, see Jan Eckel, 'Intellektuelle Transformationen im Spiegel der Widerstandsdeutungen', in Ulrich Herbert (ed.), *Wandlungsprozesse in Westdeutschland. Belastung, Integration, Liberalisierung*, Göttingen 2002, pp. 143, 145, 153–157, 161, 164; Hermann Graml and Hans Woller, 'Fünfzig Jahre Vierteljahrshefte für Zeitgeschichte 1953–2003', in *Vierteljahrshefte für Zeitgeschichte*, vol. 51, no. 1 (2003), p. 66; Roth, 'Rothfels', p. 1068–1070. As an overview of German reactions to Hans Rothfels, see Winfried Schulze, 'Hans Rothfels und die deutsche Geschichtswissenschaft nach 1945', in Christian Jansen, Lutz Niethammer and Bernd Weisbrod (eds.), *Von der Aufgabe der Freiheit. Festschrift für Hans Mommsen*, Berlin 1995, pp. 83–85. On Rothfels' views of the Potsdam Agreement, see Roth, '"Richtung halten"', p. 67.

[10]Conze, 'Hans Rothfels', pp. 339–359; Mommsen, 'Geschichtsschreibung', pp. 20–27; *idem*, 'Hans Rothfels', pp. 139–141; Roth, '"Richtung halten"', pp. 68–71, *idem*, 'Rothfels', pp. 1070–1072. See Mathias Beer, 'Die Dokumentation der Vertreibung der Deutschen aus Ost-Mitteleuropa. Hintergründe–Entstehung–Ergebnis–Wirkung', in *Geschichte in Wissenschaft und Unterricht*, vol. 50, no. 2 (1999), pp. 99, 103. On Rothfels' leading role in the foundation of the Institut für Zeitgeschichte and as editor of the *Vierteljahrshefte für Zeitgeschichte*, see esp. Horst Möller, 'Das Institut für Zeitgeschichte und die Entwicklung der Zeitgeschichtsschreibung in Deutschland', in *idem* and Udo Wengst (eds.), *50 Jahre Institut für Zeitgeschichte. Eine Bilanz*, Munich 1999, p. 26; Graml and Woller, pp. 54–61.

Although Rothfels retained his American passport until 1969 and repeatedly returned to his American refuge, his exile in the United States is not usually regarded as a crucial turning point in the development of his political values. Thus, research on his scholarship and political activities has largely focussed on the period before 1934.[11] The recent controversy about his attitudes towards the Weimar Republic has centred, at least initially, on a radio speech that Rothfels is assumed to have delivered on 30 January 1933 or earlier. This debate has led to opposing views of his role in the collapse of the first German democratic state. On the one hand, Ingo Haar has argued that Rothfels clearly aimed at a new authoritarian state; on the other hand, Heinrich August Winkler has characterised him as a reluctant, lukewarm supporter of the Weimar Republic on grounds of reason or rationality, a *Vernunftrepublikaner*.[12] Although these divergent interpretations obviously have important implications for historical assessments of Rothfels' influence in the 1950s, the development of his political views in the United States and in postwar West Germany has hitherto attracted little attention.[13]

Rothfels' enforced exile did in fact have some impact on his political views. As a German nationalist, he found it difficult to cope with the loss of his homeland and to adjust to a new life in America. But he was clearly impressed by the effectiveness of American democracy in general and by the social legislation inaugurated by Franklin Delano Roosevelt, in particular: throughout the 1920s, Rothfels had been preparing a documentation of Bismarck's social policy, which he regarded as a source of and prerequisite for a far-reaching renewal of the German state;[14] the

[11]See, for example, Ingo Haar, *Historiker im Nationalsozialismus. Deutsche Geschichtswissenschaft und 'Volkstumskampf' im Osten*, Göttingen 2000, pp. 70–91, 102; *idem*, '"Revisionistische" Historiker und Jugendbewegung: Das Königsberger Beispiel', in Peter Schöttler (ed.), *Geschichtsschreibung als Legitimationswissenschaft 1918–1945*, Frankfurt am Main 1997, pp. 52–54, 70, 72–82, 86f.; Karen Schönwälder, *Historiker und Politik. Geschichtswissenschaft im Nationalsozialismus*, Frankfurt am Main 1992, pp. 53–58, 68–72.

[12]Heinrich August Winkler, 'Hans Rothfels – ein Lobredner Hitlers? Quellenkritische Bemerkungen zu Ingo Haars Buch "Historiker im Nationalsozialismus"', in *Vierteljahrshefte für Zeitgeschichte*, vol. 49, no. 4 (2001), pp. 643–652; *idem*, 'Geschichtswissenschaft oder Geschichtsklitterung? Ingo Haar und Hans Rothfels: Eine Erwiderung', in *Vierteljahrshefte für Zeitgeschichte*, vol. 50, no. 4 (2002), pp. 635–652; Ingo Haar, 'Quellenkritik oder Kritik der Quellen? Replik auf Heinrich August Winkler', in *Vierteljahrshefte für Zeitgeschichte*, vol. 50, no. 3 (2002), pp. 497–505. The controversy has been taken up in contributions by Karen Schönwälder, Peter Thomas Walther, Karl Heinz Roth, Thomas Etzemüller, Jan Eckel, Mathias Beer and John L. Harvey in H-Soz-u-Kult (http://hsozkult.geschichte.hu-berlin.de), 14 February–4 March 2003.

[13]Peter Th. Walther, 'Emigrierte deutsche Historiker in den USA', in *Berichte zur Wissenschaftsgeschichte* 7 (1984), pp. 41–43, 47, 49–50; *idem*, 'Emigrierte deutsche Historiker in den Vereinigten Staaten, 1945–1950: Blick oder Sprung über den Großen Teich?' in Christoph Cobet (ed.), *Einführung in Fragen an die Geschichtswissenschaft in Deutschland nach Hitler 1945–1950*, Frankfurt am Main 1986, pp. 44–49. For a more critical interpretation see Roth, 'Hans Rothfels', pp. 1068–1072. See also Thomas Etzemüller, *Sozialgeschichte als politische Geschichte. Werner Conze und die Neuorientierung der westdeutschen Geschichtswissenschaft nach 1945*, Munich 2001, *passim*; Christoph Cornelißen, *Gerhard Ritter. Geschichtswissenschaft und Politik im 20. Jahrhundert*, Düsseldorf 2001, *passim*; Heinz Wolf, *Deutsch-jüdische Emigrationshistoriker in den USA und der Nationalsozialismus*, Berne 1988, *passim*; Jin-Sung Chun, *Das Bild der Moderne in der Nachkriegszeit. Die westdeutsche 'Strukturgeschichte' im Spannungsfeld von Modernitätskritik und wissenschaftlicher Innovation 1948–1962*, Munich 2000, *passim*.

[14]Lothar Machtan, 'Hans Rothfels und die Anfänge der historischen Sozialpolitik-Forschung in Deutschland', in *Internationale Wissenschaftliche Korrespondenz zur Geschichte der deutschen Arbeiterbewegung* 28 (1992), pp. 161–210.

New Deal thus appealed to him and ultimately caused a softening of his strong reservations about the United States. More importantly, Rothfels increasingly accorded the doctrine of the rule of law, one of the pillars of Western democracy, priority over state power. In fact, this reverence for legal power proved compatible with respect for the state, never entirely abandoned by Rothfels. Deeply suspicious of mass mobilisation and plebiscitary democracy, he continued to plead for a strong state capable of curbing the supposedly destructive forces of mass democracy. As Rothfels in some basic ways remained a conservative and German nationalist during his American exile, young Jewish students like Georg Iggers, who attended his classes at the University of Chicago in 1948, did not fully understand the reasons for his flight from Nazi Germany. Nevertheless, while he tended to confine democracy to community-based activities at the grass roots, he did open himself to democratic and liberal political values, even going so far as to acknowledge the American constitution as a model for the conservative and military resistance movement in Nazi Germany, represented by Carl Friedrich Goerdeler (1884–1945) and Ludwig Beck (1880–1944), for instance. By the mid-1960s, Rothfels had come to recognise that the fierce and uncompromising rejection of Western liberalism and rationalism that he had shared had lent Nazism credibility and provided the rulers of the Third Reich with considerable political support.[15]

Opting for remigration thus proved to be complex and difficult for Rothfels—and the process was made even more taxing by his expulsion having increased his self-awareness as a Jew. Hence before he returned to West Germany, he conferred about his decision with exiled Jewish historians like Fritz Epstein.[16] Nevertheless, after taking up his professorship in Tübingen, Rothfels quickly identified with the new Federal Republic. As a staunch supporter of West Germany's integration into NATO, he was able to maintain his strongly anti-communist stance on his return to Germany. At the same time, he refrained from openly discussing the support most Germans had readily lent the Nazi rulers: soul-searching and a debate on individual responsibility and guilt were clearly not his preoccupations. More importantly, Rothfels continued to hold some serious reservations about Western liberal democracy—his deep-seated suspicions regarding irresponsible impulses of the

[15]This gradual shift is neglected in Berg, *Holocaust*, pp. 188–189. For a retrospective, see Hans Rothfels, 'Die Geschichtswissenschaft in den dreißiger Jahren', in Andreas Flitner (ed.), *Deutsches Geistesleben und Nationalsozialismus. Eine Vortragsreihe der Universität Tübingen*, Tübingen 1965, p. 94. For Rothfels' anti-democratic attitudes before 1933, see Schönwälder, pp. 56f., 72. Also see Claus-Dieter Krohn, 'Geschichtswissenschaften', in *idem et al.* (eds.), *Handbuch der deutschsprachigen Emigration 1933–1945*, Darmstadt 1998, p. 757; Jean Solchany, 'Vom Antimodernismus zum Antitotalitarismus. Konservative Interpretationen des nationalsozialistischen Deutschland 1945–1949', in *Vierteljahrshefte für Zeitgeschichte*, vol. 44, no. 3 (1996), p. 393; Walther, 'Emigrierte deutsche Historiker in den Vereinigten Staaten', pp. 45, 47; Neugebauer, p. 377. For a short autobiographical reflection see Wilma and Georg Iggers, *Zwei Seiten der Geschichte. Lebensbericht aus unruhigen Zeiten*, Göttingen 2002, p. 92.

[16]Winfried Schulze, *Deutsche Geschichtswissenschaft nach 1945*, Munich 1989, pp. 141f.; *idem*, 'Refugee Historians and the German Historical Profession between 1950 and 1970', in Hartmut Lehmann and James J. Sheehan (eds.), *An Interrupted Past. German-Speaking Refugee Historians in the United States After 1933*, Cambridge 1991, pp. 218f.

masses had by no means vanished during his American years. In his view, democracy was to be framed and tamed by a strong state, his remedy for society's ills.[17] Still, he both conducted and promoted research on the rise of Nazism and the Nazi dictatorship – an academic endeavour that met strong opposition from conservative colleagues such as Gerhard Ritter. In the last resort, Rothfels was also prepared to sacrifice his cherished ideal of national unity for the sake of freedom in the new West German democracy, as his support for Chancellor Willy Brandt's new policy vis-à-vis the East German state and Germany's Eastern European neighbours signalled.[18]

All told, Rothfels appears to have been able to combine his traditional notions of a strong state and his unwavering anti-Bolshevism with selected elements of the American model of democracy. As a Jewish remigré who objected to general notions of collective guilt and shielded German history from general verdicts of long-term decay, Rothfels was almost unassailable in post-war Germany. Critics of his traditional historiography paid tribute to him as a victim of the Nazi dictatorship, and colleagues like Friedrich Meinecke, who had stayed in Germany during the Third Reich, lauded him as a bridge-builder between the old and new Germany.[19] They were also impressed by his free and open conduct, particularly vis-à-vis his new students in Tübingen, conduct that contrasted notably with that of traditional university teachers in Germany.[20] As editor-in-chief of the *Vierteljahrshefte für Zeitgeschichte* from 1952 to 1976, Rothfels also enforced rigorous methods of editing that he had become acquainted with in the United States. More significantly, having always seen himself as a scholar with a political message, he increasingly questioned the historicist ideal of 'objectivity' by insisting on clear value judgements. Although he himself largely remained devoted to political history, Rothfels supported social history as a promising new approach within West German historiography. Exile in the United States had clearly influenced the German historian's political views and his *oeuvre*; but his

[17]Georg G. Iggers, 'Die deutschen Historiker in der Emigration', in Bernd Faulenbach (ed.), *Geschichtswissenschaft in Deutschland. Traditionelle Positionen und gegenwärtige Aufgaben*, Munich 1974, pp. 108–109; Mommsen, 'Hans Rothfels', p. 142. On reservations regarding the concept of a pluralist democracy among German historians after 1945 in general, see Bernd Faulenbach, 'Historische Tradition und politische Neuorientierung. Zur Geschichtswissenschaft nach der "deutschen Katastrophe"', in Walter H. Pehle and Peter Sillem (eds.), *Wissenschaft im geteilten Deutschland. Restauration oder Neubeginn nach 1945?*, Frankfurt am Main 1992, pp. 200–201; *idem*, 'Deutsche Geschichtswissenschaft nach den beiden Weltkriegen', in Gottfried Niedhart and Dieter Riesenberger (eds.), *Lernen aus dem Krieg? Deutsche Nachkriegszeiten 1918 und 1945. Beiträge zur historischen Friedensforschung*, Munich 1992, pp. 236–237, 240.

[18]Klemens von Klemperer, 'Hans Rothfels (1891–1976)', in Hartmut Lehmann and James van Horn Melton (eds.), *Paths of Continuity: Central European Historiography from the 1930s to the 1950s*, Cambridge 1994, p. 133; Faulenbach, p. 233.

[19]Friedrich Meinecke, 'Zum Geleit', in Werner Conze (ed.), *Deutschland und Europa. Historische Studien zur Völker- und Staatenordnung des Abendlandes*, Düsseldorf 1951, p. 11. See also Graml and Woller, p. 55; Peter Th. Walther, 'Die deutschen Historiker in der Emigration und ihr Einfluss in der Nachkriegszeit', in Heinz Duchhardt and Gerhard May (eds.), *Geschichtswissenschaft um 1950*, Mainz 2002, pp. 45–47.

[20]See, for example, Theodor Eschenburg, *Letzten Endes meine ich doch. Erinnerungen 1933–1999*, Berlin 2002, pp. 200–201.

traditional reservations about democracy receded only gradually. The encounter with American liberal democracy thus clearly had a concrete, if limited, impact on Hans Rothfels.[21]

FROM 'COLLECTIVE DEMOCRACY' TO NEO-PLURALISM: ERNST FRAENKEL

Shattered by news about the persecution of Jews in Tsarist Russia, Ernst Fraenkel volunteered for military service in 1916. After the First World War, he studied law at the universities of Frankfurt and Heidelberg. He became a disciple of Hugo Sinzheimer, an expert in labour law, who impressed him deeply. After he had passed his doctoral thesis examination in 1923, Fraenkel worked as a teacher in institutions of adult education and as a lawyer, especially for trade unions. As a member of the Social Democratic Party, he criticised judicial double-standards favouring the right-wing opponents of the Weimar Republic. From 1933 to 1938, he defended Social Democrats and Communists against state prosecution. He also prepared his pathbreaking study of the internal structure of the Nazi state, which was to be published as *The Dual State* in the United States in 1942.

Finally driven into emigration in 1938, Fraenkel studied American case law at the University of Chicago from 1939 to 1941. From 1942 onwards, he wrote memoranda and comprehensive studies for the Foreign Economic Administration, the State Department and the Department of the Army, which needed information and advice regarding the prospective occupation of Germany. From 1945 to 1950, he worked as a legal adviser in the Department of Justice and in the Economic Cooperation Administration Mission to Korea. After a short period serving as a consultant to the American High Commission on Germany in 1951, Fraenkel accepted a position as lecturer at the *Deutsche Hochschule für Politik*, re-established in Berlin in 1949. Two years later, he took up a professorship at this prestigious institution, which became the Otto Suhr Institute of the Free University of Berlin in 1959. In the early 1960s, Fraenkel contributed in a major way to the same university's expansion of the Kennedy Institute for North American Studies.

Fraenkel conceived of political science as offering a broad framework for exploring both different perspectives on politics and various normative and empirical methods. In his view, a central purpose of this academic discipline in West Germany was to entrench respect for pluralism; it was thus meant ultimately to help stabilise the Federal Republic's new democracy. It is interesting that this

[21]Walter Bußmann and Günther Grünthal (eds.), *Siegfried A. Kaehler. Briefe 1900–1963*, Boppard 1993, p. 360. Also see Thomas Etzemüller, 'Kontinuität und Adaption eines Denkstils. Werner Conzes intellektueller Übertritt in die Nachkriegszeit', in Bernd Weisbrod (ed.), *Akademische Vergangenheitspolitik. Beiträge zur Wissenschaftskultur der Nachkriegszeit*, Göttingen 2002, pp. 127, 130; *idem*, *Sozialgeschichte*, pp. 238, 249–250, 252, 254; Klemens von Klemperer, 'Hans Rothfels, 1891–1976', in *Central European History*, vol. 9, no. 4 (1976), p. 383; Douglas A. Unfug, 'Hans Rothfels', in Lehmann and Van Horn Melton (eds.), pp. 153–154; Graml and Woller, pp. 60–61; Walther, 'Die deutschen Historiker in der Emigration', p. 47.

preoccupation with the West German situation did not impel Fraenkel to renounce his American citizenship.[22]

In the 1920s, Fraenkel had advocated the concept of a collective or "dialectical" democracy as a palliative to class conflict in the Weimar Republic. By integrating autonomous councils and corporations into the process of political decision-making, tensions in a society supposedly riddled with pernicious class conflicts were to be reduced. However, Fraenkel had little trust in political democracy which he tended to regard as formal and shaped by the interests of the ruling classes. It was only during his exile in the United States that he came to recognise and ultimately admire the capacity of liberal democracy to solve the pressing social, economic and political problems that had emerged in all industrialised nations after the Second World War. Roosevelt's New Deal, which fascinated Fraenkel as much as many other refugee scholars (such as Hans Rothfels and Hajo Holborn), had ameliorated living conditions for the working class, the poor and unemployed. Social conflicts, as Fraenkel saw things, could obviously be tamed by democracy and the welfare state.[23]

Just as importantly for Fraenkel, the doctrine of judicial self-restraint ruled out binding judicial decisions about politically controversial issues. This contrasted markedly with the Weimar Republic, which Fraenkel had severely criticised. As he experienced the transformation of the United States into what the Germans term a "social state", he became increasingly convinced that competitive market capitalism and political democracy were not mutually hostile but rather complemented and reinforced each other. Based on a broad but general political consensus, pluralist democracy in the United States clearly left room for competing interests, optimally to be represented in independent organisations. The common good would finally emerge as a compromise—the outcome of clashes, struggle and negotiations. This new paradigm of neo-pluralism, exerting a lasting impact on West German political science after 1945, was thus strongly influenced by Fraenkel's American experience, although in his thinking he clearly retained some elements of his earlier conception of collective democracy. In any event, a classless society, was no longer part of his political vision.[24]

[22]Falk Esche and Frank Grube (eds.), *Reformismus und Pluralismus. Materialien zu einer ungeschriebenen politischen Autobiographie*, Hamburg 1973, pp. 11–26; Gerhard Göhler and Hubertus Buchstein, 'Die ersten fünfzehn Jahre. Von der Deutschen Hochschule für Politik zum Otto-Suhr-Institut', in *Leviathan*, vol. 17 (1989), pp. 127–139; Gerhard Göhler, 'Die Wiederbegründung der Deutschen Hochschule für Politik. Traditionspflege oder wissenschaftlicher Neubeginn?', in *idem* and Bodo Zeuner (eds.), *Kontinuitäten und Brüche in der deutschen Politikwissenschaft*, Baden-Baden 1991, pp. 144–164; Ernst Fraenkel. *Gesammelte Schriften*, vol. 3, *Neuaufbau der Demokratie in Deutschland und Korea*, Baden-Baden 1999, pp. 10–19; Winfried Steffani, 'Ernst Fraenkel als Persönlichkeit', in *Zeitschrift für Politikwissenschaft*, vol. 7, no. 4 (1997), pp. 1261–1285; Wilhelm Bleek, *Geschichte der Politikwissenschaft in Deutschland*, Munich 2001, *passim*; Alfons Söllner, 'Die Gründung der westdeutschen Politikwissenschaft – ein Reimport aus der Emigration', in Krohn and von zur Mühlen (eds.), *Rückkehr*, pp. 254, 257, 270–271, 274.

[23]Schildt, pp. 29–30, 36; Lewis A. Coser, *Refugee Scholars in America. Their Impact and Their Experiences*, New Haven 1984, p. 281. On Holborn's support for the 'New Deal', see Otto Pflanze, 'The Americanization of Hajo Holborn', in Lehmann and Sheehan (eds.), p. 176.

[24]For a more detailed discussion, see Gerhard Göhler, 'Vom Sozialismus zum Pluralismus. Politiktheorie und Emigrationserfahrung bei Ernst Fraenkel', in *Politische Vierteljahresschrift*, vol. 27, no. 1 (1986), pp. 6–27. See Ernst Fraenkel, 'Strukturanalyse der moderne Demokratie', in Alexander von Brünneck (ed.), *Ernst Fraenkel. Deutschland und die westlichen Demokratien*, Frankfurt am Main 1991, pp. 326–359; Hubertus

Like Rothfels, Fraenkel became a mediator between the United States and West Germany in the 1950s. In his university teaching on the American political system and on comparative government, as well as in numerous lectures to a wider audience and many publications, he tried to abolish deeply-rooted stereotypes about American mass democracy, strong anxieties about a putatively unrestrained capitalism, and an ideological juxtaposition of Western "civilisation" and German "culture" that was proving to be almost ineradicable in the postwar period. Fraenkel also emphasised the historical roots of the political culture that had evolved in the United States, in order to counter traditional German notions about America as an "unhistorical" country. Corresponding to this basic stance, in the 1950s and early 1960s he both laboured to encourage and personally initiated close cooperation between West German and American scholars in a number of fields, in particular the various traditions of parliamentary rule as well as the institutions and values needed for a viable democracy. In Berlin his contacts with America extended to the Congress for Cultural Freedom, which had been founded in 1950 to combat communism and spread American-style consensus liberalism in Western Europe.[25]

But despite his passionate affirmation of American liberalism, Ernst Fraenkel himself rejected the idea of directly transplanting American political institutions and values to West Germany. On the contrary, his new pluralist definition of democracy encompassed respect for the *Gestalt* of each individual political culture and its underlying historical sources. Democratic values consequently needed time and patience to blossom in a society that had rejected notions of pluralist democracy in favour of authoritarian values and an adulation of state power. According to Fraenkel, even the British doctrine of "rule of law" and the American doctrine of "supremacy of law" were not fully compatible with German legal and judicial traditions. In his study of the pitfalls of the Rhineland Agreement, written in 1944 for the Carnegie Endowment for International Peace, Fraenkel argued that the military occupation of the Rhineland after the First World War had failed because it was not "based on a political philosophy that is reconcilable with the political tradition of the occupied country. In the Rhineland Agreement … American liberals, trained in Anglo-Saxon legal and political concepts, tried to transplant their own political philosophy to a government that was essentially different from their ideals and traditions". Fraenkel bluntly observed that "If the future occupation of Germany is not planned as a permanent one, the attempt must be made to give

Buchstein, 'Ernst Fraenkels Studien zu Politik und Kultur Amerikas', in *idem* and Gerhard Göhler (eds.), *Vom Sozialismus zum Pluralismus. Beiträge zu Werk und Leben Ernst Fraenkels*, Baden-Baden 2000, pp. 84–96; Esche and Grube (eds.), pp. 28–34; Bleek, pp. 298–299. On Fraenkel's criticism of the Weimar Republic, see Ernst Fraenkel, 'Cast Structure, Cast Spirit, Ghetto Parties and the Future of German Democracy' (1955), in Fraenkel, *Gesammelte Schriften*, vol. 3, pp. 615–624.

[25]See, in particular, Ernst Fraenkel, *Amerika im Spiegel des deutschen politischen Denkens. Äußerungen deutscher Staatsmänner und Staatsdenker über Staat und Gesellschaft in den Vereinigten Staaten von Amerika*, Cologne 1959, pp. 11–48, *idem*, 'Das Bild Amerikas im deutschen Bewußtsein', in Fraenkel, *Gesammelte Schriften*, vol. 4, Baden-Baden 2000, pp. 307–332; *idem*, 'Report on Lecturing Activities at the Hochschule für Politik [1953], *ibid.*, vol. 3, pp. 592–594. On Fraenkel's activities in the Congress for Cultural Freedom, see Michael Hochgeschwender, *Freiheit in der Offensive? Der Kongreß für kulturelle Freiheit und die Deutschen*, Munich 1998, p. 528.

autonomous forces inside Germany a chance to rebuild organizations of their own which may serve as cells for a reconstruction of democracy." But in his view, a political framework of individual rights and civil liberties was, nonetheless, an indispensable prerequisite for the revival of Germany's democratic traditions. Although not identical, the "Rule of Law" and the German *Rechtsstaat* were both "designed to protect the individual from arbitrary interferences by the executive branch of the government." Moreover, Fraenkel considered German labour law as constituting a strong heritage—one to be utilised as the foundation of a true democracy in postwar Germany.[26]

In general, Fraenkel envisaged the democratisation of West Germany as a long-term process to be fuelled by both German traditions and American support. German concepts of social intervention were to be combined with the path-breaking requirement of individual freedom so deeply engrained in American politics and society. As a specific type of government, "Western democracy" in Germany was seen as the outcome of political and cultural circumstances across the Atlantic. Fraenkel in any case stressed that

> Western democracy is not the invention of one nation; it is rather the result of give and take amongst various nations. Western democracy is a work of art which grew slowly in the course of many centuries. It is a strange mixture of ideas and institutions to the establishment of which … the main contribution has come from four Western nations: England, France, the United States and Germany.[27]

Rather than unequivocally proposing the American model, Fraenkel thus espoused a Western community of shared political values, with modern bureaucracy and the *Rechtsstaat* seen as the most important German ingredients. In harmony with this perspective, he believed he could observe not only a strong Americanisation of Europe but also a Europeanisation of the United States. Through mutual exchange, democracies in the Western hemisphere would ultimately draw closer to each other, if only to defend themselves against the threat from communist dictatorships, which Fraenkel saw as uncompromising foes of liberal democracies. To a certain extent, constant interchange would lead to a mutual rapprochement of democracies, but such democracies would by no means completely fuse, each political system retaining some of its characteristic features. Clearly, Fraenkel did not propose the American model as some sort of panacea. According to him, global political homogenisation was not on the horizon and not desirable.[28]

[26]Ernst Fraenkel, 'Military Occupation and the Rule of Law' (1944), in Fraenkel, *Gesammelte Schriften*, vol. 3, pp. 313, 317; Ernst Fraenkel, 'Civil Liberties in the USA and Germany' (1965), in *idem*, vol. 4, p. 922. See also the preface, *ibid.*, pp. 8–10; Göhler, 'Sozialismus', p. 22; Claus-Dieter Krohn, 'Emigranten und "Westernisierung" der deutschen Gesellschaft nach 1945. Einleitung', in *idem* and Martin Schumacher (eds.), *Exil und Neuordnung. Beiträge zur verfassungspolitischen Entwicklung in Deutschland nach 1945*, Düsseldorf 2000, p. 19; Gerhard Göhler and Dirk R. Schumann, 'Die Planungen Ernst Fraenkels zum Aufbau der Demokratie in Deutschland und Korea', in Buchstein and Göhler (eds.), *passim*; Fraenkel, *Gesammelte Werke*, vol. 3, *passim*; Esche and Grube (eds.), *passim*.

[27]Fraenkel, 'Civil Liberties', p. 923. Also see Krohn, 'Emigranten', p. 17.

[28]Ernst Fraenkel, 'Deutschland und die westlichen Demokratien', in von Brünneck (ed.), pp. 48–67; *idem*, 'Bild', pp. 312, 317, 320; *idem*, 'Civil Liberties', p. 924; *idem*, *Gesammelte Schriften*, vol. 4, pp. 36, 39, 42; *idem*, 'Das amerikanische Regierungssystem', *ibid.*, p. 448; Hochgeschwender, p. 34.

As a German Jew who had emigrated to the United States, Fraenkel was ideally suited to act as a mediator between the Old and the New Worlds after the Second World War. He did concede retrospectively that by 1940, he had largely shed his identity as a German émigré and adjusted to life in the United States. Shocked by the news about Auschwitz and the extermination of European Jewry, he deliberately cut all his ties to Germany in 1946. Only his strong friendship with the political scientist (and later mayor of West Berlin) Otto Suhr convinced him to return to his native country in 1951.[29]

BETWEEN GERMANY AND THE UNITED STATES: HANS ROSENBERG AS A SOJOURNER

Hans Rosenberg was born in Hanover in 1904. His father, who died only fourteen years later, was a Jewish merchant. His mother was a member of the Protestant Church and Rosenberg was christened. Following his school years in Hanover, Rosenberg read history and philosophy at the University of Cologne, before being drawn to the University of Berlin in 1922 by the historian Friedrich Meinecke; supervised by Meinecke, Rosenberg's doctoral thesis was on the liberal politician and publicist Rudolf Haym. Following a stay at the University of Freiburg in 1925, Rosenberg increasingly rejected the historicist traditions strongly entrenched in that and other German academic institutions. Instead, he became an early advocate of combining social history with the history of ideas—an approach still revealing Meinecke's influence.

Rosenberg's plea for historical analysis instead of description and his search for typologies in place of instances of individual motivation led him to a comprehensive study of Germany's economic crisis of 1857–1859, its social repercussions and its impact on German politics. As the theoretical and methodological approach espoused by Rosenberg was largely rejected by conservative historians, his *Habilitation*-defence in December 1932 at the University of Cologne was accepted only after strong resistance had been overcome. The young Jewish scholar found himself condemned for his unequivocal defence of the Weimar Republic against its right-wing opponents, and this condemnation had unmistakable antisemitic overtones. He consequently left for Britain even before he was deprived of his right to lecture in September 1933.[30]

During his exile in London, Rosenberg finished his work on an edition of liberal publications disseminated in Germany between 1858 and 1866. With his funds running out, he moved to the United States in September 1935. After securing a

[29]See Fraenkel's letter to Otto Suhr, 23 March 1946, *ibid*,.vol. 3, pp. 389–391.

[30]Gerhard A. Ritter, 'Hans Rosenberg 1904–1988', in *Geschichte und Gesellschaft*, vol. 15, no. 2 (1989), pp. 283–289; *idem*, 'Vorwort', in *idem* (ed.), *Entstehung und Wandel der modernen Gesellschaft. Festschrift für Hans Rosenberg*, Berlin 1970, pp. V-VI; Heinrich August Winkler, 'Ein Erneuerer der Geschichtswissenschaft. Hans Rosenberg 1904–1988', in *Historische Zeitschrift* 248 (1989), pp. 529–539; Hans-Ulrich Wehler, 'Vorwort', in *idem* (ed.), *Sozialgeschichte Heute. Festschrift für Hans Rosenberg*, Göttingen 1974, pp. 9–12; Frank Golczewski, *Kölner Universitätslehrer und der Nationalsozialismus. Personengeschichtliche Ansätze*, Cologne 1988, pp. 421–425; Otto Dann, 'Hans Rosenberg und die Universität zu Köln. Ein Nachruf', in *Kölner Universitäts-Journal*, vol. 18, no. 4 (1988), pp. 13–14.

position at Illinois College in Jacksonville in the autumn of 1936, Rosenberg taught at Brooklyn College between 1938 and 1958. He became an American citizen in 1944.[31] In 1946, he was invited to return to the University of Cologne. The following year, the university offered him a professorship. Although Theodor Schieder was the first appointee on the shortlist, an education officer for the British occupation authorities promised Rosenberg "a warm welcome, whether you come for a semester or as a definite return".[32] But due to fears of lingering antisemitism, reservations about the living conditions in destroyed Cologne and general objections on the part of his wife, Rosenberg declined the invitation in November 1947. Instead, he went to Berlin as a guest professor at the Free University in 1949–1950. The professorship in Cologne finally went to Theodor Schieder who became one of the most influential figures of the emerging West German historiography after the war.[33]

Although Rosenberg was not, in fact, a direct precursor of the influential Bielefeld School of postwar West German social historians, promising young academics like Otto Büsch, Helga Grebing and Gerhard A. Ritter were among his students in Berlin. His tenure at the University of Marburg in 1955 made less of an impact —a contrast perhaps reflected in the University of Freiburg's conservative historian Gerhard Ritter's success a few years later in preventing the publication of a German translation of Rosenberg's major book *Bureaucracy, Aristocracy and Autocracy. The Prussian Experience 1660–1915* (1958).[34] Nevertheless, after Rosenberg was appointed Shepard Professor of History at the University of California in 1959, his influence on West German historiography gradually increased. In the 1960s, his work on the relationship between German economic decline in the 1870s, the crisis of liberalism, the persistence of pre-industrial values and the predominance of the traditional élites inspired younger historians such as Hans-Ulrich Wehler to turn to social history in order to identify the roots of Germany's "special path". Rosenberg's studies, particularly his *Große Depression und Bismarckzeit* (1967), also encouraged an assimilation into history of theories and methods used in sociology and political science. Introducing West German historians to theories of social change being developed in America, Rosenberg was now established in his role as a historiographical innovator making frequent academic visits to the Federal Republic. Still, he only returned there permanently in 1977.[35]

[31] Coser, *Refugee Scholars*, p. 291.

[32] Golczewski, p. 431.

[33] On Schieder, see Rüdiger Hohls and Konrad H. Jarausch (eds.), *Versäumte Fragen. Deutsche Historiker im Schatten des Nationalsozialismus*, Stuttgart 2000, pp. 469–470; Etzemüller, *Sozialgeschichte*, pp. 234–236. See also Hans-Ulrich Wehler, 'In den Fußtapfen der kämpfenden Wissenschaft', in *Frankfurter Allgemeine Zeitung*, no. 2, 4 January 1999, p. 48.

[34] Winkler, 'Erneuerer', p. 544; Wehler, 'Vorwort', p. 17.

[35] Jürgen Kocka, *Sozialgeschichte in Deutschland seit 1945. Aufstieg–Krise–Perspektiven. Vortrag auf der Festveranstaltung zum 40-jährigen Bestehen des Instituts für Sozialgeschichte am 25. Oktober 2002 in Braunschweig*, Bonn 2002, pp. 13, 15. See also Coser, pp. 290–291; Walther, 'Die deutschen Historiker in der Emigration', p. 38; *idem*, 'Emigrierte deutsche Historiker in den USA', pp. 43, 47, 49; *idem*, Emigrierte deutsche Historiker in den Vereinigten Staaten', p. 49; Schulze, 'Geschichtswissenschaft', pp. 137–141; *idem*, 'Refugee Historians', pp. 215–217; Ritter, 'Rosenberg', pp. 289–302; *idem*, 'Vorwort', pp. VII-IX; Wehler, 'Vorwort', pp. 12–20; Winkler, 'Erneuerer', pp. 539–553; Dann, pp. 14–15; Ritter, 'Rosenberg', pp. 290–302. On Rosenberg as a mediator of American theories of social change, see Willi Oberkrome, *Volksgeschichte. Methodische Innovation und völkische Ideologisierung in der deutschen Geschichtswissenschaft 1918–1945*, Göttingen 1945, p. 228.

Looking back, Hans Rosenberg himself pointed out that the collapse of the Weimar Republic and the rise of Nazism had been crucial for the development of his political views and scholarship. However, the exhilarating experience of life and work in the United States was as important for his historical writings as the demise of the first German democracy. Although he did not voice any resentment regarding the Germans and later regretted not returning to Cologne in 1947–1948, Rosenberg clearly remained more detached from his country of birth than did Rothfels or Fraenkel. Against the traumatic backdrop of the Nazi seizure of power and his flight from the Third Reich, Rosenberg continued to harbour strong reservations about political developments in postwar West Germany.

And yet, Rosenberg never severed his strong emotional and intellectual ties to Germany—ties evident in his steady efforts to reconcile American and West German historiography. He also was interested in mediating the differences between the two democracies' political systems, which were in fact growing increasingly similar. In this respect, it is important to note that Rosenberg was also careful to stress, like Rothfels and Fraenkel, the different political traditions separating the two states. In particular, he insisted, the ambivalent legacy of Germany's authoritarian and paternalist social policies could not be neglected. More crucially, even Rosenberg's early research had made him aware of the unfulfilled promises of the 1848–1849 Revolution and German liberalism, promises crushed by monarchic and authoritarian rule.

As a lifelong liberal, Rosenberg thus pressed in the 1950s and 1960s for a thorough democratisation of Germany. Although he opposed the left-wing radicalism of the Federal Republic's student protest-movement emerging in the late sixties, he strongly sympathised with students' demands to shed authoritarian values and abolish outdated institutions. In contrast to Rothfels, Rosenberg pleaded for a democracy rooted in West German society rather than one guaranteed by the state. He also called for an open debate on the causes of the Nazi dictatorship, not only in order to purify society from the legacy of authoritarianism, militarism and expansionism, but also as the prerequisite for a viable German democracy. His unwavering support for liberal and democratic values ultimately informed his plea for a new historiography centred on the social and economic foundations of politics. Hans Rosenberg was also committed to exposing the forces behind Germany's anomalous development since the nineteenth century. In his view, political liberalism and a commitment to pluralist democracy were inseparable elements of a well-founded theoretical and methodological revisionism.[36]

GERMAN-JEWISH REMIGRÉS AND PLURALIST DEMOCRACY

Although their political views and intellectual orientations differed widely, the historian Hans Rothfels and the political scientist Ernst Fraenkel revealed a similar

[36]Hans Rosenberg, 'Rückblick auf ein Historikerleben zwischen zwei Kulturen', in *idem* (ed.), *Machteliten und Wirtschaftskonjunkturen. Studien zur neueren deutschen Sozial- und Wirtschaftsgeschichte*, Göttingen 1978, pp. 12, 18, 21–22; Wehler, 'Vorwort', p. 9; Walther, 'Emigrierte deutsche Historiker in den Vereinigten Staaten', pp. 47–48.

response to the experience of American democracy. Both remigré intellectuals selectively appropriated aspects of that democracy according to their own political convictions. In this manner they acquired specific values that, however, were compatible with their own German intellectual and cultural traditions.

For Rothfels, the idea of law to be enacted by the state proved an intellectual bridge between his German origins and the experience of pluralist democracy. Fraenkel clung to his esteem for independent intermediary organisations as an integral and indispensable element of politics. After their return to Germany, both intellectuals took pains to emphasise their rootedness in the traditional German political culture; and this capacity to acknowledge the particular context of their country of birth was the source of their credibility and of their effectiveness as mediators of American political culture. Precisely because they did *not* universalise the American model, Rothfels and Fraenkel could effectively bridge the gulf between it and the German context.

While Rothfels retained his élitist conception of democracy as a framework of legal regulations and political norms, Fraenkel came nearer to recognising pluralist democracy as a permanent process of negotiation between a multitude of social and political interest groups. Fraenkel, in contrast to Rothfels, did not regard the state as a supposedly all-embracing institutional framework separate from society. But he stuck to the concept of the common good, a notion deeply engrained in German socialist ideology. Rothfels, in his turn, still defended the entrenched ideal of the autonomous state. Despite their considerable differences as regards political ideas and convictions, holistic conceptions of democracy thus proved resilient in the minds of both German intellectuals, along with many others.[37]

Yet, as has been emphasised neither Fraenkel nor Rothfels was immune to American influences. Fraenkel, in particular, was strongly impressed by what he saw as a lively community-based democracy founded on a normative consensus about civil society. As he saw things, its essential ingredients were the recognition of a plurality of interests and views, tolerance, citizens' rights, as well as broad political participation. Rothfels, during his years in the United States, also came to cherish political freedom as a prerequisite of democracy. As eminent postwar German scholars, they both merged American models with German traditions, disseminating new, hybrid democratic variants in a country shattered by defeat, destruction and mass expulsion.[38]

[37]Hartmut Lehmann, '"Land of Divisions – Land of Culture": Anmerkungen zum amerikanischen Europabild', in Michael Salewski (ed.), *Nationale Identität und Europäische Einigung*, Göttingen 1991, p. 240; Michael Hochgeschwender, 'Remigranten im Umfeld der Zeitschrift *Der Monat* und des *Congress for Cultural Freedom* (CCF)', in Claus-Dieter Krohn and Axel Schildt (eds.), *Zwischen den Stühlen? Remigranten und Remigration in der deutschen Medienöffentlichkeit der Nachkriegszeit*, Hamburg 2002, p. 195. On the persistence of Rothfels' rootedness in German politics and culture, see Roth, '"Richtung halten"', p. 64.

[38]See, in general, Anselm Doering-Manteuffel, 'Westernisierung. Politisch-ideeller und gesellschaftlicher Wandel in der Bundesrepublik bis zum Ende der 60er Jahre', in Axel Schildt, Detlef Siegfried and Karl Christian Lammers (eds.), *Dynamische Zeiten. Die 60er Jahre in beiden deutschen Gesellschaften*, Hamburg 2000, *passim*; *idem*, 'Eine politische Nationalgeschichte für die Berliner Republik. Überlegungen zu Heinrich-August Winklers "Der lange Weg nach Westen"', in *Geschichte und Gesellschaft*, vol. 27, no. 3 (2001), p. 449.

In contrast to Rothfels and Fraenkel, Hans Rosenberg did not set about devising a postwar German democracy. Having no wish to promptly return to his native country, he offered no concrete steps for stabilising West German democracy. Although evidence in this respect is hard to come by, it appears that Rosenberg had a stronger sense of Jewish identity than either Rothfels or Fraenkel. But all told, such an identity was superseded by his self-perception as an American and a German. In this way, Rosenberg himself persistently stressed his role as a mediator between the New World and the Old. He remained a kind of sojourner, maintaining multiple identities—thus displaying, more than Fraenkel and Rothfels, the Jewish émigré's propensity to mediate across borders between nations and cultures.[39]

* * *

Such mediation was an ideal vehicle for what, in Germany's postwar context, may be considered a necessary process of subversive democratisation. The nature of this process underscores the inadequacy of such concepts as Americanisation and globalisation. Americanisation could not, in fact, be imposed on postwar Germany. The initial programmes of reeducation and reorientation were certainly a result of strong American pressure. In the transitory years immediately after the founding of the Federal Republic, democracy was imposed from above. But in the course of the 1950s, authentic democratic-pluralist political values emerged through a more subtle process of accommodation and adaptation. By studying the postwar careers of key German-Jewish remigrés, we can thus observe that, in the face of American pre-eminence, the "Americanisation" of Germany in fact involved a complex, if asymmetrical interaction.

Compared with the concept of Americanisation, that of Westernisation seems to leave more room for investigating the intricate processes of interchange themselves. However, in this author's view it remains too homogeneous and teleological a concept, one not, in the end, adequately accounting for the intermingling of different political and cultural traditions. As the cases of Rothfels and Fraenkel show, "different Germans learned different lessons from the 'West'".[40] To a considerable extent, such different images and perceptions of America on the part of the émigrés were due to their different experiences of Nazism. At one extreme and in some rare cases, even personal attraction to Nazi rulers and sympathy with their policies could be present; later, there was always the experience of exclusion and threatened persecution by the Third Reich. While the required shift in perceptions was seldom so drastic, a wide range of lived experience profoundly shaped perceptions of the United States.

[39]Martin Kirsch, 'Wissenschaftler im Ausland zwischen 1930 und 1960 – Transferbedingungen und Identitätswandel einer erzwungenen Migration', in Hartmut Kaelble, Martin Kirsch and Alexander Schmidt-Gernig (eds.), *Transnationale Öffentlichkeiten und Identitäten im 20. Jahrhundert*, Frankfurt am Main 2002, pp. 195, 201; Paul Nolte, 'Historische Sozialwissenschaft', Joachim Eibach and Günther Lottes (eds.), *Kompass der Geschichtswissenschaft*, Göttingen 2002, p. 58. On the role of sojourners in general, see Axel Schildt, *Zwischen Abendland und Amerika. Studien zur westdeutschen Ideenlandschaft der 50er Jahre*, Munich 1999, p. 177. On the 'political scholar', see Krohn, 'Einleitung', p. 20.

[40]Nolan, p. 5. Also see Philipp Gassert, 'Die Bundesrepublik, Europa und der Westen. Zu Verwestlichung, Demokratisierung und einigen komparatistischen Defiziten der zeithistorischen Forschung', in Jörg Baberowski *et al.*, *Geschichte ist immer Gegenwart. Vier Thesen zur Zeitgeschichte*, Munich 2001, pp. 68, 71.

Finally, the concept of globalisation suggests an even, all-encompassing dissemination of basically identical goods, institutions and values. *Variants* of democracy here thus become lost as much as was the case with the concepts of Americanisation and Westernisation. As the transfer of American notions of democracy to postwar Germany shows, the actual process at work here involves a steadily subtle and—as indicated—subversive mutual exchange. In this process, the experience of exile in the United States was an important source of inspiration. As cultural transmitters, remigré academics like Hans Rothfels and Ernst Fraenkel as well as sojourners like Hans Rosenberg were thus as invaluable as were refugee journalists like Hans Habe and Stefan Heym. In the end, however, they remained rooted in their national traditions. These refugee intellectuals became influential transatlantic mediators, but not members of a fully-fledged global élite.[41]

[41]Alfons Söllner, 'Normative Verwestlichung. Der Einfluß der Remigranten auf die politische Kultur der frühen Bundesrepublik', in Heinz Bude and Bernd Greiner (eds.), *Westbindungen. Amerika in der Bundesrepublik*, Hamburg 1999, p. 92. On journalists, see Jessica Gienow-Hecht, *Transmission Impossible. American Journalism as Cultural Diplomacy in Postwar Germany 1945–1955*, Baton Rouge, LA 1999, esp. pp. 30–53, 149–187; *idem*, 'Zuckerbrot und Peitsche. Remigranten in der Medienpolitik der USA und der US-Zone', in Krohn and Schildt (eds.), pp. 48–49; Krohn, 'Emigranten', p. 27. On Habe and Heym, see Robert C. Jespersen, 'Hans Habe', in John M. Spalek and Joseph Strelka (eds.), *Deutschsprachige Exilliteratur seit 1933,* vol. 1, Berne 1976, pp. 393–413;. 'Stefan Heym', *ibid.,* vol. 2, Berne 1989, pp. 358–372. The need to analyse "Europe" as discourse and social practice is emphasised by Heinz Gerhard Haupt, 'Auf der Suche nach der europäischen Geschichte: einige Neuerscheinungen', in *Archiv für Sozialgeschichte* 42 (2002).

Returning from Forced Exile: Some Observations on Theodor W. Adorno's and Hannah Arendt's Experience of Postwar Germany and Their Political Theories of Totalitarianism

BY LARS RENSMANN

In recent years, the German-Jewish theorists Theodor W. Adorno and Hannah Arendt have often been described as two of the most important social philosophers and political theorists of the twentieth century. While the former figure had gained such a status by the 1960s, which is to say already during his lifetime, it took until the 1980s and 1990s for Arendt's multi-faceted work to receive a truly broad reception. By then it had gained its place in the canon of modern political thought, in many ways surpassing Adorno's (declining) influence on American and European social and political philosophy. However, despite many biographical, intellectual and theoretical affinities, the work of Arendt and Adorno was subject to different, even mutually hostile cultures of reception. These reproduced—and certainly in part emerged from—the mutual aversion the two eminent intellectuals cultivated during their lifetime.[1] A posthumous dialogue has only recently begun.[2]

In spite of the intellectual and personal tensions between them, both Adorno and Arendt have also frequently been labelled "witnesses of a century", and for good reasons. Starting in the 1940s, each figure self-consciously acquired the position of a "public intellectual", in the full Gramscian sense: that of an active theoretician repeatedly taking sides in contemporary public and political debates. Each thus became an outstanding international commentator on a century in turmoil—a century shadowed by unprecedented social, cultural and political transformations, new and hideous forms of warfare and, indeed, human catastrophes on an unimaginable scale.

[1]The lack of mutual respect between Arendt and Adorno is documented in their limited correspondence of 1967; see Library of Congress, Manuscript division, Folder Arendt; for copies see Hannah Arendt Archive Oldenburg, General Correspondence, Theodor W. Adorno, 1967,7.1; at one point Arendt described Adorno as "a half-Jew and one of the most disgusting people that I know" and as a "string-puller" in public campaigns against Martin Heidegger; for these and other such comments on Adorno see Hannah Arendt and Karl Jaspers, *Briefwechsel 1926–1969,* Munich 1993, pp. 670, 679 and 673 (Arendt to Jaspers, 18 April 1966, 29 April 1966, 4 July 1966).

[2]The dialogue was initiated with a conference at the University of Oldenburg in 2000 ('Witnesses of a Century'); see most recently the approach put forward in Dirk Auer, Lars Rensmann and Julia Schulze Wessel (eds.), *Arendt und Adorno,* Frankfurt am Main 2003.

Theodor W. Adorno

By courtesy of the Leo Baeck Institute, New York. © Gisela Dischner

Hannah Arendt *c.* 1936

For both thinkers, the experience of forced emigration from Germany to America in a quest for refuge from Nazi persecution was crucial.[3] But, foremost, it was the catastrophe of the death camps, or rather its retrospective contemplation, that influenced most of their further thought. The Holocaust, both argued, had forced a readjustment of all philosophical and historical thinking in the West. As Arendt put it, the death camps had exploded "the continuum of our history and the terms and categories of our political thinking."[4] In this light, Nazism and modern totalitarianism soon occupied the centre of Arendt's and Adorno's theoretical endeavours and intellectual interventions. For obvious reasons, with both Adorno and Arendt deeply marked by Germany's and European Jewry's fate, the European and especially the "German problem"—coming to terms with and thinking about the road of European and German history, political culture and the continent's and Germany's future—also became an important focus of their political commentary. This article will discuss some of the reflections offered by the two émigrés in response

[3]On the "intellectual migration" of Arendt and Adorno see Anthony Heilbut's instructive *Exiled in Paradise: German Refugee Artists and Intellectuals in America from the 1930s to the Present*, Cambridge, MA 1993, pp. 160–174 (Adorno) and pp. 395–437 (Arendt).

[4]Hannah Arendt, *Elemente und Ursprünge totaler Herrschaft*, Munich 1986, p. 705. It is striking that find this passage only appears in the German edition.

to their experiences in the Germany of the late 1940s and early 1950s. The article will also consider the intellectual processing of these experiences by both intellectuals in the last decades of their careers. I will suggest that their experiences in postwar Germany induced some limited questioning of their own modernist paradigms and interpretations of the Holocaust, in particular with regard to the role of democratic and anti-democratic mentalities and traditions—but that they also point to shared tensions within their approaches to both the twentieth century's catastrophes and to ambivalences in relation to their own German cultural and intellectual heritage.

I

The analytical perspectives that Arendt and Adorno developed in their wartime American exile largely placed the Nazi dictatorship in the context of modernity. Although Arendt's political and Adorno's social theory offer quite different approaches to a critique of modernity, they also display a great deal of common ground; both theories can be viewed as representative of a critical European humanism of their time. In general, their modernist approach focused on the distinctly modern dynamics enabling totalitarian rule, Arendt and Adorno thus emerging as advocates of a "universalising" approach to Nazism and the Holocaust. Their primary focus is on the historical rise of unprecedented modes of modern capitalism, bureaucracy and imperialism. Their approaches are linked to the "modern" experience of permanent change, upheaval and catastrophic loss: an experience shared with many fellow intellectual émigrés. For all of them, the Nazi revolution was of interest less as a specific political-cultural process than as an expression of the abyss of the modern condition.

In turn, this view is marked by a consciousness of radical insecurity, with both Arendt and Adorno conceptually addressing the rapid political, cultural and social changes unfolding in the first half of the twentieth century. The phenomena and events they addressed ranged from increasingly rapid industrialisation, and the concomitant evolution of a mass society and mass culture, to the October Revolution, two world wars, and the establishment of three entirely different political orders in Germany alone: a chaotic historical dynamic transcending all previous societal limits and appearing to culminate with the Nazi state and its annihilatory project. In light of such a development, for Arendt and Adorno along with many other European intellectuals, nothing seemed predictable any more, apart from permanent discontinuity and insecurity.

From such a perspective, "modernity" came to represent new excessive constraints, permanent transformation, and the very unpredictability of the social world. With the traditional social order now dissolved, for Arendt as for Adorno, into an aggregate of reified and atomised masses, individuals, formerly agents of social action and rational reflection, were now threatened with absolute powerlessness in the face of overwhelming social processes—at its extreme, with absorption into a machinery following the principles of division of labour and instrumental logic. Totalitarianism and the "loss of the world" (Arendt) could only take hold under these distinctly modern conditions. This is the context for Arendt's famous (or, depending on one's perspective, notorious) understanding of Eichmann—and with him of the typical Nazi perpetrator—as a petty-bourgeois administrator driven by little or nothing other than a sense of blind bureaucratic purpose and petty career ambitions. It is also the context for Adorno's typological definition of the bureaucratic "manipulative character" as *the* ideal-typological Nazi organiser of genocide and, simultaneously, as the ideal type of modern subjectivity.[5]

To be sure, Arendt's idea of totalitarianism and her interpretation of the eclipse of reason followed an independent historical-genealogical path—albeit one strongly indebted to Kant and Heidegger. Arendt saw the "iron band of terror", "ice cold reasoning" and the suprahuman "logic" of "nature" (Nazism) and "history" (Stalinism),[6] as modern, totalitarian substitutes for expressions of human solidarity, interaction, and reasoning traditionally manifest in both public and private spheres. Totalitarian logic, then, was unique and unprecedented; but it was also preconditioned by modernity—a kind of "radicalization of the same loneliness it seems to have produced."[7] This loneliness—in its most modern, radical form, the experience of a vanished private and public life, indeed of not belonging to the world at all—was "the common ground for terror … closely connected with [the] uprootedness and superfluousness which have been the curse of modern masses since … the breakdown of political institutions and social traditions in our time".[8]

Adorno also pointed to a structural atomisation of the individual as a precondition for Nazism. His own emphasis was on a *loss* of individuality and individual experience, rather than on a *critique* of individualisation or privatisation (as argued by Arendt)—an emphasis deriving from a socio-economic rather than Arendt's political perspective. However, according to Adorno and similar to Arendt's general interpretation, totalitarianism is viewed as the most radical expression of the transformation of individuals into powerless masses lacking consciousness and conscience, eager to get involved in a totalitarian "dynamism". In 1946, he observed that:

> Totalitarianism means knowing no limits, not allowing for any breathing spell, conquest with absolute domination, complete extermination of the chosen foe. With regard to this meaning of fascist "dynamism", any clear-cut program would function as a limitation, a kind of guarantee even to the adversary. It is essential to totalitarian rule that nothing shall be guaranteed, no limit is set to ruthless arbitrariness.[9]

Despite the somewhat different vantage point, this analytic definition has strong similarities with Arendt's view of the inherent dynamic and drive of totalitarian movements, implicitly sharing her emphasis on the secondary role played within them by specific ideologies.

[5]See Hannah Arendt, *Eichmann in Jerusalem: A Report on the Banality of Evil,* New York 1965, pp. 21–55 and pp. 234–279; Theodor W. Adorno, Else Frenkel-Brunswik, Daniel J. Levinson, R. Nevitt Sanford, *The Authoritarian Personality,* New York 1982, pp. 355ff.

[6]Hannah Arendt, *Origins of Totalitarianism*, San Diego, CA 1966, pp. 465ff.

[7]*ibid.*, p. 474.

[8]*ibid.*, p. 475.

[9]Theodor W. Adorno, 'Anti-Semitism and Fascist Propaganda', in *idem*, *Gesammelte Schriften*, vol. 8, Frankfurt am Main 1977, pp. 397–407, here p. 400.

It is important to note that although the strong influence of Kant's three critiques marks another similarity of Adorno's mature perspective with that of Arendt,[10] Adorno was strongly influenced by the European heritage of Hegelian-Marxist dialectical materialism that Arendt categorically rejected. Nevertheless, the view of totalitarianism held by both these German-Jewish intellectuals is unmistakably stamped by Max Weber's theory of bureaucratic rationalisation—more specifically, Weber's well-known notion of an "iron cage" emerging from modern labour-oriented modes of action, administrative evolution and radical rationalisation. It is as if, in the Holocaust's wake, both Adorno and Arendt put aside Weber's emphasis on the *necessarily ambivalent* nature of this cage, its function as a metaphor of the burden always accompanying the positive aspects of democratic individualism and the modern sceptical spirit, reading it instead as a metaphoric encapsulation of a totally reified objective world. In contrast to this Weberian vision, and in spite of their belief in modernity's post-metaphysical emancipative potential, for both Arendt and Adorno, the modern condition itself, its paradigms and culture have led to an alienation between individuals nothing short of "barbarian".[11] For Adorno, the principles of modern society, organised around abstract exchange value, have fostered a subjectivity oriented at control and domination, in the process robbing the subject of essential cognitive and moral qualities. In the end, this leads to in what he terms a "subjectivity without subjectivity" within a "*totally* rationalized and socialized society", the universal condition of late capitalism, with "blinded men robbed of their subjectivity … set loose as subjects".[12]

Reflecting their shared rejection of any explanations for the Holocaust attempting to take account of particular historical conditions and dynamics within Germany, both Arendt and Adorno, emerging from exile, initially strongly defended German culture in public statements and private letters. Even later, albeit in the context of a critique of conventional research on national cultures, Adorno would lay emphasis together with Max Horkheimer on the absence of any "German problem", and of any uniquely German political-cultural issues, furnishing an explanation for either Nazi-totalitarian antisemitism or the Holocaust. In the straightforward words of Adorno and Horkheimer, "totalitarian anti-Semitism is not a specifically German phenomenon. Attempts to deduce it from a questionable entity such as 'national character'…downplay the inexplicable that needs to be understood. The problem needs a social explanation, and this is impossible in the sphere of national particularities".[13] Immediately after the Second World War, Arendt used similar if not identical language: "The real problem is not the German national character but rather the disintegration of that character, or at least the fact that this character does not play any role in German politics any more. It is as much a part of the past as German militarism and nationalism."[14]

[10]Stefan Müller-Doohm, *Adorno*, Frankfurt am Main 2003, pp. 493ff, also points out the general lack of attention to this Kantian dimension of Adorno's thinking.

[11]Max Horkheimer and Theodor W. Adorno, *Dialectic of Enlightenment*, New York 1994, p. 161.

[12]*ibid.*, p. 171 (emphasis added by L.R.).

[13]Theodor W. Adorno and Max Horkheimer, 'Vorwort zu Paul W. Massings *Vorgeschichte des politischen Antisemitismus*', in Max Horkheimer, *Gesammelte Schriften*, vol. 8, Frankfurt am Main 1985, p. 128.

[14]Hannah Arendt, 'Das "deutsche Problem": Die Restauration des alten Europa', in *idem*, *Zur Zeit: Politische Essays*, Berlin 1986, p. 31ff.

In this respect, it is noteworthy that in preparing the second volume of *Origins of Totalitarianism*, completed at the end of 1947,[15] Arendt had in fact already discussed the very specific role played by the weakness and collapse of the Weimar Republic's party system, with its peculiar coalition between the mob and the élite, in the triumph of Nazism; she had also analysed specific forms of *völkisch*-romantic imperialism centred in Germany and Russia—compensation for a lack of national unity and lost colonies—that contributed to the emergence of totalitarian dictatorship. And in 1945, she was one of the first social-political theorists to suggest that "the belated development of the Germans to become a nation" and their lack of "any sort of democratic experience" were important aspects of the Nazi rise to power.[16] This particular dimension, however, largely disappeared in Arendt's generalised theory of modern totalitarianism, as developed in volume three of the *Origins*, completed in 1950, with its strongly universal focus. This is even more the case for the work's final chapter, 'Ideology and Terror', which Arendt wrote in 1958 for its second edition. In the framework of the Cold War, a rather conventional view of totalitarianism resonates here, conceptualising and focusing on parallels between Stalinism and Nazism as mere examples of "closed" modern societies.[17] A similarly universal and generalising approach is evident in Adorno's most eloquent and sophisticated philosophical text, the *Negative Dialectics* of 1966. Here the Holocaust emerges as a "master moral paradigm",[18] one leading to a radical adaptation and postwar revision of the Kantian imperative: "In the state of their unfreedom, Hitler has superimposed a new categorical imperative on humans: to adjust their thinking and action in a way that Auschwitz will not be repeated, that nothing similar will happen."[19] Taking Auschwitz as a new, unprecedented starting point of historical perception and action, this formula is not only tied to revised Kantian cosmopolitan-universalistic premises but also embedded in the concept of a general human *Verfallsgeschichte*—an approach to modern history as a negative process reaching its negative climax with the Holocaust. Despite his relentless insistence on historical contingency and possibility and his explicit challenge to Hegel's notion of a universal history,[20] Adorno's theoretical foundations, as echoed in his *Negative Dialectics,* themselves represent a universal Hegelian historical outlook, conceptualising a general historical movement in which the Holocaust is presumably rooted.

In retrospect, it is quite clear that the approach to the Holocaust generally presented by both Arendt and Adorno reveals many of the limitations of perspective inherent in any radically generalising stance. If modern social conditions in general constitute the Holocaust's main source—more specifically, universal socioeconomic conditions (Adorno); modern paradigms of action that have destroyed the *res publica* and "being in the world" (Arendt)—then all questions of democratic and legal

[15]See Elisabeth Young-Bruehl, *Hannah Arendt: Leben, Werk und Zeit,* Frankfurt am Main 2004, p.290.
[16]*ibid.*, p. 28.
[17]See Hauke Brunkhorst, *Hannah Arendt,* Munich 1999, p. 53.
[18]On a parallel development within the American public sphere, see Jeffrey Shandler, *While America Watches: Televising the Holocaust*, Oxford 1999.
[19]Theodor W. Adorno, *Negative Dialektik*, Frankfurt am Main 1966, p. 358.
[20]*ibid.*, p. 313.

theory, the role of political culture and (anti)democratic tradition, human action and responsibility, and in this case specific German culpability, are in effect left by the wayside. It is equally evident that maintaining such a position made it far easier for Arendt and Adorno to return to Germany in the early postwar period without any strong reservations. I will now argue that although neither Arendt nor Adorno would ever abandon their basically universalistic intellectual-ethical values, the experience of this return did lead to a shift, albeit one that was limited, contradictory and fragmented, in their analysis of totalitarianism in general—and of the historical, political and cultural dynamics of the Nazi "final solution" in particular.

II

Although Arendt clearly remained attached to Germany and Europe and was concerned about the fate of both, she found her new home in America and never really intended to move back; for his part, Adorno had "never given up the hope of return" during his exile years.[21] He would later on explain that he returned because "he belonged to Europe and to Germany" and "simply wanted to return to the place of his childhood".[22] In addition, he had the feeling that in Germany he "could do some good things to help prevent a repetition of disaster".[23] He also believed that Germany would re-emerge as the place where dialectical philosophy could best be practised; he looked forward to teaching German students committed to this philosophy and initially encountered a "passionate participation regarding these questions and matters, a participation that has to make a teacher happy".[24] While Arendt herself made the decision to return to Europe, she would return only for visits: initially for a longer period—her first return to Europe after the war extended from August 1949 to March 1950—then for almost regular, sometimes substantial visits that went on for the rest of her life, albeit with no consideration of staying. In fact, during her first longer stay in postwar Germany, Arendt felt homesick for America. This visit was commissioned by Jewish Cultural Reconstruction, a newly-founded agency with a centre in Wiesbaden.[25] Working at the agency, Arendt also travelled across Germany by train and took several journeys across Europe—to France, Germany and Switzerland, where she visited Karl Jaspers in Basel.[26]

Adorno's first return lasted for three years, from the autumn of 1949 to the autumn of 1952.[27] He arrived in Frankfurt on 2 November 1949 and was

[21]Theodor W. Adorno, 'Auf die Frage: Warum sind Sie zurückgekehrt', in *idem*, *Gesammelte Schriften*, vol.20.1, Frankfurt am Main 1986, pp. 394–395, here p. 394.
[22]*ibid.*, p. 395.
[23]*ibid.*
[24]Theodor W. Adorno, 'Die auferstandene Kultur', in *idem*, *Gesammelte Schriften*, vol. 20.2, Frankfurt am Main 1986, pp. 453–464, here p. 454.
[25]See Elisabeth Young-Bruehl, *Hannah Arendt: Leben, Werk und Zeit*, Frankfurt am Main 2004, p. 344.
[26]*ibid.*, p. 337 and p. 305.
[27]See Rolf Wiggershaus, *Die Frankfurter Schule: Geschichte, theoretische Entwicklung, politische Bedeutung*, Munich 1988, pp. 507f; for a more recent and more extensive account see Detlev Claussen, *Theodor W. Adorno: Ein letztes Genie*, Frankfurt am Main 2003, pp. 240ff and Müller-Doohm, pp. 496ff.

immediately confronted with heavy professional responsibilities.[28] From the onset, his time in Frankfurt partly served to prepare his remigration and the re-establishment of the Institute for Social Research, which soon came to be envisioned as Germany's new central sociological research institution—something promised by Adorno's close friend and fellow remigré Max Horkheimer.[29] During this time Adorno taught philosophy classes and lectured at the University of Frankfurt; he also conducted or participated in several empirical studies, including a study of the community of Darmstadt and its rural surroundings and the *Group Experiment*, a qualitative study of German postwar attitudes towards Nazism, re-education, and German guilt.[30] As a naturalised American citizen, Adorno was forced to return to the United States in October 1952 in order not to lose his American citizenship which he strongly wanted to keep. Deeply committed to the idea of re-establishing the Frankfurt institute together with Horkheimer, he left "with an endlessly heavy heart",[31] travelling via Paris to New York and Los Angeles. He would only remain ten months before finally resettling in Frankfurt in August 1953, eventually being appointed "supernumerary professor for philosophy and sociology".[32] Following this "second remigration" Adorno would never return to America.

Despite all its recent horrors, Arendt and Adorno both initially arrived in Europe and Germany with a sense of hope for the possibilities of the country's political and moral renewal, and a sense of belief in the cultural and human resources for such renewal—feelings that inform several of their early postwar essays and writings.[33] Immediately after his return to the German classrooms, Adorno praised the "intellectual passion"[34] of his German philosophy students, as documented in an essay of 1950 called 'Die auferstandene Kultur' ('The resurrected culture'), though Adorno simultaneously acknowledged that the students' apolitical *Vergeistigung*, their orientation towards philosophical and spiritual matters, might be considered an ambivalent process from a democratic perspective.[35] In 1965 Adorno would look back on such early sentiments regarding his native country:

> At no moment during my emigration did I relinquish the hope of coming back. And although the identification with the familiar is undeniably an aspect of this hope, it should not be misconstrued into a theoretical identification for something that probably is legitimate only so long as it obeys the impulse without appealing to elaborate theoretical supports. That in my voluntary decision I harboured the feeling of being able to do some good in Germany, to work against the obduration, the repetition of the disaster, is only another aspect of that spontaneous identification.[36]

[28]See Claussen, p. 242.

[29]Wiggershaus, p. 514; Horkheimer to Adorno, 13 March 1953.

[30]*ibid*, p. 504 and p. 526.

[31]*ibid*, p. 508; Adorno to Horkheimer, 20 October 1952.

[32]*ibid*, p. 520.

[33]See two texts written by Arendt in 1945: 'Approaching the German Question', in *idem*, *Essays in Understanding 1930–1954*, ed. by Jerome Kohn, New York 1994, pp. 97–126; 'The Seeds of a Fascist International', *ibid.*, , pp.140–150; for Adorno see two texts written in 1949: *idem*,'Die auferstandene Kultur'; 'Toward a Reappraisal of Heine', in *idem*, *Gesammelte Schriften*, vol. 20.2, pp. 441–452.

[34]*idem*, 'Die auferstandene Kultur', p. 453.

[35]*ibid*.

[36]Theodor W. Adorno, 'On the Question: "What is German?"', in *idem*, *Critical Models: Interventions and Catchwords*, New York 1998, pp. 205–214, here p. 209.

Furthermore, at the onset of his return it appeared to Adorno, as if in Germany, of all places, "an autonomous culture would still be possible and not only a lost idealistic illusion emerging from a German tradition".[37] Adorno was not only initially enthusiastic about his new German students, these "young people, the academic youth", as he wrote to Thomas Mann in a letter dated 28 December 1949; in general, the intellectual climate in Germany appeared to him "quite seductive", as he explained to Horkheimer in a letter written one day later.[38] Adorno was looking forward to teaching German philosophy to committed native students, and *in German*, the only language he considered fully suitable for dialectical-speculative, anti-positivistic thinking.[39] Following his successful escape and survival in exile, he also hoped to finally find conditions that would, as he put it, impair his work as little as possible[40]—conditions he deemed only present in his native environment. On a theoretical and political level, it is worth noting his recollection that "the conception that the Germans as a people are guilty was alien to me" and his insistence that Nazism should not be seen as deriving from a German "national character".[41]

In contrast to Adorno, Arendt, as indicated, never seriously considered moving back to Germany permanently. Still, she herself expressed her desire and commitment to help the Germans build a new society—one based on a truthful acknowledgment and working through of the past.[42] This desire and commitment, apparently driven by a firm if ambivalent affection for her society of origin, is documented in private letters and attested to in her carefully thought out decision to return temporarily to Germany and engage in difficult *"Hundsarbeit"*[43] for Jewish Cultural Reconstruction.

In Germany, however, neither Arendt nor Adorno were offered the reception they expected, each instead encountering a society that maintained a collective narcissism of a nationalist nature: one whose basic values were still heavily influenced by Nazism and that, in fact, harboured strong hostility towards all Jewish returnees. The response to this encounter on the part of both German-Jewish intellectuals was an increasingly sharp analysis of the particular social, psychological and political dynamics manifest in the postwar West German scene; the response was presented most pointedly by Arendt in her well-known essay, 'The Aftermath of Nazi Rule: Report from Germany' (1950), and her observations concerning the Auschwitz trials, 'Der Auschwitz-Prozess' (serving as an introduction to Bernd Naumann's book *Auschwitz*, published in 1966);[44] and by Adorno in his dissection of German society

[37]Claussen, p. 243.

[38]Cited in Müller-Doohm, p. 504. On Adorno's correspondence with Thomas Mann see *ibid.*, pp. 474–489.

[39]Adorno, 'On the Question: "What is German?"', pp. 212f.

[40]See *ibid.*, p. 211. Adorno's former colleagues at the Frankfurt Institute for Social Research, Leo Löwenthal and Herbert Marcuse, chose to stay in the United States.

[41]Adorno, 'Auf die Frage: Warum sind Sie zurückgekehrt', p. 394; see also Alex Demirovic, *Der nonkonformistische Intellektuelle: Die Entwicklung der Kritischen Theorie zur Frankfurter Schule*, Frankfurt am Main 1999, p. 99f.

[42]Arendt, 'Approaching the German Question', in *idem, Essays in Understanding*, pp. 97–126, pp.114; Hannah Arendt to Karl Jaspers, 17 August 1946, in Arendt and Jaspers, *Briefwechsel*, p. 89.

[43]See Young-Bruehl, p. 344.

[44]Hannah Arendt, 'Preface', in Bernd Naumann, *Auschwitz*, New York 1966; published in German as Arendt, 'Der Auschwitz-Prozess', in *idem, Nach Auschwitz: Essays und Kommentare I*, Berlin 1989, pp. 99–136.

entitled 'Schuld und Abwehr' ('Guilt and Defensiveness') as well as his broadly received, most prominent critical intervention with the Kantian title 'Was bedeutet: Aufarbeitung der Vergangenheit' ('The Meaning of Working through the Past').[45]

In her 'Report from Germany', Arendt came to terms with her experience of living for six months in postwar Germany. She expressed shock at what she described as a particular kind of German escapism. Willingly or unintentionally, she indicated, in so far as it might harm their idealistic collective self-image, the Germans she met avoided any serious confrontation with political and historical reality, constantly displaying a continuous totalitarian relativism towards historical facts, in other words the "habit of treating facts as though they were mere opinions. For example, the question of who started the last war, by no means a hotly debated issue, is answered by a surprising variety of opinions. An otherwise quite normally intelligent woman in Southern Germany told me that the Russians had begun the war with an attack on Danzig; this is only the crudest of many examples."[46]

Arendt described time and again encountering people who still debated historical facts about the war, the concentration camps, and other historical realities in a pseudo-democratic re-enactment of public arguing. The "average German", she stated, "honestly believes this free-for-all, this nihilistic relativity about facts, to be the essence of democracy. In fact, of course, it is a legacy of the Nazi regime."[47] In general, Arendt realised that the truth about the death camps was publicly and privately ignored, and any collective or individual responsibility was fiercely denied. Arendt noted that a ubiquitous absence of response to what happened "is evident everywhere", adding that:

> It is difficult to say whether this signifies a half-conscious refusal to yield to grief or a genuine inability to feel. … And the indifference with which they walk through the rubble has its exact counterpart in the absence of mourning for the dead, or in the apathy with which they react, or, rather, fail to react to the fate of refugees in their midst. This general lack of emotion, at any rate this apparent heartlessness, sometimes covered over with cheap sentimentality, is only the most conspicuous outward symptom of a deep-rooted, stubborn, and at times vicious refusal to face and come to terms with what really happened.[48]

As a response to any references to recent history or one's own Jewish origins, Arendt observed, people "proceed to draw up a balance between German suffering and the suffering of others, the implication being that one side cancels the other and we may as well proceed to a more promising topic of conversation."[49] Hence the most common publicly expressed emotion Arendt was able to observe was self-pity, with Allied policies consistently seen as aimed at revenge, not democratisation. In

[45]Theodor W. Adorno, 'Schuld und Abwehr: Eine qualitative Analyse zum "Gruppenexperiment"', in *idem*, *Gesammelte Schriften*, vol. 9.2, Frankfurt am Main 1975, pp. 121–324; Theodor W. Adorno, 'The Meaning of Working Through the Past', in *idem*, *Critical Models*, pp. 89–104.

[46]Hannah Arendt, 'The Aftermath of Nazi Rule: Report from Germany', in *idem, Essays in Understanding*, pp. 248–269, here p. 251.

[47]*ibid.*, p. 252.

[48]*ibid.*, p. 249.

[49]*ibid.*

conclusion Arendt argued that German industriousness served as an effective tool in the country's sheltering of itself against the Nazi legacy and the political and moral challenges of the time. Indeed, this present industriousness was in reality a drive to restore an idealised past, a drive crystallised in the word *Wiederaufbau*; it fuelled Arendt's impression "at first glance" that "Germany is still potentially the most dangerous European nation."[50] Arendt encapsulated her report in an observation fusing objective history with subjective experience: "And one wants to cry out: This is not real—real are the ruins; real are the past horrors, real are the dead whom you have forgotten. But they [your addressees] are living ghosts, whom speech and argument, the glance of human eyes and the mourning of human hearts, no longer touch."[51] However, while emphasising the specificity of the German situation, Arendt's negative experience also reached, to some extent, beyond Germany's borders. In general, she was shocked by the moral chaos in Europe *in toto*, only England appearing to her as a country "that survived the war morally intact".[52]

Among Arendt's trips to Germany and elsewhere in Europe that followed her long-term sojourn, the following are particularly noteworthy: a visit to Germany from April to September 1952, this time with private funding, and with the task of helping with the reconstruction of German philosophical studies;[53] a visit to Karl Jaspers in the autumn of 1956 and a trip to Frankfurt in October 1958 to present the *laudatio* for Jaspers, who was receiving the prestigious Peace Prize of German Booksellers; a trip to Hamburg in 1959 to receive the city's prominent Lessing Prize for the humanistic and enlightened nature of her work; another trip to Darmstadt in September 1967 to receive the Sigmund Freud Prize for Academic Prose of the German Academy for Language and Poetry, awarded to Arendt not for her (very limited) admiration of Freud's work but because of her extraordinary contributions to the German language, praise she clearly appreciated;[54] and finally, a trip to Copenhagen in April 1975 to accept the Danish government's and the University of Copenhagen's prestigious Sonning Prize, awarded for major contributions to European culture. (Arendt received the award on 18 April 1975 for her work as a historian of totalitarian systems and as a political theorist; she was the first American citizen and the first woman to receive the prize.)[55] She also built new friendships with European and German colleagues, re-established some old ones—most prominently she always kept close contact with Karl Jaspers—and even participated in Germany's public and academic life through her many publications, commentaries, and speeches. Right from the start, the visits to Karl and Gertrude Jaspers in Basel had made her even "feel at home" in Europe, "both philosophically and personally,

[50]*ibid.*, p. 254.
[51]*ibid.*
[52]See Young-Bruehl, p. 345.
[53]*ibid*, p. 380 and p. 394.
[54]In a letter to Dr. Johan, the president of the academy, Arendt wrote: "I was forced to leave Germany 34 years ago; my mother tongue was everything that I could take with me from my old home, and I always made great efforts to keep this irreplaceable treasure intact and alive. The Academy's award is like a recognition that I succeeded in doing it." Arendt to Johan, 6 July 1967; quoted in Young-Bruehl, p. 535.
[55]*ibid*, p. 626 and p. 630; see also Ingeborg Nordmann, *Hannah Arendt*, Frankfurt 1994, p. 137.

especially personally".[56] At the same time, until her death in 1975 she kept a considerable distance from Germany's official policies and prevailing social mood: she strongly criticised the German government's reluctance to accept decisions by the United States and the other Allied powers (for example, the decision to build a European Defence Community in May 1952), a reluctance she began to conceptualise as stemming from an "evil nationalism" of the German people;[57] and she criticised the continuous German initiatives to legislate statutes of limitation for Nazi crimes, as well as the general lack of willingness by the German government and German courts to prosecute Nazi criminals.[58] In a letter published by the German weekly *Der Spiegel*, in 1965 she wrote that Germans might well react to the thought of living with "murderers of cab drivers" by restoring the death penalty;[59] but when it came to crimes of previously unheard of proportions, no one seemed to show any emotional reaction, let alone anger or outrage.

Adorno's experiences and analysis of the postwar mentality in Germany was strikingly similar to Arendt's. In Adorno's case, the analysis was backed up with systematic social research—the *Group Experiment,* his qualitative study of German guilt feelings and defensive mechanisms in respect to Nazi crimes—which served as the basis for a set of theoretical interpretations of postwar German reactions to the Holocaust.[60] The study involved group discussions held among Germans from various social backgrounds with a range of occupations and ages. The participants were given a letter ostensibly written by an American soldier; in the letter he both criticised German authoritarianism and the way Germans had been dealing with the recent past and praised the Germans for their cultural achievements and capabilities. The general response to the letter revealed strong affective reactions—in particular what Adorno defined as a collective defensiveness regarding German national guilt and political responsibility, as well as the guilt of specific German perpetrators. The response appeared to be as strong among participants who were evidently personally "innocent" as among former members of the Nazi party, and efforts to deny collective, national responsibility appeared even more affectively loaded than those to deny personal guilt.

In his analysis of the findings, Adorno discerned seven major themes and differentiated between two major reaction-patterns among the participants. On the one hand, the vast majority had a strong sense of German national identity and reacted defensively and aggressively when confronted with German crimes. All farmers participating in the study, as well as virtually all academics, denied any guilt on the part of Germany or the Germans. Almost ninety per cent of the latter group

[56]Hannah Arendt to Fritz Fränkel, 20 December 1950, Library of Congress, Manuscript Division, Arendt folder.

[57]Hannah Arendt to Heinrich Blücher, 30 May 1952, *ibid.*

[58]See, for example, Arendt's preface to Karl Jaspers, *The Future of Germany,* Chicago 1967.

[59]Hanna Arendt to editors of *Der Spiegel* 12 February 1965, Hannah Arendt Archive Oldenburg, Catalogue: Publishers, *Der Spiegel* 1965–1970, 32.5.

[60]For a brief overview of the study's empirical results see Lars Rensmann, 'Collective Guilt, National Identity, and Political Processes in Contemporary Germany', in Nyla Branscombe and Bertjan Doosje (eds.), *Collective Guilt: International Perspectives*, Cambridge 2004 [forthcoming]; for a more extensive analysis see Lars Rensmann, *Kritische Theorie über den Antisemitismus,* Hamburg 1998, pp. 231–288.

was either somewhat or radically antisemitic—although academics were often reluctant to speak up about the topic.[61] On the other hand, a small minority of those interviewed identified less with the national collective. While itself revealing defensive reactions to a lesser degree, this minority (sixteen per cent) was relatively open to acknowledging German guilt and more frequently supported the idea of compensation for the victims. But despite these scattered exceptions the study underscored a widespread pattern of defensive strategies such as equating the Holocaust with "crimes committed by the others". These strategies were accompanied by continued strong identification with Germany as a self-evidently superior nation, as well as frequent projection of personal guilt onto both the Allied forces and, above all, the Jewish victims and survivors: a process expressed in what Adorno defined as a *secondary antisemitism* motivated by identifying the Jews as representatives of an unwanted and unmastered memory. Adorno argued that Germans holding such attitudes in fact simultaneously clung to authoritarianism and deep-seated prejudices and clichés regarding virtually every minority, while every statement about "the Germans" is defensively rejected as an illegitimate "false generalisation".[62] A cognitive incapacity to judge and evaluate historical processes or even get the basic historical facts straight, strong national identifications and high levels of prejudice, a general lack of empathy towards the victims, a high degree of national and individual self-pity to the point of viewing the Germans as the "real victims" of Nazism and the Second World War —such traits, Adorno concluded, amounted to nothing less than a general "social tendency" towards an irrational, aggressive defensiveness, a "transsubjective factor" characterising early postwar, post-totalitarian West German society and culture.[63] Adorno thus discovered what he termed a social "objective spirit", amounting to a new "German ideology".[64]

It is striking that interspersed throughout Adorno's two hundred-page empirical material, we find expressions of personal anger, and even shock, at the responses of various participants in his study. Like Arendt, Adorno, who as indicated had celebrated the capabilities of his new German students a short time before, was unmistakably surprised and affected by the level of aggression, prejudice and denial he encountered on an unexpectedly broad scale. It was as if, as Arendt later put it in *Eichmann in Jerusalem*, German society and its prevailing moral system were "not shared by the outside world"[65] and were still a world apart from the rest of contemporary civilisation.

For Adorno, it appears that things did not get better in the 1950s; he experienced this static situation both personally and, more so, in his professional life in which he had invested so much hope. Against his expectations, he was not welcomed home by Germany's academic community: like many other German-Jewish academic exiles, he initially received no adequate professional appointment (though he was invited to teach classes at the Philosophy faculty of the Johann Wolfgang Goethe University of

[61]Wiggershaus, p. 490.
[62]Adorno, 'Schuld und Abwehr', pp. 121–324, here pp. 218f.
[63]*ibid.*, p. 138 and p. 146.
[64]Draft manuscript by Adorno cited in Wiggershaus, p. 489.
[65]Hannah Arendt, *Eichmann in Jerusalem*, p. 103.

Frankfurt between 1949 and 1952),[66] and was finally offered a "supernumerary chair" in August 1953 by Frankfurt University as a result of pressure exerted by Max Horkheimer after Adorno had spent another year in the US. Addressing Adorno's Jewish background and émigré status, the dean of the philosophical faculty declared that such a chair would be established for Adorno "solely for reasons of restitution".[67] A number of his university colleagues, many appointed by Nazi university presidents, viewed Adorno's position as a privilege granted because he was Jewish; his "restitution chair" thus became a *Judenprofessur*—a "Jews' professorship".[68] In any event, until July 1957 his hopes of becoming a regular full professor remained unfulfilled.

In February 1956, Adorno was forced to remind the dean of philosophy of his right to become a full professor according to the third revision of the Law for the Restitution of National Socialist Injustice. Many colleagues in the Philosophy faculty (which, following the German tradition, included the humanities in their entirety) objected. One of the most distinguished colleagues, Hellmut Ritter, a professor of oriental history, claimed in a meeting of the commission founded to deal with the "Adorno case" that "in Frankfurt you only need to be promoted by Mr. Horkheimer and to be a Jew in order to have a career".[69] Ritter's voice was representative of many, and of a generally hostile climate facing Jews in the Philosophy faculty and in various departments throughout the university.[70] This climate largely shattered Adorno's hopes for a fresh start for German society and culture that could revive its best traditions; the steady frustration caused by experiences of ostracisation and inflicted resentment soon led to a fading of the high ambitions tied to the re-establishment of the Frankfurt institute. In May 1956, Adorno's friend and mentor Horkheimer officially applied for retirement because of the "hatred against Jews" expressed by his colleagues.[71] To be sure, both Adorno and Horkheimer seemed to be encountering more hostility within the academy than outside it, where Adorno quickly re-established old friendships and formed new ones.[72] Still, even when he finally received his *Ordinarius* title on 1 July 1957, he did not enjoy an ordinary professorship at Frankfurt; and at that point, he was not fully satisfied with the appointment, as its terms could not be improved on through the presence of similar offers from other German universities (he would receive no such offers during the remaining years of his career).[73] In 1959, Adorno laid out the conclusions drawn from his previous research, and even more so, from his accumulated experience inside the academy and in German society as a whole during the 1950s in his essay 'Was bedeutet: Aufarbeitung der Vergangenheit' ('The Meaning of Working through the Past'), an essay that remains one of the most radical critiques of postwar West Germany's approach to coming to terms with the

[66]See Müller-Doohm, *Adorno,* p. 507.
[67]Wiggershaus, p. 520.
[68]*ibid.*
[69]*ibid.*, p. 521.
[70]*ibid.*
[71]*ibid.*
[72]Müller-Doohm, p. 526.
[73]Wiggershaus, p. 521.

past. Adorno here drew a stark portrait of a society in which "National Socialism lives on", where "even today we still do not know whether it is merely a ghost of what was so monstrous that lingers on after its own death, or whether it has not yet died at all, whether the willingness to commit the unspeakable survives in people as well as in the conditions that enclose them".[74] Within this framework, he criticised an omnipresent desire to "break away from the past", with its concomitant full-scale public "destruction of memory"[75]—a widespread indifference towards what had transpired that he identified with as much acuity and indignation as had Arendt almost a decade earlier. Adorno argued:

> There is much that is neurotic in the relation to the past: defensive postures where one is not attacked, intense affects where they are hardly warranted by the situation, an absence of affect in the face of the gravest matters, not seldom simply a repression of what is known or half-known. ... We are also familiar with the readiness today to deny or minimize what happened—no matter how difficult it is to comprehend that people feel no shame in arguing that it was at most only five and not six million Jews who were gassed.

Responsibility for Hitler's crimes and the Nazi disaster, he continued, "is shifted onto those who tolerated his seizure of power [i.e. England and America] and not to the ones who cheered him on. The idiocy of all this is truly a sign of something that psychologically has not been mastered, a wound, although the idea of wounds would be rather more appropriate for the victims".[76] What had not been mastered, he concluded, was a persistent "collective narcissism": an ongoing identification with an idealised image of the nation as a huge collective self. Secretly, smouldering "unconsciously and therefore all the more powerfully", Adorno suggested, the "identifications" and "collective narcissism" stamping the Hitler years were thus "not destroyed at all, but continue to exist".[77]

Although in many respects Hannah Arendt's interpretation of the Holocaust, totalitarianism, and the post-totalitarian constellation in Germany did differ from Adorno's, as has been suggested in these pages, in other respects we can also find striking similarities in relation to the "German problem", some of these apparently related to similar postwar observations and experiences. On the one hand, her time in postwar Germany did not induce her to revise her view of the modern condition, and of totalitarianism as to a great extent a modern phenomenon, rooted in universal modern developments such as imperialism and atomisation in mass society. She continued to interpret antisemitism as an essentially supranational political ideology that needed to be approached in terms of its general social and political origins, in other words as a powerful weapon in organising the rootless, atomised masses of modernity.[78] With the publication of her Eichmann book in 1963, she even seemed to go so far as to describe the Holocaust as essentially an abstract administrative procedure carried out by thoughtless bureaucrats, rather than by

[74]Theodor W. Adorno, 'The Meaning of Working Through the Past', p. 90.
[75]*ibid.*, pp. 89 and 91.
[76]*ibid.*, p. 91.
[77]*ibid.*, p. 96.
[78]See Richard J. Bernstein, *Hannah Arendt and the Jewish Question*, Cambridge, MA 1996, p. 70.

fanaticised followers of a demented political and cultural ideology. Some of her observations on Germany in the wake of the Holocaust appear to reflect her thesis that a totalitarian system destroys the moral and cognitive competence of its members: the situation in postwar Germany, Arendt argued, also demonstrates that "totalitarian rule is something more than merely the worst form of tyranny".[79] The experience of totalitarianism, Arendt claimed, had robbed the Germans "of all spontaneous speech and comprehension, so that now, having no official line to guide them, they are, as it were, speechless, incapable of articulating thoughts and adequately expressing their feelings".[80]

On the other hand, it is possible to discern a new epistemological position in Arendt's writings of the postwar period: an insight into the importance of socio-cultural, political, anti-democratic traditions, and, in particular into the unwillingness of most Germans to deal with the Nazi legacy; the isolation of a contemporary West German predisposition to coldness, indifference and insensitivity that she defined as anti-democratic.[81] The "deep moral confusion" apparent in Germany today, then, "is more than amorality and has deeper causes than mere wickedness. The so-called good Germans are often as misled in their moral judgements of themselves and others as those who simply refuse to recognize that anything wrong or out of the ordinary was done by Germany at all."[82] In such passages, Arendt expressed her own surprise at the depth of the destruction of Germany's prewar public and private life[83]—at the extent of the anti-democratic traits maintained by "accomplices to unspeakable crimes",[84] and especially at the widespread repression of recent history and outright hostility she encountered as a German-Jewish exile.[85] In an attempt to link her general theory of totalitarianism to an analysis of specific historical traits and traditions, Arendt critically reconstructed these particular attitudes, for example as manifest in a prevailing bustling activity that she saw not as the reflection of a fixed national character but rather as one symptom of a deep-seated historically determined mentality.[86] It was "a well-known fact," she indicated, "that Germans have for generations been overfond of working".[87] However, watching "the Germans busily stumble through the ruins of a thousand years of their own history, shrugging their shoulders at the destroyed landmarks or resentful when reminded of the deeds of horror that haunt the whole surrounding world, one comes to realize that busyness has become their chief defence against reality".[88] For Arendt, then, such bustle and "escape from responsibility"[89] and associated postwar defensiveness in the face of industrial mass

[79]Arendt, 'The Aftermath of Nazi Rule', p. 269.
[80]*ibid.*, p. 253.
[81]*ibid*, p. 268.
[82]*ibid*, p. 259.
[83]*ibid.*, p. 259f.
[84]*ibid.*, p. 261.
[85]Hannah Arendt to Fritz Fränkel, 4 February 1950, Manuscript Division, Folder Arendt, Library of Congress.
[86]Arendt, 'The Aftermath of Nazi Rule', p. 261.
[87]*ibid.*
[88]*ibid.*, p. 254.
[89]*ibid.*, p. 250.

murder corresponded to the process through which the Nazi murder machine kept going.[90] At one point, she ironically remarked to Fritz Fränkel that "The Germans are working their brains off" (*die Deutschen arbeiten sich dumm und dämlich*).[91]

In Adorno's postwar writing, and in light of his postwar experiences, one likewise finds elements of an increasingly specified approach to the interlinking questions of how to define the role of German antidemocratic traditions and what caused the Holocaust. As the following remarks reveal, this development culminated in a complex and critical version of the *Sonderweg* thesis that was rooted in social psychology:

> Because historically German unification was belated, precarious, and unstable, one tends, simply so as to feel like a nation at all, to overplay the national consciousness and irritably avenge every deviation from it. In this situation it is easy to regress to archaic conditions of a pre-individualistic disposition, a tribal consciousness, to which one can appeal with all the greater psychological effectiveness the less such consciousness actually exists.[92]

In the same context, Adorno juxtaposed Germany's dominant "blind dependencies, which include the unreflected supremacy of the national" with another, universalistic tradition originating with Kant, whose thought "centered upon the concept of autonomy, the self-responsibility of the reasoning individual."[93] In the years after his return to Germany, Adorno's focus would correspondingly turn to the specific relationship between anti-modern sentiments and authoritarian ideologies anchored in German political-cultural history, on the one hand, and the processes of capitalist modernisation and totalisation of the "iron cage" of modernity in the twentieth century, on the other.

In a manner clearly reflecting insights gained since remigration, Adorno thus came to define Nazism as an anti-modern German movement based on the political mobilisation of specifically national cultural residues, these nonetheless interacting with modern conditions and preconditioned by modernity's drastic transformations. The nineteenth- and twentieth-century German social model, he explained, was the civil servant fulfilling his duties to authority, not the free entrepreneur operating according to the laws of the market.[94] A society still at some distance from the modern laws of commodification and rationalisation could easily be swept into the Nazi vortex, he suggested (this, of course, stands in sharp contrast to his general theory of Nazism as the product of the totalisation of instrumental reason and capitalist modernity); while Hitler could "hardly be ascribed to the German national character as its fate, it was nonetheless hardly a coincidence that he rose to power in Germany".[95]

Such arguments are found only in some works by the late Adorno and mark a clear, though not consistent, indeed rather exceptional, shift from his earlier dialectic

[90] *ibid.*

[91] Hannah Arendt to Fritz Fränkel, 20 December 1949, Manuscript Division, Folder Arendt, Library of Congress.

[92] Adorno, 'On the Question: "What is German?"', p. 206.

[93] *ibid.*, p. 206.

[94] Adorno argued in 1965 that in Germany commercialisation "had not flourished as widely as in the advanced capitalist countries" which caused a *lack* of intellectual, cultural and democratic modernisation; *ibid.*, p. 207.

[95] *ibid.*

social theory with both a general stance and specific orientation towards the modern condition that was highly universal in orientation. By the 1960s, he had concluded that totalitarian antisemitism was not simply a product of a modern rationalisation process gone mad. German culture was, at its innermost core, and particularly where it believed itself to be most cultivated, "interspersed with anti-Semitic prejudices".[96] In the essays he wrote shortly before his death, once more Adorno laid stress on the persistence of anti-democratic ideologies in Germany after the Holocaust: a prevailing collective conformity, self-idolisation, a political culture stamped by an absence of self-reflection and self-criticism. He observed an increasingly widespread "completely imagined international ostracism of the German, or a no less fictive lack of that national self-esteem that so many would like to incite again". "Imperceptibly," he argued in 1965, "an atmosphere is slowly taking shape that disapproves of the one thing most necessary: critical self-reflection. Once again one hears the ill-fated proverb of the bird that dirties its own nest, whereas those who grouse about the bird themselves tend to be birds of a feather who flock together".[97] While Adorno may well have been mainly referring here to his own situation, his remarks also defined the fate of many of his fellow Jewish survivors who had returned to the land of their former persecution.

Although in its details, Adorno's analysis is strikingly similar to Arendt's, the theoretical postulates informing it mark a far more dramatic shift in stance. Nevertheless, for Adorno as for Arendt, one finds no abandonment of their "grand theory" of modernity as a central underlying concept and the primary source of explanation for the Holocaust. In spite of some considerable reconfigurations and shifts, in this important respect both thinkers remained, unmistakably, in strong debt to the intellectual heritage of the Weimar Republic.

III

When Adorno returned to Germany in 1949, he had finished *Minima Moralia* two years before. Begun during the last years of war and completed after the Holocaust's dimensions had started to surface, this collection of aphorisms conveyed some hope in the midst of a critique of what Adorno viewed as modern civilisation's dialectic of destruction. One of Adorno's purposes was to explore the concept of an emancipated society that "would not be a unitary state but the realisation of universality in the reconciliation of differences". These differences would not be subsumed under the imperative of the general or subject to a unitary tolerance excluding refractory groups; instead, the good state was to be conceived as "one in which people could be different without fear".[98] And the last of the aphorisms goes so far as to reformulate a messianic idea of history unmistakably inspired by Walter Benjamin: a redemption of all previous history through a process of dialectical

[96]Theodor W. Adorno, 'Zur Bekämpfung des Antisemitismus heute', in *idem*, *Gesammelte Schriften*, vol. 20.1, Frankfurt am Main 1986, pp. 382f.

[97]*idem*, 'On the Question: "What is German?"' p. 206.

[98]*idem*, *Minima Moralia: Reflections from Damaged Life*, London 1974, p. 103.

turnover, grounded in the possibility that total negativity "delineates the mirror-image of its opposite".[99]

We can understand Adorno's move to Germany as reflecting a sense that perhaps paradoxically, this 'place of catastrophe' was the location where he could best re-ignite such a messianic motif in temporary suspension. He hoped to do so through his work; in seeing this as most realisable in a country that had abandoned him he was, it seems, following his messianic principle that "consummate negativity, once squarely faced, delineates the mirror-image of its opposite". Germany was, for sure, the site of total social negativity, hence the site of utmost hope—this concept formulated at a time when most surviving German Jews were expressing "the impossibility of staying in their 'fatherland' after all that had happened".[100]

In a similar manner, although more in political than general social terms, Hannah Arendt first dreamt after the war of the rise of a new German republic—an exemplary site of freedom, political agency, and plurality "in which every Jew, no matter where he was born, could become a full citizen any time if he wishes, simply by virtue of his Jewish nationality, without abandoning being Jewish".[101] Such a republic, she felt in 1945, could become a model for a new Europe, where a truly civil society had come to terms legally and ethically with past problems such as statelessness and persecution of national minorities.[102] But with her visits of 1949 and 1950 and occasional ones thereafter, this political vision melted into air.

For both Adorno and Arendt, the sense of political disillusionment followed the shock generated by news of the Nazi genocide; this shock had led to a more general disillusionment with their fellow Germans for their collaboration and their murderous deeds. The subsequent political disillusionment involved a painful realisation that the German society and culture both thought they had known and had as a "home" had apparently been destroyed to the core, and to a much higher degree than they had expected; and an equally painful realisation that most of those who had been part of it would not acknowledge the crimes, rather harbouring all the old resentments, their coldness—their Nazi world-view.

The initial postwar ideals and hopes of both Arendt and Adorno were rooted in the Weimar Republic's destroyed intellectual and cultural environment. With the experience of modern American society now a crucial part of their intellectual-experiential arsenal,[103] it would seem that in face of the postwar German scene, both figures became sharply aware of a set of deeply-grounded differences between their world of exile and their world of origin. Despite their own set of theoretically elaborated political-historical concepts, each moved—albeit only in some rather marginal writings hardly undermining their general theoretical focus on universal-totalitarian modernity—towards a reflection of their experience and thus towards partial theoretical reconfigurations; each moved beyond exclusively blaming the

[99] *ibid.*, p. 247.

[100] See Michael Brenner, 'East European and German Jews in Postwar Germany, 1945–50', in Y. Michal Bodemann (ed.), *Jews, Germany, Memory*, Ann Arbor, MI 1996, pp. 49–64, here p. 57.

[101] Hannah Arendt to Karl Jaspers, 17 August 1946, in Arendt and Jaspers, *Briefwechsel* , p. 89.

[102] Arendt, 'Approaching the German Question', pp. 111ff.

[103] See Joanna Vecchiarelli Scott, 'Die amerikanische Erfahrung: Arendt, Adorno und das Exil in den USA', in Auer, Rensmann and Wessel (eds.), pp. 57–73.

"final solution" on the modern condition or indeed on life spent within a totalitarian order. At least in the margins, both Adorno and Arendt now acknowledged the important role of anti-democratic traditions, and the centrality in historical events of active human agents driven by specific sets of ideas and emotions. Largely autobiographical in nature, the writings in which this shift is manifest represent a fascinating dialogue between subjective experience and theoretical abstraction: a dialogue *not* subsuming particular history under an abstract theoretical notion.[104]

Nevertheless, it sometimes seems that the tension between strictly modernist interpretations of the twentieth century's catastrophes, from Stalinism to Nazism, interpretations criticising the modern atomisation of man and the structures of the modern bureaucratic apparatus, and more contingent interpretations of the specific political and cultural conditions of European and German society, remains unresolved in the writings of both thinkers.

When Adorno wrote about the totality of late capitalism in the 1960s and when Arendt published her theory of the bureaucratic perpetrator in *Eichmann in Jerusalem*, they were reflecting, on parallel epistemological horizons, on the crucial role of the particular in history—a role that had escaped their critical model of modernity. The two theoretical narratives represented in their work, the general critique of modernity and the critique of particular traditions, appear especially irreconcilable, disparate, fragmented. Such ambivalence and ambiguity is, in fact, broadly characteristic of their postwar work. Without essentialising German national identity, Arendt and Adorno were increasingly critical of German society, while nevertheless remaining deeply attached to its intellectual heritage, as well as empathising with its potential and identifying with its fate—just as they remained harsh critics of modernity while endorsing its prospects.

In any event, the postwar German experiences of each thinker did prompt some clear-cut shifts of perception—a partial reconsideration of the Holocaust's significance and a shared fading of hopes invested in both a German and European postwar order. For Arendt and even for Adorno, the critic of the American culture-industry, if there was any remaining potential for freedom and democracy in the Western World, this potential came to lie rather in America, and certainly not in Germany. It was, in fact, the American experience that showed both thinkers a different side to the dialectics of modernity. Modern, cut-throat capitalist America now represented a concrete and symbolic site of refuge, civilised values and democratic stability—this in itself represented an implicit challenge to all Holocaust-aetiologies that focused on universal conditions tied to modernity. One thus finds Arendt eventually identifying the emergence of isolated masses susceptible to totalitarian ideologies as an essentially *European* condition: these masses, she explained, were "a result of the disintegration of the class system", a process unknown in America.[105] As announced most eloquently in *On Revolution*, Arendt,

[104]This is the way Moishe Postone critically assesses the bulk of Hannah Arendt's oeuvre. See *idem*, 'Hannah Arendts *Eichmann in Jerusalem*: Die unaufgelöste Antinomie von Universalität und Besonderem', in Gary Smith (ed.), *Hannah Arendt Revisited: "Eichmann in Jerusalem" und die Folgen*, Frankfurt am Main 2000, p. 284.

[105]Arendt to George Ackerman, 21 February 1974, Hannah Arendt Archive Oldenburg, Miscellany, 1954–1975 and undated, 7.1.

now a New York intellectual who had been recognised since her early *Aufbau* writings[106] as a prominent if controversial member of the New York émigré community, had developed a strong belief in the ideals and legacy of the American Revolution and the American republic. In light of the fact that Adorno never stopped loathing American popular culture, and indeed never went back to his land of exile or wrote anything in English after his return to Germany, it is perhaps more surprising that Adorno himself came around, in his reflections on his "Scientific experiences of a European Scholar in America" (1968), to praising the political and social climate of the oldest modern Western democracy:

> Over there I became acquainted with a potential for real humanitarianism that is hardly to be found in old Europe. The political form of democracy is ultimately closer to the people. American everyday life, despite the often lamented hustle and bustle, has an inherent element of peaceableness, good-naturedness, and generosity, in sharpest contrast to the pent-up malice and envy that exploded in Germany between 1933 and 1945. … I do not want to imply by this that America is somehow immune to the danger of veering toward totalitarian forms of domination. Such a danger lies in the modern condition per se. But probably the power to resist fascist currents is stronger in America than in any European country, perhaps with the exception of England.[107]

Correspondingly, throughout the 1950s and 1960s both Arendt and Adorno attacked both European anti-Americanism in general and its German variant in particular as symptoms of the continued strength of anti-modernist and anti-democratic ideas on the old continent. In 1954 Arendt wrote as follows in three essays on anti-Americanism which resulted from a lecture at Princeton University:

> Anti-Americanism, its negative emptiness notwithstanding, threatens to become the content of a European movement. If it is true that each nationalism (though, of course, not the birth of every nation) begins with a real or fabricated common enemy, then the current image of America in Europe may well become the beginning of a new pan-Europeanism. Our hope that the emergence of a federated Europe and the dissolution of the present nation-state system will make nationalism itself a thing of the past may be unwarrantedly optimistic.

That the remnants of European fascism had joined the fight for European federation, Arendt added, "reminds everybody that after Briand's futile gestures at the League of Nations it was Hitler who started the war with the promise that he would liquidate Europe's obsolete nation-state system and build a united Europe. The widespread and inarticulate anti-American sentiments find their political crystallisation point precisely here".[108] In the 1950s, Arendt developed elements of a theory of European anti-Americanism, one of this theory's basic assumptions being

[106]See Hannah Arendt, *Vom Antisemitismus ist man nur auf dem Monde sicher: Beiträge für die deutsch-jüdische Emigrantenzeitung "Aufbau" 1941–1945*, Munich 2000.

[107]Theodor W. Adorno, 'Scientific Experiences of a European Scholar in America', in *idem*, *Critical Models*, pp. 215–242, here p. 240.

[108]Hannah Arendt, 'Dream and Nightmare', in *idem*, *Essays in Understanding*, pp. 409–417, here pp. 416f; on Arendt's critique of anti-Americanism see Lars Rensmann, *European Political Identity, the Problem of Anti-Americanism, and the Future of Transatlantic Relations: An Arendtian View*, New Haven 2004.

that in the postwar European order anti-American ideas would serve as a source of identity-creation and as a means of projecting difficulties in confronting the realities of present-day modernity and past totalitarianism onto the New World:

> As long as Europe remains divided, she can afford the luxury of dodging these very disturbing problems of the modern world. She can continue to pretend that the threat to our civilization comes to her from without. ... Both anti-Americanism and neutralism are, in a sense, clear signs that Europe is not prepared at this moment to face the consequences and problems of her own development."[109]

In an analogous way, Adorno insisted again and again that in "Germany, arrogance against America is inappropriate. By misusing a higher good, it only serves the mustiest of instincts",[110] as he wrote in 1965. In 1968, denouncing an apparently rising anti-Americanism in Germany during this period[111] and contrasting the "substantiality of democratic forms" in American political and cultural traditions to the problematic traditions of Europe, and of Germany in particular, Adorno noted that in America democratic modes of self-understanding "have seeped into life itself, whereas at least in Germany they were, and I fear still are, nothing more than formal rules of the game".[112] Similar to Arendt's approach to the subject, Adorno's critical theory of anti-Americanism, which he developed during the 1960s, conceptualises anti-Americanism as a particular, personifying expression of discontent with modernity as such. In this context, Russell Berman has argued that "for Adorno, the issue is ... the difference between the American culture of freedom, on the one hand, and the German, or more broadly European, regime of regulatory statism, on the other. ... This is why he has long been rejected by the German Left for his anti-collectivism and by the German nationalist Right for his pro-Americanism".[113] Here, again, a postwar re-evaluation and reconfiguration of the role of specific (democratic) political cultures within the horizon of modernity is visible.

Both Arendt and Adorno, who had found refuge in America and in the end endorsed its democratic political culture, began to see German anti-Americanism as just another expression of the problematic, unmastered, and in particular collectivist features and traditions of postwar German society—a society towards which they had become steadily more sceptical. Although affectively the two intellectual figures remained strongly tied to their German cultural and intellectual heritage, they simultaneously felt alienated in Germany as it had become. Having taken markedly different biographical paths, they now shared a common sense of "permanent exile" because of the experience of a far-reaching alienation from their original home—a sense of continued exile shared with many other returned German-Jewish intellectuals.[114]

[109]Hannah Arendt, 'Europe and the Atom Bomb,' in *idem, Essays in Understanding,* pp. 418–422, here p. 422.

[110]Adorno, 'On the question: "What is German"', p. 210.

[111]Cf. Russell A. Berman, *Anti-Americanism in Europe: A Cultural Problem,* Stanford 2004, p. 141.

[112]Adorno, 'Scientific Experiences of a European Scholar in America', p. 239f.

[113]Berman, *Anti-Americanism in Europe,* p. 143.

[114]See Martin Jay, *Permanent Exiles: Essays on the Intellectual Migration from Germany to America,* New York 1986.

Embodied in different ways by the postwar lives of Arendt and Adorno, the status of such "permanent exile" reflects the biographical reality of both forced emigration and confrontation with a culture that was once familiar but has turned unfamiliar. Their former home could not be fully regained. But such status likewise signifies a general theoretical position. On both a personal and broader cultural level, both Arendt and Adorno increasingly came to perceive that the wound left by the Holocaust would never close. It seems that the perception was reinforced by the postwar experiences of each of these thinkers, experiences largely shattering the continued hope in a revived German tradition, while bringing home the loss of friends, community, a portion of humanity itself. Rendered even more acute through a specific form of *eingeholte Erfahrung* of the unexpected level of German society's moral destruction—realising that most of their fellow Germans had at least accepted the Nazi's genocidal project—such a sense of loss could not fail to leave high universalistic hopes untouched. In part this explains the tensions, and indeed the despair, that we can find in some of Arendt's and Adorno's postwar writings: a despair transforming the Kantian imperative's direction from a hope for universal freedom, which is still reflected in their continued engagement with an intellectual ideal of universal enlightenment, increasingly into the defensive, if not resigned hope of a "never again". It thus appears that in a certain sense, the return to Germany of both Arendt and Adorno made them both homeless in this world once and for all. On a theoretical level, their postwar insights into the role of political culture foster a more complex, multifaceted, and indeed more advanced approach to interpreting the Holocaust, one that takes account of the specific interactions between rapid social modernisation, politics, and cultural mentality. In doing so, Arendt and Adorno also further enhance our general understanding of the complex relationship between democracy, culture, and modernity.

Hidden Memory and Unspoken History: Hans Rothfels and the Postwar Restoration of Contemporary German History

By Nicolas Berg

I. "NEGLECTED QUESTIONS": DEBATES WITHIN GERMAN ACADEMIC HISTORY SINCE THE 1990s

Over the past decade, a number of extensive studies in German historiography have examined a fundamental problem: what was the specific form in which historiographical conceptions stemming from the pre-1945 period entered postwar German historical writing? Almost all these studies were intended as contributions to a more encompassing question: after the demise of Nazism, how did historians confront the Nazi legacy within their own profession? What were the "paths of continuity", if any were present?[1] In this dynamic process of reflection the field of contemporary history (what the Germans term *Zeitgeschichte*) has emerged as a paradigm of the discipline as a whole, its approach to National Socialism serving, as it were, as an emblem of the credibility and integrity of an entire branch of scholarly inquiry.[2]

A number of themes and methods have been focused on within this conceptual framework. A key methodological question has centred around the meaning and impact of the concept of *Volksgeschichte* (national or "folk" history) both in Weimar Germany and under National Socialism.[3] Other enquiries have focused on the distinctive variant of German social history as it crystallised in the early 1950s, slowly penetrating the methodological self-identity of the historians' guild.[4] In thematic terms, interest has partly revolved around the defensive perception of "modernity" by exponents of German "structural history", and their (re)interpretation

The original version of this article was translated from the German by Bill Templer.

[1] Hartmut Lehmann and James van Horn Melton (eds.), *Paths of Continuity. Central European History from the 1930s to the 1950s*, Cambridge 1994.

[2] For an introduction to the general context see Martin H. Geyer, 'Im Schatten der NS-Zeit. Zeitgeschichte als Paradigma einer (bundes-)republikanischen Geschichtswissenschaft', in Alexander Nützenadel und Wolfgang Schieder (eds.), *Zeitgeschichte als Problem. Nationale Traditionen und Perspektiven der Forschung in Europa*, Göttingen 2004, pp. 25–53.

[3] Willi Oberkrome, *Volksgeschichte. Methodische Innovation und völkische Ideologisierung in der deutschen Geschichtswissenschaft, 1918–1945*, Göttingen 1993; for an earlier study, see Winfried Schulze, 'Von der "politischen Volksgeschichte" zur "neuen Sozialgeschichte"', in *idem*, *Deutsche Geschichtswissenschaft nach 1945*, Munich 1989, pp. 281–301.

[4] Thomas Etzemüller, *Sozialgeschichte als politische Geschichte. Werner Conze und die Neuorientierung der westdeutschen Geschichtswissenschaft nach 1945*, Munich 2001.

of this "modernity";[5] and around the special challenge the Nazi mass crimes against the European Jews represented for the field of history in general—and how it sought to do justice to this challenge.[6] Closely intertwined with these questions but not identical with them are a number of controversies and disputes about the role played by individuals or specific groups within this conceptual nexus. This is not surprising. The moving force behind the new effort at better understanding has not been "scholarship" or the "profession as a whole", but what has been termed "refractions of biography and scholarship".[7] What is here being foregrounded is a re-evaluation of self-interpretations and autobiographies as valuable sources, sharpening an awareness of the social construction of reality within the realm of the history of scholarship. For this reason, the new approaches have been especially useful in conjunction with biographic research projects such as the voluminous biography of the Freiburg historian Gerhard Ritter by Christoph Cornelißen.[8] In any event the "return of biography"[9] has not always galvanised internal debate in the profession. On the contrary: it has become clear in connection with Cornelißen's study that Ritter's personality is in fact no longer controversial enough to spark a fresh contemporary debate, and that the material collated in this study harbours few fundamental surprises.

In marked contrast with the case of Ritter, *deutschnational* in his convictions and commitments, some astonishment has indeed been generated by new studies of the "*Volksgeschichte*" of the late 1920s, 30s and 40s, although the recognition that a historiography largely defining itself as "*völkisch*" was fully consonant with Nazi ideology of that time is in itself nothing new. Bitter debates and stubborn disputes thus recently erupted over the manner in which leading historians such as Theodor Schieder and Werner Conze had played an active, even propagandistic role in this ideological confluence, as well as over the extent of this participation.[10] It has become clear, as the

[5]Jin-Sung Chun, *Das Bild der Moderne in der Nachkriegszeit. Die westdeutsche Strukturgeschichte im Spannungsfeld von Modernitätskritik und wissenschaftlicher Innovation 1948–1962*, Munich 2000.

[6]Nicolas Berg, *Der Holocaust und die westdeutschen Historiker. Erforschung und Erinnerung*, Göttingen 2003.

[7]Konrad H. Jarausch and Rüdiger Hohls, 'Brechungen von Biographie und Wissenschaft. Interviews mit deutschen Historiker/innen der Nachkriegsgeneration', in *idem* (eds.), *Versäumte Fragen. Deutsche Historiker im Schatten des Nationalsozialismus*, Stuttgart and Munich 2000, pp. 15–54.

[8]Christoph Cornelißen, *Gerhard Ritter. Geschichtswissenschaft und Politik im 20. Jahrhundert*, Düsseldorf 2001; on the positive re-evaluation of autobiographical self-interpretations in the framework of historiography see Volker Depkat, 'Autobiographie und die soziale Konstruktion von Wirklichkeit', in *Geschichte und Gesellschaft*, vol. 29, no. 3 (2003), pp. 441–476; Dagmar Günther, '"And now for something completely different." Prolegomena zur Autobiographie als Quelle der Geschichtswissenschaft', in *Historische Zeitschrift*, vol. 272 (2001), pp. 25–61; Nicolas Berg, 'Zwischen individuellem und historiographischem Gedächtnis. Der Nationalsozialismus in Autobiographien deutscher Historiker', in *BIOS. Zeitschrift für Biographieforschung und Oral History*, vol. 13, no. 1 (2000), pp. 181–207.

[9]See *Kursbuch*, no. 148 (2002), special issue on "the return of biography".

[10]Karl Heinz Roth and Angelika Ebbinghaus, 'Vorläufer des "Generalplans Ost". Eine Dokumentation über Theodor Schieders Polendenkschrift vom 7. Oktober 1939', in *1999*, vol. 7, no. 1 (1992), pp. 62—94; cf. Götz Aly, '"Daß uns Blut zu Gold werde". Theodor Schieder, Propagandist des Dritten Reiches', in *Menora. Jahrbuch für deutsch-jüdische Geschichte*, vol. 9 (1998), pp. 13–27; idem, 'Theodor Schieder und Werner Conze oder die Vorstufen der physischen Vernichtung', in Winfried Schulze and Otto G. Oexle (eds.), *Deutsche Historiker im Nationalsozialismus*, Frankfurt am Main 1998, pp. 163–182; by contrast, see Hans Ulrich Wehler, '"In den Fußtapfen der kämpfenden Wissenschaft"', in *Frankfurter Allgemeine Zeitung*, 4 January 1999, p. 48; against Wehler, see Götz Aly, '"Stakkato der Vertreibung, Pizzikato der Entlastung". Welche Sprache ersetzt die Rhetorik der Raumordnung? Eine Antwort auf Hans Ulrich Wehler', in *Frankfurter Allgemeine Zeitung*, 3 February 1999, p. 36. The volume *Versäumte Fragen* also goes back to a highly charged session on 'German

historian Reinhard Rürup aptly observes, that precisely the prominent authorities in the field succeeded in "placing an almost total seal" on the file of memories regarding their own Nazi past. And it has become just as clear that it is now up to their pupils to discuss and illuminate their own "neglected questions", as the above-cited title to an anthology of essays on the topic has phrased it: to ask questions their teachers had failed to raise.[11] In any event, the tendency in the postwar period for West German academic historians to view the Holocaust as a topic of secondary importance, to neglect or deflect the German mass murder, is no longer a matter of dispute. As Dirk van Laak has recently noted, the postwar process of "therapeutic forgetting" did not begin to be drained of its "political-cultural hegemony" until well into the 1970s[12]—and then only slowly and with great effort. In this respect, three particular questions have been the occasion for highly controversial assessments of the topography of postwar historiography: (1) to what extent was the long duration of such a defensive ploy driven by underlying biographical factors? (2) Did the ploy extend, as something like an epistemological given, far down into what Paul Nolte has termed the "long generation" of West German historians, signifying those born around 1930[13]—a generation including prominent figures such as Martin Broszat and Hans Mommsen? (3) Was there an associated exclusion of Jewish perspectives on the topic inside the German historians' guild?[14]

Historians in National Socialism' at the Conference of German Historians held in Frankfurt in 1998, in which the debate on Conze and Schieder caused a sensation, both inside the profession and for the broader public; see also Schulze and Oexle (eds.); on the conference itself, see the precise and differentiated report by Werner Lausecker, 'Bericht über einige Wahrnehmungen. Zur Sektion "Deutsche Historiker im Nationalsozialismus" am Deutschen Historikertag 1998 in Frankfurt am Main', in *Österreichische Zeitschrift für Geschichtswissenschaft* vol.10, no. 1 (1999), pp. 147–156.

[11]See interview with Reinhard Rürup, 'Das Dritte Reich hatte kein Problem mit den deutschen Historikern' in Jarausch and Hohls (eds.), pp. 267–280, here p. 279; Manfred Hettling, 'Schweigen im Konsens. Erst jetzt fragen deutsche Historiker nach der Rolle ihres Faches im "Dritten Reich"', in *Die Zeit*, 27 July 2000, p. 43.

[12]Dirk van Laak, 'Der Platz des Holocaust im deutschen Geschichtsbild', in Konrad Jarausch and Martin Sabrow (eds.), *Die historische Meistererzählung: Deutungslinien der deutschen Nachkriegsgeschichte nach 1945*, Göttingen 2002, pp. 163–193; Raphael Gross, 'Die verspätete Holocaustforschung', in *Tages-Anzeiger* (Zurich), 8 October 2001, p. 11.

[13]Paul Nolte, 'Die Historiker der Bundesrepublik. Rückblick auf eine lange Generation', in *Merkur* 53 (1999), pp. 413–423. Cf. Ulrich Herbert, 'Drei politische Generationen im 20. Jahrhundert', in Jürgen Reulecke (ed.), *Generationalität und Lebensgeschichte im 20. Jahrhundert*, Munich 2003, pp. 95–114.

[14]See, for example, Peter Longerich, 'Der Fall Martin Broszat', in *Die Zeit*, 14 August 2003; Rainer Blasius, 'Keiner wäscht weißer. Ja, nein, weiß nicht: Der Disput um den Historiker Martin Broszat', in *Frankfurter Allgemeine Zeitung*, 20 September 2003, p. 35; for a contrary position, see Norbert Frei, 'Hitler-Junge, Jahrgang 1926. Hat der Historiker Martin Broszat seine NSDAP-Mitgliedschaft verschwiegen—oder wusste er nichts davon?', in *Die Zeit*, 11 September 2003, p. 50; Hans Mommsen, 'Täter und Opfer—ein Streit um die Historiker', in *Die Welt*, 13 September 2003, p. 9. The controversy was sparked by the following article: Nicolas Berg, 'Die Lebenslüge vom Pathos der Nüchternheit. Subjektive jüdische Erinnerung und objektive deutsche Zeitgeschichtsforschung? Joseph Wulf, Martin Broszat und das Institut für Zeitgeschichte in den 60er Jahren', in *Süddeutsche Zeitung*, 17 July 2003, p. 14. A parallel dispute recently erupted over personal knowledge by various, sometimes prominent professors of German literature of their own Nazi Party membership. See Karl Otto Conrady, 'In den Fängen der Vergangenheit. Der neue Streit über Germanisten und ihre Mitgliedschaft in der NSDAP', in *Die Zeit*, 4 December 2003, p. 49; that dispute was triggered by Christoph König (ed.), *Internationales Germanistenlexikon 1800–1950*, 3 vols., Berlin 2003. For a more general view, see Frank-Rutger Hausmann, 'Schien die Sonne auch für Nazis? Braunhemden unter Talaren sind für keinen Skandal mehr gut', in *Frankfurter Allgemeine Zeitung*, 27 November 2003; Armin Nolzen, 'Nur zu illustrativen Zwecken. In der NS-Forschung sind zukünftig neue Schwerpunktsetzungen vonnöten: Einwurf zur Debatte um die Mitgliedschaft führender bundesdeutscher Intellektueller in der NSDAP', in *Frankfurter Rundschau*, 4 February 2004.

Discussion of the new insights that have emerged from these debates regarding leading historians such as Theodor Schieder and Werner Conze, Hermann Aubin and Karl Dietrich Erdmann, Hermann Heimpel and Reinhard Wittram would go beyond the scope of this essay. Such discussion has taken place elsewhere, more or less exhaustively, sometimes in concentrated form as defensive essays.[15] Some detailed studies—several announced for the near future, including one on Aubin[16]—have elevated the general debate to a new level. Nevertheless, many questions remain open—still debated and inadequately answered—for instance that of the intellectual legacy of Karl Dietrich Erdmann.[17] For some questions no answers will be forthcoming in the foreseeable future, since essential archival material will not be accessible for another ten or fifteen years. (The stagnating discussion regarding Hermann Heimpel is the result of such a situation).[18]

The vehemence apparent in all these controversies can be explained by a postponed dispute regarding two key, interrelated questions: How can the history of a scholarly domain be properly addressed in a biographical framework?[19] And to what extent can the exemplary illustration of the ties between life and scholarly labour serve as a cognitive tool?[20] Seen from this vantage-point, neither the context nor its evaluation is in fact under dispute, but rather the personalities: who stands inside this context, who outside it?

[15]See, for example, Wolfgang J. Mommsen, '"Gestürzte Denkmäler"? Die "Fälle" Aubin, Conze, Erdmann und Schieder', in Jürgen Elvert and Susanne Krauß (eds.), *Historische Debatten und Kontroversen im 19. und 20. Jahrhundert*, Wiesbaden 2003, pp. 96–109 (with references to further literature).

[16]The director of the Herder Institute, Eduard Mühle, is working on a biography of Hermann Aubin; he has published several preliminary essays: Eduard Mühle, 'Hermann Aubin, der "deutsche Osten" und der Nationalsozialismus—Deutungen eines akademischen Wirkens im Dritten Reich', in Hartmut Lehmann and Otto Gerhard Oexle (eds.), *Nationalsozialismus in den Kulturwissenschaften. Band 1: Fächer – Milieus – Karrieren*, Göttingen 2003, pp. 523–584; *idem*, 'Weltkriegserlebnis an der galizisch-polnischen Ostfront 1914/15. Zur Wahrnehmung des Ostens in Feldpostbriefen des Ostforschers Hermann Aubin', in *Zeitschrift für Ostmitteleuropa-Forschung* vol. 51, no. 4 (2002), pp. 529–576. On Aubin see also Hans-Erich Volkmann, 'Historiker aus politischer Leidenschaft. Hermann Aubin als Volks-, Kulturboden- und Ostforscher', in *Zeitschrift für Geschichtswissenschaft* vol. 49, no. 1 (2001), pp. 32–49.

[17]The debate on Erdmann has subsided. For its onset see Martin Kröger and Roland Thimme, *Die Geschichtsbilder des Historikers Karl Dietrich Erdmann. Vom Dritten Reich zur Bundesrepublik*, Munich 1996. For a contrasting view see Eberhard Jäckel and Agnes Blänsdorf, 'Karl Dietrich Erdmann und der Nationalsozialismus', in *Geschichte in Wissenschaft und Unterricht*, vol. 48, no. 4 (1997), pp. 224–240. For a reply see Martin Kröger and Roland Thimme, 'Karl Dietrich Erdmann im "Dritten Reich". Eine Antwort auf Eberhard Jäckel und Agnes Blänsdorf', *ibid.*, pp. 462–478; *idem*, Karl Dietrich Erdmann, 'Utopien und Realitäten', in *Zeitschrift für Geschichtswissenschaft* vol. 46, no. 7 (1998), pp. 603–621.

[18]Hermann Heimpel's papers will remain closed for a long time to come. For a critique of the available interpretations of Heimpel (interpretations offered by his students) see Klaus Sommer, 'Eine Frage der Perspektive? Hermann Heimpel und der Nationalsozialismus', in Tobias Kaiser, Steffen Kaudelka, and Matthias Steinbach (eds.), *Historisches Denken und gesellschaftlicher Wandel. Studien zur Geschichtswissenschaft zwischen Kaiserreich und deutscher Zweistaatlichkeit*, Berlin 2004, pp. 199–215.

[19]Claus Leggewie, 'Mitleid mit Doktorvätern oder: Wissenschaftsgeschichte in Biographien', in *Merkur*, vol. 53, no. 5 (1999), pp. 433–444.

[20]See Hans-Harald Müller, 'Ein Magazin voller Geschichten zur deutschen Philologie. Das "Internationale Germanistenlexikon" und das Leben. Eine Veranschaulichung', in *Süddeutsche Zeitung*, 1 March 2004, p. 14.

II. ON THE PROBLEM OF SPLIT EPISTEMOLOGY: HANS ROTHFELS AS AN HISTORICAL CHALLENGE

These are key problems emerging from the border-zone between contemporary history and the culture of memory and generating questions of split or schizoid epistemology: an epistemology challenging historians to analyse specific processes at work within the history of German scholarship, as well as the individual's location within these processes. In regard to transformations within various scholarly disciplines in Germany after 1945, the problems will likely require even greater scrutiny.[21] Mitchell G. Ash, Otto G. Oexle and Bernd Weisbrod have all recently pointed to the double aspect of the problem of post-totalitarian self-understanding within academic scholarship—an understanding that had to guarantee the individual both a capacity for change *and* personal authenticity. In other words, he (or she) had to first be disentangled from complicity or collaboration with the old system, past achievements transposed to new temporal and spatial loci within the framework of a new status quo. And this had to be done with distinct stress placed on supposed continuities. An individual had to be willing and able to learn—while remaining the same familiar person.[22]

* * *

Among the various scholarly disciplines, the history of historiography is challenged in a special way by the singular, exemplary figure of Hans Rothfels.[23] In the above-cited discussions, hardly any name came up more frequently than his (although this was frequently through intimation) in reference to the broader context. Conversely, hardly any figure in the field of contemporary history better illustrates the intertwining of the new and the old, of positions before 1933 and after 1945, of transformations in the rhetorical cloak of the old and continuities appearing as seeming innovations. The dominance he established within his discipline is becoming ever clearer. Even in the retrospective interviews contained in Jarausch and Hohls' *Versäumte Fragen*, it sometimes appears impossible for those historians being interviewed to render fair judgement on Rothfels' students Schieder and Conze, as well as on contemporary German history in postwar Germany in general, without first turning to the life and ideas of their teacher.

[21]See Konrad H. Jarausch and Martin Sabrow (eds.), *Verletztes Gedächtnis. Erinnerungskultur und Zeitgeschichte im Konflikt*, Frankfurt am Main 2002.

[22]Mitchell G. Ash, 'Verordnete Umbrüche—Konstruierte Kontinuitäten: Zur Entnazifizierung von Wissenschaftlern und Wissenschaften nach 1945', in *Zeitschrift für Geschichtswissenschaft*, vol. 43, no. 10 (1995), pp. 903–923; Bernd Weisbrod, 'Dem wandelbaren Geist. Akademisches Ideal und wissenschaftliche Transformation in der Nachkriegszeit', in *idem* (ed.), *Akademische Vergangenheitspolitik. Beiträge zur Wissenschaftskultur der Nachkriegszeit*, Göttingen 2002, pp. 11–35, here pp. 30f.; Otto G. Oexle, '"Zusammenarbeit mit Baal". Über die Mentalität deutscher Geisteswissenschaftler 1933—und nach 1945', in *Historische Anthropologie. Kultur, Gesellschaft, Alltag*, vol. 8, no. 1 (2000), pp. 1–27; *idem*, 'Zweierlei Kultur. Zur Erinnerungskultur deutscher Geisteswissenschaftler nach 1945', in *Rechtshistorisches Journal*, vol. 16 (1997), pp. 358–390.

[23]On Rothfels as a "special case" see interview with Rürup, in Jarausch and Hohls (eds.), pp. 278 f.

In controversies centred on such history, observations by Hans Rothfels had foundational importance. In this light, Rothfels' presence on the postwar West German historiographical scene relativises the thesis, proposed on occasion, that the influence of emigrant historians on that scene was basically minor.[24] At the same time, the basic thrust of both personal recollections of Rothfels and assessments of his place in scholarship is highly disparate. For example, Wolfram Fischer's emphasis on Rothfels' role as an educator in the period after his remigration is not without a certain undertone of discontent. Many of his students from Tübingen in the 1950s themselves describe a generally "distanced" demeanour and the "dry", "wooden" and basically "old-fashioned" tenor (Hartmut Lehmann) of his lectures.[25] But within the smaller circle composed of his doctoral candidates and assistants in Königsberg before the Second World War, Rothfels' word was authoritative. In that circle, he was revered as a kind of "deity", his books as "scripture" (Wolfgang Mommsen).[26] Over the span of several recent decades, testimonials from these different periods—from his pupils in the 1930s and again in the 1950s and 60s—shaped Rothfels' image. But there was, in fact, no genuinely historical (or even historiographical) interest in his writings or person, aside from work by Peter Thomas Walther: a doctoral thesis on Rothfels appearing in the USA in 1989; two short essays published in the mid-1980s, dealing in part with Rothfels, but then precisely and knowledgeably, hence with lasting value.[27] In any case, for a considerable time after Rothfels' death in 1976, articles by Werner Conze and Hans Mommsen had the strongest influence on the general understanding of Rothfels.[28] These articles were based in part on unpublished material, but were still written in the basically adulatory spirit of the collection of open letters presented to Rothfels on the occasion of his seventieth birthday.[29] Examinations of Rothfels' historiography had to wait until the 1990s,

[24]Sebastian Conrad, *Auf der Suche nach der verlorenen Nation. Geschichtsschreibung in Westdeutschland und Japan 1945–1960*, p. 344; for a contrary view, see Claus-Dieter Krohn, 'Unter Schwerhörigen? Zur selektiven Rezeption des Exils in den wissenschaftlichen und kulturpolitischen Debatten der frühen Nachkriegszeit', in Weisbrod (ed.), p. 118.

[25]See the interviews with Wolfram Fischer and Hartmut Lehmann, in Jarausch and Hohls (eds.), pp. 101 and 322. Hans Rothfels recalls his own mentor, Otto Hintze, as a "knight in armour"; see *idem*, 'Erinnerungen an Otto Hintze', Ms. [3 S.], in Bundesarchiv Koblenz, NL 213, No. 36 (dated "Tübingen, July 1965").

[26]Interview with Wolfgang J. Mommsen, in Jarausch and Hohls (eds.), pp. 196 and 203.

[27]Peter Thomas Walther, 'Von Meinecke zu Beard? Die nach 1933 emigrierten deutschen Neuzeithistoriker', doctoral thesis, State University of New York 1989; *idem*, 'Emigrierte deutsche Historiker in den USA', in *Berichte zur Wissenschaftsgeschichte* vol. 7 (1984), pp. 41–52; *idem*, 'Emigrierte deutsche Historiker in den Vereinigten Staaten, 1945–1950: Blick oder Sprung über den Großen Teich?', in Christoph Cobet (ed.), *Einführung in Fragen an die Geschichtswissenschaft in Deutschland nach Hitler 1945–1950*, Frankfurt am Main 1986, pp. 41–50.

[28]Hans Mommsen, 'Geschichtsschreibung und Humanität. Zum Gedenken an Hans Rothfels', in Wolfgang Benz and Hermann Graml (eds.), *Aspekte deutscher Außenpolitik im 20. Jahrhundert*, Stuttgart 1976, pp. 10–27; *idem*, 'Hans Rothfels', in Hans-Ulrich Wehler (ed.), *Deutsche Historiker*, vol. 9, Göttingen 1982, pp. 127–147; Werner Conze, 'Hans Rothfels', in *Historische Zeitschrift*, vol. 237 (1983), pp. 311–360.

[29]Theodor Schieder, 'Hans Rothfels zum 70. Geburtstag am 12. April 1961', in *Vierteljahrshefte für Zeitgeschichte* vol. 9, no. 1 (1961), pp. 117–123.

when a handful of studies on specialised questions appeared,[30] along with initial efforts at a synthesis; such efforts have taken an increasingly critical position regarding Rothfels.[31]

This shift—an acknowledgment of the "all too positive image of Rothfels in the postwar generation"[32]—occurred in close connection with the above-discussed debates. It was first manifest mainly in efforts to explore the milieu of the so-called Rothfels group, the most outstanding example being Ingo Haar's study of historians under National Socialism, which deals extensively although not exclusively with Rothfels and several of his Königsberg pupils, along with their networks.[33] Attention has also been paid to the power of his personality to forge a community of like-minded individuals after his return to the University of Tübingen. Thus in his study of German postwar historiography published in 2001, Thomas Etzemüller repeatedly refers to Rothfels as a "father figure", characterising his role, in the Foucaultian sense, as that of group "spokesperson", or "mentor" or "patriarch".[34] Gerhard Ritter, coining the term "Rothfelsians", had already expressed his surprise at the group's coherence around their guiding light in 1962.[35]

Nevertheless, despite such scholarly evolution, no comparably intensive research has yet been undertaken on Rothfels' function as a scholar and historian in the postwar era. There have been recent signs that a "Rothfels debate" is emerging.[36]

[30]Lothar Machtan, 'Hans Rothfels und die Anfänge der historischen Sozialpolitikerforschung in Deutschland', in *Internationale Wissenschaftliche Korrespondenz zur Geschichte der Arbeiterbewegung* vol. 28, no. 2 (1992), pp. 161–210; Wolfgang Neugebauer, 'Hans Rothfels Weg zur vergleichenden Geschichte Ostmitteleuropas, besonders im Übergang von früher Neuzeit zur Moderne', in *Berliner Jahrbuch für Osteuropäische Geschichte* vol. 3, no. 1 1996), pp. 333–378.

[31]See, for example, Karen Schönwälder, *Historiker und Politik. Geschichtswissenschaft im Nationalsozialismus*, Frankfurt am Main—New York 1992, pp. 53 ff.; Oberkrome, pp. 95ff. and 133ff.

[32]Peter Schöttler, 'Einleitende Bemerkungen', in *idem* (ed.), *Geschichtswissenschaft als Legitimationswissenschaft 1918–1945*, Frankfurt am Main 1997, pp. 7–30, here p. 23.

[33]Ingo Haar, *Historiker im Nationalsozialismus. Deutsche Geschichtswissenschaft und der "Volkstumskampf" im Osten*, Göttingen 2000 (2nd rev. edn. 2002), esp. pp. 70ff.; see also *idem*, '"Revisionistische" Historiker und Jugendbewegung: Das Königsberger Beispiel', in Schöttler (ed.), pp. 52–103.

[34]Etzemüller, *Sozialgeschichte als politische Geschichte*, pp. 11, 25 f., 32 ("father figure"), 45 ("patriarch"), 47 ("authority"), 134 ("mentor"), 213 ("chieftain).

[35]For citation see *ibid.*, p. 46.

[36]Volker Ullrich, 'Der Fall Rothfels. Der Streit um den berühmten Zeithistoriker und die Versäumnisse der Geschichtswissenschaft', in *Die Zeit*, 24 July 2003, p. 38. The article comments on two conferences on Rothfels held simultaneously at the Centre Marc Bloch in Berlin ('Hans Rothfels 1891–1976—ein "Wanderer zwischen den Welten"?') and at the Institute for Contemporary History in Munich ('Hans Rothfels und die deutsche Zeitgeschichte') in the summer of 2003; see also the preceding discussion in the H-Net Portal 'H-Soz-u-Kult', with contributions by Peter Thomas Walther, 'Eine kleine Intervention und ein bescheidener Vorschlag in Sachen Rothfels'; Karl Heinz Roth, 'Hans Rothfels: Neokonservative Geschichtspolitik diesseits und jenseits des Atlantiks'; Thomas Etzemüller, 'Suchen wir Schuld oder wollen wir Gesellschaft analysieren? Eine Anmerkung zur aktuellen Debatte um Hans Rothfels'; Karen Schönwälder, 'Repräsentant der Übergänge'; Jan Eckel, 'Historiographie als Personalgeschichte. Bemerkungen zu einer neuen Diskussion über deutsche Historiker'; Mathias Beer, 'Wo bleibt die Zeitgeschichte? Fragen zur Geschichte einer Disziplin' (in http://hsozkult.geschichte.hu-berlin.de/forum/id=281&type=diskussionen). See now most recently: Karsten Borgmann (ed.), *Historisches Forum*, vol. 1 (2004): 'Hans Rothfels und die Zeitgeschichte' (publications of Clio-online, no. 2); http://edoc.hu-berlin.de/e_histfor/1/PDF/HistFor_1-2004.pdf. This volume includes an extensive bibliography compiled by Nina Balz: 'Zitierte und ergänzte Literatur zum "Rothfels-Streit"', pp. 95–106.

But now as before, the discussion is dominated by the question of Rothfels' presumed proclivities towards Nazi ideology and the politics he articulated before his forced emigration in 1938.[37] Karl Heinz Roth, in several articles appearing over recent years, has been the only scholar to examine Rothfels as a "politician of history"; he has advanced the thesis that Rothfels worked to rehabilitate two separate discredited phases of past German history, and did so in two separate periods: after the First World War, and after 1945. In this manner, Roth argues, Rothfels' influence helped "delay by decades" the formulation of decisive questions about Nazi society and rule.[38] Such an approach sharpens the critique Winfried Schulze levelled in a far more cautious manner in an essay published in 1995 in a festschrift for Hans Mommsen. Already here, significant stress was laid on Rothfels as a "strategic personality" for the postwar period. In his analysis Schulze moved significantly forward from his earlier position, elaborating a wide-ranging study of postwar German historiography.[39] Schulze has criticised the approach manifest in even the most recent debates, arguing that Rothfels and his "key function" were being sorely neglected; he has emphasised the need for a "critical biography of Rothfels".[40]

III. A FRACTURED UNITY: LIFE AND SCHOLARSHIP IN THE CAREER OF ROTHFELS

One can assume that such a biography would pay due attention to the "unusual development of a conservative-revolutionary Prussian who had had scant scholarly impact in the United States into a magnanimous grandseigneur of professional historians in West Germany".[41] Indeed, writing in 1986, Peter Thomas Walther

[37] See the recent debate between Heinrich August Winkler and Ingo Haar with the following contributions: Heinrich August Winkler, 'Hans Rothfels – ein Lobredner Hitlers? Quellenkritische Bemerkungen zu Ingo Haars Buch "Historiker im Nationalsozialismus"', in *Vierteljahrshefte für Zeitgeschichte*, vol. 49, no. 4 (2001), pp. 643–652; Ingo Haar, 'Quellenkritik oder Kritik der Quellen? Replik auf Heinrich August Winkler', *ibid.*, vol. 50, no. 3 (2002), pp. 497–505; Heinrich August Winkler, 'Geschichtswissenschaft oder Geschichtsklitterung? Ingo Haar und Hans Rothfels: Eine Erwiderung', *ibid.*, vol. 50, no. 4 (2002), pp. 635–651.

[38] Karl Heinz Roth, 'Geschichtspolitische Doktrinen im Wandel der Zeiten. Weimar—NS-Diktatur—Bundesrepublik', in *Zeitschrift für Geschichtswissenschaft* vol. 49, no. 12 (2001), pp. 1061–1073; *idem*, '"Richtung halten": Hans Rothfels und die neo-konservative Geschichtsschreibung diesseits und jenseits des Atlantik', in *Sozial.Geschichte. Zeitschrift für historische Analyse des 20. und 21. Jahrhunderts*, new series, vol. 18, no. 1 (2003), pp. 41–71.

[39] Winfried Schulze, 'Hans Rothfels und die deutsche Geschichtswissenschaft nach 1945', in *Von der Aufgabe der Freiheit. Politische Verantwortung und bürgerliche Gesellschaft im 19. und 20. Jahrhundert. Festschrift für Hans Mommsen*, ed. by Christian Jansen, Lutz Niethammer and Bernd Weisbrod, Berlin 1995, pp. 83–98; cf. *idem*, *Deutsche Geschichtswissenschaft nach 1945*, Munich 1989.

[40] *ibid.*, p. 86; see also interview with Winfried Schulze, in Jarausch and Hohls (eds.), pp. 417f. A comprehensive research project on Rothfels led by Jan Eckel is currently underway at the University of Freiburg: 'Hans Rothfels. Biographie eines Intellektuellen im 20. Jahrhundert'; see also *idem*, 'Intellektuelle Transformationen im Spiegel der Widerstandsdeutungen', in Ulrich Herbert (ed.), *Wandlungsprozesse in Westdeutschland. Belastung, Integration, Liberalisierung 1945–1980*, Göttingen 2002, pp. 140–176. For some time, the Technische Universität Chemnitz has been announcing the forthcoming publication of a volume of selected letters of Rothfels, edited by Günther Grünthal: see http://www.tu-chemnitz.de/phil/nng/Archiv/Arch_pro/fb_98.html

[41] Walther, 'Von Meinecke zu Beard?' p. 49.

sensed that Rothfels' career trajectory was marked by a "certain irony", since as an "emigrant and Jew", he had become a veritable "figure of legitimation" for postwar German historiography.[42] At the time, Walther did not pursue this line of inquiry; but he did call attention to the fundamentally contrary nature of Rothfels' influence: after his remigration and his "encouragement of research on contemporary history", he in effect paved a road for the, as Walther termed it, "antiquated guild" (*verkrustete Zunft*) to begin critically examining the political and academic views of those to whom Rothfels had been closely allied before 1933, making them the object of its sharpest critique. Shortly after Rothfels' death in 1976, Konrad Kwiet termed it a "rewarding research-task" to probe his attitude towards Judaism. Kwiet was correctly assuming that the fact of Rothfels' "Jewish origins" was "little known". Yet his assimilation, Kwiet stressed even then, was apparently "so total that it did not allow for any ties whatsoever to Judaism. At best it allowed some memories to be aired, in an intimate circle, of the earlier discrimination he had experienced as a student and historian".[43] However, Kwiet's suggestion did not bear fruit at the time: no detailed methodological-epistemological study followed—one that would have taken appropriate account of memory, perspectivity and emotion.[44]

In this context, from a present-day viewpoint an apparent contradiction seems provocative: namely that in previous discussions of Rothfels, the dominant opinion has been that he succeeded, in an especially reflective manner, in fusing the key biographical questions of the century with his chosen agenda of research, producing a striking harmony of the personal and professional. Hence Hans Mommsen refers to his "ability … to overcome the dissonances between his own world of experience and his intellectual character, achieving a unity of private life and scholarly work, and this despite a chain of interlinking personal and general perils".[45] Hans Mommsen, in any case, does not further analyse this "ability" or relate it to his mentor's forced emigration and exile. Likewise, in his eulogy for Rothfels, and drawing on Rothfels' own autobiographical writings, Theodor Schieder has placed special emphasis on Rothfels' "unobtrusively pre-shaped unity of scholarship and way of living" (*unaufdringlich vorgeprägte Einheit von Wissenschaft und Lebenshaltung*). In Schieder's view, Rothfels "repeatedly sought to reconstitute" this unity "whenever he confronted new situations".[46] Such an assessment may be accurate in regard to Rothfels' image of Bismarck, or his ideas regarding nationhood and nationalities in Eastern Europe—a theme that his Königsberg professorship had helped make highly

[42]*ibid.*

[43]Konrad Kwiet, 'Judenverfolgung und Judenvernichtung im Dritten Reich. Ein historiographischer Überblick', in *Militärgeschichtliche Mitteilungen*, vol. 27, no. 1 (1980), pp. 149–192; cited from the article's revised version published in Dan Diner (ed.), *Ist der Nationalsozialismus Geschichte? Zu Historisierung und Historikerstreit*, Frankfurt am Main 1987, p. 295.

[44]As an initial approach see Nicolas Berg, 'Perspektivität, Erinnerung und Emotion. Anmerkungen zum "Gefühlsgedächtnis" in Holocaustdiskursen', in Gerald Echterhoff and Martin Saar (eds.), *Kontexte und Kulturen des Erinnerns. Maurice Halbwachs und das Paradigma des kollektiven Gedächtnisses. Mit einem Geleitwort von Jan Assmann*, Constance 2002, pp. 225–251.

[45]Hans Mommsen, 'Geschichtsschreibung und Humanität', p. 11.

[46]Theodor Schieder, 'Betroffenheit einer Generation. Zum Tode des Historikers Hans Rothfels', in *Rheinischer Merkur*, 2 July 1976.

topical—but not in regard to Nazism and antisemitism. Although he felt "a sense of bitterness over the forced separation", and gratitude for the "enrichment which the American environment had meant for him", in his relationship to Germany and the Germans, "he had nonetheless never drawn that inner line of separation", as another famous pupil of his, Werner Conze, put it in his eulogy for Rothfels.[47]

The failure to draw that "internal line of separation" had a significant impact on the development of postwar German historiography. Hans Rothfels repeatedly referred to his reacquisition of a "community of experience" (*Erlebnisgemeinschaft*) with the Germans. And he tried to achieve this not only in the private realm, but also in that of academic history, in the form of a return to the old "community of interpretation". However, since Rothfels' view of himself and his pupils' view of their teacher have prevailed in both general evaluations in newspapers and professional journals and specialised studies in postwar German historiography, we need to look more carefully at the problem of revoking the "inner line"—or the refusal to draw it in the first place. Although not discussed until now, this problem lies at the heart of all previous interpretations of Rothfels. Can his historiography be read as part of a *Jewish* narrative, beyond any political provenance, through which the Nazis' victims helped shape the postwar scholarly and public image of the terrible recent events and their meaning? Is a cognitive vector inscribed in his historical works—a vector addressing his personal historical experiences, or at least preserving and protecting them?

* * *

A central premise of this discussion is that in Rothfels' case, a unity of life and work was anything but uniform. Rothfels had a decisive impact on the emerging field of contemporary history in the German Federal Republic. In doing so, he excluded a significant portion of his "bitter personal experience" from the problems meriting inquiry: namely, the portion encompassing topics such as antisemitism, Aryanisation, expulsion, exile and the mass-murder of the European Jews. These were, to be sure, topics that contemporary history in West Germany dealt with only hesitatingly, generally favouring the topic of German resistance to Nazism, foregrounding the many and diverse apologies formulated on behalf of the German nation-state and its traditions, and favourably emphasising the role of the bourgeois élites. This tendency was bolstered by Rothfels' opinion-shaping historical studies. In this manner Rothfels' "function as a bridge" in the politics of the past—his role in

[47]Werner Conze, 'Geschichte in Ideen und Personen. Zum Tode von Hans Rothfels', in *Frankfurter Allgemeine Zeitung*, 25 June 1976. In a similar vein, in his famous lecture at the Mannheim conference of historians in 1976, Conze noted that Rothfels brought "his own bitter personal experiences to bear on research in contemporary history". In Rothfels' methodologically pioneering introduction to the first volume of the *Vierteljahrshefte für Zeitgeschichte*, Conze stressed, he had "objectified" his experiences in a classic manner; see *idem*, 'Die deutsche Geschichtswissenschaft seit 1945', in *Historische Zeitschrift*, vol. 225 (1977), pp. 1–28, here p. 15.

generating a "restitution of German questions in the realm of scholarship"[48]—was an option whose personal legitimacy and biographical consequences require more probing scrutiny than is possible here. But as its significance was not only private and personal, in coming to terms with the meaning of Rothfels' career one needs to take account of the impact of both an unarticulated process of remembering and an unstated experience of history.

In exploring such factors, one must avoid hasty prejudgements regarding specific life-decisions Rothfels made in the course of his career, since we still know far too little about them. Rather, our interest here will be focused on Rothfels the returned emigrant as founder of a German postwar historiographical discourse—on his enduring importance for both the history of his profession and the image its members articulated, in Germany for Germans, over a span of nearly three decades. One argument that will be made in this essay is that through his important role in constructing this image, Rothfels served, despite his own recent exile, to marginalise the experiences of those who had fled Germany or been persecuted by the Nazi regime.

It is now possible to confirm Hans Mommsen's 1982 assessment of an "elemental relation to history" in Rothfel's writing in a different way than was originally intended: such a relation is indeed present in Rothfels' generation as a whole; their work before 1933 and after 1945 was indeed significantly shaped by their ability to "ultimately harmonise historical knowledge and individual self-discovery".[49] But "historical knowledge" and "individual self-discovery" were possible in Rothfels' case—and in that of German contemporary historiography as a whole—because neither Rothfels nor his discipline were prepared to transpose specifically Jewish experiences of history onto an epistemological plane in an effort to grasp historical meaning and forge forms of individual self-knowledge.

IV. RESENTMENT AGAINST RETURNED EMIGRANTS—HANS ROTHFELS AS AN EXCEPTION

Born in 1891 in Kassel, Rothfels was a student of Friedrich Meinecke in Freiburg before the First World War. He also studied with Max Lenz, Hans Delbrück and Otto Hintze in Berlin and Heidelberg, where he wrote a doctoral dissertation on Clausewitz under the supervision of Hermann Oncken; in the years of crisis of the Weimar Republic he wrote his Habilitation thesis for Meinecke in Berlin on the social policies of Theodor Lohmann.[50] Rothfels had returned home from the front with a serious injury that would leave him handicapped for the rest of his life. In 1926 he received a professorship at the University of Königsberg, where he devoted his research to nationality problems in Eastern Europe. He filtered his views on the history of the

[48]See Berg, *Holocaust*, pp. 143–192.

[49]Hans Mommsen, 'Hans Rothfels', in Hans-Ulrich Wehler (ed.), *Deutsche Historiker*, vol. 9, Göttingen 1982, pp. 127–147, here p. 129.

[50]Hans Rothfels, *Theodor Lohmann und die Kampfjahre der staatlichen Sozialpolitik (1871–1905). Nach ungedruckten Quellen bearbeitet*, Berlin 1927.

state through the prism of the new *Volksgeschichte,* now espousing a programme of "integrated folk history" *(ganzheitliche Volksgeschichte)* to supplant the concept of the state as *Machtstaat.*[51] In respect to this conceptual focus, Rothfels would later write to his colleague Reinhard Wittram that he felt he basically shared some responsibility for the rise of Nazism: "Didn't the Nazis have a certain diabolical skill for slithering inside everything that was 'genuine'? ... In part, we assisted them in that, and I don't exclude myself from this blame".[52]

Although Rothfels converted to Protestantism in 1910 at the age of nineteen, as the son of Jewish parents he would become a victim of Nazi racial policy. The fact that he was not immediately subject in 1933 to the "Law on the Restoration of the Professional Civil Service" was due to his war injury. In the eyes of the Nazi Party, Rothfels was a "Judenprofessor". It was "totally unacceptable that a person of alien blood should teach the coming generation of young Germans about German history".[53] In an open letter, his students defended "all of Prof. Rothfels' work in teaching and research", and his "attacks against the destructive tendencies mentioned and against ruinous individualism". They considered him one of the "very best now paving the way for a new spirit in scholarship".[54] Moreover, the university's *Kurator,* who had no reservations about seeing Rothfels as "one of those now preparing the path for the new Germany", wrote to the Ministry of Science, Art and National Education in Berlin to praise Rothfels for the "always genuine German courage of his convictions". He suggested creating exceptions to the pending "de-Judaisation (*Entjudung*) of the German university system, noting that in Königsberg, Rothfels had "constructed a world of ideas basically identical with the one which has created the new Germany". The *Kurator* indicated in closing that "our new state is so strong that it can easily place itself behind a man like Rothfels".[55] Yet despite such testimonials on his behalf, the Protestant and Prussian conservative was dismissed from his post and stripped of his title and honours. He always regarded this as an "error", and in taking leave from his students he articulated something like an oath of allegiance or alliance: "Allow us to be in essence something resembling a community of the intellect [*eine intelligible Gemeinschaft*]".[56]

[51]For a detailed overview cf. Haar, '"Revisionistische" Historiker und Jugendbewegung', pp. 52–103; *idem,* 'Historiker im Nationalsozialismus', *passim.*

[52]Hans Rothfels to Reinhard Wittram, 25 October 1946, quoted in Roth, '"Richtung halten"', pp. 41f.; see also Hans Rothfels, 'Die Geschichtsschreibung in den dreißiger Jahren', in Andreas Flitner (ed.), *Deutsches Geistesleben und Nationalsozialismus. Eine Vortragsreihe der Universität Tübingen,* Tübingen 1965, pp. 90–107, here p. 106: He too, Rothfels confirmed, had himself "for a time been entangled"; nevertheless his lecture's basic thrust is to protect his colleagues (see p. 106).

[53]Representative of the party's central office to the deputy of the Führer, 2 July 1934, in Bundesarchiv Koblenz (BAK), Nachlass (NL) Rothfels 213, no. 20.

[54]Open letter to Hans Rothfels, 2 July 1934, *ibid.* A letter from the students to Rothfels himself, likewise from early July 1934, contained the following sentences: "In recent weeks we have experienced with you the beginning of a new Germany, and have welcomed the long-hoped-for change. ... Under your guidance, the insight into national and social questions has broadened our perspective on the development and essence of the new Reich". (*ibid.*)

[55]*Kurator* of the Albertus University Königsberg to the Minister for Science, Art and National Education, 8 April 1933, in BAK, NL Rothfels 213, no. 20.

[56]Hans Rothfels, 'Abschiedsworte beim Zusammensein mit dem Seminar in Juditten', 25 July 1934, in BAK, NL Rothfels 213, 20 (unnumbered, p. 6).

What followed Rothfels' academic expulsion was the then familiar chain of events: initially, the *Historische Zeitschrift* spurned his reviews. Later, during the November 1938 nation-wide pogrom, he was arrested. But in his case luck played its part and he was released.[57] That same year he left Germany and headed for England, where after the outbreak of the war he was detained as a German and sent to an internment camp on the Isle of Man. Eventually he was offered a professorship at Brown University in Providence, Rhode Island, and after the war he was appointed to one of the most respected chairs at the University of Chicago. Still in the states, he wrote what is probably his most famous book, *The German Opposition to Hitler* (published in 1948 by the Henry Regnery company in Hinsdale, Illinois, near Chicago) which would pave the way for his return to Germany: initially as a guest lecturer in Tübingen and Göttingen, and then from 1951 onwards as full professor in Tübingen.

In debates on Rothfels, it has at times been possible to gain an impression that the various phases of his life could be separated into five different sections representing five layers of memory and time within German history, each individually negotiable: *Kaiserreich*, Weimar Republic, National Socialism, emigration and Federal Republic. But the different character of Rothfels' life within these phases of evolving experience is not what has made him a key personality in German postwar and scholarly history. Rather, this has emerged from his labour to bridge biographical breaks and gullies, to distil something that endures in the midst of change. To begin to grasp the meaning of Rothfel's career, one must consider the way in which his work of historical interpretation was counterposed to these ruptures in historical flow—especially his influential reading of the Third Reich, which resonated powerfully within the self-understanding of the early Federal Republic, indeed helping it to formulate its sense of identity. By contrast, defining Rothfels as a representative of a "unique patriotism of German-Jewish symbiosis" (*einzigartiger Patriotismus deutsch-jüdischer Symbiose)*[58] merely serves to distort the nature of the discursive-communicative historical path that Rothfels travelled. Put briefly, such a definition disregards the fact that Rothfels' function in the years after 1945 lay in an interplay of perspectives. It is true that as a foreigner, emigré and expelled Jew, he was ascribed special importance. This was not, however, because of any new perspective he championed, but rather because of his re-importation of old views, his formulations of the positions of a German patriot that his colleagues could no longer afford to profess.

Contemporaries very consciously perceived and used this unique function of Rothfels for the postwar discipline of contemporary German history. Siegfried A. Kaehler, before the remigration of his friend—a move he constantly tried to dissuade him from taking—spoke quite bluntly about Rothfels' situation. His "current position between two spheres of Western scholarship is so unique and special that it

[57]Interview with Hans Rothfels by Viktor v. Oertzen and Hubert Locher for the Südwestfunk broadcasting corporation (n.d.), in BAK, NL Rothfels 213, No. 20.

[58]Erich Kosthorst, 'Mein Weg durch die Zeitgeschichte', in Hartmut Lehmann and Gerhard G. Oexle (eds.), *Erinnerungsstücke. Wege in die Vergangenheit. Rudolf Vierhaus zum 75. Geburtstag gewidmet*, Vienna—Cologne—Weimar 1997, pp. 139f.

is presumably more in the German interest if he remains in his new workplace *looking after our intellectual concerns* [*geistige Belange*] *from that vantage*".[59] After the war, Friedrich Meinecke officially referred to Rothfels as a "bridge builder". In his introduction to the Rothfels festschrift, he explicitly praises his "masterfully balanced 1949 Munich lecture on Bismarck", extolling Rothfels' "striving" for "unification" as the "leitmotif of your life and work as a teacher and scholar".[60] Meinecke here makes no explicit reference to the events in Rothfels' life linked to Nazi "*Entjudung*". Instead, he praises his former student for his ability "to combine, with a strong sense of character, loyalty towards everything good in your German past with an inner obligation to your new environment". "Germany," Meinecke declares, "will never forget that you were able to write the book *The German Opposition to Hitler*. ... You were in a position to dare to venture forth as a defender of German values—because now you were observing things from a higher vantage-point than that offered by a merely national-historical perspective."[61]

What becomes clear here is the entire paradox of a national exculpation for which one was meant to be emphatically grateful—because, although it involved a "defence" of German values, it seemed to spring from a "higher vantage-point" than that of the mere "national-historical perspective" that historians who had remained in Germany might have been expected to share. In view of the interpretative model of German national history that prevailed in the Nazi period, Meinecke explicitly acknowledged the exculpatory utility inherent in Rothfels' "inner universalism", which he glossed as follows:

> Today, in this shattering time of transition for the world and its peoples [*in der heutigen erschütternden Zeit einer Völker- und Weltenwende*] how bitterly we need such an inner universalism. A universalism which, rooted in respect for the positive values of one's own people, turns into respect for the positive values and common ground of all peoples, *building bridges* to everything that is truly and universally human in them. *You have become such a bridge builder.*[62]

Of course Meinecke also wrote similar lines to other star students of his who had emigrated, such as Hajo Holborn and Gerhard Masur. But he did not thank anyone else as emphatically for their work as he had thanked Rothfels. For example, in reference to Rothfels' English essay treating the mass flight of Germans from the east Meinecke commented: "the fact that you, precisely, have written this is a deed for which I warmly shake your hand. Let our motto be *Treue um Treue* [faithfulness everlasting]."[63] The history of a specific discourse unfolds in such private letters. The "handshake" Meinecke offered Rothfels accurately signalled the programme of return that was successfully implemented later. From the emphatic expression of

[59]Siegfried A. Kaehler to Friedrich Meinecke, 20 April 1950, in Friedrich Meinecke, *Ausgewählter Briefwechsel*, ed. and introduced by Ludwig Dehio and Peter Classen, Stuttgart 1962, p. 557 (emphasis added).

[60]Friedrich Meinecke, 'Zum Geleit', in Werner Conze (ed.), *Deutschland und Europa. Historische Studien zur Völker- und Staatenordnung des Abendlandes. Festschrift für Hans Rothfels*, Düsseldorf 1951, pp. 9–11, here p. 10.

[61]*ibid.*

[62]*ibid.*, p. 11.

[63]Friedrich Meinecke to Hans Rothfels, 3 June 1946, in Meinecke, *Ausgewählter Briefwechsel*, p. 250 (emphasis added).

gratitude for the essay at the start, to Meinecke's suggestive invocation of "closeness", "consoling elements" and "our deeper shared common ground", conciliation is not so much pleaded for or negotiated, but rather proclaimed. What remained implicit was the highly consequential tacit agreement to remain silent about differences, conflicts, contrary perceptions.

* * *

Feelings of resentment against returning emigrants were widespread in postwar Germany;[64] from the start their judgements were regarded as skewed. In indicating that "whoever wishes to speak about Germany and pass judgement has to have remained here", Gottfried Benn offered an accurate formulation of this view.[65] Following the defeat of Germany, the Munich social and economic historian Friedrich Lütge published a long memorandum on the relation between "party members" and "non-party members" addressed to the American occupiers.[66] At the memorandum's beginning, he explicitly excluded information on Germany offered by emigrants before and during the Nazi period as, *a priori,* devoid of value—an extreme hypostasising of the Third Reich's "internal development" typical of the text as a whole. In order to reinstall the "goddess of justice" to her throne, Lütge argued, the only acceptable basis for assessment was "*insight* into the internal situation", the "*internal* events", "*internal* development", "*inner* attitude" and a most "deep and personal conviction". The only adequate yardstick for evaluation was "the honest will" (*ehrlicher Wille*), the "feeling of social responsibility", the "pangs of conscience" of individuals during the war, as well as their constant efforts to "mitigate and improve" the situation—not any "superficial" formal party membership or modes of social action demanded under compulsion by "terrorists in the party".

In a letter to Carl Schmitt in 1950, the sociologist Helmut Schelsky expressed a sweeping and pejorative rejection of "remigratory scholarship [*remigratorische Wissenschaft*]".[67] Even such a liberally-minded historian as Franz Schnabel was capable, at the end of the 1950s, of commenting as follows on Eric Voegelin's appointment to a newly created chair in political science at the University of Munich: "Well, now they've hauled the emigration's last flotsam and jetsam [*das letzte Strandgut der Emigration*] back onto dry land".[68]

[64]Marita Krauss, *Heimkehr in ein fremdes Land. Geschichte der Remigration nach 1945*, Munich 2001; Krohn, pp. 97ff.

[65]Gottfried Benn to Friedrich Wilhelm Oelze, 19 March 1945, in Gottfried Benn, *Briefe an Oelze (1882–1945)*, Wiesbaden and Munich 1977, p. 388; see Nicolas Berg, 'Intellektuelle Distanzen. Versuch über Gottfried Benn, Peter de Mendelssohn und die Frage nach dem Gegenteil von Gedächtnis', in *Freiburger Literaturpsychologische Gespräche*, vol. 23 (2004), pp. 111–124.

[66]Friedrich Lütge, 'Parteigenosse—Nichtparteigenosse', in *Zeitschrift für Politik*, new series, vol. 10, no. 2 (1963), pp. 170–191. The following citations are from this source.

[67]Helmut Schelsky to Carl Schmitt, 28 September 1950, quoted in Dirk van Laak, '"Nach dem Sturm schlägt man auf die Barometer ein…" Rechtsintellektuelle Reaktionen auf das Ende des "Dritten Reiches"', in *Werkstatt Geschichte*, vol. 6, no. 17 (September 1997), pp. 25–44, here p. 37.

[68]Quoted in Hans Maier, 'Ein Schwieriger zwischen den Fronten. Erinnerungen an Eric Voegelin', in *Frankfurter Allgemeine Zeitung*, 8 April 2000.

Emigrants defended themselves at times against such "selective perception"—against a dictum that Germany could only be understood by Germans who had stayed in the country under the Nazis, itself equivalent to a form of epistemological marginalisation. But that notwithstanding, returnees frequently either found themselves confronted with ever-stronger feelings of resentment or were praised with such strategic exuberance that their role in the system was narrowly circumscribed and their position rigidly fixed right from the start. Of course, some returnees gladly withheld any critical observations, thus fulfilling the special hopes invested in them by colleagues who had remained in Germany. This was the case, for example, with Arnold Bergstraesser, a colleague of Rothfels at the University of Chicago, whose anthology *Deutsche Beiträge zur geistigen Überlieferung*, published in Chicago in 1947, was enthusiastically welcomed by Ludwig Dehio in a review in the *Historische Zeitschrift*, where it was referred to as "tidings from the old Germany" and a "monument of German intellectual life overseas".[69] This particular sort of "coming home" characterised Rothfels' career to a far greater degree (his contribution to Bergsträsser's *Beiträge* recommended the "timelessness" of the Prussian reformers to those calling for a political "reawakening").[70] Heinrich Ritter v. Srbik clearly sensed this would be so, that should Rothfels return to Germany, it would be "a ray of sunlight in the darkness of the hour".[71]

Thus Rothfels was, and not only in Meinecke's eyes, an exception to the prejudical rule established by German historians against their newly-returned Jewish colleagues. Nor was Meinecke the only one to note Rothfels' strategic position as someone spared from the prejudice otherwise directed against emigrés. When plans were afoot at the Institute for Contemporary History to establish a new periodical (the *Vierteljahrshefte für Zeitgeschichte*), Rothfels was also regarded as "*the* right man" to direct it as Hellmuth Becker, a member of the journal's new advisory board, put it. Similarly, in a testimonial for Rothfels submitted to the board, Otto Vossler indicated that "there is someone else who is downright predestined for this job, Mr. Rothfels in Tübingen. He is *the* obvious and absolutely ideal solution. What more could one possibly want?"[72]

V. FULFILLED EXPECTATIONS AND THE RESTORATION OF THE "COMMUNITY OF EXPERIENCE": *THE GERMAN OPPOSITION* (1948)

So how did Rothfels provoke such German expectations? And, in particular, how did he fulfill them? To answer these questions, let us note for a start his remark, made while commenting on the American public, that "only a few foreigners were

[69]Arnold Bergstraesser (ed.), *Deutsche Beiträge zur geistigen Überlieferung*, vol. 1, Chicago 1947; untitled review of the volume by Ludwig Dehio in *Historische Zeitschrift*, vol. 169 (1949), pp. 339f.

[70]Hans Rothfels, 'Stein und die Neugründung der Selbstverwaltung', in Bergsträsser (ed.), pp. 154–167 (reproduced in *Zeitschrift für Religions- und Geistesgeschichte*, vol. 1 (1948), pp. 210–221).

[71]Heinrich Ritter v. Srbik to Hans Rothfels, 10 February 1949, in Heinrich Ritter v. Srbik, *Die wissenschaftliche Korrespondenz des Historikers, 1912–1945*, ed. by Jürgen Kämmerer, Boppard am Rhein 1988, pp. 563–565.

[72]Hellmut Becker to Hermann Mau, 24 February 1951, in archives of the Institute for Contemporary History: IfZ/Gründungsunterlagen ID 101, vol. 1; Otto Vossler to Hermann Mau, 19 October 1951, *ibid.*

prepared to realise that Germany after 1933 was an 'occupied country'."[73] Rothfels' description of Nazi Germany as "occupied" in fact both defined and sanctioned an entire style of thought. This style is also manifest in Rothfels' studies of the German resistance to Nazism, where he wished to demonstrate, in his forthright words, "the fiction of any identity between what is German and what is National Socialist".[74] The German resistance had shown itself to be a "moral rebellion against evil as such". Foregrounding a concept of "man" and his "humanity" that was universalistic in a specific way. Rothfels established a concept of resistance that, viewed politically, was pronouncedly opportunistic: resistance as the "legacy of humanness in extremis" (*Vermächtnis des Menschentums in extremis*) and as a "breakthrough into freedom" (*Durchbruch ins Freie*) opposed to the "arrogance of totalitarianism in all its colours, brown or red".[75]

The English version of *German Opposition*, its plea, explicitly directed at the American public, for recognition of a better Germany, turned out on closer scrutiny to have two sets of addressees. In fact, the book implicitly targeted a German audience, and Rothfels had more success with it in Germany than in America. There a book by Allen Welsh Dulles had already been published in 1947 with the suggestive title *Germany's Underground*, and Rothfels' review of the book is revealing. He praised both the author's "insight into the conditions and problems faced by an opposition under the totalitarian form of rule" and his "spirit of uninhibited analysis and evaluation". But Rothfels' complaints are more instructive. He particularly criticised Dulles' concept of "opposition" for being too narrow, adding that "anonymous forces and the problems of a silent or potential opposition are hardly touched on". As a whole, what he found lacking in the study was insight into the overall character of the resistance movement, which in Rothfels' view had crossed all boundaries between classes, professions and parties. And he viewed the book as lacking, not least of all, clear criticism of the United States. In short, Rothfels here offered a blueprint for his own upcoming book, its appearance announced in the last sentence of the review, concluding with an exclamation mark.[76]

Germany had been discussing its resistance to Hitler without waiting for Rothfels to give the go-ahead. Even before the book's original version began to make the rounds in Germany, the *Historische Zeitschrift* had published a long review essay on the topic;[77] Rothfels' book was given a separate review in the journal, by none other than Gerhard Ritter, in addition to its mention in this essay.[78] The force of his voice from

[73]Rothfels, *Die deutsche Opposition gegen Hitler*, p. 20.

[74]Hans Rothfels, 'Das politische Vermächtnis des deutschen Widerstands', in *Vierteljahrshefte für Zeitgeschichte* vol. 2, no. 3 (1954), pp. 329–343, p. 333; this article appeared under the same title as an offprint published by the Bundeszentrale für Heimatdienst (untitled series, no. 14, Bonn 1955).

[75]*ibid.*, p. 334, 337, 341 and 343; see also: Hans Rothfels, 'Zum 20. Jahrestag der Erhebung des 20. Juli 1944', in *Aus Politik und Zeitgeschichte*, no. 29, 15 July 1964, pp. 3–6, here p. 6.

[76]Hans Rothfels, untitled review of Allen Welsh Dulles, *Germany's Underground*, New York 1947, in *Historische Zeitschrift*, vol. 169 (1949), pp. 133–135, here p. 135.

[77]Paul Kluke, 'Der deutsche Widerstand. Eine kritische Literaturübersicht', *ibid.*, pp. 136–161; on the broader framework of this body of texts see Eckel, 'Intellektuelle Transformationen'.

[78]Gerhard Ritter, untitled review of Rothfels, *German Opposition*, in *Historische Zeitschrift*, vol. 169 (1949), pp. 402–405.

"outside" was thus immediately acknowledged, Ritter now setting to work arranging a translation of the book into German. With this volume, Rothfels not only opened up the field of "contemporary history" for himself personally, but had also prepared the way for his return to Germany. As a preliminary step, he mailed no fewer than a hundred copies to colleagues.[79] In the above-cited radio interview with Rothfels by Viktor v. Oertzen and Hubert Locher, he emphasised his good fortune in finding a topic "which went beyond being merely a welter of *flagellation* and *self-accusations*, although these were naturally unavoidable".

But this mode of inquiry did not constitute historical research. Rather, it involved the construction of an "invented autobiography" to use a phrase once aptly coined by Ulrich Raulff.[80] Through such a project, Rothfels transformed the general apologetic reflexes of the Germans after 1945 into an academic discipline. The "justified" resistance of would-be assassins to Hitler was now expanded to cover Germany and the German people as a whole. As early as 1947, Rothfels noted in a letter to Siegfried A.Kaehler, that "it was necessary to make substantial modifications [when it came] to the so-called failure of the German intelligentsia", and that he hoped to "do something along those lines in a pamphlet on the resistance movement".[81] "Justice towards a collectively discriminated nation" was important for him.[82] Rothfels' use of the ciphers Buchenwald, Oranienburg, Dachau was reductionistic to an extreme degree, since these ciphers were being used to refer explicitly to *German* victims. He talked about the sense of outrage in the postwar years, the "indescribable atrocities" in the camps in Russia and Poland, continuing with the following breathtaking statement: "When these proofs of 'German bestiality' appeared, little was said about the great number of *Germans* among the victims".[83] And alongside some biting remarks on the French "camps" in southern Germany and the American war against the native American Indians, Rothfels could not resist offering his own explanation of the facts:

> All available evidence and the results of sober and unbiased examination will demonstrate *that modern mass civilisation produces from its own depths a reservoir of dark forces whose release spells pure and naked barbarism, while by the same token it should also be clear that potential material for both torturers and martyrs is present in every nation, should a politics of hatred and revenge choose to overlook this.*[84]

The conclusion was left unstated but crystal clear: to talk about the camps meant to perpetuate a "politics of hatred and revenge". The overwhelming pathos in Rothfels' book, his constant invocation of the essence of humanness (*das Menschliche*)"in the borderline situation as such",[85] is in significant measure a result of the fact that he

[79]Hans Rothfels to Friedrich Meinecke, 24 September 1948, Geheimes Staatsarchiv Preußischer Kulturbesitz, NL Meinecke, Rep. 92, Nr. 221.

[80]Ulrich Raulff, 'Erträumte Autobiographie', in *Frankfurter Allgemeine Zeitung*, 11 July 1994.

[81]Hans Rothfels to Siegfried A. Kaehler, 17 November 1947, in Niedersächsische Staats- und Universitätsbibliothek Göttingen (NStUB), correspondence Kaehler-Rothfels, no. 268.

[82]Rothfels, *Die deutsche Opposition gegen Hitler*, p. 24.

[83]*ibid.*, p. 22.

[84]*ibid.*, pp. 23ff. (emphasis added).

[85]*ibid.*, p. 24.

had to depart from the concrete plane where such "humanity" had actually been negated in order to legitimise his self-chosen theme of "resistance" in the first place. At the same time, he suggestively juxtaposed scholarship with politics, spoke up for conciliation, took distance from revenge—indeed co-opted an affirmation of Enlightenment in opposition to repression, speaking in the name of "truth" against "ideology".[86] In this way, a model of German resistance was established in German historiography and German memory.

As its yardstick, the model had concepts such as "resistance", "courage", "the power of suffering", "steadfastness", "composure", "martyrdom", "moral self-assertion", and "Christianity as a 'saving anchor' in chaos". These concepts appear within three consecutive pages of *German Opposition*. In concord with the historians who had remained in Germany, Rothfels made no attempt whatsoever to ask any questions about the expulsion, expropriation, despoiling, destruction and murder of the Jews. Returnees who wished to be properly recognised in Germany had to toe the line: they could only speak about the German past within the accepted German forms of discourse. In Rothfels' words, remigration to Germany was a "return to the nature-given locus".[87] Rothfels was convinced that any true pedagogical effectiveness had to be grounded in the "community of experience", the recurrent metaphor for the loss and restoration of this community, through a "filling in of the gaps in experience" which clearly and unequivocally foregrounded the question of one's own identity and sense of belonging. In June 1947, he explained his doubts about a possible return to Germany by the fact that he had not been inside the "positive and negative community of experience of the past eight years" and that it was difficult to bridge over these "gaps in experience".[88] Rothfels responded to this gap—solving the task of returning to Germany and constructing through scholarship an image of it he could sustain—with his book on the German resistance. And a short time later, having ascertained through guest professorships at several German universities that "a ten-year absence is no problem in my relationship to the present generation of students",[89] the gap had apparently closed; it seemed that re-establishing the *Erlebnisgemeinschaft* was not much of a problem. But the process drew on and tapped memories that were "German", not "Jewish". If it indeed succeeded, this was in the general way we have noted between Meinecke and Rothfels: as a strange offer of alliance held out by Germans to Jewish emigrants, an offer that emphasised acceptance of the thematic canon of German traditions. Valorising the "other Germany" had become a prerequisite for speaking at all about German history.

[86]*ibid.*, pp. 19–26.

[87]Quoted in Schulze, *Deutsche Geschichtswissenschaft*, p. 136; *idem*, 'Hans Rothfels und die Deutsche Geschichtswissenschaft nach 1945', p. 84.

[88]Hans Rothfels to Freiherrn v. Guttenberg, 1 June 1947, in BAK, NL Rothfels 213, no. 20; see also Hans Rothfels to Siegfried A. Kaehler, 12 October 1946, in NStUB, Correspondence Kaehler-Rothfels [Cod. Ms., Nr. 1, 144, d.]. It is striking that Hans Mommsen does not cite the concept of "gap in experience" (Erlebnislücke) in his 1976 portrait of Rothfels, but rather cites (probably mistakenly) another expression, "gap of knowledge" (Wissenslücke). But for Rothfels—as for other returned emigrants—the problem was not to gain insight and knowledge as rapidly as possible (one could do that on one's own); rather, it was centred on the task of restoring community—and for this one of course needed an alliance with the other side. See Hans Mommsen, *Geschichtsschreibung und Humanität*, p. 21.

[89]Rothfels, letter to Paul Kluckhohn, November 1949 (transcript), in Kaehler-Rothfels correspondence, NStUB Göttingen, Nr. 286.

VI. "COUNTER-IMAGES": THE RECEPTION AND MEANING OF HANS ROTHFELS' WORK AS A HISTORIAN

Against this backdrop, the enthusiastic reception of *German Opposition* serves as a typical element in the reception of his work in general, since it was itself one of the programmatic documents of the restoration in progress at the time. The reviews of the book by Gerhard Ritter and Karl Dietrich Erdmann in, respectively, the first volume of the *Historische Zeitschrift* and the first issue of *Geschichte in Wissenschaft und Unterricht* put forward the official reading.[90] Ritter did not skimp on honesty and effort, sketching in his first sentence the framework within which he saw the book's importance:

> The literature by German emigrants in America and England on the German problem has given rise to more confusion than enlightenment. *A feeling of resentment, where it reigns unchecked, is not favourable soil for sober and objective historiography, and estrangement over many years from German soil easily leads to a distorted view of reality.*[91]

This precisely identified the consensus of German historiography of the time: emigrants did not write "soberly and objectively", but rather in a fashion distorted by "resentment". The exception represented by Rothfels' book was all the more "heartening", noted Ritter. In his view, the book combined "noble humanism" and a "masterful control" of the subject. Although the author had been "tested by suffering", he was completely free of "blind passion and bitterness". And although Rothfels had himself suffered heavily from being persecuted as a Jew, "he is able to render his judgements with admirable objectivity, far removed from making the entire German people responsible for [the] atrocities". According to Ritter, Rothfels' exacting approach, precision, caution and intellectual mastery of the material led to his book's persuasive basic premise, which with "great clarity illuminates the political and moral emphasis of this opposition movement, while proving the working notion that all Germans obeyed the Hitler tyranny [*die Hitlertyrannei*], offering no resistance, to be a legend".

In Ritter's eyes, a "just assessment" meant focusing on the breadth of the movement, the depth of its motives, the truth of its basic religious convictions and the "fateful and mysterious nature" of the failed assassination attempts, while looking at both the church and the military "with a deep sense of understanding" for their position. In the course of his review, he formulated what amounted to an official welcoming speech for Rothfels on behalf of the German historians' profession, lauding the ethos and ability "of our old colleague and friend, whose voice we are pleased to hear once again, after such a long period of silence, coming now from across the sea". Ritter continued by asserting that there can "hardly be better proof of the fact that the scholarly maturity of the genuine historian leads to a reflective highground where the bickering of daily politics fades into silence".

[90]For Ritter's review see note 78; Karl Dietrich Erdmann, untitled review, in *Geschichte in Wissenschaft und Unterricht*, vol. 1, no. 6 (1950), p. 313.

[91]This and the following from Ritter, untitled review of Rothfels, *German Opposition*, p. 402 (emphasis added).

Friedrich Meinecke, Karl Dietrich Erdmann, Werner Conze, Theodor Schieder and Siegfried Kaehler all stressed that Rothfels could not possibly be partisan—that he looked at recent history from a healthy distance, able to demonstrate objectively, in Kaehler's words, the "exculpation" (*Rechtfertigung*) of "substantial sections of the German people".[92] In this connection, Kaehler spoke of the assassination plot of 20 July 1944 as a genuine "German freedom movement". Meinecke, "deeply moved", called the book an "air bridge" (*Luftbrücke*) linking the U.S.A. with Germany.[93] The "bridge" metaphor, symbolically so important for Rothfels' historiographical architecture, here naturally involved a wordplay, referring as it did to a concrete contemporary event—the Berlin blockade and General Lucius D. Clay's airlift to the city, with up to a thousand daily flights between 1948 and 1949, representing the first great confrontation of the Cold War. Meinecke went on to note that when reading Rothfels' description of events linked to the German resistance, "all my conversations with Kaiser and Beck came vividly back to me. Yes, it was exactly like that; it seemed to us a simple human obligation of conscience to eliminate the monster [Hitler] and then rebuild an ethically purer Germany [*ein ethisch reineres Deutschland*]."[94]

This citation makes clear how Rothfels regularly imparted to both his colleagues who had stayed in Germany and his readership what they had—or wished they had—experienced. But it was not only his fellow professional historians who praised the book, its topic and premises and the ethos of its author. Eventually, the German Foreign Office itself would voice sincere gratitude for a work that had served, for so many, as a form of "liberation", a work that had understood the tasks of politics.[95] The similar reception of Rothfels' book by professional historians and the public, running across the political spectrum, illuminates a German longing for a narrative of resistance: a longing whose expression must be termed an "invention of tradition", because the narrative was not shaped for the sake of genuine history but was meant to serve as a great counter-narrative to Nazism. Rothfels' "little book", as he put it, "had many peculiar effects", provoking a response by readers that amounted to a "barely endurable burden of correspondence".[96] He answered the deep longing generated by his ideas as best he could: through manifold encounters with his former colleagues, industrious correspondence with friends, and numerous scholarly publications. In a letter to Kaehler, he once termed this continuous activity "laying emergency footbridges over the old pillars".[97]

Rothfels' exchanges with Kaehler makes it clear that he maintained correspondences with others for one main purpose: to promote "matters of

[92]Siegfried A. Kaehler, 'Der 20. Juli im geschichtlichen Rückblick', in *Die Sammlung* vol. 9 (1954), pp. 440 and 442; see also Werner Conze, 'Die deutsche Opposition gegen Hitler', in *Neue Politische Literatur*, vol. 2, no. 3 (1953), cols. 719–721; Theodor Schieder, *Hans Rothfels zum 70. Geburtstag*, p. 123.

[93]Friedrich Meinecke to Hans Rothfels, 22 August 1948, in *idem*, *Ausgewählter Briefwechsel*, pp. 293f.

[94]*ibid.*

[95]Martin Krapf to Hans Rothfels, 16 July 1965, in BAK, NL Rothfels 213, No. 36; Theo Kordt to Hans Rothfels, 23 May 1951, in BAK, NL Rothfels 213, No. 158.

[96]Hans Rothfels to Siegfried A. Kaehler, n.d. (1948?), in NStUB, Correspondence Kaehler—Rothfels (Cod. Ms., Nr. 1, 144, d).

[97]Hans Rothfels to Siegfried A. Kaehler, 7 April 1947, in Siegfried A. Kaehler, *Briefe 1900–1963*, ed. by Walter Bußmann and Günther Grünthal (*Deutsche Geschichtsquellen des 19. und 20. Jahrhunderts*, vol. 58), Boppard am Rhein 1993, p. 336.

importance within the framework of internal German discussion".[98] At one point Kaehler confirmed to Rothfels, innocently but accurately, that in reading his letters he had the feeling that "the past years had not really taken place and today was directly attached to the day before yesterday".[99] It is evident that such bridges spanning the Nazi period—presented paradigmatically in this private correspondence—were a basic part of the politics of scholarship and science of their time. Rothfels had no doubt that the emphasis on equating Nazis and Germans was created to legitimate "Potsdam"—i.e. that treaty's ceding to Poland of the formerly German territory on the other side of the Oder-Neisse Line—and that the concentration camps were a "piece of propaganda" designed to legitimate the division of Germany.[100] As in his book, Rothfels here implied that the concentration camps were largely a means of compulsion used by the state against Germans; and the fact that after the Allied victory they had been instrumentalised a second time against Germany now called for "counter-images".[101]

Rothfels was dedicated to the task of formulating such "counter-images". In the private sphere, he had repeatedly sought new beginnings, "built bridges", strung out "emergency footbridges" and proclaimed the need for conciliation. In 1949, commenting on Ernst Jünger's diary *Strahlungen*, Peter de Mendelssohn had diagnosed Jünger's "total blindness" and "complete inability to see the other side".[102] From our present perspective, the same diagnosis would seem to apply to Rothfels, illuminating his pivotal role in postwar German academic life with Rothfels acting like a magnetic field—someone around whom the hopes, interests and intentions of the historians who had stayed in Germany were concentrated. In turn, exploring this role supplies some answers to the question of why in the immediate postwar period German historians were unable to perceive the Jewish catastrophe.

VII. CONCLUSION: A "SENSE FOR HISTORY" AND THE "TASK OF MEMORY"

This essay has proceeded from two central premises, the first related to the impact of Hans Rothfels' remigration, the second to the question of how this impact can be precisely understood. As an example of interaction between former academic exiles and colleagues who had stayed in Germany, it is clear that Rothfels' experience marks a significant exception, his own return being nothing less than a great success. But looked at soberly, it is clear that the success came at very great cost: that of something like a discursive erasure. In contrast to other emigrant colleagues, Rothfels did not hesitate to pay this form of tribute; his contribution to

[98]Hans Rothfels to Siegfried A. Kaehler, 8 May 1948, in NStUB, Correspondence Kaehler—Rothfels, No. 271, p. 2.

[99]Siegfried A. Kaehler, letter, 12 November 1946, *ibid.*

[100]Hans Rothfels to Siegfried A. Kaehler, 7. February 1947, *ibid.*

[101]*ibid.*

[102]Peter de Mendelssohn, 'Gegenstrahlungen. Ein Tagebuch zu Ernst Jüngers Tagebuch', in *Der Monat*, vol. 2, no. 14 (1949), pp. 149–174, here p. 157.

historiography can be understood as confirming an intellectual alliance with the German élites in which their offer of acceptance was combined with his reaction to it. The foundation underpinning this alliance was a concept of Nazism as the "absolute other" within German history. The true Germany, Rothfels suggested, in the process acting somewhat like a stage prompter whispering lines to his grateful German colleagues, had been the Germany that resisted and opposed Hitler.

Against this backdrop, one can cogently argue that none of the key figures in postwar German historiography chose "articulate silence" (or "communicative silence")[103] as consciously as did Hans Rothfels. Stigmatised as a Jew in the Third Reich and forced to emigrate despite his pronouncements of loyalty, Rothfels constituted the greatest potential threat to the discipline of German history at a time when it was trying to found itself anew. He was one of the most respected German historians abroad, and as a consequence of his shabby and scandalous expulsion from Germany now occupied an ideal position. But neither publicly nor privately did he use his position to formulate probing questions, let alone rebuke his countrymen. His approach to Nazism was a form of de-historicisation, pushing historical problems aside or supplanting them with moral pathos. His postwar efforts at bridge-building were not orientated around the German-Jewish divide, but rather around a divide he believed was present within German history. Put otherwise, these efforts were concrete acts of suppression, based on a view of the years between 1933 and 1945 as years that needed to be "bridged over", and on a refusal to juxtapose the historical experiences emerging from their murderous matrix.

* * *

In his recent autobiography, the historian Georg Iggers reminisces about his studies in Chicago, where he had attended two seminars taught by Rothfels, one in the winter of 1948–1949 on the Prussian reforms of Freiherr von Stein and another the following summer on the Frankfurt-based German national parliament of 1848–1849. Iggers expresses surprise that Rothfels was so "conservative and German-national" in his thinking. And he comments that as a young man, he had never understood why Rothfels had in fact emigrated. "Only later did I learn that he had been raised in a Jewish home."[104] The Chicago encounter between Iggers and Rothfels was marked by decided feelings of antipathy. Iggers recalls that Rothfels told him "straight to his face" that it would be wise to give up his studies since "I had no sense for history".[105]

This meeting between two emigrants from Germany shortly after the end of the Second World War has only been preserved in the mode of a personal memory. Whatever the reason for their mutual antipathy during the late 1940s, and whatever

[103]On the concept of "articulate silence", see Max Picard, *Die Welt des Schweigens*, Erlenbach/Zürich 1948, p. 89. For the formulation "communicative silence", see Hermann Lübbe, 'Der Nationalsozialismus im deutschen Nachkriegsbewußtsein', in *Historische Zeitschrift*, vol. 236 (1983), pp. 579–599.

[104]Wilma and Georg Iggers, *Zwei Seiten der Geschichte. Lebensbericht aus unruhigen Zeiten*, Göttingen 2002, p. 92.

[105]*ibid.*

led Rothfels to make the assessment he did about Iggers as a student—from today's perspective the space between them takes on more than anecdotal interest. It might, in fact, serve as an emblem for the analysis presented in this essay.

Georg G. Iggers was born in 1926 in Hamburg as Georg Igertsheimer; his parents changed their name when they emigrated in 1938. Iggers, who would live in America for many years, dates the "transition … from a patriotic German who identified completely with the other kids at school and the teacher to a nationally-minded and religious Jew" to the years preceding his flight from Germany.[106] Expelled from Königsberg in 1938 without telling his children at the time why,[107] and returning to Germany shortly after the end of the war, Rothfels experienced no comparable confrontation with his Jewish origins. His devotion, as a conservative German nationalist, to the putative gap between National Socialism and the German nation forms a stark contrast to Iggers' attempt to fathom the overburdened traditions of German history over the *longue durée*.[108] Rothfels became the doyen of German contemporary history, head of the German Association of Historians, board member of the German Institute for Contemporary History, editor of its *Vierteljahrshefte für Zeitgeschichte*, author of programmatic studies reflective of the era of restoration in the Federal Republic. Iggers, on the other hand, devoted himself to fundamental studies in the history of historiography, historicising his own doubts about the dignity and integrity of the historical profession in Germany. Put briefly: Rothfels represented the dominant line in the foundational discourse of postwar German historical studies, and Iggers embodied the sceptical resistance to that line.

Indeed, the contrast between Rothfels—born in Wilhelminian Germany—and Iggers—35 years his junior—could not be more pronounced. Rothfels was a full professor, holding one of the most respected chairs in American academia, while Iggers was supporting himself at the time by working part-time as a lift operator in the University of Chicago library.[109] The fundamental difference of generation and status helps account for the two men's divergent paths—their views on history express entirely different times, values, interests, perspectives. In this light, it is not surprising that Rothfels misread Iggers's criticism of the traditions of the nation-state—traditions that he himself still represented as a veteran of the First World War—as a basic inability "to think historically"; nor perhaps is it surprising that one of the earliest criticisms of Rothfels' function and role in postwar West German historiography would be formulated by Iggers two decades later. Initially, this criticism was conveyed in a broader context of Iggers' questioning of nationalist

[106]Georg Iggers, 'Eine Kindheit in Deutschland. Erinnerungen 1926–1938', in *Sozialwissenschaftliche Informationen*, vol. 18, no. 3 (1989), pp. 170–176, here p. 172; see also *idem* and Wilma Iggers, *Zwei Seiten der Geschichte*, pp. 51–65; Franz Fillafer, 'Gespräch mit Georg G. Iggers', in *Sozial.Geschichte. Zeitschrift für historische Analyse des 20. und 21. Jahrhunderts*, new series, vol. 19, no. 1 (2004), pp. 84–99.

[107]See the comments by Hans Mommsen in Jarausch and Hohls (eds.), p. 172.

[108]Georg G. Iggers, *The German Conception of History. The National Tradition of Historical Thought from Herder to the Present*, Middletown, CT. 1968, (German transl., *Deutsche Geschichtswissenschaft. Eine Kritik der traditionellen Geschichtsauffassung von Herder bis zur Gegenwart*, Vienna—Cologne—Weimar 1997 [revised and expanded version of first German edition of 1971]).

[109]Iggers, *Zwei Seiten der Geschichte*, p. 93.

traditions with German historiography as a whole.[110] It was then articulated more clearly and directly in later writings.[111]

Nevertheless, the differences between the two historians cannot be sufficiently explained through a gap in chronology and career. This was not a private conflict, the reflection of a purely generational difference discharging itself in personal animosity. Rather, a real clash was at work here between very different views of the Nazi period, indeed of that period's prehistory. In understanding the latter in the framework of a crisis-charged continuum of German history itself, Iggers gave theoretical expression to Jewish historical experience, thus locating the expulsion of Germany's Jewish minority in an epistemological space.[112] In Rothfels' case, just the opposite is true. Starting with his participation as an enlisted soldier in the First World War, his dominant historical experiences remained *national-deutsch*, subsequently attached to the Imperial German model of German history—a model that by no means became antiquated or invalid in the Weimar period.[113] Consequently, when it came to Rothfels' self-identity, he always remained—before, during and after his emigration from Germany—a Prussian conservative in the Protestant tradition and that of Bismarck's nation state. He may well have considered his "Jewish extraction", as defined by National Socialist racialist ideology, as a type of misunderstanding; in any event, he rarely expressed himself in public on the matter, thus leaving it in the realm of "implicit memory" or "unarticulated history". Because his perception as a "Jew" came in the form of an externally imposed and denigrating stigmatisation through Nazi ideology, the continuity of his own self-perception is not something incomprehensible or counterintuitive. Seen in these terms, Rothfels perceived the de facto experiences he endured of

[110]Iggers, *Deutsche Geschichtswissenschaft*, pp. 309f., 339 and 364 (on Rothfels′ conservative nationalist views); pp. 318, 322 and 326 (on his assessments of the role of the historical sciences in National Socialism); pp. 345ff. (on the reductionist approach taken in his book *Die deutsche Opposition*); pp. 350 (on his apologia for Bismarck); pp. 357f. (on "defensive" research in contemporary history at the Institute for Contemporary History).

[111]See, for example, Georg Iggers, 'Die deutschen Historiker in der Emigration', in Bernd Faulenbach (ed.), *Geschichtswissenschaft in Deutschland. Traditionelle Positionen und gegenwärtige Aufgaben*, Munich 1974, pp. 97–111, here p. 103; on the broader picture see Ernst Schulin, 'Deutsche und Amerikanische Geschichtswissenschaft. Wechselseitige Impulse im 19. und 20. Jahrhundert', in *idem*, *Arbeit an der Geschichte. Etappen auf dem Weg zur Moderne*, Frankfurt am Main—New York 1997, pp. 164–191, here p. 190.

[112]Heinz Wolf, *Deutsch-jüdische Emigrantenhistoriker in den USA und der Nationalsozialismus*, Frankfurt am Main—New York—Paris 1988, p. 179.

[113]See Bernd Faulenbach, *Ideologie des deutschen Weges. Die deutsche Geschichte in der Historiographie zwischen Kaiserreich und Nationalsozialismus*, Munich 1980; on the fundamental impact of the Great War on subsequent German historiography, for a persuasive description of the young Gerhard Ritter by Christoph Cornelißen see, 'Der Erste Weltkrieg: Fronterfahrung und historisch-politisches Denken', in *idem*, *Gerhard Ritter. Geschichtswissenschaft und Politik im 20. Jahrhundert*, Düsseldorf 2001, pp. 65–105. Referring to Siegfried A. Kaehler's expression "spiritual comradeship on the march", (1950) Cornelißen notes (*ibid.*, p. 8) that generation-specific experiences structure the experiential process itself and are not some sort of confection of retrospective historiography. On the broader context, see also Fritz Stern, 'Die Historiker und der Erste Weltkrieg. Privates Erleben und öffentliche Erklärung', in *Transit*, vol. 5, no. 8 (1994), pp. 116–134.

"Aryanisation"—dismissal, expulsion, antisemitic and racist rejection—as elements incompatible with his own self-understanding, an alien ascription.

This experience was, then, basically incongruous with Rothfels' own being, with his political views, education and impressive career as a historian in Germany. Thus, on the level of individual formation of memory, his ideological choices were no more or less than those West German postwar society had made in general—and which contemporary German historiography had opted for in particular.

Comment

By Gabriel Motzkin

Remigrés are never greeted with open arms on their return. Literature's first remigré, Odysseus, has to kill his wife's suitors, and even she, Penelope, does not recognise him until he discloses the secret of their marriage bed.

Remigrés are viewed at best as living anachronisms incarnating a half-forgotten past, but one which is too close to be either eulogised or to be fossilised as nostalgia. The first modern remigrés, the aristocrats who followed the Bourbons into exile, were not received with enthusiasm after twenty years of absence from France. While they were readmitted into the corridors of power by their remigré kings, Louis XVIII and Charles X, they did not get their lands back. And the most conspicuous of long-term remigrés, the Jews returning to their Holy Land, were not greeted with local cheer.

The remigrés themselves also had to struggle with the reciprocal coherence of their contradictory pasts. Holocaust survivors often had two such different pasts, their prewar lives and their sufferings in the war-years. Sometimes the task was too much and they felt compelled to choose between these pasts, either obliterating the Holocaust from their memory, or suppressing prewar memories that had grown painful, peopled as they were by loved ones whose lives had ended so tragically.

German-Jewish remigrés also had opposing pasts between which they had to mediate. Those who chose permanent exile by suppressing their German past have not been mentioned here, for they are not remigrés, but we should not forget that this alternative of suppression of one's past was ever-present for the émigré. Remembering his or her past was a conscious choice. Those who sought to obliterate their years of exile were at the other end of the spectrum.

Here too there was a division of pasts: did the bridge to the past go through the experience of exile, the "real" Germany surviving in the Pacific Palisades? Or was Nazi Germany the "real" Germany, an experience that had to be integrated into the German historical narrative? Those, like Hans Rothfels, who were so concerned with the question of the bridge to the past, found it in the German resistance, thus integrating exile in its allegedly internal form with the historical experience of Nazism. But as these papers have shown so lucidly, the opportunities for bad faith and self-deception lurked in every choice, in every story that both the remigrés and their somewhat embarrassed German hosts told themselves. Even in his own eyes the remigré enjoyed a somewhat dubious legitimacy. Having been delegitimised once, the remigré cannot obliterate the experience of exile and Diaspora so easily. Hans Rosenberg could only *retire* to Germany; having chosen the United States he did not attempt to reinvent himself once more.

What could the remigreé bring to their old homes? Arnd Bauerkämper points out that it was not the remigrés who brought Americanisation to postwar Germany.

Those then-younger German historians who were looking to America as a sensed palliative for the failure of their own traditions had to seek out the émigrés in their new abode, while those exiles who returned to Germany could only bring back their prewar Germanys, whether it was Rothfels' conservatism, which was used by historians to provide postwar Germany with an alternative historical narrative, or Adorno's Marxist humanism which promised to revitalise the German left that was bereft of a narrative after the Nazi years.

After 1968 Adorno's lineage was self-evident to a generation of Germans who could not stand the suppression of unarticulated memories so typical for post war Germany. The more interesting case, however, is Rothfels, partly because of the rebirth of conservative hankerings implicit in the current fashions for Leo Strauss and Carl Schmitt. Could a reckoning with the choices of conservatives and traditionalists take place within the conservative tradition itself, or has the memory of Nazism so corrupted the conservative discourse that its framework is indistinguishable from Nazism itself? Is Hans Rothfels' apologia for the German past through glorifying conservative resisters not an apologia for coming to terms with the Nazi regime? Or could German conservatism discern a different and relevant past? Or can German conservatism only then cleanse itself when it casts off both the German mandarins and the conservative remigrés of the 1950s?

German conservatism was always marked by anti-capitalist adherence to communitarian corporatism. But the American quality of exile could not further this allegiance, since America was stamped with the hallmark of capitalism, and most exiled German intellectuals could not befriend this individualistic underpinning of American social organisation. Hannah Arendt's critique of totalitarianism could almost as easily be read as a critique of capitalism: few postwar intellectuals were prepared to imagine that American anomie *is* the productive engine of that society.

It is the nature of anomie that it is silent. Nicolas Berg points out that silences are indistinguishable, and therefore should not be romanticised into a (non)-rhetoric of authenticity. Sincerity can only be judged through language, and even silence can only be evaluated through words. But the postwar German silence into which the remigrés were received was not just the ambiguous silence of a living but of an undigested past. It is the nature of the social manifestation of tacit counterfeelings to the discourse of the day that it does not let itself be vocally expressed. Thus, as Arnd Bauerkämper indicates, social meanings in our contemporary social contexts are not as "globalised" as it might appear from the published discourse of globalisation.

In a way, as shown by the quotations from Meinecke and Rothfels, German nationalism survived the Nazi experience in somewhat better shape than prewar multinationalism. The ideology survived, but the prewar context in which it derived its meaning from the nationalities problem on Germany's eastern frontier no longer applied and it sank into a general anti-Communism that could cloak the aversion to the eastern nationalities in the rhetoric of aversion to the internationalist threat issuing from the Communist east. It was with some sense of familiar surprise that one first learned of Conze's schooling in Eastern nationalist polemics.

Thus the conclusion must be that nationalism could not appear as such, and that its only permitted outlet was the interpretation of the past: hence the importance accorded to historical debate in the culture of the nascent Federal Republic.

However, this history did not focus on the actual history that concerned historians in the prewar period, but rather on the question of the bridges between past and present, for which much of the past historical debate was deemed irrelevant. The burden of seeking historical continuity meant that past historical contexts had to be discarded as being discontinuous. Thus the memory of National Socialism, for example, could not survive together with its context, but rather had to be separated from its context in order to be integrated into the continuous history that was viewed as a necessary component of national identity.

Rothfels thus emerges as the quasi-historicist in this group. Rosenberg was engaged in a kind of social deconstruction of the past, a revisionary history that had 1933 as its *terminus ad quem*, whereas Rothfels was interested in projecting the past into the present. In contrast, Hannah Arendt emerges as resolutely antihistoricist, a view that corresponded well to her rejection of postwar German national consciousness, which, as portrayed, she viewed as disingenuous and hypocritical. However, my point is that Arendt, no less than the others, with the exception of Rosenberg, subscribed to some kind of organic view of community, to which she contrasted the abstract forces of modernity. Indeed, in one sense she was the least liberal and reconstructed of these thinkers, for the reason that she did not really have to reconstruct her view of the world to fit historical reality. This was so not only because of her basic ahistoricity, but also because her categories of thinking could be applied to contemporary societies simply by changing the object of criticism from one kind of anti-communitarian hyperstate to another. Her task was not to query the survival of national identity, but rather the possibilities for a humane universalism.

These different attitudes are well exposed in relation to the *Sonderweg* thesis: Arendt and Adorno did not subscribe to it at first, only moving towards it once it had become well entrenched in the *Zeitgeist*. In their hands, however, the *Sonderweg* thesis does not imply the failure of Germany to be like other nations in the West, but rather the failure of the drive to universalism in German national consciousness. The Germans were not as global or as cosmopolitan as they should have been. This inherent ambiguity in the *Sonderweg* thesis (modernisation v. universalisation) is sometimes neglected. For Arendt, the hidden drive perhaps was the yearning that all Jews should be Germans, and should be accepted as such, just as Jews in America could become American. Her rejection of remigration stemmed perhaps from the perception that the Germans were still failing in universalism. In some ways, she was perhaps not as far from Meinecke, despite the vast difference in tone, as might at first appear: both believed in the hegemony of the cultural, and both believed in the need for manifesting the universal in the particular.

Thus Germany moved Hannah Arendt in the book on Eichmann towards an inner despair, the despair of the emigrée who can neither return nor be fully at home in the oblivion of her new world where exiles were pressured to forget the old one. Perhaps that suspension between worlds reveals the motive for remigration: not so much the search for the past, as the need for a future. It was clear that what moved both Rothfels and Adorno was the question of which future they wanted to share: such émigrés did not return hoping to find a past, but they did seek to bind together their past and their future. Perhaps Germans of different generations accepted Rothfels and Adorno not so much because they could explain the past but because they showed how the past could be used in designing a future: to some degree the Germans of the 1950s succumbed to repressed hysteria about the past because they were so unsure about their concept of the future. Not only does memory relate to a past and to a present, it also has a relationship with the future. As Heidegger foresaw, apparent forgetting renders anxieties about the future more palatable.

The past which Rothfels and Adorno sought to bind to the future was not their remembered past. Unlike aristocratic émigrés they did not really seek a return of the Old Regime. Their concern was rather a historical past, whether Bismarck or Marx, and their question was not one of memory, but rather one of the relation between history and future. Thus for them the Nazis had made memory difficult, but had not made historiography impossible, whereas both Rosenberg and Arendt in different ways queried the possibility of continuing their history, a history to which they did not wish to return because they were less sanguine about that history's possible value for the future.

The Haskalah

The German-or-Yiddish Controversy within the Haskalah and the European "Dialogue of the Dead": Tuvyah Feder's Kol Meḥazezim *versus Mendel Lefin's Translation of the Book of Proverbs*

By Moshe Pelli

INTRODUCTION

The inclination of the first Hebrew *maskilim* [enlighteners] in Germany to adhere to either pure Hebrew or pure German and their opposition to the use of Yiddish has been accepted by most scholars.[1] Apparently, some *maskilim* deviated from the norm, as manifested in the German-Yiddish controversy that became a literary dispute between two well-known *maskilim*, Tuvyah Feder (1760–1817) and Mendel Lefin (1749–1826). Tuvyah Feder wrote his satiric *Kol Meḥazezim* (*The Voice of the Archers*) in 1813; it is, in effect, a diatribe against Mendel Lefin's translation into Yiddish of the Book of Proverbs.

The Feder-Lefin dispute signals the emergence of a debate among Germany's *maskilim* concerning whether the Hebrew Haskalah, which started as a movement of and for the élite, should reformulate its Enlightenment goals in more populist terms, aiming its general enterprise at the masses. Was the movement to continue catering to those *maskilim* who had adopted their aesthetic standards from German culture and were demanding a use of the German language, in all its purity? Or was it to abandon such a linguistic ideal for the sake of a practical need to translate biblical books into Yiddish, the common language used by the Jewish masses in Eastern Europe?

Tuvyah Feder continued to express the viewpoint of the early Haskalah in Germany; in the matter of biblical translation, he seemed to be a dedicated disciple of Moses Mendelssohn, arguing that literary German should be used for such translation rather than Yiddish. Like the German *maskilim*, he considered the latter language used, for example, by Polish Jews, to be a corrupt form of German. Most of the early *maskilim* in Germany knew German, were familiar with German culture,

[1]I distinguish between Hebrew *maskilim* who created mostly in Hebrew and those whose intellectual and creative energies were mostly in German. The Hebrew *maskilim* rejected the use of Yiddish, either by traditionalists or East European Jews, which they considered a faulty language, as compared to German or Hebrew.

On Hebrew during the Haskalah, see Moshe Pelli, *Dor Hame'asfim Beshaḥar Hahaskalah* (*The Circle of* Hame'asef *Writers at the Dawn of the Haskalah*), Tel Aviv 2001. A Hebrew version of the present article appears in my book *Sugot Vesugyot Besifrut Hahaskalah Ha'ivrit* (*Genres of Haskalah Literature: Types and Topics*), Tel Aviv 1999.

and tried to adhere to German cultural goals. Many of them were bilingual, and they did not indicate the presence of any tension between the Hebrew and German languages—only between the use of proper German and the use of Yiddish. As indicated, Lefin's translation into Yiddish signals a later development within the Haskalah aiming the movement's resources and efforts at the masses. On the surface, Feder was fully loyal to Mendelssohn's school; he does not directly raise the issue of the Haskalah's overall orientation towards populism or elitism. His view of Lefin's translation as corrupt is presented as an indisputable premise.

THE DIALOGUE OF THE DEAD AS A LITERARY GENRE

The vehicle that Feder used to express his criticism was a so-called dialogue of the dead, one of the most popular literary genres in eighteenth- and nineteenth-century French, English and German literatures. Taking manifold forms—satirical, religious and philosophical, political, biographical—hundreds of such dialogues were published during this period. A list of some five hundred were compiled for German literature alone. The genre was already manifest in the dialogues of the second-century satirist Lucian, and literary scholars have examined the impact translations of these texts had on its subsequent development in the work of writers such as Bernard Fontenelle and François Fenelon in France, George Lyttleton and Henry Fielding in England, and David Fassmann and Christoph Wieland in Germany.[2] Fassmann is considered the author who introduced the genre into German literature, in his long dialogues published between 1718 and 1739.[3] However, the genre's more prominent and long-lasting influence is owed to Wieland, who translated Lucian into German starting in 1780 and published his own *Dialogues in the Elysium* in 1800.[4]

The dialogues of the dead left their mark on the literature of the Haskalah much after the genre's high-point in European literature. Its first manifestation in Hebrew was Aaron Wolfssohn's *Siḥah Be'eretz Haḥayim* (*Dialogue in the Land of the Living* [Afterlife]), published in *Hame'asef* from 1794 to 1797.[5] Several other Hebrew dialogues were also published, some of them satiric—including Feder's *Kol Meḥazezim*. Published in 1793, Joseph Ha'efrati's dialogue *Alon Bachut* (*Oak of Weeping*) was in a very different vein, being an elegiac treatment of the death of Rabbi

[2]On the dialogues of the dead, see Benjamin Boyce, 'News From Hell', *Publications of the Modern Language Association of America*, vol. 58 (1943), pp. 402–437; John W. Cosentini, *Fontenelle's Art of Dialogues*, New York 1952; Frederick M. Keener, *English Dialogues of the Dead*, New York 1973; John Rutledge, *The Dialogue of the Dead in Eighteenth-Century Germany*, Berne–Frankfurt am Main 1974. Boyce lists some two hundred texts—not all dialogues—taking place in the world of the dead. Keener has a selective list of 277 dialogues, and Rutledge, p. 129 and in the appendix, lists about 500 German dialogues.

[3]Rutledge, pp. 27ff.

[4]*ibid.*, pp. 86–87. See Christoph Martin Wieland, 'Gespräche im Elysium' in *idem*, *Sämmtliche Werke*, vol. 27, Leipzig 1839, pp. 389–421. For an eighteenth-century English rendition of Wieland's translation of Lucian into German, accompanied by an introduction, see *Lucian of Samosata. From the Greek. With The Comments and Illustrations of Wieland*, London 1820. Wieland (Introduction, p. xii) asserts that Lucian established this genre, combining Socratic dialogue with Aristophanian drama.

[5][Aaron Wolfssohn], '*Siḥah Be'eretz Haḥayim*', in *Hame'asef*, vol. 7, (1794–1797), pp. 53–67, 120–153, 203–228, 279–298. I discuss Wolfssohn's text in *Sugot*, pp. 48–72.

Yehezkel Landau. There were also didactic dialogues of the dead, such as Shlomo Löwisohn's *Siḥah Be'olam Haneshamot* (*Dialogue in the World of the Souls*) focused on the Hebrew language (1811) and Juda Mises's dialogue of the same title, included in his *Kine'at Ha'emet* (*Zeal for the Truth*) (1828).[6] Works in this genre in various European languages and Hebrew continued to be published throughout the nineteenth century and into the twentieth century.[7]

One can gain insight into the emergence of Hebrew dialogues of the dead by examining both their counterparts in the Western European languages and their cultural, social, and political backdrop. Critics hypothesise that dialogues come into literary vogue in times of historical upheaval, thus reflecting the unfolding of profound spiritual change. This would seem to hold true for the German, French, and English dialogues of the dead, which received their enthusiastic reception in a time of religious decline and loss of faith. Readers are no longer fearful of any punishment after death and thus feel free to enjoy this genre with few inhibitions.[8] With the Haskalah marking the start of a major transformation in modern Jewish cultural history, this theory would seem to apply as well to the dialogues of the dead in Haskalah literature.

For John Cosentini, the European dialogue of the dead serves as a weather vane for whatever ideological conditions surround its writing.[9] Other scholars have asserted that the genre's popularity was largely due to the eighteenth-century interest in subjects such as the existence of spirits, the afterlife, and immortality of the soul, as well as legends about an entrance to hell putatively found in Ireland.[10] At the same time, it is important not to forget that the inherent literary worth of these texts would have contributed as much as such ideological and thematic concerns to the popular interest in them. In light of all these factors, it becomes clear that although the emergence of such an esoteric literary form in literature of the Haskalah may seem odd to the modern reader, it appeared natural, relevant and attractive to readers of the time. For one thing, the *maskilim* had a strong interest in the themes of death and immortality—an interest intensified by Moses Mendelssohn's highly influential book on the immortality of the soul, *Phaedon,* published in German in 1767 and in Hebrew in 1787.[11] The *maskilim* were likewise engaged in an intense controversy over the

[6]Joseph Ha'efrati, *Alon Bachut*, Vienna 1793; Shlomo Löwisohn, *Siḥah Be'olam Haneshamot*, in *Hame'asef*, vols. 9 and 10 (1810–1811); Juda Mises, *Kine'at Ha'emet*, Vienna 1828. Meir Halevi Alter published his own *Siḥah* in *Bikurei Ha'itim* (*First Fruits of the Times*), vol. 6 (1825–1826), pp. 5–24. A shorter *siḥah* by Itzik Aurbach was published in *Hame'asef*, vol. 8, no. 1 (1809), pp. 93–95.

[7]*Siḥot* [plural of Siḥah] were published by Peretz Smolenskin (in *Hashaḥar* [*Dawn*], vol. 1, no. 3 (1869), p. 28); Judah Leib Gordon (*ibid.* vol. 8 (1877), pp. 205–225); as did Yaakov Sobel, *Haḥozeh Ḥezyonot Be'arba'ah Olamot* (*He Who Sees Visions in Four Worlds*), Odessa 1872; In 1988, J. H. Biletzki published a dialogue of the dead in Hebrew, *Mifgshim Mehasug Hasifruti* (*Encounters of the Literary Kind*), Tel Aviv 1988.

[8]Boyce, p. 407 (citing J. S. Egilsrud) and Rutledge, p. 19 (citing Rudolph Herzel).

[9]Cosentini, p. 19.

[10]See Boyce, p. 405; Keener, p. 8. On the concept of the Garden of Eden in the Kabbalah, see Moshe Idel, 'Hamasa Legan Eden: Gilgulav Shel Motiv Mehamitos Hayevani Liteḥum Hayahadut' ('The Voyage to the Garden of Eden: the Transformation of a Motif from the Greek Mythology to the Realm of Judaism'), in *Meḥkerei Yerushalayim Befolklor Yehudi* 2, Jerusalem 1982, pp. 7–16.

[11]Moshe Midessau (Moses of Dessau; Mendelssohn), *Phaedon Hu Sefer Hasharat Hanefesh* (*Phaedon, A Book on Immortality of the Soul*), Berlin 1787. Wolfssohn, in his *Siḥah*, pp. 204–205, notes that Mendelssohn's words were cited from the German edition of *Phaedon* as spoken by Socrates.

burial of the dead, supporting the delayed burial as demanded by the authorities as opposed to the Jewish custom of immediate burial upon death which the traditionalists desired to follow. Their articles on the subject occupied many pages in *Hame'asef* while also being published as separate pamphlets.

Like many of the other genres, this genre, too, attests to the orientation of Haskalah literature towards contemporary European literatures especially in Germany, and their various styles and genres, which they attempted to emulate. Indeed, this genre was part and parcel of the cultural and spiritual milieu of the intellectual elite, and its adoption was emblematic of the desire of the authors of Haskalah to integrate into the spiritual and cultural climate of European Enlightenment.

A study of this literary genre, as part of the endeavour to map and analyse the literary genres of early Hebrew Haskalah, will enrich our knowledge and understanding of this literature, and provide much-needed insight into its aesthetic and literary perception. In addition, insight may be gained into the relationship between Hebrew and European literatures, and the interconnection between this genre and some others which this author has discussed elsewhere, such as satire, travelogues and so on.

Some of the Hebrew dialogues of the dead were discussed previously by Shmuel Werses as part of his work on Haskalah satire, especially the impact of Lucian's satire on Hebrew satire. Afterwards, Friedlander discussed Wolfssohn's Dialogue of the Dead also as part of Haskalah satire. This was the first time in Hebrew criticism that the dialogues of the dead were discussed as a unique genre.[12]

Haskalah literature was strongly orientated towards developments in contemporary Western European literature—especially in Germany. With the genre firmly entrenched in the cultural and spiritual milieu of Europe's intellectual élite, its adoption by Haskalah authors reflects their desire to share the cultural climate of the European Enlightenment.

DIALOGUES OF THE DEAD AND OTHER LITERARY DIALOGUES

In a general manner, dialogues of the dead are rooted in classical mythology and the classical philosophical dialogue. The genre's more modern form was in debt to literature treating, for instance, imaginary voyages, letters from hell, visits to the netherworld, and conversations between the living and the dead.[13] At the same time,

[12]The kernel of this article was originally delivered as a lecture at the Eighth World Congress of Jewish Studies in 1981, and it was published in the proceedings of the congress, *Divrei Hacongress Ha'olami Shashmini Lemada'ei Hayahadut* (*Proceedings of the Eighth World Congress of Jewish Studies*), vol. III Jerusalem 1982. It was also published in *Hado'ar* in 1982. An early version of this article was published first in Hebrew in my book *Sugot Vesugyot Besifrut Hahaskalah Ha'ivrit*. Also see Shmuel Werses, 'Hedei Hasatirah Shel Lucian Besifrut Hahaskalah Ha'ivrit' ('Echoes of Lucian's Satire in Hebrew Haskalah Literature'), in *Bikoret Ufarshanut* (*Criticism and Interpretation*), vols. 11–12 (1978), pp. 84–119; reprinted in *idem*, *Megamot Vetzurot Besifrut Hahaskalah* (*Trends and Forms in Haskalah Literature*), Jerusalem 1990, pp. 223–248. Also see Yehuda Friedlander, *Perakim Basatirah Ha'ivrit Beshilhei Hame'ah Ha-18 Begermanyah* (*Chapters in Hebrew Satire at the End of the 18th Century in Germany*), Tel Aviv 1980, pp. 121–200.

[13]See sources cited in note 2.

typical features of other forms of literary dialogues—features that eighteenth century authors found particularly attractive—are naturally at work in the dialogues of the dead as well. Hence the present-tense of the dialogic form, along with its inherent compactness—due to the absence of superfluous material—conveys a sense of immediacy and authenticity; the form is thus inclined towards dialectic contrast and a presentation of ideas from varying perspectives. Because of this conceptual and formal variability literary dialogues have great didactic potential.[14]

It stands to reason, then, that a dialogue, whether dramatic or satirical, is more than a conversation or just two monologues following each other. The dialogue form has its own rhythm and the participants have their own style, sentence structure, and rhetorical devices which characterise each speaker individually. The dialogues of the dead possess all these characteristics except that they take place in the other world and therefore also allow for the possibility of dialogues among the dead from different historical periods searching for true knowledge, a quality that was already mentioned in *The Dialogues of Plato.*[15]

In a comment on *Gulliver's Travels*, Samuel Johnson observes that once an author has thought of making the dead speak to each other, the rest is easy enough.[16] In this respect, one thing that dialogues of the dead can do far more easily than other literary genres is call upon distinguished historical figures from various times and countries to debate contemporary issues, express learned opinion, at times pass judgment. Within the limits of historical credibility, the author here enjoys full poetic licence, none of the dead being in a position to complain of the portrait painted of them.[17]

Indeed, they may express their authoritative views unequivocally on contemporary controversies. The ability to discuss issues and to pass judgment on matters related to both this world and the world-to-come is typical of this genre, which is located in the place of judgment, the world of ultimate peace and truth. Taking place in *Olam Ha'emet* ("world of truth" or afterlife), the dialogues tend to be quite intriguing and more open than in this world, free, as it were, from the shackles of earthly conventions and customs. Thus, the views expressed in these dialogues retain an air of ultimate truth, supported by an ostensible stamp of authority. Although the dialogues take place in the other world, they clearly focus on matters related to this world.

The dialogues may be satirical, such as the Lucian dialogues, or ethical and philosophical. As the modern genre evolved, other forms of dialogues emerged: historical, political, biographical, philosophical, and religious, that contributed to the enrichment of the genre.

[14]See Pelli, *Sugot,* pp. 48–52; 91–93.

[15]In the "Apology" Socrates says: "But if death is the journey to another place, and there, as men say, all the dead abide. ... What would not a man give if he might converse with Orpheus ... and Homer? ... I shall then be able to continue my search into true and false knowledge; as in this world, so also in the next; and I shall find out who is wise, and who pretends to be wise, and is not. ... What infinite delight would there be in conversing with them and asking them questions.", see "Apology", *The Dialogues of Plato,* II, transl. by B. Jowett, London 1931, p. 134.

[16]Keener, p. 11.

[17]Those still living may, of course, complain on their behalf, as was in fact the case with several readers who campaigned against *Hame'asef* and its editor's portrayal of characters in *Siḥah Be'eretz Haḥayim,* accusing him of taking liberties in his dialogue and misrepresenting the characters. See *Hame'asef,* vol. 7, no. 4 (1797), pp. 299–360.

KOL MEḤAZEZIM

Published in the wake of Wolfssohn's *Siḥah Be'eretz Haḥayim*, Tuvyah Feder's *Kol Meḥazezim* is the second Hebrew dialogue of the dead. Feder could not publish this satire during his lifetime because of the interference by the *maskilim*, led by Yaakov Shmuel Byk;[18] it was only published posthumously forty years after its writing, in 1853, a second edition appearing twenty-two years later. This work was discussed in 1978 by Werses as part of his study of Haskalah satire.[19]

In 1981, Yehuda Friedlander published an annotated version of a manuscript of *Kol Meḥazezim* that was copied by an anonymous *maskil* in 1830.[20] Friedlander characterised this satire as exemplifying "*riv haleshonot*", the language conflict between Hebrew and Yiddish.[21] Unfortunately this manuscript, which is located in the New York Public Library, represents a version that deviates from the printed text.

At the centre of *Kol Meḥazezim* is Feder's acrimonious critique of Lefin's translation of Proverbs, which was published in 1813. Feder argues that Lefin's translation is inferior and corrupt because it deviates from Mendelssohn's school of *be'ur*, the Haskalah project of biblical translation into German and biblical commentary, and from that school's adherence to grammatically correct and idiomatic German. Indeed, Feder goes so far as to assert that Lefin's translation is in effect a translation into Yiddish, thus following in the footsteps of earlier Yiddish translations that had been severely criticised by Mendelssohn.

The first part of *Kol Meḥazezim* consists of a four-page diatribe against Lefin's translation; the second part is in effect Feder's dialogue of the dead. Feder "recruits" some of the leading Haskalah figures, headed by Moses Mendelssohn, as the dialogue's major protagonists. He is here most likely following in the footsteps of Wolfssohn's *siḥah*, in which Mendelssohn plays a central role. Feder was also probably influenced by Löwisohn's didactic *siḥah*, in which the noted *maskil*-grammarian Joel Brill-Loewe (1760–1802), an active member of the circle of *Hame'asef*'s writers, converses with the medieval grammarian and Bible commentator David Kimḥi on

[18]Byk's letter to Feder, dated *Tevet* 1815 and published in *Kerem Ḥemed*, vol. 1 (1833), pp. 96–99, attempts to dissuade the author from publishing his book because it attacks Mendel Lefin "with invectives not related to the criticism". Byk suggests that Feder apologise to Lefin. Feder indicates in reply that he is willing to burn the manuscript if he is compensated for the printing expenses, and argues conversely that the injuries he has inflicted on Lefin are done by a "loving person" (*ibid.*, pp. 99–102). For a description of the controversy among the *maskilim* and a discussion of Feder's editions of *Kol Meḥazezim*, see Joseph Klausner, *Historiah Shel Hasifrut Ha'ivrit Haḥadashah* (*History of Modern Hebrew Literature*), vol. 1, third edn., Jerusalem 1960, pp. 239–246. Additional discussions on this issue may be found in Werses, *Megamot Vetzurot Besifrut Hahaskalah*, pp. 110–159, 338–355; Simḥah Katz, 'Targumei Tanach Me'et M. M. Lefin MiSatanov', ('Biblical Translations by M.M. Lefin of Satanow'), in *Kirjath Sepher*, vol. XVI, no. 1 (1939), pp. 114–133, especially p. 114; A[vraham] M[eir] Habermann, *Masechet Sofrim Vesifrut* (*Tractate on Authors and Literature*), Jerusalem 1977, pp. 30–40.

[19]See Werses, 'Hedei Hasatirah'.

[20]Yehuda Friedlander, 'Tuvyah Gutmann Feder—Kol Meḥazezim, in *Zehut*, vol. 1 (1981), pp. 275–303.

[21]*idem*, 'Riv Haleshonot Bemizraḥ Eiropah Beresheetah Shel Hame'ah Hatesha Esreh' ('The Language Conflict in Eastern Europe in the Beginning of the 19th Century'), in *Min Hakatedra* (*Ex Cathedra*) (1981), pp. 5–34. Both the annotated text and this article appear in *idem*, *Bemisterei Hasatirah (In the Hiding of Satire*), Ramat Gan 1984, pp. 13–75. *Kol Meḥazezim* was discussed earlier by Shmuel Werses in his article 'Hedei Hasatirah'.

Hebrew grammar. In spite of the resemblances to Wolfssohn's *siḥah,* that of Lefin is markedly different from it in its concentration on a single topic, namely the quality of biblical translation, whereas the earlier dialogue covered many important Haskalah topics.

As mentioned above, Friedlander attempted to view this literary piece as heralding the language dispute between Hebrew and Yiddish. However, that dispute in fact only emerged at the end of the nineteenthth century and is related to a late phenomenon of the tension between the languages, which was not prevalent in the second decade of the nineteenth century, the time of the actual writing of this dialogue.

As already mentioned, the Feder-Lefin controversy revolves around the question of whether the Haskalah should orientate itself towards the masses, through the use of Yiddish, or towards a Jewish cultural élite, through the use of German. Feder maintains Mendelssohn's position—that embodying the early Haskalah in Germany—advocating the consistent use of German. The use of dialogues of the dead for internal maskilic dispute was a new phenomenon, although there had been various other disputes among *maskilim,* sometimes heated in nature, such as the disputes between Wolfssohn and Satanow, between Feder himself and Wolfssohn, and between Naḥman ben Simḥa and the editors of *Hame'asef.*[22] There also appears to have been some considerable tension between Naphtali Hartwig Wessely and Isaac Euchel.[23] It was only natural that such disputes would be expressed in a literary medium when breaking out between literati—to the general enrichment of Hebrew literature.

AN INVECTIVE INTRODUCTION TO FEDER'S DIALOGUE

The text's introductory exposition occupies approximately four of its the sixteen pages. Replete with redundancy and verbiage and at times rhymed, it addresses Feder's adversary directly in an invective critique of his translation. The aesthetic and linguistic criteria to which Feder appeals are, as indicated, those of Mendelssohn and his school of biblical exegetes and translators. In this manner, no ideological revelation need be introduced in the following dialogue; but the reader's curiosity is aroused regarding the *method* Feder will use to attack Lefin's translation.

The introduction was intended by Feder to create covert ties to and a backdrop for the actual dialogue, thus creating a framework for the ensuing dialogue. Likewise,

[22]See Naḥman ben Simḥa, *Ein Mishpat* [Fountain of Justice], Berlin 1796, pp. 4–5, and his harsh attack on the editors of *Hame'asef,* especially Wolfssohn, who, in turn, attributed its authorship to Satanow. Feder's own dispute with Wolfssohn and Satanow had its literary representation in his book *Lahat Haḥerev* (*The Fiery Sword*), Vilna 1867, originally published in 1804. See also Pinḥas Argosi de Silva [Baruch Jeiteles], *Sefer Ha'orev* (*Book of the Ambusher*), Saloniki [?] 1795, pp. 2a–2b, and his criticism of the editors of *Hame'asef.*

[23]For Wessely vs. Euchel, see Moshe Pelli, *The Age of Haskalah,* p. 194, note 11.

such an introductory exposition was used by some authors of dialogues of the dead to explain how they got hold of the dialogues, which purportedly had taken place in the other world. However, in Lucian's thirty classical dialogues there is no frame story nor any attempt to explain how the author came by these writings in this world.[24] In this unique genre, the reader is expected to acknowledge the literary convention that these dialogues took place in another realm, either in hell, in Eden, or in any other supernatural world. He is not expected to ask questions.[25]

Apart from having the purpose of explaining how authors obtained the dialogues, the introductory expository frameworks were also sometimes used to foreshadow two motifs in the dialogue linked to the topic of death. The first of these centres on the fact that Mendelssohn could not complete his project of translating the Bible in his lifetime; in his wisdom and foresight, Feder explains, he had assembled a group of *maskilim* and prepared them for the completion of the task.[26] Like many *maskilim* before him, Feder here employs imagery equating Moses Mendelssohn with the original Moses, thus relating Moses's bestowal of the Torah on the Israelites to Mendelssohn's translation of and commentary on the Torah. Both the earlier and later Moses are portrayed as sweetening the bitter water so that the Israelites might drink it (Ex. 15:23–25), and as planting and cultivating a vineyard so that in time it will bear fruit.[27] The second anticipatory passage appears at the end of the introduction where Feder turns to his adversary, Lefin, urging him to go out and collect copies of his book to bury or burn them. By this act, Feder suggests, Lefin will cleanse himself, so that he may now wear clean instead of soiled clothing. Feder then asks Lefin rhetorically how he will face his creator on the day of judgment , and what he will say to the inhabitants of Eden—to Mendelssohn and his students.[28]

These examples of foreshadowing are somewhat misleading. For even if Feder would have liked to see his adversary in the other world, at the time of the writing, Lefin was still very much alive (he died in 1826). Thus, the author could not have brought him to the other world even in a fictional work, unless he were to write a dialogue between the living and the dead. In the dialogue itself, Lefin is not even allowed to defend himself, the deliberations and argumentation being conducted on the basis of criteria established by the first generation of *maskilim* without any serious attempt to defend Lefin's way of translating. As the substitution for a defence, Feder

[24]Lucian's classical dialogues have no introductory framework, the reader being expected to simply acknowledge the other-worldly locus. This is the case as well with the dialogues of Fontenelle, Lyttleton, Wieland and Matthew Prior; see also Rutledge, p. 16.

[25]The same applies to the dialogues of Fontenelle, Lyttleton and Wieland. See *Lucian's Dialogues*, transl. by Howard Williams, London 1900, pp. 86–167 and 'Conferences of the Dead', in Wieland, *Lucian of Samosata*, comments [by]: Wieland edited by William Tooke, vol. 1, London 1920, pp. 382–443; Bernard Fontenelle, *Nouveaux Dialogues des Morts*, edited by Jean Dagen, Paris 1971; George Lyttleton, *Dialogues of the Dead*, London 1760; facsimile edn., New York 1970; Wieland, 'Gespräche im Elysium', pp. 389–421; see also Matthew Prior's dialogues, *The Literary Works of Matthew Prior*, London 1959, pp. 599–663. See also Rutledge, p. 16.

[26]Tuvyah Feder, *Kol Meḥazezim*, Lemberg 1853, p. 14; *ibid.*, Lemberg, 1875, p. 10. Henceforth the two editions will be cited by page numbers alone, in the above order.

[27]*ibid.* See Moshe Pelli, *Moshe Mendelssohn: Bechavlei Masoret* (*Moses Mendelssohn: Bonds of Tradition*), Tel Aviv 1972, pp. 91–94.

[28]p. 15; p. 11.

cites an approbation of the translation by another writer of the old school, Reb Elyakim Melamed ben Jacob Schatz, whose book *Melamed Si'aḥ* (*Teaching Dialogue*) contains the translation into Yiddish of words and passages from the Torah and the "five scrolls". But this approbation itself constituted incriminating testimony in the eyes of the *maskilim*; it is intended as a device for ridiculing both Lefin and Elyakim Melamed—the latter figure serving as a substitute for Lefin himself.

Feder's dialogue is different from Wolfssohn's in several respects with possible relevance for the genre's development in Hebrew literature. To begin, Feder's presentation of his characters at the start of the dialogue, as if they were acting in a play, is an innovation. The presentation is in order of appearance, with verbs and adverbs used to describe the characters' action, the sequence of events, and the flow of time. Wessely, for instance, arrives "reciting a poem" while Euchel is "approaching", Brill "following him" and "[Judah Loeb] Ben Ze'ev being the last one".[29] Connected to this, Feder describes his characters' actions much more extensively than does Wolfssohn in his *siḥah*. Thus, as Wessely approaches, Feder inserts a parenthetical statement functioning as something like stage directions: "[NHW approaches, reciting a poem as he walks]".[30] Such statements can occupy a few lines of smaller print, at times in parentheses, as in the following example: "[Moshe Ḥayim] Luzzatto, Menashe ben Israel, Mendelssohn and Wessely are strolling in Eden towards the Lord of Glory, and behold Euchel is approaching and he seems enraged; Wessely was happy to see him and he greeted him".][31] Euchel, we learn, is very angry about the inept translation of the Book of Proverbs—a book that he had in fact himself translated:[32] "(Euchel is an arrow's throw away, he walked and sat across [from the others], crying for the great calamity that befell this generation, and Wessely returned to his place [next to the others] to rejoice in love together with Moses [Mendelssohn], his chosen one, and with the sages that were with him)".[33] This sort of description is also manifest in the following shorter passage: "(They came to the gate and the cherubim were looking at his [Joel Brill's] face, and observing that he was happy and content, they opened [the gate for him])".[34]

To make *Kol Meḥazezim* more interesting and colourful, Feder incorporates some action between the fragments of the dialogues, which are generally not as long as those in Wolfssohn's *siḥah* (sometimes consisting of long monologues). Characters come and go; Mendelssohn and Wessely expel their colleague, Euchel, to the far end of Eden because he has cursed the sage (*ḥacham*) Mendel Lefin;[35] Brill is visible as he draws near,[36] followed by Ben Ze'ev,[37] who later faints upon hearing Mendelssohn's harsh words. Ben Ze'ev is asked to read Lefin's translation of Proverbs, which he

[29]pp. 15–16; pp. 11–12.
[30]p. 16; p. 12. Some of the descriptions are in brackets while the longer ones are in parentheses.
[31]p. 18; p. 14.
[32]*Mishlei*, transl. by Isaac Euchel, Berlin 1789. See also Euchel's *Darchei No'am* (*Pleasant Ways*), Dessau 1804.
[33]p. 19; p. 15.
[34]pp. 21–22; p. 18.
[35]p. 20; p. 16.
[36]p. 21; p. 17.
[37]p. 22; p. 19.

holds in his hands.[38] Duma, the overseer of the lower section of the other world, is instructed by Mendelssohn to bring the author of *Melamed Si'aḥ* from the underworld; he does so in order that he testify in Mendelssohn's court, then taking him back to his abode.[39]

Taken together, these passages connect various components of the dialogue and contribute towards its narrative synchronisation. The passages help clarify the psychological situation and feelings of the dialogue's characters—for instance, "and his heart foretold him that his time has come"[40]—offering a comment on both their cultural and spiritual condition. Interestingly, at one point—towards the dialogue's end—there is a merger of a dialogical exchange with a piece of narrative itself containing dialogue. In other words, the author abandons his dialogue, embarking on a narrative that contains fragmentary statements presented in direct speech:

> And Duma hurried up and took it [the book] and gave it to him and said: raise your voice so that you will become known to all the inhabitants of Eden. The [author of] *Melamed Si'aḥ* called and screamed till his voice became hoarse and his eyes bulged, and before the sun set he had read it from beginning to end, and he was happy, jumping, hopping, and leaping, and he said: now I know that my wisdom is still alive, this is my Torah [teaching].[41]

Feder does not describe manners of speech in the "stage directions" as Wolfssohn does. Instead, actions are described in the fragmentary connecting narratives. In comparison to Wolfssohn's own *siḥah*, in the *siḥah* of Feder Wessely's speeches and poetical discourse mark an exception to the general brevity of the dialogic exchanges. In this respect, both in their length and formal characteristics, Wesseley's dialogical passages are in concert with the poems he published in *Hame'asef* and with his biblical epic *Shirei Tiferet* (*Songs of Glory*), thus functioning as something other than strict declamation. All in all, Feder's *siḥah* lacks the vital ideological tension present in Wolfssohn's dialogue—more specifically, in the confrontation between Rabbi Ploni, the traditionalist, and Moses Mendelssohn, the *maskil.* It is an echo of an inner rift within the circle of *maskilim*—albeit a significant echo, in that, as something like a judgment-day drama, it represents the emergence of a new form of the dialogue of the dead within Hebrew literature.

FEDER'S SETTING: JUDGMENT DAY AT THE HEAVENLY COURT

Since Feder's *Kol Meḥazezim* does not constitute a dispute between two ideological rivals in the world-to-come, it may be classified as a judgment day scene. It is a subdivision in the genre of the dialogues of the dead. Feder contributed a new form to the genre of the dialogue of the dead in Hebrew literature in counterdistinction to Wolfssohn and Löwisohn.

[38] p. 23; p. 20.
[39] pp. 24, 26; pp. 21, 23.
[40] p. 25; pp. 21–22.
[41] p. 25; p. 22.

The portrayal of Mendelssohn in *Kol Meḥazezim* is important because it addresses his image as conceptualised and portrayed by the *maskilim*. In Wolfssohn's *siḥah,* Mendelssohn is introduced on the day of his arrival in Eden; he is portrayed as having doubts and apprehensions concerning the reception he may receive, in light of the traditionalists' attacks on him during his life. In fact, he is welcomed warmly into Eden. In contrast, Feder describes Mendelssohn as a well-established resident there, and his position and stature have changed dramatically. At the end of Wolfssohn's *siḥah,* God himself embraces Mendelssohn, acknowledging his cultural contributions and welcoming him as one of the chosen élite. In Feder's *siḥah,* he is portrayed as the supreme judge of the court, surrounded by his fellow *maskilim*—Wessely, Euchel, Brill and Ben Ze'ev—who act in accordance with his commands, and as the only figure seated on a chair, ben Israel and Luzzatto standing to his left and right respectively.[42] Thus for Feder Mendelssohn's centrality in the Jewish world is an established fact.

Even though there is an interesting development in Feder's portrayal of Mendelssohn in comparison to the other dialogue, there is no major change from his portrayal by the early *maskilim* in his lifetime, and after his death.[43] Since this is a dialogue that belongs to a sub-group of the dialogue of the dead, namely, to the judgment day scene, Mendelssohn's figure is conceived and portrayed here as a supreme judge, who has the final word in all matters including the evaluation of Lefin's translation. Mendelssohn is further depicted as deciding the fate of the author of *Melamed Si'aḥ*, who is being returned to his original place in the lower world. He is also portrayed as having the authority to condemn one to the damnation of hell.[44]

In Wolfssohn's *siḥah*, God plays an important role, furnishing Mendelssohn with his stamp of approval. In Feder's *siḥah*, God's role is more limited—He merely welcomes Wessely into heaven. Only His voice is heard, interestingly in rhymed Hebrew, not unlike the Hebrew of a *maskil* such as Wessely.[45] Mendelssohn opens Feder's dialogue with a monologue about the *be'ur* project that he has started, expressing his satisfaction at having trained a generation of translators who will follow in his footsteps.[46] In this manner Feder establishes a backdrop for the condemnation of Lefin, who was once among Mendelssohn's followers but has now gone astray and rejected Mendelssohn's legacy—the accusation levelled by Feder in his introduction.[47]

* * *

The author capitalises on the genre's unique trait of assembling personalities from different historical periods and letting them express their views on controversial issues. Letting historical figures comment on contemporary topics makes the

[42]p. 15; p. 12.
[43]See Pelli, *Moshe Mendelssohn,* pp. 88–114.
[44]p. 20; p. 16.
[45]In Friedlander's published text of the manuscript (see text near note 21), God is not included, the voice of the seraphim being heard instead.
[46]p. 16; p. 12.
[47]p. 13; p. 9.

dialogue interesting and intriguing. Their authority, each one in his respective field, is mobilised to pass judgment in areas which are not necessarily in their field of expertise. In this dialogue, Feder has Menashe ben Israel and Moshe Ḥayim Luzzatto recalled from oblivion, placing them, as customary in the genre, in the company of the *maskilim*.

One may suppose that Feder's choice of two scholars of Sephardic ancestry from an earlier period, neither very likely to have spoken Yiddish, yet asked to express their views on issues of language and translation involving Yiddish, was not made on the basis of their spiritual authority or linguistic talents, but rather tongue in cheek. The other positively viewed figures are taken from the ranks of the Hebrew *maskilim* and grammarians, especially those who translated or wrote commentaries on the Bible as part of the Mendelssohnian school of *be'ur.* In order of their appearance in Feder's text (and of their listing at the head of the dialogue), these figures are Wessely, Euchel, Brill, and Ben Ze'ev.

Dialogues of the dead usually take place upon the death of an important personality and his entry into the world-to-come. It is worth noting that despite the tendency of Hebrew dialogues of the dead to mark a distinguished figure's transition from death to the afterlife, the order of their appearance is here that of their earthly dates of birth[48]—with the exception of Mendelssohn, who is treated differently as the text's central personality. In this manner, the hierarchy of earthly age continues to count within the afterlife reality.

Such transfer of earthly temporality to the hereafter is characteristic of the genre. Wessely's poetic locution immediately suggests that he has just arrived in the latter locus,[49] where he is indeed welcomed by God, as He welcomed Mendelssohn in Wolfssohn's dialogue, and Wessely now meets Mendelssohn and the other *maskilim* in the afterlife. The author passes over an unmistakable anachronism: while the action does in fact take place following the earthly departure of Wessely in 1805, it predates the death of Ben Ze'ev in 1811. (Although, by the time Feder wrote the dialogue in 1813, Ben Ze'ev was in fact dead). Anachronism, Feder appears to be suggesting, does not play a role in the perception of time in the world-to-come.

Elyakim Melamed, author of *Melamed Si'aḥ*, and the unnamed author of *Aluf Omer* (Master of Speech)—the eighteenth-century, traditionalist, non-Haskalah figures in Feder's dialogue—are placed permanently in Sheol (with the exception of Elyakim Melamed's heavenly court appearance), as befitting the Haskalah concept of who deserves to be accepted in the spiritual world-to-come. These figures are doomed specifically because of the old-fashioned, non-enlightened nature of their biblical translations and commentaries—texts Feder aligns with Lefin's own outmoded translation. As far as the dialogue's remaining figures are concerned, they are the functionaries in the upper world, and then there is Duma in the lower world.

[48]Ben Israel (1604–1657), Luzzatto (1707–1747), Wessely: 1725–1805; Euchel: 1758–1803; Brill: 1760–1802; Ben Ze'ev: 1764–1811.

[49]p. 16; p. 12.

THE STATURE OF THE CHARACTERS IN *KOL MEḤAZEZIM* AND THEIR PORTRAYAL

As would be expected, the stature of the characters in Feder's text in the afterlife is similar to that which they held in this world. Wessely, for instance, remains the poet *par excellence*, typified by both his verse and florid speech. He is described as singing before the Almighty—in Jewish sources a characterisation of the righteous in Eden.[50] Similarly, Euchel's eloquence, too, is sometimes conveyed through his speaking in rhymed verse. Feder expresses consistent respect for the *maskilim* by referring to them with honorific acronyms: interestingly, the titles found in the manuscript published by Friedlander are different from those found in the Lemberg edition of 1853. In the latter edition, Wessely is *MHRNHW* (*Morenu Harav Reb Naphtali Herz Weisel*), the full honorific *Morenu Harav* ("our teacher, the Rabbi") being used only in his case; Mendelssohn is *RMD* (Rabbi Moshe Dessau), as he was referred to in Hebrew by the *maskilim*; Euchel is *RAA* (R. Aleph Aleph, the acronym of Isaac Euchel's name in Hebrew characters), or else simply *R. Itzik Euchel*; Brill is either *R. Joel Brill* or *RJ Brill*; and Menashe ben Israel and Moshe Ḥayim Luzzatto receive either the honorific *R.* or the abbreviations *MBI* and *RMḤL*, respectively. Only Ben Ze'ev is not referred to by any honorific title, but simply by his name— perhaps a token of him not being considered one of the founding fathers of the Haskalah.[51]

Wessely is also characterised by Feder through the contents of his prosaic statements. At one point, for example, he praises himself for walking in Luzzatto's footsteps and like him helping to revive the Hebrew language—this self-praise sounding very much like Feder's own words resounding in Wessely's mouth.[52] It would thus appear that in the world to come truth matters more than the party conveying it. Feder likewise reveals Wessely's high degree of optimism regarding the future of the Haskalah through that *maskil*'s observation that many young people are now following the early *maskilim*. This optimism also seems manifest in Wessely's initial response to Euchel's complaint about Lefin's translation of Proverbs—an expression of faith in Lefin's spiritual and maskilic leadership. But once he hears Brill's and then Ben Ze'ev's testimony regarding the translation, he reverses his position: a reversal perhaps expressing Feder's sense that individual viewpoints are not static or frozen in time, that they can at least change in the world beyond. In any event, the main function of Wessely's initial position in Feder's dialogue is tactical (and certainly no effort to convey factual reality), enabling the other *maskilim* to establish that Lefin's translation is indeed defective.

It is notable that in line with the basic Haskalah ethos, not only Wessely but in fact all of Feder's positive characters, the *maskilim*, are capable of undergoing spiritual change, of developing their personality and making intellectual progress. Predictably, the negative characters, the traditionalists, display no capacity for any change, hence

[50]p. 16; p. 12. See 'Seder Gan Eden', in Aharon Jellinek (ed.) *Beit Hamidrash* (*House of Learning*), vol. 3, third edn., Jerusalem 1967, p. 133: "All *tzadikim* [righteous people] sing in the rising morning."

[51]In Friedlander's manuscript, Mendelssohn is referred to as *RMBMN* (Rabeinu Moshe ben Menaḥem), another honorific term used by the *maskilim* for Mendelssohn.

[52]p. 18; p. 14.

being cut off in Sheol from wisdom and learning. Euchel, like Wessely, thus undergoes some change: he is temporarily punished for the anger sparked in him by Lefin's work, as in the world-to-come there is no place for such an unbecoming earthly trait. However, once Wessely and Mendelssohn realise that Euchel has indeed been correct in rejecting a corrupt translation, he is restored to his proper place in Eden.

In contrast, as the embodiment of a "negative" character, Elyakim Melamed remains intellectually static, despite his aspiration to "become free at last",[53] that is to be raised from the lower to the upper world through his judges' recognition of his own role in the biblical translation, and despite his own temporary move on high when summoned to the heavenly court of the *maskilim*. For in Feder's work, in distinction to Wolfssohn's, there is not even an effort to persuade the "negative" character to change his mind.

As a compliment to the various more or less indirect ways of characterising the *maskilim* in their pursuit of wisdom (*ḥochmah*) and knowledge, Feder makes use of a satirical device that one also finds in Wolfssohn: a presentation of the *maskilim* through the eyes of their adversaries, the rabbis and traditionalist authors. Elyakim Melamed, for instance, describes the *maskilim* as "clean-shaven, baring their backsides".[54] The absence of a beard is simply a stereotypical attribute of a modern *maskil*. On the other hand, the image of "bare backsides" (in other words, uncovered buttocks), based on Isaiah 20:4, may be of more than passing interest, as something other than a sardonic reference to the short, modern coats worn by *maskilim*.[55] It is possible that, aside from being a derogatory phrase, it may indicate some influence of the antique and European dialogues of the dead, with their characters occupying Elysium in appropriately scant antique clothing.[56]

Finally, we need to note that in Feder's dialogue as in Wolfssohn's before him, psychological reactions and inner feelings are depicted through vividly described facial expression in the bracketed description. Euchel, upset as he enters the scene, reveals this mood in an angry face.[57] Ben Ze'ev's face "turns green" as he trembles, and his face is "blackened".[58] Such descriptions of facial expressions are in line with the general use of an "earthly" language abounding with figurative speech.

FEDER'S DESCRIPTION OF THE HEAVENLY ABODE

Descriptions of the heavenly landscape in various dialogues of the dead are, as perceived by the writer, of great interest as they reveal the writer's mindset and his

[53]p. 26; p. 22.

[54]pp. 24–25; pp. 22–23.

[55]Ha'efrati's *Alon Bachut* features a title page with an illustration of Rabbi Yeḥezkel Landau embracing and kissing Mendelssohn in Eden. The two figures' paradisical clothes are identical with their presumed earthly ones, Landau wearing a rabbinical robe and Mendelssohn a modern European suit. (See copy of this illustration on the front plate of Pelli, *Age of Haskalah*.)

[56]In Lucian's dialogues of the dead, the shades remove their clothes and other earthly status symbols; see *Lucian's Dialogues*, transl. by Howard Williams, London 1900, p. 105.

[57]p. 18; p. 14.

[58]p. 23; p. 19.

special treatment of the genre. In his own dialogue, Wolfssohn bases his depiction of the heavenly locus on Jewish tradition, more specifically on biblical descriptions of Eden and especially on the Midrash. Allusions to the depiction in Genesis are abundant, trees thus being described as "pleasing to the sight and good for food" (Genesis 2:9), with many souls sitting in joy and friendship in their shade.[59] By contrast, Feder's dialogue is rather pale in its depiction of the same setting, lacking any description of the heavenly scenery in the "stage instructions" provided in parentheses. All told, there is hardly an effort in Feder's *siḥah* to portray the reality of the heavenly locale, whether in metaphysical, spiritual or physical terms. It is possible that Feder assumed that any such description would no longer be necessary, being so well known now to readers of Hebrew dialogues of the dead. Readers are thus required to fill in the missing details, whether from their own imaginations or based on the literary conventions of the genre.

Similarly, in contrast to Wolfssohn's approach in his *siḥah*, there is very little reference by the characters themselves to their heavenly environment, which, following Jewish tradition, is signified simply as *Gan Eden* in an identification of that locus with the world to come,[60] but without any vivid or definitive description. But there are several exceptions. Wessely, for example, refers to the locale as the "dwelling place of *Moshe*, your servant",[61] thus playing on the identification—established already in the introduction—of Moses Mendelssohn with his illustrious namesake, both figures being presented as equals in stature in the world-to-come. In doing so he capitalises on the ambivalent identity of Moshe as either Moshe the lawgiver or Moses Mendelssohn. The reader is now engaged in an identity riddle: is it Mendelssohn or Moses? The result is that these great personalities are presented as equals in stature in the world-to-come. This ambivalence is already referred to in the introduction as the author mentions the great opposition to Mendelssohn's *Be'ur*, using the expression "but Moshe, His servant, was successful", a term that is customarily applied to Moses the lawgiver, but now is reassigned to Moses Mendelssohn.[62] The solution to the identity riddle does identify "Moses, His servant" as Moses Mendelssohn. This repeated phrase places Mendelssohn at the center of reality in the maskilic Eden, as perceived by Feder, paralleling the stature of Moses, the lawgiver and the "Master of all prophets". This juxtaposition became a permanent feature in the perception and the portrayal of Mendelssohn in the early part of Haskalah during Mendelssohn's lifetime and immediately after his death.[63]

The transition from earthly life to the heavenly one, discussed in the critical literature on the dialogues of the dead, is depicted by Feder through Wessely using clichés such as "from darkness to light" and "release from prison to freedom".[64] These expressions are very general and do not contribute significant insight into the

[59]Wolfssohn, 'Siḥah Be'eretz Haḥayim', p. 54.
[60]p. 17; p. 13.
[61]*ibid.*
[62]p. 14; p. 10.
[63]See discussion about the identification of Moses Mendelssohn and Moses in Pelli, *Moshe Mendelssohn*, pp. 91–94.
[64]p. 16; p.12

author's concept of the afterlife beyond the known conventional notions of "darkness-light" (the latter representing the light of wisdom and Haskalah) and "prison-freedom".

It is clear that Feder did not make use of descriptive options inherent in the genre that might have furthered his satiric purposes. Nor did he endow his dialogue with either realistic or super-realistic detail. Nevertheless, there is an apparent focus in the dialogue on one physical object in the Garden of Eden, a "gate"—although this is itself referred to rather than described. As the shades arrive at the gate, a "voice from up high" is heard saying, "This gate is closed and will not be open; an enraged heart may not enter here, only a happy one will". And, indeed, as the shades approach the gate the angels ascertain whether the new soul, that of Joel Brill, is happy and content; at first he is refused entry but eventually he is allowed through the gate into Eden.[65] The gate again appears as a metaphor in Wessely's poetic utterances: "Eden, open up your doors"[66] and "lift up your heads, O gates, lift them up, you everlasting doors",[67] which is based on Psalms 24: 7, 9. The source of the gate's importance is rather apparent: it marks a distinct separation between the sections in the world to come, at the same time ideologically demarcating the separation between the *maskilim* and their opponents.[68]

Of the heavenly bodies, only the setting sun is mentioned in Feder's dialogue,[69] a continuation in heaven of the earthly temporal cycle (a prominent theme in Feder's satire), and an expression of the need to complete all business in Eden, especially the trial, before sunset. This theme may be related to that of *Yom Hadin*, the day of judgment. It should be noted that the metaphor of closing the "evening gates" already appears in Löwisohn's *Siḥah Be'olam Haneshamot*, where it signifies the dialogue's end.[70]

Even Feder's depiction of the heavenly world's nonmaterial, *spiritual* aspects is rather one-dimensional, happiness being the dominant feature of the reality of Eden. As Wessely indicates, in Eden "there is no anger, no jealousy and no sadness",[71] features common throughout the European dialogue of the dead.[72] One must be happy and content to be allowed into Eden, as has been seen in the cases of Joel Brill and Isaac Euchel: at first "sullen and displeased", he follows Wessely's advice to change his attitude and is then allowed in. Euchel, unhappy about Lefin's translation, is likewise temporarily excluded from Eden's bliss.

As mentioned earlier, when the *maskil* Joel Brill is about to enter the gate, the cherubim are checking to see whether he is happy in order to ascertain that he deserves to enter Eden.[73] Brill, who at first was "sullen and displeased", he follows Wessely's advice to change his attitude and is then allowed in. and indeed once he does, the

[65]p. 21; p. 18.
[66]p. 21; p. 17.
[67]p. 21; p. 18.
[68]Gates are naturally abundantly present in the Jewish sources; see, for example, 'Seder Gan Eden', p. 134.
[69]p. 25; p. 22.
[70]Löwisohn, *Siḥah Be'olam Haneshamot,* p. 38a.
[71]p. 18; p. 14; cf. p. 19; p. 15.
[72]Wieland's Elysium, for instance ('Gespräche im Elysium', pp. 394–395), is likewise depicted as a place lacking jealousy or a desire for vengeance.
[73]p. 21; p. 18

cherubim allow him to enter the gate to Eden. Euchel, on the other hand, who is portrayed as being very depressed while expressing critical remarks about Lefin's translation, is temporarily excluded from Eden's bliss and is held back. He is not permitted to enter Eden, where "there is no anger, no jealousy and no sadness" (p. 18; p. 14), according to Wessely's specification. Thus Wessely establishes the characteristics of the afterlife as peaceful, full of friendship, lacking jealousy, anger, and sadness.[74]

While this thematic emphasis may reflect Feder's debt to the non-Hebraic European genre, he may have also drawn his sources from Hebraic works such as Immanuel Haromi's *Maḥberot Immanuel*, where Eden is graced with "everlasting happiness and ceaseless rejoicing"[75]—states of mind that, however, Haromi does not further delineate. Another aspect of the afterlife, which is discussed in the critical literature of the genre, is the question of memory. Importantly, in this Hebrew piece, memory continues in the other world, and the shades do not forget their past earthly experience.[76]

While both Wolfssohn and Feder portray Eden as a locus of total peace and harmony, Feder, unlike Wolfssohn, does not connect this harmonious locus to an idea of ultimate truth. This difference emerges from the very nature of the disputes in the two dialogues. In Wolfssohn's *Siḥah Be'eretz Haḥayim*, the dispute between the *maskilim* and Reb Ploni, a traditionalist rabbi, who has been cited above, is in fact aimed at arriving at a sense of the maskilic truth; Wolfssohn thus emphasises truth as the afterlife's dominant feature. By contrast, in Feder's *Kol Meḥazezim* the dispute is among the *maskilim* themselves, the maskilic truth thus being known and widely recognized. Although at one point Euchel, complaining that he has been sent to the outskirts of Eden, exclaims "Arise, Truth, for you I have fought"[77], for Feder the dominant trope is peace, the struggle to achieve tranquillity among the *maskilim*.

Nevertheless, as each of the *maskilim* appears on the heavenly scene, he is characterised as upset, angry or depressed. Against the backdrop of the required heavenly harmony, their anger is initially perplexing, its explanation not revealed at once, since the dialogue follows a principle of gradual disclosure: at first, there is the position espoused by Wessely, who is unwilling to believe the other *maskilim*'s complaints about Lefin's translation. Inevitably, this disbelief raises doubts in the reader as well regarding these complaints. But confronted by the weight of the testimony directed against Lefin, Wessely eventually changes his mind. The tradition-bound Elyakim Melamed continues to vouch for the excellence of Lefin's translation—but at this point his words have the opposite of the intended effect.

THE WORLD AS IT IS AND THE WORLD-TO-COME

As befits the European dialogue of the dead in general, Feder's *Kol Meḥazezim* does not take place in a realm detached from earthly events. The author does not desire

[74]p. 19; p. 15

[75]Immanuel Haromi, *Maḥberot Immanuel* (*Immanuel's Books*), vol. 2, Jerusalem 1957, ed. by Dov Yardeni, p. 539.

[76]p. 22; p. 18.

[77]p. 20; p. 17.

to depict the world-to-come as existing in some sort of ivory tower. On the contrary, the other-worldly reality is closely related to the this-worldly reality. Indeed, like his maskilic colleagues, Mendelssohn, for example, is portrayed in the opening of the dialogue's first scene as having "his heart in the studies of *ḥochmah*".[78] Feder does not really explain what the study of *ḥochmah* is or how Mendelssohn's labours are related to those of the other *maskilim*. But in their preoccupation with *ḥochmah*, the *maskilim* in Eden are, of course, maintaining the same Haskalah ideal they preached on earth, an ideal thus defined as worthy of Eden as well. In general these *maskilim* are very much interested in occurrences back on earth. Feder dwells on both the information they receive in that regard and their reaction to it. Thus Feder presents his *maskilim* as interested in the progress of the Enlightenment on earth and in the continuity there of their Haskalic projects—a clear reflection of the author's own earthbound focus, the celestial Haskalah of the *maskilim* itself representing the utopian aspirations of an earthly ideal.

While earthly objects are generally wanting in the heavenly venue, one such object that does appear there is Lefin's controversial book itself. Already in Wolfssohn's *siḥah*, as well as in the anti-Chassidic satires that are to appear later in Haskalah literature, books, as objects, play an important role.[79] Feder depicts Ben Ze'ev as approaching, "an open book [i.e. Lefin's book] in his hand".[80] In doing so he wishes to reinforce the justification of his critique through a resort to proven Talmudic method, as encapsulated in the injunction "let us get the book and examine it" (*neitei sefer veneḥezei*). The verdict of corrupt translation will thus not emerge from mere hearsay, even hearsay on the part of *maskilim* not meant to be suspected of bias, but from the very text at issue. Ben Ze'ev, the biblical scholar, is now asked by Mendelssohn, the initiator and editor of the *be'ur*, to read several passages from the book he is holding, both Wessely—until now unwilling to heed the complaints of his colleagues—and Mendelssohn—sitting in judgment, hence bound to objectivity—now being compelled to adapt a critical stance in its regard. Quoting from texts is a common feature in European dialogues of the dead;[81] Wolfssohn used the device (citing from Mendelssohn's *Phaedon*) before Feder.

Another object in Feder's dialogue is brought to Eden in mysterious ways. It is the text of a poem, composed by Elyakim Melamed in the other world in praise of Lefin's translation. Lefin is referred to as "Menaḥem Mendel of Satanow", citing the Yiddish version of his name for satirical purpose. And the poem, which is handed to Duma to be forwarded to Lefin, parodies a mixture of Hebrew and Aramaic, in an archaic, rabbinic fashion. This communication between the upper and lower worlds, or between the world-to-come and this world, lacks detail, and it is difficult to decide whether Feder is treating it as one of the features of the genre. If it were a message

[78]p. 15; p. 11.

[79]See Pelli, *Sugot*, pp. 169, 195 (on the satire of Saul Berlin and Isaac Erter). See also Shmuel Werses, *Sipur Veshorsho* (*The Story and Its Root*), Ramat Gan 1971, p. 42, and Baruch Kurzweil, *Bama'avak Al Erchei Hayahadut* (*Struggling over Judaic Values*), Jerusalem and Tel Aviv 1970, pp. 55–95 (on Joseph Perl's satire). See also Ben Ami Feingold, 'Hasefer Vahasifrut Kenose Basiporet Hamaskilit' ('The Book and Literature as Subjects in Haskalah Fiction'), in *Meḥkarim Besifrut Ivrit, Te'udah*, vol. 5, Tel Aviv 1986, pp. 85–100.

[80]p. 22; p. 19.

[81]See Rutledge, p. 90.

from the *maskilim*, the author would have emphasised it as the word of the departed Haskalah fathers to their followers on earth. There is, however, no indication this is the case, and it seems depositing the poem with Sheol's custodian is simply meant to hint at Lefin's destiny upon departing from earth to hell, where the message will await him.

As mentioned before, the author enlists two Jewish scholars of world renown, Menashe ben Israel and Moshe Ḥayim Luzzatto, who were not necessarily known for their expertise in Yiddish, to testify and identify the language of Lefin's translation. Mendelssohn himself has difficulties identifying that language ("I don't know, perhaps it is a language unknown to me"[82]). Then the two pundits have doubts about its identity, saying: "[The] Italian [language] says, it is not mine, and the Arab [language] says, it is not with me, perhaps it is the language of the scapegoats and Azazels, the neighing of a horse or a whooping of a crane."[83] Ostensibly, Yiddish is not perceived to be one of the accepted languages of cultured people.

But Feder is not content with such scholarly testimony and enlists an ideological rival to express his traditional views, which will serve the purpose of the author. Thus the traditionalist author of *Melamed Si'aḥ*, who also translated passages from the Torah into Yiddish in his book, is summoned to provide his "professional" view of Lefin's translation. In order to prepare the reader for the "expert" testimony of Elyakim Melamed, Feder places him on the lower level of the world to come, as appropriate to someone who himself has used Yiddish in his biblical translations. An additional device Feder employs, the characterisation of spiritual through physical attributes, while common in Haskalah literature, is uncommon in modern European dialogues of the dead, whose figures, inhabiting Eden or Elysium, tend to be incorporeal, to lack distinct physical characterisation. Here the single physical portrayal is of the traditionalist author, and the description is something less than complimentary: "He is a very terrible old man, a span in height, his saliva on his beard, and his beard down to his navel, he is a hunchback having crushed testes, crawling on his belly, his hairlocks are black, wherein numerous small and big insects abide."[84]

FEDER'S CHARACTERISATION OF "PLUTO BEN ḤLAVNA"

In the above-cited passage, Feder presents Elyakim Melamed—referring to him as "Pluto ben Ḥlavna"—through a series of biblical allusions which serve as metaphors for his spiritual traits. His description of Pluto as a dwarf ("a span in height") is in

[82]p. 24; pp. 20–21.

[83]*ibid.*

[84]p. 25; p. 22. A more positive exception is found in Wolfssohn's *siḥah*, p. 151, in the figure of Socrates, embodying wisdom as a high value in Eden. See Pelli, *Sugot*, chap. 2a, on Wolfssohn, p. 62. It should be pointed out that placing non-Jewish righteous people in Eden and exhibiting a positive attitude toward them is not unique to Haskalah. In *Seder Gan Eden*, the Righteous Among the Nations are depicted as situated between the garden's second and third walls, but not within Eden's confines themselves; they are moved to the abyss towards evening (Jellinek [ed.], vol. 3, p. 131). On the other hand, it cannot be said that there is a dominant influence of Haromi on Feder. For the latter could have used Haromi's method by bringing in King Solomon, who, according to tradition, composed the Book of Proverbs, to testify on the translation, as did Immanuel in his *Maḥbarot*, p. 548.

direct contrast to the giant Goliath, whose height was "six cubits and a span tall" (I Samuel 17:4). He implies that Pluto is mad ("his saliva on his beard), which is based on the depiction of David (when "sore afraid of Achish the king of Gath") as letting "his saliva run down his beard" (I Samuel 21:14). He further suggests that, because of his deformity, he is permanently excluded from the priesthood (as a "hunchback having crushed testes"), which alludes to the relevant injunction in Leviticus (21:20) regarding anyone who is "crook-backed, or a dwarf … or hath his stones crushed". He also portrays Pluto as an impure insect ("crawling on his belly"), which is based on the injunction in Leviticus (11:42) that "whatsoever goeth upon the belly" or "upon all fours, or whatsoever hath many feet … them ye shall not eat; for they are a detestable thing". (Curiously, the expression "black hairlocks", a reference to Song of Songs 5:11, is given a drastically different valence here). The lower level of the other world is depicted as inhabited by lowly individuals who were placed there as part of their punishment. They are associated with lower creatures, their spiritual status being depicted by the insects that nest on their bodies.[85]

Depicting reality in Hell in a corporeal manner in this work is no different from its depiction in the traditional Jewish and in general literature. The portrayal of punishment in Hell in the Midrash and by Immanuel Haromi and Moshe Zaccut are based on corporeal punishment that requires a body.[86] Obviously, Feder did not undertake to describe the punishment of this resident in Hell as the dwellers of the abyss were previously portrayed in Jewish literature.

Predictably enough, Feder's dialogue reaches its climax in a confrontation between representatives of the two opposing viewpoints, traditional and maskilic, regarding the appropriateness of translation into Yiddish. Although Feder invites Elyakim Melamed to leave the abyss and testify in Eden, he also establishes clear physical and spiritual boundaries between these two worlds and between the unenlightened and enlightened perspectives they represent. Upon his arrival in Eden, Elyakim tries to approach the group of *maskilim*, which includes Mendelssohn, but Duma keeps him at a sufficient distance from Mendelssohn,[87] thus establishing the marked gap that separates them.[88] This is a physical as well as a spiritual gap, which the author attempts to highlight. It reflects the wide gulf that separates the enlightened world of Haskalah and a backward element in Judaism—strictly from a maskilic point of view. In the author's mind, Lefin has manifested his association with this anti-maskilic element by the very translation that he had done. Lefin appears to belong to this group of Haskalah adversaries, as will be shown below.

The author of *Melamed Si'aḥ* is now asked to first examine, then assess Lefin's translation. In his description of this assessment, Feder makes use of satiric allusions to the Bible and other sources that could be readily identified by contemporary

[85]p. 26; p. 23.

[86]See Elijah ben Moshe de Vidas, 'Masechet Gehinom' ('Tractate Gehenna'), in *Reisheet Ḥochmah* (*The Beginning of Wisdom*), Amsterdam 1708, facsimile edn., chap. 13. See also Immanuel Haromi, *Maḥberet Hatofet Veha'eden* (*The Book of Tofet and Eden*), Berlin 1922, and Moshe Zaccut, *Tofteh Aruch* (*Readied Tofet*), Berlin 1922, and additional references in Pelli, *Sugot*, chap. 2b, pp. 85–86, n. 30.

[87]p. 25; p. 22.

[88]*ibid.*

readers. For example, he describes Elyakim Melamed as having read Lefin's book from beginning to end before sunset and as being joyful, "leaping and whirling"[89]—the phrase *veyefazez veyechrker* being a reference to the episode in II Samuel (6: 16) where Michal, daughter of Saul, sees David "leaping and dancing before the Lord" after smiting the Philistines. In reaction to David's joyful motions, we read in the same verse, Michal "despised him in her heart", and Feder is clearly suggesting a similar response of the *maskilim* to Elyakim. In another passage of the dialogue Elyakim joyfully exclaims that, "Now I know my wisdom is still alive; this is my teaching, this is my rhetoric, this is my riddle, this translator's name will go forth throughout the land."[90] This is a verbal irony as Feder, through his protagonist, refers to the the language of *kaparot*, expiatory prayers, in the Jewish liturgy: *Zeh ḥalifati, zeh temurati, zeh kaparati, zeh hatarnegol yelech lemitah va'ani elech ve'ekanes leḥayim tovim arukim uleshalom*—"this is my replacement, this is my substitute, this is my atonement, this rooster will go to death and I will go and enter a good and long life and peace".[91] The textual parallel, not grasped by Elyakim himself, alludes to Lefin's fate, and perhaps ironically to the "good" life Elyakim can expect in the abyss.

A last episode involves Elyakim's effort to follow in the footsteps of the maskilic poets (who are referred to early in the dialogue) by declaiming a poem in honour of Lefin's new translation, Duma then being asked to take the poem to Lefin. Feder characterises this approbation as written in a corrupt language abounding with Aramaisms, in contrast to the elegant poem Wessely recites upon arriving on the scene, itself based on the purity of biblical Hebrew. The content of the author of *Melamed Si'aḥ*'s poetic approbation is contrary to the maskilic ideal that is now realised in Eden. This author's aspirations are not wisdom and learning as was the goal of Mendelssohn and Wessely; instead, he yearns for the midrashic legendary goose of Bar Ḥanah,[92] and for the preserved wine and the leviathan,[93] promised, according to the Midrash, to the righteous in Eden.The reaction of the *maskilim* to the approbation is derisive laughter, directed at both the poet's work and his appearance.[94] Obviously, the traditionalist author's support of Lefin is intended for its verbal irony, because his positive assessment of Lefin's translation is conceived by the *maskilim* as an incriminating testimony against Lefin. Finally, Mendelssohn orders Duma to take him back to Hell, the place that befits him best.

The peculiar name of the author of *Melamed Si'aḥ* is no doubt of significant interest. He is referred to as "Pluto ben Ḥlavna" by Duma, in charge of the abyss, according to Feder,[95] and by Mendelssohn as well.[96] Friedlander attempted to interpret the name only to admit that his explanation was just a conjecture, perhaps

[89] *ibid.*
[90] *ibid.*
[91] *ibid.*
[92] Rabah bar bar Ḥanah was known for his exaggerated stories; see Talmud Bavli, Baba Batra 73 on his geese, and 75 on the leviathan.
[93] p. 26; p22.
[94] p. 26; p. 23.
[95] p. 25; p. 21.
[96] p. 26; p. 23.

even somewhat tenuous.[97] The name Pluto in Greek mythology refers to the god who rules Hades, but its appearance in *Kol Meḥazezim* may be traced to the dialogues of the dead. In Lucian's dialogues of the dead, as well as in other dialogues, Pluto is one of the main figures who plays an important role.[98] Feder's use of the name is intended for ironical purpose: Pluto is an exalted, lofty name, yet it is attributed here to the resident of the lower abyss. With the perceived association of Pluto with Hell (for Pluto is, in effect, in charge of that region), there emerges an incongruity between that sublime name and the lowly situated person.

The name Ḥlavna is an uncommon Yiddish name for women and for men. In its application to men, Ḥlavna serves as a Yiddish nickname for the Hebrew name 'Lapidot'.[99] The allusion Ḥlavna=Lapidot ridicules this inhabitant of Sheol, whose punishment is burning in fire (*Lapidot, lapid*, implies a torch).[100] There may be a different meaning that ironically alludes to 'Eshet Lapidot' (the wife of Lapidot, based on Judges 4:4), referring to a mighty woman (such as Deborah), whereas the wretched description of the author of *Melamed Si'aḥ* is a far cry from the folklore notion of the powerful 'Eshet Lapidot'. In addition, Feder creates another incongruity stemming from the equation of the lofty Greek name Pluto and the esoteric and rare Yiddish name Ḥlavna. The combination of the two names creates a sense of dissonance, a disharmony leading to ridicule.

It should be noted that the function of the author of *Melamed Si'aḥ* is intended to criticise Lefin for deviating from the enlightened paths of Haskalah and walking in the footsteps of the *maskilim*'s adversaries. Lefin is to be condemned because he did not follow Mendelssohn's spiritual will—this is the fundamental premise of the author of this *siḥah*. The suggested notion that the author of *Melamed Si'aḥ* was modeled on the figure of the Polish rabbi, Reb Ploni, Mendelssohn's main adversarial character in Wolfssohn's *Siḥah*, ought to be rejected.[101] For the author of *Melamed Si'aḥ* is not a viable adversary at all, but is somewhat of a twin image, an alter ego, of Lefin himself, whom Feder could not have transferred prematurely to the other world. His wretched character is but a distorted mirror image of Lefin. The poem that the traditionalist author wrote in honor of Lefin reads like an enthusiastic

[97]Friedlander, in his article in *Zehut*, I, p. 302, and in his book *Bemisterei Hasatirah*, p. 70, refers to it as quite an unclear name. In the edition of the manuscript he published, the name is read as "Pilta", and consequently Friedlander interprets the name as based on Shir Hashirim Rabah, meaning oil. Another suggestion by Friedlander that relates Pluto to the planet does not explain its use here. At any rate, if indeed the name is Pilta, it is a nickname of Elimelech (see *Sefer Tiv Gitin* [*Book of Divorce*] by Menaḥem Mannes, Vilna 1849, p. 6a). However, the right name is Pluto, which in the context of the dialogues of the dead is a common figure.

[98]See *Lucian's Dialogues*, dialogues v and vi, pp. 95–99, and Sir Fleetwood Sheppard's dialogues in Keener, pp. 180–184.

[99]As to the identity of the name Ḥlavna, see *Sefer Tiv Gitin*, p. 23a. Also, Shlomo Gansfried, *Ohalei Shem* (*Tents of Shem*), Lemberg 1907, p. 86a. That this name was known—though rare—at that time is apparent from Aaron Wolfssohn's article on foreign names among Jews in *Hame'asef*, vol. VI (1790), p. 252.

[100]*Sefer Tiv Gitin*, p. 23a, explains that the firewood called Hlavna is erroneously named Ḥlavna, as the author cites several sources where the name is related to 'Lapidot'.

[101]Friedlander found alleged traces of Wolfssohn's influence on Feder in the depiction of the traditional author, but did show also the difference between them. Yet, he insisted that there is no doubt that Reb Ploni served as model to Feder's character. See, 'Riv Haleshonot Bemizraḥ Eiropah Beresheetah Shel Hame'ah Hatesha Esreh', in *Min Hakatedra*, pp. 30–31 and his book *Bamisterei Hasatirah*, pp. 31–32.

approbation of the translation and as a declaration of a total identification with and sympathy for him. The use of the language structure of the *kaparot* style, as cited above, "this is my teaching, this is my rhetoric",[102] purports to point out the affinity in mentality and creative endeavor of the traditionalist speaker with his protégé. And the echo of the alluded style of *kaparot* indeed supports the notion that the author of *Melamed Si'aḥ* is but a double ("this is my replacement, this is my substitute") of Lefin.

DUMA AND HIS ENVIRONMENT

Feder's *siḥah* manifests some development in the Hebrew genre of the dialogues of the dead. Although Feder does not offer a topography of the Garden of Eden itself, his dialogue nevertheless presents a picture of the relation between Sheol and Eden different from what one finds in Wolfssohn, for whom the lower world only exists through implication (Mendelssohn expresses his fear of not being accepted into the upper chamber).[103] Hence Wolfssohn does not transfer Reb Ploni to the lower world, rather leaving him by himself once Moses and God proceed on their way. In contrast, Feder's portrayal of the reality of after-life does acknowledge the existence of the lower level and also tells a little about its residents. As part of this concept, a figure associated with the lower level of afterlife appears in Feder's *siḥah* and is in addition to the cherubim, the angels of the upper level, who play a role in both Wolfssohn's *siḥah* and at the beginning of Feder's. As mentioned before, he is Duma, in charge of the nether world (Hebrew: 'ḥatzar mavet'), who is well versed with all the inhabitants of the world.[104]

As a counterpart to the upper world's angels (appearing in both of Wolfssohn's dialogues as well), Sheol's most prominent resident in Feder's dialogue is Duma, the region's custodian. In his choice of a name for the functionary in charge of Sheol, Feder once again draws on Judaic sources such as the Zohar, where Duma is in charge of Gehenna ("Tofta", the burning fire in "the valley of the son of Hinom", to the south of Jerusalem, mentioned in both 1 Kings [11:7] and 2 Kings [23:10], where children were sacrificed in ritual fire[105] (now reinterpreted as the equivalent of hell); the souls of the wicked being handed to him to be placed there and be judged by him. In some sources, Duma is described as possessing all information on all the dead, his main duty being to report to the Almighty about them. He is also described as being responsible for announcing, on behalf of the Almighty, the future resurrection of a given body at its appointed time, as well as the identity of the righteous ones who will be resurrected in the world-to-come.[106] The name of Duma's dwelling place 'ḥatzar

[102]p. 25; p. 22.

[103]Wolfssohn, '*Siḥah*', pp. 203–205.

[104]p. 24; p. 21.

[105]See *Beit Hamidrash*, vol. 1, p. 147; *ibid.*, vol. 5, p. 49; *Reisheet Ḥochmah*, p. 42a, 47b, 42b.

[106]Duma and his role are described in early talmudic sources such as Shabat 152b and Sanhedrin 94a, in midrashim such as Tanḥuma and Shoḥer Tov, and in late sources such as the Zohar. These midrashim were collected, in part, in *Reisheet Ḥochmah*, and in Jellinek (ed.) as well as in Judah David Eisenstein, *Otzar Midrashim* (*A Treasure of Midrashim*), New York 1915. The sources dealing with Duma are found in Reuven Margaliyot, *Malachei Elyon* (*The Angels of the Almighty*), Jerusalem 1964, pp. 225–229. Friedlander argues that Duma is named after the name of his section in Hell. See *idem*, *Bamisterei Hasatirah*, p. 69.

mavet,' the nether world, appears in Jewish sources; it is the place where all dead spirits abide.[107]

Duma, following Mendelssohn's command and in his capacity as the angel knowing the location of every human being, summons Elyakim Melamed "to the place which I shall show you". Elyakim reacts with joyful anticipation ("He hurried up, his heart telling him that his time to join the residents of Eden was coming close"[108])—a reaction that can be understood in light of Duma's role in Jewish sources as heralding redemption from Sheol. The terms used in this episode to describe the netherworld—*Alukah*, *Taḥtit*, *Tofta* and *Gay ben Hinom*, and of course *Sheol*[109]—themselves naturally stem from various Jewish sources.[110]

Werses, who checked the sources of influence on Feder's descriptions, is of the opinion that he is indebted to the German dialogues and not the Jewish sources. Werses assumes that Wieland's translation of Lucian's works (1788–1789) most probably was known to Feder. While he admits to some influence from the Jewish sources, Werses argues that the greatest influence came from external sources. Friedlander cites Werses, but does not reach any conclusion as to the sources of influence on Feder.[111]

Our discussion so far leads us to conclude that in selecting the names of sections of the netherland and the name of the person in charge of Gehenna and his responsibilities, Feder used the Jewish literary tradition. Yet, the genre of the dialogues of the dead is always in his mind as a model. The final product of his *siḥah* is determined by the ideological need and the effectiveness of the satiric device on the reader. The name Pluto ben Ḥlavna, borrowed from both internal and external sources, best shows Feder's way of writing.

* * *

It is thus apparent that in his dialogue Feder is in strong debt to the Jewish literary tradition, on the one hand, the European dialogues of the dead, on the other. One theme above all is at work in the dialogue, connecting its parts, accounting for its wider implications, and exemplifying its spirit. This is the involvement and the interest of the founding fathers of the Haskalah in seeing—through both biblical translation and exegetical labour—to the movement's ideological continuity, and to the continuity of the Mendelssohnian school, beyond their deaths. This central concept exemplifies the spirit and essence of the dialogue. Not only are the *maskilim* characterised as interested in biblical translations done after their death, following up

[107]'Gan Eden Vegehinom' ('Garden of Eden and Gehenna'), in Jellinek (ed.), vol. 5, pp. 44–45, and esp. *ibid.* p. 50 where 'ḥatzar mavet' is given as one of the names of Gehenna. See also Margaliyot, p. 225.

[108]p. 25; pp. 21–22.

[109]Friedlander's manuscript offers variants (*passim*).

[110]For *Alukah* as a reference to Gehenna, see Avodah Zarah 17a. On *Alukah*, *Toftah*, and other terms, see Maimonides, 'Hilchot Teshuvah' ('The Laws of Repentance') in *Mishneh Torah* (Deuteronomy), Jerusalem 1957, p. 247. Eiruvin 19a cites seven names for Gehenna, among them *Sheol* and *Tzalmavet*.

[111]Friedlander, 'Riv Haleshonot', p. 30; *idem*, *Bemisterei Hasatirah*, p. 30.

on their own exegetical work, but also they are portrayed as extremely interested posthumously in the continuous progress of Hebrew Haskalah.

Feder can thus be understood as arguing for the centrality of these founding fathers, and for the seminal importance of the early Haskalah, in German-Jewish history during the age of Enlightenment—and he urges his contemporary *maskilim* to follow along the fathers' pathway. The dialogue attempts to renew and enforce the ideological principles of the first *maskilim* and to continue the golden chain of early Haskalah in the manner set by the early *maskilim.* More than anything else he wishes to impart a sense of continuity in Haskalah ideology in particular and the *Weltanschauung* of continuity and succession in general.

By using a European literary genre, Feder proves himself a student of early German Haskalah. Following the early *maskilim* he combines European and Hebrew sources to enhance the ideology of Hebrew Enlightenment.

Dissertation Abstracts

REFORMATION AND JUDAISM

ACHIM DETMERS

The Reformation began at a point in time when nearly all of the Jewish communities in Western Europe had been subjected to over four hundred years of massive persecution. In most European countries and smaller territories edicts of expulsion had brought the once flourishing Jewish life and culture to near extinction. The Jews had almost completely vanished from public life, but not from common knowledge. The deeply rooted anti-Jewish stereotypes that had developed over the previous centuries still determined the general attitude towards Judaism. Correspondingly, the pictures people had of Judaism were not the result of direct social contact. The theology of the sixteenth century, in particular, was dependent on the generally accepted prejudices reflected in the Christian anti-Jewish traditions and the *Adversus Judaeos* literature. For this reason the theological judgement of sixteenth-century Judaism and its religious practices maintained a momentum of its own that had little to do with the actual Judaism of the age—that is, a changing and multi-facetted Judaism.

In addition, few Jews lived in areas where the Reformation was a dominant force, and even fewer had a rabbinic education. Under these conditions it is hardly surprising that intensive exchanges with Jews were seldom and that only on rare occasions did the Reformers take up a direct discussion with Jewish partners or their texts. While some Jews—mostly converts—did serve the Reformers as teachers of Hebrew, only the fewest Reformers had experienced Jewish life and piety personally. Exceptions to the rule were Andreas Osiander, Wolfgang F. Capito, Sebastian Muenster and Paul Fagius. Intensive discussions with Jews were only tolerated if they had Jewish conversion as their goal. So the participants of such exchanges were under pressure to justify these contacts. The Hebrew studies of certain Reformers were eyed with suspicion, and not only by Roman Catholics: the Protestant side also warned against a new "judaising" tendency. As a result, the first Christian studies of Jewish sources were labelled a useless and dangerous science and fell into disrepute. After an initial openness to the *Hebraica veritas*, the Reformers felt it necessary to dissociate themselves from the Jewish faith in order to protect their flanks against the virulent accusation that they were "Judaisers".

This development stands opposed to the expectations raised by Luther's first writing on the Jews: *Das Jhesus Christus eyn geborener Jude sey* (1523). In this work Luther massively criticised the anti-Jewish politics of the Roman Church. The "pro-Jewish" tendencies of this work raised high expectations on the part of the Jews. Above all, the anticlerical and iconoclastic characteristics of the Reformation with its intensified interest in the Hebrew Bible caused many Jews to expect a change in the anti-Jewish direction of Christian theology. However, the effect which the Reformation had on the situation of the Jews was minimal. By the mid-1520s the newly awakened interest in Judaica began to diminish and in the following decades the Jews were not spared from further expulsions and discriminatory measures.

Because of the inner-Christian debate over the Reformation the Jews largely disappeared from public interest until 1529. The role that they did play during the conflicts surrounding the Reformation was marginal—Protestants and Roman Catholics accused one another of "judaising". This changed in 1529 when the Ottomans besieged Vienna and Jews were accused of collaborating with them. When certain "judaising" heresies (Sabbatarianism, Antitrinitarianism, Millenarianism) appeared at the beginning of the 1530s, the relationship between the Jews and Christians further deteriorated. The Jews were suspected of being responsible for these inner-Protestant phenomena. This led, together with legal and economic questions, to certain consequences at the end of the 1530s: the Jews were driven out of important Protestant territories (Electorate of Saxony 1536) or they were tolerated, but only under unbearable conditions (Hesse 1539).

That the effect of the Reformation on the relationship between Jews and Christians can be described as somehow positive is out of the question. Especially Luther pulled back in the 1530s from the "pro-Jewish" tendencies of his early work and now spoke against toleration of the Jews. His later writings on the Jews (1543) contributed to an intensification of the anti-Jewish atmosphere: anti-Jewish measures were implemented in Hesse and the area around Strasbourg, and the Jews were expelled from the *Neue Mark*, the Electorate of Saxony, Silesia and Brunswick.

Achim Detmers, *Reformation und Judentum. Israel-Lehren und Einstellungen zum Judentum von Luther bis zum frühen Calvin*, Stuttgart: Kohlhammer 2001, vii, 392 pp., ill. (paperback). Includes bibliographical references and indexes.

Doctoral thesis, Giessen University, 2000; ISBN/ISSN:3170169688.

SOURCES: Edited and non-edited letters, tracts, biblical commentaries, pamphlets and leaflets.

DR. HORST FISCHER IN AUSCHWITZ AND ON TRIAL IN THE GERMAN DEMOCRATIC REPUBLIC IN 1966

CHRISTIAN DIRKS

Dr. Horst Fischer (born 1912) was a concentration-camp doctor from 1942 until 1945 in the main sub-camp of IG Farben, the Monowitz Camp, located at Auschwitz (I.G. Farben had a total of forty sub-camps). In the summer of 1943, Fischer was appointed chief medical deputy to his friend and mentor, head physician Eduard Wirths, at Auschwitz. During his service, Fischer participated in the annihilation of at least 70,000 deportees and concentration-camp prisoners. Fischer was also a profiteer from injustice: there were a number of medical authorities among the prisoners at Auschwitz, and he used their expertise to increase his own academic standing. The motivation for his criminal deeds thus involved a blend of antisemitism, indifference to the fate of the prisoners, careerism and corruption.

After the Second World War Fischer lived for almost 20 years in East Germany. Parallel to the Auschwitz Trials in Frankfurt am Main (1963–1966) he was put on trial before the German Democratic Republic Supreme Court. He was convicted of committing crimes against humanity according to Article 6c of the International Military Tribunal. Fischer received the death penalty and was executed by guillotine at the beginning of July 1966 in Leipzig.

Christian Dirks: *'Die Verbrechen der anderen'. NS-Prozesse in der DDR. Das Verfahren gegen den KZ-Arzt Dr. Horst Fischer*

Doctoral thesis, Freie Universität Berlin, 2004.

SOURCES: Various documents in the archives of the East German State Security Services, Berlin, the German Federal Archives, Berlin, the Fritz Bauer Institute, Frankfurt am Main, and the Archives of the Auschwitz State Museum.

EDUARD ARNHOLD (1849–1925). A BIOGRAPHICAL INVESTIGATION

MICHAEL DORRMANN

This study both fills a gap in the research on the Jewish business elite during the German Empire and contributes to scholarship on upper-class philanthropy in the nineteenth and twentieth centuries. It traces the life of Eduard Arnhold, who was the son of a physician in Dessau and grew up in a large family of modest means, and who became one of the richest, most powerful philanthropists in the German Empire.

Arnhold's business activities revolved around coal from Upper Silesia. Toward the end of the nineteenth century, his company, Caesar Wollheim, together with Emanuel Friedlaender & Co., succeeded in monopolising the market for the second-largest coal-mining area in Germany. The study follows Arnhold as he expanded his power by becoming a board member of various corporations—including AEG and the Dresdner Bank—and by working together with trade and industry lobbies. As an influential businessman Arnhold was also a welcome guest of the Prussian government bureaucracy. Although he clearly identified with the political system in the German Empire, he became the only unbaptised Jew ever to be appointed by Wilhelm II to the Prussian upper chamber, and was repeatedly decorated for his service to his country. This biographical study rejects characterising Arnhold as a *Kaiserjude*.

Arnhold's activity in promoting the fine arts is one important reason for such a rejection: his interests in this area were diametrically opposed to the established taste in art, as well as to the aesthetic preferences of the emperor. Thus Arnhold was one of the principal defenders of Hugo von Tschudi, director of the Berlin National Gallery, whom Wilhelm II had forced to resign after he had opened the doors of his museum to artistic modernism. Arnhold himself not only collected impressionist art—this study reconstructs his collection, which, with its many paintings by Edouard Manet and Max Liebermann, was known far beyond Berlin—but also donated numerous works of art to the National Gallery and other museums. His friends and advisers within the art scene of Wilhelminian Berlin included Max Liebermann, Paul Cassirer and the sculptor Louis Tuaillon.

His most famous project as a patron of the arts, however, was the "Villa Massimo", a residential studio for German students of art in Rome. Arnhold had it built at his own expense and then donated it to the Prussian state shortly before the outbreak of the First World War. In the field of social policy he was primarily interested in child and youth welfare. Together with his wife Johanna he founded a girls' orphanage on the outskirts of Berlin. It was home to nearly a hundred girls and known for its progressive educational methods. Privately funded scientific research could also count on Arnhold's support; the "Kaiser-Wilhelm-Gesellschaft zur Förderung der Wissenschaften" was only one of his beneficiaries in this domain.

This study reconstructs the basic conditions and structures that made philanthropy and entrepreneurship possible during the German Empire. In addition, it offers insight into the way of life and the social integration of a self-assured, influential Jewish member of the German upper class around 1900.

Michael Dorrmann, *Eduard Arnhold (1849–1925). Eine biographische Untersuchung zu Unternehmer- und Mäzenatentum im Deutschen Kaiserreich*, Berlin: Akademie Verlag 2002, 413 pp., ill. (hardcover). Includes bibliographical references and indexes.

Doctoral thesis, Humboldt UniversityBerlin, 2002; ISBN/ISSN:3-05-003748-2.

SOURCES: Numerous archival collections including the estate of Eduard Arnhold, the Geheimes Staatsarchiv PK, the Political Archives of the German Foreign Office, the Central Archives of the Berlin State Museums, and the Leo Baeck Institute, New York.

JEWS IN THE COUNTY OF BURGUNDY IN THE MIDDLE AGES

ANNEGRET HOLTMANN

This study treats different aspects of Jewish life in the thirteenth and fourteenth centuries in the county of Burgundy, a region attached to the German empire in this period. First, the history of Jewish settlement in the region is outlined, with particular emphasis on the events surrounding the persecutions and expulsions of the Jews in the fourteenth century. The main body of the book is devoted to the analysis of the Jews' economic activities. This focus emerges from unique source material, namely two Hebrew account books from a Vesoul merchants' company presumably led by Héliot of Vesoul. The two large fragments date from the first and second decades of the fourteenth century and allow insight into Jewish credit transactions with members of the aristocracy and the rural population in the villages surrounding Vesoul. Other segments of the account books deal with Jewish trade in wine and cloth. Combined with further source material, it is possible to appreciate the importance of the Jews' activities both for the aristocracy and the economic development of the county of Burgundy.

Annegret Holtmann, *Juden in der Grafschaft Burgund im Mittelalter*, Hannover: Hahnsche Buchhandlung 2003 (*Forschungen zur Geschichte der Juden*, [section] A, [vol.] 12), X, 502 pp. (hardcover). Includes maps, bibliographical references and index.

Doctoral thesis, University of Trier, 2000.

SOURCES: This thesis is mainly based on departmental archives of Haute-Saône (Vesoul), Doubs (Besançon) and Côte d'Or (Dijon).

JEWISH HISTORY AND CULTURE IN MUSEUMS. NON-JEWISH MUSEOLOGY OF JUDAICA IN GERMANY

JENS HOPPE

The way general museums of cultural history present Jewish history and culture reveals whether a society is prepared to commemorate minorities in a museum framework. Museums have been very special areas that have shown to what degree Jews have been integrated into German society. Both Jews and non-Jews can gain insight here.

This study covers the period from the middle of the nineteenth century to the end of the 1980s. Amongst other things it examines the origins of collections of Jewish works in famous museums such as the German National Museum in Nuremberg and in less familiar places such as the Bergwinkel Museum in Schlüchtern (Hesse); it also treats individual themes such as how Judaica reached the museums and what happened to these during the Nazi period; and it considers the question of non-Jews exhibiting Jewish history and culture. In considering such work by non-Jews one chapter also examines the Jewish museology of Jewish culture There is a striking difference here between the two approaches as up to the 1970s non-Jews quite strictly limited their understanding of Jewish culture to its religious aspects.

The thesis shows that starting in the nineteenth century various cultural-historical museums began collecting Judaica as specific objects of Jewish history and culture. Deeper presentations of the Jewish world by non-Jews, generally supported and furnished with advice by Jews, were not apparent until the end of the nineteenth century; such presentations began to flourish around 1910 when numerous museums started to set up special Jewish departments. The First World War marked an end to such projects but in the 1920s museums again turned to Jewish culture, often building on the efforts made during the reign of the Kaiser. The Nazis degraded all Judaica, declaring such items of no exhibition-interest, leading to its disappearance from German museums. Jewish works again became a topic for discussion in West Germany at the end of the 1950s, becoming a mass phenomenon towards the end of the 1970s. Since then, Judaica has been collected continuously, with ongoing efforts to connect the various initiatives.

It is clear that at least a part of Germany's democratic society wants general museums to include Jewish history and culture and to deal with both in more depth. Any such initiatives have to be based on a sense by Jews in Germany that they are an integral part of the larger society; with such a sense they are willing to donate Judaica and support the museums in their efforts. In the framework of such past efforts, the history of Germany's museums points to the depth of Jewish integration during both the *Kaiserreich* and, especially, the Weimar Republic—this despite the reality of antisemitism, and in stark contrast to the persecution and destruction that followed 1933. The Shoah of course also had a great impact on the work of the museums in this domain: after the defeat of Nazi Germany it took almost three decades for Jewish history to return to German museums as part of regional history, and for visitors to be able to regard Judaica as part of their own past and present.

Jens Hoppe, *Jüdische Geschichte und Kultur in Museen. Zur nichtjüdischen Museologie des Jüdischen in Deutschland*, Waxmann: Münster, New York, Munich, Berlin 2002, 395 pp., ill. (paperback). Includes archival and bibliographical references and an index.

Doctoral thesis, University of Münster, 2001; ISBN/ISSN: 3830911785.

SOURCES: State and municipal archives, museum archives, Judaica in museum collections, Jewish newspapers, and interviews.

SPEAKING ABOUT STRANGERS. DISCOURSE ON "FOREIGN INFILTRATION" AND EXCLUSION IN SWITZERLAND, 1900–1945

PATRICK KURY

Following Michel Foucault's theory of discourse, this thesis analyses the construction of one of the most important catchwords of the political language in Switzerland, so-called *Überfremdung* ("foreign infiltration") and its influence on Switzerland's anti-Jewish refugee-policy during the Second World War.

The term *Überfremdung* is found for the first time in an article by Carl Alfred Schmid, chief of the poor-relief fund of the canton of Zurich, in 1900. Yet, shortly before the First World War political debates in Switzerland were increasingly influenced by discussions concerning the threat by foreigners; *Überfremdung* was the catchphrase during this decade. Already in 1914, this problematic term found its way into internal papers of the Federal Department for Domestic Affairs. Around 1910 there were plenty of articles, booklets and pamphlets published concerning so-called *Überfremdung*. During the First World War the Federal Council founded the *Eidgenössische Fremdenpolizei* (Swiss Foreign Police), a special police unit that formed part of the immigration office. The policy of this new police unit was predominantly aimed at Eastern Jews, who were considered incapable of assimilation.

Überfremdung also had an influence on Swiss naturalisation policies: In the 1920s, Heinrich Rothmund, chief of the Swiss Federal Foreign Police, stated in a letter to the Zurich authorities that what he termed "typical Eastern Jews would not be eligible for naturalisation when they were first-generation immigrants. The fight against *Überfremdung* increasingly developed into a collective phobia. In the internal guidelines concerning the new law of asylum of 1931, the concept is cited as a reason for forbidding permanent residency to all foreigners not able to "present valid and convincing reasons a permit may be granted"—this in the context of Switzerland's purported overly-dense population.

Überfremdung increasingly was also cloak for antisemitism. In September 1938, Rothmund again cited the concept in a letter to his superior, Federal Councillor Baumann, in which he asserted that the *Fremdenpolizei* had succeeded in preventing the "judaising" (*Verjudung*) of Switzerland through "systematic and careful work." This is an example of the close ties between xenophobia and antisemitism in Switzerland before the Second World War. Hostility towards Eastern Jews had became publicly legitimised when the 'foreign question' was taken up as a highly respectable theme in national debates on domestic policy. On the brink of the Second World War the refugee question once again became a political issue, with antisemitism now being directed without mercy against all Jews from abroad, not only against those from Eastern Europe.

Patrick Kury, *Über Fremde reden. Überfremdungsdiskurs und Ausgrenzung in der Schweiz 1900–1945,* Zurich: Chronos Verlag 2003, 271 pp., ill. (hardback). Includes bibliographical references and indexes.

Doctoral thesis, University of Basel, 2002; ISBN/ISSN:3-0340-0646-2.

SOURCES: The thesis is mainly based upon the sources of the Swiss Foreign Police (*Eidgenössische Fremdenpolizei*), a part of the Department of Justice in the Swiss Federal Archives in Berne.

THE VIENNA SCHOOL APPROACH TO SINGLE FAMILY HOUSING 1910–1938

IRIS MEDER

Otto Wagner was the dominant figure in Viennese architecture after 1900. Jews, however, did not attend Wagner's master class at the Vienna Academy of Fine Arts because the Academy was considered antisemitic. They preferred the Technical College and its director Carl König who was himself of Jewish origin. König and his neo-baroque late-historicist architecture, however, could not influence his students the way Wagner did. This gave them the opportunity to develop new architectonical concepts. Around 1910, a young group of Jewish architects, following their studies with König, began their work. The concept of Oskar Strnad, Josef Frank, and Oskar

Wlach had as little in common with their teacher's historicism as with Otto Wagner and Josef Hoffmann. Like Adolf Loos, they were influenced by the theories of Camillo Sitte, whose principles of urbanism they also applied to housing. The starting point of the design process was the movement towards, into, and within the building. Gradually increasing room dimensions lead to the living space, the "piazza" of the house. No claim was made that this was artistic; the house was meant to hold all kinds of possibilities without imposing any of them on the inhabitant. A certain disorder was here regarded as a symptom of a dynamic process, represented by life and its reflection, the house. The house itself could also display signs of this process as the result of planning changes or conversions. At the same time, the house was expected, like a civilised person, to "behave properly" towards its environment and not loudly sell its modernity. With this undogmatic philosophy Strnad and Frank offered a contrast in the 1910s to the aestheticism of the *Wiener Werkstätte*. From the second half of the 1920s, Frank especially distanced himself from the dogmatic international functionalism of the Bauhaus and Le Corbusier. Soon Strnad, Frank, and Wlach were surrounded by an ever-growing circle of like-minded fellow students. They came almost exclusively from the liberal, assimilated Jewish bourgeoisie. The clients belonged to the same class as the architects; often they were friends or relatives. The (mostly Jewish) students of Adolf Loos formed an important part of the Vienna School, too. The influence of Loos was here combined with that of Strnad and Frank. The Vienna School regarded architecture as an open system; that is changes, conversions and extensions were as much a part of the concept as the buildings' ability to age. All possibilities of living were left open to the inhabitants; the house was the background to their life and supported them in an open, dialectical view of the world. This open attitude as the principle of the design process also implied a political dimension; the members of the Vienna School were mostly Social Democrats. The Vienna School could operate more freely with the given facts than "classical" functionalism, which denied any questions of form *per se*. In this study, a description focussing on the stylistic criteria of the Vienna School is followed by a concise catalogue of architects listing their works and theoretical writings.

Iris Meder, *Offene Welten—die Wiener Schule im Einfamilienhausbau 1910–1938*. (This thesis will be published on OPUS, the digital dissertation system of the Stuttgart university library).

Doctoral thesis, University of Stuttgart, 2003.

SOURCES: Archives including those of the Vienna Technical University, the Vienna Academy of Fine Arts, The Vienna University of Applied Arts, the Jewish Community of Vienna, the Documentary Archives of the Austrian Resistance and the "Vermögensanmeldungsakten" ("Arianisation" Files) in the Austrian State Archive.

FROM CHARLOTTENBURG TO CENTRAL PARK WEST. HENRY LOWENFELD AND PSYCHOANALYSIS IN BERLIN, PRAGUE AND NEW YORK

THOMAS MÜLLER

Heinrich Julius Löwenfeld had little to worry about in the years he spent at his Berlin *Gymnasium*. He had decided to give in to one of his passions and study art history. Little evidence exists that would disprove Peter Gay, who wrote in 1987 that one cannot "resent" a German Jew "for showing optimism" in the *Kaisserreich*. With his two sisters, Heinrich Löwenfeld grew up in an environment that was financially secure and rich in culture. His father Raphael had initiated the foundation of the *Centralverein deutscher Staatsbürger jüdischen Glaubens* through a newspaper announcement, published the first complete German edition of Tolstoy, which brought fame as well as a lawsuit, and founded and then made famous the Schiller Theater in Charlottenburg. However, his father died when Heinrich was still young, and as a matter of course he enlisted as a soldier for the German Reich in the First World War. Notably, his falling ill with tuberculosis quickly ended his deployment at the front and thus possibly saved his life. His father's death and his wartime experience caused a crisis in Löwenfeld's sense of the meaning of life; emerging from this was an ethically-motivated decision to study medicine. In the course of his studies, he quickly developed an interest in neurology. The neuro-somatic focus he had initially chosen soon gave way to psychiatry and, unavoidably for a young physician in the Weimar Republic who oriented himself around the modern and successful trends in this science, led him to psychoanalysis which he studied at the Berlin Psychoanalytic Institute. He initially responded to the increasingly powerful Nazis with self-defence training, then with membership of a political association, the *Verein Sozialistischer Ärzte*. The fact that he rather quickly decided to leave Germany together with his psychoanalytically-trained wife, the pediatrician Yela Herschkowitz, and his son Andreas reflected a realistic appraisal of Nazism and the antisemites. He fled to Prague via France and Switzerland, where until 1938 he was associated with a psychoanalytic, Freudian-Marxist oriented group around the theorist of psychoanalysis Otto Fenichel. In 1938 he and his family arrived in New York City. In the U.S. his earlier tuberculosis prevented his enlistment during the Second World War. Although it was difficult for emigrés to establish themselves as medical doctors in America, Löwenfeld's psychoanalytic training facilitated his—it would turn out eminently successful—integration into the country's health system. Berlin, Prague, and New York were stations in Löwenfeld's life and cornerstones in the history of psychoanalysis.

The loss of *Heimat* was a continuing source of pain to Henry Lowenfeld, as he now called himself. In the 1960s Germany's leading post-war psychoanalyst Alexander Mitscherlich suggested that Lowenfeld relocate to Frankfurt am Main instead of himself, in order to take over the Frankfurt psychoanalytic institute. However, with members of the family having been murdered in the Holocaust, his wife and son were unwilling to move back to Germany permanently. His contact with the country of his birth thus remained limited to German-language publications and visits.

Thomas Müller, *Von Charlottenburg zum Central Park West. Henry Lowenfeld und die Psychoanalyse in Berlin, Prag und New York,* Frankfurt am Main: Sigmund Freud-Buchhandlung 2000 (*Edition déjà-vue*, 1), 344 pp., ISBN: 3-9805317-5-9.

Doctoral thesis, Greifswald University, 1998.

SOURCES: A wide range of archives in Germany, the United States, England, Israel, France, and the Czech Republic

GERMAN-JEWISH HISTORIOGRAPHY AFTER THE SHOAH: THE FOUNDATION AND EARLY HISTORY OF THE LEO BAECK INSTITUTE

RUTH NATTERMANN

In 1955, exiled German-Jewish historiography created its most important forum in the *Leo Baeck Institute* (Jerusalem, London, New York), named after the last representative of German Jewry, Rabbi Leo Baeck (1873–1956). But in spite of the extraordinary cultural-historical significance and the far-reaching influence on specialist historiography in Germany, German-Jewish historiography in exile has been taken note of by historians only in recent years. As far as the *Leo Baeck Institute* (LBI) is concerned, there existed only a few articles which dealt rather marginally with the prehistory and the circumstances of its foundation as well as with the early stage of its existence.

This thesis seeks to fill the gap in scholarship by focusing deliberately on the prehistory, the foundation, and the first decade of the institute. The study concludes with the year 1965, as the publication of *Entscheidungsjahr 1932* introduced a new period during which the LBI experienced a profound change with regard to its members and central ideas.

The thesis is based on the premise that the foundation of the LBI and the beginning of German-Jewish historiography in the countries of emigration fulfilled more than a purely academic interest: after the *Shoah*, the record of German-Jewish history was also perceived as a monument for the destroyed Jewish community in Germany. Considering themselves as the true and last heirs of this community, the founders of the LBI felt that it was their duty to save their memories from oblivion. In fact, among the people who formed the institute in its first decade, there was no predominance of emigré scholars of the *Wissenschaft des Judentums*. It was, rather, a professionally and ideologically heterogeneous group of leading German-Jewish organisations' representatives and intellectuals that brought the LBI into being.

The structure of the thesis is organised according to three central aspects: first, the motives for starting German-Jewish historiography outside Germany; second, the people involved and the self-conception of the institute's first generation; third, the early institute's reconstruction of the past.

The thesis demonstrates that the foundation of the LBI meant the realisation of a concept which had been developed by individual German-Jewish scholars in exile from the beginning of the 1940s. In all these projects, the combination of academic interests with commemorative intention prevailed. From this starting point, the early LBI created an image of the past which—based on the memories of its members—emphasised the cultural achievements of German Jews, while excluding themes like antisemitism and persecution.

It was not until the first generation was replaced by the second one that the commemorative function of the institute lost its significance. Only then did it become possible to get closer to more problematic and formerly excluded issues.

Ruth Nattermann, *Deutsch-jüdische Geschichtsschreibung nach der Shoah: Die Gründungs- und Frühgeschichte des Leo Baeck Institute* (forthcoming publication autumn 2004, Essen: Klartext Verlag, 256 pp., ISBN 3-89861-331-3).

Doctoral thesis, University of Düsseldorf, 2003.

SOURCES: Archives of the major German-Jewish refugee organisations, personal papers, correspondence, minutes, and publications of the early Leo Baeck Institute, as well as several interviews with contemporaries, among others with Professor Esra Bennathan, Dr. Arnold Paucker and Professor Herbert A. Strauss.

THE JEWISH NOTION OF HONOUR IN EIGHTEENTH CENTURY SOUTH WEST GERMANY

MONIKA PREUSS

Based on Homi Bhabha's concept of "location of culture" this study attempts to analyse the specific Jewish concept of honour. Honour was one of the most essential values to classify groups and/or individuals in early modern Europe. Whereas in theory Christian concepts of honour depicted Jews as being without honour, in everyday life the conduct of Jews was measured according to the standards of honesty. And, vice versa, Jews acted and classified persons according to their norms of honour.

The majority of early modern German Jews lived in rural settlements. This study focuses on a group of Jews living in the South West German Kraichgau region in the eighteenth century.

According to Bhabha, cultural differences cannot be detected in exterior differences like religious ceremonies, colour of skin, and so on. Culture, Bhabha maintains, can be detected in in-between spaces, in moments of dislocation. Adapting Bhabha's concept to historical research this study approaches the concept of Jewish honour from three perspectives.

1. Analysing the Christian point of view that Jews are dishonest and contrasting this with the 'certificates of good character' that were issued by bailiffs or burgomasters and required evidence of honour (the Christian point of view).

2. Exploring Jewish perceptions of honour and honesty and their representation in Hebrew epitaphs (the Jewish point of view).
3. Investigating quarrels about the loss of honour and its public restitution to Jewish individuals (moments of dislocation).

A specific Jewish habitus of honour could be traced in two major fields, the right to participate in public worship and the attitude towards responsibility for sexual morality. Jewish perceptions of participating in public worship were mainly viewed as a purchasable right. This right was fiercely fought for, not only verbally but also physically. Combining cultic participation with a purchasable right was opposed to Protestant understanding (the majority of Christians in this region were Protestants) of cultic practices in their own tradition such as, for instance, receiving Holy Communion. Jews quarrelled in the presence of the open scroll of law, Protestants felt that one had to have a 'pure heart' when receiving Holy Communion. These cultural differences wer reinforced by anti-Jewish stereotypes of associating Jews with money and being preoccupied with financial gain. Regarding sexual morality Jews held both sexes responsible in cases of illegitimate pregnancies; Christians, who exclusively blamed women, did not even realise that Jewish morals were different. Investigations of pregnant unmarried Jewish women by the local bailiff demonstrate the limitations of crossing cultural boundaries. Jewish and Christian discourses of morality led to no common ground and the differences were not even realised. This thesis shows both the cultural divisions and the limitations of attempts to overcome them.

Monika Preuß, "*… aber die Krone des guten Namens überragt sie.*" *Jüdische Ehrvorstellungen im 18. Jahrhundert im Kraichgau.* (This thesis will be published in the Schriftenreihe der Kommission für geschichtliche Landeskunde Baden-Württemberg in autumn 2004).

Doctoral thesis, Heidelberg University, 2003.

SOURCES: Badisches Generallandesarchiv Karlsruhe.

GEORG SIMMEL'S POLITICAL THOUGHT. THE ORPHANS OF EUROPE

CÉCILE ROL

The main aim of this thesis is to analyse the political thought in the work of the sociologist and philosopher Georg Simmel (1858–1918). Despite being regarded as an "unpolitical" scholar, to use Max Weber's description, Georg Simmel's political insights have had a remarkable influence on many European scholars. A detailed analysis of Simmel's works, war writings and correspondences show his insights into politics to be quite considerable in three different areas:

1. At the margins of the political philosophy and the political sciences of his time, Simmel developed a kind of political concept which stood at a great epistemological distance to the general concept of politics. Illustrating the lack of this concept in order to understand the problems of socialism and of normation, Simmel proposed an anthropological approach to politics, where the "Other" is the transcendental basis that makes the human being, as a *zoon politikon*, possible—a concept which is also to be found in Buber's or Arendt's writings.
2. On the basis of these thoughts, Simmel proposed a political sociology which—often exploited but rarely explicitly acknowledged—played an important part in the emergence of this discipline. He developed a tripartite socio-political scheme, *Wechselwirkung—Kompromiss—Tausch* and used this epistemological frame to construct a sociological analysis of democracy, in which compromise may be considered the core concept of Simmel's political sociology since it not only shapes its subject but also defines its methods and its tools.
3. Finally, this study focuses on the influence Simmel's political insights had in Europe after his death. This part is particularly interesting from the perspective of the history of German-speaking Jewry. Indeed, associated with his project of developing a philosophical culture, which Simmel partly realised through the international journal *Logos*, his political thought caught the attention of Jewish and Slav scholars. Thus he came to influence several circles in Prague such as that around Berta Fanta (which included Felix Weltsch, Emil Utitz and Hugo Bergman), the "Losgoscy"-circle and the young Jewish Russian students who organised the *Logos* in Prague (Boris Jakovenko, Fedor Stepun, and Sergius Hessen). Vladimir Jankélévitch's role is considered in this context. An important question discussed is how members of these various groups met and came to be receptive to Simmel's political approach. Although these issues are not dealt with exhaustively in this thesis, they nevertheless draw attention to hitherto unknown or neglected fields of research in the history of German-speaking Jewry and in European sociology. Orphans of Europe, Simmel's heirs also indicate the fruitfulness of his contribution to the European debate on contemporary democracy: how to commit oneself and how to resist.

Cécile Rol, *La problématique politique de Georg Simmel. Les orphelins d'Europe*

Doctoral thesis, Universities of Bielefeld (Germany) and Caen (France) 2003.

SOURCES: Georg Simmel Archives, Bielefeld University; Georg Simmel Gesamtausgabe.

WALTHER RATHENAU IN HISTORICAL CONTEXT: A BIOGRAPHY

CHRISTIAN SCHÖLZEL

This thesis presents a biography of Walther Rathenau (1867–1922) which focuses on his life and work. Rathenau's complex life as an entrepreneur, industrial "system-builder", politician, *homme de lettres* and as a Jew is analysed in the context of his times. This study uses different approaches from political, social, cultural and gender history and also employs methods inspired by social psychology. It shows how Rathenau dealt in all parts of his life with the contradictions he encountered, such as for instance those between "Jewishness" and "Deutschtum", Liberalism and conservative attitudes, the forces of the market economy and the trends towards Socialism or "Gemeinwirtschaft".

Christian Schölzel, *Walther Rathenau in Auseinandersetzung mit den Widersprüchen seiner Zeit. Eine Biographie*

Doctoral thesis, Leipzig University, 2002.

SOURCES: Material from eighty-five archives in Europe, Israel and the US was used, in particular documents from the Osobyi archive in Moscow where the private papers of Walther Rathenau are located.

BERTHA BADT-STRAUSS (1885–1970). A BIOGRAPHY

MARTINA STEER

Bertha Badt-Strauss was born in Breslau on 7 December 1885. She was descended from a well known family of Jewish scholars and studied literature, languages and philosophy in Breslau, Berlin and Munich. One of the first women awarded a doctoral degree in Prussia, she worked as a researcher and publisher. Like her brother Herman Badt and her sister Lotte Prager she became a fierce Zionist and was deeply involved in the Jewish Renaissance. After the First World War Badt-Strauss contributed to the aims of the Jewish Renaissance, that is the creation of a Jewish community with a special Jewish culture. With her husband Bruno Strauss, a teacher and expert on Moses Mendelssohn, she lived in Berlin from 1913 onwards. In 1921 their only son, Albrecht, was born. Shortly after his birth Badt-Strauss fell ill with multiple sclerosis. In spite of this she continued writing numerous articles for Jewish publications like the *Jüdische Rundschau* or the *Israelitische Familienblatt*, and also for leading non-Jewish newspapers like the *Vossische Zeitung* and the *Berliner Tageblatt*. She also co-edited the fist scholarly edition of Annette von Droste-Hülshoff's works and translated and edited volumes of works by Gertrud Mars, Profiat Duran, Süßkind von Trimberg, Heinrich Heine, Rahel Varnhagen, and Moses Mendelssohn. She contributed to the *Jüdisches Lexikon* and the *Encyclopaedia Judaica*, wrote short stories, a serial novel, and a collective biography of Jewish women. Her last editorial work in Germany (together with her husband) was an anthology of letters by Hermann Cohen.

Unlike some other German Jews whose ties with the Jewish community were strengthened by traumatic experiences during and after the First World War and who felt they had to distance themselves from everything German and from assimilated Jews, Badt-Strauss, as a religious Jew, did not share this feeling. She participated in the German women's movement, wrote about German literature and included (alleged) "Assimilanten" and converts like Moses Mendelssohn or Heinrich Heine in her agenda. She tried to reinterpret the return of prominent Jews to Judaism as a self-determined step in the right direction and offered new role models for identification.

Badt-Strauss' intensive engagement with Jewish women, partially derived from feminist consciousness, should also be attributed to her aim of creating new role models. The predominantly male protagonists of the Jewish Renaissance had a somewhat reductive image of Jewish women: the bad "Westjüdin" versus the good "Ostjüdin". As a religious German-Jewish woman Badt-Strauss could not identify with either of these two images and did not believe that such an attitude would motivate women to reflect on their Judaism. Instead, in her articles and books she presented a series of Jewish women, from diverse backgrounds and historical periods, without judging their lifestyle. Her only belief was in the need to return to Judaism and eventually to Eretz Israel. By not specifying too narrowly what this return should be like and which role women had to play in Judaism and in the *Yishuv*, she invited women to take part in the creation of a Jewish community that had not seen women's role in this context because of the rigid male definition of Jewish femininity.

Badt-Strauss was most successful with her individual interpretation of the Jewish Renaissance—her list of publications includes more than six hundred editions and articles. However, whether her work affected German Jewry in the way it was meant to do is a question which cannot easily be answered. The National Socialists brought the Jewish Renaissance prematurely to an end.

In 1939 Badt-Strauss emigrated to the United States where her husband became a professor at Centenary College in Shreveport, Louisiana. She continued writing for several American Jewish publications and published a biography of the American Zionist Jessie Sampter. She died in Chapel Hill, North Carolina, on 20 February 1970.

Martina Steer, *Bertha Badt-Strauss (1885–1970). Eine Biographie*

Doctoral thesis, University of Vienna, 2002.

SOURCES: Leo Baeck Instiute, New York [Collection Elisabeth Bab, Julius Bab, Leo Baeck, Fritz Bamberger, David Baumgardt, Hermann Cohen, Richard A. Ehrlich, Kurt Eisner, Ludwig Feuchtwanger, Siegfried Guggenheim, Georg Hermann, Hannah Karminski, Jakob Picard, Franz Rosenzweig, Hans Schaeffer, Bertha Badt-Strauss, Bruno Strauss]; Leo Baeck Institute, Jerusalem [Collection Isaac Prager]; Deutsches Literaturarchiv, Marbach [Collection Eduard Berend, Manfred George, Oskar Walzel, Karl Wolfskehl, Archive of the Albert Langen Publishing House]; Private Collection of Albrecht Strauss, Chapel Hill (NC); Interview with Albrecht Strauss. November 2000, Chapel Hill (NC).

LIBERALISM, NATIONALISM AND ANTISEMITISM IN THE 'BERLIN ANTISEMITISM DISPUTE' OF 1879/1880

MARCEL STOETZLER

This thesis analyses the series of newspaper and journal articles and pamphlets published in 1879/1880 which constitute what came to be called the 'Berlin Antisemitism dispute'. They were written by the German historian and politician Heinrich von Treitschke and some of the political and academic figures who responded to his anti-Jewish statements, and they discuss the antisemitic movement and the place of Jews in German society at that time.

Treitschke's texts have been seen as crucial to both the development of modern antisemitism in Germany and the emergence of a distinctly German form of nationalism. But the debate which they provoked also reveals a great deal about social and political thought at that time, and in particular the relationship between antisemitism and liberalism; most of the contributors were liberals like Treitschke, or opponents of liberalism.

As well as providing a close reading of the debate in a full-length study (something which has not been done before) this thesis also analyses it in terms of the wider issues of nationalism and liberalism. What emerges from this material is a conceptual weakness of liberalism in its relation to antisemitism and Jewish emancipation. Both Treitschke's support for antisemitism and the ambivalence evident in the views of his opponents are shown here to be rooted in the contradiction between inclusionary and exclusionary tendencies inherent in the nation-form. To the extent that liberal society constitutes itself in the form of a *national state*, it has to guarantee, or produce, some degree of homogeneity or conformity of a *national culture*. This necessity leads Treitschke to embrace, and his critics to be unable to fully oppose, antisemitism. In this respect the thesis aims to provide a starting point for a critical assessment of current debates on nationalism versus patriotism, ethnic minorities and the 'multicultural society'.

Doctoral thesis, Middlesex University, 2004.

SOURCES: British Library and the Institute for German Jewish History in Hamburg.

THE AUSTRIAN SECOND REPUBLIC'S TREATMENT OF VICTIMS OF NATIONAL SOCIALISM AND THE AUSTRIAN "*STÄNDESTAAT*" FROM 1945 TO 1964

ANDREA STRUTZ

This thesis focuses on the treatment of victims of the Austrian "Ständestaat" (1934–1938) and of Austria under National Socialism (1938–1945). Such treatment was based on the "Opferfürsorgegesetz", a special welfare law for the victims of persecution between 1933 and 1945, which was passed in Austria (Second Republic) in 1947. This law was one of the first national measures concerning *Wiedergutmachung* and defines as victims those who where persecuted between 1933 and 1945 for political reasons, for reasons of descent (e.g. Jews, Roma and Sinti), religion or nationality (e.g. Slowenes). A condition for application was Austrian citizenship as well as domicile within the national borders.

For the empirical evaluation a sample of 2,637 cases (out of a total of 9,723) from the province of Styria (in the period from 1945 to 1964) was analysed and processed in a database, taking into account both quantitative and qualitative aspects. Thus biographical data of the victims such as the reasons for their persecution and the place and time of their imprisonment or exile were evaluated. The process of acknowledgment and the receipt of compensation (e.g. pensions, compensation for imprisonment or for loss of income) were also a significant part of the analysis as were other factors such as reasons for refusal by the authorities. This in turn showed how Austrian authorities classified applicants and which kinds of administrative barriers they put in place. The analysed cases for the province of Styria indicate that 83% of applications were made because of political persecution, approximately 8% because of descent (7% Jewish descent, 1% Roma and Sinti), 1% because of religion and roughly 8% for other reasons.

The Austrian Second Republic granted compensation for the victims only hesitatingly and to a relatively small material extent for the period of the investigation. Triggered by the "Waldheim-Debate" in 1986, the Austrian state began to realise its responsibility for involvement in National Socialism and established additional funds in the following years but the "Opferfürsorgegesetz" must still be regarded much more as a welfare measure than as "*Wiedergutmachung*" (restitution). Some victims of Nazi persecution were not taken into account when the initial legislation was drawn up, therefore the law had to be reformed repeatedly, and to this day some groups have still not been granted eligibility for compensation.

Andrea Strutz, *Wieder gut gemacht? Der Umgang der Zweiten Republik mit den Opfern von Nationalsozialismus und "Ständestaat" am Beispiel der Opferfürsorge in der Steiermark von 1945 bis 1964*

Doctoral thesis, University of Graz, 2003. (This thesis will be published by the Mandelbaum Verlag, Vienna in winter 2004/2005 or spring 2005).

SOURCES: Files regarding "Opferfürsorge" (2,637 single cases) of the Provincial Archives of Styria (Steiermärkisches Landesarchiv), Subject: StLA L. Reg. 405; Federal Law on "Opferfürsorge" 4 July 1947 (Bundesgesetz über die Fürsorge des Kampfes um ein freies, demokratisches Österreich und die Opfer politischer Verfolgung vom 4. Juli 1947, BGBl. 183) and other material relating to the Opferfürsorgegesetz" (OFG/47) from 1947 to 2002.

'PROTEST AND PRAYER': RABBI DR. SOLOMON SCHONFELD AND ORTHODOX JEWISH RESPONSES IN BRITAIN TO THE NAZI PERSECUTION OF EUROPE'S JEWS 1942–1945

CHANAN TOMLIN

Recent scholarship has researched the reactions and responses of Jews in the free world to the Holocaust. Most historians have concentrated on the roles that secular leaders and institutions played in assisting refugees and the attempts they made to persuade governments to assist the Jews. In the past two decades Orthodox journalists and historians have written about the efforts of Orthodox activists during the war. These two schools have produced differing and at times conflicting accounts of this aspect of the historiography of that time. The Orthodox, or *Haredim*, for their part, claim that the activities of the Orthodox have been consistently overlooked, or at least marginalised by secular historians. The secular camp has either ignored or downplayed the roles of the Orthodox, with the claim that the Orthodox communities in the free world were insignificant and the efforts of their leaders negligible.

The purpose of this thesis is to examine the reactions of the Orthodox community and its leadership in Britain during the war. It is limited to the years 1942–1945, years that most would consider the apogee of the Holocaust and focuses on the efforts of Solomon Schonfeld, who was the leader of the *Haredi* community in Britain at the time and who was exceptionally devoted to assisting Europe's beleaguered Jews. He was the rabbi of Adath Israel and the Union of Orthodox Hebrew Congregations – organisations that were primarily made up of descendants of German-speaking Jews. He was one of the organisers of the 'kindertransports'. This study concentrates on the community's efforts on behalf of Jews on the Continent as opposed to the assistance of refugees in Britain, a subject that has already been well documented. It analyses the obstacles that were faced by both the Orthodox and secular leaders, and evaluates their joint and individual responses both in isolation and in comparison to each other. It also analyses the responses of Orthodox laymen in Britain and compares the opportunities available to them with those available to their leaders.

This thesis conveys and analyses the responses of Orthodox Jews in Britain to the Holocaust as opposed to analysing the results they achieved. Many of the difficulties and obstacles that they and their secular counterparts encountered were insurmountable and they should not be judged solely on their accomplishments but also on their efforts.

Doctoral thesis, Southampton University, 2004.

SOURCES: Agudat Israel World Organisation Archives, London; Agudat Israel World Organisation Archives, New York; Archives and Manuscripts—Special Collections Division, Hartley Library, Southampton University, Southampton; Central Zionist Archives, Jerusalem; Israel State Archives, Jerusalem; London Metropolitan Archives; Yeshiva University Archives, New York.

Publications on German-speaking Jewry

A Selected and Annotated Bibliography of Books and Articles 2003

Compiled by

BARBARA SUCHY and ANNETTE PRINGLE

The Bibliography is supported by grants from:

Friends of Bat Hanadiv Foundation

Sheldon and Suzanne Nash Fund

Robert Bosch Stiftung

Leo Baeck Institute
4 Devonshire Street
London W1W 5LB

BIBLIOGRAPHY 2003

The Bibliography of the *Leo Baeck Institute Year Book XLIX* includes books and articles published in 2003 as well as some published in 2002 and in a few exceptional cases even earlier. It always happens that some of these titles "surface" only some years after their publication to the level of the Deutsche Bibliothek or come otherwise to our attention. We have decided to include them if we thought they would be important for the readers of our Bibliography.

With 1,472 entries this year's Bibliography lists a record number of books and articles. The rising trend we mentioned last year seems to continue—quite apart from the additional factor of outstanding anniversaries (we included a selection of "only" about fifteen titles for Theodor W. Adorno's anniversary ....). Something else, however, is worth mentioning: we have found articles related to the history of German-speaking Jewry in at least twenty-two *Festschriften*. This seems to be significant in two ways: *Festschriften* are very popular and their number is increasing year by year; and that generation of German historians, born before or during the Second World War, has now reached the age for being honoured with a *Festschrift*. In addition, the contributions on a Jewish theme integrated into so many of these volumes indicate that interest in and knowledge of Jewish aspects of German history have spread considerably among these scholars, their colleagues and their students. This, of course, can also be clearly seen in the vast number of conference volumes. Unthinkable that a symposium would take place without ensuing publication. And—it has to be acknowledged—many of them are based on new research and of real interest, as are the articles in the ever-growing number of exhibition catalogues. They certainly deserve to be listed in full detail, but there is a limit to the space allocated to the Bibliography and we therefore have to be selective. In future we shall again have to curtail some sections appreciably.

Much effort and care is taken in the editing process of the bibliography. Over many years Sylvia Gilchrist, the former assistant editor of the *Year Book*, has helped us unselfishly in eliminating not only incorrect English, but also all other errors from factual mistakes down to the minutiae of punctuation and spelling. We are much indebted to her and would like to express our heart-felt gratitude. Luckily we have found in Marion Koebner a very able successor.

Again, we would like to thank those authors who have informed us directly about their publications, and we encourage others to do so likewise (info@leobaeck.co.uk).

B.S.

CONTENTS

I. HISTORY

A. General

42206. BATTENBERG, J. FRIEDRICH: *Hofjudenschaft und Waffenbesitz in der Vormoderne.* [In]: Von Enoch bis Kafka. Festschrift für Karl E. Grözinger zum 60. Geburtstag [see No. 43050]. Pp. 93–104, footnotes.

42207. BAUMGART, PETER: *Jüdische Minorität und von der Aufklärung erfaßte Reformstaaten im Reich am Vorabend der Emanzipation.* [In]: Menschen und Strukturen in der Geschichte Alteuropas. Festschrift für Johannes Kunisch zur Vollendung seines 65. Lebensjahres, dargebracht von Schülern, Freunden und Kollegen. Hrsg.: Helmut Neuhaus [et al.]. Berlin: Duncker und Humblot, 2002. (Historische Forschungen, Bd. 73.) Pp. 341–358.

42208. BENZ, WOLFGANG: *Jüdische Erfahrungen in Deutschland in der Zwischenkriegszeit.* [In]: "Habt den Mut zu menschlichem Tun". Die Jüdin und Demokratin Jeanette Wolff in ihrer Zeit (1888–1976) [see No. 43486]. Pp. 75–84.

——— BERTRAMS, OLIVER: *Religion, Territorium und Genealogie: Exklusions- und Inklusionsargumente von Christen und Juden im Streit um die Judenemanzipation (1781–1823).* [See in No. 43123.]

42209. *Der "Berliner Antisemitismusstreit" 1879–1881.* Eine Kontroverse um die Zugehörigkeit der deutschen Juden zur Nation. Kommentierte Quellenedition im Auftrag des Zentrums für Antisemitismusforschung bearb. von Karsten Krieger. München: Saur, 2003. 2 vols., XLV, 901 pp., bibl., chronol., index. [Incl.: Einleitung (Wolfgang Benz, VII-IX).] [Cf.: Der "Berliner Antisemitismusstreit"—als der Antisemitismus gutbürgerlich wurde (Brigitte Mießner) [in]: Die Mahnung, Jg. 51, Nr. 2, Berlin, 1. Feb. 2004, p. 5. Der "Einbruch des Judentums in das deutsche Leben". Eine neue Quellenedition dokumentiert den "Berliner Antisemitismusstreit" um Heinrich von Treitschke (Michael Philipp) [in]: Aufbau, Vol. 69, No. 24, New York, Dec. 11, 2003, p. 17.]

42210. BRÄMER, ANDREAS: *The dilemmas of moderate reform: some reflections on the development of conservative Judaism in Germany 1840–1880.* [In]: Jewish Studies Quarterly, Vol. 10, No. 1, Tübingen, 2003. Pp. 73–87, footnotes. [Focuses on Rabbi Zacharias Frankel.]

42211. CARLEBACH, ELISHEVA: *Divided souls: the convert critique and the culture of Ashkenaz, 1750–1800.* New York: Leo Baeck Institute, 2003. 24 pp., notes. (The Leo Baeck Memorial Lecture, 46.) [Discusses the role of several German converts in disseminating the Christian critique of Judaism within the Jewish world.]

42212. CASTRITIUS, HELMUT, ed.: *Themenschwerpunkt: Juden und Waffen* [section title of] Aschkenas, Jg. 13, H. 1, Tübingen, 2003. [Incl.: Waffenbesitz und Militärdienst der Juden von der römischen Antike bis zur Aufklärung. Zur Einführung (ed., 1–2). Militärdienst und Wehrhaftigkeit der Juden in der Spätantike (ed., 3–12). Das Thema Waffen aus der rabbinischen Perspektive (Israel Yuval, 13–16). 'Waffenrecht' und 'Waffenverbot' für Juden im Mittelalter—zu einem Mythos der Forschungsgeschichte (Christine Magin, 17–34). Von jüdischen Rittern und anderen waffentragenden Juden im mittelalterliche Deutschland (Markus J. Wenninger, 35–82). Juden und Waffen im 16. und 17. Jahrhundert—Anmerkungen zu einem Alltagsphänomen (Stefan Litt, 83–92). "... gleich anderen dero Diener einen Degen zu tragen ...". Reflexionen zum sozialen Rang der Hofjudenschaft in vormoderner Zeit (J. Friedrich Battenberg, 93–106).]

42213. CLUSE, CHRISTOPH/HAVERKAMP, ALFRED/YUVAL, ISRAEL J., eds.: *Jüdische Gemeinden und ihr christlicher Kontext in kulturräumlich vergleichender Betrachtung von der Spätantike bis zum 18. Jahrhundert.* Hannover: Verlag Hahnsche Buchhandlung, 2003. VII, 569 pp., footnotes, indexes. (Forschungen zur Geschichte der Juden, Abt. A: Abhandlungen, Bd. 13.) [Conference vol. resulting from an int. conference held at Trier Univ., Oct. 1999. Cont. the sections: 1. Orientierungen; cont.: Jüdische Gemeinden und ihr christlicher Kontext: Konzeptionen und Aspekte (Alfred Haverkamp, 1–32). Christliche Zeit und jüdische Zeit: Das Paradox einer

Übereinstimmung (Israel J. Yuval, 33–48). Das Konzept der Rasse in der Forschung über mittelalterlichen iberischen Antijudaismus (David Nirenberg, 49–75). 2. Wandlungsprozesse in Spätantike und Frühmittelalter; cont. essays by Oded Irshai and Friedrich Lotter (75–150). 3. Regionale Kontexte im europäischen Mittelalter; cont. essays on French, Spanish, Polish, Anglo and Italian Jewish communities by Sonja Benner, Alexander Reverschon, Juan Carrasco, Jürgen Heyde, Robin R. Mundill, Alessandra Veronese (151–294). 4. Mittelalterliche Judengemeinden in lokalen Kontexten; cont.: Jüdische und christliche Gemeinde im Kölner Kirchspiel St. Laurenz (Matthias Schmandt, 295–308). Jüdische Gemeinde und christliche Stadtgemeinde im spätmittelalterlichen Worms (Gerold Bönnen, 309–340). Die Prager Judengemeinde im hussitischen Zeitalter (1389–1485) (Frantisek Smahel, 341–364). Stadt und Judengemeinde in Regensburg im späten Mittelalter: Das "Judengericht" und sein Ende (Christoph Cluse, 365–388). 5. Jüdische Organisationsformen im hohen und späten Mittelalter; cont.: "Kehillot Schum": Zur Eigenart der Verbindungen zwischen den jüdischen Gemeinden Mainz, Worms und Speyer bis zur Mitte des 13. Jahrhunderts (Rainer Barzen, 389–404). 'A suis paribus et non aliis iudicentur': jüdische Gerichtsbarkeit, ihre Kontrolle durch die christliche Herrschaft und die 'obersten rabi gemeiner Judenschafft im heilgen Reich' (Yacov Guggenheim, 405–440). Community and super-community in Provence in the Middle Ages (Joseph Shatzmiller, 441–450). Die jüdischen Gemeinden in den 'Medinot Aschkenas' zwischen Spätmittelalter und Dreißigjährigem Krieg (Stefan Rohrbacher, 451–464). Über das Wesen der 'Takkonaus', der jüdischen Gemeindeordnungen: Von der Provence bis Metz (13.-17. Jahrhundert) (Simon Schwarzfuchs, 465–504). Selbstverständnis einer polnischen Judengemeinde des 16. Jahrhunderts: Die 'Taqanot Qraqa' aus dem Jahr 1595 (Heidemarie Petersen, 505–512). Christlich-jüdische "Doppelgemeinden" in den Dörfern der Markgrafschaft Burgau während des 17./18. Jahrhunderts (Rolf Kießling/Sabine Ullmann, 513–534).]

42214. DAVID, ABRAHAM: *The Lutheran Reformation in sixteenth-century Jewish historiography.* [In]: Jewish Studies Quarterly, Vol. 10, No. 2, Tübingen, 2003. Pp. 124–139, notes.

——— EHRENPREIS, STEFAN/GOTZMANN, ANDREAS/WENDEHORST, STEPHAN: *Probing the legal history of the Jews in the Holy Roman Empire—norms and their application.* [See in No. 42564.]

42215. ELON, AMOS: *Zu einer anderen Zeit. Porträt der deutsch-jüdischen Epoche (1743–1933).* Aus dem Amerik. von Matthias Fienbork. München: Hanser, 2003. 423 pp., notes (393–416), index. [For American orig. edn. see No. 40848/YB 48.] [Cf.: Von der Leibsteuer zur Reichsfluchtsteuer. Amos Elon über die jüdische Assimilation in Deutschland (Stefana Sabin) [in]: 'NZZ', Nr. 116, Zürich, 21. Mai 2003, p. 36; publ. also with the title: Die Vergeblichkeit des Ganzen [in]: Tribüne, Jg. 42, H. 167, Frankfurt am Main, 2003, pp. 186–188. Der große Kummer. Amos Elon erzählt die bewegende Geschichte von Glanz und Elend der jüdischen Emanzipation (Michael Naumann) [in] Die Zeit, Nr. 17, Hamburg, 16. April 2003, p. 45.]

42216. *L'Europe et les juifs.* Édité par Esther Benbassa [et al.]. Genève: Labor et Fides, 2002. 216 pp., footnotes. (Religions en Perspectives, No. 11.) [Selected essays: L'Europe et les juifs. Introduction (Pierre Gisel, 7–24). La Réforme et les juifs (Lucie Kaennel, 79–94; on the Age of Reformation, incl. Luther, Calvin and the Jews). Raison et conflits de traditions (Esther Starobinski-Safran, 95–116). Vers d'autres lumières. Les juifs et la raison (Dominique Bourel, 117–128). La formation des identités juives modernes en Europe (Esther Benbassa, 129–140). Rejet identitaire et quête de "spiritualité": Raissa Maritain, Edith Stein, Simone Weill (Sylvie Courtine-Denamy, 141–166). L'Allemagne nazie et les juifs (Philippe Burrin, 167–174). Israel en Europe: réflexions sur la modernité juive (Pierre Bouretz, 175–186). Quel avenir pour les juifs et le judaisme en Europe? (David Banon/François Garai, 187–200). Conclusion: Vers une Europe unie et plurielle? (Esther Benbassa, 201–204).]

42217. *Ex Oriente: Isaak und der weiße Elefant.* Eine Reise durch drei Kulturen um 800 und heute. Hrsg. von Wolfgang Dreßen, Georg Minkenberg und Adam C. Oellers. Katalogbuch in drei Bänden zur Ausstellung in Rathaus, Dom und Domschatzkammer Aachen vom 30. Juni bis 28. Sept. 2003. [Mainz: Zabern, 2003]. 3 vols., illus., facsims. [Vol. 1 entitled 'Die Reise, Bagdad: 800 und heute' incl.: Die Reise des Isaak und die politische Situation um 800 (Hans Altmann, 28–35). Juden und Friesen als Hoflieferanten Karls des Grossen (Detlev Ellmers, 56–65). Vol. 2 entitled 'Aachen, der Westen: 800 und heute' incl.: Das Judentum von der Spätantike bis zur Zeit Karls des Grossen

(Karl Leo Noethlichs, 68–77). Fremde, Verbündete, Gegner? Muslime und Juden im Verständnis Karls des Grossen (Lioba Geis, 78–93). Das Vermächtnis und die Legende Karls des Grossen in hebräischen Schriften des Mittelalters (Aryeh Grabois, 122–143). Mehr als ein Fragezeichen: Die Zukunft der jüdischen Gemeinden in Deutschland (Andreas Nachama, 190–197).]

42218. FEINER, SHMUEL: *The Jewish enlightenment in the eighteenth century.* Jerusalem: The Zalman Shazar Center for Jewish History, 2002. 410 pp., bibl., index.

42219. FISCHER, BERND: *Jüdische Emanzipation und deutsche Nation: Von Mendelssohn zu Auerbach.* [In]: 1848 und das Versprechen der Moderne. Hrsg. von Jürgen Fohrmann [et al.]. Würzburg: Königshausen & Neumann, 2003. Pp. 147–164, footnotes.

42220. *Germania Judaica.* Bd. III, 1350–1519. Hrsg. von Arye Maimon s.A., Mordechai Breuer und Yacov Guggenheim im Auftr. der Hebr. Univ. in Jerusalem. 3. Teilband: Gebietsartikel, Einleitungsartikel und Indices. Tübingen: Mohr Siebeck, 2003. XI, pp. 1753–2591. [Incl.: Vorwort (Mordechai Breuer, Yacov Guggenheim, VII-X). Die Gebietsartikel Abensberg—Württemberg (1753–2078). Die jüdische Gemeinde, Gesellschaft und Kultur (Yacov Guggenheim, 2079–2138). Die wirtschaftliche Tätigkeit (Michael Toch, 2139–2164). Die Rechtsstellung der Juden (Dietmar Willoweit, 2165–2207). Steuern und Abgaben (Eberhard Isenmann, 2208–2281). Die Kirche und die Juden (Peter Moraw, 2282–2297). Die Verfolgungen des Spätmittelalters (Michael Toch, 2298–2327). For previous vol., publ. 1995, see No. 32483/YB XLI.]

42221. *Geschichte des jüdischen Alltags in Deutschland. Vom 17. Jahrhundert bis 1945.* Hrsg. im Auftrag des Leo Baeck Instituts von Marion Kaplan. Mit Beiträgen von Marion Kaplan, Robert Liberles, Steven M. Lowenstein und Trude Maurer. Übers. aus dem Engl. von Friedrich Griese, Georgia Hanenburg und Alice Jakubeit. München: Beck, 2003. 638 pp., illus., gloss., notes (473–574), indexes (persons, places, subjects, 625–638). [Cont.: Einführung (ed., 9–17). Erster Teil. An der Schwelle zur Moderne: 1618–1780 (Robert Liberles, 19–122). Zweiter Teil. Anfänge der Integration 1780–1871 (Steven M. Lowenstein, 123–224). Dritter Teil. Konsolidierung eines bürgerlichen Lebens im kaiserlichen Deutschland 1971–1918 (Marion Kaplan, 225–344). Vierter Teil. Vom Alltag zum Ausnahmezustand: Juden in der Weimarer Republik und im Nationalsozialismus 1918–1945 (Trude Maurer, 345–470).] [Cf.: Bespr. (Michael Wildt) [in]: Vierteljahrschrift für Sozial- und Wirtschaftsgeschichte, Bd. 90, H. 4, Stuttgart, 2003, pp. 475–476.]

42222. GILOMEN, HANS-JÖRG: *Städtische Sondergruppen im Bürgerrecht.* [In]: Neubürger im späten Mittelalter. Migration und Austausch in der Städtelandschaft des alten Reiches (1250–1550). Hrsg. von Rainer Christoph Schwinges. Red. Roland Gerber u. Barbara Studer. Berlin, 2003. Pp. 125–167, footnotes. [Deals mainly with the Jews.]

42223. GOTZMANN, ANDREAS: *Eigenheit und Einheit. Modernisierungsdiskurse des deutschen Judentums der Emanzipationszeit.* Leiden; Boston: Brill, 2002. IX, 314 pp., footnotes, bibl., index. (Studies in European Judaism, Vol. 2.) [Cont. the sections: Teil 1: Judentum zwischen Erziehung und Umerziehung. Teil 2: Geschichte als Deutungssystem der Moderne. Teil 3: Nation und Religion.] [Cf.: Bespr. (Thomas Meyer) [in]: Zeitschrift für Geschichtswissenschaft, Jg. 51, H. 9, Berlin, 2003, p. 858.]

——— GYSSLING, WALTER: *Mein Leben in Deutschland vor und nach 1933 und Der Anti-Nazi: Handbuch im Kampf gegen die NSDAP.* Hrsg. und eingeleitet von Leonidas Hill. Mit einem Vorwort von Arnold Paucker. [See No. 43586.]

42225. HAMBROCK, MATTHIAS: *Die Etablierung der Außenseiter. Der Verband nationaldeutscher Juden 1921–1935.* Köln: Böhlau, 2003. VII, 787 pp., footnotes, bibl. (735–768), index (769–787). [Cf.: Dazugehören um jeden Preis (Ludger Heid) [in]: Jüdische Allgemeine, Jg. 58, Nr. 23, Berlin, 6. Nov. 2003, p. 14. Dazugehören um jeden Preis. Von den Widersprüchen nationaldeutscher Juden (Michael Brenner) [in]: Süddeutsche Zeitung, Nr. 167, München, 23. Juli 2003, p. 16.]

42226. HECHT, CORNELIA: *Deutsche Juden und Antisemitismus in der Weimarer Republik.* Bonn: Dietz, 2003. 428 pp., illus., facsims., footnotes, bibl. (409–422), index. (Reihe: Politik- und Gesellschaftsgeschichte, Bd. 62.) Zugl.: Tübingen, Univ., Diss.

——— *In Breslau zu Hause? Juden in einer mitteleuropäischen Metropole der Neuzeit.* [See No. 42313.]

42227. JAEGER, ACHIM/TERLAU, WILHELM/WUNSCH, BEATE: *Positionierung und Selbstbehauptung.* Debatten über den Ersten Zionistenkongreß, die 'Ostjudenfrage' und den Ersten Weltkrieg in der deutsch-jüdischen Presse. Hrsg. von Hans Otto Horch. Tübingen: Niemeyer, 2003. X, 155 pp., footnotes, index. (Conditio Judaica, 45.)

42228. *Jewish emancipation reconsidered. The French and German models.* Ed. by Michael Brenner, Vicki Caron and Uri R. Kaufmann. Tübingen: Mohr Siebeck, 2003. VI, 245 pp., footnotes, index (Eine Veröff. der Wiss. Arbeitsgemeinschaft des Leo Baeck Instituts in der Bundesrepublik Deutschland.) [Cont. papers presented at a conference held in Tutzing, May 2001 titled "Two paths of emancipation? The German and French Jewish models reconsidered". Incl.: Introduction (Michael Brenner, 1–4). Alsace and Southern Germany: The creation of a border (Simon Schwarzfuchs, 5–26; comment by Silvie Anne Goldberg). Jewish enlightenment in Berlin and Paris (Frances Malino, 27–38; comment by Dominique Bourel). Wissenschaft des Judentums in Germany and the science of Judaism in France in the nineteenth century: tradition and modernity in Jewish scholarship (Perrine Simon-Nahum, 39–54; comment by Nils Römer). Celebrating integration in the public sphere in Germany and France (Richard I. Cohen, 55–78; comment by Jakob Vogel). The Jewish fight for emancipation in France and Germany (Uri R. Kaufmann, 79–92; comment by Ulrich Wyrwa). Kultur and civilisation after the Franco-Prussian war: debates between German and French Jews (Silvia Cresti, 93–110; comment by Sandrine Kott). Two communities with a sense of mission: the Alliance Israélite Universelle and the Hilfsverein der deutschen Juden (Eli Bar-Chen, 111–128; comment by Aron Rodrigue). Modern Antisemitism and Jewish responses in Germany and France 1880–1914 (Christian Wiese, 129–154; comment by Vicki Caron). Citizenship and acculturation: some reflections on German Jews during the Second Empire and French Jews during the Third Republic (Jacques Ehrenfreund, 155–168; comment by Paula Hyman). In the academic sphere: the cases of Emile Durkheim and Georg Simmel (Pierre Birnbaum, 169–198; comment by Peter Pulzer). Towards the phenomenology of the Jewish intellectual: the German and French cases compared (Steven E. Aschheim, 199–220; comment by Nancy L. Green). Epilogue: French and German Jewries in the New Europe: convergent itineraries? (Diana Pinto, 221–236).]

42229. *Judenemanzipation und Antisemitismus in Deutschland im 19. und 20. Jahrhundert.* Ein Tagungsband. Hrsg. von Wolfgang Michalka und Martin Vogt. Eggingen: Ed. Isele, 2003. 165 pp., bibl. (Bibliothek europäischer Freiheitsbewegungen, Bd. 3.) [Based on a conference held by the Militärgesch. Forschungsamt and the Bundesarchiv in Rastatt, Oct. 2000; cont.: Geleitwort (Hartmut Weber, 7–8). Gibt es einen deutschen Antisemitismus? (Martin Vogt, 9–38). Deutsche jüdische Soldaten. Von der Epoche der Emanzipation bis zum Zeitalter der Weltkriege (Chana C. Schütz, 39–44). Juden 1848/49—Fortschritt oder Rückschritt? (Irmtraud Götz v. Olenhusen, 45–56). Die Entstehung des bildungsbürgerlichen Antisemitismus im Deutschen Kaiserreich. Zur Wirkungsgeschichte der Vereine Deutscher Studenten (Norbert Kampe, 57–104). Zwischen Patriotismus und Judenzählung: Juden und Militär während des Ersten Weltkrieges (Wolfgang Michalka, 105–116). Zwischen Normalität und Vertreibung. Die deutschen Juden in den zwanziger und dreißiger Jahren (Aleksandar-S. Vuletic (117–138). Wehrmacht, Krieg und Holocaust (Jürgen Förster, 139–160).]

42230. *Jüdische Geschichte: Alte Herausforderungen, neue Ansätze.* Hrsg. von Eli Bar-Chen und Anthony D. Kauders. München: Utz Verl., 2003. 208 pp., footnotes, bibl. (194–205). (Münchner Universitätsschriften, Philos. Fakultät für Geschichts- und Kunstwissenschaften; Münchner Kontaktstudium Geschichte, Bd. 6.) [Incl.: Vorwort (eds., 9–12). Orchideenfach, Modeerscheinung oder ein ganz normales Thema? Zur Vermittlung von Jüdischer Geschichte und Kultur an deutschen Universitäten (Michael Brenner, 13–24). Die Juden unter dem Halbmond (Eli Bar-Chen, 25–34). 'Israel' und Diaspora in der jüdischen Geschichtsschreibung (Marcus Pyka, 35–46). Juden und Geld. Mythos und Historiographie (Gideon Reuveni, 47–58). Die Familie Feuchtwanger und die Tradierung von jüdischer Religiosität und Identität im 19. und 20. Jahrhundert (Heike Specht, 59–76). Judentum und Religion & "Tallit oder Pallium?"—jüdischer Gebetsmantel oder Philosophenmantel? Einige Überlegungen zur "Jüdischen Philosophie" (Michael Heinzmann, 77–90; 91–102). Also essays on the Jews in the Ottoman Empire (Eli Bar-Chen), Hebrew language (Rachel Perets), the Vilna ghetto (Mirjam Triendl). Further essays are listed according to subject.]

42231. *Jüdische Geschichte lesen. Texte der jüdischen Geschichtsschreibung im 19. und 20. Jahrhundert.* Hrsg. und kommentiert von Michael Brenner, Anthony Kauders, Gideon Reuveni und Nils Römer. München: Beck, 2003. 447 pp., gloss., bibl., index. [Cont.: Einleitung: Lesarten jüdischer Geschichte (eds., 9–18). I. Konstruktionen jüdischer Geschichte (19–96; cont. introd. and texts by Isaak Markus Joost, Heinrich Graetz, Simon Dubnow, Salo W. Baron, Raphael Mahler, Haim Hillel Ben-Sasson). II. Jüdische Geschichte und Weltgeschichte (97–154; cont. introd. and texts by Wilhelm Roscher, James Darmesteter, Moritz Lazarus, Franz Rosenzweig, Eugen Täubler, Ben-Zion Dinur, Arnold J. Toynbee, Jacob L. Talmon, Salo W. Baron). III. Israel und die Diaspora (155–213; cont. introd. and texts by Heinrich Graetz, Abraham Geiger, Simon Dubnow, Jizchak Fritz Baer, Simon Rawidowicz, Yosef Hayim Yerushalmi, Michael Galchinsky). IV. Integration und Bewahrung (214–280; cont. introd. and texts by Yehezkel Kaufmann, Simon Dubnow, Salo W. Baron, Gerson D. Cohen, Jacob Katz, Paula Hyman, Amos Funkenstein). V. Judenfeindschaft und jüdische Identität (281–336; cont. introd. and texts by Leopold Zunz, Cecil Roth, Jean-Paul Sartre, Hannah Arendt, Shmuel Almog, Sander L. Gilman, Emil L. Fackenheim, Saul Friedländer). VI. Rekonstruktionen und Dekonstruktionen jüdischer Geschichte (337–414; cont. introd. and texts by Leopold Zunz, Immanuel Wolf, Ismar Elbogen, Gershom Scholem, Yosef Hayim Yerushalmi, Amos Funkenstein, Susannah Heschel, Laurence J. Silberstein).] [Cf.: Einladung zum Diskurs (Thomas Meyer) [in]: Jüdische Literatur [Beilage von] Jüdische Allgemeine, Jg. 58, Nr. 26, Berlin, Winter 2003, p. 29.]

42232. KAPLAN, MARION: *'Unter uns': Jews socialising with other Jews in Imperial Germany.* [In]: Leo Baeck Institute Year Book 2003, Vol. XLVIII, Oxford; New York, 2003. Pp. 41–65, illus., footnotes.

42233. KAPLAN, MARION: *Redefining Judaism in Imperial Germany: practices, mentalities, and community.* [In]: Jewish Social Studies, Vol. 9, No. 1, Bloomington, IN, Fall 2002. Pp. 1–33, notes.

42234. KAUFMANN, URI: *Kleine Geschichte der Juden in Europa.* Berlin: Cornelsen Scriptor, 2003. 112 pp., illus., chronol., gloss., index (Pocket Thema.)

42235. KLEIN, BIRGIT E.: *Wohltat und Hochverrat. Kurfürst Ernst von Köln, Juda bar Chaijim und die Juden im Alten Reich.* Hildesheim; New York: Olms, 2003. 549 pp., bibl., index. (Netiva, Wege deutsch-jüdischer Geschichte und Kultur, Bd. 5.) [Deals with the 1603 Frankfurt rabbinical assembly, and Levi of Bonn/Löb Krauß, whose denunciation led the archbishop of Cologne to instigate proceedings at the Imperial Court (Reichskammergericht) in 1606, accusing the Jews of high treason against Emperor Rudolf II. Cont. the sections: 1. Einleitung. 2. Die kurkölnischen Juden und der Streit um den Aufseher Levi von Bonn. 3. Von der Denunziation zur Hochverratsklage—Levis Strafverfolgung gegen Wolf von Koblenz. 4. Der Hochverratsprozess gegen die Juden im Reich. 5. Levi von Bonn nach jüdischen Quellen.] [Cf.: Löw Kraus ist Levi von Bonn (Robert Jütte) [in]: 'FAZ', Nr. 27, Frankfurt am Main, 2. Dez. 2004, p. 39.]

42236. *Die Landjudenschaften in Deutschland als Organe jüdischer Selbstverwaltung von der frühen Neuzeit bis ins neunzehnte Jahrhundert.* Eine Quellensammlung. Hrsg. von Daniel J. Cohen. Bd. 3. [Besorgt durch Shmuel Reem und Stefan Litt.] [Göttingen]: [Wallstein, 2003]. VIII, 1370–2033. [Imprint on title page: Jerusalem 2001. Israel. Akad. d. Wiss; Akad. d. Wiss. zu Göttingen; incl.: Vorbemerkung (Stefan Litt, V-VI).] [Corrected entry of No. 40872/YB XLVIII. A fourth vol. with indexes to the three vols. will follow.]

42237. MALKIEL, D.: *Jewish-Christian relations in Europe, 840–1096.* Historiographical essay. [In]: Journal of Medieval History, Vol. 29, Amsterdam, 2003. Pp. 55–83, footnotes. [Discusses the period between efflorescence and stability under the Carolingians and the massacres during the First Crusade questioning hitherto common interpretations.]

42238. MARTIN, BERND: *Assimilation, Integration oder Zwangsanpassung? Streiflichter zur Geschichte der Juden in Deutschland, Baden und Freiburg in der Zeit des Deutschen Reiches (1871–1945).* [In]: Freiburger Universitätsblätter, Jg. 42, H. 162, Freiburg, Dez. 2003. Pp. 91–105, footnotes.

42239. MAURER, TRUDE: *Der Centralverein in neuer Perspektive? Zur "ideengeschichtlichen" Monographie des Sozialhistorikers Avraham Barkai.* [In]: Aschkenas, Jg. 13, H. 2, Tübingen, 2003. Pp. 519–529, footnotes. [Review essay on Avraham Barkai: "Wehr Dich!" Der Centralverein deutscher Staatsbürger jüdischen Glaubens (C.V.) 1893–1938. München: Beck, 2002; see No. 40836/YB XLVIII.]

42240. MIRON, GUY: *Emancipation and assimilation in the German-Jewish discourse of the 1930s.* [In]: Leo Baeck Institute Year Book 2003, Vol. XLVIII, Oxford, 2003. Pp. 165–189, footnotes. [Covers the debates between 1931–1937.]

42241. *1928–2003. Liberales Judentum in Deutschland: Entfaltung, Zerstörung, Erneuerung/Liberal Judaism in Germany: genesis, destruction, renewal.* The World Union for Progressive Judaism. [Jerusalem; Berlin], 2003. 40 pp. [Addresses and other contribs. on the occasion of the 75th anniversary of the first conference (in Berlin, 1928) of the World Union for Progressive Judaism held in Berlin, July 10, 2003; incl.: Das liberale Judentum in Deutschland und die Weltunion für Progressives Judentum. Ein kurzer historischer Überblick (Michael A. Meyer, 12–15).]

42242. NIRENBERG, DAVID: *The Rhineland massacres of Jews in the First Crusade.* Memories medieval and modern. [In]: Medieval concepts of the past. Ritual, memory, historiography. ed. by Gerd Althoff [et al.]. Washington, DC: German Historical Institute; Cambridge Univ. Press, 2002. Pp. 279–309, footnotes.

42243. *Le patrimoine juif Européens.* Actes du colloque international tenu à Paris, au Musée d'art et d'Histoire du Judaisme, les 26, 27 et 28 janvier 1999. Édité par Max Polonovski. Paris: Collection de la Revue des Études juives, 2002. 348 pp., footnotes. [Incl.: La centralisation des informations concernant les projets de documentation d'inscriptions funéraire sur le territoire de la République Fédérale Allemande (Peter Honigmann, 105–112; on the project of the Zentralarchiv, Heidelberg). Documentation de l'ancien cimetière de Francfort-sur-le-Main (Michael Brocke, 113–124). Jewish heritage in Bavaria: The Jewish Museums (Otto Lohr, 165–179).]

42244. PAUCKER, ARNOLD: *Verteidigung der Republik.* [In]: Deutsche Juden im Kampf um Recht und Freiheit [see No. 43407]. Pp. 91–126, notes.

42245. PULZER, PETER: *Jews and the German state: the political history of a minority, 1848–1933.* Detroit: Wayne State Univ. Press, 2003. XVII, 370 pp., footnotes, tabs., maps, bibl. (351–359), index. [Reprint, with new introd.; orig. publ. in 1992, see No. 29033/YB 38; cont. the sections: Why was there a Jewish Question in Imperial Germany? Religion and judicial appointments in Imperial Germany. Jews in German politics. Jews and the crisis of German Liberalism. The beginning of the end.]

42246. PULZER, PETER: *Einheit und Differenz—Über deutsche und deutsch-jüdische Geschichte.* [In]: Leipziger Beiträge zu jüdischen Geschichte und Kultur, Bd. I, München, 2003. Pp. 13–26, footnotes. [Discusses since when and how Jewish history became an integrated part of German history.]

42247. RASPE, LUCIA: *Ein legendärer Sänger: Amnon von Mainz.* [In]: Kalonymos, Jg. 6, Duisburg, 2003. Pp. 1–5. [On a medieval legend in the context of Jewish hagiography.]

42248. RICHARZ, MONIKA: *Frauenforschung und jüdische Geschichte.* Frau, Religion und Gesellschaft in der Neuzeit. [In]: Irene Dinge, ed.: Feministische Theologie und Gender-Forschung. Bilanz—Perspektiven—Akzente. Leipzig: Evangelische Verlagsanstalt, 2003. Pp. 137–154, footnotes.

42249. ROOS, LENA: *"God wants it!" The ideology of martyrdom of the Hebrew crusade chronicles and its Jewish and Christian background.* Uppsala: Uppsala Universitet, 2003. 259 pp., footnotes, bibl. (241–259). [Deals with the ideology of martyrdom of the Hebrew chronicles written in response to the persecutions of the Rhineland Jews during the First Crusade in 1096; stresses the importance of taking the non-Jewish background into account when studying medieval Jewish texts.]

42250. SCHAPKOW, CARSTEN: *"Mit stets neuer Bewunderung"—Iberisch-sephardische Topoi im deutsch-jüdischen Diskurs des 19. Jahrhunderts.* [In]: Leipziger Beiträge zur jüdischen Geschichte und Kultur, Bd. I, München, 2003. Pp. 199–216, footnotes.

42251. SCHMIDT, CHRISTOPH: *Zur Typologie jüdischer Integration in West und Ost.* [In]: Geschichte in Wissenschaft und Unterricht, Jg. 54, H. 3, Stuttgart, 2003. Pp. 140–153, footnotes. [Deals with Amsterdam and Vilna, Frankfurt am Main and Cracow, Berlin and Budapest.]

42252. SIMMS, NORMAN: *The radical transformation of Jewish childrearing after the massacres of the first two crusades: A problem in multi-generational post-traumatic stress.* [In]: Journal of Psychohistory, Vol. 30, No. 2, New York, 2002. Pp. 164–189, notes, bibl.

42253. STAUDINGER, BARBARA: *Von den Rechtsnormen zur Rechtspraxis. Eine Stellungnahme zu einem Forschungsvorhaben zur Rechtsgeschichte der Juden im Heiligen Römischen Reich.* [In]: Aschkenas, Jg. 13, H. 1, Tübingen, 2003. Pp. 107–116.

42254. TOCH, MICHAEL: *Peasants and Jews in medieval Germany.* Aldershot; Burlington, VT: Ashgate, 2003. XIV, 328 pp., illus., maps, diagr., tabs., bibl., index. (Variorum Collected Studies Series, 757.) [Cont. 14 previously publ. papers.]

42255. *Towards normality? Acculturation and modern German Jewry.* Ed. by Rainer Liedtke and David Rechter. Tübingen: Mohr Siebeck, 2003. XI, 353 pp., footnotes, index. (Schriftenreihe wissenschaftlicher Abhandlungen des Leo-Baeck-Instituts, Bd. 68.) [Incl.: Obituary: Professor Werner Eugen Mosse, 1918–2001 (Peter Pulzer, V-VIII). Introduction: German Jewry and the search for normality (eds., 1–12). German Jewry's path to normality and assimilation: complexities, ironies, paradoxes (Michael A. Meyer, 13–26). Constructing Jewish modernity: Mendelssohn jubilee celebrations within German Jewry, 1829–1929 (Christhard Hoffmann, 27–52). "... durch Fluten und Scheiterhaufen": persecution as a topic in Jewish historiography on the way to modernity (Johannes Heil, 53–76). Struggling for normality: the apologetics of 'Wissenschaft des Judentums' in Wilhelmine Germany as an anti-colonial intellectual revolt against the Protestant constructions of Judaism (Christian Wiese, 77–102). The troubling dialectic betrween reform and conversion in Biedermeier Berlin (Deborah Hertz, 103–126). The emergence of a middle-class religiosity: social and cultural aspects of the German-Jewish reform movement during the first half of the nineteenth century (Simone Lässig, 127–158). Germanising the Jewish male: military masculinity as the last stage of acculturation (Gregory A. Caplan, 159–184). Segregation or integration? Honour and manliness in Jewish duelling fraternities (Lisa Swartout, 185–200). "Nothing more German than the German Jews"? On the integration of a minority in a society at war (Ulrich Sieg, 201–216). A "West-östlicher Divan" from the front: Moritz Goldstein beyond the 'Kunstwart' debate (Elisabeth Albanis, 217–236). Divergent paths of national integration and acculturation: Jewish and Catholic educational strategies in nineteenth century Hesse-Darmstadt (Keith H. Pickus, 237–250). Jewish political behaviour and the 'Schächtfrage', 1880–1914 (Robin Judd, 251–270). German and Austrian Jews' concept of culture, nation and 'Volk' (Silvia Cresti, 271–290). Jewish identities and acculturation in the province of Salzburg in the shadow of antisemitism (Helga Embacher, 291–308). Exceptionalism and normality: "German Jews" in the United States 1840–1880 (Tobias Brinkmann, 309–328). Towards abnormality: assimilation and degeneration in German-Jewish social thought (Mitchell B. Hart, 329–246).]

42256. VOLKOV, SHULAMIT: *The magic circle—Germans, Jews and antisemites.* [In Hebrew.] Tel Aviv: Am Oved, 2002. 261 pp., notes, indexes.

42257. WALLENBORN, HILTRUD: *Bekehrungseifer, Judenangst und Handelsinteresse. Amsterdam, Hamburg und London als Ziele sefardischer Migration im 17. Jahrhundert.* Hildesheim; New York: Olms, 2003. 572 pp., footnotes, bibl. (532–566), index. (Haskala, Wissenschaftliche Abhandlungen, Bd. 27.)

42258. WALTER, HANS-ALBERT: *Deutsche Exilliteratur 1933–1950. Band 1: Die Vorgeschichte des Exils und seine erste Phase. Band 1.1: Die Mentalität der Weimardeutschen. Die "Politisierung" der Intellektuellen.* Stuttgart: Metzler, 2003. 781 pp., notes (689–763), index. [Incl. the sections: "Jüdische Zersetzung" (256–292). Exkurs: Die Mentalität der deutschen Juden (357–455; incl. Assimilationsstreben und Antisemitismusangst (394–404). Jüdische Störer der Assimilation? (405–428).]

——— WASSERMANN, HENRY: *False start. Jewish studies at German universities during the Weimar Republic.* [See No. 42567.]

42259. WILKE, CARSTEN: *"Den Talmud und den Kant". Rabbinerausbildung an der Schwelle zur Moderne.* Hildesheim; New York: Olms, 2003. 726 pp., footnotes, index. (Netiva, Wege deutsch-jüdischer Kultur, Bd. 4.) [Book documents the development of rabbinical studies in their European context, incl. also Prussian and Russian Poland, Alsace-Lorraine, Bohemia and Moravia,

Hungary, the Netherlands and Northern Italy; cont. the sections: I. Jeschiwot im Schatten der Aufklärung. II. Der "studierte Rabbiner" im Sinne der Staatsreformer. III. Rabbinerqualifikation im Zeitalter des Historismus.]

42260. WYRWA, ULRICH: *Juden in der Toskana und in Preußen im Vergleich. Aufklärung und Emanzipation in Florenz, Livorno, Berlin und Königsberg i.Pr.* Tübingen: Mohr Siebeck, 2003. IX, 491 pp., illus., footnotes, bibl. (436–482), index. (Schriftenreihe wiss. Abhandlungen des Leo Baeck Instituts, 67.)

42261. WYRWA, ULRICH, ed.: *Judentum und Historismus. Zur Entstehung der jüdischen Geschichtswissenschaft in Europa.* Frankfurt am Main; New York: Campus, 2003. 256 pp., footnotes, index. [Incl.: Die europäischen Seiten der jüdischen Geschichtsschreibung. Eine Einführung (ed., 9–36). Erinnerungspolitik und historisches Gedächtnis: Zur Entstehung einer deutsch-jüdischen Wissenschaft im Kaiserreich (1870–1914) (Jacques Ehrenfreund, 39–61). Die 'Verbürgerlichung' der jüdischen Vergangenheit: Formen, Inhalte, Kritik (Christhard Hoffmann, 149–171). Jüdische Theologie im Taumel der Geschichte: Religion und historisches Denken in der ersten Hälfte des 19. Jahrhunderts (Andreas Gotzmann, 173–202). Identitätssuche ohne Modell: Geschichte und Erinnerung im jüdisch-historischen Roman des frühen 19. Jahrhunderts (Gabriele von Glasenapp, 200–231). Historisches Denken im deutsch-jüdischen Familiengedächtnis (Miriam Gebhardt, 233–245; on the patterns of unpubl. memoirs written between 1890 and 1932). Also essays related to England, France, Italy and Poland by Mitchell B. Hart, Perrine Simon-Nahum, Gadi Luzzatto-Voghera, Francois Guesnet.]

——— ZUMBINI, MASSIMO FERRARI: *Die Wurzeln des Bösen. Gründerjahre des Antisemitismus: Von der Bismarckzeit zu Hitler.* [See No. 43635.]

Linguistics/Western Yiddish

42262. ALTHAUS, HANS PETER: *Kleines Lexikon deutscher Wörter jiddischer Herkunft.* München: Beck, 2003. 216 pp., bibl., index. Orig.-Ausg. [Incl. an essay on Western Yiddish (7–26).] [Cf.: Die verlorene Sprache (Stefana Sabin) [in]: 'NZZ', Nr. 268, Zürich, 18. Nov. 2003, p. 37.]

——— *Die altjiddischen (jüdisch-deutschen) Drucke der Universitätsbibliothek Rostock.* [See No. 42562.]

42263. APTROOT, MARION: *Yiddish, Dutch and German among late 18th-century Amsterdam Jewry.* [In]: Dutch Jewry: its history and secular culture (1500–2000). Ed. by Jonathan Israel and Reinier Salverda. Leiden; Boston: Brill, 2002. (Brill's Series in Jewish Studies, Vol. 29.) Pp. 201–211, footnotes.

42264. GRUSCHKA, ROLAND/APTROOT, MARION: *The manuscript versions of Isaac Euchel's 'Reb Henokh oder vos tut me damit'* [In]: Zutot 2001, Dordrecht, 2002. Pp. 165–179, footnotes. [On an Enlightenment comedy written in Yiddish and German in 1792/1793.]

42265. BUTZER, EVI: *Die Anfänge der jiddischen 'purim shpiln' in ihrem literarischen und kulturgeschichtlichen Kontext.* Hamburg: Buske, 2003. XII, 237 pp., footnotes, bibl. (Jidische Schtudies. Beiträge zur Geschichte der Sprache und Literatur der aschkenasischen Juden, Bd. 10.). [Analyses Purim plays of the 16th and 17th cent., their parodistic allusions to the Hebrew liturgy and to the rites and ceremonies of the Jews in South Germany.]

——— DAXELMÜLLER, CHRISTOPH: *Elia Levita Bachur, Italien und die Volkskultur.* [See in No. 42340.]

42266. EGGERS, ECKHARD: *Einflüsse slavischer Sprachen auf Morphologie und Grammatik des Jiddischen.* [In]: Wolfgang Gladrow, ed.: Die slawischen Sprachen im aktuellen Funktionieren und historischen Kontakt. Beiträge zum XIII. internationalen Slawistenkongress vom 15. bis 21. August 2003 in Ljubljana. Frankfurt am Main; New York: Lang, 2003. Pp. 99–110, footnotes.

42267. GROSSMAN, JEFFREY: *"Die Beherrschung der Sprache": Funktionen des Jiddischen in der deutschen Kultur von Heine bis Frenzel.* [In]: 1848 und das Versprechen der Moderne. Hrsg. von Jürgen Fohrmann [et al.]. Würzburg: Königshausen & Neumann, 2003. Pp. 165–178, footnotes.

——— GRUSCHKA, ROLAND: *Von Parodien deutscher Dichtung, dem Nachleben von Isaak Euchels 'Reb Henoch' und anderen Lesestoffen der Berliner Juden: Die Kolportagereihe 'Gedichte und Scherze in jüdischer Mundart'.* [See No. 42293.]

42268. HOMANN, URSULA: *Versunkene Welt? Das Jiddische hat sein letztes Wort noch nichts gesprochen.* [In]: Tribüne, Jg. 42, H. 165, Frankfurt am Main, 2003. Pp. 160–168, bibl. [Also on Western-Yiddish and the study of Yiddish at German universities.]

42269. *Die jiddischen Glossen des 14.–16. Jahrhunderts zum Buch "Hiob" in Handschriftenabdruck und Transkription.* Hrsg. von Walter Röll unter Mitarb. von Gabriele Brünnel [et al.]. Tübingen: Niemeyer, 2002. 2 vols. (Texte und Textgeschichte, 52.) [Teil 1: Einleitung und Register. VIII, 381 pp., facsims., bibl. Teil 2: Edition. 835 pp.]

——— KLEPSCH, ALFRED: *Die Reste des Jiddischen in Mittelfranken.* [See in No. 42340.]

42270. PRZYBILSKI, MARTIN: *Frauen in Büchern für Frauen—Zur altjiddischen Mussarliteratur.* [In]: Leipziger Beiträge zur jüdischen Geschichte und Kultur, Bd. I, München, 2003. Pp. 65–82, footnotes.

42271. STARK, FRANZ: *Deutsch in Europa. Geschichte seiner Stellung und Ausstrahlung.* Sankt Augustin: Asgard, 2002. 231 pp., bibl. (219–231). (Sprachen und Sprachenlernen, Bd. 309.) [Incl. sections on Western Yiddish.]

——— SÜß, HERMANN. *Ernstes und Heiteres aus der altjiddischen (Jüdisch-deutschen) Literatur.* [See in No. 42340.]

42272. TIMM, ERIKA: *An den Quellen des Jiddischen. Ergebnisse eines Forschungsprojektes.* [In]: Von Enoch bis Kafka. Festschrift für Karl E. Grözinger zum 60. Geburtstag [see No. 43050]. Pp. 105–115, footnotes.

42273. *Travels among Jews and Gentiles: Abraham Levie's travelogue Amsterdam 1764.* Edition of the text with introduction and commentary by Shlomo Berger. Leiden; Boston: Brill, 2002. XII, 207 pp., footnotes, notes (145–190), lists, bibl., map. (Hebrew Language and Literature Series.) [Incl. the annot. edition of the Yiddish manuscript of A.L. born near Lemgo (Westphalia), who later lived in Amsterdam and travelled widely in Germany, Austria and Italy.]

42274. WEINSTEIN, MIRIAM: *Jiddisch: eine Sprache reist um die Welt.* Aus dem Amerik. von Mirjam Pressler. Berlin: Kindler, 2003. 350 pp., illus., bibl. [For American edn. see No. 40911/YB XLVIII.]

——— *Le yidich en Alsace: textes et documents.* [See No. 42460.]

42275. ZWIERS, ARIANE DIGNA: *Kroniek van het Jiddisj. Taalkundige aspecten van achttiende-eeuws Nederlands Jiddisj.* Delft: Uitgeverij Eburon, 2003. 602 pp., footnotes, bibl. [Incl. Engl. summary (597–602).]

B. **Communal and Regional History**

1. **Germany**

42277. AHLEM. BUCHHOLZ, MARLIS/SCHMID, HANS-DIETER: *Kafka und Ahlem.* [In]: Hannoversche Geschichtsblätter, Bd. 54, Hannover, 2003. Pp. 87–96, illus., facsims., footnotes. [On various visitors to Ahlem, and letters of Kafka to a young woman seeking agricultural training in Ahlem.]

42278. ALTENKIRCHEN (KREIS). MARENBACH, WALTER: *Juden in der Bürgermeisterei Weyerbusch.* [In]: Heimat-Jahrbuch des Kreises Altenkirchen und der angrenzenden Gemeinden 2003, Jg. 46, Altenkirchen, 2002. Pp. 104–106, illus. [Article is followed by a poem entitled 'Kristallnacht' (Hanna B. Hurst-Duetzer, 107).]

42279. AMBERG. DÖRNER, DIETER: *Juden in Amberg—Juden in Bayern.* Pressath: Verlag der Buchhandlung Bodner, 2003. 345 pp., illus., facsims., notes, bibl. [Covers the period 1861–1947.]

42280. ANHALT. *Anhalt, deine Juden* ... Materialien des Dessauer Herbstseminars 2002 zur Geschichte der Juden in Deutschland. Im Auftrag der Moses-Mendelssohn-Gesellschaft hrsg. von Bernd G. Ulbrich. Dessau: M.-Mendelssohn-Ges., 2002. 154 pp., illus., notes. [Cont.: Anhalt, deine Juden ... Ein Vorwort (ed., 3–9). Die jüdischen Buchschätze der Anhaltischen Landesbücherei Dessau (Martine Kreißler, 11–20). Juden als Mitgestalter des gesellschaftlichen Lebens in Sandersleben (Peter Puschendorf, 21–38). Jüdisches Erbe in Anhalt-Bernburg (Joachim Grossert, 39–50). Zur Geschichte der jüdischen Gemeinde von Nienburg/Saale (Erich Vogel, 51–58). Kindheit und Jugend Chajim Heymann Steinthals (1823–1899) (Marion Méndez, 59–68). Zur Geschichte der Juden in Köthen (Viktor Samarkin, 69–88). Erinnerungen an die jüdische Gemeinde von Zerbst (Walter Briedigkeit, 89–98). Dreimal Cohen—eine jüdische Familie aus Coswig, ihre Lebenswege und Wirkungen (Hans-Günter Lindemann, 99–108). Zur Geschichte der Dessauer Synagoge (Werner Grossert, 109–126). Erfahrungen beim Bau eines Modells der Dessauer Synagoge (Werner Bormann, 127–130). "... der Gottheit als heiliger Tempel, den Menschen als heilige Stätte der Anbetung"—jüdische Ritualbauten des 18. und 19. Jahrhunderts in Anhalt (Ulrich Knufinke, 133–148; with a preliminary remark by Eva J. Engel, 131–132).]

42281. ANSBACH. RIES, ROTRAUD: *Bridging the gaps—Reflections on the trial of a court Jew and a modern concept of Jewish history in Germany.* [In]: Zutot 2001, Dordrecht, 2002. Pp. 148–162, footnotes. [On Elkan Fränkel, Jew at the court of the Margrave of Ansbach, early 18th cent.]

42282. AUGSBURG. CRAMER, ERNST: *Die Botschaft eines "Wiederbeschenkten".* Auszüge aus der Rede des Publizisten Ernst Cramer anlässlich seiner Ernennung zum Ehrenbürger von Augsburg am 16. Oktober 2003. [In]: Aufbau, Vol. 69, No. 20, New York, Oct. 16, 2003. P. 3, port. [Author, b. 1918 in Augsburg, emigr. 1939 to the US, returned 1945 with the US army, instrumental in building up a free and democratic press in post-war Germany; lives in Berlin.]

42283. BADEN. EXNER, KONRAD: *Marie Bernays—einer der ersten badischen Parlamentarierinnen Mannheims.* [In]: Badische Heimat, Jg. 83, H. 3, Freiburg, 2003. Pp. 507–513, port. [M.B., 1883 Munich—1939 Beuron/Danube, Politician (DVP), member of the Baden Landtag, Social Reformer, Director of the Soziale Frauenschule, Mannheim, dismissed 1933.]

——— BADEN. FRANK, WERNER L.: *Legacy. The saga of a German-Jewish family across time and circumstance.* [See No. 43084.]

42284. BADEN. MÜLLER, LEONHARD: *Finanzpolitik im Großherzogtum Baden.* Zum 175. Geburtstag von Moritz Ellstädter (1827–1905). [In]: Badische Heimat, Jg. 81, H. 4, Freiburg, 2001. Pp. 724–728, port. [M.E., Minister of Finance in Baden 1868–1893.]

42285. BADEN-WÜRTTEMBERG. KRAISS, EVA MARIA/REUTER, MARION: *Bet Hachajim—Haus des Lebens. Jüdische Friedhöfe in Württembergisch Franken.* Künzelsau: Swiridoff, 2003. 144 pp., illus., notes, bibl. [On cemeteries in Schopfloch, Landkreis Schwäbisch Hall, Hohenlohekreis, Main-Tauber-Kreis.]

42286. BALHORN. ARING, PAUL-GERHARD: *"Gute Nachbarn". Christen und Juden im Kurhessischen.* [In]: Jahrbuch 2004 Landkreis Kassel, Kassel, 2003. Pp. 131–133. [On the missionarising "Verein für Israel" in Balhorn, 19th cent.]

42287. BAVARIA. ECKSTEIN, ADOLF: *Haben die Juden in Bayern ein Heimatrecht? Eine geschichtswissenschaftliche Untersuchung mit kriegsstatistischen Beilagen.* [Bamberg, Viktor-von-Scheffel-Str. 32]: C. Fiebig, 2002. 120 pp., name lists. [Reprint of the 2nd, revised edn., Berlin, 1929.]

42288. BAYREUTH (MARKGRAFENTUM). HAAS, HELMUT: *Die Lage der Juden des 14./15. Jahrhunderts im Land ob dem Gebirg.* [In]: Archiv für Geschichte Oberfrankens, Bd. 81, Bayreuth, 2001 [publ. 2002]. Pp. 153–171, facsims., docs., footnotes, bibl.

42289. BEERFELDEN. KAUFMANN, URI: *Die Beerfeldener Juden.* Hrsg.: Stadt Beerfelden. Beerfelden: Stadt Beerfelden, 2003. 134 pp., illus., facsims., footnotes, bibl. [Beerfelden: in Hesse, nr. Michelstadt. Covers the period from the Middle Ages to the present day. Incl. name list entitled: Die verfolgten, vertriebenen und ermordeten Beerfeldener Juden (117–122); English summary (113–115).]

42290. BERLIN. BUSCHBOM, JAN/EGGERS, ERIK: *"So wird ein guter Sportsmann gewöhnlich auch ein guter Staatsbürger sein ...". Deutsche Juden in den bürgerlichen Sportvereinen der Weimarer Republik—Das Fallbeispiel Tennis Borussia Berlin.* [In]: SportZeiten, Jg. 3, H. 2, Göttingen, 2003. Pp. 7–30, footnotes, bibl.

42291. BERLIN. DERICUM, CHRISTA: *"Die Zeit und die Zeit danach". Eine Spurensuche auf den Friedhöfen Berlins.* Mit Fotografien von Isolde Ohlbaum. Berlin: Nicolai, 2003. 194 pp., illus. [Incl.: VIII: Jüdische Friedhöfe (163–184).]

42292. BERLIN. *Geschichte des Finanzplatzes Berlin.* Mit Beiträgen von Hartmut Berghoff [et al.]. Hrsg. im Auftrag des Wissenschaftlichen Beirats des Instituts für bankhistorische Forschung e.V. von Hans Pohl. Frankfurt am Main: Fritz Knapp Verlag, 2002. 321 pp., illus., tabs., footnotes, bibl., indexes. [The first four chaps., covering the period from the 16th cent. up to 1945, by Ilja Mieck, Hartmut Berghoff, Christoph Buchheim, Harold James, incl. passim numerous references to court Jews, Jewish bankers and "aryanisation".]

42293. BERLIN. GRUSCHKA, ROLAND: *Von Parodien deutscher Dichtung, dem Nachleben von Isaak Euchels 'Reb Henoch' und anderen Lesestoffen der Berliner Juden: Die Kolportagereihe 'Gedichte und Scherze in jüdischer Mundart'.* [In]: Aschkenas, Jg. 13, H. 2, Tübingen, 2003. Pp. 485–499, footnotes. [On a series of more than 20 issues publ. in Berlin between 1859 and 1877 by Eduard Bloch.]

42294. BERLIN. *Jews in Berlin.* Ed. by Andreas Nachama, Julius H. Schoeps, Hermann Simon. Transl. by Michael S. Cullen and Allison Brown. Berlin: Henschel, 2002. 263 pp., illus., chronol., bibl., index. [For orig. German edn. and contents see No. 39656/YB XLVII.]

——— BERLIN. KAMPE, NORBERT: *Freiheitliche Kunstpolitik und reaktionäre Künstler. Die Berliner Akademie der Künste unter Max Liebermanns Präsidentschaft 1920–1932.* [See in No. 43134.]

——— BERLIN. KRIEGER, KARSTEN: *Judentum und Antisemitismus im wilhelminischen Berlin.* [See in No. 43595.]

——— BERLIN. LEVENSON, THOMAS: *Einstein in Berlin.* [See No. 43280.]

——— BERLIN. MALINO, FRANCES: *Jewish enlightenment in Berlin and Paris.* [See in No. 42228.]

42295. BERLIN. MIECK, ILJA: *Der Aufstieg Berlins zum preußisch-deutschen Finanzplatz.* [In]: Ein gefüllter Willkomm. Festschrift für Knut Schulz zum 65. Geburtstag. Hrsg. von Franz J. Felten [et al.]. Aachen: Shaker, 2003. Pp. 629–645, footnotes. [Emphasizes the importance of court Jews and Jewish "marchand-banquiers" during the 18th cent.]

——— BERLIN. NADOLNY, STEN: *Ullsteinroman.* [See No. 43471.]

42296. BERLIN. PAUCKER, ARNOLD: *Das Berliner liberale jüdische Bürgertum im "Centralverein deutscher Staatsbürger jüdischen Glaubens".* [In]: Deutsche Juden im Kampf um Recht und Freiheit [see No. 43407]. Pp. 161–180, notes.

42297. BERLIN. SCHÄFER, BARBARA: *Berliner Zionistenkreise. Eine vereinsgeschichtliche Studie.* Unter Mitarbeit von Saskia Krampe. Berlin: Metropol, 2003. 176 pp., footnotes (minima judaica, Bd. 3.).

42298. BERLIN. SCHÄFER, BARBARA: *Das Jüdische Volksheim.* [In]: Kalonymos, Jg. 6, H. 3, Duisburg, 2003. Pp. 4–7, illus., notes. [On an institution initiated by Siegfried Lehmann, Martin Buber et al. and founded by "students and women", among them Felice Bauer, Franz Kafka's fiancée, in 1916.]

42299. BERLIN. SIMON, HERMANN: *Jüdisches Berlin.* Museen, Gedenkstätten, Synagogen, Friedhöfe, Restaurants, Cafés, Shopping, Business. Berlin: Jüd. Presse, 2003. 1 map. (Kultur-Karte.) [With illus. and texts; also publ. in English.]

42300. BERLIN. TALBAR, ADIN: *Schuljahre in einem zionistischen Biotop.* [In]: Jüdischer Almanach [2003] des Leo Baeck Instituts, Frankfurt am Main, 2003. Pp. 46–51. [Author recalls his school days in Berlin.]

42301. BERLIN. WYRWA, ULRICH: *Berlin and Florence in the Age of Enlightenment: Jewish experiences in comparative perspective.* [In]: German History, Vol. 21, No. 1, London, 2003. Pp. 1–28, footnotes.

——— BERLIN. WYRWA, ULRICH: *Juden in der Toskana und in Preußen im Vergleich. Aufklärung und Emanzipation in Florenz, Livorno, Berlin und Königsberg i.Pr.* [See No. 42260.]

42302. BERLIN. WYRWA, ULRICH: *Juden in Paris und Berlin. Zur Berichterstattung über die Französische Revolution in Berliner Zeitungen und Zeitschriften (1789–1791).* [In]: Aschkenas, Jg. 13, H. 2, Tübingen, 2003. Pp. 425–439, footnotes. [On the reception of debates about the emancipation of the Jews in the French National Assembly by Berlin Jewish intellectuals.]

42303. BERLIN, JEWISH MUSEUM. HOPP, ANDREA: *Musealisierte Vergangenheit nach dem Holocaust: das Jüdische Museum Berlin.* [In]: Ein Leben für die jüdische Kunst. Gedenkband für Hannelore Künzl. Hrsg. v. Michael Graetz. Heidelberg: Winter, 2003. Pp. 181–194.

42304. BERLIN, JEWISH MUSEUM. LAUTZAS, PETER: *Das Jüdische Museum in Berlin.* [In]: Geschichte in Wissenschaft und Unterricht, Jg, 54, H. 1, Stuttgart, 2003. Pp. 70–72. [A response to this article, also in 'GWU': Stellungnahme zum Bericht "Das Jüdische Museum in Berlin" von Peter Lautzas (Ute Becker) [in]: H. 7/8, 2003. Pp. 477–479, to which Peter Lautzas responds (479).]

42305. BERLIN-PANKOW. LAMMEL, INGE: *Das Jüdische Waisenhaus in Pankow.* Seine Geschichte in Bildern und Dokumenten. Mit einem Geleitwort von Hermann Simon. [Berlin]: [Verein der Förderer und Freunde des ehemaligen Jüdischen Waisenhaus in Pankow e.V.], 2001. 103 pp., illus., facsims., maps.

42306. BERLIN-WANNSEE. *Zurück am Wannsee: Max Liebermanns Sommerhaus.* Hrsg. von Nina Nedeykov und Pedro Moreira. Mit Beiträgen von Reinald Eckert, Klaus-Henning von Krosigk, Anna Teut und Wolf Borwin Wendlandt. Berlin: Transit, 2003. 128 pp., illus., notes. [Deals also with the successful efforts of the Max-Liebermann-Gesellschaft Berlin to acquire and restore the summer house and garden and make it accessible to the public.]

42307. BIEBESHEIM. *Familienbuch der Biebesheimer Juden.* [Issue title of] Biebesheimer Geschichtsblätter, H. 5, Biebesheim, 2003. [Hrsg.: Heimat- und Geschichtsverein Biebesheim e.V.] 34 pp., index. [Incl. a preface by Thomas Schell.]

42308. BONN. BEMMELEN, NICOLE: *Die Neue Judengasse in Bonn—Entstehung und Zerstörung.* [In]: Bonner Geschichtsblätter, Bd. 51/52, Bonn, 2001/2002 [publ. 2003]. Pp. 197–284, illus., facsims., footnotes, bibl. [On the recent excavations.]

42309. BORKEN. RIDDER, THOMAS: *Die jüdischen Friedhöfe in Borken.* [In]: Westmünsterland. Jahrbuch des Kreises Borken 2003. Bocholt, 2002. Pp. 127–136.

42310. BRANDENBURG. WENNINGER, MARKUS J.: *Die Judensteuerliste Markgraf Albrechts von Brandenburg aus dem Jahr 1461.* [In]: Aschkenas, Jg. 13, H. 2, Tübingen, 2003. Pp. 361–424, footnotes.

42311. BRANDENBURG (LAND). WEISSLEDER, WOLFGANG: *Der Gute Ort—Jüdische Friedhöfe im Land Brandenburg.* Hrsg.: Verein zur Förderung antimilitaristischer Traditionen in der Stadt Potsdam e.V. [Potsdam]: [Verein z. Förd. antimilit. Trad. i.d. Stadt Potsdam], 2002. 131 pp., illus., maps., bibl., index.

42312. BREMEN. MARKREICH, MAX: *Geschichte der Juden in Bremen und Umgebung.* Ediert von Helge-Baruch Barach-Burwitz. Hrsg. von "Erinnern für die Zukunft e.V." Mit einem Vorwort von Hans Koschnick. Bremen: Ed. Temmen, 2003. 275 pp., frontis., footnotes. (Schriftenreihe Erinnern für die Zukunft, Bd. 1.) [First publ. of a manuscript held in the LBI New York, completed by the author in 1955; incl.: Max Markreich: ein Manuskript und ein Autor, die in Bremen Geschichte machten (Bettina Decke, 257–268).] [M.M., 1881 Leer–1962 San Francisco, lived from the 1890s in Bremen, emigr. 1938 via Trinidad to the US.]

42313. BRESLAU. *In Breslau zu Hause? Juden in einer mitteleuropäischen Metropole der Neuzeit.* Hrsg. von Manfred Hettling, Andreas Reinke, Norbert Conrads. Hamburg: Dölling und Galitz Verlag, 2003. 264 pp., illus., tabs., notes (185–258), index. (Studien zur jüdischen Geschichte, Bd. 9.) [Incl.: I. Einleitung. Handlungslogiken und Sinnkonstruktionen. Juden im Breslau der Neuzeit (eds., 7–21). II. Geduldet und teilweise geschützt; cont.: Die Predigttätigkeiten des Giovanni di Capistrano in Breslau und Krakau 1453/54 und ihre Auswirkungen auf die dortigen Judengemeinden (Heidemarie Petersen, 22–29). Die Juden in Glogau im frühneuzeitlichen Konfessionalisierungsprozeß (Jörg Deventer, 30–45). Die Juden Breslaus im 18. Jahrhundert (Arno Herzig, 46–62). Jüdische Schriftsteller im Breslau des späten 18. Jahrhunderts (Gunnar Och, 63–73). III. Religion zwischen Tradition und Reform; cont.: Das Ende der rabbinischen Gerichtsbarkeit in Breslau (um 1750) (Anne Brenker, 74–80). Der Geiger-Tiktin-Streit—Trennungskrise und Publizität (Andreas Gotzmann, 81–98). Die Anfangsjahre des Jüdisch-Theologischen Seminars. Zum Wandel des Rabbinerberufs im 19. Jahrhundert (Andreas Brämer, 99–112). IV. Emanzipiert und partiell integriert; cont.: Sozialstruktur und politische Orientierung der jüdischen Bevölkerung im Kaiserreich (Manfed Hettling, 113–130). Gemeinde und Verein. Formen jüdischer Vergemeinschaftung im Breslau des 19. und beginnenden 20. Jahrhunderts (Andreas Reinke, 131–147). Mut, Mensur und Männlichkeit. Die "Viadrina", eine jüdische schlagende Verbindung (Lisa Fetheringill Swartout, 148–166). "Das Judenthum isoliren!" Antisemitismus und Ausgrenzung in Breslau (Olaf Blaschke, 167–184).]

42314. BRETZENHEIM. WITTKOPF, HELGA: *Spurensuche—die jüdische Gemeinde in Bretzenheim.* [In]: 1250 Jahre Bretzenheim. Hrsg. vom Verein für Heimatgeschichte Bretzenheim und Zahlbach. Mainz: Verein für Heimatgesch. Bretzenheim und Zahlbach, 2002. Pp. 151–154, illus., facsims. [Also in this vol.: Die Bretzenheimer Synagogen (Erich Zehnder, 54–57).]

42315. BROMBERG. COHN, ALFRED: *Erinnerungen an Bromberg.* Hrsg. von Elzbieta Alabrudzinska [et al.]. Torun: Wydawnictwo Adam Marszalek, 2002. 202 pp., illus. [Memoirs of Jewish life in Bromberg (after 1919: Bydgoszczy) and Krone an der Brahe before and during World War I; book incl. an introd. in Polish.] [Cf.: Bespr. (Stefan Hartmann) [in]: Zeitschrift für Ostmitteleuropaforschung, Jg. 52, N.F., H. 3, Marburg, 2003, pp. 455–456.] [A.C., 1901 Bromberg–1961 Wroclaw (before 1945: Breslau), in 1920 went with his family to Berlin, after the war lived in Wroclaw.]

42316. BRUCHSAL. OBERBECK, REINER: *Die Synagoge Bruchsal 1881–1938.* [In]: Badische Heimat, Jg. 82, H. 2, Freiburg, 2002. Pp. 360–363, illus., notes.

42317. BUCHAU. MAYENBERGER, CHARLOTTE: *Jüdisches Bad Buchau: Einladung zu einem Rundgang.* [Hrsg.: Stadt Bad Buchau]. Haigerloch: Medien und Dialog, Schubert, 2003. 18 pp., illus., map. (Orte jüdischer Kultur.)

42318. BUCHAU. MAYENBERGER, CHARLOTTE: *Moritz Vierfelder. Leben und Schicksal eines Buchauer Juden.* Bad Buchau: Federsee-Verlag, 2000. 102 pp., ports., illus., facsims. (Geschichte und Kultur, Landkreis Biberach. Bd. 4.). [On the Jews of Buchau and the life of the confectioner M.V. (1877–1961), chairman of the congregation; emigr. in 1940 to the US.]

42319. BURGHOLZHAUSEN. PEILSTÖCKER, M.: *Der jüdische Friedhof in Burgholzhausen.* [In]: Friedrichsdorfer Schriften, Jg, 2, 2002/2003, Friedrichsdorf, 2003. Pp. 65–71.

—— BUTTENHEIM. DOUBEK, KATJA: *Blue Jeans. Levi Strauss und die Geschichte einer Legende.* [See No. 42515.]

42320. CASTROP-RAUXEL. ASCHOFF, DIETHARD: *Juden in Castrop-Rauxel im Vergleich zu anderen Kommunen Westfalens vor allem im Ruhrgebiet.* [In]: Kultur und Heimat, Jg. 54, Nr. 1/2, Castrop-Rauxel, 2003. Pp. 33–52, notes.

42321. CHAM. BULLEMER, TIMO: *"Die hiesigen Juden sind in Cham alteingesessen".* Aus der Geschichte der jüdischen Gemeinde vom Mittelalter bis zur Gegenwart. Cham: Selbstverlag des Stadtarchivs Cham, 2003. 128 pp., illus., facsims., bibl., index. (Bausteine zur Geschichte und Kultur der Stadt Cham, Bd. 1.) [Incl. list of Nazi victims; also on the DP Camp.]

42322. CHEMNITZ. *Spurensuche: Jüdische Mitbürger in Chemnitz. Stätten ihres Lebens und Wirkens, Orte der Erinnerung.* [Hrsg.: Stadtarchiv Chemnitz. Autoren: Jutta Aurich et al.] Chemnitz: Stadtarchiv Chemnitz, 2002. 80 pp., illus. [A guide, publ. on the occasion of the inauguration of the new synagogue.]

42323. COLOGNE. BALTRUSCH, ERNST: *Die konstantinische 'lex generalis' von 321 an die Stadt Köln und die Juden.* [In]: Ein gefüllter Willkomm. Festschrift für Knut Schulz zum 65. Geburtstag. Hrsg. von Franz J. Felten [et al.]. Aachen: Shaker, 2002. Pp. 1–15, footnotes.

42324. COLOGNE. MEYER, MARTIN: *Vom J.T.V.02 zum TuS Makkabi. 100 Jahre jüdischer Sport in Köln.* Köln: [Privately printed], 2002. 183 pp., facsims., docs., footnotes, bibl. [Available at the Bibliothek Germania Judaica, Cologne. Incl. reprint of "Festschrift zum 25-jährigen Jubiläumsfest des JTV Köln" (1927).]

42325. COLOGNE. SCHMIDT, KLAUS: *Andreas Gottschalk: Armenarzt und Pionier der Arbeiterbewegung. Jude und Protestant.* Köln: Greven, 2002. 168 pp., illus., chronol., bibl., index. [A.G., Feb. 28, 1815 Düsseldorf–Sept. 8, 1849 Cologne, physician, lived from 1825 in Cologne, converted to Protestantism in 1844, actively involved in the 1848 revolution.]

42326. CREGLINGEN. *Wurzeln und Wege.* Eine Dauerausstellung für das Jüdische Museum Creglingen. Hrsg.: Stiftung Jüd. Museum Creglingen. Text: Myrah Adams [et al.]. [Creglingen]: Jüd. Museum Creglingen, [2003?]. 32 pp., illus. [Opened in Nov. 2000.]

42327. DIESPECK. VOGEL, ILSE: *Koscher oder trefa.* Wie das Neben- und Miteinander von Juden und Christen in Diespeck zweihundert Jahre lang eine Dorfkultur schuf. Scheinfeld: Hans Meyer Verlag, 2003. 339 pp., illus., facsims., name lists, bibl., map [attached to back cover]. [Title on book cover also in Hebrew. Diespeck on Aisch: in Franconia, nr. Erlangen. Book focuses on the 18th and 19th centuries.]

42328. DORSTEN-LEMBECK. COSANNE-SCHULTE-HUXEL, ELISABETH: *Ein Besuch bei einem Nachkommen der Lembecker Familie Lebenstein.* [In]: Heimatkalender der Herrlichkeit Lembeck und der Stadt Dorsten, Jg. 62, Dorsten-Lembeck, 2003. Pp. 69–72.

42329. DRIBURG. BECKER, WALDEMAR: *Geschichte der Driburger Juden.* Bad Driburg: Heimatverein Bad Driburg, 2003. 110 pp., notes, bibl. (Aus der Heimatkunde der Stadt Bad Driburg, Nr. 29.) [Documents about thirty families or individuals.]

——— DÜLKEN. TAPKEN, HERMANN: *Von der Ratinger Kinderärztin zur prominenten amerikanischen Wissenschaftlerin—Hilde Bruch, ein jüdisches Schicksal.* [See No. 43251.]

42330. DÜLMEN. WERP, WOLFGANG: *Das Textilunternehmen Bendix in Dülmen.* [In]: Dülmener Heimatblätter, Jg. 50, H. 1, Dülmen, 2003. Pp. 2–34, illus., notes. [On the Bendix textile mills and the family (baptised in 1909) from 1800 to the post-1945 era.]

42331. DÜLMEN. WERP, WOLFGANG: *Zur Geschichte der Dülmener Textilindustrie.* [In]: Dülmener Heimatblätter, Jg. 49, H. 2, Dülmen, 2002. Pp. 50–72, illus., notes. [Deals with three families and their textile mills, two of whom were Jewish: Weberei L. & S. Leeser and Weberei und Spinnerei Paul Bendix.]

42332. DÜREN (KREIS). *Juden im Kreis Düren.* Texte: Willi Dovern [et al.]. Red.: Bernd Hahne. 2. Aufl. Düren: [Arbeitsgemeinschaft der Geschichtsvereine im Kreis Düren], 2002. 1 vol. (Unterrichtsmaterialien, 1.)

42333. DÜSSELDORF. BERNARD, BIRGIT/SCHUMACHER, RENATE: *Fritz Worm oder der obsolet gewordene Bildungsauftrag.* [In]: StadtLandFluß. Urbanität und Regionalität in der Moderne. Festschrift für Gertrude Cepl-Kaufmann zum sechzigsten Geburtstag [see No. 43138]. Pp. 109–128, notes. [F.W., 1887 Loebschütz/Upper Silesia – 1940 Rio de Janeiro, book dealer, author, broadcaster, lived from 1910 in Düsseldorf, member of the Immermannbund, emigr. in 1934 to Brazil.]

–42334. DÜSSELDORF. JAKOBS, HILDEGARD [et al.]: *Zeitspuren in Düsseldorf 1930–1950.* Ein Stadtführer. Hrsg. vom Förderkreis der Mahn- und Gedenkstätte Düsseldorf. 2. Aufl. Düsseldorf: Die Qualitaner, 2003. 160 pp., illus. [Incl. numerous aspects of Jewish life in Düsseldorf.]

42335. DÜSSELDORF. WELLING, MARTIN: *"Wie ein böser Spuk". Düsseldorfer Juden in Krieg und Revolution 1914–1920.* [In]: Aschkenas, Jg. 13, H. 1, Tübingen, 2003. Pp. 167–188, footnotes.

42336. EMDEN. SCHRÖDER, WILT ADEN: *Zur Geschichte und Entwicklung einer jüdischen Familie vom Ende des 18. bis ins 20. Jahrhundert: die Ärzte Joseph Calmer (1805–1854) und Carl Joseph Norden (1836–1903) sowie der Rabbiner Joseph Norden (1870–1943).* [In]: Emder Jahrbuch für historische Landeskunde Ostfrieslands, Jg. 82, Aurich, 2002. Pp. 80–121, geneal. [J.N., 1870 Hamburg–1943 Theresienstadt, rabbi in Elberfeld, father of Albert Norden; see also No. 43038.]

42337. ESSEN. EIDEN, CHRISTIAN: *Sanierung der jüdischen Trauerhalle.* [In]: Denkmalpflege im Rheinland, Jg. 19, Nr. 1, Essen, 2002. Pp. 24–30, illus., notes. [On a burial hall in Essen-Huttrop built in 1931 by Ernst Bode and Hermann Finger.]

42338. FLÖRSHEIM/MAIN. SCHIELE, WERNER: *Die neu entdeckte Mikwe in Flörsheim am Main.* [In]: Zwischen Main und Taunus, Jg. 11, Hofheim a.Ts., 2003. Pp. 185–190.

42339. FRANCONIA. FLEISCHMANN, JOHANN, ed.: *Mesusa 3: Spuren jüdischer Vergangenheit an Aisch, Aurach, Ebrach und Seebach.* Die jüdischen Friedhöfe von Zeckern, Walsdorf, Aschbach, Uehlfeld, Mühlhausen, Lisberg, Burghaslach und Reichmannsdorf. [Hrsg.: Arbeitskreis "Jüdische Landgemeinden an Aisch, Aurach, Ebrach und Seebach"]. 96171 Mühlhausen: Selbstverlag REG D. Fleischmann [R.-Matthes-Str. 9], 2002. 392 pp., illus., gloss., index. [Incl. Hebrew inscriptions with transl. and annotations.]

42340. FRANCONIA. *Jüdisches Leben in Franken.* Hrsg. von Gunnar Och und Hartmut Bobzin. Würzburg: Ergon, 2002. 244 pp., illus., facsims., footnotes, indexes. (Bibliotheca Academica, Reihe Geschichte, Bd. 1.) [Cont. papers, most of which were presented at a symposium at Erlangen-Nürnberg Univ. in coop. with the Jewish Museum Franken in autumn 1999. Cont.: Vorwort (eds., 7–9). Elia Levita Bachur, Italien und die Volkskultur (Christoph Daxelmüller, 11–32, bibl.; on a scholar b. in 1468 in Ipsheim nr. Neustadt, who lived from the late 15th cent. in Padua and Venice as a translator and editor of 'Bovo Bukh' and other works). Judenfeind oder Judenfreund? Der Altdorfer Gelehrte Johann Christoph Wagenseil (Hartmut Bobzin, 33–51). Jüdische Lektoren an der Universität Altdorf im 17. und 18. Jahrhundert (Hermann Süß, 53–67). Bodenschatz' Kirchliche Verfassung der heutigen Juden—Interkulturelle Mittlerschaft und frühe emanzipatorische Ansätze (Gerda Heinrich, 69–84). Purimspiel und Familiengemälde—Theaterstücke von Fürther Juden aus dem 18. und 19. Jahrhundert (Jutta Strauss, 85–114). Jüdische Landgemeinden in Franken zwischen Aufklärung und Akkulturation (Eva Groiss-Lau, 115–155, illus.). Beziehungen zwischen Juden und Nichtjuden: Beobachtungen zur Alltagsgeschichte Frankens (Trude Maurer, 157–175; from the late 19th to the Nazi period). Zion, Heimat, Golus—Jakob Wassermann zwischen jüdischer Selbstbesinnung, Assimilation und Antisemitismus (Gunnar Och, 177–195). Jüdisches Leben in Franken nach 1945 am Beispiel der Gemeinde Fürth (Monika Berthold-Hilpert, 197–212). Die Reste des Jiddischen in Mittelfranken (Alfred Klepsch, 213–225). Ernstes und Heiteres aus der altjiddischen (jüdisch-deutschen) Literatur (Hermann Süß, 227–236).]

42341. FRANKFURT AM MAIN. BACKHAUS, FRITZ: *"Daß die Begünstigung der Juden und Bluthunde so groß sei ...". Juden und Patriziat im alten Frankfurt.* [In]: Archiv für Frankfurts Geschichte und Kunst, Bd. 68, Frankfurt am Main, 2002. Pp. 125–150, illus., footnotes. [On mid-15th to early 17th cent.]

42342. FRANKFURT AM MAIN. EIBACH, JOACHIM: *Frankfurter Verhöre. Städtische Lebenswelten und Kriminalität im 18. Jahrhundert.* Paderborn: Schöningh, 2003. 476 pp., illus., footnotes, tabs., graphs, bibl. (435–464), index. [Incl. passim conflicts with Jews.]

——— FRANKFURT AM MAIN. KOHRING, ROLF/KRAFT, GERALD, eds.: *Tilly Edinger. Leben und Werk einer jüdischen Wissenschaftlerin.* [See No. 43275.]

42343. FRANKFURT AM MAIN. LUSTIGER, ARNO, ed.: *Charles Hallgarten*. Leben und Wirken des Frankfurter Sozialreformers und Philanthropen. Mit Beiträgen von Jens Friedemann [et al.] und einem Vorwort von Klaus Töpfer. Frankfurt am Main: Societäts-Verlag, 2003. 174 pp., frontis., illus., facsims., notes (150–174). [Incl.: Ein Wort des Herausgebers (Arno Lustiger, 11–12). Charles L. Hallgarten (Hans-Otto Schembs, 13–88). Der gemeinnützige Wohnungsbau: Vom Mittelalter bis ins 21. Jahrhundert (Jens Friedemann, 89–112). Charles Hallgartens Jahre in New York (Ulrich Stascheit, 113–126). Charles Hallgartens reichsdeutsche und internationale Aktivitäten (Arno Lustiger, 127–144). Stammbaum der Familie Hallgarten (145–149).] [Cf.: Vor der Geschichte Zeugnis ablegen. Auszüge aus der Rede von Julius Schoeps zur Verleihung der Ehrendoktorwürde der philosophischen Fakultät der Universität Potsdam an Arno Lustiger [in]: Illustr. Neue Welt, Wien, Aug./Sept. 2003, p. 15.] [Ch.H., Nov. 18, 1838 Mainz–April 19, 1908 Frankfurt am Main, philanthropist, social reformer.]

42344. FREIBURG. BLÜMLE, GEROLD/GOLDSCHMIDT, NILS: *Robert Liefmann als Ökonom*. [In]: Freiburger Universitätsblätter, Jg. 41, H. 162, Freiburg, Dez. 2003. Pp. 119–143, footnotes. [Also in this issue: Die Geschwister Liefmann (Kathrin Clausing, 107–114; on Else L., paediatrician, Robert L., economist and jurist, and Martha L., all baptised, deported 1940 to Gurs and later to Auschwitz.) Gedichte (Else Liefmann, 115–118).]

42345. FRIEDBERG. *Kehilat Friedberg*. Hrsg. von Andreas Gotzmann. Band 1: Cilli Kasper-Holtkotte: Jüdisches Leben in Friedberg (16.-18. Jahrhundert). Friedberg: Verlag der Bindernagelschen Buchhandlung, 2003. XVI, 451 pp., footnotes, bibl. (275–283), index. (Wetterauer Geschichtsblätter, 50.) [Incl.: Einleitung (ed., IX-XVI; deals with general historiographical aspects). Quellen zur Geschichte der Juden Friedbergs (289–451).]

42346. FÜRTH. BERTHOLD-HILPERT, MONIKA/FLECKENSTEIN, JUTTA: *Jüdische Stiftungen in Fürth: Einladung zu einem Rundgang*. Haigerloch: Medien und Dialog, Schubert, 2003. 22 pp., illus., map. (Orte jüdischer Kultur.)

42347. FÜRTH. *nurinst 2002. Beiträge zu deutschen und jüdischen Geschichte*. Bd. 1: Schwerpunktthema: Jüdisches Leben in Fürth. Jahrbuch des Nürnberger Instituts für NS-Forschung und jüdische Geschichte des 20. Jahrhunderts. Hrsg. von Jim G. Tobias und Peter Zinke. Nürnberg: Antogo, 2002. 147 pp., notes. [Incl. (titles abbr.): Synagogen in Fürth (17. bis 20. Jh.) (Monika Berthold-Hilpert, 97–112). Jüdische und antijüdische Vereine in Fürth 1871–1914 (Heike Scharf, 113–126). Further essays are listed according to subject.]

42348. GÖTTINGEN. MAURER, TRUDE: *Balten, Polen, Juden—und strebsame Frauen. Die "russischen" Studenten Göttingens um die Wende vom 19. zum 20. Jahrhundert*. [In]: Russland und die "Göttingische Seele": 300 Jahre St. Petersburg. Ausstellung in der Paulinerkirche Göttingen. Hrsg.: Elmar Mittler [et al.]. Göttingen: Niedersächsische Staats- und Univ.-Bibliothek, 2003. Pp. 453–473, footnotes.

42349. GOSLAR. *Zwischen den Mauern. Der jüdische Friedhof zu Goslar an der Glockengießerstraße*. Dokumentation der Grabstädten und Inschriften. Hrsg.: Stadt Goslar, Fachbereich Kultur und Stadtgeschichte. Bearb. von Berndt Schaller, Jens Behnsen. Fotogr. von Friedhelm Geyer. Goslar: Stadt Goslar [2003]. 216 pp., illus.

42350. HAIGERLOCH. SCHÄFER, RALF: *Die Rechtsstellung der Haigerlocher Juden im Fürstentum Hohenzollern-Sigmaringen von 1634–1850: eine rechtsgeschichtliche Untersuchung*. Frankfurt am Main; New York: Lang, 2002. XXXV, 209 pp., footnotes. (Rechtshistorische Reihe, Bd. 254.) Zugl.: Tübingen, Univ., Diss., 2001.

42351. HAMBURG. BRADEN, JUTTA: *Die Hamburger Judenpolitik und die lutherisch-orthodoxe Geistlichkeit im 17. Jahrhundert*. [In]: Zeitschrift des Vereins für Hamburgische Geschichte, Bd. 89, Hamburg, 2003. Pp. 1–40, illus., footnotes.

42352. HAMBURG. BRÄMER, ANDREAS: *The dialectics of religious reform: The 'Hamburger Israelitische Tempel' in its local context 1817–1938*. [In]: Leo Baeck Institute Year Book 2003, Vol. XLVIII, Oxford; New York, 2003. Pp. 25–37, footnotes.

42353. HAMBURG. BÜTTNER, ANNETT: *Hoffnungen einer Minderheit: Suppliken jüdischer Einwohner an den Hamburger Senat im 19. Jahrhundert.* Münster: Lit, 2003. 157 pp., bibl. (147–157). (Veröff. des Hamburger Arbeitskreises für Regionalgeschichte, Bd. 18.)

42354. HAMBURG. *Hamburgische Biografie.* Personenlexikon. Hrsg. von Franklin Kopitzsch und Dirk Brietzke. Hamburg: Christians, 2001; 2003. 2 vols., 368; 478 pp. [Both vols. incl. many contribs. on Jews.]

42355. HAMBURG. LIEBERMAN, JULIA R.: *Sermons and the construct of a Jewish identity: the Hamburg Sephardic community in the 1620s.* [In]: Jewish Studies Quarterly, Vol. 10, No. 1, Tübingen, 2003. Pp. 49–72, footnotes, illus.

42356. HAMBURG. MÜHLFRIED, KLAUS: *Martin Hallers Sicht vom Adel und Judentum im Spiegel seiner Döntjes.* [In]: Zeitschrift des Vereins für Hamburgische Geschichte, Bd. 88, Hamburg, 2002. Pp. 89–123, ports., footnotes. [Deals with a Hamburg architect (1835–1925), grandson of a converted Hamburg Jew.]

42357. HAMBURG. OETTERMANN, STEPHAN/SEFFINGA, JAN J.: *Adolph Friedländer Lithos. Ein Verzeichnis nach Nummern.* Zweite, verm. und verb. Aufl. Unter Mitarbeit von Hans W. Bäumer [et al.]. Gerolzhofen: Steingrabenstr. 44: S. Oettermann, 2002. 186 pp., illus., facsims., footnotes, index. (Studien und Quellen zur Geschichte der Vergnügungskultur. H. 4.) [A.F., 1851 Hamburg–1904 Hamburg, book and poster printer, lithographer, first owner of the Adolph Friedländer Buch- und Plakatdruckerei (1872–1935).]

42358. HAMBURG. SON, HERBERT VAN: *The tobacco road: Hamburg, Kentucky, Shanghai. The collected letters of Herbert van Son 1908–1929.* Transl. from the German to Hebrew by Miriam Ron; transl. from Hebrew to Engl. by Dorothea Shefer-Vanson. [Israel]: Shefer Publ., [2003]. XII, 267 pp., illus., facsims., notes, index. [Incl. letters written by a young man, son of a Hamburg Jewish tobacco merchant family, from his business travels to Kentucky, Tennessee and Carolina from early 1928 until his mysterious death in Shanghai, May 1929; incl. also an introd. by his niece Dorothea Shefer-Vanson (I-III).] [Cf.: Bespr. (Batya Rabin-Emanuel) [in]: 'MB', Jg. 71, Nr. 185, Tel Aviv, Sept./Okt. 2003, p. 15.]

——— HAMBURG. WALLENBORN, HILTRUD: *Bekehrungseifer, Judenangst und Handelsinteresse. Amsterdam, Hamburg und London als Ziele sefardischer Migration im 17. Jahrhundert.* [See No. 42257.]

42359. HAMM. ASCHOFF, DIETHARD: *Ein Dolberger Pastor vor dem Reichskammergericht.* Temmo Lethmathe aus Dolberg prozessiert gegen den Juden Moises von Hamm. Teil 1 & 2. [In]: Der beflügelte Aal, Bd. 21, Ahlen, 2002. Pp. 99–105, notes & Bd. 22, 2003. Pp. 116–119.

42360. HAMM. ASCHOFF, DIETHARD: *Hamm als Vorort der westfälischen Juden und die Frankfurter "Rabbinerverschwörung" von 1603.* [In]: Märkisches Jahrbuch für Geschichte, Bd. 102, Dortmund, 2002. Pp. 42–80, footnotes. [Using trial documentation of the Reichskammergericht, deals with the case of Moises von Hamm; incl. docs. (64–80).]

42361. HANOVER. BARDELLE, THOMAS: *Der Konkurs des jüdischen Bankhauses Salomon Michael David & Söhne.* [In]: Hannoversche Geschichtsblätter, Bd. 54, Hannover, 2003. Pp. 57–66, footnotes. [Deals with the first decade of the 19th cent.]

42362. HEIDELSHEIM. MAISCH, STEFFEN: *Das jüdische Schulwesen in Heidelsheim im 19. Jahrhundert.* [In]: Badische Heimat, Jg. 82, H. 2, Freiburg, 2002. Pp. 370–376, illus., notes.

42363. HERSFELD. ABBES, OTTO: *Hersfelds jüdische Geschichte 1330 bis 1970. Die über 600-jährige Geschichte der Ausgrenzung, Duldung und Verfolgung der Juden in Hersfeld.* Eine Dokumentation. Hersfeld: Verein f. Hess. Geschichte u. Landeskunde e.V.; Kassel, Zweigverein Bad Hersfeld, 2003. 242 pp., illus., facsims., footnotes, docs., bibl. (Verein für Hessische Geschichte und Landeskunde e.V. Kassel—Zweigverein Bad Hersfeld, Bd. 5.)

42364. HESSE. LOTZE, SIEGFRIED: *Niederhessische Juden in Freimaurerlogen (1803–1866).* [In]: Jahrbuch 2003 Landkreis Kassel, Kassel, 2002. Pp. 41–52, illus., notes. [Mainly on freemasonry in Kassel.]

42365. HILDESHEIM. REYER, HERBERT/OBENAUS, HERBERT, eds.: *Geschichte der Juden im Hildesheimer Land.* Hildesheim; New York: Olms, 2003. X, 115 pp., footnotes, index. [Cont.: Einleitung (eds., VII-IX). Städtische und landesherrliche Judenpolitik in Hildesheim im 15. und 16. Jahrhundert (Peter Aufgebauer, 1–14). Jüdisches Leben in Hildesheim vom 16. bis zum 18. Jahrhundert im Überblick. Rechtliche, soziale und wirtschaftliche Aspekte (Herbert Reyer, 15–28). Vom Schutzjuden zum gleichberechtigten Staatsbürger. Ein Beitrag zur Geschichte der Kleinstadt Gronau (Andrea Baumert, 29–44). Politisches Engagement und Protestverhalten jüdischer Gemeinden im Vormärz am Beispiel der Gemeinde Hildesheim (1817–1832) (Rainer Sabelleck, 45–72). Zwischen Assimilation und Akkulturation. Aspekte jüdischen Vereinslebens in Hildesheim 1871–1942 (Jörg Schneider, 73–88). Jüdisches Leben in Niedersachsen nach dem Holocaust (Herbert Obenaus, 89–108).]

42366. HILDESHEIM. SCHNEIDER, JÖRG: *Die jüdische Gemeinde in Hildesheim 1871–1942.* Hildesheim: Stadtarchiv, 2003. 547 pp., illus., tabs., footnotes, bibl. (524–547). (Schriftenreihe des Stadtarchivs und der Stadtbibliothek Hildesheim, Bd. 31.)

42367. HÖSBACH. HEEG-ENGELHART, INGRID: *Von Hösbach nach Israel.* Claire Keveházi geb. Löwenthal (1905–2002) in memoriam. [In]: Mainfränkisches Jahrbuch für Geschichte und Kunst, Jg. 55, Würzburg, 2003. Pp. 143–148, port., footnotes. [On the family of Lazarus Löwenthal, cattle trader in Hösbach nr. Aschaffenburg.]

42368. HOLSTEIN (DUCHY). REHN, MARIE-ELISABETH: *Juden in Süderdithmarschen. Fremde im eigenen Land Herzogtum Holstein 1799–1858.* Hrsg. von Erhard Roy Wiehn. Konstanz: Hartung-Gorre, 2003. 154 pp., footnotes.

42369. HOLZMINDEN (KREIS). GELDERBLOM, BERNHARD: *Jüdisches Leben im mittleren Weserraum zwischen Hehlen und Polle. Von den Anfängen im 14. Jahrhundert bis zu seiner Vernichtung in der nationalsozialistischen Zeit.* Ein Gedenkbuch. [Hrsg. vom Heimat- und Geschichtsverein für Landkreis und Stadt Holzminden]. Holzminden: Mitzkat, 2003. 304 pp., illus., bibl.

42370. HOPSTEN. ALTHOFF, GERTRUD: *Nun bleibt uns nur zu gedenken. Geschichte der jüdischen Hopstener.* Rheine: [Selbstverlag] 2003. 50 pp., footnotes. [Hopsten: nr. Ibbenbüren, Westphalia.]

42371. JÜLICH. JAEGER, ACHIM: *Ein "Zeichen der Zeit". Zum Ritualmord-Vorwurf gegen die Eheleute David (Jülich 1840).* [In]: Neue Beiträge zur Jülicher Geschichte, Bd. XIV, Jülich, 2003. Pp. 127–141, footnotes.

42372. KAPPELN. PHILIPSEN, BERND: *Erfolgreicher Unternehmer und großmütiger Philanthrop. Leben und Wirken des Jacob Moser (Kappeln/Bradford).* [In]: Jahrbuch des Heimatvereins der Landschaft Angeln 2002, Kappeln, 2002 [?]. Pp. 121–148.

42373. KASSEL. THIERLING, MAGDA: *Sein statt Schein. Anmerkungen zum Lebensbild eines herausragenden Menschen. Dr. Ludwig Goldschmidt (1895–1970).* [In]: Jahrbuch 2004 Landkreis Kassel, Kassel, 2003. Pp. 141–152, illus., notes. [Also on other members of the Goldschmidt family.] [L.G., 1895 Kassel–1970 Kassel, jurist, judge, emigr. 1939 to the UK, returned to Kassel 1948.]

42374. KIEL. GOLDBERG, BETTINA: *Kleiner Kuhberg 25—Feuergang 2. Die Verfolgung der schleswig-holsteinsichen Juden im Spiegel der Geschichte zweier Häuser.* [In]: Informationen zur Schleswig-Holsteinischen Zeitgeschichte, H. 40, Kiel, Juli 2002. Pp. 3–21, illus., facsims., notes. [Deals with Eastern-Jewish families and their houses, used after their expulsion as "Judenhäuser".]

42375. KIPPENHEIM. KALLMANN, ERNEST: *More than a book review: Gedächtnis aus Stein: Die Synagoge in Kippenheim, 1852–2002.* [In]: Avotaynu, Vol. 19, No. 2, Bergenfield, NJ, Summer 2003. Pp. 34–40, illus., notes. [For book of the same title see No. 40990/YB XLVIII; article also covers the history of the synagogue.]

42376. KIPPENHEIM. STEIN, PETER: *Grußwort zur Vorstellung des Buches über die Synagoge Kippenheim, vorgetragen am 10. November 2002.* [In]: Die Ortenau, Bd. 83, Offenburg, 2003. Pp. 69–76, facsims. [Speech given by a descendant of Kippenheim Jews on his 80th birthday dealing with the Stein family; for the book on the Kippenheim synagogue see No. 40990/YB XLVIII.]

42377. KIRCHZARTEN. ALTHAUS, HERMANN: *Der Markenhof in Kirchzarten und seine Synagoge.* [In]: Badische Heimat, Jg. 80, H. 2, Freiburg, 2000. Pp. 259–267, illus., notes. [On a Zionist agricultural school founded in 1919 by Konrad Goldmann.]

——— KÖNIGSBERG. WYRWA, ULRICH: *Juden in der Toskana und in Preußen im Vergleich. Aufklärung und Emanzipation in Florenz, Livorno, Berlin und Königsberg i.Pr.* [See No. 42260.]

42378. KREFELD. BROCKE, MICHAEL/POMERANCE, AUBREY: *Steine wie Seelen. Der alte jüdische Friedhof Krefeld. Grabmale und Inschriften.* Textband & Bildband. Unter Mitarbeit von Barbara Mattes. Hrsg.: Stadt Krefeld. Der Oberbürgermeister; Salomon Ludwig Steinheim-Inst. für deutsch-jüd. Gesch. Krefeld: [Stadtarchiv Krefeld], 2003. 2 vols. [Vol. I (text) (500 pp., illus., facsims., bibl., docs., name lists, index, plan) incl. short essays dealing with historical and artistic aspects (3–61). Second part entitled Die Inschriften (68–424) cont. Hebrew inscriptions with German transl. and detailed annotations. Vol. II (illustrations) (208 pp., indexes) cont. photographs of all gravestones.]

42379. KREFELD. SCHUPETTA, INGRID: *Vor 150 Jahren: Eröffnung der Synagoge an der Petersstraße.* [In]: Die Heimat. Krefelder Jahrbuch, Jg. 74, Krefeld, 2003. Pp. 13–15, notes.

42380. LAGE. HANKEMEIER, MARTIN: *Zur Geschichte der Juden in Lage.* 2. veränd. und erheblich erw. Aufl. Detmold: Gesellschaft für Christlich-Jüdische Zusammenarbeit in Lippe e.V., 2003. 300 pp., illus., facsims. (Panu Derech, Bd. 12.) [Documents 15 families; incl. (unpag.) 14 family trees and bibl.]

42381. LEIPZIG. BUCHOLTZ, ERIKA: *Musikverleger—Jüdischer Bürger—Mäzen: Henri Hinrichsen (1868–1942) und der Verlag C.F. Peters in Leipzig.* [In]: Zeitschrift für Geschichtswissenschaft, Jg. 51, H. 4, Berlin, 2003. Pp. 301–317, footnotes.

42382. LEIPZIG. LANG, HUBERT: *Das gescheiterte Duell oder: Muß der Anwalt den Richter grüßen?* Von einer Auseinandersetzung unter Juristen und ihrem antisemitischen Hintergrund. [In]: Leipziger Blätter, H. 43, Leipzig, Herbst 2003. Pp. 74–75, illus. [On the lawyer Paul Werthauer (1858 Leipzig–1933 Berlin).]

42383. LOWER SAXONY. BERG, MEIKE: *Jüdische Schulen in Niedersachsen.* Tradition—Emanzipation—Assimilation. Die Jacobson-Schule in Seesen (1801–1922). Die Samsonschule in Wolfenbüttel (1807–1928). Köln: Bohlau, 2003. XIV, 287 pp., footnotes, bibl. (260–287). (Beiträge zur Historischen Bildungsforschung, Bd. 28.)

——— LÜBECK. KLATT, INGABURGH: *Judentum und Antisemitismus zwischen 1870 und 1890 in Lübeck.* [See in No. 43595.]

42384. MAINZ. SIMON, PAUL: *Paul Simon (1884–1977). Meine Erinnerungen.* Das Leben des jüdischen Deutschen Paul Simon, Rechtsanwalt in Mainz. Bearb. von Tillmann Krach. Hrsg. von Tillmann Krach in Verbindung mit dem Verein für Sozialgesch. Mainz e.V. Mainz: [Verein für Sozialgesch.], 2003. 120 pp., illus., facsims. (Mainzer Geschichtsblätter, Sonderheft.) [P.S., 1884 Mainz–1977 New York, lawyer, member of the DDP, emigr. 1939 via Switzerland to the US.]

42385. MANNHEIM. BAYER, TILDE: *Der Platz in der Synagoge.* Sitzordnung im religiösen Raum, jüdische Sozialordnung und städtische Topographie in Mannheim um 1860. [In]: Stadt und Land. Bilder, Inszenierungen und Visionen in Geschichte und Gegenwart. Wolfgang von Hippel zum 65. Geburtstag. Hrsg. von Sylvia Schraut und Bernhard Stier. Stuttgart: Kohlhammer, 2001. (Veröffentlichungen der Kommission für geschichtliche Landeskunde in Baden-Württemberg, Reihe B, Forschungen, Bd. 147). Pp. 239–253, footnotes.

42386. MÖNCHENGLADBACH. HABRICH, HEINZ: *Kirchen und Synagogen. Denkmäler aus der Zeit von 1850 bis 1916 in Mönchengladbach.* Hrsg. vom Münster-Bauverein e.V. Mönchengladbach:

[Stadtarchiv Mönchengladbach], 2002. 102 pp., illus., footnotes. [Incl. the synagogues of Mönchengladbach, Rheydt and Odenkirchen.]

42387. MOHRUNGEN (EAST PRUSSIA). VOGELSANG, ERNST: *Auszüge aus den Hauptregistern des Standesamts Mohrungen 1874–1900 zur dortigen Synagogengemeinde.* [In]: Altpreußische Geschlechterkunde, N.F., Bd. 32, Hamburg, 2003 [?]. Pp. 265–279.

42388. MÜHRINGEN. *Gräber im Wald. Dokumentation des Friedhofs, der über 300 Jahre in Mühringen ansässigen jüdischen Gemeinde und des Rabbinats Mühringen.* [Above title: Lebensspuren auf dem jüdischen Friedhof in Mühringen]. Hrsg. vom Stadtarchiv Horb und vom Träger- und Förderverein Ehemalige Synagoge Rexingen. Mit Beiträgen von Renate Karoline Adler [et al.]. Stuttgart: Theiss, 2003. XI, 424 pp., illus., plan, index, bibl. (Jüdische Friedhöfe der Stadt Horb, Bd. II.) [For vol I (Rexingen) see No. 34847/YB XLIII.]

42389. MÜLHEIM AN DER RUHR. KAUFHOLD, BARBARA: *Juden in Mülheim an der Ruhr I: 500 Jahre Juden in Mülheim an der Ruhr.* [In]: Mülheim an der Ruhr. Jahrbuch 2004, Jg. 59, Mülheim, 2003. Pp. 274–279, illus., notes.

42390. MÜNSTER. SCHLAUTMANN-OVERMEYER, RITA: *Ein Aktenfund in Hamburg zur Geschichte der jüdischen Gemeinde Münster.* [In]: Westfälische Forschungen, Bd. 53, Münster, 2003. Pp. 419–427, footnotes. [Deals also with new documents relating to Oldenburg, Detmold and Lippe.]

42391. MÜNSTERLAND. ALLKÄMPER, URTE: *"Grausam ermordet im Kampf um ihre Tugend ...". Volkskundliche Aspekte eines Sexualmordes im Münsterland des späten 19. Jahrhunderts.* [In]: Rheinisch-westfälische Zeitschrift für Volkskunde, Bd. 58, Bonn, 2003. Pp. 55–84, footnotes. [Abbr. version of M.A. Thesis, Univ. of Münster; deals with a murder near Enniger in 1873, and an unsubstantiated allegation against a local Jew of the murder.]

42392. MUNICH. HOSER, PAUL: *Der jüdische Bankier: Simon von Eichthal.* [In]: Wilhelm Liebhart, ed.: König Ludwig I. von Bayern und seine Zeitgenossen. Biographische Essays. Frankfurt am Main; New York: Lang, 2003. Pp. 259–266, port., bibl. [On Simon Aron Freiherr von Eichthal (1787–1854), orig. Simon Aron Seligmann, banker, philanthropist, co-founder of the Bayerische Hypotheken- und Wechselbank.]

42393. MUNICH. JANKRIFT, KAY PETER: *Jüdische Heilkundige im Münchener Medizinalwesen des 14. und 15. Jahrhunderts.* [In]: Medizin, Gesellschaft und Geschichte, Jg. 2002, Bd. 21. Stuttgart, 2003. Pp. 9–22, notes.

42394. MUNICH. PETERSDORF, INGRID: *Lebenswelten. Jüdische bürgerliche Familien im München der Prinzregentenzeit.* Hamburg: Verlag Dr. Kovac, 2003. 573 pp., footnotes, bibl. (545–573). (Studien zur Zeitgeschichte, Bd. 32.) Zugl.: Regensburg, Univ., Diss., 2002.

42395. MUNICH. SCHIRNDING, ALBERT VON:...*"die unlitterarischste Stadt par excellence" ... Thomas Mann und das München der Familie Pringsheim.* [In]: Thomas Mann Jahrbuch, Bd. 15, Frankfurt am Main, 2002. Pp. 201–208, footnotes.

42396. MUNICH. WIESEMANN, FALK: *Die nationaljüdische Antwort: 'Das Jüdische Echo. Bayerische Blätter für jüdische Angelegenheiten' (1913–1933).* [In]: Le milieu intellectuel conservateur en Allemagne, sa presse et ses réseaux (1890–1960)/Das konservative Intellektuellenmilieu in Deutschland, seine Presse und seine Netzwerke (1890–1960). Etudes réunies par/Hrsg. von Michel Grunewald [et al.]. Bern: Lang, 2003. Pp. 219–238, footnotes.

42397. NEUENKIRCHEN (WESTPHALIA). LINNEMEIER, BERND-WILHELM: *"Da Wohltaten die Stützen der Welt sind ...". Die "Zunft der Heiligkeit" jüdischer Junggesellen und Knechte zu Neuenkirchen und ihre Nachfolgerin.* Ein Beitrag zur inneren Verfassung jüdischer Landgemeinden Ostwestfalens im 18. Jahrhundert. [In]: Rheinisch-westfälische Zeitschrift für Volkskunde, Bd. 46, Bonn, 2001. 239–274, footnotes.

42398. NEUWIED. ANHÄUSER, GERD: *Jüdisches Neuwied: Orte und Spuren.* Haigerloch: Medien und Dialog, Schubert, 2003. 42 pp., illus. (Orte jüdischer Kultur.)

42399. NORDERNEY. PAULUHN, INGEBORG: *Zur Geschichte der Juden auf Norderney. Von der Akzeptanz zur Desintegration.* Mit zahlreichen Bildern, Dokumenten und historischen Materialien. Oldenburg: Igel Verlag Wissenschaft, 2003. 74 [56] pp., frontis., illus., facsims., tabs., docs., bibl. [Incl. the Nazi period.]

42400. NUREMBERG. BERLIN, LUDWIG C./JOSEPHTAL, SENTA: *Berlin, Metzger, Josephtal: Sechs exemplarische Biographien von Mitgliedern bedeutender jüdischer Familien aus Nürnberg.* Bearb. von Gerhard Jochem. [In]: Mitteilungen des Vereins für Geschichte der Stadt Nürnberg, Bd. 89, Nürnberg, 2002. Pp. 181–199, illus.

42401. OELDE. TILLMANN, WALTER: *Ausgegrenzt—anerkannt—ausgelöscht. Geschichten, Berichte, Episoden und Anekdoten aus dem Leben und dem Untergang der jüdischen Minderheit in Oelde.* Hrsg.: Kreisgeschichtsverein Beckum-Warendorf e.V. Warendorf: Kreisarchiv Warendorf, 2003. XI, 302 pp., illus., footnotes, bibl., indexes. (Quellen und Forschungen zur Geschichte des Kreises Warendorf, Bd. 41.)

42402. OFFENBURG. RUCH, MARTIN: *Der Salmen. Geschichte der Offenburger Synagoge. Gasthof—Synagoge—Spielstätte.* Offenburg: KulturAgentur [Dr. Martin Ruch], 2002. 108 pp., illus., notes, bibl. [Herst.: Books on Demand GmbH.] [On the historical inn and dance hall "Salmen", a synagogue between 1875 and 1938, today a culture centre and memorial site.]

42403. OLDENBURG. MEINERS, WERNER: *Jüdisches Leben im Oldenburger Land vom Ende des 17. Jahrhunderts bis 1827.* [In]: Das Oldenburger Land, Nr. 113/114, III./IV. Quartal, Oldenburg, 2002. Pp. 16–18, notes.

42404. OLPE. WERMERT, JOSEF, ed.: *Olpe. Geschichte von Stadt und Land.* Bd. 1: Von den Anfängen bis zum Ende des Ersten Weltkrieges. Red.: Günther Becker [et al.]. Olpe: Stadt Olpe, 2002. 968 pp., illus., maps, tabs. [Incl.: Jüdische Familien: Neuenkleusheim—Oberveischede—Rhode, Stadt Olpe (Gretel Kemper, 723–730; incl. tab. of names; the Lenneberg family).]

42405. ORTENAU. RUCH, MARTIN: *Drei jüdische Gemeindebibliotheken aus der Ortenau (Offenburg, Kippenheim, Lahr).* [In]: Die Ortenau, Bd. 83, Offenburg, 2003. Pp. 77–82, facsims., notes.

42406. PALATINATE. BLASTENBREI, PETER: *Die kurpfälzischen Judenkonzessionen von 1744. Entstehung, Bedingungen, Folgen.* [In]: Mannheimer Geschichtsblätter, N.F., Bd. 9, Heidelberg, 2003. Pp. 155–175, footnotes, docs.

42407. PALATINATE. MAAS, WERNER: *Das Leben meines Vaters: 1888–1936. Ein Bild jüdischen Lebens in der Rheinpfalz zwischen Emanzipation, Integration, Vertreibung und Vernichtung.* Hrsg. vom Arbeitskreis für Neuere Jüdische Geschichte in der Pfalz. Speyer: Evang. Presseverl. Pfalz, 2003. 151 pp., illus., bibl.

42408. PALATINATE. MARX, WERNER J.B.: *Circumstances: a family history.* Schenectady, NY: Northeast Color Laboratory, Werner Marx, 2003. XII, 100 pp., illus., ports., facsims., map, geneal. tabs. [On two related families from the Palatinate: The Marx families from Sohren and Marienthal, the Freiberg family from Steinbach, Rockenhausen and the related Dreyfuss and Deutsch families; from the 18th century to the emigration to many different US states, 19th and 20th cent.]

42409. PALATINATE. STAB, FRANZ: *Die angebliche Ersterwähnung von Juden in der Pfalz im Jahr 831.* Zur Interpretation des Liber Aureus von Prüm. [In]: Mitteilungen des Historischen Vereins der Pfalz, Bd. 100, Speyer, 2002. Pp. 79–86, facsims., footnotes.

42410. POMERANIA. *Jewish life in Pomerania.* Stories researched, translated and written by Stephen Cameron Jalil Nicholls with a foreword by Sir Martin Gilbert C.B.E. D.Litt. Burgess Hill, West Sussex RH15 8JG: Stephen C.J. Nicholls, 2002. 56 pp., illus., facsims., maps, notes. [Book is dedicated to Julius Carlebach (1922–2001).]

42411. POSEN. LUFT, EDWARD DAVID: *Using Polish magnate records for Posen.* [In]: Avotaynu, Vol. 19, No. 3, Bergenfield, NJ, Fall 2003. Pp. 25–27, notes. [Explains how to find archival material on the Jews in Posen.]

42412. POSEN. PAKULA, ZBIGNIEW: *The Jews of Poznan.* Transl. by William Brand. London; Portland, OR: Vallentine Mitchell, 2003. VI, 199 pp. (Library of Holocaust testimonies.) [Contains individual family histories under the Nazis; also discusses the history of the Jews generally, going back to the Middle Ages.]

42413. REGENSBURG. DIRMEIER, ARTUR: *Die Schierstatt von Regensburg. Frühe jüdische Siedlungsspuren.* [In]: Staat und Verwaltung in Bayern. Festschrift für Wilhelm Volkert zum 75. Geburtstag. Hrsg. von Konrad Ackermann und Alois Schmid. München: Beck, 2003. Pp. 37–42, footnotes. [Deals with a document dated 981.]

42414. REGENSBURG. FISCHER, KLAUS: *Regensburger Hochfinanz. Die Krise einer europäischen Metropole an der Wende zur Neuzeit.* Regensburg: Univ.-Verl. Regensburg, 2003. 203 pp., illus., footnotes, bibl., index. (Regensburger Studien und Quellen zur Kulturgeschichte, 14.) Zugl.: Nürnberg-Erlangen, Univ., Diss., 1990. [Incl. a chap. on Jews (96–101).]

42415. REGENSBURG. WITTMER, SIEGFRIED: *Regensburger Synagogen. Eine bewegte Geschichte vom 12. Jahrhundert bis heute.* [In]: Regensburger Almanach, Jg. 37, Regensburg, 2003. Pp. 142–249.

42416. REINHARDSWALD. ALBRECHT, EBERHARD/LOTZE, SIEGFRIED: *Gedenkstätte Judenbaum am Auerhahnkamp im Reinhardswald.* [In]: Jahrbuch 2004 Landkreis Kassel, Kassel, 2003. Pp. 153–155, illus., map. [On the plaque recently affixed, commemorating the murder of "Samuel von Schwartzkirchen auß Polen" in 1668, the event forming the backdrop to Annette von Droste-Hülshoff's 'Judenbuche'.]

42417. RHEINE. ALTHOFF, GERTRUD/ALTHOFF, WERNER: *Die drei jüdischen Friedhöfe in Rheine: kleine Einführung in jüdische Totenbräuche.* Deutsche und hebräische Grabsteininschriften mit deutscher Übersetzung. Kurze Lebensdaten der Verstorbenen. [Rheine, Sperberweg 16]: G. Althoff, [2002]. 105 pp., illus.

42418. RHINELAND. *Die Tante mit der Synagoge im Hof: aus dem Leben rheinischer Landjuden.* Produktion: Landschaftsverband Rheinland, Medienzentrum Rheinland im Auftr. des Kulturamtes des Landschaftsverbandes. Buch und Regie: Barbara Stupp. Red.: Monika Grübel. Sprecherin: Hannelore Hoger. Köln: LVR, 2002.

42419. RHINELAND. ZITTARTZ-WEBER, SUZANNE: *Zwischen Religion und Staat. Die jüdischen Gemeinden in der preußischen Rheinprovinz 1815–1871.* Essen: Klartext, 2003. 419 pp., footnotes, bibl. (383–415), gloss. (Düsseldorfer Schriften zur neueren Landesgeschichte und zur Geschichte Nordrhein-Westfalens, Bd. 64.) [Incl. the sections: I. Einleitung. II. Die 'Kehila' und das Rheinland vor 1815. III. Die jüdische Gemeindeorganisation im Rheinland vom Beginn der preußischen Herrschaft bis 1840. IV. Das Gesetz vom 23.7.1847 und die Entwicklung des jüdischen Kulturwesens bis 1870. V. Die Religiosität der rheinischen Juden zwischen Kontinuität und Veränderung.]

42420. RHINELAND & HUNSRÜCK. PIES, CHRISTOF: *Jüdisches Leben im Rhein-Hunsrück-Kreis.* Mit Beiträgen von Hans-Werner Johann, Gustav Schellack, Doris Spormann, Hildburg-Helene Thill, Willi Wagner, Hilde Weirich, Doris Wesner. [Simmern]: Hunsrücker Geschichtsverein, [2003?]. 336 pp., illus., facsims., bibl. (Schriftenreihe des Hunsrücker Geschichtsvereins e.V., Nr. 40.) [Incl. lists of names, chaps. on the synagogues and cemeteries.]

42421. RHINELAND & WESTPHALIA. DENEKE, BERNWARD: *Zur Amtstracht der jüdischen Kultusbeamten, vornehmlich in Westfalen und im Rheinland.* [In]: Rheinisch-westfälische Zeitschrift für Volkskunde, Bd. 47, Bonn, 2002. Pp. 139–166, illus., facsims., footnotes. [Deals with the adaptation of robes of office of rabbis and cantors and the resulting discussions in the 19th cent. Also, by same author, in this periodical: Zwischen Anpassung und Differenz. Bemerkungen zu Chanukkafeiern in Bielefeld im 19. Jahrhundert. Bd. 46, Bonn, 2001. Pp. 275–290.]

42422. ROTHENBURG OB DER TAUBER. MATTES, BARBARA: *Jüdisches Alltagsleben in einer mittelalterlichen Stadt. Responsa des Rabbi Meir von Rothenburg.* Berlin; New York: de Gruyter, 2003. XII, 322 pp., footnotes, bibl. (293–312), indexes. (Studia Judaica, Bd. 24.) Zugl.: Duisburg, Univ., Diss., 2001.

42423. RÜTHEN. GRUN, ULRICH: *Der "Judenhagen" in Rüthen. "Wichtiger als eine Synagoge"—Seit 1625 Begräbnisstätte.* [In]: Heimatkalender des Kreises Soest, 2003. Soest, 2002. Pp. 76–77, illus.

42424. SAXONY. WILDE, MANFRED: *Jüdische Wohnplätze und Freihöfe im Spätmittelalter. Sonderrechtsbereiche in nordsächsischen Städten.* [In]: Jahrbuch für Regionalgeschichte, Bd. 22, Stuttgart, 2003. Pp. 7–57, illus., footnotes.

——— SCHLESWIG-HOLSTEIN. WULF, PETER: *"Jüdische Weltherrschaftspläne". Antisemitismus in bürgerlichen und bäuerlichen Parteien und Verbänden in Schleswig-Holstein zu Beginn der Weimarer Republik.* [See No. 43633.]

42425. SCHNAITTACH. KRODER, KARL/KRODER-GUMANN, BIRGIT: *Schnaittacher Häuserchronik—"seit unfürdenklichen Zeiten".* Gewidmet allen Einwohnern, die im Rad der Zeit von Vergangenheit, Gegenwart und Zukunft Schnaittach behaus(t)en... Nürnberg, Selbstverlag der Gesellsch. f. Familienforschung in Franken, 2002. 645 pp., illus., facsims., bibl., indexes, gloss. (Quellen und Forschungen zur fränkischen Familiengeschichte, Bd. 11.) [Incl. passim the Jews as house and shop owners; also a chap.: Geschichte der jüdischen Gemeinde von Schnaittach (88–99).]

42426. SCHNAITTACH. PURIN, BERNHARD: *Judaica aus der Medina Aschpah. Die Sammlung des Jüdischen Museums Franken in Schnaittach.* Fürth: Jüd. Museum Franken—Fürth und Schnaittach, 2003. 88 pp., illus., bibl. [With Engl. summary.]

42427. SCHWELM. ASCHOFF, DIETHARD: *"Levi zue Schwelm" in Nöten. Zur Frühgeschichte der Juden in Schwelm.* "Jacob Jude" und sein Sohn, die ersten bekannten Juden zu Schwelm. [In]: Beiträge zur Heimatkunde der Stadt Schwelm und ihrer Umgebung, H. 52, Schwelm, 2003. Pp. 49–60, notes. [Deals with the late 16th/early 17th cent.]

42428. SEGEBERG (Bad). GLEISS, FRIEDRICH: *Jüdisches Leben in Segeberg vom 18. bis 20. Jahrhundert.* Gesammelte Aufsätze aus zwei Jahrzehnten mit über 100 Fotos und Dokumenten. Vorwort von Miriam Gillis-Carlebach. Unter Mitarb. von Torsten Mußdorf und Manfred Neumann. Bad Segeberg, Selbstverlag Fr. Gleiss, 2002. 228 pp., illus., facsims. [Cf.: Bespr. (Ole Harck) [in]: Zeitschrift der Gesellschaft für Schleswig-Holsteinische Geschichte, Bd. 128. Neumünster, 2003, pp., 266–268.]

42429. SELIGENSTADT. FIRNER, INGRID: *Jüdisches Leben in Seligenstadt am Main im späten 18. Jahrhundert.* [In]: Archiv für hessische Geschichte und Altertumskunde, N.F., Bd. 60, Darmstadt, 2002. Pp. 129–157, notes.

42430. SIEGEN. STETTNER, HEINER: *23. Juli 1903—Grundsteinlegung für die Synagoge in Siegen. Eine erläuternde Dokumentation.* [In]: Siegener Beiträge. Jahrbuch für regionale Geschichte. Siegen, 2003. Pp. 169–174, notes, illus., facsims.

42431. SOLINGEN. ROSENBAUM, WILHELM: *Jenny Gusyk. Jüdin, Türkin, Solingerin.* [Solingen: W. Rosenbaum; Stadtarchiv Solingen, 2003.] 147 pp., illus. [Documents the story of Jenny Stucke née Gusyk, and her family of Turkish nationality, orig. from Wilkowischky/Vilkaviskis, Lithuania, who grew up in Solingen, studied in Cologne at the Handelshochschule, later lived in Berlin; denounced in June 1943, murdered in Auschwitz Jan. 1944.]

42432. THURINGIA. *Die jüdischen Friedhöfe in Heinrichs und Suhl.* Dokumentation. Erarbeitet von Ulrike Jähnichen. Suhl: Stadtverwaltung, 2002. 315 pp., illus., facsims., chronol., bibl. [Documents the gravestones and their inscriptions; incl. name lists.]

42433. THURINGIA. LITT, STEFAN: *Juden in Thüringen in der Frühen Neuzeit (1520–1650).* Köln: Böhlau, 2003. VIII, 251 pp., footnotes, maps, bibl. (231–244), index. [Diss., Hebrew Univ. Jerusalem, 2001.]

42434. THURINGIA. OLBRISCH, GABRIELE: *Landrabbinate in Thüringen 1811–1871. Jüdische Schul- und Kultusreform unter staatlicher Regie.* Köln: Böhlau, 2003. X, 506 pp., footnotes, tabs., bibl. (471–499), indexes. (Veröff. der Hist. Kommission für Thüringen, Kleine Reihe, Bd. 9.)

42435. THURINGIA. SCHRAMM-HÄDER, ULRIKE: *Jeder erfreut sich der Gleichheit vor dem Gesetze, nur nicht der Jude.* Die Emanzipation der Juden in Sachsen-Weimar-Eisenach (1823–1850). München: Urban und Fischer, 2001. 298 pp., footnotes, bibl. (263–287), index. (Veröffentlichungen der Historischen Kommission für Thüringen: Kleine Reihe, Bd. 5.) Zugl.: Jena, Univ., Diss., 2000 u.d.T.: Zwischen Pro und Contra, die Emanzipation der Juden in Sachsen-Weimar-Eisenach. [Incl. chap. on Jews at Jena University.] [Cf.: Bespr. (J. Friedrich Battenberg) [in]: Archiv für hessische Geschichte und Altertumskunde, N.F., Bd. 60, Darmstadt, 2002, pp. 495–496.]

42436. TRIER. HALLER, ANNETTE: *Der Jüdische Friedhof an der Weidegasse in Trier und die mittelalterlichen jüdischen Grabsteine im Rheinischen Landesmuseum Trier.* Hrsg. im Auftrag der Trierer Gesellschaft für christlich-jüdische Zusammenarbeit von Gunther Franz. Trier: Paulinus Verl. u. Trierer Gesellsch. f. christl.-jüd. Zusammenarbeit, 2003. XXIX, 384 pp., frontis., illus., footnotes, bibl. [Docs. Hebrew inscriptions with German transl.; incl. lists of names.].

42437. TRIER. RASKIN, VLADIMIR, ed.: *Themen des Judentums. Juden im Trierer Land.* [Trier]: Paulinus, 2003. 215 pp., illus. [Title and texts also in Russian; incl.: short contribs. on several aspects of Jewish life in Trier through the ages: the Nazi period (Klaus Fischer, Anne Retza), ancient Trier (Hans-Joachim Kann), Adolf and Alexander Altmann (Norbert Hinske, Giuseppe D'Alessandro), new research at Trier Univ., medieval Jewish history and Yiddish (Christoph Cluse, Simon Neuberg), Jewish immigration to Germany and problems of integration (Heinrich Reuter, Wladimir Tarantul, Wladimir Stalski, Yoram Moyal, Leo Korchemny), the medieval cemetery (Lukas Clemens), Judaica at the Stadtbibliothek Trier, Rheinisches Landesmuseum Trier, Bibliothek des bischöflichen Priesterseminar, Stadtarchiv Trier (Gunther Franz, Hans-Peter Kuhnen, Michael Embach, Bernhard Schmitt, Reiner Nolden); also contribs. on Christian-Jewish relations.]

42438. UNNA. REDEL, M.: *Der jüdische Friedhof in Unna.* [In]: Roland, Zeitschrift der genealogisch-heraldischen Arbeitsgemeinschaft Roland zu Dortmund, e.V., Bd. 12, Jg. 35, H. 2 & 4, Dortmund, 2001. Pp. 36–42 & 80–87. [Part 1 & 2; incl. alphabetical name lists.]

42439. VIERSEN. NUSSBAUM, ISRAEL: *"Gut Schabbes!" Jüdisches Leben auf dem Lande. Aufzeichnungen eines Lehrers (1869–1942).* Ein Textauszug—ausgew. und eingel. von Arie Nabrings. [In]: Heimatjahrbuch des Kreises Viersen, Jg. 55, Viersen, 2003. Pp. 171–175, illus. [For complete edn. see No. 41054/YB XLVIII.]

42440. WARENDORF. SANDMANN, LAURENZ: *Die Synagoge in Warendorf. Zur Baugeschichte des jüdischen Gotteshauses.* [In]: Der Warendorfer Kiepenkerl, Nr. 40, Warendorf, Juni 2002. Pp. 7–10, illus.

42441. WEHEN. WEINBERGER, HANS CHRISTOPH: *Über die Juden in Wehen.* [Taunusstein: Im Hängl 13]: Privately printed, [2003]. 63 pp., illus. [Available at the Bibliothek Germania Judaica, Cologne. Wehen: nr. Wiesbaden.]

42442. WERNE. FERTIG-MÖLLER, HEIDELORE: *Der Jüdische Friedhof in Werne. "Stätte des Lebens" unter Schatten spendendem Grün.* [In]: Jahrbuch Kreis Unna 2002, Unna, [2001]. Pp. 58–61, illus.

42443. WEST PRUSSIA. NOWAK, ZENON HUBERT: *Das Bild der Juden in der deutschen und polnischen Gesellschaft Westpreußens bzw. Pommerellens bis 1939.* [In]: Stereotyp, Identität und Geschichte: die Funktion von Stereotypen in gesellschaftlichen Diskursen. Hrsg.: Hans Henning Hahn [et al.]. Frankfurt am Main; New York: Lang, 2002. Pp. 227–248, footnotes. [Also in this vol.: Das Bild der Juden in der Slowakei in Folklore, Jahrmarktdrucken und in der Literatur (Eva Krekovicová, 249–272).]

42444. WESTPHALIA. FREUND, SUSANNE/REININGHAUS, WILFRIED: *Das "Handbuch der jüdischen Gemeinden und Gemeinschaften in Westfalen und Lippe"—ein neues Projekt der Historischen Kommission für Westfalen.* [In]: Westfälische Forschungen, Bd. 53, Münster, 2003. Pp. 412–417, footnotes.

42445. WESTPHALIA. MINNINGER, MONIKA: *"... olim Judaeus". Jüdische Konvertiten in Ostwestfalen und Lippe 1480–1800.* [In]: Kloster—Stadt—Region. Festschrift für Heinrich Rüthing. Mit einem Geleitwort von Reinhart Koselleck. Hrsg. von Johannes Altenberend [et al.]. Bielefeld: Verlag für

Regionalgesch., 2002. (Sonderveröff. des Hist. Vereins für die Grafschaft Ravensberg, 10.) Pp. 265–290, footnotes.

42446. WESTPHALIA. MÖLLENHOFF, GISELA: *Die 'Allgemeine Zeitung des Judentums' und das 'Israelitische Familienblatt' als historische Quellen zur jüdischen Gemeinde- und Personengeschichte Westfalens.* [In]: Westfälische Forschungen, Bd. 53, Münster, 2003. Pp. 429–445, footnotes.

42447. WESTPHALIA. NAARMANN, MARGIT: *Eine "vernünftige" Auswanderung. Geseke, Paderborn, Amerika: Aufstieg, Verfolgung und Emigration der Familie Grünebaum.* Paderborn: Takt-Verlag, 2002. 222 pp., illus., facsims., gloss., notes. [First part of book incl. memoirs of Ernst Grünebaum (1861–1944), a judge, about family life in Geseke and Paderborn, written before and shortly after emigr. to England; second part deals with Siegmund Grünebaum, owner of the department store Steinberg & Grünebaum, and his family's emigr. to the US. Incl. family tree.]

42448. WESTPHALIA. RIEKER, YVONNE/ZIMMERMANN, MICHAEL: *Zur Geschichte der Juden in Westfalen.* [In]: "Habt den Mut zu menschlichem Tun". Die Jüdin und Demokratin Jeanette Wolff in ihrer Zeit" (1888–1976) [see No. 43486]. Pp. 25–42, notes.

42449. WILDUNGEN (BAD). GRÖTECKE, JOHANNES: *Spurensuche. Ein Rundgang über den jüdischen Friedhof in Bad Wildungen.* 34537 Bad Wildungen: [Druckerei Blind], 2003. 29 pp., illus., facsims. [Also on hotels and shops owned by Jews.]

42450. WORMS. REUTER, FRITZ: *Kirchhöfe, Gottesäcker und Kommunalfriedhöfe in Worms—Zum 100jährigen Bestehen des Friedhofs auf der Hochheimer Höhe 1902–2002.* [In]: Der Wormsgau, Bd. 22, Worms, 2003. Pp. 145–200, illus., docs., footnotes. [Incl. sections on the old and new Jewish cemeteries.]

42451. WÜRTTEMBERG. *Jüdische Gotteshäuser und Friedhöfe in Württemberg.* Hrsg. vom Oberrat der Israelitischen Religionsgemeinschaft Württembergs. Haigerloch: Medien und Dialog Klaus Schubert, 2002. 143 pp., illus. [Reprint edn., orig. publ.: Frankfurt am Main: J. Kauffmann Verlag, 1932.]

——— WÜRTTEMBERG. MÜLLER, HANS PETER: *Antisemitismus im Königreich Württemberg zwischen 1871 und 1914.* [See No. 43610.]

42452. WÜRTTEMBERG. WILSON, PETER H.: *Der Favorit als Sündenbock. Joseph Süß Oppenheimer (1698–1738).* [In]: Der zweite Mann im Staat. Oberste Amtsträger und Favoriten im Umkreis der Reichsfürsten in der Frühen Neuzeit. Hrsg. von Michael Kaiser und Andreas Pecar. Berlin: Duncker & Humblot, 2003. (Zeitschrift für Historische Forschung, Beih. 32.) Pp. 155–176, footnotes.

42453. WÜRZBURG. STEIDLE, HANS: *Jakob Stoll und die Israelitische Lehrerbildungsanstalt—eine Spurensuche.* [Hrsg.: Israelitische Kultusgemeinde Würzburg]. Würzburg: Königshausen & Neumann [Vertrieb], 2002. 127 pp., illus., bibl. [Focuses on the history of the Orthodox teacher training college during the final years of the Weimar Republic and the Nazi period until its closure, and on its last director, Jakob Stoll; also on Seligmann Bär Bamberger, the founder, and other rabbis and teachers at the ILBA.] [J.St., 1876 Massbach (Unterfranken)–1962 New York, educationist, emigr. 1938 to the US, spiritual leader of the German-Jewish refugee congregation Olav Sholaum in Washington Heights.]

42454. WULFEN. KLEIMANN, JÜRGEN: *Der jüdische Friedhof. Ein fast vergessener Ort am Rande Wulfens.* [In]: Heimatkalender der Herrlichkeit Lembeck und Stadt Dorsten 2002, Jg. 61, Dorsten-Lembeck, [2001]. Pp. 145–146, notes.

42455. WUPPERTAL. *"Niemand hat mich wiedererkannt ...". Else Lasker-Schüler in Wuppertal.* Ausgew. und kommentiert von Ulrike Schrader. Hrsg. vom Trägerverein Begegnungsstätte Alte Synagoge Wuppertal [et al.]. Wuppertal: [Begegnungsstätte Alte Synagoge], 2003. 112 pp., illus., facsims., chronol., bibl.

42456. ZEHDENICK. WERNER, HANSJÜRGEN: *Eine SteinZeit Geschichte. Der "Gute Ort" der Kinder von Zehdenick.* Mit einem Vorwort von Paul Spiegel. Blieskastel: Gollenstein, 2002. 188 pp., illus., facsims., gloss., bibl. [Documents the work of pupils of an elementary school in Zehdenick/Brandenburg, who over several years, guided by their teacher, restored the forgotten and neglected cemetery (officially closed 1898).]

42457. ZWICKAU. PESCHKE, HERBERT: *Der Zwickauer Schocken-Konzern.* Anlässlich der Gründung der fünftgrößten Kaufhauskette Deutschlands vor 100 Jahren. [In]: Sächsische Heimatblätter, H. 6, Dresden, 2001. Pp. 319–332, illus., facsims., notes.

1a. **Alsace and Lorraine**

42458. KORNWEITZ, JOSEF ARIE/WALESCH-SCHNELLER, CHRISTIANE/BOLL, GÜNTER: *Zone 30. Rückkehr aus dem Exil.* Freiburg: Modo, 2003. 123 pp., illus. [All texts also in French and Engl.; incl.: Der jüdische Friedhof bei Mackenheim im Unterelsass (Günter Boll, 15–26). Türen, die sich öffnen (Christiane Walesch-Schneller, 35–84); on the Förderverein Ehemaliges Jüdisches Gemeindehaus Breisach e.V.]

42459. LÉVY, MONIQUE: *De l'usage des archives privées. Entre la France et l'allemagne: itinéraire d'un Juif lorrain.* [In]: Archives Juives, No. 36/1, Paris, 2003. Pp. 119–126, port.

——— SCHWARZFUCHS, SIMON: *Alsace and Southern Germany. The creation of a border.* [In]: Jewish emancipation reconsidered. The French and German models [see No. 42228]

42460. *Le yidich en Alsace: textes et documents.* Éd. par Astrid Starck. Mulhouse: Publ. du Credyo, 2003. 241 pp. (Les cahiers du Credyo, 4.)

2. **Austria**

42462. BADEN. MEISSNER, HANS/FLEISCHMANN, KORNELIUS: *Die Juden von Baden und ihr Friedhof.* Baden: Verlag Grasl, 2002. 293 pp., illus., footnotes, bibl., index, plan [attached to book cover]. [Baden: nr. Vienna. Cont.: Geschichte der Badener Juden 1800 bis 1945. Eine Einführung (Hans Meissner, 9–116). Der jüdische Friedhof in Baden (Kornelius Fleischmann, 117–288; incl. German transl. of Hebrew inscriptions; also two name lists.)

42463. BUNZL, MATTI: *Austrian Zionism and the Jews of the New Europe.* [In]: Jewish Social Studies, Vol. 9, No. 2, Bloomington, IN, Winter 2003. Pp. 154–173, notes.

42464. HÖDL, SABINE/STAUDINGER, BARBARA: *"Ob mans nicht bei den juden [...] leichter und wolfailer bekommen müege"? Juden in den habsburgischen Ländern als kaiserliche Kreditgeber (1520–1620).* [In]: Finanzen und Herrschaft. Materielle Grundlagen fürstlicher Politik in den habsburgischen Ländern und im Heiligen Römischen Reich im 16. Jahrhundert. Hrsg. von Friedrich Edelmayer [et al.]. München: Oldenbourg, 2003. Pp. 246–269, footnotes. [On the attempts of Emperor Rudolf II. to finance, with the help of Jewish merchants and bankers the war against the Ottoman Empire and the expenses of the Imperial court.]

42465. *Jiddische Kultur und Literatur aus Österreich.* Hrsg. von Armin Eidherr und Karl Müller im Auftrag der Theodor Kramer Gesellschaft. Wien: Th. Kramer Ges./Drava Verlag, 2003. 275 pp., illus., facsims., notes. (Zwischenwelt 8.) [Incl.: Zentren der jiddischen Kultur in Österreich (Czernowitz, Lemberg, Krakau, Wien) (Armin Eidherr, 19–32). Jiddische Dichter im Wien der Zwischenkriegszeit: Jiddische Gedichte mit Übersetzung (34–43). Tracing Yiddish theatre in Cracow before 1918 (Miroslawa Bulat, 44–56). Jiddische Dramen aus Wien (Brigitte Dalinger, 57–71). Eugen Hoeflich (M.Y. Ben-Gavriêl) und die jiddische Kultur in Wien (Armin A. Wallas, 72–102). Stefan Zweig, Jiddisch und die ostjüdische Kultur (Mark Gelber, 103–115). Franz Kafka als Kritiker und Kenner des jiddischen Theaters und der ostjüdischen Kultur (Marisa Romano, 115–130). Bemerkungen zu Itzik Mangers Czernowitzer Umfeld (Alexander Spiegelblatt (131–142). Itzik Manger, der Prinz der jiddischen Literatur (Edith Silbermann, 143–153). Das

Bild Wiens in der jiddischen Literatur (Gabriele Kohlbauer-Fritz, 154–166). Aspekte jiddischer Prosa am Beispiel von Abraham Mosche Fuchs (Karl Müller, 167–184). Schalom Asch und Wien (Evelyn Adunka, 185–198). Die Verwertung rabbinischer Texte in Schaloms Aschs Roman 'Der Nazarener' ('The Nazarene') (Gerhard Bodendorfer, 199–222). Die Budapester Orpheumgesellschaft (Georg Wacks, 223–249). Zwischen Partei- und Selbstverlag: Die jiddische Literatur und Publizistik in Wien (Thomas Soxberger, 250–263).]

——— SALZBURG. EMBACHER, HELGA M.: *Jewish identities and acculturation in the province of Salzburg in the shadow of antisemitism.* [In]: Toward normality. Acculturation and modern German Jewry [see No. 42255]

42466. ST. PÖLTEN. LIND, CHRISTOPH: *"... sind wir doch in unserer Heimat als Landmenschen aufgewachsen ...".* Der "Landsprengel" der Israelitischen Kultusgemeinde St. Pölten: Jüdische Schicksale zwischen Wienerwald und Erlauf. Linz: Landesverlag, 2002. 399 pp., illus., notes, bibl. (Jüdische Gemeinden, Bd. 3.) [Incl. "aryanisation" and restitution; personal recollections about deportation and concentration camps; "mixed marriages"; Hungarian-Jewish slave labourers; name lists.]

42467. VIENNA. BOTZ, GERHARD/OXAAL, IVAR/POLLAK, MICHAEL/SCHOLZ, NINA, eds.: *Eine zerstörte Kultur. Jüdisches Leben und Antisemitismus in Wien seit dem 19. Jahrhundert.* 2., neu bearb. und erw. Aufl. Wien: Czernin, 2002. 447 pp., frontis., illus., index. [Orig. publ. in 1990, see No. 27115/YB XXXVI; this edn. incl. seven new contribs., eleven are revised. Cont. (some titles abbr.): Einleitung (eds., 13–34). Juden in Österreich vor 1867 (Klaus Lohrmann, 35–46). Die Juden im Wien des jungen Hitler (Ivar Oxaal, 47–66). Soziale Schicht, Kultur und die Wiener Juden um die Jahrhundertwende (Steven Beller, 67–84). "Niemand hat je gefragt, wer jetzt gerade ein Jude oder ein Nichtjude war". Ein Interview mit Hermine Koebl (Ernst Gombrich, 85–96). Kulturelle Innovation und soziale Identität im Wien des Fin de Siècle (Michael Pollak, 97–112). Die Wiener jüdische Kultur und die jüdische Selbsthass-Hypothese (Allan Janik, 113–128). Spezifische Momente und Spielarten des österreichischen und des Wiener Antisemitismus (Peter Pulzer, 129–146). Die Auseinandersetzung zwischen dem Rabbiner Joseph Samuel Bloch und dem Theologen August Rohling (Michael Ley, 147–164). Nuancen in der Sprache der Judenfeinde (Sigurd Paul Scheichl, 165–186). Sozialdemokratie, Antisemitismus und die Wiener Juden (Robert S. Wistrich, 187–198). Die Politik der Jüdischen Gemeinde Wiens zwischen 1890 und 1914 (Walter R. Weitzmann, 197–226). Segregation, Anpassung und Identitäten der Wiener Juden vor und nach dem Ersten Weltkrieg (Marsha L. Rozenblit, 227–240). Politischer Antisemitismus im Wien der Zwischenkriegszeit (Bruce F. Pauley, 241–260). Katholischer Antisemitismus in der Ersten Republik (Anton Staudinger, 261–282). Antisemitismus in den Wiener Pfarren (Nina Scholz, 283–302). Die assimilierte jüdische Jugend im Wiener Kulturleben um 1930 (Richard Thieberger, 303–314). Ausgrenzung, Beraubung und Vernichtung (Gerhard Botz, 315–340). Österreichisch-jüdische Vertriebene in den USA (Albert Lichtblau, 341–356). Jüdisches Leben nach der Schoah (Helga Embacher, 357–374). Letzter Walzer in Wien—ein Nachtrag (George Clare, 375–382). Zur Identität der Wiener Juden nach der Schoah (Ruth Beckermann, 383–442).]

42468. VIENNA. DALINGER, BRIGITTE: *Quellenedition zur Geschichte des jüdischen Theaters in Wien.* Tübingen: Niemeyer, 2003. 281 pp., notes (167–258), indexes. (Conditio Judaica, 42.) [Incl. 79 German and Yiddish texts (transl. into German); also texts dealing with antisemitism.]

42469. VIENNA. ENGEL, AVI: *Making the connection.* [In]: Avotaynu, Vol. 19, No. 4, Bergenfield, NJ, Winter 2003. Pp. 52–54, illus. [On the author's family research leading her to the Jewish cemetery in Vienna.]

42470. VIENNA. FELSENBURG, CLAIRE: *Flüchtlingskinder.* Erinnerungen. Vorwort von Elfriede Jelinek. Bearb. von Rosemarie Schulak. Wien: Theodor Kramer Gesellschaft; Aktionsradius Augarten, 2002. 193 pp., illus. [C.F., 1911 Lemberg–2002 Denver, Colorado, in 1914 fled with her family to Vienna, in 1938 via Switzerland, UK to the US.]

42471. VIENNA. GRUBER, KARLHEINZ [et al.]: *Ernst Epstein 1881–1938—der Bauleiter des Looshauses als Architekt.* Wien: Holzhausen, 2002. 195 pp., illus. (Wiener Persönlicheiten, Bd. 3.) [Catalogue for exhibition with the same title held at the Jewish Museum in Vienna in cooperation with the Albertina, Summer 2002.] [E.E., 1881–1938 Vienna (suicide), architect of more than a hundred buildings in Vienna.]

42472. VIENNA. JACOBS, NEIL G.: *Soirée bei Kohn: Jewish elements in the repertoire of Hermann Leopoldi.* [In]: Zutot 2002, Dordrecht, 2003. Pp. 200–208, footnotes. [H.L., 1888–1959, orig. Hermann Hersch Kohn, popular Viennese "Klaviersänger", emigr. 1939 to the US, returned to Vienna 1947 resuming his career.]

——— VIENNA. KUSCHEY, BERNHARD: *Die Ausnahme des Überlebens. Ernst und Hilde Federn.* Eine biographische Studie und eine Analyse der Binnenstruktur des Konzentrationslagers. [See No. 43290.]

42473. VIENNA. LILLIE, SOPHIE: *Was einmal war. Handbuch der enteigneten Kunstsammlungen Wiens.* Wien: Czernin Verlag, 2003. 1446 pp., illus., bibl., index. (Bibliothek des Raubes, Bd. VIII.) [Incl.: Vorwort (13–20). Documents the art collectors, their biographies, and their looted collections.] [Cf.: Canaletto and the toastmaster (Leo A. Lensing) [in]: TLS, London, Feb. 27, 2004. Was einmal war (Evelyn Adunka) [in]: Illustrierte Neue Welt, Nr. 2/3, Wien, Feb./März 2004, p. 21.]

42474. VIENNA. LOHRMANN, KLAUS: *Jüdisches Wien.* Museen, Gedenkstätten, Synagogen, Friedhöfe, Restaurants, Cafés, Shopping, Business. Berlin: Jüd. Presse, 2003. 1 map. (Kultur-Karte.) [With illus. and texts; Engl. edn.: Jewish Vienna, 2003.]

42475. VIENNA. MALLEIER, ELISABETH: *Jüdische Frauen in Wien 1816–1938. Wohlfahrt—Mädchenbildung—Frauenarbeit.* Wien: Mandelbaum, 2003. 352 pp., illus. Zugl.: Wien, Univ., veränd. Diss., 2000. [Focuses on women's organisations; also on antisemitism.] [Cf.: Jüdische Frauen in Wien (Thierry Elsen) [in]: Zwischenwelt, Jg. 20, Nr. 2, Wien, Sept. 2003, p. 82.]

42476. VIENNA. *Quasi una fantasia. Juden und die Musikstadt Wien.* Hrsg. von Leon Botstein und Werner Hanak im Auftr. des Jüdischen Museums Wien mit Textbeiträgen von Karl Albrecht-Weinberger [et al.]. Wien: Wolke, 2003. 206 pp., illus., facsims., bibl., index, 2 CDs. [Catalogue publ. for the exhibition with the same title at the Palais Eskeles, May 14–Sept. 21 2003. Selected essays (some titles abbr.): Vorwort: "Über einen Juden können Sie bei mir nicht promovieren" (Karl Albrecht-Weinberger, 7–10). Einführung: Tragödie und Ironie des Erfolgs: Juden im Wiener Musikleben, (Leon Botstein, 11–22). Juden und Musik in Wien 1870–1938 (Leon Botstein, 43–64). Jüdische Familien, Komponisten und Musiker in der Wiener Musikszene der ersten Hälfte des 19. Jahrhunderts (Otto Biba, 65–76). Die Verherrlichung Wiens in den Werken jüdischer Operettenkomponisten und -librettisten & Charles Kalman im Gespräch (Sara Trampuz/Wolfgang Dosch, 107–114; 115–122). Frauen und bürgerliche Musikkultur (Elisabeth Derow-Turnauer, 123–130). Erica Morini (Elena Ostleitner, 131–138). Wiens Musikleben der Zwischenkriegszeit (Hartmut Krones, 139–152). Orpheus Trust—Verein zur Erforschung und Veröffentlichung vertriebener und vergessener Kunst (Primavera Gruber, 159–168). Two further essays are listed according to subject.]

——— VIENNA. RAGGAN-BLESCH, MICHAELA: *Der "fehlende Ort". Frauenbewegte Jüdinnen zwischen Antisemitismus und Antifeminismus im Wien der Jahrhundertwende.* [See in No. 43591.]

42477. VIENNA. ROSSBACHER, KARLHEINZ: *Literatur und Bürgertum. Fünf Wiener jüdische Familien von der liberalen Ära zum Fin de Siècle.* Wien: Böhlau, 2003. 667 pp., illus., footnotes, geneal., indexes. (Literatur und Leben, Bd. 64.) [On the Wertheimstein, Gomperz, Todesco, Auspitz and Lieben families.]

42478. VIENNA. SINGER, PETER: *Pushing time away: my grandfather and the tragedy of Jewish Vienna.* New York: Ecco, 2003. XI, 254 pp., illus., ports., genealogy, notes, bibl. [Deals with the author's family history in Vienna, focusing on the grandparents David Ernst Oppenheim (1881 Brünn–1943 Theresienstadt), a high school teacher, and Amalia Pollack, a physicist; also on O.s membership of Freud's weekly salon.] [Cf.: Philospher Peter Singer writes a family history (Ilya Marritz) [in]: Aufbau, Vol. 69, No. 7, New York, April 3, 2003, p. 16.]

42479. VIENNA. *Literature in Vienna at the turn of the centuries: continuities and discontinuities around 1900 and 2000.* Ed. by Ernst Grabovszki and James Hardin. Rochester, NY: Camden House, 2003. VIII, 232 pp., illus., ports., notes, bibl., index. (Studies in German literature, linguistics, and culture.) [Incl. chap.: "Wien bleibt Wien": Austrian-Jewish culture at two fins de siècle. Also on Sigmund Freud, Hugo von Hofmannsthal, Karl Kraus.]

42480. VIENNA. Winterstein, Stefan: *Wien- London und nur halb zurück.* Erich Fried und der Alsergrund. [In]: Wiener Geschichtsblätter, Beih. 3, Wien, 2001. Pp. 16–19, illus. [Also in this issue: "... er war und ist und bleibt ein Urwiener". Das Schnitzler-Memorial im Bezirksmuseum Alsergrund (Wilhelm Urbanek, 20–22).]

3. **Central Europe**

——— BOHEMIA. *Kafkas Fabriken.* [See No. 43339.]

42482. BOHEMIA. Wlaschek, Rudolf M.: *Biographia Judaica Bohemiae.* Bd. 3. Dortmund: Forschungsstelle Ostmitteleuropa, 2003. IX, 56 pp. (Veröffentlichungen der Forschungsstelle Ostmitteleuropa an der Universität Dortmund, Reihe B., Bd. 74.)

42483. BUKOWINA. Hausleitner, Mariana: *Gegen die Zwangsrumänisierung. Die Kooperation von Bukowiner Deutschen, Juden und Ukrainern in der Zwischenkriegszeit.* [In]: WerkstattGeschichte, Jg. 11, H. 32, Hamburg, Nov. 2002. Pp. 31–43, footnotes.

42484. BUKOWINA. Motzan, Peter: *Die ausgegrenzte Generation. Voraussetzungen literarischer Produktion und Barrieren der Rezeption: Alfred Margul-Sperber und seine Bukowiner Weggefährten im Jahrzehnt 1930–1940.* [In]: Deutsche Literatur in Rumänien und das "Dritte Reich". Vereinnahmung—Verstrickung—Ausgrenzung. Hrsg. von Michael Markel und Peter Motzan. München: IKGS Verlag, 2003 (Wissenschaftliche Reihe (Literatur- und Sprachgeschichte), Bd. 94.). Pp. 193–229, footnotes.

42485. CZECHOSLOVAKIA. Nemec, Mirek: *'Die Provinz'. Ein Versuch kultureller Vermittlung zwischen Deutschen und Tschechen.* [In]: Brücken, N.F. 9–10, Prag, 2003. Pp. 221–240, footnotes. [On a short-lived periodical publ. by his publ. company in Weimar in 1924 by Bruno Adler (b. 1888 in Karlsbad).]

42486. CZECHOSLOVAKIA. Srubar, Helena: *Juden in der Tschechoslowakei. Eine Analyse lebensgeschichtlicher Interviews.* München: Osteuropa-Institut, 2002. 127, [53] pp., footnotes, bibl. (Osteuropa-Institut München, Mitteilungen, Nr. 47.) [Two of the four interviewees originate from German-speaking families.]

42487. CZECHOSLOVAKIA. Veselská, Magda: *Oskar Federer—Unternehmer und Kunstsammler.* [In]: Theresienstädter Studien und Dokumente 2003, Prag, 2003. Pp. 240–247, footnotes. [On the director of the Wittkowitzer Eisenwerke.]

42488. CZERNOWITZ. Heymann, Florence: *Le crépuscule des lieux. Identités juives de Czernowitz.* Paris: Stock, 2003. 443 pp.

42489. CZERNOWITZ. *Zwischen Pruth und Jordan.* Lebenserinnerungen Czernowitzer Juden. Von Gaby Coldewey [et al.]. Köln: Böhlau, 2003. XIII, 176 pp., illus., map, gloss. [Incl. 7 chaps. covering life in Czernowitz and Transnistria before, during and after the Second World War, and later life in Palestine/Israel, based on about 50 interviews with men and women from Czernowitz now living in Israel.]

42490. GALICIA. Sadowski, Dirk: *Maskilisches Bildungsideal und josephinische Erziehungspolitik—Herz Homberg und die jüdisch-deutschen Schulen in Galizien 1787–1806.* [In]: Leipziger Beiträge zur jüdischen Geschichte und Kultur, Bd. I, München, 2003. Pp. 145–168, footnotes.

42491. GALICIA. SINKOFF, NANCY: *The 'maskil', the convert, and the 'agunah': Joseph Perl as a historian of Jewish divorce law.* [In]: AJS Review, Vol. 27, No. 2, Nov. 2003. Pp. 281–299, notes. [Deals with the treatise "Über die Modifikation der Mosaischen Gesetze" written by Joseph Perl in Lemberg in the 1830s focusing on a moderate reform of rabbinic law.]

42492. HAUSLEITNER, MARIANA: *Varianten jüdischer Geschichtserfahrung—Moldau, Bukowina, Bessarabien.* [In]: Jahrbuch des Simon-Dubnow-Instituts, Jg. II, München, 2003. Pp. 23–46, footnotes. [Also in this vol.: Port Jews of Odessa and Trieste—a tale of two cities (Patricia Herlihy, 183–198).]

42493. HECKER, HANS/ENGEL, WALTER, eds.: *Symbiose und Traditionsbruch.* Deutsch-jüdische Wechselbeziehungen in Ostmittel- und Südosteuropa (19. und 20. Jahrhundert). Essen: Klartext, 2003. 316 pp., footnotes, index. [Cont. papers presented at a conference at Düsseldorf Univ., Nov. 2000: Symbiose und Traditionsbruch. Deutsch-jüdische Wechselbeziehungen in Ostmittel- und Südosteuropa (19.-20. Jahrhundert). Ein Versuch (Hans Hecker, 9–22). Polen, Tschechen, Deutsche, Juden. Tausend Jahre Nachbarschaft, Rivalität, Vertreibung und Tod (Ferdinand Seibt, 23–32). Die Beziehungen zwischen den Juden und den Sachsen in Siebenbürgen im Zeitalter der Emanzipation (1790–1867) (Ladislau Gyémánt, 33–46). Langzeitwirkungen der deutsch-jüdischen Kulturgemeinschaft in der Bukowina (Emanuel Turczynski, 47–64). Kubbi Wohl—ein Dichter aus der Bukowina im Spannungsfeld deutscher und jiddischer Kultur (Inge Blank, 65–80). Das Verhältnis der Juden in Westgalizien zur polnischen und deutschen Kultur an der Wende vom 19. zum 20. Jahrhundert (Leszek Hondo, 81–94). "Deutsch" und "jüdisch": Wahrnehmungen des anderen und ihre Bedeutung im soziokulturellen Umfeld am Beispiel Galizien (um 1900) (Desanka Schwara, 95–110). Die positive Grenzerfahrung. Lebenslaufperspektiven von Juden an der preußisch-litauischen Grenze (Ruth Leiserowitz, 111–122). Baltendeutsche und jiddische Sprachkontakte im Baltikum (Anna Verschik, 123–134). Wie "deutsch" war die "fortschrittliche" jüdische Bourgeoisie im Königreich Polen? Antworten anhand einiger Beispiele aus Warschau und Lodz (Jürgen Hensel, 135–172). "man sprach deutsch und fühlte nichtmagyarisch ...". Assimilationsprozesse in der deutschen und jüdischen Bevölkerung von Pest-Buda im 19. Jahrhundert (Péter Varga, 173–182). Deutsch oder tschechisch—Entscheidung oder Vorgabe? Zur sprachlichen und politischen Orientierung der Juden in Böhmen im 19. Jahrhundert (Vera Leininger, 183–191). Judentum und Prager deutsche Literatur. Brod, Kafka, Werfel, Kisch (Jürgen Born, 191–200). Deutsch-jüdische Kontakträume in den Ländern der ungarischen Krone vom 18. bis zum beginnenden 20. Jahrhundert. Der städtische Kontaktraum Temeswar (Josef Wolf, 201–310, tabs.).]

42494. HUNGARY. ARNSTEIN, GEORGE: *Jewish life in Eastern Hungary during the 18th century.* [In]: Avotaynu, Vol. 19, No. 3, Bergenfield, NJ, Fall 2003. Pp. 34–38. [Refers also to the Jews who had come from Franconia.]

42495. HUNGARY. EINHORN, IGNAZ: *Die Revolution und die Juden in Ungarn.* Von Ignaz Einhorn (Eduard Horn). Bevorwortet von Dr. Julius Fürst. Nachwort von Ambrus Miskolczy. Hrsg. von Ambrus Miskolczy unter Mitwirkung von Michael K. Silber. Budapest: Universitas Budapest, 2001. 189 pp. footnotes. (Europica Varietas.) [Orig. publ. in Leipzig, 1851. Incl.: Nachwort: Ein Lebenskampf für die Freiheit (ed., 181–189).] [I.E. (1825–1875), rabbi, author, changed his name to Eduard Horn, lived for some years in France, left Judaism without converting.]

42496. HUNGARY. *In the land of Hagar: the Jews of Hungary: history, society and culture.* Ed. by Anna Szalai. Tel Aviv: Beth Hatefutsoth, The Nahum Goldmann Museum of the Jewish Diaspora; Ministry of Defense Publ. House, 2002. 303 pp., illus., ports., facsims., maps.

42497. PETERSEN, HEIDEMARIE: *Judengemeinde und Stadtgemeinde in Polen: Lemberg 1356–1581.* Wiesbaden: Harrassowitz, 2003. VII, 161 pp., footnotes, bibl., index. (Forschungen zur osteuropäischen Geschichte, Bd. 61.) [Covers the numerous connections with German lands.]

42498. PRAGUE. CERMÁK, JOSEF: *Das Kultur- und Vereinsleben der Prager Studenten. Die Lese- und Redehalle der deutschen Studenten in Prag.* [In]: Brücken, N.F. 9–10, Prag, 2003. Pp. 107–190, footnotes. [Describes also the role of German-speaking Jews as mediators between Germans and Czechs; also the growing influence of antisemites. Also in this issue: Franz Kafka und der Mythos (Michel Riffet, 191–204). Modernekritik und literarischer Messianismus bei Max Brod (Ekkehard W. Haring, 205–220).]

42499. PRAGUE. CERMÁK, JOSEF: *Kafka und Prag.* [In]: Deutsche und Tschechen [see No. 42648.] Pp. 217–253.

42500. PRAGUE. HAVRÁNEK, JAN: *Die Juden zwischen Tschechen und Deutschen in Prag.* [In]: Figuren und Strukturen. Historische Essays für Hartmut Zwahr zum 65. Geburtstag. Hrsg. von Manfred Hettling [et al.]. München: Saur, 2002. Pp. 413–422, footnotes, tabs.

42501. PRAGUE. WELLING, MARTIN: *"Von Haß so eng umkreist". Der Erste Weltkrieg aus der Sicht der Prager Juden.* Frankfurt am Main; New York: Lang, 2003. 246 pp., footnotes, bibl. (220–242), index (persons, subjects). (Europäische Hochschulschriften, Reihe III: Geschichte und ihre Hilfswissenschaften, Bd. 957.) Zugl.: Düsseldorf, Univ., Diss., 2003.

42502. PRAGUE. WÖLL, ALEXANDER: *Der Golem: Kommt der erste künstliche Mensch und Roboter aus Prag?* [In]: Deutsche und Tschechen [see No. 42648]. Pp. 153–245.

42503. PRAGUE. ZIMMERMANN, HANS DIETER: *Zwei Prager Philosophen: Felix Weltsch und Tomas Garrigue Masaryk.* [In]: Von Enoch bis Kafka. Festschrift für Karl E. Grözinger zum 60. Geburtstag [see No. 17, von]. Pp. 323–342, illus., notes. [Also on the Hilsner affair and Masaryk's fight against antisemitism; incl. reprint of M.'s review of "Mein Kampf", April 30, 1933.]

4. **Switzerland**

42505. BASLE. MÜLLER, ESTHER: *"Grosse Not uns zu lindern vergönnt war ...". 1903 beherbergte das Schweizerische Israelitische Waisenhaus seine ersten Zöglinge.* [In]: tachles, Jg. 3, Nr. 52/1, Zurich, Dec. 24, 2003. Pp. 6–8, illus.

42506. *Contemporary Jewish writing in Switzerland: an anthology.* Ed. by Rafael Newman. Lincoln: Univ. of Nebraska Press, 2003. XXI, 264 pp., notes, bibl. [Incl. writings by Daniel Ganzfried, Charles Lewinsky, Serguei Hazanov, Gabriel Markus, Luc Bondy, Miriam Cahn, and Stina Werenfels.]

42507. DEJUNG, CHRISTOF/GULL, THOMAS/WIRZ, TANJA: *Landigeist und Judenstempel. Erinnerungen einer Generation 1930–1945.* Mit Fotoporträts von Hans Peter Jost [et al.] Zürich: Limmat, 2002. 503 pp., ports. [Excerpts from a Swiss oral-history project called Archimob. Incl.: "Wir haben rübergeschaut ins Gelobte Land". Ruth Schwob-Bloch, geboren 1919 in Neckarbischofsheim, Deutschland, Flucht vor der nationalsozialistischen Verfolgung, Heirat in der Schweiz (41–49). "Die Nazis urinierten in die Konfitüren". Kurt Bigler, geboren 1925 in Mannheim, nach Frankreich deportiert, Flüchtling, Student, später Gymnasiallehrer in Ins (117–126); also a collection of memoirs entitled 'Antisemitismus in der Schweiz'.]

42508. GROSS, RAPHAEL/LEZZI, EVA/RICHTER, MARC R., eds.: *"Un monde qui avait perdu sa réalité ...".* Survivants juifs de l'Holocauste en Suisse. Traduction de Sophie Pavillon. Lausanne: Ed. Antipodes, 2003. 237 pp., illus., gloss., notes. [For German orig. edn. see No. 37388/YB XLV.]

42509. KURY, PATRICK: *Der "Ostjude" als Zeichen des "ganz Anderen". Ausschlussprozesse in der Schweiz der Zwischenkriegszeit.* [In]: Comparativ, Jg. 13, H. 3, Leipzig, 2003. Pp. 98–113, footnotes.

42510. MANETSCH, RACHEL: *Wer hat die Hausaufgaben nicht gemacht? Antisemitismus in der Schweiz.* [In]: tachles, Jg. 3, Nr. 30, Zürich, 25. Juli 2003. Pp. 6–8.

42511. ZURICH. REISS, ROGER: *Fischl und Chaye. Szenen aus dem Zürcher Stetl.* Berlin: Philo, 2003. 153 pp., illus., gloss. [A collection of stories, partly autobiographical, about Eastern Jewish life in Zurich during the 1950s and 1960s. Also on this topic: Livio Piatti: Schtetl Zürich. Von orthodoxen jüdischen Nachbarn. Mit Texten von Ralph Weingarten [et al.]. Zürich: Offizin, 2001. 175 pp.; cont. mainly photographs of Jewish life in Zurich in the 1990s. Leaflet with Engl. transl. of texts attached to book.] [Cf.: Das jüdische Zürich von einst. Der gebürtige Zürcher Roger Reiss nähert sich seiner eigenen Biografie an (Bettina Spoerri) [in]: tachles, Jg. 3, Nr. 52/1, Zürich, 24. Dez. 2003, pp. 10–12, illus.

42512. ZWEIG-STRAUSS, HANNA: *David Farbstein (1868–1953). Jüdischer Sozialist—sozialistischer Jude.* Zürich: Chronos, 2002. 281 pp., illus., notes (203–232), bibl., index. [Incl. selected speeches and articles by D.F (245–275).] [D.F., Aug. 12, 1868 Warsaw–April 1953, Zurich, lawyer, Zionist activist, Socialist, lived from the 1890s in Zurich, co-organiser of the First Zionist Congress in Basle.]

C. **German-Speaking Jews in Various Countries**

42513. *Auswanderung, Flucht, Vertreibung, Exil im 19. und 20. Jahrhundert.* [Hrsg.: Haus der Geschichte Baden-Württemberg. Red.: Anna-Ruth Löwenbrück]. Berlin: Philo, 2003. 229 pp., notes, index. (Laupheimer Gespräche 2001.) [Selected essays pertaining to German-Jewish history: Jüdische und christliche Immigranten aus Deutschland in den USA 1820–1914 (Avraham Barkai, 73–84). Deutschland verlassen—Auswanderungsmuster von Juden und Nichtjuden in der Weimarer Republik (Doron Niederland, 85–116). Further essays are listed according to subject.]

42514. BOAS, FRANZ. KAUFMANN, DORIS: *"Rasse und Kultur". Die amerikanische Kulturanthropologie um Franz Boas (1858–1942) in der ersten Hälfte des 20. Jahrhunderts—ein Gegenentwurf zur Rassenforschung in Deutschland.* [In]: Rassenforschung an Kaiser-Wilhelm-Instituten vor und nach 1933. Hrsg. von Hans-Walther Schmuhl. Göttingen: Wallstein, 2003. (Geschichte der Kaiser-Wilhelm-Gesellschaft im Nationalsozialismus, Bd. 4.) Pp. 309–327, footnotes. [On Franz Boas see also in No. 42532.] [F.B., 1858 Minden–1942 New York, ethnologist, anthropologist, founding father the American cultural anthropology, lecturer in Geography at Berlin Univ., in 1887 went to New York, 1899–1933 Prof. of Anthropology at Columbia Univ.]

——— BOUREL, DOMINIQUE: *Von Glogau nach Paris: Deutsch-jüdische Gelehrte in der französischen Kultur.* [See in No. 43180.]

42515. DOUBEK, KATJA: *Blue Jeans. Levi Strauss und die Geschichte einer Legende.* München: Piper, 2003. 360 pp., illus. [Based on biographical and archival material, tells the story of Löb/Levi Strauss from Buttenheim near Bamberg, who emigr. 1847 to the US to become as the "inventor" of jeans, one of the most successful manufacturers of his time.]

42516. ESSER, BARBARA: *Sag beim Abschied leise Servus: eine Liebe im Exil.* Wien: Kremayr und Scherlau, 2002. 349 pp., illus., bibl. [On Fred S. Tysh and his wife, Ilse Lönhardt.] [Fred. S. Tysh, orig. Salomon Siegfried Tisch, 1905 Tornow (Galicia), librettist, lived from 1915 in Vienna, in June 1938 deported to Dachau, later to Buchenwald, emigr. 1939 to the UK, resumed his career as a librettist ("My heart and I").]

42517. EXILE. *Adressat Fritz Lang, Hollywood* [issue title of] Filmexil 17, München, Mai 2003. 71 pp., illus., facsims., notes. [Part of this issue deals with several people who wrote to Fritz Lang asking for help; incl.: "Und lass Dir die Hand drücken". Adolf Edgar Licho (Wolfgang Jacobsen, 4–8). Wege des Ruhms. Albert und Elsa Bassermann (Heike Klapdor, 9–16). "Die Menschen reden so viel u. helfen so wenig!" Hanns Brodnitz (Wolfgang Jacobsen, 20–32). Also in this issue: Vier Charakteristika. Rudolf Arnheim (Thomas Meder, 39–43). "Columbus discovered America, and I discovered Hollywood". Otto Katz und die Hollywood Anti-Nazi League (Marcus G. Patka, 44–65).]

42518. EXILE. ANDRESS, REINHARD: *"Der Inselgarten"—das Exil deutschsprachiger Schriftsteller auf Mallorca, 1931–1936.* Amsterdam: Rodopi, 2001. VIII, 208 pp. (Amsterdamer Publikationen zur Sprache und Literatur, 144.) [Incl.: Martha Brill. Die Beschäftigung mit Marannen (110–122, notes); see also No. 43505.]

42519. EXILE. *Deutschsprachige Exilliteratur seit 1933.* Bd. 3, Teil 4: USA. Hrsg. von John M. Spalek, Konrad Feilchenfeldt und Sandra H. Hawrylchak. Zürich: Saur, 2003. XI, 557 pp. [Cont. the sections: Autoren (3–335); incl.: Erich Heller (Volker Dürr, 57–77). Siegfried Kracauer (Ingrid

Belke, 78–126). Heinz Liepman (Wilfried Weinke, 127–151). Eugene Vale (Richard Benter/Johannes Evelein, 225–248; orig. Jakob Hermann Weissmann). Sammel- und thematische Aufsätze (336–557); selected essays: Deutschsprachige Buchillustrationen im US-amerikanischen Exil (Rosamunde Neugebauer, 336–356; incl. Grete Bernheim Weiskopf). Papagei und Mamagei—Kinder und Jugendliteratur im amerikanischen Exil (Ursula Seeber, 357–374). Exil-Kabarett in New York (Regina Thumser/Christian Klösch, 375–415). Religiöser Konfessionswechsel im Exil und 'Apologia pro vita sua' als Beitrag zur Exilliteratur (Robert McFarland, 416–440). Doppelte Verbannung: Politisches Renegatentum im Exil (Andrea Reiter, 469–499; on Ruth Fischer, Hans Sahl et al.). Das Bild Roosevelts im deutschsprachigen Exil in den USA (Richard Critchfield, 500–513). Die Hollywood Anti-Nazi League 1936–1940. Eine "Volksfront" in Amerika (Johanna W. Roden, 514–531). Alice in Wonderland: deutschsprachige Künstler im amerikanischen Black Mountain College (1933–1956) (Karl-H. Füssl, 532–557.).]

42520. EXILE. *Deutschsprachige Exilliteratur seit 1933*. Bd. 3, Teil 3: USA. Hrsg. von John M. Spalek, Konrad Feilchenfeldt und Sandra H. Hawrylchak. Bern: Saur, 2002. IX, 541 pp., notes. [For previous two vols. with the title Deutsche Exilliteratur seit 1933 see Nos. 39230/YB XLVI and 40428/YB XLVII. Incl. the sections: Autoren (3–216; contribs. on exile writers). Sammel- und thematische Aufsätze; cont.: Lyrikerinnen im amerikanischen Exil (Sigrid Bauschinger, 217–242). Der Aphorismus im Exil (Friedmann Spicker, 243–271). Die deutschsprachige Verlegeremigration in den USA nach 1933 (Ernst Fischer, 272–306). Vortragstätigkeit der Exilschriftsteller in den USA (Helga Schreckenberger, 307–333). Gibt es eine Rückkehr aus dem Exil? (Wulf Köpke, 334–363). Dorothy Thompson. Eine Schlüsselfigur der Welt des Exils (Kerstin Feller, 364–409). Anti-Nazi-Filme des deutschen Exils (Jan-Christopher Horak, 410–426). Die Rezeption der Exilliteratur in der marxistischen deutsch-amerikanischen Presse (Reinhard K. Zachau, 427–440). Wartesaal Lissabon 1940–1941 (Christina Heine Texeira (441–481). "Jewish Club of 1933, Inc."—ein deutsches Kulturzentrum am Pazifischen Ozean (Johanna W. Roden, 482–494). The American Guild for German Cultural Freedom und die Deutsche Akademie im Exil (Brita Eckert/Werner Berthold, 495–525). Congress for Cultural Freedom (Michael Hochgeschwender, 526–541).]

42521. EXILE. *Film and exile*. [Issue title of] New German Critique, No. 89, Ithaca, NY, Spring-Summer 2003. 1 issue, footnotes. [Incl.: A stranger in the house: Fritz Lang's Fury and the cinema of exile (Anton Kaes, 33–58). Space out of joint: Ernst Lubitsch's To be or not to be (Gerd Gemünden, 59–80). Doubling the double: Robert Siodmak in Hollywood (Lutz Koepnick, 81–104). Hollywood's terror films: do they reflect an American state of mind? (Siegfried Kracauer, 105–111). Siegfried Kracauer, "Hollywood terror films," and the spatiality of film noir (Ed Dimendberg, 113–142). Homeward bound? Peter Lorre's The lost man and the end of exile (Jennifer M. Kapczynski, 145–171). Also incl. as documents: What's wrong with anti-Nazi films (Klaus Mann, first publ. in 1941). Are Jewish themes "Verboten?" (Ruth Karp, first publ. in Aufbau, Aug. 27, 1943, p. 11.) What our immigration did for Hollywood—and vice versa (Hans Kafka, first publ. in Aufbau, Dec. 27, 1944, p. 40–41).]

——— EXILE. *Intellektuelle im Exil*. [Section title of] Arendt und Adorno. Hrsg. von Dirk Auer, Lars Rensmann und Julia Schulze Wessel. [See No. 43212.]

42522. EXILE. KLÖSCH, CHRISTIAN/THUMSER, REGINA: *"From Vienna". Exilkabarett in New York 1938 bis 1950*. Österreichische Exilbibliothek. Wien: Picus, 2002. 176 pp., illus., facsims., bibl., index. [Book publ. for an exhibition with the same title, held at the Literaturhaus, Vienna. Incl. short biographies of the artists/authors.]

42523. EXILE. NAMAL, ARIN: *Prof. Dr. Max Sgalizer (1884–1974). Ein österreichischer Leiter des Radiologischen Instituts der Universität Istanbul*. [In]: Zeitgeschichte, Jg. 30, H. 1, Salzburg, Jan./Feb. 2003. Pp. 37–49, notes. [Based on documents at Istanbul University's archives, article deals with M.S.'s five years at Istanbul Univ. after his expulsion from Vienna Univ. in 1938.]

42524. EXILE. *Österreicher im Exil: Mexiko 1938–1947*. Eine Dokumentation. Hrsg.: Dokumentationsarchiv des österreichischen Widerstandes. Einl., Ausw. und Bearb.: Christian Kloyber, Marcus G. Patka. Mit einem Geleitwort von Friedrich Katz. Wien: Deutecke, 2002. 704 [14] pp., illus., chronol., bibl., index.

42525. EXILE. *Refugees from the Third Reich in Britain.* [Issue title of] Yearbook of the Research Centre for German and Austrian Exile Studies. Vol. 4. Ed. by Anthony Grenville. Amsterdam: Rodopi, 2002. VII, 217 pp., illus., notes, index. [Cont.: 'A noteworthy contribution in the fight against Nazism': Hubertus Prinz zu Löwenstein im Exil (Elke Seefried, 1–26). 'A wandering scholar' in Britain and the USA, 1933–45: the life and work of Moritz Bonn (Patricia Clavin, 27–42). 'England find ich gut!': Facetten aus Leben und Werk des Autors Robert Muller (Wilfried Weinke, 43–72). 'Es soll diese Spur doch bleiben ...': Hans Jacobus: exile, national socialism and the Holocaust (Steven W. Lawrie, 73– 96). Eulenspiegel to Owlyglass: the impact of the work of the exiled illustrators Walter Trier and Fritz Wegner on British children's literature (Gillian Lathey, 97–116). 'Although he is Jewish, he is M & S': Jewish refugees from Nazism and Marks & Spencer from the 1930s to the 1960s (Ulrike Walton-Jordan, 117–133). Into exile: Ernst Sommer in London (Jennifer Taylor, 135–149). Exil in Grossbritannien: die Keramikerin Grete Loebenstein-Marks (Ursula Hudson-Wiedenmann, 151–172). Selma Kahn: a provincial exile (Andrea Hammel, 173–186). AJR Information in the context of German-language exile journal publication, 1933–1945 (Jon Hughes, 187–198). Listening to refugee voices: the Association of Jewish Refugees. Information and research on the refugees from Hitler in Britain (Anthony Grenville, 199–211).]

42526. EXILE. SCHRECKENBERGER, HELGA: *Ästetiken des Exils.* Amsterdam; New York: Rodopi, 2003. 403 pp., footnotes. (Amsterdamer Beiträge zur neueren Germanistik, Bd. 54—2003.) [Cont. papers given at a conference at the Univ. of Vermont, Sept. 1998. Selected essays (some titles abbr.): Einleitung (ed., 9–14). Aesthetics of internment art in Britain during the Second World War (Jutta Vinzent, 71–92). Anti-Nazi-Cartoons deutschsprachiger Emigranten in Großbritannien (Rosamunde Neugebauer, 93–122). Alfred Kerr's unknown film scripts written in exile (Deborah Vietor-Engländer, 123–140). Der "kleine Mann" als Übermensch in Stefan Heyms Thriller 'Hostages' (1942) (Reinhard Zachau, 141–156). Mascha Kalékos Exil im Exil (Karina von Tippelskirch, 157–172). Das Exil als biographischer und ästhetischer Kontinuitätsbruch: Von Hans Sochaczewer zu José Orabuena (Thomas Schneider, 173–186). Rückbesinnung auf jüdische Traditionen im amerikanischen Exil am Beispiel der Künstlerin Lulu Kayser-Darmstädter (Petra Weckel, 187–208). Wurde Lion Feuchtwanger durch das Exil zum Trivialautor? (Karl Kröhnke, 251–264). Drei Exil-Gedichte Erich Frieds aus den frühen 40er Jahren (Jörg Thunecke, 265–286). Zur Funktion der Erinnerung in Anna Seghers Erzählung "Der Ausflug der toten Mädchen" (Heike Doane, 287–300). Reise-Erinnerungen—die nachgetragenen Exilerfahrungen Fred Wanders (Hannes Krauss, 319–332). Zur deutschsprachigen Rezeption von Jakov Lind (Ursula Seeber, 333–352). Hilde Domins Rückkehr aus dem Exil als Ursprung und Voraussetzung ihrer Poetologie (Dieter Sevin, 353–364). Paul Celans Bremer Rede (Leonard Olschner, 365–386). The impact of rescued artists on European and American culture (Guy Stern, 387–403).]

——— EXILE. UBBENS, IRMTRAUD: *Aus meiner Sprache verbannt: Moritz Goldstein, ein deutsch-jüdischer Journalist und Schriftsteller im Exil.* [See No. 43303.]

42527. FLESCH, CARL F.: *"Woher kommen Sie?" Hitlerflüchtlinge in Großbritannien damals und heute.* Hamburg: Krämer, 2003. 230 pp. (Beiträge zur deutschen und europäischen Geschichte, Bd. 30.) [Incl. a preface by Wolf D. Gruner (9–13; on the author's biography). Personal memoirs combined with reflections on the situation of "refugees" past and present. For Engl. orig. edn. see No. 39849/YB XLVII.] [C.F.Flesch, b. 1910 in Austria, insurance agent, author, grew up in Germany, emigr. to UK in 1934, lives in London.]

42528. GARNHAM, ALISON: *Hans Keller and the BBC: the musical conscience of British Broadcasting, 1959–79.* Aldershot; Burlington, VT: Ashgate, 2003. XII, 194 pp., illus., notes, index. [H.K., Vienna 1919–London 1985, musician, music critic, emigr. to UK in 1938, violin and viola player in various orchestras and string ensembles, music adviser to the British Film Institute, co-founder of 'Music Survey', 1959–1979 member of BBC Music Division.]

42529. JACOB, WALTER, ed.: *Gardening from the bible to North America.* Essays in honor of Irene Jacob. Pittsburgh, PA: Rodef Shalom Press, 2003. VI, 138 pp., frontis., illus., bibl. I.J. [I.J., née Loewenthal, b. April 20, 1928 in Hamburg, horticulturist, ethnobotanist, plant therapist, garden designer, wife of Walter Jacob (see No. 43022).]

42530. *German-Jewish identities in America.* Ed. and introd. by Christof Mauch and Joseph Salmons. Madison, WI: Univ. of Wisconsin, Max Kade Institute for German- American studies, 2003. XI, 171 pp., illus., footnotes, bibl., index. [Papers presented at a conference held Oct. 2000 at the Max Kade Institute, Univ. of Wisconsin. Incl. chaps.: German Jews and the American-Jewish synthesis (Henry Feingold, 8–20). Franz Boas as German, American, and Jew (Mitchell B. Hart, 88–105). German Jews and American show business: a reconsideration (Harley Erdman, 106–116). German Jews and Ostjuden in the American South: Alfred Uhry's Last night of Ballyhoo (Thomas Kovach, 117– 132; on a play depicting the life of German Jews in the South). "I always thought I was a German—it was Hitler who taught me I was a Jew": National-Socialist persecution, identity, and the German language (Monika S. Schmid, 133–151, tabs., facsims.). German Jew or Jewish German?: post-immigration questions (Manfred Kirchheimer, 154–162).]

42531. GRILL, TOBIAS: *Odessa's German rabbi—The paradigmatic meaning of Simon Leon Schwabacher (1881–1888).* [In]: Jahrbuch des Simon-Dubnow-Instituts, Jg. II, München, 2003. Pp. 199–222, footnotes.

42532. GRÖLL, BARTHOLOMÄUS: *Momente der Entscheidung, 28: Herr der Diamanten. Globalisierung brutal: Wie Ernest Oppenheimer ein Edelstein-Imperium schuf.* [In]: Die Zeit, Nr. 41, Hamburg, 1. Okt. 2003. P. 34, illus. [E.O., 1880 Friedberg–1957 South Africa, diamond tycoon, chief executive of De Beers, went to South Africa in 1902.]

42533. KAPP, YVONNE: *Time will tell: memoirs.* Ed. by Charmian Brinson and Betty Lewis. With a preface by Alison Light. London: Verso, 2003. XV, 296 pp., illus., ports., facsims. [First part of book deals with the author's various German-Jewish ancestors from Bielefeld, Cologne, Worms and Karlsruhe, one of whom, a wool merchant, emigr. to the UK in the 1870s.] [Y.K., née Mayer, London 1903–Bradford 1999, journalist, political activist, novelist; was very active on behalf of German-Jewish refugees.]

42534. KUBISCH, BERND: *Der Weg zur Synagoge führt über Vulkane.* Wie aus zwei Schulbuben aus Deutschland erfolgreiche Firmenchefs in Ecuadors Anden wurden. [In]: tachles, Jg. 3, Nr. 30, Zürich, 25. Juli 2003. Pp. 28–30, illus. [On Kurt Dorfzaun, orig. from Bavaria, and Kurt Heimbach, orig. from Westphalia, both now living in Cuenca.]

42535. KÜPPERS, TOPSY: *Wolf Messing. Hellseher und Magier.* München: Langen Müller, 2002. 374 pp., illus., index. [On the magician and clairvoyant (1899 Gora Kalvaria–1974 Moscow) who had a successful career in Poland, Germany, Austria, Hungary, France, and finally in the Soviet Union.]

42536. LUBICH, FREDERICK A.: *Twilight memories: the eclipse of German Jewish culture in Argentina.* [In]: The Germanic Review [with the issue title] A Festschrift to Inge Halpert [see No. 43307]. Pp. 55–61, notes.

42537. PAUCKER, ARNOLD: *Speaking English with an accent.* [In]: Deutsche Juden im Kampf um Recht und Freiheit [see No. 43407]. Pp. 339–353, notes. [On problems of integration; incl. the author's own experiences in England, his home for more than fifty years.]

42538. PERRY, YARON/LEV, EFRAIM: *The medical activities of the London Jews' Society in nineteenth-century Palestine.* [In]: Medical History, Vol. 47, No. 1, London, 2003. Pp. 67–88, footnotes. [Incl. Jews, resp. converted Jews, from Germany.]

42539. POLLAK, JOAN F.: *Bridging a century's divide.* [In]: Avotaynu, Vol. 19, No. 4, Bergenfield, NJ, Winter 2003. Pp. 59–62, ports. [Researches into the author's ancestors, Gerson Heilbroner and his family, who came from Bavaria and went to the US in the 1840s.]

42540. RICH, MICHAEL W.: *Henry Mack: An important figure in nineteenth-century American Jewish history.* [In]: Stammbaum, Issue 23, New York, Summer 2003. Pp. 1–10, notes. [Deals with the textile merchant and early leader of the American Jewish Reform movement, H.M., orig. Elkan M., b. 1820 in Demmelsdorf nr. Bamberg, who in 1839 emigr., together with his brother Abraham, to the US and settled in 1846 in Cincinnati, followed by other members of the family.]

42541. SCHMIED, IRENE KATZENSTEIN: *For the children. A memorial to the Kindertransport in London.* [In]: Aufbau, Vol. 69, No. 20, New York, Oct. 16, 2003. P. 12, illus. [On the unveiling ceremony of a sculpture at London's Liverpool Street Station.]

42542. SÖLLNER, ALFONS: *Jüdische Emigranten in den USA: Ihr Einfluss auf die amerikanische Deutschlandpolitik 1933–1949.* [In]: "Gegen alle Vergeblichkeit". Jüdischer Widerstand gegen den Nationalsozialismus [see No. 42899]. Pp. 365–387, footnotes.

42543. *'Stimme der Wahrheit': German-language broadcasting by the BBC.* [Issue title of] Yearbook of the Research Centre for German and Austrian Exile Studies. Vol. 5. Ed. by Charmian Brinson and Richard Dove. Amsterdam; New York: Rodopi, 2003. XV, 250 pp., footnotes, index. [Incl. papers from a conference on the German-language broadcasting of the BBC, held in London in 2002. Section headings: 'London calling': broadcasting to the enemy. Broadcasting for a Post-war Germany. The BBC German Service remembered. Selected essays: Grete Fischer: 'outside writer' for the BBC (Jennifer Taylor, 43–56). 'Ein Urviech und eine Seele von Mensch': Erich Fried at the BBC (Steven Lawrie, 117–138). Über alle Hindernisse hinweg: London-Remigranten in der westdeutschen Rundfunkgeschichte (Hans-Ulrich Wagner, 139–158). Changing the guard: the transition from emigrés to recruits on the staff of the BBC's German Service (Alfred Starkmann, 185–196).]

42544. ZWEIG, STEFANIE: *Strangers in a strange land.* [In]: The Guardian, London, March 21, 2003. P. 9. [Author describes how, as Jewish refugees from Nazi Germany, her family found sanctuary in Kenya and then returned to Germany after the war. The story was made into the film "Nowhere in Africa".]

II. RESEARCH AND BIBLIOGRAPHY

A. **Libraries and Institutes**

42545. ARCHIV BIBLIOGRAPHIA JUDAICA, FRANKFURT: *Dokumentation zur jüdischen Kultur in Deutschland 1840–1940.* [Mikroform]. Die Zeitungsauschnittssammlung Steininger/Archiv Bibliographia Judaica e.V. ed.: Abt. 5, Teil 2 = Lfg. 2. Rabbiner. Suppl. München: Saur, 2003. 39 Microfiches. [Also issued in 2003: Abt. 6, Persönlichkeiten des öffentlichen Lebens, Lfg. 1. 32 Mikrofiches (incl. 2 index fiches).] [Cf.: Im Zweifel Frankfurt fragen. Das Archiv Bibliographia Judaica leistet seit zwanzig Jahren literaturhistorische Forschung (Katharina Sommer) [in]: Jüdische Allgemeine, Jg. 58, Nr. 26, Berlin, 27. Nov. 2003, p. 13.]

42546. CENTRAL ZIONIST ARCHIVES, JERUSALEM: *Guide to the archival record groups and collections.* Jerusalem: [Central Zionist Archives], July 2003. 60 & 51 pp. [Text and title also in Hebrew.]

42547. DEUTSCHES EXILARCHIV 1933–1945/DIE DEUTSCHE BIBLIOTHEK, FRANKFURT AM MAIN: *Deutsches Exilarchiv 1933–1945 und Sammlung Exil-Literatur 1933–1945.* Katalog der Bücher und Broschüren. [Bearb.: Mechthild Hahner. Wiss. Leitung: Brita Eckert]. Stuttgart: Metzler, 2003. XVIII, 614 pp., indexes (571–614). (Deutsches Exilarchiv 1933–1945, Bd. 2.) [Lists all publs. up to 1995, year of purchase; first vol. publ. 1989.]

42548. ERNST, WOLFGANG: *Im Namen von Geschichte. Sammeln—Speichern—Er/zählen. Infrastrukturelle Konfigurationen des deutschen Gedächtnisses.* München: Fink, 2003. 1140 pp., footnotes, bibl. (1067–1106), index. [Deals with the "MGH", archives, museums, libraries, inventories, statistics; incl.: Kontraststudie: Museum oder Grab? Das "Zentralmuseum jüdischer Altertümer" in Prag (421–443). Kehrseite: Jüdische Archivlektüren und Gedächtnislöschung (728–756).]

42549. FRITZ-BAUER-INSTITUT, FRANKFURT AM MAIN DECKER, JUDITH: *Unrecht am eigenen Leib erfahren.* Fritz Bauer 1903–1968. [In]: Tribüne, Jg. 42, H. 167, Frankfurt am Main, 2003. Pp. 71–75. [On Fritz Bauer, the Fritz-Bauer-Institut and the Fritz-Bauer prize, instituted in 1968 after B.'s death.]

42550. GERSMANN, GUDRUN: *Spurensuche: Portale zur jüdischen Geschichte im Internet.* [In]: Geschichte in Wissenschaft und Unterricht, Jg. 54, H. 3, Stuttgart, 2003. Pp. 179–181. [A review of eight internet sites.]

42551. GERMANIA JUDAICA, COLOGNE: *Deutschsprachige Zeitungen aus Palästina und Israel/German newspapers from Palestine and Israel.* Mikroficheausgabe. Hrsg. von Friedrich Reichenstein und der Germania Judaica—Kölner Bibliothek zur Geschichte des deutschen Judentums e.V. Abt. 1: Palästina 1935–1948. München: Saur, 2003. 345 Fiches. [Incl.: 'Jedioth Chadashot' and 'Yedioth Hayom'. Will be continued.]

42552. HEBREW UNIVERSITY, JERUSALEM. DISSELNKÖTTER, ANDREAS/ZABEL, HERMANN: *Deutsch in Israel: Eine Bestandsaufnahme.* Aachen: Shaker, 2002. 162 pp. [First part of book deals with the "Walter-A.-Berendsohn-Sammlung für Exilliteratur an der Deutschen Abteilung der Hebräischen Universität Jerusalem".]

42553. INSTITUT TEREZINSKÉ INICIATIVY/INSTITUT THERESIENSTÄDTER INITIATIVE, PRAG: *Theresienstädter Studien und Dokumente 2003.* Hrsg.: Jaroslava Milotová, Ulf Rathgeber, Michael Wögerbauer. Prag: Sefer, 2003. 395 pp., frontis., illus., facsims., tabs., footnotes, index. [Also publ. in Czech. Individual contribs. are listed according to subject.]

42554. LANDESARCHIV BERLIN. HALLE, ANNA SABINE: *Über Nichtglaubensjuden—Anmerkungen zu einem Begriff und einem Archivbestand.* [In]: Exil, Jg. 23, No. 1, Frankfurt am Main, 2003. Pp. 89–96, notes. [On a collection, orig. from the Quakers, relating to "non-Aryans".]

42555. LEO BAECK INSTITUTE: *Jüdischer Almanach* [2003] *des Leo Baeck Instituts* [with the issue title] Kindheit. Hrsg. von Gisela Dachs. Frankfurt am Main: Jüd. Verlag im Suhrkamp Verlag, 2003. 176 pp., illus. [Articles pertaining to German-speaking Jewry are listed according to subject.]

42556. LEO BAECK INSTITUTE: *LBI Information.* Nachrichten aus den Leo Baeck Instituten in Jerusalem, London, New York und der Wissenschaftlichen Arbeitsgemeinschaft des LBI in Deutschland. Hrsg. von den Freunden und Förderern des LBI e.V. in Frankfurt/Main. Frankfurt am Main: [Privately printed], 2003. 101 pp., XX pp. [Incl.: Editorial (Georg Heuberger, 5–6). Wir nähern uns fünfzig Jahren (Michael A. Meyer, 7–8). Also reports on the three institutes and on publications and conferences. Incl., as an appendix: Deutsch-jüdische Geschichte im Unterricht. Orientierungshilfe für Lehrplan- und Schulbucharbeit sowie Lehrerbildung und Lehrerfortbildung (XX pp.), see No. 42979.]

42557. LEO BAECK INSTITUTE, LONDON: *Leo Baeck Institute Year Book 2003*, Vol. XLVIII. J.A.S. Grenville, Raphael Gross, eds., Joel Golb, Gabriele Rahaman, manuscript eds. Oxford: Berghahn Books, 2003. X, 448 pp., frontis., illus., facsims., footnotes, bibl. (249–433), general index (437–448). [Cont.: Preface (eds., IX-X). Essays are arranged under the sections: I. Religious renewal. II. Jewish social life. Antisemitism and Jewish reactions in Imperial Germany and during the Weimar Republic. III. Shattered hopes under National Socialism. IV. Yad Vashem and the German "righteous". Individual contribs. are listed according to subject.]

42558. LEO BAECK INSTITUTE, NEW YORK. BLOCH, TALIA: *Listening to the Jewish Voice.* A conference at the Leo Baeck Institute in New York City. [In]: Aufbau, Vol. 69, No. 19, New York, Oct. 2, 2003. P. 18, illus. [On a conference entitled 'The Jewish voice in German-American relations', focusing on the contemporary Jewish community in Germany.]

42559. LEO BAECK INSTITUTE, JERUSALEM. WEIGERT, REUVEN: *Memories, documents, diaries until mid-19th century.* [In Hebrew.] Jerusalem: LBI Jerusalem, 2002. 1 vol. [Summaries of the archival files at the LBI Jerusalem. Also, by same author: Memories, documents, diaries 1850–1993. Jerusalem: LBI Jerusalem, 2003. 1 vol.]

42560. LEO BAECK INSTITUTE, NEW YORK/BERLIN: *Overview 2003.* [New York]: [LBI New York], 2003. 57 pp. [On recent activities, projects and developments.]

42561. NIEDERSÄCHSISCHE LANDESBIBLIOTHEK, HANNOVER: *Christlich-jüdischer Dialog in der Frühen Neuzeit.* Kostbarkeiten aus der Judaica-Sammlung der Niedersächsischen Landesbibliothek. Eine Ausstellung im Rahmen der Israelischen Kulturwochen in Niedersachsen vom 15. Mai bis 12. Juli 2003 in Hannover. [Text: Verena Dohrn unter Mitarb. von Anke Griesbach] [Hannover]: Nieders. Landesbibliothek, [2003]. 87 pp., notes.

——— NÜRNBERGER INSTITUT FÜR NS-FORSCHUNG UND JÜDISCHE GESCHICHTE DES 20. JAHRHUNDERTS: *nurinst 2002. Beiträge zur deutschen und jüdischen Geschichte.* [See No. 42347.]

42562. ROSTOCK UNIVERSITY LIBRARY: *Die hebräischen Drucke. Teil 1: Die altjiddischen (jüdisch-deutschen) Drucke der Universitätsbibliothek Rostock.* Bearb. von Hermann Süß. Erlangen: Fischer, 2003. 172 pp., indexes (155–172, titles, authors, publishers and printers, print locations). (Kataloge der Univ. Rostock, Bd. 3.) [Mostly from the private collection of Oluf Gerhard Tychsens.]

42563. SIMON-DUBNOW-INSTITUT LEIPZIG: *Leipziger Beiträge zur jüdischen Geschichte und Kultur.* Bd. I, 2003. Simon-Dubnow-Institut für jüdische Geschichte und Kultur an der Universität Leipzig. [Red.: Christoph Böwing, Übers. ins Engl.: William Templer.] München: Saur, 2003. 408 pp., illus., footnotes. [Cont.: Editorial (Dan Diner, 9–10). Essays are arranged under the sections: Begriff und Geschichte (13–62). Frühe Zeiten (65–119). Zeit der Aufklärung (123–195). Räume und Topoi (199–279). Zeit der Finsternis (283–346). Orte des Bewahrens (349–382). Wege der Forschung (385–396). Incl. abstracts (397–403). Individual essays pertaining to German-speaking Jewry are listed according to subject.]

42564. SIMON-DUBNOW-INSTITUT, LEIPZIG: *Jahrbuch des Simon-Dubnow-Instituts/Simon Dubnow Institute Yearbook.* [Red.: Christoph Bowing, Übers. aus dem Engl.: William Templer]. Bd. II, München, Deutsche Verlags-Anstalt, 2003. 599 pp., footnotes. [Cont.: Editorial (Dan Diner, 9–12). Zwischen Triest, Saloniki und Odessa—Über balkanische und angrenzende Judenheiten (15–150). Schwerpunkt: Das jüdische Odessa (mithrsg. und betreut von Guido Hausmann, 151–386). Jüdische Historiker (387–408). Aus der Forschung; cont.: Probing the legal history of the Jews in the Holy Roman Empire—norms and their application (Stefan Ehrenpreis/Andreas Gotzmann/Stephan Wendehorst, 409–412). At home in many worlds? Thoughts about new concepts in Jewish legal history (Andreas Gotzmann, 413–436). Imperial spaces as Jewish spaces. The Holy Roman Empire, the Emperor and the Jews in the Early Modern Period. Some preliminary observations (Stephan Wendehorst, 437–474). Legal spaces for Jews as subjects of the Holy Roman Empire (Stefan Ehrenpreis, 475–487). Diskussion (491–518). Dubnowiana (519–546). Literaturbericht (547–590). Further contribs. pertaining to German-speaking Jews are listed according to subject.]

42565. STADT- UND UNIVERSITÄTSBIBLIOTHEK FRANKFURT AM MAIN & GERMANIA JUDAICA KÖLN: *Jüdische Periodika im deutschsprachigen Raum/German Jewish periodicals.* Das Fachportal für Jüdische Zeitschriften/A gateway to Jewish periodicals. Ein Kooperationsprojekt von Lehr- und Forschungsgebiet Deutsch-jüdischer Literaturgeschichte, RWTH Aachen, Stadt- und Universitätsbibliothek Frankfurt am Main, Germania Judaica Köln. www.compactmemory.de [The project, sponsored by Deutsche Forschungsgemeinschaft, provides global internet access to the major (German-language) Jewish periodicals (fulltext). The current list (2003/2004) cont. 25 periodicals; more titles will be added, incl. Hebrew and Yiddish ones, up to 2006.]

42566. VATICAN, ROME. WENDEHORST, STEPHAN: *Die Römische Inquisition, der Index und die Juden—Neue Materialien und Perspektiven.* [In]: Leipziger Beiträge zur jüdischen Geschichte und Kultur, Bd. I, München, 2003. Pp. 385–396, footnotes. [On the opening (in 1998) of the Archivio della Congregazione per la Dottrina delle Fede (ACDF), and its implications for research in the field of Jewish history.]

42567. WASSERMANN, HENRY: *False start. Jewish studies at German universities during the Weimar Republic.* New York: Humanity Books, 2003. 253 pp., notes, bibl., index. [Deals with the universities at Leipzig, Halle, Hamburg, Giessen, Bonn and Breslau; also on the lack of awareness that the new field of study might profit from the experience of established rabbinical seminaries which had taught "Wissenschaft des Judentums" with impressive results.]

42568. YAD VASHEM, JERUSALEM. *Fraenkel, Daniel* :The German "Righteous among the Nations". An historical appraisal. [In]: Leo Baeck Institute Year Book 2003, Vol. XLVIII, Oxford, 2003. Pp. 223–247, illus., facsim., footnotes. [On German rescuers, based on the Yad Vashem database.]

42569. ZEITZEUGEN TV GMBH, BERLIN: *Erinnerung als Verantwortung. Das Zeitzeugen-Archiv in Text und Bild.* Katalog. Hrsg. von Thomas Grimm. Berlin: Parthas, 2003. 298 pp., ports., indexes. [Documents most of the collection of the Zeitzeugen TV GmbH, Berlin. Incl. numerous Jews.]

42570. ZENTRUM FÜR ANTISEMITISMUSFORSCHUNG, BERLIN: *Jahrbuch für Antisemitismuforschung 12.* Hrsg. von Wolfgang Benz für das Zentrum für Antisemitismusforschung der Technischen Universität Berlin. Red.: Werner Bergmann, Johannes Heil, Mona Körte. Geschäftsführende Red.: Juliane Wetzel. Berlin: Metropol, 2003. 350 pp., footnotes. [Incl.: Vorwort (Wolfgang Benz, 9–12). Essays are arranged under the sections: Die Entstehung von Feindbildern im Konflikt um Palästina (15–146). Antisemitismus (147–258). Gewalt und Rassismus (259–306). Besprechungsessays (307–342). Selected articles pertaining to German-speaking Jews and antisemitism in German-speaking lands are listed according to subject.]

B. **Bibliographies, Catalogues and Reference Books**

42571. ADORNO, THEODOR W. BEHRENS, ROGER: *Adorno-ABC.* Leipzig: Reclam, 2003. 248 pp., bibl., index. Orig.-Ausg. [From Abgebrochensein, Abschaffung, Absterben, Adornitisch, Adornesk to Zwergobst, Zwitschern, Zwölftonmusik, Zwutsch.]

——— BRUHNS, MAIKE: *Kunst in der Krise. Künstlerlexikon Hamburg 1933–1945. Verfemt, verfolgt—verschollen, vergessen.* [See No. 42708.]

——— *Buch der Erinnerung. Die ins Baltikum deportierten deutschen, österreichischen und tschechoslowakischen Juden.* Book of Remembrance. The German, Austrian and Czechoslovakian Jews deported to the Baltic States. Bearb. von Wolfgang Scheffler und Diana Schulle. [See No. 42602.]

——— *Buchgestaltung, Typografen und Buchillustratoren aus Deutschland und Österreich im Exil 1933–1950.* Eine Biobibliografie. [See No. 43150.]

42572. COHEN, SUSAN SARAH, ed.: *Antisemitism: an annotated bibliography. Vol. 16 (2000).* [Publ. by] The Vidal Sassoon International Center for the Study of Antisemitism/The Hebrew Univ. of Jerusalem. München: Saur, 2003. 450 pp., indexes. (The Felix Posen Bibliographic Project on Antisemitism.)

42573. *Deutsche biographische Enzyklopädie (DBE).* Hrsg. von Walther Killy und Rudolf Vierhaus. Unter Mitarb. von Dietrich von Engelhardt [et al.]. 13 vols., München: Saur, 1995–2003. 13 vols. [Vol. 11, 1: Supplement, index (persons), 11, 2: index (persons). Vol. 12, 1: index (places), 12, 2: index (places, professions). Vol. 13: Supplement, ed. by Rudolf Vierhaus only. All vols. incl. numerous articles on Jewish personalities.]

——— *Germania Judaica.* Bd. III: 1350–1519. 3. Teilband: Gebietsartikel, Einleitungsartikel und Indices. [See No. 42220.]

42574. HIRSCHFELD, GERHARD [et al.], eds.: *Enzyklopädie Erster Weltkrieg.* Paderborn: Schöningh, 2003. 1001 pp., illus. [Incl.: Antisemitismus (Ulrich Sieg, 335–336). Sigmund Freud (Bernd Ulrich, 505–506). Hugo Haase (Walter Mühlhausen, 539). Judentum, Judenzählung (Ulrich Sieg, 599–600). Rosa Luxemburg (Walter Mühlhausen, 692). Walther Rathenau (Martin Sabrow, 786–787). Reichsbund jüdischer Frontsoldaten (Ulrich Sieg, 790). Theodor Wolff (Christoph Cornelissen, 973). Arnold Zweig (Thomas F. Schneider, 981–982).]

42575. *Holocaust literature: an encyclopedia of writers and their work.* Ed. by S. Lillian Kremer. New York: Routledge, 2003. 2 vols. XLVII, 1499 pp., maps, appendixes, bibl., index. [Incl. both Jewish and non-Jewish writers.]

42576. *Jewish writers of the twentieth century.* Ed. by Sorrel Kerbel. Asst. eds. Muriel Emanuel, Laura Phillips. New York: Fitzroy Dearborn, 2003. XVIII, 695 pp., bibl., index. [Cont. chronol. list of writers, incl. many German-Jewish ones. Also chap. on Holocaust writing.]

42577. *Lexikon deutschmährischer Autoren.* Hrsg. von Ingeborg Fiala-Fürst und Jörg Krappmann. Olomouc: Univ. Palackého, 2002. 658 pp., illus., bibl. (Beiträge zur mährischen deutschsprachigen Literatur, Bd. 5.) [Incl. Otto Abeles, Meir Marcell Faerber, Oskar Rosenfeld, Ernst Sommer, Hermann Ungar, Ludwig Winder, Max Zweig.] [Cf.: "Mährischen Volkes Weisen". Das Olmützer "Lexikon deutschmährischer Autoren" (Hans Otto Horch) [in]: Aschkenas, Jg. 13, H. 2, Tübingen, 2003, pp. 531–534.]

——— LILLIE, SOPHIE: *Was einmal war. Handbuch der enteigneten Kunstsammlungen Wiens.* [See No. 42473.]

42578. *List of Germany's synagogues of the 20th century.* Foreword by Meir Schwarz. Comp. by Benjamin Rosendahl [et al.]. 2nd draft. Jerusalem: Synagogue Memorial, Beth Ashkenaz, 2003. III, 64 pp., illus.

42579. LIPPE, CHAIM DAVID: *Bibliographisches Lexikon der gesammten jüdischen und theologisch-rabbinischen Literatur der Gegenwart mit Einschluss der Schriften über Juden und Judenthum.* Hildesheim; New York: Olms, 2003. XXXII, 496 pp. (Bibliothek des Deutschen Judentums, Abt. 1: Quellensammlungen, Lexika, Bibliographien und Zeitschriften.) [Facsim. reprint of the edn. publ. in Vienna in 1899; incl.: Einleitung (Ch.D.L., VII-XXXII; book incl. literature publ. between 1830 and 1889.]

42580. *Medieval Jewish civilization: an encyclopedia.* Ed. by Norman Roth. New York, London: Routledge, 2003. XXI, 701 pp., illus., maps, gloss., bibl., indexes. [Incl. many German-Jewish communities; also Christian attitudes to these communities.]

42581. *Metzler Lexikon jüdischer Philosophen.* Hrsg. von Andreas B. Kilcher und Otfried Fraisse unter Mitarb. von Yossef Schwartz. Stuttgart: Metzler, 2003. XXXI, 476 pp., bibl. notes, index. [Incl. more than 100 philosophers from Philon of Alexandria to Sarah Kofman; incl.: Zum Begriff der jüdischen Philosophie (Andreas B. Kilcher, VII-XVIII). Zur Geschichte der jüdischen Philosophie (Yossef Schwartz, XIX-XXII).]

——— NEUGEBAUER, ROSAMUNDE: *Zeichnen im Exil—Zeichen des Exils? Handzeichnung und Druckgraphik deutschsprachiger Emigranten ab 1933.* [See No. 43146.]

42582. *Publications on German-speaking Jewry.* A selected and annotated bibliography of books and articles 2002. Compiled by Barbara Suchy and Annette Pringle. [In]: Leo Baeck Institute Year Book 2003, Vol. XLVIII. Oxford, 2003. Pp. 249–433, index (names, places, subjects, periodicals, 393–433).

42583. *Quellen zur Geschichte der Juden in polnischen Archiven.* Im Auftrag der Berlin-Brandenburgischen Akademie der Wissenschaften hrsg. von Stefi Jersch-Wenzel. Bd. 1: Ehemalige preußische Provinzen: Pommern, Westpreußen, Ostpreußen, Preußen, Posen, Grenzmark Posen-Westpreußen, Süd- und Neuostpreußen. Bearb. von Annekathrin Genest und Susanne Marquardt. Red.: Stefan Grob und Barbara Strenge. München: Saur, 2003. XLIV, 632 pp., indexes. (Quellen zur Geschichte der Juden in polnischen Archiven, Bd. 1.)

42584. *Reference guide to Holocaust literature.* Ed. by Thomas Riggs. Introd. by James E. Young. Detroit: St. James Press, 2002. XLI, 714 pp., maps, bibl., indexes.

42585. SINGERMAN, ROBERT: *Jewish given names and family names.* A new bibliography ed. by David L. Gold. Leiden: Brill, 2001. 245 pp. [Incl. 3040 titles, part VI (128–174) cont. literature about European names (Germany: pp. 140–156).] [Cf.: Bespr. (Andreas Angerstorfer) [in]: Beiträge zur Namenforschung, Jg. 38, H. 3, Heidelberg, 2003, pp. 352–354.]

42586. TAITZ, EMILY/HENRY, SONDRA/TALLAN, CHERYL: *The JPS guide to Jewish women, 600 B.C.E–1900 C.E.* Philadelphia: The Jewish Publication Society, 2003. XXVIII, 354 pp., illus., ports., geneal. tab., bibl. (325–346), index. [Incl. Jewish women from Breslau, Prague, Regensburg, i.a.]

——— WLASCHEK, RUDOLF M.: *Biographia Judaica Bohemiae*. Bd. 3. [See No. 42482.]

III. THE NAZI PERIOD

A. General

42587. AACHEN. CLAHSEN, HELMUT: *Mama, was ist ein Judenbalg? Eine jüdische Kindheit in Aachen 1935–1945*. Aachen: Helios, 2003. 257 pp.

42588. ADAM, UWE DIETRICH: *Judenpolitik im Dritten Reich*. Düsseldorf: Droste, 2003. 405 pp., bibl. (255–272), notes (273–392), index. (Droste Taschenbuch Geschichte.) [Incl.: Vorwort zur Neuausgabe (Günther B. Ginzel, 9–13). Orig. publ. in 1972.]

42589. ADAMO, HANS: *Zuckermanns Tochter.* Stärker als Liebe war der Tod. Ein dokumentarischer Bericht unter Mitarbeit von Gaby Rehnelt. Essen: Klartext, 2003. 189 pp., illus., facsims., notes, bibl. [Documents the life of Elisabeth (Liesl) Will, née Klein, 1901 Vienna–Dec. 1942 Auschwitz; moved with her non-Jewish husband, the artist Heinrich Will (executed in Preungesheim Feb. 1943) in the early 1930s from Vienna to Gießen, both denounced in 1942.]

42590. AHLEN. OFFELE-ADEN, HILDEGARD: *"Und wo sind die anderen?" Therese Münsterteicher.* [In]: Der beflügelte Aal, Bd. 21, Ahlen, 2003. Pp. 52–54, illus. [On the November pogrom in Ahlen and the friendship between a young Christian woman and the Moszkowicz family. Also in this issue: Vom Aal, der eine Ahle sein sollte (Imo Moszkowicz, 91–94, illus.; recollections of childhood in Ahlen and the author's father, a poor cobbler). See also No. 43399.]

42591. ALEXANDER, EDWARD: *Hitler's professors, Arafat's professors.* [In]: Judaism, Vol. 52, Nos. 1–2, New York, Winter-Spring 2003. Pp. 95–102, notes. [Compares the anti-Jewish boycott by Nazi professors with today's boycott of Israeli scientists and scholars by some pro-Palestinian academics.]

42592. ALY, GÖTZ: *Hitlers Volksstaat. Anmerkungen zum Klassencharakter des Nationalsozialismus.* [In]: "Gegen alle Vergeblichkeit". Jüdischer Widerstand gegen den Nationalsozialismus [see No. 42899]. Pp. 133–141, footnotes. [Incl. the looting of Jewish property.]

42593. ALY, GÖTZ: *Rasse und Klasse. Nachforschungen zum deutschen Wesen.* Frankfurt am Main: S. Fischer, 2003. 254 pp. [Incl.: Die Fahrt ins Blaue. Alfred Döblin und die Berliner "Listenkranken" (99–113). Zur Schonung des Steuerzahlers. Massenmord als Technik staatlicher Umverteilung (114–120). Im Dienste des Volkes. Der kleine Kaufrausch an der Heimatfront (135–138). Planungssicherheit für den Holocaust. Hitlers Geheimrede vom 12. Dezember 1941 (155–163). One essay is listed according to subject.]

42594. ANDERS, EDWARD/DUBROVSKIS, JURIS: *Who died in the Holocaust?: recovering names from official records.* [In]: Holocaust and Genocide Studies, Vol. 17, No. 1, Oxford, Spring 2003. Pp. 114–138, notes. [Uses the example of the town of Liepa, Latvia to show how the use of a variety of sources, incl. census records, police and camp records can increase accurate data information for thousands of Jewish victims.]

42595. APPELIUS, STEFAN, ed.: *"Der Teufel hole Hitler". Briefe der sozialdemokratischen Emigration.* Essen: Klartext, 2003. 406 pp., illus., footnotes. [Cont. letters mostly written by or addressed to the (non-Jewish) Social Democrat Fritz Heine (1904–2002) between 1940 and Nov. 1942 when he was active in the Resistance and in the rescue of refugees in Marseille and Lisbon. Incl. numerous letters from Jewish SPD friends/letters addressed to them; also other reports and documents related to this period.]

42596. AUSCHWITZ. ALLEN, MICHAEL THAD: *Anfänge der Menschenvernichtung in Auschwitz, Oktober 1941. Eine Erwiderung auf Jan Erik Schulte.* [In]: Vierteljahrshefte für Zeitgeschichte, Jg. 51, H. 4, München, Sept. 2003. Pp. 565–573, footnotes. [Engl. abstract on p. 614; response to an article, see No. 41189/YB XLVIII.]

42597. AUSCHWITZ. *The last expression: art and Auschwitz.* Ed. by David Mickenberg, Corinne Granof, and Peter Hayes. Evanston, IL: Northwestern Univ. Press, 2003. XV, 272 pp., illus., notes, bibl., index. [Catalogue of some 200 artworks created at Auschwitz and other concentration camps and first shown at the Block Museum of Art in Chicago before touring other American cities.]

42598. AUSCHWITZ TRIAL. HERZINGER, RICHARD: *Am Anfang der Wahrheit.* Mit dem Frankfurter Auschwitz-Prozess vor 40 Jahren drang der organisierte Judenmord erstmals wirklich in das deutsche Bewusstsein. [In]: Die Zeit, Nr. 51, Hamburg, 11. Dez. 2003. P. 82, illus.

42599. AUSTRIA. ZALMON, MILKA: *Forced emigration of the Jews of Burgenland: a test case.* [In]: Yad Vashem Studies, Vol. 31, Jerusalem, 2003. Pp. 287–323, footnotes. [On the expulsion of Jews from Burgenland between March and October 1938, immediately after the "Anschluss".]

42600. BADEN. KISSENER, MICHAEL: *"Betr.: Maßnahmen aus Anlass des Krieges".* Ein Dokument über die Veräußerung jüdischen Vermögens in Baden 1940. [In]: Mannheimer Geschichtsblätter, N.F., Bd. 9, Heidelberg, 2003. Pp. 553–560, footnotes. [Incl. a document relating to the confiscation and auctioning of chattels and real estate of the Jews deported to Gurs, Oct. 1940.]

42601. BADEN. KISSENER, MICHAEL: *Jüdische Richter in Baden 1933–1945.* [In]: Festschrift 200 Jahre Badisches Oberhofgericht—Oberlandesgericht Karlsruhe. Hrsg. von Werner Münchbach. Heidelberg: Müller Verlag, 2003. Pp. 93–116. [Also in this vol.: Das Oberlandesgericht in der Nazidiktatur (Christof Schiller, 67–91).]

42602. BALTIC STATES. *Buch der Erinnerung. Die ins Baltikum deportierten deutschen, österreichischen und tschechoslowakischen Juden.* Bearb. von Wolfgang Scheffler und Diana Schulle. Hrsg. vom "Volksbund Deutsche Kriegsgräberfürsorge e.V." und dem "Riga-Komitee der deutschen Städte" gemeinsam mit der Stiftung "Neue Synagoge Berlin—Centrum Judaicum" und der Gedenkstätte "Haus der Wannsee-Konferenz". München: Saur, 2003. 2 vols., XVI, 1072 pp., tabs., index, bibl. [Titles and essays also in Engl. Incl. deportations to Kovno (Lithuania), Riga (Latvia), Raasiku/Reval (Estonia); lists also survivors; essays by Wolfgang Scheffler, Klaus Dettmer, Gerhard Ungar, Diana Schulle, Vojtech Blodig, Ekkehard Hübschmann, Jürgen Sielemann, Erich Koch, Horst Matzerath, Monica Kingreen, Barbara Materne, Gisela Möllenhoff, Rita Schlautmann-Overmeyer, Monika Minninger, Peter Schulze, Ellen Bertram, Markus Gryglewski, Günther Högl, Thomas Kohlpoth.] [Cf.: Bespr. (Matthias M. Ester) [in]: Westfälische Forschungen, Bd. 53, Münster, 2003, pp. 717–720.]

42603. BAMBERG. *Erinnerung an jüdische Schülerinnen und Schüler Bambergs.* Ein Schülerprojekt der Berufsoberschule Bamberg, des Eichendorff-Gymnasiums Bamberg und des Franz-Ludwig-Gymnasiums Bamberg. Hrsg. von Ursula Schember [et al.]. Bamberg: Collibri-Verl., 2001. 88 pp., notes.

42604. *Banken und "Arisierung" in Mitteleuropa während des Nationalsozialismus* [Issue title of] Geld und Kapital. Jahrbuch der Gesellschaft für mitteleuropäische Banken- und Sparkassengeschichte, Bd. 5. [Ed.: Dieter Ziegler.] Stuttgart: Steiner, 2002. 236 pp., footnotes. [Cont.: Einleitung: Banken und "Arisierung" in Mitteleuropa (ed., 5–14). Die "Germanisierung" und "Arisierung" der Mercurbank während der Ersten Republik Österreich (Dieter Ziegler, 15–42). Enteignungen und Säuberungen—Die österreichischen Banken im Nationalsozialismus (Peter Eigner/Peter Melichar, 43–118). Die Nationalbank in den Jahren 1939–1945 und die "Arisierung" im Protektorat Böhmen und Mähren (Jiri Novotny/Jiri Sousa, 119–142). Die "Arisierungsaktivitäten" der Böhmischen Escompte Bank im Protektorat Böhmen und Mähren 1939–1945 (Drahomir Jancik, 143–174). Die Verwaltung von konfisziertem und sequestriertem Vermögen—eine spezifische Kategorie des "Arisierungs-Profits": Die Kreditanstalt der Deutschen Bank und ihre Abteilung "F" (Eduard Kubu, 175–210). Kredite für den Holocaust—Die Deutsche Bank und J.A.Topf & Söhne, Erfurt 1933–1945 (Monika Dickhaus, 211–234).]

42605. BARTOV, OMER: *Germany's war and the Holocaust: disputed histories.* Ithaca: Cornell Univ. Press, 2003. XXI, 248 pp., footnotes, bibl., index. [Incl. chaps.: Germans as Nazis: Goldhagen's Holocaust and the world. Jews as Germans: Victor Klemperer bears witness. Germans as Jews: representations of absence in post-war Germany.]

42606. BAYREUTH. *Denk Steine setzen. Über die Wiedergewinnung der Erinnerung an die ermordeten Juden von Bayreuth.* Eine Dokumentation von Irene Hamel. Geschichtswerkstatt Bayreuth. Bayreuth: Bumerang, 2003, 98 pp. [Documents a project of several Bayreuth high schools to research the fate of Bayreuth Jews.]

42607. Benz, Wolfgang/Distel, Barbara, eds.: *Instrumentarium der Macht. Frühe Konzentrationslager 1933–1937.* Red.: Angelika Königseder, Verena Walter. Berlin: Metropol, 2003. 277 pp., footnotes. (Geschichte der Konzentrationslager 1933–1945, Bd. 3.) [A collection of 15 articles.]

42608. Benz, Wolfgang/Reif-Spirek, Peter, eds.: *Geschichtsmythen. Legenden über den Nationalsozialismus.* Berlin: Metropol, 2003. 168 pp., footnotes, indexes. [Selected essays: Die "jüdische Kriegserklärung" an Deutschland. Judenvernichtung aus Notwehr? (Wolfgang Benz, 11–26). Die Auschwitzlüge (Juliane Wetzel, 27–42). Matthaeus Parisiensis, Henry Morgenthau und die "Jüdische Weltverschwörung" (Johannes Heil, 131–150). One further essay is listed according to subject.]

42609. Bergen, Doris: *War and genocide: a concise history of the Holocaust.* Lanham, MD: Rowman & Littlefield, 2002. XI, 263 pp., illus., maps., bibl. (229–241), notes, index. (Critical issues in history.) [Incl. antisemitism in pre-Nazi Germany.]

42610. BERLIN. FIGES, EVA: *Tales of innocence and experience: an exploration.* New York: Bloomsbury: Distrib. by Holtzbrinck Publ., 2003. 183 pp. [Story explores the relationship between a grandmother and her granddaughter evoking the author's own childhood in Nazi Berlin and subsequent escape to England.]

42611. BERLIN. Gruner, Wolf: *The factory action and the events at the Rosenstrasse in Berlin: facts and fictions about 27 February 1943—sixty years later.* [In]: Central European History, Vol. 36, No. 2, Boston; Leiden, 2003. Pp. 179–208, footnotes.

42612. BERLIN. Heesch, Johannes: *Berliner Facetten: Jüdischer Kulturbund.* [In]: Neue Gesellschaft/Frankfurter Hefte, Jg. 50, H. 10, Frankfurt am Main, 2003. Pp. 70–73.

42613. BERLIN. Höppner, Wolfgang: *Das Berliner Germanische Seminar in den Jahren 1933 bis 1945.* Kontinuität und Diskontinuität in der Geschichte einer wissenschaftlichen Institution. [In]: Literaturwissenschaft und Nationalsozialismus. Hrsg. von Holger Dainat [et al.]. Tübingen: Niemeyer, 2003. (Studien und Texte zur Sozialgeschichte der Literatur, Bd. 99.) Pp. 87–106, footnotes. [Deals also with the expulsion of Jewish academics and the involvement of colleagues with the Nazi régime and its antisemitism 1933.]

42614. BERLIN. Jochheim, Gernot: *Frauenprotest in der Rosenstraße Berlin 1943.* Berichte, Dokumente, Hintergründe. [Erweiterte Neuausg.] Berlin: Hentrich & Hentrich, 2002. 220 pp., frontis., illus., facsims., docs., index.

42615. BERLIN. Lovenheim, Barbara: *Überleben im Verborgenen. Sieben Juden in Berlin.* Aus dem Amerik. von Doris Gerstner. Mit einem Nachwort von Barbara Schieb. Berlin: Siedler, 2002. 222 pp., illus. [For American edn. see No. 41215/YB XLVIII.]

42616. BERLIN. Schmidt, Monika: *Die "Arisierung" des Berliner Zoologischen Gartens.* [In]: Jahrbuch für Antisemitismusforschung 12. Berlin, 2003. Pp. 211–229, footnotes.

42617. BERLIN. Silver, Daniel B.: *Refuge in hell: how Berlin's Jewish hospital outlasted the Nazis.* Boston: Houghton Mifflin, 2003. XXII, 311 pp., illus., ports., gloss. notes, bibl. (279–283), index. [On the Jewish Hospital at Iranische Straße, Wedding, still housing some 800 survivors (mainly Jews in mixed marriages) when the Soviet army liberated it in April 1945; also on its controversial director Walter Lustig.] [Cf.: Double dealing Dr Dr (Walter Laqueur) [in]: TLS, London, Sept. 28, 2003. Reviving a forgotten story (Cecilia Rothschild) [in]: Aufbau, Vol. 69, No. 19, New York, Oct. 2, 2003, p. 17.]

42618. BERLIN. Süss, Peter: *"Ist Hitler nicht ein famoser Kerl?". Graetz. Eine Familie und ihr Unternehmen vom Kaiserreich bis zur Bundesrepublik.* Paderborn: Schöningh, 2003. 356 pp., illus., facsims., tabs., notes

(271–327), bibl., indexes. [Author's doctoral thesis, Berlin, Freie Univ., 2001; chap. III. Im Dritten Reich (113–247) incl. Jewish forced labour and the deportation of Jewish workers, Feb. 1943. See also No. 42621.]

42619. BERLIN. WÖRMANN, HEINRICH-WILHELM: *Widerstand 1933–1945. Berlin. Schöneberg und Tempelhof.* Berlin: Gedenkstätte Deutscher Widerstand, 2002. 352 pp., ports., illus., bibl., indexes. (Widerstand 1933–1945. Berlin. Gedenkstätte Dt. Widerstand, Bd. 13.)

42620. BERLIN & BRANDENBURG. GAILUS, MANFRED: *Die vergessenen Brüder und Schwestern. Zum Umgang mit Christen jüdischer Herkunft im Raum der evangelischen Kirche Berlin-Brandenburg.* [In]: Zeitschrift für Geschichtswissenschaft, Jg. 51, H. 11, Berlin, 2003. Pp. 973–995, footnotes.

42621. BERLIN-TREPTOW. *Jüdische Zwangsarbeiter bei Ehrich & Graetz, Berlin-Treptow.* Hrsg. von Aubrey Pomerance. Köln: Dumont, 2003. 271 pp., illus., facsims., notes, bibl. [Incl.: Eine Schachtel voller Schicksale. Passfotos von jüdischen Zwangsarbeiterinnen und Zwangsarbeitern bei Ehrich & Graetz (ed., 6–27). Von der "Schikanepromenade" in die Zwangsarbeit. Der Arbeitseinsatz der Berliner Juden 1938–1943 und die Erinnerungen der Volkswirtin Elisabeth Freund (Carola Sachse/Ulrike Baureithel, 28–51). Die Firma Ehrich & Graetz in der Zeit des Nationalsozialismus (Jana C. Reimer, 52–65). Biografien (contribs. by Simone Erpel, Gisela Freydank, Beate Kosmala, Aubrey Pomerance and Sylvia Rogge-Gau on ten former forced labourers, 66–139). Dokumentation (Jana C. Reimer, 141–253, incl. photographs and data of 534 workers). See also No. 42618.] [Cf.: Vor der Fabrikaktion. Zeitzeugnisse zum Schicksal jüdischer Zwangsarbeiter in Berlin (Monika Richarz) [in]: Aufbau, Vol. 69, No. 24, New York, Dec. 11, 2003, p. 21.]

42622. BERLIN-WEDDING. SANDVOSS, HANS RAINER: *Widerstand in Wedding und Gesundbrunnen.* Berlin: Gedenkstätte Deutscher Widerstand, 2003. 352 pp., illus., facsims., bibl., indexes. (Reihe Widerstand in Berlin von 1933 bis 1945, Bd. 14.) [Incl.: 10. Kapitel: Verfolgung der Juden/Hilfe für "Untergetauchte" (289–319); other chaps. incl. also Jews and help for Jews.]

42623. BERLER, WILLY: *Durch die Hölle. Monowitz, Auschwitz, Groß-Rosen, Buchenwald.* Aufgezeichnet und historisch kommentiert von Ruth Fivaz-Silbermann. Mit einem Vorwort von Simon Wiesenthal. Augsburg: Ölbaum, 2003. 226 pp., illus., notes (200–226), bibl. [Orig. publ. with the title 'Itinéraire dans les ténèbres', Paris, 1999; author, b. 1918 in Czernowitz, studied in Belgium, from where he was deported in 1943. Lives in Brussels and on Gran Canaria.]

42624. BEUEL. SCHLETTE, RUTH: *"Ich hoffe trotzdem bald in Palästina ein neues Leben anfangen zu können". Ruth Hadassah Herz aus Beuel (1925–1942) und ihre Briefe.* [In]: Bonner Geschichtsblätter, Bd. 51/52, Bonn, 2001/2002 [publ. 2003]. Pp. 123–176, footnotes. [Cont. an introd. and annot. letters written by a young girl between March 1938 and the deportation of her family; Beuel: since 1969 part of Bonn.]

42625. BILLERBECK. MEYER-RAVENSTEIN, VERONIKA: *Zersplitterte Steine. Erinnerungen an jüdische Familien und ihre Zeit.* [Hrsg.: Förderverein Mahnmal Billerbeck e.V.] Dülmen: Typ. Werkstatt & Verl. Stegemann, 2002. 258 pp., illus. [Billerbeck: nr. Coesfeld (Münsterland).]

42626. BÖHLE, INGO: *Die "Judenfrage" in der privaten Krankenversicherung (PKV) im Nationalsozialismus.* "Ganz allgemein hat allerdings die private Krankenversicherung feststellen müssen, dass Nichtarier unversicherbar sind [...]." [In]: Zeitschrift für Unternehmensgeschichte, Jg. 48, H. 2, München, 2003. Pp. 164–195, footnotes.

42627. BOEHM, ERIC H.: *We survived: fourteen stories of the hidden and hunted in Nazi Germany.* As told to Eric H. Boehm. Rev. and updated edn. Boulder, CO: Westview Press, 2003. XXV, 326 pp., maps. [Incl. chap. on Leo Baeck: A people stands before God. For earlier edns. and details see No. 23227/YB XXXII.]

42628. BONN. NUSSBAUM, CARL: *Ein Lebenslauf von der Geburt bis zum Ende des Dritten Reichs.* [In]: Bonner Geschichtsblätter, Bd. 51/52, Bonn 2001/2002 [publ. 2003]. Pp. 97–122, illus., facsims. [Author, b. 1921 in Bonn, son of Adolf N., Prof. of Surgery at Bonn Univ., writes about his upbringing in Bonn and the fate of his "partly Jewish" family after 1933.]

42629. BROWDER, GEORGE C.: *Perpetrator character and motivation: an emerging consensus?* [In]: Holocaust and Genocide Studies, Vol. 17, No. 3, Oxford, Winter 2003. Pp. 480–497, notes.

42630. BROWNING, CHRISTOPHER R.: *Collected memories: Holocaust history and postwar testimony.* Madison: Univ. of Wisconsin Press, 2003. X, 105 pp., notes. (George L. Mosse series in modern European cultural and intellectual history.) [Deals with survivors' and perpetrators' testimonies; incl.: Perpetrator testimony: another look at Adolf Eichmann (3–36).]

42631. BRUCHSAL. EXNER-SEEMANN, KONRAD: *Die Deportation der Bruchsaler Juden in das Vernichtungslager Gurs 1940.* [In]: Badische Heimat, Jg. 82, H. 2, Freiburg, 2002. Pp. 364–369, illus. [Incl. list of names, based on the research of students from the Bruchsal Balthasar-Neumann-Schule.]

——— BUCHENWALD. KUSCHEY, BERNHARD: *Die Ausnahme des Überlebens. Ernst und Hilde Federn.* Eine biographische Studie und eine Analyse der Binnenstruktur des Konzentrationslagers. [See No. 43290.]

42632. BÜCHLER, YEHOSHUA R.: *"Unworthy behaviour": the case of SS officer Max Täubner.* [In]: Holocaust and Genocide Studies, Vol. 17, No. 3, Oxford, Winter 2003. Pp. 409–429, notes. [Discusses the only known case in which an SS officer was punished by Nazi authorities for killing Jews.]

42633. *Bücherverbrennung Mai 1933—Geschichte und Wirkung* [Issue title of] Zeitschrift für Geschichtswissenschaft, Jg. 51, H. 5, Berlin, 2003. 1 issue. [Incl. (titles abbr.): Traditionen und Wirkungen der Bücherverbrennung des 10. Mai 1933 (Wolfgang Benz, 398–406). Bücherverbrennungen in Altertum und Mittelalter: eine Skizze (Johannes Heil, 407–420). Der Sturm auf Magnus Hirschfelds Institut für Sexualwissenschaft (Herbert Wiesner, 421–429). Bücherverbrennungen und ihre Wirkung in der Literatur (Mona Körte, 430–438). Die "Bilderverbrennung" 1939—ein Pendant? (Angelika Königseder/Juliane Wetzel, 439–446; discusses whether or not paintings were destroyed). Erinnerungszeichen und Denkmäler für die Bücherverbrennung (Stefanie Endlich, 447–455).]

42634. BUKOWINA. *Blaueule Leid.* Bukowina 1940–1944. Eine Anthologie. Hrsg. und kommentiert von Bernhard Albers. Aachen: Rimbaud, 2003. 159 pp. (Orig.-Ausg.) [Incl. autobiographical texts mostly by Jewish authors, also some poems and short biographies.]

42635. CASTROP-RAUXEL. UELNER, KARL-HEINZ: *Ilse Löwenwärter, 12 Jahre, Jüdin.* [In]: Kultur und Heimat, Jg. 53, Nr. 3/4, Castrop-Rauxel, 2003. Pp. 129–132. [The author's personal recollections are supplemented by Dietmar Scholz: Ilse Löwenwärter, 16 Jahre, jüdisches Opfer. In: Kultur und Heimat, Jg. 54, Nr. 1/2, 2003. Pp. 53–58.]

42636. CHURCH. BACHARACH, WALTER ZVI: *Antisemitism, Holocaust and the Holy See: an appraisal of new books about the Vatican and the Holocaust.* Transl. from the Hebrew by Martin Friedlander. [In]: Yad Vashem Studies, Vol. 31, Jerusalem, 2003. Pp. 365–388, footnotes.

42637. CHURCH. FELDKAMP, MICHAEL F.: *Goldhagens unwillige Kirche: Alte und neue Fälschungen über Kirche und Papst während der NS-Herrschaft.* München: Olzog, 2003. 178 pp., footnotes, bibl., index.

42638. CHURCH. *Goldhagen, der Vatikan und die Judenfeindschaft* [issue title of] Menora 2003, Jg. 14, Berlin, 2003. 284 pp., notes, index. [Incl. the sections: Einführung (Julius H. Schoeps/Karl E. Grözinger/Willi Jasper/Gert Mattenklott, 9–13). I. Goldhagen in der Kritik (17–100; 13 reviews). II. Dokumente und Aufsätze (101–278; essays by Pater Groothuis, Gerhard Besier, Olaf Blaschke, David Kertzer, Julius H. Schoeps, Klaus Berger, Rudolf Kreis).]

42639. CHURCH. GRIECH-POLELLE, BETH A.: *Bishop von Galen: German Catholicism and National Socialism.* New Haven: Yale Univ. Press, 2002. 259 pp., appendix, notes, index. [Incl. a chap. on von Galen and the Jews.]

42640. CHURCH. KALTEFLEITER, WERNER: *Der Vatikan öffnet sein Geheimarchiv.* [In]: Freiburger Rundbrief, N.F., Jg. 10, H. 3, Freiburg, 2003. Pp. 162–169, footnotes. [Incl. reprint of a letter from Edith Stein addressed to Pope Pius XI in March 1933 reporting aggressive antisemitism.]

42641. CHURCH. LINDEMANN, GERHARD: *Antijudaismus und Antisemitismus in den evangelischen Landeskirchen während der NS-Zeit.* [In]: Geschichte und Gesellschaft, Jg. 29, Göttingen, 2003. Pp. 575–607, footnotes. [Also in this issue: Die "Deutschen Christen" 1933–1945: Ganz normale Gläubige und eifrige Komplizen? (Doris L. Bergen, 542–574; deals also with Jews). Protestantische Pfarrer und Nationalsozialismus in der Region. Vom Ende der Weimarer Republik bis zum Beginn des Zweiten Weltkrieges (Thomas Fandel, 512–541).]

42642. CHURCH. MILLER, PAUL B.: *Daniel Goldhagen and the role of the Catholic Church in the Holocaust.* [In]: Midstream, Vol. 49, No. 3, New York, April 2003. Pp. 37–39, notes.

42643. CHURCH. SÁNCHEZ, JOSÉ M.: *Pius XII. und der Holocaust. Anatomie einer Debatte.* Aus dem Amerik. übers. von Karl Nicolai. Paderborn: Schöningh, 2002. XXI, 167 pp., footnotes, bibl., index. [For American edn. see No. 39930/YB XLVII.]

42644. CHURCH. ZUCCOTTI, SUSAN: *L'Osservatore Romano and the Holocaust, 1939–1945.* [In]: Holocaust and Genocide Studies, Vol. 17, No. 2, Oxford, Fall 2003. Pp. 249–277, notes. [Author argues that the Vatican newspaper could have done more; as an example she contrasts the reporting of Soviet atrocities with the lack of reporting of the Nazi genocide.]

42645. COLOGNE. *Köln unterm Hakenkreuz. Die Jahre 1933—1945 in der Domstadt.* Hrsg. von Harald W. Jürgensohn. Köln: Dumont, 2003. 95 pp., illus., facsims. [Incl.: Die "Kristallnacht" (24–29).]

42646. COLOGNE. SERUP-BILFELDT, KIRSTEN: *Stolperstein. Vergessene Namen, verwehte Spuren.* Wegweiser zu Kölner Schicksalen in der NS-Zeit. Mit einem Beitrag von Elke Heidenreich. Köln: Kiepenhauer & Witsch, 2003. 160 pp. [A collection of biographical stories, several about Jews.]

42647. CZECHOSLOVAKIA. BRUCHOVÁ, TEREZA/NEKULA, MAREK: *Die bildliche Darstellung der Juden in der Zeitung 'Der Neue Tag', 1939–1945.* [In]: Brücken, N.F. 9–10, Prag, 2003. Pp. 241–255, illus., footnotes. [On Prague's German language daily newspaper, and its antisemitism; also in this issue: Emigrantenschicksale. Drei Beispiele aus der böhmisch-mährischen Lebenswelt (Peter Becher, 281–302; incl. a Jewish girl, Ruth Weisz, from Moravia).]

42648. CZECHOSLOVAKIA. *Deutsche und Tschechen.* Geschichte, Kultur, Politik. Hrsg. von Walter Koschmal [et al.] mit einem Geleitwort von Václav Havel. München: Beck, 2001. 727 pp., index. [Incl.: Die Juden zwischen Deutschen und Tschechen (Miroslav Kárny, 117–124). Das Ghetto Theresienstadt 1941–1945 (Karl Braun, 125–133). Two further essays are listed according to subject.]

42649. CZECHOSLOVAKIA. EIGNER, RUTH: *Nazis, Jews, Czechs in Sudetenland: a memoir.* [In]: Judaism, Vol. 52, Nos. 1–2, New York, Winter-Spring 2003. Pp. 61–70. [Author now lives in San Diego.]

42650. CZECHOSLOVAKIA. SHLAIN, MARGALIT: *Jakob Edelsteins Bemühungen um die Rettung der Juden aus dem Protektorat Böhmen und Mähren von Mai 1939 bis Dezember 1939.* Eine Korrespondenzanalyse. [In]: Theresienstädter Studien und Dokumente 2003, Prag, 2003. Pp. 71–94, footnotes.

42651. DACHAU. ZÁMECNIK, STANISLAV: *Das war Dachau.* Hrsg. von der Stiftung Comité International de Dachau. [Luxemburg]: [St. Zámecnik], 2002. 435 pp., footnotes, bibl. (414–425), index.

42652. DANZIG. BERENDT, GRZEGORZ: *Die Judenfrage in der Freien Stadt Danzig und die Rolle Hermann Rauschning 1933–1934.* [In]: Hermann Rauschning—Materialien und Beiträge zu einer politischen Biographie. Hrsg. von Jürgen Hensel [et al.]. Warszawa: Oficyna Wdawn. Volumen, 2002. (Einzelschriften der Hist. Kommission für Ost- und Westpreußische Landesforschung; Brostiana, 6.) Pp.71–89.

42653. DAVID, RUTH: *Child of our time: a young girl's flight from the Holocaust.* London; New York: I.B. Tauris; distrib. in the US by Palgrave Macmillan, 2003. XIII, 170 pp., illus., ports. [For 1996 German edn. and data see No. 34026/YB XLII.]

42654. DENMARK. WERNER, EMMY E.: *A conspiracy of decency: the rescue of the Danish Jews during World War II.* Boulder, Col.: Westview Press, 2002. XII, 212 pp., illus. [Also on this topic: Auf Fischkuttern in die Freiheit. Vor sechzig Jahren retteten die Dänen ihre jüdischen Mitbürger vor der Deportation durch die Deutschen (Arne Melchior) [in]: 'FAZ', Nr. 249, Frankfurt am Main, 27. Okt. 2003. P. 42; deals also with Georg Ferdinand von Duckwitz, an employee at the German Embassy, who helped in these rescue operations.]

——— *Dennoch leben sie. Verfemte Bücher, verfolgte Autorinnen und Autoren. Zu den Auswirkungen nationalsozialistischer Literaturpolitik.* Hrsg. von Reiner Wild [et al.]. [See No. 43135.]

42655. DINER, DAN: *Gedächtniszeiten. Über jüdische und andere Geschichten.* München: Beck, 2003. 293 pp., notes. [Cont. a collection of previously publ. essays; selected essays: "Meines Bruders Wächter"—Zur Diplomatie jüdischer Fragen (113–124; on the Damascus affair and its European repercussions). Zweierlei Emanzipation—Westliche Juden und Ostjuden gegenübergestellt (125–134; on the November Pogrom against the background of the Evian Refugees Conference). Jenseits des Vorstellbaren—Der "Judenrat" als Grenzsituation (135–151). Angesichts des Zivilisationsbruchs—Max Horkheimers 'Aporien der Vernunft' (152–179). Schulddiskurse und andere Narrative—Epistemisches zum Holocaust (180–200). Geschichte der Juden—Paradigma einer europäischen Geschichtsschreibung (246–262).]

42656. DÖSCHER, HANS-JÜRGEN: *Das Attentat auf den deutschen Diplomaten Ernst vom Rath am 7. November 1938.* [In]: Geschichte in Wissenschaft und Unterricht, Jg. 54, H. 4, Stuttgart, 2003. Pp. 241–246, footnotes.

42657. DORA. SELLIER, ANDRÉ: *A history of the Dora camp.* Transl. from the French by Stephen Wright and Susan Taponier. With a foreword by Michael J. Neufeld and an afterword by Jens-Christian Wagner. Chicago: Ivan R. Dee in association with the United States Holocaust Memorial Museum, 2003. 547 pp., illus., ports., maps, bibl. (501–504), index. [Subtitle on dust jacket: the story of the Nazi slave labor camp that secretly manufactured V-2 rockets. For German edn. see No. 38773/YB XLVI.]

42658. DREYER, FELIX: *Kurt Gerstein. Vom Täter zum Widerstandskämpfer. Der Rehabilitierungsprozess Kurt Gersteins im Wandel der Beurteilung von Widerstand in der Nachkriegszeit.* [In]: Jahrbuch für Westfälische Kirchengeschichte, Bd. 98, Bielefeld, 2003, pp. 315–367, footnotes. [Abbr. version of the author's M.A. thesis (Bielefeld).]

42659. DUBROVSKY, GERTRUDE: *Six from Leipzig.* London: Vallentine Mitchell, 2003. 256 pp., ports. [Deals with Jewish children who went to England on a Kindertransport organised by the Cambridge Refugee Children's Committee.]

42660. DÜREN. JOHANNSEN, LORENZ PETER: *Dr. Karl Leven, Kinderarzt. Lebensspuren—Todesspur.* Mit Grußworten von Paul Larue, Bürgermeister der Stadt Düren und Pfarrerin Cornelia Kenke. Hrsg. aus Anlass des Besuches ehemaliger jüdischer Mitbürger in Düren, 29. Juni bis 6. Juli 2003. Düren: Evangelische Gemeinde zu Düren, 2003. 210 pp., illus., chronol., family tree, bibl. [Abbr. preprint; available at the Bibliothek Germania Judaica, Cologne. In part an account by the author, a paediatrician in Düren, of his years of research into the life of K.L., b. 1895 in Düren, deported with his family to Izbica in June 1942.]

42661. DÜSSELDORF. *Augenblick.* Berichte, Informationen und Dokumente der Mahn- und Gedenkstätte Düsseldorf. Nr. 24/25. Red.: Angela Genger, Barbara Materne. Düsseldorf, 2003. 48 pp., illus., facsims., notes. [Incl.: "Liebe, nicht Fanatismus, ist die Antwort auf die Probleme der Welt". Humanist, Historiker und Publizist: Helmut Hirsch (Mechthild Keller, 24–28; eulogy held in the Heine-Institut on the occasion of H.H.'s 95th birthday). Letters from Düsseldorf Jews; also obits. (29–45).]

——— DÜSSELDORF. JAKOBS, HILDEGARD [et al.]: *Zeitspuren in Düsseldorf 1930–1950. Ein Stadtführer.* [See No. 42334.]

42662. DÜWELL, SUSANNE/SCHMIDT, MATTHIAS, eds.: *Narrative der Shoah. Repräsentationen der Vergangenheit in Historiographie, Kunst und Politik.* Paderborn: Schöningh, 2002. 306 pp., footnotes. [Most contribs.

to this vol. are based on a conference with the title Vergangenheitspolitik und Narrative der Shoah, Bonn, Feb. 2001; selected essays: Geschichte und Erinnerung: Über Saul Friedländer (Steven E. Aschheim, 15–48). Geschichte und Restitution—oder die Begründung einer europäischen Erinnerung (Dan Diner, 71–76). Inszenierung 'authentischer' Erinnerung. Die fiktionale Holocaust-Autobiographie von Binjamin Wilkomirski (Susanne Düwell, 77–90). Von 'Hitler' zu 'Holokaust'. Die Thematisierung des Holocaust in den Geschichtsdokumentationen der ZDF-Redaktion Zeitgeschichte (Judith Keilbach, 127–142). "Von heute her gesehen, ist es zumindest verwunderlich ...". Der Blick auf den literarischen Zionismus durch das Perspektiv der Shoah. Ein Projektbericht (Alexandra Pontzen, 245–254). Von Schuld und Sühne, Versagen und Erneuerung: Zu Theorie und Praxis christlicher Annäherung an den Staat Israel (Matthias Schmidt, 265–280). Shoah als Politik (Moshe Zimmermann, 281–292). Israel und der Holocaust: Die Ideologisierung einer Wende (Moshe Zuckermann, 293–302).]

42663. DUISDORF. REY, MANFRED VAN: *Zum Schicksal der jüdischen Bürger des Amtes Duisdorf unter nationalsozialistischer Gewaltherrschaft.* [In]: Bonner Geschichtsblätter, Bd. 51/52, Bonn, 2001/2002 [publ. 2003]. Pp. 177–196, illus., footnotes. [Duisdorf: since 1969 part of Bonn.]

42664. EINHORN, LENA: *Menschenhandel unterm Hakenkreuz.* Aus dem Schwedischen von Wolfgang Butt. Stuttgart: Klett-Cotta, 2002. 560 pp., notes (511–553), bibl., index. [Orig. publ. in Stockholm 1999; tells the story of Gilel Storch and his negotiations with German spies, Swedish senior government clerks, representatives of the Allied Forces, Raoul Wallenberg, Folke Bernadotte, attempting to "buy" Jewish inmates from the concentration camps and bring them to Sweden.]

42665. ELLGER, HANS: *Gespräche mit Überlebenden des Holocaust—eine Chance der dritten Generation.* [In]: Lebendige Sozialgeschichte. Gedenkschrift für Peter Borowsky [see No. 43599]. Pp. 454–463, footnotes.

42666. EPHRAIM, FRANK: *Escape to Manila: from Nazi tyranny to Japanese terror.* Foreword by Stanley Karnow. Urbana: Univ. of Illinois Press, 2003. XII, 220 pp., illus., ports., maps, facsims., notes, bibl. (195–211), index. [Testimonies of 36 refugees who describe their escape to the Philippines, life there amongst an existing Jewish community, and the hardships under Japanese occupation.] [E.F., b. in Berlin 1931, emigr. to Manila in 1939 with his family, went to the US in 1946, where he made a career in the US Department of Transportation.]

42667. ERLANGER, PINCHAS: *Erinnerungen—meine Jugend in Deutschland und die Auswanderung nach Palästina.* [In]: Auswanderung, Flucht, Vertreibung, Exil im 19. und 20. Jahrhundert [see No. 42513]. Pp. 145–170. [Author, b. 1926 in Ravensburg, son of the agriculturist Ludwig Erlanger, educated at Landschulheim Herrlingen, emigr. with his family in 1939 to Palestine; lives in Shavey Zion.]

42668. ESSEN. HELD, HEINZ JOACHIM: *Zuflucht unter den Trümmern der Reformationskirche—Hilfe für jüdische Mitbürger in letzter Stunde.* Zugleich eine persönliche Erinnerung an den Essener Pfarrer Johannes Böttcher und seinen jüdischen Freund Josef Anschel. [In]: Essener Beiträge, Beiträge zur Geschichte von Stadt und Stift Essen, Bd. 115, Essen, 2003. Pp. 187–251, footnotes.

42669. *Experience and expression: women, the Nazis, and the Holocaust.* Ed. by Elizabeth R. Baer and Myrna Goldenberg. Detroit: Wayne State Univ. Press, 2003. XIV, 321 pp., illus., notes, bibl., index. [Incl. the treatment of Jewish women in Nazi Germany. Deals with both Jewish and non-Jewish womens' experiences as camp inmates, slave labourers, in the resistance movement, and as perpetrators; also on the post-war depiction of women in the Holocaust through film, fiction, and the arts.]

42670. FANGERAU, HEINER: *Etablierung eines rassenhygienischen Standardwerkes 1921–1941: der Baur-Fischer-Lenz im Spiegel der zeitgenössischen Rezensionsliteratur.* Frankfurt am Main; New York: Lang, 2003. 298 pp., footnotes, tabs., bibl. (253–290), index. (Marburger Schriften zur Medizingeschichte, Bd. 43.) Zugl.: Bochum, Univ., Diss., 2000. [Incl. a section entitled: Rezensionen zum "Judentum" im BFL (195–210).]

42671. FILM. BATHRICK, DAVID: *Filmische Perspektiven auf den "Holocaust". Die Kindergeschichten.* [In]: Babylon, H. 20, Frankfurt am Main, 2002. Pp. 95–112. [Deals with 'Mutters Courage', 'Life is beautiful', 'Jakob der Lügner'.]

42672. FILM. CORMICAN, MURIEL: *Aimée und Jaguar and the banality of evil.* [In]: German Studies Review, Vol. 26, No.1, Tempe, AZ, Feb. 2003. Pp. 105–119, notes. [Deals with the reception and criticism of the book and film of the love affair between Elisabeth Wust and Felice Schragenheim; for the book by Erica Fischer see No. 32836/YB XLI.]

42673. FILM. GIESEN, ROLF: *Nazi propaganda films: a history and filmography.* Jefferson, NC: McFarland, 2003. VII, 287 pp., illus., notes, filmography (185–232), bibl., index. [Incl. chap. on antisemitic films incl. "Der ewige Jude".]

42674. FILM. INSDORF, ANNETTE: *Indelible shadows: film and the Holocaust.* 3rd ed. Cambridge; New York: Cambridge Univ. Press, 2003. XIX, 410 pp., illus., filmography (313–365), notes, bibl., index. [For orig. edn. in 1983 see No. 20119/YB XXIX. Author has added five new chaps. to cover recent trends in "Holocaust films"; incl. information about over 100 titles from around the world.]

42675. FILM. *Medien—Politik—Geschichte* [Issue title of] Tel Aviver Jahrbuch für deutsche Geschichte, Jg. 13. Göttingen: Wallstein, 2003. 447 pp., graphs, footnotes. [Selected essays (titles partly abbr.): Die Darstellung der "Endlösung" in den Sendungen des Zweiten Deutschen Fernsehens (Wulf Kansteiner, 253–286). Zur Inszenierung von Zeitzeugen in bundesdeutschen Fernsehdokumentationen über den Nationalsozialismus (Judith Keilbach, 287–306). 'Holocaust' revisited—Lesarten eines Medienereignisses zwischen globaler Erinnerungskultur und nationaler Vergangenheitsbewältigung (Oliver Marchart/Vrääth Öhner/Heidemarie Uhl, 307–334). Tragische Märchen? Deutsche Generationendramen (Hanno Loewy, 335–360). Further essays are listed according to subject.]

42676. FILM. PETERS, CHRISTIAN: *"Wir werden dies nicht dulden!"—Veit Harlan oder die Auseinandersetzung um eine nationalsozialistische Filmkarriere.* [In]: Mannheimer Geschichtsblätter, N.F., Bd. 9, Heidelberg, 2003. Pp. 453–468, facsims., footnotes.

42677. FILM. WYDRA, THILO: *Rosenstraße: die Geschichte, die Hintergründe, die Regisseurin. Ein Film von Margarethe von Trotta.* Berlin: Nicolai, 2003. 191 pp., bibl., filmogr. [On the film about the protest in Berlin of non-Jewish wives against the deportation of their spouses (Germany, 2003).]

42678. FINAL SOLUTION. BROWNING, CHRISTOPHER: *Die Entfesselung der "Endlösung".* Nationalsozialistische Judenpolitik 1939–1942. Mit einem Beitrag von Jürgen Matthäus. München: Propyläen, 2003. 832 pp., maps., notes (626–777), bibl. (778–814), indexes (places; persons, 815–832).] [Publ. simultaneously with the title 'The origins of the Final Solution'. Jerusalem: Yad Vashem. Incl.: 7. Das "Unternehmen Barbarossa" und der Beginn der Judenvernichtung, Juni–Dezember 1941 (Jürgen Matthäus, 360–448).] [Cf.: Hitler gab das Signal (Daniel Koerfer) [in]: Zeitliteratur & Musik [Beilage von] Die Zeit, Jg. 58, Nr. 47, Hamburg, Nov. 2003, pp. 29–30. Vor der Kriegswende beschlossen (Christoph Klessmann) [in]: 'FAZ', Nr. 59, Frankfurt am Main, 10. März 2004, p. 11.]

42679. FINAL SOLUTION. JERSAK, TOBIAS: *A matter of foreign policy: "final solution" and "final victory" in Nazi Germany.* [In]: German History, Vol. 21, No. 3, London, 2003. Pp. 369–391, footnotes. [Examines Hitler's changing policy when prioritising "final victory" or the "final solution".]

42680. FINAL SOLUTION. MATTHÄUS, JÜRGEN/KWIET, KONRAD/FÖRSTER, JÜRGEN/BREITMAN, RICHARD: *Ausbildungsziel Judenmord?* "Weltanschauliche Erziehung" von SS, Polizei und Waffen-SS im Rahmen der "Endlösung". Frankfurt am Main: Fischer Taschenbuch Verlag, 2003. 219 pp., footnotes, docs. (143–204), bibl., index. Orig.-Ausg. (Die Zeit des Nationalsozialismus.) [Incl.: Einleitung (eds., 7–17). Teil I; cont.: "Gegner Nummer eins". Antisemitische Indoktrination in Himmlers Weltanschauung (Richard Breitman, 21–34). Die "Judenfrage" als Schulungsthema von SS und Polizei. "Inneres Erlebnis" und Handlungslegitimation (Jürgen Matthäus, 35–86). Die weltanschauliche Erziehung der Waffen-SS. "Kein totes Wissen, sondern lebendiger Nationalsozialismus" (Jürgen Förster, 87–113). Von Tätern zu Befehlsempfängern. Legendenbildung und Strafverfolgung nach 1945 (Konrad Kwiet, 114–138).]

—— FÖRSTER, JÜRGEN: *Wehrmacht, Krieg und Holocaust.* [See in No. 42229.]

42681. FORCED LABOUR. KARAY, FELICJA: *HASAG-Leipzig slave labour camp for women: the struggle for survival.* Told by the women and their poetry. Transl. from the Hebrew by Sara Kitai. London; Portland, OR: Vallentine Mitchell, 2002. XVII, 261 pp., illus., ports., map, notes, bibl., index. (The library of Holocaust testimonies.)

42682. FRANCE. BOITEL, ANNE: *Les enfants juifs internés au camp de Rivesaltes entre 1941 et 1942.* [In]: Revue d'histoire de la Shoah, No. 179, Paris, Sept.-Déc. 2003. Pp. 225–268, footnotes, tabs. [Incl. German-Jewish refugee children.]

42683. FRANCE. SAMUEL, VIVETTE: *Rescuing the children: a Holocaust memoir.* Transl. and with an introd. by Charles B. Paul. With a foreword by Elie Wiesel. Madison: Univ. of Wisconsin Press, 2002. XXXV, 220 pp., illus., map, facsims., notes, index. [Author describes her work with the French organisation OSE which operated initially legally, then illegally, to save Jewish children from the Nazis, incl. many German-Jewish refugee children.]

42684. FRANCONIA. *Wege in die Vernichtung. Die Deportation der Juden aus Mainfranken 1941–1943.* Begleitband zur Ausstellung des Staatsarchivs Würzburg und des Instituts für Zeitgeschichte München-Berlin in Zusammenarbeit mit dem Bezirk Unterfranken. [Gesamtred. des Begleitbandes: Albrecht Liess]. München: [Generaldirektion der Staatlichen Archive Bayerns]: 2003. 199 pp., illus., facsims., bibl. [Incl. contribs. by Alexander M. Klotz, Dieter Pohl, Herbert Schott on the deportations; also: Das Strafverfahren wegen der Deportation der Juden aus Unter- und Mittelfranken nach 1945 (Edith Raim, 178–192).]

42685. FRANK, ANNE. *Anne Frank Tagebuch.* Fassung von Otto H. Frank und Mirjam Pressler. Aus dem Niederl. von Mirjam Pressler. [Der vorliegende Band bietet die einzig autorisierte und ergänzte Fassung vom 'Anne Frank Tagebuch']. Frankfurt am Main: S. Fischer, 2003. 316 pp.

42686. FRANK, ANNE. HANSEN, JENNIFER, ed.: *Anne Frank.* San Diego: Greenhaven Press, 2003. 218 pp., illus., map, notes, bibl., index. (People who made history.) [Anthology of essays dealing both with her diary and with her skills as a writer, and her legacy.]

42687. FRANK, ANNE . *Searching for Anne Frank: letters from Amsterdam to Iowa.* By Susan Goldman Rubin in collaboration with the Simon Wiesenthal Center—Museum of Tolerance Library and Archives. New York: Harry N. Abrams, 2003. 144 pp. [Tells the story of Anne Frank's pen-friend Juanita Wagner, a 10 year-old girl from Danville, Iowa, with whom A.F. exchanged two letters in 1939.]

42688. FRANKENTHAL, HANS: *The unwelcome one: returning home from Auschwitz.* In collaboration with Andreas Plake, Babette Quinkert, and Florian Schmaltz. Transl. from the German by John A. Broadwin. Evanston, IL: Northwestern Univ. Press, 2003. XII, 169 pp. [For details and orig. edn. see No. 38802/YB XLVI.]

——— FRAENKEL, DANIEL: *The German "Righteous among the Nations": an historical appraisal.* [See No. 42568.]

42689. FRIEDMANN, DAVID: *Nach der Befreiung. Tagebuchnotizen auf dem Weg von Krakau nach Prag.* [In]: Dachauer Hefte, Jg. 19, H. 19, Berlin, Nov. 2003. Pp. 152–169, footnotes. [Excerpts from a diary held in the LBI New York; author, 1893 Mährisch Ostrau–1980 St. Louis, Missouri, graphic artist, deported to Litzmannstadt/Lodz in 1941, liberated in Blechhammer Jan. 25, 1945.]

42690. FÜRTH. SCHOPFLOCHER, ROBERT: *Kindheitsheimat.* [In]: Jüdischer Almanach [2003] des Leo Baeck Instituts, Frankfurt am Main, 2003. Pp. 52–59. [Author, who has lived in Argentina since 1937, recalls his childhood in Fürth.]

42691. FÜRTH. SPONSEL, UDO/STEINER, HELMUT: *Jüdisches Sportleben in Fürth 1933–1938.* [In]: nurinst 2002. Beiträge zur deutschen und jüdischen Geschichte, Bd. 1, Nürnberg, 2002. Pp. 85–96, notes.

42692. GALLANT, MARY J.: *Coming of age in the Holocaust: the last survivors remember.* Lanham, MD: Univ. Press of America, 2002. 323 pp., notes, appendixes, bibl., index. [18 interviews with people from

Austria, Czechoslovakia, Germany, Hungary and other countries who either survived in hiding or in camps.]

42693. GARZ, DETLEF/LEE, HYO-SEON: *"Mein Leben in Deutschland vor und nach dem 30. Januar 1933". Ergebnisse des wissenschaftlichen Preisausschreibens der Harvard University aus dem Jahre 1939.* Forschungsbericht. [In]: Jahrbuch 2003 zur Geschichte und Wirkung des Holocaust. Frankfurt am Main; New York, 2003, Pp. 333–358, notes. [See also No. 43494.]

42694. GILBERT, MARTIN: *Geistliche als Retter—auch eine Lehre aus dem Holocaust.* Übers. von Alexandra Riebe. Hrsg. von Eilert Herms. Tübingen: Mohr Siebeck, 2003. 104 pp., notes. [Text also in Engl. Address on the occasion of the 2003 Dr. Leopold-Lucas-Award.]

42695. GOLDHAGEN DEBATE. KÖNIG, HELMUT: *Die Zukunft der Vergangenheit. Der Nationalsozialismus im politischen Bewußtsein der Bundesrepublik.* Frankfurt am Main: Fischer Taschenbuch Verlag, 2003. 192 pp. (Die Zeit des Nationalsozialismus.) Orig.-Ausg. [Incl.: Goldhagen und die Deutschen (120–143).]

42696. GOTTWALDT, ALFRED: *Die Deutsche Reichsbahn und ihre jüdischen Eisenbahner.* [In]: Jahrbuch für Eisenbahngeschichte, Bd. 34, Werl, 2002. Pp. 85–88, ports., footnotes. [Also on discrimination against Jewish passengers and the deportation of Jews.]

42697. GREAT BRITAIN. BOLCHOVER, RICHARD: *British Jewry and the Holocaust.* Oxford, Portland, OR: Littman Library of Jewish Civilization, 2003. XLIV, 210 pp., notes, bibl. (188–203), index. [Paperback edn. of No. 30341/YB XXXIX, publ. in 1993.]

42698. GREAT BRITAIN. DECKER, KAROLA: *Divisions and diversity: the complexities of medical refuge in Britain, 1933–1948.* [In]: Bulletin of the History of Medicine, Vol. 77, No. 4. Baltimore, MD, Winter, 2003. Pp. 850–873, footnotes.

42699. GREAT BRITAIN. GOULD, JONATHAN S.: *The OSS and the London "Free Germans".* [In]: Studies in Intelligence, Vol. 46, No. 1, Washington, D.C., 2002. Pp. 11–29, notes. [Incl. Jürgen Kuczynski (1904–1997), and his sister Ursula Kuczynski (1907–2000), alias Ruth Werner, a Soviet spy (code name Sonja).]

42700. GREAT BRITAIN. STEINERT, JOHANNES-DIETER/WEBER-NEWTH, INGE, eds.: *European immigrants in Britain 1833–1950.* München: Saur, 2003. 224 pp., footnotes, index. [Cont. contribs. to the int. conference at the German Historical Inst. in London, Dec. 2000. Incl.: European immigrants in Britain, 1933–50 (eds., 7–16). Context; cont. the sections: Immigrants and refugees. Keynote address (Albert H. Friedlander, 19–27). The historiography of European immigrants in Britain during the twentieth century (Panikos Panayi, 29–42). Immigrants and immigration policy in Britain from the nineteenth to the twentieth centuries (Andreas Fahrmeier, 43–54). Refugees from Nazi-Germany; cont.: Exclusion, persecution, expulsion: National Socialist policy against undesirables (Wolfgang Benz, 57–72). Britain and refugees from Nazism: policies, constraint, choices (Louise London, 73–86). Jewish refugees in Britain (Marion Berghahn, 87–104). The repatriation of German political émigrés from Britain (Lothar Kettenacker, 105–118). The impact of war; cont.: Jewish Holocaust survivors between liberation and resettlement (Eva Kolinsky, 121–136). The Displaced Persons problem: repatriation and resettlement (Wolfgang Jacobmeyer, 137–150). Also four contribs. on DPs, Poles, Italians, Germans.]

42701. GREAT BRITAIN. STEWART, JOHN: *Angels or aliens? Refugee nurses in Britain, 1938 to 1942.* [In]: Medical History, Vol. 47, No. 2, London, April 2003. Pp. 149–172, footnotes.

42702. GREAT BRITAIN. STONE, DAN: *Responses to Nazism in Britain, 1933–1939: before war and Holocaust.* Basingstoke; New York: Palgrave Macmillan, 2003. XI, 269 pp, notes, index. [Deals with British public opinion of the events in Nazi Germany, esp. the treatment of the Jews, incl. attitudes of writers, politicians, historians. Also discusses the admiration many Britons had for the Nazis.]

42703. GREAT BRITAIN. SÉNÉCAL, PEGGY: *Le dévoilement de la "solution finale" (1941–1943): les réactions de la Grande-Bretagne.* [In]: Revue d'histoire de la Shoah, No. 179, Paris, Sept.-Déc. 2003. Pp. 208–224.

42704. GREAT BRITAIN & USA. PAUCKER, ARNOLD: *Die Haltung Englands und der USA zur Vernichtung der europäischen Juden im Zweiten Weltkrieg.* [In]: Deutsche Juden im Kampf um Recht und Freiheit [see No. 43407]. Pp. 293–308, notes.

42705. GUBAR, SUSAN: *Poetry after Auschwitz: remembering what one never knew.* Bloomington, IN: Indiana University Press, 2003. XXI, 313 pp., illus., bibl. (281–299), index. (Jewish Literature and Culture.)

42706. GÜNZBURG. KELLER, SVEN: *Günzburg und der Fall Josef Mengele.* Die Heimatstadt und die Jagd nach dem NS-Verbrecher. München: Oldenbourg, 2003. 211 pp., footnotes, bibl. (195–205), index. (Schriftenreihe der Vierteljahrshefte für Zeitgeschichte, Bd. 87.)

——— HALLE, ANNA SABINE: *Über Nichtglaubensjuden—Anmerkungen zu einem Begriff und einem Archivbestand.* [See No. 42554.]

42707. HAMBURG. BÖHLE, INGO: *"Juden können nicht Mitglieder der Kasse sein". Versicherungswirtschaft und die jüdischen Versicherten im Nationalsozialismus am Beispiel Hamburg.* Hamburg: Landeszentrale für politische Bildung, 2003. 50 pp., illus.

42708. BRUHNS, MAIKE: *Kunst in der Krise.* Band 1: Hamburger Kunst im "Dritten Reich". Band 2: Künstlerlexikon Hamburg. Verfemt, verfolgt—verschollen, vergessen. Hamburg: Dölling und Galitz, 2001. 2 vols., 661 pp., illus., facsims., plates, notes, docs., index; 454 pp., ports., index. [Vol. 1 cont. essays, some dealing with the persecution and and expulsion of artists; Vol. 2 incl. 212 biographies, very many among them of Jewish artists or artists classified by the Nazis as "Jews".]

42709. HAMBURG. MEYER, BEATE: *"A conto Zukunft". Hilfe und Rettung für untergetauchte Hamburger Juden.* [In]: Zeitschrift des Vereins für Hamburgische Geschichte, Bd. 88, Hamburg, 2002. Pp. 205–233, illus., footnotes.

42710. HAMBURG. MORISSE, HEIKO: *Jüdische Rechtsanwälte in Hamburg.* Ausgrenzung und Verfolgung im NS-Staat. Hamburg: Christians, 2003. 192 pp., illus., facsims., tabs., notes, bibl., index. (Hamburger Beiträge zur Geschichte der deutschen Juden, Bd. XXVI.) [Incl.: Biographischer Teil (113–176); documents the fate of 235 lawyers.]

——— HAMBURG. MÜLLER-WESEMANN, BARBARA: *Auf der Suche nach der gestohlenen Jugend. Zu Leben und Werk des Hamburger Schriftstellers Robert Muller (1925–1998).* [See No. 43404.]

42711. HAMM. BURBACH, BRIGITTE: *Jüdische Familien aus Hamm unter dem Nationalsozialismus.* [In]: Heimat-Jahrbuch des Kreises Altenkirchen und der angrenzenden Gemeinden 2004, Jg. 47, Altenkirchen, 2003. Pp. 238–245, illus., notes.

42712. HANOVER. OPPENHEIMER, LORE: *"... und eigentlich wissen wir selbst nicht, warum wir leben ...".* Aus dem Tagebuch von Lore Oppenheimer, geb. Pels. [Hannover: Region Hannover, 2002. Red.: Gabriele Lehmberg, Martina Mußmann]. 83 pp., frontis., illus., facsims., footnotes, map. (Schriftenreihe der Mahn- und Gedenkstätte Ahlem, Bd. 1.) [Incl.: Geleitwort (Michael Arndt, 3–4). Recollections and letters dealing with the Pels family, deported in Dec. 1941 from Hanover via Ahlem to Riga; L.O. lives in the US.]

42713. HAUCH, GABRIELLA , ed.: *Industrie und Zwangsarbeit im Nationalsozialismus. Mercedes Benz—VW—Reichswerke. Hermann Göring in Linz und Salzgitter.* Unter Mitarb. von Peter Gutschner und Birgit Kirchmayr. Innsbruck: StudienVerlag, 2003. 252 pp., footnotes, tabs. (Studien zur Gesellschaft- und Kulturgeschichte, Bd. 13.). [Cont. 12 essays.]

——— HELLIG, JOCELYN: *The Holocaust and antisemitism; a short history.* [See No. 43597.]

42714. HESSE, KLAUS: *Sichtbarer Terror—Öffentliche Gewalt gegen deutsche Juden 1933–1936 im Spiegel fotografischer Quellen.* [In]: WerkstattGeschichte, Jg. 11, H. 32, Hamburg, Nov. 2002. Pp. 44–56, footnotes.

42715. HEYER, HELMUT: *10. Mai 1933: "Ehrentag der freien deutschen Literatur".* [In]: Bonner Geschichtsblätter, Bd. 51/52, Bonn, 2001/2002 [publ. 2003]. Pp. 285–328, footnotes. [On the bookburning.]

42716. HICKMAN, HANNAH: *Let one go free.* Newark: Quill Press, 2003. XI, 119 pp., illus. [Author, orig. Hannah Weinberger, b. 1928 in Würzburg, tells the story of her childhood in Würzburg, her escape to England on a Kindertransport and subsequent life there with adoptive parents.]

42717. HILBERG, RAUL: *The destruction of the European Jews.* Third edn. New Haven: Yale Univ. Press, 2003. 3 vols. 1440 pp., diagrs., maps, tabs., notes, bibl., index. [For the 1985 edn. see No. 22134/YB XXXI.]

42718. HISTORIOGRAPHY. BERG, NICOLAS: *Der Holocaust und die westdeutschen Historiker.* Erforschung und Erinnerung. Göttingen: Wallstein, 2003. 766 pp., footnotes, bibl. (663–761). (Moderne Zeit, Bd. III.) [Abbr. and revised dissertation (Freiburg Univ., 2001). Cf.: Bespr. (Alexandra Przyrembel) [in]: Historische Anthropologie, Jg. 11, H. 3, Köln, 2003, pp. 482–485. Forschung ohne Erinnerung. Nicolas Bergs Buch über den Holocaust und die deutschen Historiker sorgt für Streit (Volker Ullrich) [in]: Die Zeit, Nr. 29, Hamburg, 10. Juli 2003, p. 39. Beware the moral high ground (Ian Kershaw) [in]: 'TLS', London, Oct. 10, 2003.]

42719. HISTORIOGRAPHY. BERG, NICOLAS: *Ein Außenseiter der Holocaustforschung—Joseph Wulf (1912–1974) im Historikerdiskurs der Bundesrepublik.* [In]: Leipziger Beiträge zu jüdischer Geschichte und Kultur, Bd. I, München, 2003. Pp. 311–346, footnotes.

42720. HISTORIOGRAPHY. BERG, NICOLAS: *Lesarten des Judenmords.* [In]: Wandlungsprozesse in Westdeutschland. Belastung, Integration, Liberalisierung 1945–1980. Hrsg. von Ulrich Herbert. Göttingen: Wallstein, 2002. Pp. 91–139, footnotes.

42721. HISTORIOGRAPHY. BRINKMANN, TOBIAS: *Amerika und der Holocaust: Die Debatte über die "Amerikanisierung des Holocaust" in den USA und ihre Rezeption in Deutschland.* [In]: neue politische literatur, Jg. 48, H. 2, Frankfurt am Main, 2003. Pp. 251–270.] [Review essay.]

42722. HISTORIOGRAPHY. INGRAO, CHRISTIAN: *Conquérir, aménager, exterminer. Recherches récentes sur la Shoah.* [In]: Annales HSS, Tome 58, No. 2, Paris, 2003. Pp. 417–438, footnotes. [Review essay.]

42723. HISTORIOGRAPHY. KAUTZ, FRED: *Die Holocaust-Forschung im Sperrfeuer der Flakhelfer: vom befangenen Blick deutscher Historiker aus der Kriegsgeneration.* 2., erw. Aufl. Frankfurt am Main: Verlag Ed. AV, 2002. 172 pp., bibl. [English edn.: The German historians: Hitler's willing executioners and Daniel Goldhagen. Transl. from the German by the author. Montreal; London, Black Rose, 2003. 204 pp. For details of the orig. edn. with the title Gold-Hagen und die "hürnen Sewfriedte" see No. 36299/YB XLIV.]

42724. HISTORIOGRAPHY. MICHMAN, DAN: *Holocaust historiography: a Jewish perspective, conceptualizations, terminology, approaches, and fundamental issues.* London; Portland, OR: Vallentine Mitchell, 2003. X, 435 pp., notes, index. (Parkes-Wiener series on Jewish studies.) [A collection of articles publ. previously; the Hebrew edn. of this book was publ. in 1998. Articles are arranged in the sections: I. 'The Holocaust'. II. The 'Final Solution'. III. Fascism and National-Socialism. IV. Judenrat. V. Relief, rescue, foresight. VI. Resistance. VII. Religious Jewry and the Jewish religion. VIII. Holocaust and rebirth. IX. Holocaust historiography: History and problems.]

42725. HISTORIOGRAPHY. PÄTZOLD, KURT: *Ausgewählte neuere Literatur zur Geschichte von Judenverfolgung und Judenmord. Anzeige und Kommentar.* [In]: Bulletin für Faschismus- und Weltkriegsforschung, H. 20, Berlin, 2003. Pp. 56–84, footnotes. [On publs. from the 1980s to the present.]

42726. HISTORIOGRAPHY. STONE, DAN: *Constructing the Holocaust.* Foreword by Jonathan Webber. London; Portland, OR: Vallentine Mitchell, 2003. XX, 308 pp., notes, index.

——— HISTORIOGRAPHY. WASSERMANN, HENRY: *On the construction of anti-semitism.* [See No. 43628.]

42727. HITLER, ADOLF. CARRIER, RICHARD C.: *Hitler's table talks: troubling finds.* German Studies Review, Vol. 26, No. 3, Tempe, AZ, Oct. 2003. Pp. 561–576, notes. [Discusses the authenticity and the different versions of the 'table talks'.]

42728. HITLER, ADOLF. DORPAT, THEODORE L.: *Wounded monster: Hitler's path from trauma to malevolence.* Lanham, MD: Univ. Press of America, 2002. XXIII, 344 pp., notes, bibl., index.

42729. HITLER, ADOLF. REUTH, RALF GEORG: *Hitler.* Eine politische Biographie. München: Piper, 2003. 685 pp., illus., notes (651–670), index. [Incl.: "Die jüdische Weltverschwörung" als Erklärung für die deutsche Not (1918–20), (67–114).] [Cf.: Bespr. (Hans Rudolf Wahl) [in]: Zeitschrift für Geschichtswissenschaft, Jg. 52, H. 2, Berlin, 2004, pp. 190–191.]

42730. HITLER, ADOLF. SAUER, CHRISTOPH: *Rede als Erzeugung von Komplizentum. Hitler und die öffentliche Erwähnung der Judenvernichtung.* [In]: Hitler der Redner. Hrsg. von Josef Kopperschmidt in Verb. mit Johannes G. Pankau. München: Fink, 2003. Pp. 413–440, footnotes.

42731. HOFFMANN, DANIEL: *Ariadnefaden und Auschwitznummer. Cordelia Edvardsons Errettung aus Elisabeth Langgässers Mythenkosmos.* [In]: Arcadia, Int. Zeitschrift für Literaturwissenschaft, Bd. 38, H. 1, Berlin; New York, 2003. Pp. 39–54, footnotes. [On C.E.'s autobiographical novel 'Burned child seeks the fire'. Incl. English abstract.]

42732. HOFMANN, MICHAEL: *Literaturgeschichte der Shoah.* Münster: Aschendorff, 2003. 153 pp., notes, bibl. (Literaturwissenschaft, Theorie & Beispiele, Bd. 4.)

42733. HOLOCAUST. BARON, L.: *The Holocaust and American public memory, 1945–1960.* [In]: Holocaust and Genocide Studies, Vol. 17, No. 1, Oxford, Spring 2003. Pp. 62–88, notes. [Article suggests that, in the US, heightened awareness of the Holocaust only began in the 1960s with the Eichmann trial.]

42734. HOLOCAUST. BOLKOSKY, SIDNEY M.: *Searching for meaning in the Holocaust.* Westport, CT: Greenwood Press, 2002. XV, 128 pp., bibl., index. (Contributions to the Study of Religion, No. 69.)

42735. HOLOCAUST. LANG, BEREL: *Act and idea in the Nazi genocide.* Syracuse, NY: Syracuse Univ. Press. 2003. XXVII, 258 pp., notes, bibl., index. (Religion, theology, and the Holocaust.) [For orig. edn. in 1990 see No. 27291/YB XXXVI.]

42736. HOLOCAUST. MCKALE, DONALD M.: *Hitler's shadow war: the Holocaust and World War II.* New York: Cooper Square Press: Distrib. by National Book Network, 2002. XVII, 541 pp., illus., notes, index. [Cont.: 1. Germany and the rise of Hitler. 2. The Nazi revolution and German Jews, 1933. 3. The revolution ends?: between anti-Jewish violence and legislation, 1933–36. 4. Foreign aggression and the "Jewish Question", 1936–38. 5. The final steps to war and intensification of Jewish persecution, 1938–39. 6. The beginning of racial war, 1939–40. 7. Expanding the racial war, 1940. 8. The racial war in the east, 1941. 9. Repercussions of the war and decision for the final solution. 10. The killing centers and deportations of Polish Jewry, 1942. 11. Attempted revolts, Auschwitz, and the beginning deportations of European Jewry, 1942. 12. Growing Jewish resistance and continued deportations, 1943. 13. Expansion of Auschwitz, Allied victories, and more deportations, 1943–44. 14. The final solution amid German defeat, 1944–45. 15. Bystanders: the world and the Holocaust, 1942– 44. 16. Rescue, relief, and war crimes trials. 17. The perpetrators: types, motives, and the post-war era. 18. The victims: destruction, resistance, and memory. 19. Learning from the Holocaust.]

42737. HOLOCAUST. TEC, NECHAMA: *Resilience and courage: women, and men, and the Holocaust.* New Haven: Yale Univ. Press, 2003. VII, 438 pp. [Deals with the psychological impact of the Holocaust on women; incl. Jewish resistance, interviews with survivors.]

42738. HOLOCAUST. WISTRICH, ROBERT S.: *Hitler und der Holocaust.* Aus dem Engl. von Sabine Schulte. Berlin: Berliner Taschenbuch Verlag, 2003. 414 pp., notes (337–390), chronol., maps, index. Deutsche Erstausgabe. [Orig. publ. 2001 with the title Hitler and the Holocaust, see No. 40027/YB XLVII; incl. a chap. on Great Britain, the USA and the Holocaust (259–294).]

42739. HOLOCAUST DENIAL. MAYER, ELKE: *Verfälschte Vergangenheit.* Zur Entstehung der Holocaust-Leugnung in der Bundesrepublik Deutschland unter besonderer Berücksichtigung rechtsextremer Publizistik von 1945 bis 1970. Frankfurt am Main; New York: Lang, 2003. 291 pp., footnotes, bibl. (275–291). (Europäische Hochschulschriften, Reihe III: Geschichte und ihre Hilfswissenschaften, Bd. 927.) Zugl.: Augsburg, Univ., Diss., 2001.

42740. HUNGARY. BLAIKIE, EVI: *Magdas's daughter: a hidden child's journey home.* Introd. by Bella Brodzki. New York: Feminist Press at the City Univ. of New York, 2003. XX, 277 pp., illus., notes. (The Helen Rose Scheuer Jewish women's series.) [Deals with author's childhood, first in France, then in hiding in Hungary where her Hungarian parents, then living in France, had sent her to escape the German occupation. Lives in the US.]

42741. HUNGARY. COLE, TIM: *Holocaust city: the making of a Jewish ghetto.* New York: Routledge, 2003. XV, 303 pp., illus., notes, bibl., index. [Author focuses primarily on the Budapest ghetto.]

42742. HUNGARY. FENYVESI, CHARLES: *When angels fooled the world: rescuers of Jews in wartime Hungary.* Madison: Univ. of Wisconsin Press, 2003. XLI, 302 pp., illus., notes, bibl.

42743. *The impact of Nazism: new perspectives on the Third Reich and its legacy.* Ed. by Alan E. Steinweis and Daniel E. Rogers. Lincoln: Univ. of Nebraska Press, 2003. XVII, 260 pp., notes, bibl., index. [Incl. chaps.: Antisemitic scholarship in the Third Reich and the case of Peter-Heinz Seraphim (Alan E. Steinweis, 68–80; refers to S.'s antisemitic publications). A reassessment of Volksdeutsche and Jews in the Volhynia-Galicia-Narew resettlement (Valdis P. Lumans, 81–100). The Chancellors of the Federal Republic of Germany and the political legacy of the Holocaust (Daniel E. Rogers, 231–247).]

42744. *"... ist uns noch allen lebendig in Erinnerung". Biografische Porträts von Opfern der nationalsozialistischen "Euthanasie-"Anstalt Pirna-Sonnenstein.* Bearb. und eingel. von Boris Böhm und Ricarda Schulze. Dresden: Stiftung Sächsische Gedenkstätten zur Erinnerung an die Opfer politischer Gewaltherrschaft, 2003. 154 pp., ports., illus., facsims., footnotes. (Lebenszeugnisse—Leidenswege, H. 14.) [Incl.: "... dass er ein hochgebildeter Intellektueller war, liberal gesinnt ...". Arnold Grünfeld (1887–1941) (118–129, port., illus., footnotes).] [A.G., rabbi in Eger and Iglau.]

42745. ITALY. VILLANI, CINZIA: *Zwischen Rassengesetzen und Deportation: Juden in Südtirol, im Trentino und in der Provinz Belluno 1933–1945.* Aus dem Ital. von Michaela Heissenberger. Bearb. von Hugo Seyr. Mit einem Vorwort von Klaus Voigt und Federico Steinhaus. Innsbruck: Wagner, 2003. 208 pp., illus., facsims., tabs., footnotes, bibl., index. (Veröff. des Südtiroler Landesarchivs, Bd. 15.) [Focuses on the fate of the refugees.]

42746. IZBICA. KUWALEK, ROBERT: *Das Durchgangslager in Izbica.* [In]: Theresienstädter Studien und Dokumente 2003, Prag, 2003. Pp. 321–352, footnotes.

42747. JAMES, HAROLD: *Die Deutsche Bank im Dritten Reich.* Aus dem Engl. übers. von Karin Schambach und Karl Heinz Siber. München: Beck, 2003. 267 pp., notes (228–252), bibl., indexes. [Incl. the section: III. Antisemitismus und die deutschen Banken (42–84); also a chap. entitled Jüdische Bankkonten (196–204).]

42748. JOSHI, VANDANA: *Gender and power in the Third Reich: female denouncers and the Gestapo (1933–45).* Basingstoke; New York: Palgrave Macmillan, 2003. XX, 229., tabs., notes, bibl. (215–223), index. [Incl. chap.: Fishing troubled waters?: gender perspectives on denouncers and their Jewish victims; also incl. the Gestapo's treatment of Jews, as well as specific case files on Düsseldorf.]

42749. *Jüdischer Buchbesitz als Beutegut.* Eine Veranstaltung des Niedersächsischen Landtages und der Niedersächsischen Landesbibliothek. Symposium im Niedersächsischen Landtag am 14. November 2002. [Hannover]: Landtag Niedersachsen, 2003. 87 pp., footnotes (Schriftenreihe des Niedersächsischen Landtages zu Themen, die für die Öffentlichkeit von Interesse sind, H. 50.) [Focuses on Lower Saxony, Hesse and Baden. Incl. essays by Peter Schulze, Klaus-Dieter Lehmann, Anja Heuß, Veronica Albrink, Jürgen Babendreier, Bernd Reifenberg, Ingo Toussaint, Berndt von Egidy.]

42750. KALTHOFF, MECHTHILD: *Manfred Weil—Sein oder Nichtsein*. Köln: Elen Verlag, 2002. 262 pp., illus. [The story of the artist M.W.'s childhood in Cologne, flight to Belgium in 1939, and his survival, after deportation to Gurs and going into hiding, as a "Belgian" forced labourer in Germany; lives in Meckenheim; for his wife's story see No. 39454/YB 46.]

42751. KATER, MICHAEL H., ed.: *Music and Nazism: art and tyranny, 1933–1945*. Laaber: Laaber Verlag, 2003. 328 pp., illus., facsims., notes, bibl., index. [Proceedings of a conference at the Canadian Centre for German and European Studies, York University, Toronto, Oct. 1999. Selected essays: Stefan Wolpe: broken sequences (Austin Clarkson). Stefan Zweig and the fall of the Reich Music Chamber President, Richard Strauss (Albrecht Riethmüller).]

42752. KATZ, BRUNO (BRUNO J. KEITH): *Mein Kampf ums Überleben in einer Welt der Vorurteile als Teil der Geschichte Barntrups in Lippe oder Die Schwierigkeiten und Ängste eines Barntruper Juden während der Zeit zwischen den zwei Weltkriegen*. Hrsg. v. Erika und Martin Böttcher. Übers. v. Karl-Heinz Richter. Detmold: Ges. f. Christl.-Jüd. Zusammenarbeit, 2002. 282 pp., illus. (Panu Derech—Bereitet den Weg, Ges. f. Christl.-Jüd. Zusammenarbeit in Lippe e.V., Bd. 22.) [Author, b. 1911 in Barntrup/Lippe-Detmold, teacher at Jewish schools in Ahlem, Beelitz and Altona, emigr. 1939 to Shanghai, 1947 to the US. Memoirs written in 1998.]

42753. KATZ, ZWI: *Von den Ufern der Memel ins Ungewisse. Eine Jugend im Schatten des Holocaust*. Mit einem Geleitwort von Ernst Holthaus und einem Nachwort von Christoph Dieckmann. Zürich: Pendo, 2002. 173 pp., illus. [Author, b. 1927 into a German-speaking family in Kovno, survived several concentration camps and the death march from Dachau to Waakirchen; after liberation emigr. illegally to Palestine. Now lives in Israel.]

42754. KELLER, STEFAN: *Die Rückkehr. Joseph Springs Geschichte*. Zürich: Rotpunktverlag, 2003. 236 pp., illus., notes (221–236). [Tells the story of Joseph Spring (orig. Sprung), b. 1927 in Berlin, who as a young boy fled through several countries, in Nov. 1943 was delivered to the Gestapo by the Swiss border police and deported to Auschwitz. Also his unsuccessful lawsuit against the Swiss government sixty years later, alleging its complicity in genocide. J.S. lives in Melbourne.]

42755. KINDERTRANSPORT. *Die Kindertransporte 1938/39. Rettung und Integration*. Mit Beiträgen von Ilse Aichinger [et al.]. Übers. aus dem Engl. und Amerik. von Claudia Curio und Andrea Nagel. Hrsg. von Wolfgang Benz, Claudia Curio und Andrea Hammel. Frankfurt am Main: Fischer Taschenbuch Verlag, 2003. 253 pp., gloss., notes. (Die Zeit des Nationalsozialismus.) [Cont.: Emigration als Rettung und Trauma. Zum historischen Kontext der Kindertransporte nach England (Wolfgang Benz, 9–16). Kindheit im Exil. Ein Forschungsdesiderat (Marianne Kröger, 17–33). Kindertransport. Geschichte und Erinnerung (Rebekka Göpfert, 34–43). Klassenzugehörigkeit als Faktor der sozialen Adaption. Sozialmilieus im deutschen Judentum (Susan Kleinman/Chana Moshenska, 44–59). "Unsichtbare" Kinder. Auswahl- und Eingliederungsstrategien der Hilfsorganisationen (Claudia Curio, 60–81). Meist war es eine "Sie". Die Rolle britischer Frauen bei der Rettung und Versorgung jüdischer Flüchtlingskinder (Sybil Oldfield, 82–101). Identitätsbildung und Integration. Exilschulen in Großbritannien (Hildegard Feidel-Mertz, 102–119). Bildung oder Ausbildung? Das Jawne-Gymnasiuzm und die ORT-Schule in Deutschland und England (Monica Lowenberg, 120–135). Traumatisierung durch Trennung. Familien- und Heimatverlust als kindliche Katastrophen (Ute Benz, 136–155). Familiengedächtnis. Erste und zweite Generation in der therapeutischen Praxis (Ruth Barnett, 156–170). Armband, Handtuch, Taschenuhr. Objekte des letzten Augenblicks in Erinnerung und Erzählung (Mona Körte, 171–185). Familienbilder im Spannungsfeld. Autobiographische Texte ehemaliger Kindertransport-Teilnehmer (Andrea Hammel, 186–202). Erinnerungen (203–246; contribs. by Ilse Aichinger, Helga Aichinger-Michie, Iris Guske, Vernon Saunders, Fred Jordan).]

42756. KITTEL, SABINE: *Erinnerungen an die Befreiung—Jüdische Überlebende erzählen über die letzten Kriegstage*. [In]: Kriegsende 1945 in Deutschland. Im Auftrag des Militärgesch. Forschungsamtes hrsg. von Jörg Hillmann [et al.]. München: Oldenbourg, 2002. (Beiträge zur Militärgeschichte, Bd. 55.) Pp. 223–238, footnotes.

42757. KOONZ, CLAUDIA: *The Nazi conscience*. Cambridge, MA: Belknap Press of Harvard Univ. Press, 2003. 362 pp., illus., map, facsims., tabs., notes, index. [On antisemitic propaganda, the "Jewish

Question", Nazi racial theories and laws, and how they were made acceptable to the German people, including intellectuals, by stressing ethnic pride and loyalty to Volk and Fatherland.]

42758. KRAFT, ROBERT N.: *Memory perceived: recalling the Holocaust.* Westport, CT: Praeger, 2002. [Based on 200 hours of testimonies of Holocaust survivors.]

42759. KREFELD-HÜLS. MELLEN, WERNER: *Juden in Krefeld-Hüls: Gegen das Vergessen.* Mit einem Beitrag von Ingrid Schupetta: "Deportationsziel Riga". Krefeld: Kronsbein, 2003. 144 pp., illus. (Niederrheinische Regionalkunde, 3.) [Incl. a documentation of the cemetery in Hüls (names and biogr. data only).]

42760. KULTURBUND. HAASE, RICARDA: *Goethe im Getto.* Zum Selbstverständnis des "Kulturbundes deutscher Juden" (1933–1935). [In]: Tribüne, Jg. 42, H. 167, Frankfurt am Main, 2003. Pp. 138–147.

42761. LAASPHE. OPFERMANN, ULRICH FRIEDRICH: *Die Ausschreitungen vom 9. und 10. November 1938 in einer ländlichen Kleinstadt und ihre Wahrnehmung und Rezeption nach 1945. Das Beispiel Laasphe.* [In]: Siegener Beiträge. Jahrbuch für regionale Geschichte. Jg. 8, Siegen, 2003. Pp. 175–216, notes, illus., facsims.

42762. LANDÉ, PETER: *Jewish emigration training centers in Germany.* [In]: Stammbaum, Issue 22, New York, Winter 2003. Pp. 20–22. [Article is followed by reminiscences of Hans Hirsch about the training farm in Gross-Breesen/Silesia (22–23).]

42763. LANGER, PHIL C.: *Schreiben gegen die Erinnerung? Autobiographien von Überlebenden der Shoah.* Hamburg: Krämer, 2002. 195 pp., illus., footnotes, bibl. (164–194). [On the memoirs of Ruth Elias, Ruth Klüger and Anita Lasker-Wallfisch.]

42764. LAQUEUR, WALTER: *Der Exodus der jüdischen Jugend nach 1933.* [In]: Auswanderung, Flucht, Vertreibung, Exil im 19. und 20. Jahrhundert [see No. 42513]. Pp. 133–144.

42765. LARGE, DAVID CLAY: *And the world closed its doors: the story of one family abandoned to the Holocaust.* New York: Basic Books, 2003. XXIII, 278 pp., illus., notes, bibl. (257–264), index. [Deals with the Allies' restrictive refugee policies, using the example of Max Schohl and his family who were turned away by Britain, the US, Chile and Brazil.] [M. Sch., 1884 Pirmasens–1943 Auschwitz, owner of a chemical factory.]

42766. LAUBE, STEFAN: *"Nach einer Mitteilung unserer Geschäftsstelle vom 20. Mai soll Herr Oppenheimer Jude sein".* Über den Umgang mit Lebensversicherungspolicen im Dritten Reich. Ein vernachlässigtes Thema und seine Quellen. [In]: Vierteljahrshefte für Zeitgeschichte, Jg. 51, H. 3, München, Juli 2003. Pp. 339–361, footnotes. [Engl. abstract on p. 477; deals with German insurance companies and their Jewish clients.]

42767. *The legacy of the Holocaust: children and the Holocaust.* Ed. by Zygmunt Mazur [et al.] Cracow: Jagiellonian Univ. Press, 2002. 459 pp., illus., notes. [Proceedings of the conference 'The Legacy of the Holocaust: children and the Holocaust' held at the Jagiellonian Univ. in Cracow and on the site of the former Auschwitz Concentration Camp, May 24–27, 2001.]

42768. LEICHTER, OTTO: *Briefe ohne Antwort. Aufzeichnungen aus dem Pariser Exil für Käthe Leichter 1938–1939.* Hrsg. von Heinrich Berger [et al.] und mit einem Nachwort von Henry O. Leichter. Wien: Böhlau, 2003. 348 pp., footnotes. [Incl. letters found in 1996 in the Moscow "Special Archives". Nachwort (Henry O. Leichter (323–340; son of O. and K.L.). See also No. 43368.] [Käthe L. née Pick, 1895 Vienna–March 17, 1942 Bernburg concentration camp; O.L., data see No. 40582/YB XLVII.]

42769. LEIPZIG. HEINTZE, BEATRIX: *Walter Cramer, die Kammgarnspinnerei Stöhr & Co in Leipzig und die sogenannte "Judenfrage".* Materialien zu einer Gratwanderung zwischen Hilfe und Kapitulation. Leipzig: Leipziger Universitätsverlag, 2003. 143 pp., frontis., illus., facsim., footnotes, bibl., index. (Sächsisches Wirtschaftsarchiv e.V. Erinnerungen, Bd. 3.) [W.C., industrialist, executed as member of the resistance in Berlin-Plötzensee, Nov. 1944, tried to evade implementing laws concerning deportation and murder of Jewish slave workers.]

42770. LEIPZIG. HELD, STEFFEN: *Carl Goerdeler in Leipzig—Antisemitismus und Kommunalverwaltung 1933–1936.* [In]: Leipziger Beiträge zur jüdischen Geschichte und Kultur, Bd. I, München, 2003. Pp. 283–310, footnotes.

42771. LEIPZIG. KABUS, SYLVIA: *Wir waren die Letzten ... Gespräche mit vertriebenen Leipziger Juden.* Mit Essays von Sylvia Kabus. Porträtfotografien von Karin Wieckhorst. Beucha: Sax Verlag, 2003. 212 pp., frontis., ports., footnotes. [Incl. 12 memoirs; essays on Leipzig-Rosenthal, the expulsion of the Polish Jews, deportations a.o.]

42772. LEICHSENRING, JANA, ed.: *Frauen und Widerstand.* Münster: Lit, 2003. 165 pp., footnotes, bibl., index. (Schriftenreihe der Forschungsgemeinschaft 20. Juli, Bd. 1.) [Selected essays pertaining to Jews and aid for Jews: Der Einsatz von Katharina Staritz für Menschen jüdischer Herkunft im Kontext der schlesischen Vertrauensstelle der "Büro Pfarrer Grüber" (Hannelore Erhart, 55–73). Der "Versuch, in der Wahrheit zu leben" und die Rettung von jüdischen Angehörigen durch deutsche Frauen im "Dritten Reich" (Nathan Stoltzfus, 74–95). Das Frauenkonzentrationslager Ravensbrück (Sigrid Jacobeit, 96–104).]

42773. LITHUANIA. *Holocaust in Litauen. Krieg, Judenmorde und Kollaboration im Jahre 1941.* Hrsg. von Vincas Bartusevicius, Joachim Tauber und Wolfram Wette. Mit einem Geleitwort von Ralph Giordano. Köln: Böhlau, 2003. VI, 337 pp., illus., docs., notes, indexes. [Cont. 22 contribs.; incl.: Feldwebel Anton Schmid. Judenretter in Vilnius 1941–1942 (Arno Lustiger, 185–198).]

42774. LITHUANIA. KOUDYTÉ, DALIA/STANKEVICIUS, RYMANTAS: *Whoever saves one life ... The efforts to save Jews in Lithuania between 1941 and 1944.* [Engl. edn. ed. by Alexander Fortescue]. Vilnius: Garnelis, 2002. 231 pp., illus. [Orig. publ. in 1990. Cf.: Bespr. (Klaus-Peter Friedrich) [in]: Zeitschrift für Ostmitteleuropa-Forschung, Jg. 52, H. 4, Marburg, 2003, pp. 615–616.]

42775. LITHUANIA. TAUBER, JOACHIM: *"Juden, Eure Geschichte auf litauischem Boden ist zu Ende!" Litauen und der Holocaust im Jahr 1941.* [In]: Osteuropa, Jg. 52, Bd. 9/10. Stuttgart, 2002. Pp. 1346–1360, footnotes.

——— LITHUANIA. WETTE, WOLFRAM/HOFFMANN, DETLEV, eds.: *Litauen 1941 und 2001. Auf den Spuren des SS-Massenmörders Karl Jäger.* Erlebnisberichte von Freiburger Schülern und Studenten. [See No. 43003.]

42776. LÖRRACH. CYBINSKI, NIKOLAUS: *Vier Fotos aus Lörrach.* [In]: Badische Heimat, Jg. 82, H. 4, Freiburg, 2002. Pp. 693–696, illus. [On photographs documenting the deportation of Jews from Lörrach to Gurs in Oct. 1940.]

42777. LOMMATZSCH, ERIK: *Hans Globke und der Nationalsozialismus.* Eine Skizze. [In]: Historisch-Politische Mitteilungen, Jg. 10, Köln, 2003. Pp. 95–128, footnotes. [Incl. Engl. summary, p. 384. Discusses G.s different positions as a civil servant, esp. his influence on legislation and his participation in commentating the Nuremberg laws.]

42778. LOWER SAXONY. OBENAUS, HERBERT: *Die Bestattung von sowjetischen Kriegsgefangenen auf jüdischen Friedhöfen in Deutschland während des Zweiten Weltkriegs.* [In]: Die Welt querdenken. Festschrift für Hans-Heinrich Nolte zum 65. Geburtstag. Hrsg. von Carl-Heinz Hauptmeyer [et al.]. Frankfurt am Main; New York, 2003. Pp. 235–245, footnotes. [Focuses on cemeteries in the Hanover and Weser-Ems regions.]

42779. MAINZ. *Stadtführer: Auf den Spuren des Nationalsozialismus durch Mainz.* Sonderheft der Mainzer Geschichtsblätter hrsg. vom Verein für Sozialgeschichte Mainz e.V. in Zusammenarbeit mit der Stadt Mainz. Bearb. von Jan Storre. Mainz: [Stadt Mainz], 2002. 63 pp., illus., bibl., plan.

42780. MANNHEIM. CAROLI, MICHAEL: *Die Bücherverbrennung "Wider den undeutschen Geist" in Mannheim am 19. Mai 1933.* [In]: Mannheimer Geschichtsblätter, N.F., Bd. 9, Heidelberg, 2003. Pp. 441–451, footnotes.

42781. MANNHEIM. KELLER, VOLKER: *Mannheim—Große Merzelstr. 7.* Ein "Judenhaus" in der NS-Zeit. [In]: Badische Heimat, Jg. 83, H. 3, Freiburg, 2003. Pp. 451–459. [Incl. list of names.]

42782. MARTIUS, GOETZ-ALEXANDER: *1933–1945. Auch das geschah in Deutschland: Martius zum Beispiel.* [In]: Genealogie, Jg. 52, Bd. XXVI, H. 1/2, Neustadt/Aisch, Jan.-Feb. 2003. Pp. 402–411, footnotes. [Also on the Martius family by the same author: Das Hitlerfoto [in]: Genealogie, Sonderheft 2002/2003, pp. 42–45, illus.; Hedwig Conrad-Martius [in]: Genealogie, Jg. 52, Bd. XXVI, März-April 2003, pp. 469–484; final part of the series; for previous parts see No. 41402/YB XLVIII.]

42783. MAURER, TRUDE: *Kunden, Patienten, Nachbarn und Freunde. Beziehungen zwischen Juden und Nichtjuden in Deutschland 1933–1938.* [In]: Geschichte in Wissenschaft und Unterricht, Jg. 54, H. 3, Göttingen, 2003. Pp. 154–166, footnotes.

——— MAURER, TRUDE: *Vom Alltag zum Ausnahmezustand: Juden in der Weimarer Republik und im Nationalsozialismus 1918–1945.* [See in No. 42221.]

——— MEYER ZU UPTRUP, WOLFRAM: *Kampf gegen die "jüdische Weltverschwörung": Propaganda und Antisemitismus der Nationalsozialisten 1919 bis 1945.* [See No. 43608.]

42784. MINSK. PROJEKTGRUPPE BELARUS IM JUGENDCLUB COURAGE KÖLN E.V., ed.: *"Existiert das Ghetto noch?". Weißrussland: Jüdisches Überleben gegen nationalsozialistische Herrschaft.* [Projektgruppe: Andreas Hollender et al.] Berlin: Assoziation A, 2003. 319 pp., illus., chronol., gloss. [Incl. interviews with/memoirs of survivors in Belarus, essays on Belarus Jewish history; also excerpts from the memoirs of Heinz Rosenberg (172–192). Selected essays: Das Minsker Ghetto (Daniel Romanowsky, 211–233). Trostenez—das Vernichtungslager bei Minsk (Paul Kohl, 234–249). Die Täter: Zur justiziellen Aufarbeitung von NS-Verbrechen (Heiner Lichtenstein, 295–307).]

42785. MIRON, GUY: *The emancipation 'pantheon of heroes' in the German-Jewish public memory in the 1930s.* [In]: German History, Vol. 21, No. 4, London, 2003. Pp. 476–504, footnotes. [Discusses how German Jewry was forced to reevaluate the history of emancipation, and the influence of figures such as Moses Mendelssohn, Gabriel Riesser, Rahel Varnhagen in the light of events of the 1930s.]

——— MIRON, GUY: *Emancipation and assimilation in the German-Jewish discourse of the 1930s.* [See No. 42240.]

42786. MOGULOF, MILLY: *Foiled: Hitler's Jewish Olympian: the Helene Mayer story.* Oakland, CA: RDR Books, 2002. 253 pp., illus., notes, index. [Tells the story of the "half-Jewish" German fencing champion who had won a gold medal at the 1928 Olympics and participated in the 1936 Olympics.]

42787. MORLOCK, BERND: *Der Geschichte ein Gesicht geben: Zeitzeugen berichten.* [In]: Badische Heimat, Jg. 82, H. 2, Freiburg, 2002. Pp. 335–343. [On oral history projects and their outcomes; incl. witnesses from Israel.]

42788. MÜLLER, BERNHARD: *Alltag im Zivilisationsbruch. Das Ausnahme-Unrecht gegen die jüdische Bevölkerung in Deutschland 1933–1945.* Eine rechtstatsächliche Untersuchung des Sonderrechts und seiner Folgewirkungen auf den "Alltag" der Deutschen jüdischer Abstammung und jüdischen Bekenntnisses. München: Allitera Verlag; Norderstedt: Books on Demand, 2003. 696 pp., chapter notes, bibl. (672–691). Zugl.: Bielefeld, Univ., Diss., 2002. [Incl. the sections: I. Teil: Der Aufbruch in das Unrechtssystem. II. Teil: Die Vernichtung der beruflichen Existenz. III. Teil: Die "Entjudung" der deutschen Wirtschaft. IV. Teil: Vom Angriff auf das Vermögen bis zu dessen gänzlicher Einverleibung. V. Teil: Die Rechtsgebiete. VI. Teil: Die "rassisch" motivierte Diskrimination. VII. Teil: Kompensation und Selbsthilfe (on the Reichsvertretung and Reichsvereinigung, Jewish daily life, resistance, emigration, illegal life).]

42789. MÜLLER, INGO: *Aus demokratischem Recht wird Willkür. Juristen und die nationalsozialistische Judenverfolgung.* [In]: "Gegen alle Vergeblichkeit". Jüdischer Widerstand gegen den Nationalsozialismus [see No. 42899]. Pp. 129–132, footnotes.

42790. MUNICH. *Biographisches Gedenkbuch der Münchner Juden 1933–1945.* Band 1 (A-L). Hrsg. vom Stadtarchiv München. Erarbeitet von Andreas Heusler, Brigitte Schmidt, Eva Ohlen, Tobias Weger und Simone Dicke. München: Stadtarchiv, 2003. 871 pp. [Incl. prefaces by Christian Ude, Richard Bauer; Geleitwort (Charlotte Knobloch, 11–13). Einleitung (Andreas Heusler, 15–24, notes).]

42791. MUNICH. DRECOLL, AXEL: *Finanzverwaltung und Judenfrage. Die Rolle des Fiskus bei der Entziehung, Verwaltung und Verwertung jüdischen Vermögens, dargestellt am Beispiel jüdischer Ärzte Münchens.* [In]: Jüdische Geschichte: Alte Herausforderungen, neue Ansätze [see No. 42230]. Pp. 143–166, footnotes.

42792. *Nazi Europe and the Final Solution.* Ed. by David Bankier and Israel Gutman. Jerusalem: Yad Vashem, the Holocaust Martyrs' and Heroes' Remembrance Authority, the International Institute for Holocaust Research, 2003. 572 pp., illus., footnotes, indexes (names, places). [Collection of articles based on papers delivered at an int. conference in Warsaw, Aug. 1999. Section I deals with Germany; cont.: Signaling the Final Solution to the German people (David Bankier, 15–39). Exclusion as a stage in persecution: the Jewish situation in Germany, 1933–1941 (Wolfgang Benz, 40–52). The boycott campaign as an arena of collective violence against Jews in Germany, 1933–1938 (Michael Wildt, 53–72). Customers, patients, neighbors and friends: relations between Jews and non-Jews in Germany, 1933– 1938 (Trude Maurer, 73–92). The rescue of Jews, 1941–1945: resistance by quite ordinary Germans (Beate Kosmala, 93–107). Other sections deal with Poland, the Soviet Union, Czechoslovakia, Romania, France, Benelux, Italy, Denmark.]

42793. NETHERLANDS. CASTAN, JOACHIM: *Hans Calmeyer und die Judenrettung in den Niederlanden.* Mit einem Grußwort von Johannes Rau und vertiefenden Beiträgen von Johann Cornelis Hendrik Blom, Gerhard Hirschfeld, Mathias Middelberg und Peter Niebaum hrsg. von Thomas F. Schneider. Göttingen: V&R unipress, 2003. 128 pp., illus., facsims., side notes. [Book accompanying an exhibition at the Erich Maria Remarque-Friedenszentrum, Osnabrück, Summer 2003; deals with H.C., a lawyer from Osnabrück and 1941–1945 a German administrator in the occupied Netherlands, who saved numerous Jews from deportation by classifying them as non-Jews.]

42794. NETHERLANDS. HÁJKOVÁ, ANNA: *The making of a Zentralstelle. Die Eichmann-Männer in Amsterdam.* [In]: Theresienstädter Studien und Dokumente 2003, Prag, 2003. Pp. 353–382, footnotes.

42795. NETHERLANDS. ROMIJN, PETER: *The experience of the Jews in the Netherlands during the German occupation.* [In]: Dutch Jewry: its history and secular culture (1500–2000). ed. by Jonathan Israel and Reinier Salverda. Leiden; Boston: Brill, 2002. (Brill's Series in Jewish Studies, Vol. 29.) Pp. 253–271, footnotes. [Also in this vol.: Anne Frank and her diaries (Gerrold van der Stroom, 301–314, footnotes). Another contrib. from this vol. is listed according to subject.]

42796. NEUENAHR (BAD). GINZLER, HILDEGARD: *"Hoffnung darauf, dass es mal wieder besser wird". Vom Überlebenskampf der Neuenahrer Jüdin Ruth Preiss nach 1933.* [In]: Heimat-Jahrbuch 2004 Kreis Ahrweiler. Jg. 61, Monschau, 2003. Pp. 195–201, illus., notes.

42797. NOLZEN, ARMIN: *The Nazi Party and its violence against the Jews, 1933–39: violence as a historiographical concept.* [In]: Yad Vashem Studies, Vol. 31, Jerusalem, 2003. Pp. 245–285, tabs., footnotes.

42798. NOVEMBER POGROM. FRIEDLANDER, HENRY: *Eine Berliner Pflanze: an unusual Kristallnacht story.* [In]: German Studies Review, Vol. 26, No.1, Tempe, AZ, Feb. 2003. Pp. 1–14, notes. [Deals with German post-war trials, in particular with an incident in a village in Friesland where non-Jews had been persecuted for helping Jews during the November Pogrom.]

42799. NOVEMBER POGROM. KNOBLOCH, HEINZ: *Der beherzte Reviervorsteher: ungewöhnliche Zivilcourage am Hackeschen Markt.* Mit einem Nachwort von Hermann Simon. Berlin: Jaron, 2003. 201 pp., illus. [New edn., for orig. edn. publ. in 1990 see No. 28238/YB XXXVII.]

42800. NOVEMBER POGROM. LICHTENSTEIN, HEINER: *Der 9. November vor 65 Jahren.* [In]: Tribüne, Jg, 42, H. 167, Frankfurt am Main, 2003. Pp. 60–66.

42801. NUREMBERG. ZINKE, PETER: *Flucht nach Palästina. Lebenswege Nürnberger Juden.* [Im Auftrag des Nürnberger Instituts für NS-Forschung und jüdische Geschichte des 20. Jahrhunderts]. Nürnberg: Antogo, 2003. 317 pp., illus., notes, bibl., gloss. [Incl. chaps. on Zionism and antisemitism in Nuremberg (13–62); 38 interviews with Israelis orig. from Nuremberg and surroundings.] [Cf.: Treffen in Nürnberg. Das Haus der Familie Nussbaum war bis 1933 ein Zentrum der deutschen zionistischen Bewegung (Jim G. Tobias) [in]: Aufbau, Vol. 69, No. 13, New York, July 10, 2003, p. 12.]

42802. ORANIENBURG. *Konzentrationslager Oranienburg.* Augenzeugenberichte aus dem Jahr 1933. Gerhart Seger, Reichstagsabgeordneter der SPD. Max Abraham, Prediger aus Rathenow. [Neu hrsg. von Irene A. Diekmann und Klaus Wettig.] Potsdam: Verlag für Berlin-Brandenburg, 2003. 191 pp., illus., gloss. (Neue Beiträge zur Geistesgeschichte, Bd. 4.) [Seger's account first publ. in Karlsbad 1934, with a foreword by Heinrich Mann. Abraham's report first publ. in Teplitz-Schönau 1934, orig. entitled 'Juda verrecke. Ein Rabbiner im Konzentrationslager'.]

42803. *Orte des Grauens. Verbrechen im Zweiten Weltkrieg.* Hrsg. von Gerd R. Ueberschär. Darmstadt: Primus, 2003. XIV, 270 pp., map, notes, index. [Incl. contribs. on Auschwitz, Kovno, Riga.]

42804. OSWALD, RUDOLF: *"Ein Gift, mit echt jüdischer Geschicklichkeit ins Volk gespritzt (Guido von Mengden): Nationalsozialistische Judenverfolgung und das Ende des mitteleuropäischen Profifußballes, 1938–1941.* [In]: SportZeiten, Jg. 2, H. 2, Göttingen, 2002. Pp. 53–67, footnotes. [Focuses on Vienna and Bohemia (Czechoslovakia).]

——— PADERBORN. NAARMANN, MARGIT: *Eine "vernünftige" Auswanderung. Geseke, Paderborn, Amerika: Aufstieg, Verfolgung und Emigration der Familie Grünebaum.* [See No. 42447.]

42805. PAUCKER, ARNOLD: *Juden und Deutsche im Vorkriegsdeutschland 1930–1939.* [In]: "Gegen alle Vergeblichkeit". Jüdischer Widerstand gegen den Nationalsozialismus [see No. 42899]. Pp. 10–119, footnotes.

42806. PAUCKER, ARNOLD: *Zum Selbstverständnis jüdischer Jugend in der Weimarer Republik und unter der nationalsozialistischen Diktatur.* [In]: Deutsche Juden im Kampf um Recht und Freiheit [see No. 43407]. Pp. 183–204, notes.

42807. PAUL, GERHARD: *Täterbilder—Täterprofile—Taten. Ergebnisse der neueren Forschung zu den Tätern des Holocaust.* [In]: "Gegen alle Vergeblichkeit". Jüdischer Widerstand gegen den Nationalsozialismus [see No. 42899]. Pp. 142–164, footnotes.

42808. PIRMASENS. SCHWERIN, ALFRED: *Von Dachau bis Basel. Erinnerungen eines Pfälzer Juden an die Jahre 1938 bis 1940.* Im Auftrag des Bezirksverbands Pfalz bearbeitet von Roland Paul. Kaiserslautern: Institut für pfälzische Geschichte und Volkskunde, 2003. 208 pp., frontis., illus., footnotes, bibl. [A.Sch., 1892 Buchen/Odenwald–1977 Cincinnati, lived in Pirmasens until 1939, fled to Switzerland in 1940, emigr. to the US in 1948.]

42809. PIRNA. *Unsere Heimat unterm Hakenkreuz. Ein Beitrag zu nationalsozialistischer Gewaltherrschaft, Verfolgung und antifaschistischem Widerstand in Amtshauptmannschaft und Kreis Pirna von 1933 bis 1945.* Erarb. von Dr. Boris Böhm [et al.]. Pirna: Verband der Verfolgten des Naziregimes—Bund der Antifaschisten e.V. im Freistaat Sachsen, Kreisverband Sächsische Schweiz, 2003. 368 pp., illus., ports., facsims., footnotes, bibl., index. [Incl.: Antisemitismus und Rassismus (Hugo Jensch, 243–254; on the persecution of the Jews in Pirna).]

42810. *Politics and culture in twentieth-century Germany.* Ed. by William Niven and James Jordan. Rochester, NY: Camden House, 2003. VI, 274 pp., notes, index. (Studies in German literature, linguistics, and culture.) [Selected essays: "In the exile of internment" or "Von Versuchen, aus der Not eine Tugend zu machen": German-speaking women interned by the British during the Second World War (Charmian Brinson, 63–87). Stefan Heym and GDR cultural politics (Reinhard K. Zachau, 125–142). "Wie kannst Du mich lieben?" Normalizing the relationship between Germans and Jews in the 1990's films *Aimée und Jaguar* and *Meschugge* (Stuart Taberner, 227–243).]

42811. POPKIN, JEREMY D.: *Holocaust memories, historians' memoirs: first-person narrative and the memory of the Holocaust.* [In]: History and Memory, Vol. 15, No. 1, Bloomington IN, Spring/Summer 2003. Pp. 49–84, notes. [Deals with autobiographies by mainly German-Jewish historians incl. Saul Friedländer, Helmut Eschwege, Peter Gay, Raul Hilberg, Georg Iggers, Walter Laqueur, George Mosse, Gershom Scholem, Herbert Strauss o.a. Also discusses the special problems they face, due to their own personal experiences, when writing histories of the Nazi period.]

42812. POTSDAM. BERGEMANN, HANS/LADWIG-WINTERS, SIMONE: *Für ihn brach die Welt, wie er sie kannte, zusammen ...* Juristen jüdischer Herkunft im Landgerichtsbezirk Potsdam. Köln: Verlag Dr. Otto Schmidt, 2003. 156 pp., illus., facsims., bibl., notes. [Incl. 32 short biographies (85–142).]

42813. PRAGUE. *Adolf Kohn: painter of the Prague Ghetto.* Exhibition at the Jewish Museum in Prague, Robert Guttman Gallery, 14 Aug.-27 Oct., 2002. Text and catalogue preparation by Arno Parik. Transl. by Stephen Hattersley. Prague: Jewish Museum, 2002. 48 pp., illus., port., map. [Catalogue, deals also with the fate of his family.] [A.K., 1868 Prague–1953 Prague, artist, survived the Nazi period in Prague.]

42814. PRZYREMBEL, ALEXANDRA: *'Rassenschande'. Reinheitsmythos und Vernichtungslegitimation im Nationalsozialismus.* Mit 13 Abbildungen und 13 Tabellen sowie einem Dokumentenanhang. Göttingen: Vandenhoeck & Ruprecht, 2003. 568 pp., illus., tabs., bibl. (539–565). (Veröff. des Max-Planck-Instituts für Geschichte, Bd. 190.) [Diss., Berlin, Techn. Univ., 2001.]

42815. RAVENSBRÜCK. APEL, LINDE: *Jüdische Frauen im Konzentrationslager Ravensbrück 1939–1945.* Berlin: Metropol, 2003. 423 pp., tabs., footnotes, bibl. (393–421). [Incl. forced labour in the satellite camps.]

42816. RAVENSBRÜCK. STREBEL, BERNHARD: *Das KZ Ravensbrück. Geschichte eines Lagerkomplexes.* Mit einem Geleitwort von Germaine Tillion. Paderborn: Schöningh, 2003. 615 pp., maps, tabs., bibl. (575–598), indexes, footnotes.

42817. RAYMES, FREDERICK: *Are the trees in bloom over there?: thoughts and memories of two brothers.* Transl. from Hebrew by Shulamit Berman. Jerusalem: Yad Vashem, 2002. 235 pp., illus., ports., facsims., map. [Story of two brothers, F. Raymes orig. Manfred Mayer, a US rocket scientist, and Menachem Mayer, orig. Heinz Mayer, an Israeli educationist, who fled with their family from Germany to France, imprisoned in Drancy, rescued by the Jewish organisation OSE; lived in orphanages in France and Switzerland, later became separated.]

——— *Rechtsextreme Ideologien in Geschichte und Gegenwart.* Hrsg. von Uwe Backes. [See No. 43617.]

42818. REFUGEE POLICY. SCHUBERT, GÜNTER: *Der Fleck auf Uncle Sams weißer Weste. Amerika und die jüdischen Flüchtlinge 1938–1945.* Frankfurt am Main; New York: Campus, 2003. 283 pp., footnotes, bibl., index.

42819. REFUGEE POLICY. WYMAN, DAVID S./MEDOFF, RAFAEL: *A race against death: Peter Bergson, America, and the Holocaust.* New York: New Press; W.W. Norton, 2002. XVI, 269 pp., illus., facsims., notes, bibl., index. [On Hillel Kook alias Peter Bergson (1915 Lithuania–Aug. 18, 2001 Jerusalem), moving force behind the U.S. War Refugee Board, instrumental in various rescue efforts to save the European Jews; book is based on an interview with P.B. in 1973 in Amherst, MA.]

42820. REISS, HANS: *Geisteswissenschaften in the Third Reich: some reflections.* [In]: German History, Vol. 21, No. 1, London, 2003. Pp. 86–103, footnotes. [Historiographical review essay on the fate of the humanities during the Nazi regime. Incl. the dismissal of Jews, book burnings.]

42821. *Representing the Holocaust: essays in memory of Bryan Burns.* Ed. by Sue Vice and Bryan Burns. London; Portland, OR: Vallentine Mitchell, 2003. 280 pp., notes. [Incl.: Holocaust refugees in Great Britain and the Research Centre for German and Austrian Exile Studies in London (J.M. Ritchie, 63–77; on the recent work and research projects of the Centre). Fiction of the real: Shoah and documentary (Bryan Burns, 81–88; incl. Lanzmann's 'Shoah'). Benjamin

Wilkomirski's fragments and Holocaust envy: 'Why wasn't I there too?' (Sue Vice, 249–268). One further essay is listed according to subject. All essays in this vol. are also publ. as a "Special Issue" of Immigrants & Minorities, Vol. 21, Nos. 1–2, London, 2002.]

42822. RESCUE OF JEWS. Benz, Wolfgang, ed.: *Selbstbehauptung und Opposition. Kirche als Ort des Widerstandes gegen staatliche Diktatur.* Berlin: Metropol, 2003. 212 pp., footnotes. [Selected essays pertaining to Jews and rescue of Jews: Widerstand im Nationalsozialismus am Beispiel Dietrich Bonhoeffers (Juliane Wetzel, 79–94; incl. his opposition to the persecution of Jews and help for Jewish refugees). "Wo ist Dein Bruder Israel?" Pfarrer Adolf Freudenbergs Einsatz für die Rettung von Juden (Katrin Rudolph, 95–122; deals with Berlin). Die mutigen Frauen in einer kirchlichen Männergesellschaft. Anmerkungen zur Frauen- und Geschlechtergeschichte am Beispiel des Berliner "Kirchenkampfes" (Manfred Gailus, 145–174; on women's efforts to help persecuted Jews).]

42823. RESCUE OF JEWS. Bronowski, Alexander: *Es waren so wenige. Retter im Holocaust.* [Aus dem Hebr. übers. von Zeev Eshkolot]. Holzgerlingen: Hänssler, 2002. 254 pp., illus. [New edn., for first German edn. see No. 28243/YB XXXVII.]

42824. RESCUE OF JEWS. Gilbert, Martin: *The righteous: the unsung heroes of the Holocaust.* New York: Henry Holt, 2003. XXVI, 529 pp., illus., maps, notes, bibl. (463– 478), index. [Incl. chaps. on rescuers in Germany and Austria, incl. Berlin; also on Germans who helped Jews in occupied countries.]

42825. RESCUE OF JEWS. Polevoy, Nancy: *My family's connection to Schindler's list.* [In]: Avotaynu, Vol. 19, No. 4, Bergenfield, NJ, Winter 2003. Pp. 47–51. [On the author's research into her German-Jewish family, discovering that parts of her family had survived the Holocaust thanks to Oskar Schindler's "list".]

42826. RESCUE OF JEWS. Smith, Dabba Frank: *Elsie's war.* Foreword by Henri Cartier-Bresson. London: Frances Lincoln, 2002. 128 pp., illus. [Photographic history of Elsie Kühn-Leitz, a member of the Leica camera family, who was imprisoned during the war for helping Jewish slave labourers in the Leitz factory.]

42827. RHEINBACH. Mies, Horst: *Sie waren Nachbarn: zur Geschichte der Juden in Rheinbach im Dritten Reich.* Mit einem Anhang: "Weggekommen"! Aber: Wer? Wohin? Welches Schicksal? von Peter Mohr. Rheinbach: CMZ-Verl., 2002. 109 pp., illus., footnotes, bibl.

42828. RHEINE. Czekalla, Martin: *Die Reichspogromnacht in Rheine und wie es soweit kommen konnte.* [In]: Unser Kreis 2002, Jahrbuch für den Kreis Steinfurt, 2002 [?]. Pp. 243–249, illus., notes.

42829. RIGA. *Von Hünfeld Über Kassel in das Ghetto Riga. Bericht von Lilli Strauß über ihre Verschleppung im Dezember 1941.* Kommentiert von Monica Kingreen. [In]: Jahrbuch 2004 Landkreis Kassel, Kassel, 2003. Pp. 134–140, notes. [A letter written by L.St. from Sweden shortly after liberation.]

42830. Rivka, Elkin: *The heart beats on. Continuity and change in social work and welfare activities of German Jews under the Nazi regime, 1933–1945.* [In Hebrew.] Jerusalem: Yad Vashem; LBI Jerusalem, 2003. 403 pp., bibl., index.

42831. Rigg, Bryan Mark: *Hitlers jüdische Soldaten.* Mit einem Geleitwort von Eberhard Jäckel. Aus dem Amerik. übers. von Karl Nicolai. Paderborn: Schöningh, 2003. XXI, 439 pp., illus., notes, bibl., index. [For American orig. edn. see No. 41451/YB XLVIII.] [Cf.: Wenn Spekulationen zu Tatsachen werden. Bryan Riggs Buch über jüdische Soldaten ist eine Mogelpackung (Beate Meyer) [in]: Die Zeit, Nr. 46, Hamburg, 6. Nov. 2003, p. 49.]

42832. ROTHENBURG OB DER TAUBER. Ollendorff, Valli: *Fate did not let me go: a mother's farewell letter.* Foreword by Stephen A. Ollendorff. Text in German and English. Gretna, LA: Pelican Publishing, 2003. 1 vol., illus., [Letter written by V.O. to her son Ulrich on Aug. 24, 1942 in Rothenberg just prior to being deported to Theresienstadt where she died; ed. by her grandson, an attorney in New York, adding biogr. material about the family.]

42833. ROTH, MARKUS: *Theater nach Auschwitz. George Taboris 'Die Kannibalen' im Kontext der Holocaust-Debatten.* Frankfurt am Main; New York: Lang, 2003. 187 pp., notes (145–168), bibl. (Historisch-Kritische Arbeiten zur Deutschen Literatur, Bd. 32.) [On the play, first performed in the US in 1968, in Europe (Berlin), Dec. 1969; also other plays in Germany.]

42834. ROTHBERG, MICHAEL & STARK, JARED: *After the witness: a report from the twentieth anniversary conference of the Fortunoff Video Archive for Holocaust testimonies at Yale.* [In]: History and Memory, Vol. 15, No. 1, Bloomington, Spring/Summer 2003. Pp. 85–96. [Under the title "The contribution of oral testimony to Holocaust and Genocide studies" the conference was held from Oct. 6 to 8, 2002.]

42835. RUHR. FEYEN, MARTIN: *Verbotene Liebe. Die Verfolgung von "Rassenschande" im Ruhrgebiet 1933–1945.* [In]: Essener Beiträge. Beiträge zur Geschichte von Stadt und Stift Essen, Bd. 115, Essen, 2003. Pp. 99–186, footnotes, tabs.

42836. RUPNOW, DIRK: *"Der Judenmord". Bausteine zur Lektüre eines 'Stürmer'-Artikels.* [In]: nurinst 2002, Beiträge zur deutschen und jüdischen Geschichte, Bd. 1, Nürnberg, 2002. Pp. 38–52, notes.

42837. *Salvaged pages: young writers' diaries of the Holocaust.* Collected and ed. by Alexander Zapruder. New Haven: Yale Univ. Press, 2002. XVIII, 481 pp., appendix, notes, index. [Incl. several German-Jewish writers.]

42838. SACKS, ADAM J.: *Kurt Singer's shattered hopes.* [In]: Leo Baeck Institute Year Book 2003, Vol. XLVIII, Oxford, 2003. Pp. 191–203, illus., footnotes. [Analyses Singer's involvement with the Kulturbund; incl. two of his letters (transl. into English) written in Amsterdam in Dec. 1938.]

42839. SCHLESWIG-HOLSTEIN. GÖHRES, ANNETTE [et al.], eds.: *Als Jesus "arisch" wurde. Kirche, Christen, Juden in Nordelbien 1933–1945.* Eine Ausstellung in Kiel. Bremen: Ed. Temmen, 2003. 280 pp., frontis., footnotes. [Incl. addresses and sermons relating to Christian-Jewish relations, Christian apologias, "Vergangenheitsbewältigung"; selected contribs. dealing with Jewish history/antisemitism (some titles abbr.): Wurzeln der Judenfeindschaft (Siegfried Bergler, 105–116). Martin Luther und die Juden (Jörgen Sontag, 117–131). Antisemitismus in der schleswig-holsteinischen Landeskirche (Stephan Linck, 132–146). Halfmanns Schrift "Die Kirche und der Jude" von 1936 (Klauspeter Reumann, 147–161; on a brochure by Wilhelm Halfmann publ. in Breklum). "Entjudung der Kirche" (Hansjörg Buss, 162–186). Jüdische Kinder und Jugendliche in Schleswig-Holstein unter dem NS-Regime (Bettina Goldberg, 187–202). Die mühsamen Schritte der evangelischen Kirche zur Anerkennung ihrer Mitschuld an der Judenverfolgung (Jörgen Sontag, 229–255).]

42840. SCHREIBER, MARION: *Silent rebels: the true story of the raid on the 20th train to Auschwitz.* London: Atlantic Books, 2003; New York: Grove Press, 2004. XII, 308 pp., illus., bibl. [For German edn. and more details see No. 39011/YB XLVI.]

42841. SCHMITZ, WALTER, ed.: *Erinnerte Shoah. Die Literatur der Überlebenden/The Shoah remembered, Literature of the survivors.* Dresden: Thelem bei w.e.b., 2003. 533 pp., illus., facsims., footnotes. (Lesecher ... Judentum in Mitteleuropa, Bd. 1.) [Papers presented with the same title at an int. conference, Dresden, May 2000; selected contribs. relate to authors from/in German-speaking countries: Nachträglichkeit des Schreibens in der "Post-Holocaust-Ära". Literatur von Überlebenden der Shoah (Andreas Disselnkötter, 42–60). Erinnerung und Authentizität. Der Fall Binjamin Wilkomirski (Andrea Reiter, 64–73). Biblische Erzählmuster in den Erinnerungen Überlebender des Holocaust (Barbara Mahlmann-Bauer, 91–119). 'Im eigenen Hause' ... 'vom eigenen Ich'. Holocaust autobiography and the quest for 'Heimat' and self (Erin Heather McGlothlin, 120–134). Erinnern an die Shoah und die Literatur des Überlebenden. H.G. Adler (1910–1988) (Franz Hocheneder, 137–152). "... and the dream took on a face ...". Cordelia Edvardson's Vorstudie zu ihrem Roman 'Gebranntes Kind sucht das Feuer' (Anthony W. Riley, 153–164; followed by the text: And the dream took on a face, 165–172). Lagerliteratur lesen lernen. Zu Jurek Beckers Roman 'Jakob der Lügner' (Thomas Taterka, 173–185). "Kommen wir jemals aus dem KZ heraus?" Die 'Erinnerungsbücher' von Fred Wander (186–202). Erzählen, Erinnern und Moral. Ruth Klügers 'weiter leben. Eine Jugend' (1992) (Dagmar von Hoff/Herta Müller, 203–222). Jean Améry's Autorschaft im Zeichen eines gebrochenen Vertrages (Klaus

Schuhmacher, 223–235). "Dichter sind unsere Erinnerungen". Zu den Shoah-Romanen von Edgar Hilsenrath (Michael Braun, 396–402). "Wir waren der Wind, der im Steppengras faucht". Tragik des jüdischen Schicksals und Mythologisierung des Todes in der Holocaust-Lyrik von Immanuel Weißglas (Peter Rychlo, 403–419). "Es lebe die krummnasige Kreatur". Der etwas andere Celan (Jürgen Wertheimer, 420–434). Erinnerte Shoah? Literaturwissenschaftliche Anmerkungen zur Literatur der Überlebenden (ed., 497–521).]

42842. SHANGHAI. HOCHSTADT, STEVE: *Jüdische und nichtjüdische Vertriebene aus Nazi-Deutschland in Shanghai.* [In]: Auswanderung, Flucht, Vertreibung, Exil im 19. und 20. Jahrhundert [see No. 42513]. Pp. 117–132.

42843. SHAVIT, ZOHAR: *Was lasen jüdische Kinder im "Dritten Reich"?* [In]: Jüdischer Almanach [2003] des Leo Baeck Instituts, Frankfurt am Main, 2003. Pp. 74–82, notes.

42844. SIEGEN. SCHILDE, KURT: *"Ankauf von Synagogengemeinde Siegen". Üblicher Liegenschaftsvorgang oder "Arisierung"?* [In]: Siegener Beiträge. Jahrbuch für regionale Geschichte. Jg. 8, Siegen, 2003. Pp. 217–228, notes, illus., facsims. [Also in this issue: "... beschuldigt, ... die Synagoge in Siegen in Brand gesetzt zu haben". Das 1948 gesprochene Urteil des Landgerichts Siegen gegen die Brandstifter und ein Kommentar (Kurt Schilde, 229–252). Kurt Gerstein—Leben im Widerstand (Bernd Hey, 253–266).]

42845. *Sie durften nicht mehr Deutsche sein: jüdischer Alltag in Selbstzeugnissen 1933–1938.* Hrsg.: Margarete Limberg, Hubert Rübsaat. Berlin: Aufbau-Taschenbuch-Verl., 2003. 320 pp. (AtV, Bd. 8103.). [Incl. 33 memoirs from the 1939 Harvard Univ. competition established by Gordon W. Allport and from the LBI New York.]

42846. *Silence of God.* [Issue title of] Philosophia. Philosophical Quarterly of Israel, Vol. 30, Nos. 1–4, Bar-Ilan Univ., Ramat-Gan, March 2003. 218 pp., notes. [Incl.: Introduction (Asa Kasher, 3–5). The silence of God in the thought of Martin Buber (Robert Merrihew Adams, 51–68). The place of the Shoah in history: uniqueness, historicity, causality (Francois Bédarida, 69–86). Religious Jewish education and the Holocaust: the theological dimension (Michael Rosenak, 189–218).]

42847. SILESIA. CARTARIUS, JULIA: *Jewish persecution in Western Upper Silesia 1933–1943.* London: Univ. College London, 2003. 43 pp. [M.A. Diss., available at the Zentralarchiv zur Erforschung der Geschichte der Juden in Deutschland, Heidelberg.]

42848. SLOVAKIA. BARAK-RESSLER, ALYZA: *Cry little girl: a tale of the survival of a family in Slovakia.* Transl. from the Hebrew by Ralph Mandel. Jerusalem: Yad Vashem, 2003. 241 pp., illus. [Author's story of her and her family's survival in hiding in Nazi-occupied Slovakia. In 1947 she went to Palestine.]

42849. SLOVAKIA. GOSSMAN, EVA: *Good beyond evil: ordinary people in extraordinary times.* London; Portland, OR: Vallentine Mitchell, 2002. XIII, 134 pp., illus. (Library of Holocaust testimonies.) [Author's story of her and her brother's life in Slovakia under the Nazis when they lived in hiding, and later with assumed Christian identities, shielded by a young woman.]

42850. SLOVAKIA. KAMENEC, IVAN: *Die Grundzüge des Arisierungsprozesses in der Slowakei.* [In]: Theresienstädter Studien und Dokumente 2003, Prag, 2003. Pp, 307–320, footnotes.

42851. SONNENFELDT, RICHARD W.: *Mehr als ein Leben. Vom jüdischen Flüchtlingsjungen zum Chefdolmetscher der Anklage bei den Nürnberger Prozessen.* Aus dem Amerik. von Theda Krohm-Linke. [Frankfurt am Main]: Scherz, 2003. 288 pp., frontis., illus. [R.W.S., b. 1923 in Gardelegen, electrical engineer, instrumental in developing colour television, emigr. 1938 to the UK, in 1940 deported to Australia on the 'Dunera', in 1941 went to the US; lives in Port Washington, Long Island.]

42852. SOUTH AFRICA. *Seeking refuge: German Jewish immigration to the Cape in the 1930s including aspects of Germany confronting its past.* Designed and comp. by Linda Coetzee [et al.]. Cape Town: Cape Town Holocaust Centre, 2003. 56 pp., illus.

42853. STEINBURG (KREIS). PAUL, GERHARD: *"Die jüdischen Bewohner der meerumschlungenen Provinz sind fast nur auf sich selbst angewiesen." Juden und Judenverfolgung in Schleswig-Holstein im allgemeinen und im Kreis Steinburg im besonderen.* [In]: Steinburger Jahrbuch, Jg. 4, Itzehoe, 2002. Pp. 13–35.

42854. STEIGMANN-GALL, RICHARD: *Rethinking Nazism and religion: "How anti-Christian were the pagans"?* [In]: Central European History, Vol. 36, No. 1, Boston; Leiden, 2003. Pp. 75–105, footnotes. [Incl. anti-Judaism]

42855. STEIGMANN-GALL, RICHARD: *The Holy Reich: Nazi conceptions of Christianity, 1919–1945.* Cambridge; New York: Cambridge Univ. Press, 2003. XVI, 294 pp., illus., notes, bibl., index. [Incl. Christian antisemitism.]

42856. STIER, OREN BARUCH: *Committed to memory: cultural mediations of the Holocaust.* Amherst: Univ. of Massachusetts Press, 2003. XVI, 277 pp., illus., notes, bibl. (257–269), index.

42857. STRUK, JANINA: *Photographing the Holocaust: interpretations of the evidence.* London: I.B. Tauris, 2003. 256 pp., illus.

42858. *Survival. Holocaust survivors tell their stories.* Foreward by Sir Martin Gilbert. Ed. by Wendy Whitworth. Retford, UK: Quill Press in assoc. with The Aegis Inst., 2003. XX, 427 pp., ports., illus., map, index. [Incl.: Introduction (Marina H. Smith, XV-XVI); cont. 46 memoirs collected by the Holocaust Centre Beth Shalom in Laxton nr. Nottingham, UK; incl. also "Notes for teachers" (411–412).]

42859. SWITZERLAND. ERLANGER, SIMON: *Order versus education: the aims of the Swiss labor camps for refugees.* [In]: Yad Vashem Studies, Vol. 31, Jerusalem, 2003. Pp. 175–200, footnotes. [Discusses the Swiss attitude to Jewish refugees from Nazi Germany, their internment in labour camps and so-called 'homes' for women and children.]

42860. SWITZERLAND. NARBEL, NATHALIE: *Un ouragon de prudence. Les églises protestantes vaudoises et les réfugiés victimes du nazisme (1933–1949).* Préface d'André Lasserre. Genève: Labor et Fides, 2003. 211 pp. [Cf.: Review essay (Peter Aerne) [in]: Schweizerische Zeitschrift für Geschichte, Vol. 53, Nr. 3, Bern, 2003, pp. 363–367; also on other related publs.]

42861. SWITZERLAND. SPECK, ANTON-ANDREAS: *Der Fall Rothschild. NS-Judenpolitik, Opferschutz und "Wiedergutmachung" in der Schweiz 1942–1962.* Zürich: Pendo, [2003 ?]. 204 pp., notes (175–200), bibl. (Beiträge zur Geschichte und Kultur der Juden in der Schweiz, Schriftenreihe des Schweizerischen Israelitischen Gemeindebundes.) [Incl.: Geleitwort (Jacques Picard, 7–9). Deals with the deportation of Selma Rothschild and her children, Swiss nationals, from occupied France to Auschwitz and the failure of the Swiss authorities to intervene on their behalf; also on restitution in this matter.]

42862. SWITZERLAND (JEWISH ASSETS). SCHAPIRO, JANE: *Inside a class action: the Holocaust and the Swiss banks.* Madison: Univ. of Wisconsin Press, 2003. XII, 292 pp., notes, index. [Deals with the class action which the World Jewish Congress brought against Swiss banks.]

42863. SWITZERLAND (JEWISH ASSETS) . *La place financière et les banques suisses á l'époque du national-socialism: les relations des grandes banques avec l'Allemagne (1931–1946).* Ed. Marc Perrenoud et al. Publié par la Commission Indépendante d'Experts Suisse—Second Guerre Mondiale. Lausanne; Zürich: Editions Payot; Chronos, 2002. 724 pp., tabs., diagrs. (Publications de la Commission Indépendante d'Experts Suisse—Second Guerre Mondiale, Vol. 13.)

42864. TENT, JAMES F.: *In the shadow of the Holocaust: Nazi persecution of Jewish- Christian Germans.* Lawrence: Univ. Press of Kansas, 2003. XVI, 280 pp., notes, bibl. (257–260), index. (Modern War Studies.) [Deals with individual histories of Christians of Jewish descent.]

——— THERESIENSTADT. AMBROS, PETER: *Leben vom Blatt gespielt. Eine dramatische Lebenspartitur.* [See No. 43347.]

42865. THERESIENSTADT. FEDOROVIC, TOMÁS: *Der Theresienstädter Lagerkommandant Siegfried Seidl.* [In]: Theresienstädter Studien und Dokumente 2003, Prag, 2003. Pp. 162–210. [Also in this vol.: Die Geschichte eines Briefes. Eingeschriebene Postsendungen ins Ghetto Theresienstadt und die Postverwaltung des Protektorats Böhmen und Mähren (Patricia Tosnerová, 211–239).]

42866. THERESIENSTADT. WÖGERBAUER, MICHAEL: *Kartoffeln—Ein Versuch über Erzählungen zum Ghettoalltag.* [In]: Theresienstädter Dokumente 2003, Prag, 2003. Pp. 95–144, footnotes. [On the misery of daily Ghetto life as reflected in the stories of Hans Günther Adler and Josef Taussig.]

42867. THERESIENSTADT. ZGEBANINA (IVAN POLÁK): *Wie entsteht der 'Kamarád?* [In]: Jüdischer Almanach [2003] des Leo Baeck Instituts, Frankfurt am Main, 2003. Pp. 83–89. [On a periodical produced by the author, as a young boy, during his imprisonment in Theresienstadt.]

42868. THURINGIA. *Heimatgeschichtlicher Wegweiser zu Stätten des Widerstandes und der Verfolgung 1933–1945.* Bd. 8: Thüringen. Hrsg. vom Thüringer Verband der Verfolgten des Naziregimes—Bund der Antifaschisten und dem Studienkreis deutscher Widerstand 1933–1945. Red.: Ursula Krause-Schmitt, Heinz Koch. Frankfurt am Main: VAS—Verlag für Akademische Schriften, 2003. 380 pp., illus., facsims., bibl., index. [Incl. the persecution of Jews.]

42869. *To life: 36 stories of memory and hope: a living memorial to the Holocaust.* Ed. by the Museum of Jewish Heritage [New York]. Foreword by Robert M. Morgenthau. Preface and historical essay by David G. Marwell. Boston, MA: Bulfinch Press, 2002. XV, 174 pp., illus., facsims., index. [Incl. an essay on Leo Baeck, celebrating Purim in Theresienstadt, and an illus. of the Megillah used by Baeck; also on other German-Jewish survivors.]

42870. TRAPP, FRITHJOF: *Der Geist der "völkischen Bewegung" und die Bücherverbrennungen vom Mai 1933.* [In]: Exil, Jg. 23, Frankfurt am Main, 2003. Pp. 5–15, notes.

42871. TRAVERSO, ENZO: *The origins of Nazi violence.* Transl. by Janet Lloyd. New York: New Press, 2003. VII, 200 pp., notes, bibl. (167–186), index. [First publ. in French, 2002. German edn. with the title: Moderne und Gewalt. Eine europäische Genealogie des Nazi Terrors. Karlsruhe: Neuer ISP Verlag, 2003. [Incl. chaps. on antisemitism.]

42872. TRESS, WERNER: *"Wider den undeutschen Geist". Bücherverbrennung 1933.* Berlin: Parthas Verlag, 2003. 247 pp., frontis., illus., footnotes, maps, bibl., index. [Incl.: "Schwarze Listen", distributed among the students for bookburning (228–235).]

42873. *Überleben im Dritten Reich. Juden im Untergrund und ihre Helfer.* Hrsg. von Wolfgang Benz. München: Beck, 2003. 349 pp., illus., notes (315–336), bibl. [Cont.: I. Prolog: Juden im Untergrund und ihre Helfer (ed., 11–48). II. Anständige Leute; cont.: Berlin Wielandstraße 18—Ein ehrenwertes Haus (Marion Neiss, 51–66). Donata und Eberhard Helmrich, zwei Helfer ohne Eigennutz (Cornelia Schmalz-Jacobsen, 67–82). "Können wir uns noch in die Augen sehen, wenn wir hier nicht das tun, was uns möglich ist?" (Marie-Luise Kreuter, 83–96). "Er ist gemein zu unseren Freunden ...". Das Retternetz der Gruppe "Onkel Emil" (Karin Friedrich, 97–109). III. Kräfte der Milieus; cont.: Zuflucht in Potsdam bei Christen der Bekennende Kirche (Beate Kosmala, 113–130). Hilfe im katholischen Milieu. Das Überleben der Konvertitin Annie Kraus (Andreas Mix, 131–142). Rettung im Bordell (Christina Herkommer, 143–152). Flucht über das Meer. Illegal von Danzig nach Palästina (Dennis Riffel, 153–156). Herzensfragen. Überleben im Nonnenkloster (Mona Körte, 166–181). IV. Unterschiedliche Motive. Bezahlte Hilfe, Risiko und Eigennutz; cont.: Die Vermieterin (Isabel Enzenbach, 185–197). "Herr Obersturmführer lässt daran erinnern, dass die Rate noch nicht da ist". Eine Rettung nach Abzahlung (Marion Neiss, 198–204). Fluchtziel Schweiz. Das Hilfsnetz um Luise Meier und Josef Höfler (Claudia Schoppmann, 205–219). Gegenleistungen. Stationen eines Kirchenasyls zwischen Weserbergland und Lausitz (Wolfgang Benz, 220–228). Von einem Quartier zum nächsten. Eine Odyssee im Berliner Untergrund (Christine Zahn, 229–238). "Jüdische Fahnder". Verfolgte, Verfolger und Retter in einer Person (Doris Tausendfreund, 293–256). V. Zivilcourage und Heldenmut. Vom Risiko der Helfer; cont.: Der Druckereibesitzer Theodor Görner. Helfer aus antifaschistischer Gesinnung (Frank Görlich, 259–277). Die Kunst der Frechheit. Ein Maler und das Überleben in München (Peter Widmann, 278–286). Robert Eisenstädts Flucht aus dem KZ

Majdanek. Über Frankfurt am Main in die Schweiz (Beate Kosmala, 287–298). VI. Epilog: Karriere nach der Rettung. Charlotte Knoblochs Weg zur Vizepräsidentin der Juden in Deutschland (Juliane Wetzel, 301–311).] [Cf.: Die Kraft des Anstands. Ein neues Buch zeigt: Es gab mehr Helfer für die verfolgten Juden im "Dritten Reich" als oft angenommen (Klaus Harpprecht) [in]: Zeitliteratur [Beilage von] Die Zeit, Hamburg, Sept. 2003, pp. 39–40.]

42874. UNTERFRANKEN. SCHMITTNER, MONIKA: *Verfolgung und Widerstand 1933 bis 1945 am bayerischen Untermain.* Aschaffenburg: Alibri-Verlag, 2002. 414 pp., illus., bibl. [Cf.: Bespr. (Herbert Schott) [in]: Mainfränkisches Jahrbuch für Geschichte und Kunst, Jg. 55, Würzburg, 2003, pp. 385–387.]

42875. *Verbrannt, geraubt, gerettet! Bücherverbrennungen in Deutschland.* Eine Ausstellung der Bibliothek der Friedrich-Ebert-Stiftung anlässlich des 70. Jahrestages. [Red.: Erhard Stang]. Mit Beiträgen von Detlev Brunner [et al.]. Bonn: Bibl. der Fr.-Ebert-Stiftung, 2003. 56 pp., illus. (Veröff. der Bibl. der Fr.-Ebert-Stiftung, Bd. 13.)

42876. VICE, SUE: *'I feel torn': hidden children in the Holocaust and the Catholic Church.* [In]: The Jewish Quarterly, Vol. 50, No. 2, London, Summer 2003. Pp. 45–48, illus. [Deals with children who were hidden by the Church and were given Catholic identities.]

——— VIENNA. BOTZ, GERHARD [ET AL.], eds.: *Eine zerstörte Kultur. Jüdisches Leben und Antisemitismus in Wien seit dem 19. Jahrhundert.* [See No. 42467.]

42877. VIENNA. JAHODA, MOSHE H.: *Erlebte Geschichte—Fragen an Gott und Mensch.* [In]: Zwischenwelt, Jg. 19, Nr. 4, Wien, Feb. 2003. Pp. 16–20, port., notes. [Personal memoirs of the Israeli diplomat and current director of the Vienna office of the Claims Conference, b. 1926 in Vienna, about childhood in Vienna and life in Palestine/Israel; also on matters of restitution and other problems related to Israeli policies.]

42878. VIENNA. PAMMER, MICHAEL: *Jüdische Vermögen in Wien 1938.* Wien: Oldenbourg, 2003. 151 pp., footnotes, tabs., bibl. (Veröff. der Österreichischen Historikerkommission. Vermögensentzug während der NS-Zeit sowie Rückstellungen und Entschädigungen seit 1945 in Österreich, Bd. 8.)

42879. VIENNA. RATH, ARI: *Mein Bar-Mizwa-Fahrrad.* [In]: Jüdischer Almanach [2003] des Leo Baeck Instituts, Frankfurt am Main, 2003. Pp. 61–69. [Author, the former editor-in-chief of the 'Jerusalem Post', recalls his childhood in Vienna.]

42880. VIENNA. SPRING, CLAUDIA: *Staatenloses Subjekt, vermessenes Objekt: Anthropologische Untersuchungen an staatenlosen Juden im September 1939.* [In]: Zeitgeschichte, Jg. 30, H. 3, Salzburg, Mai/Juni 2003. Pp. 163–170, notes. [Deals with the arrest of 440 stateless Jews in Vienna, Sept. 1939, anthropologically measured by members of the Natural History Museum before their deportation to Buchenwald.]

42881. VLOTHO. *Wir wollen weiterleben ...* Das Schicksal der jüdischen Familie Loeb—dokumentiert in Briefen und Selbstzeugnissen. Im Auftrag der Mendel-Grundmann-Gesellschaft e.V. Vlotho hrsg. von Manfred Kluge. Bielefeld: Verlag für Regionalgeschichte. 232 pp., illus., facsims., index, bibl. (Quellen zur Regionalgeschichte, Bd. 10.) [Incl. letters written between 1938 and 1941 by members of the Loeb family, owners of a textile department store in Vlotho until 1938. Part 2 deals with the fate of surviving family members in the US and their visits to Vlotho, esp. Stephen H. Loeb, who was given the freedom of the town of Vlotho in 1991.]

42882. WAGNER, FRANZ-JOSEF: *Die Deutsche Reichspost und die Juden.* [In]: Heimat-Jahrbuch des Kreises Altenkirchen und der angrenzenden Gemeinden 2003, Jg. 46, Altenkirchen, 2002. Pp. 96–99, facsims.

42883. WARSAW GHETTO. *Sixtieth anniversary of the Warsaw Ghetto uprising. The testament of youth.* [Issue title of] Dialogue and Universalism, Vol. 13, Nos. 3–4, Warsaw, 2003. 1 issue. [Incl. contribs. on and by Marek Edelman, other eyewitness accounts, also essays on the impact of the Holocaust on philosophy and Judaism.]

42884. WEGNER, GREGORY PAUL: *Anti-semitism and schooling under the Third Reich.* New York; London: RoutledgeFalmer, 2002. XIV, 262 pp., illus., facsims., tabs., glossary, appendixes, notes, bibl. (241–255), index. (Studies in the history of education.) [Covers the development of racial antisemitism in the 19th cent. and its application to educational philosophy under the Nazis. Discusses antisemitic textbooks and teachers' manuals used in schools in the Third Reich.] [Cf.: Review (Katherine T. Carroll) [in]: Education Review, Tempe, AZ, Aug. 24, 2003, www.edrev.asu.edu.]

42885. WEINBERG, AVRAHAM S.: *Wilkomirski & Co. Im Land der Täter, im Namen des Volkes.* Berlin: Kronen-Verl.-ges., 2003. 153 pp., illus., bibl. [On the Wilkomirski affair.]

42886. WEINBERG, KERRY: *Scenes from Hitler's 1000–year Reich: twelve years of Nazi terror and the aftermath.* Amherst, NY: Prometheus Books, 2003. 169 pp., illus., ports., notes, bibl. (165–166), index. [Author, b. in Trier to an orthodox family, sets her own life experiences in the context of a number of interviews with survivors.]

42887. WESTPHALIA. PALKA, CHRISTOPH: *Antisemitisches Handeln ohne Anordnung der NS-Führung.* [In]: Mitteilungen des Vereins für Geschichte an der Universität Paderborn, Nr. 16, H. 2, Paderborn, 2003. Pp. 80–102, footnotes. [Deals with incidents in the Detmold/Paderborn area.]

42888. *Why didn't the press shout?: American and international journalism during the Holocaust.* Ed. by Robert Moses Shapiro. Introd. by Marvin Kalb. New York: Yeshiva Univ. Press, in association with KTAV Publ., Jersey City, NY., 2003. XX, 665 pp., notes, bibl., index. [Collection of papers orig. presented at an int. conference at Yeshiva Univ., Oct., 1995.]

42889. WIESBADEN. KINGREEN, MONICA: *Die gewaltsame Verschleppung der Juden aus den Dörfern und Kleinstädten des Regierungsbezirks Wiesbaden (1942–1945).* [In]: Nassauische Annalen, B. 114, Wiesbaden, 2003. Pp. 305–351, footnotes, tabs. [Incl. name lists of the deportees.]

42890. WIECK, MICHAEL: *A childhood under Hitler and Stalin: memoirs of a "certified Jew".* Foreword by Siegfried Lenz. Transl. by Penny Milbouer. Madison: Univ. of Wisconsin Press, 2003. 293 pp., illus., ports., glossary, appendixes, bibl. [Author, b. 1912 in Königsberg, tells the story of his childhood under both Nazi and Soviet regimes. For German edn. and data see No. 40048/YB XLVII.]

42891. WIND, RUTH: *Im Schatten des Holocaust. Ich warte nicht mehr auf dich, Mama.* Moers: Ges. für Christl.-Jüd. Zusammenarbeit, 2002. 167 pp., frontis., illus. [Orig. publ. with the title 'Non ti aspetto più Mamma', Milano: Alexa Edizioni, 2000. A collection of letters written by the author (1913 Moers–2002 Milan) between 1943 and 1949 in Northern Italy, but never posted.]

42892. WOLFHAGEN. SOLTAU, PETER: *9. November 2000 in Wolfhagen—ein Kreis schließt sich.* In]: Jahrbuch 2002 Landkreis Kassel, Kassel, 2001. Pp. 53–54, illus. [On the Kann family.]

42893. WUPPERTAL. OKROY, MICHAEL: *Volksgemeinschaft, Erbkartei und Arisierung.* Ein Stadtführer zur NS-Zeit in Wuppertal. Hrsg. vom Trägerverein Begegnungsstätte Alte Synagoge Wuppertal e.V. Wuppertal: [Begegnungsstätte Alte Synagoge e.V.], 2002. 164 pp., illus., facsims., bibl., index.

42894. ZACHAU, REINHARD K.: *Sacred memory or relics? Should Holocaust documents be altered?* [In]: Arcadia, Int. Zeitschrift für Literaturwissenschaft, Bd. 38, H. 2, Berlin; New York, 2003. Pp. 359–362, notes. [On Wolfgang Koeppen's novel 'Jakob Littners Aufzeichnungen aus einem Erdloch'.]

42895. ZEE, NANDA VAN DER: *The roommate of Anne Frank.* Soesterberg: Aspekt, 2003. 94 pp., illus. [Orig. publ. in the Netherlands in 1990; deals with Fritz Pfeffer, a German-born dentist (in A.F.'s diary called "Dussel", correcting the image that A.F. gave of him.]

42896. ZIMMERMANN, CLEMENS: *Der Wissenschaftsverlag Carl Winter im Nationalsozialismus.* [In]: Regionen Europas—Europa der Regionen. Festschrift für Kurt-Ulrich Jäschke zum 65. Geburtstag. Hrsg. von Peter Thorau [et al.]. Köln: Böhlau, 2003. Pp. 247–263, footnotes. [Deals also with the exclusion of about a hundred Jewish authors/editors.]

42897. ZIMMERMANN, MOSHE: *Die deutschen Juden in der Geschichte der Shoah: Keine Exklave!* Übers. von Alexandra Riebe, hrsg. von Eilert Herms. Tübingen: Mohr Siebeck, 2002. 124 pp., notes. [All texts also in Engl.; incl.: Ansprache bei der Verleihung des Dr. Leopold-Lucas-Preises 2002 (ed., 88–122).]

42898. ZINKE, PETER: *"Es besteht nach wie vor dringender Bedarf". Die Haar-Verwertung der KZ-Opfer am Beispiel der Firma Alex Zink in Roth bei Nürnberg.* [In]: nurinst 2002. Beiträge zur deutschen und jüdischen Geschichte, Bd. 1, Nürnberg, 2002. Pp. 71–84, notes.

B. **Jewish Resistance**

42899. ERLER, HANS/PAUCKER, ARNOLD/EHRLICH, ERNST LUDWIG, eds.: *"Gegen alle Vergeblichkeit". Jüdischer Widerstand gegen den Nationalsozialismus.* Frankfurt am Main; New York: Campus, 2003. 456 pp., footnotes. [Incl.: Vorwort: "Alle Völker im Reiche fügten sich dem, früher oder später, nur dieses Volk nicht" (Hans Erler, 11–19). Rede zum 60. Jahrestag des Warschauer Ghettoaufstandes (Paul Spiegel, 20–29). Einleitung: Die Idee des Widerstands im Judentum (Ernst Ludwig Ehrlich, 30–37). Zur Problematik des Widerstandes deutscher Juden gegen den Nationalsozialismus (Arnold Paucker, 38–52). Teil 1: Die Lage: Herausforderung von Widerstand (55–164). Teil 2: Widerstand in Deutschland; cont.: "Charakterinseln im Schlammsee des Dritten Reiches". Assimilierte Juden im liberalen Widerstand (167–186). Zwischen den Fronten: Linke politische Kleingruppen im Widerstand 1933–1939/40 [&] Die Widerstandsgruppe "Org." ("Neu Beginnen") 1929–1935 (Jan Foitzik, 187–195; 196–205). Jüdische Jugendliche gegen den Nationalsozialismus in Deutschland: Widerstand oder Opposition? (Kurt Schilde, 206–227). Schule—Exodus—Krieg. Persönliche Erinnerungen an die Nazi-Zeit (Werner T. Angress, 228–249). Teil 3: Widerstand in Europa; cont.: Einige Aspekte des jüdischen Widerstandes in Europa: Die Juden hatten mehr Gründe zum Widerstand als die nichtjüdischen Menschen (Arno Lustiger, 253–260). Jüdische Frauen im Widerstand im besetzten Europa (Ingrid Strobl, 261–277). Jüdischer Widerstand in Frankreich und Belgien. Der Anteil der deutschsprachigen Juden (Lucien Steinberg, 278–296). Der Aufstand im Warschauer Ghetto (Arno Lustiger, 308–316). Die Teilnahme der Juden am italienischen Widerstand (Viviana Ravaioli, 317–322). Der Anteil der Juden am Sieg der Alliierten im Zweiten Weltkrieg: Jüdische Soldaten im Kampf gegen den Faschismus [&] Stalin und die Juden. Die tragische Geschichte des Jüdischen Antifaschistischen Komitees (Arno Lustiger, 323–340; 341–362). Teil 4: Der (Wieder-)Aufbau der Demokratie in Deutschland (365–431). Statt eines Nachworts: "Hier wird der Kampf des Menschen exemplarisch ausgefochten" (Hans Erler, 432–448). Further contribs. are listed according to subject.] [Cf.: Der Kampf um Würde (Thomas Kreuder) [in]: Frankfurter Rundschau, Nr. 286, Frankfurt am Main, 8. Dez. 2003, p. 12.]

42900. LANDAUER, HANS in Zusammenarbeit mit ERICH HACKL: *Lexikon der österreichischen Spanienkämpfer 1936–1939.* Wien: Verlag der Theodor Kramer Gesellschaft, 2003. 258 pp., illus., chronol., bibl., index (places). [Incl. numerous Jewish fighters. Cf.: Buch der Verluste und der Lebensräume. Ein paar Worte über das "Lexikon der österreichischen Spanienkämpfer" (Erich Hackl) [in]: Zwischenwelt, Jg. 20, Nr. 3, Wien, Dez. 2003, pp. 27–29; also in this issue: "Es ist faszinierend und irritierend zugleich ..." (Hans Landauer, 30–32). Zur Bedeutung des Lexikons der österreichischen Spanienkämpfer (Bernhard Kuschey, 77–78).]

42901. PAUCKER, ARNOLD: *Deutsche Juden im Widerstand 1933–1945. Tatsachen und Probleme.* 2., erw. und verb. Aufl. der 1999 unter demselben Titel veröff. Broschüre. [Red.: Johannes Tuchel, Anneke de Rudder.] [Berlin]: Gedenkstätte Deutscher Widerstand, 2003. 67 pp., footnotes. (Beiträge zum Widerstand 1933–1945.) [Incl.: Exkurs: Österreich (57–61).]

42902. PAUCKER, ARNOLD: *Jüdischer Abwehrkampf* [section title of] Deutsche Juden im Kampf um Recht und Freiheit [see No. 43407]. [Incl.: Kampf gegen den Nationalsozialismus (127–160). Also in this vol.: Deutsche Juden im Widerstand 1933–1945. Tatsachen und Probleme (205–289, notes). Abwehr, Widerstand und jüdische Verhaltensweisen unter der NS-Diktatur (309–327, notes).]

——— WÖRMANN, HEINRICH-WILHELM: *Widerstand 1933–1945. Berlin. Schöneberg und Tempelhof.* [See No. 42619.]

IV. POST-1945

A. General

——— AUSTRIA. EMBACHER, HELGA: *Die Restitutionsverhandlungen mit Österreich aus der Sicht jüdischer Organisationen und der Israelitischen Kultusgemeinde.* [See No. 42950.]

——— BAROTH, HANS DIETER: *Jugendtraum: Vorsitzender. Der DGB-Vorsitzende Ludwig Rosenberg.* [See in No. 43421.]

42903. BENSIMON, DORIS: *Jews in today's Germany.* [In]: The Jewish Journal of Sociology, Vol. 45, Nos. 1–2, London, 2003. Pp. 20–33, notes.

42904. BENSIMON, DORIS: *Juifs en Allemagne aujourd'hui.* Paris: L'Harmattan, 2003. 223 pp., maps, notes, gloss., bibl., index.

42905. BERGEN-BELSEN. KÖNIGSEDER, ANGELIKA/WETZEL, JULIANE: *Displaced Persons. Zwischen Lagerexistenz und internationaler Politik: DB Camp Bergen-Belsen 1945–1950.* [In]: Dachauer Hefte, Jg. 19, H. 19, Berlin, Nov. 2003. Pp. 201–216, footnotes. [Also, in this issue, on Bergen-Belsen: "Germany's gayest and happiest town"? Bergen-Belsen 1945–1950 (Rainer Schulze, 216–238).]

42906. BERLIN. BROWN, LOUISE: *School ties. Germany's first Jewish-American university.* [In]: Aufbau, Vol. 69, No. 19, New York, Oct. 2, 2003, port. [On Touro College Berlin, and its director, Sara Nachama.]

42907. BERLIN. *Jüdische Berliner. Leben nach der Schoa.* 14 Gespräche. Hrsg.: Ulrich Eckhardt/Andreas Nachama. Fotografie: Elke Nord. Berlin: Jaron Verlag, 2003. 288 pp., ports. [Book accompanying an exhibition held at the Centrum Judaicum in Berlin.]

42908. BERLIN. LAUFER, PETER: *Exodus to Berlin: the return of the Jews to Germany.* Chicago: Ivan R. Dee, 2003. XII, 237 pp., maps, ports., notes, bibl. (225– 228), index. [Deals with different aspects of the recent Jewish immigration to Germany, especially to Berlin, a large proportion of which originates from the former Soviet Union and other Eastern European countries. Also covers present-day antisemitism, Neo-Nazism, and aspects of integration and coexistence.]

42909. BERLIN. RIESENBURGER, MARTIN: *Das Licht verlöschte nicht. Ein Zeugnis aus der Nacht des Faschismus.* Hrsg. und mit Beiträgen zur Erinnerung an ein Berliner Rabbinerleben von Andreas Nachama und Hermann Simon. Teetz: Hentrich & Hentrich, 2003. pp., illus., footnotes. (Jüdische Memoiren, Bd. 5.) [Incl.: Martin Mosche ben Chajim Riesenburger (1896–1965) (Hermann Simon, 7–34; personal recollections; also how M.R. survived the war in Berlin). In Deiner Hand sind meine Zeiten (Ps.31,16) (Andreas Nachama, 35–52). Das Licht verlösche nicht. Ein Zeugnis aus der Nacht des Faschismus & Ausgewählte Predigten (Martin Riesenburger, 53–102; 103–164).] [M.R., May 14, 1896 Berlin–1965 Berlin, piano teacher, actor, cantor, from 1953 rabbi in Berlin (East).]

42910. BERLIN. SCHÜTZE, YVONNE: *Migrantennetzwerke im Zeitverlauf—Junge russische Juden in Berlin.* [In]: Berliner Journal für Soziologie, Jg. 13, H. 2, Opladen, 2003. Pp. 239–253.

——— BLOCH, TALIA: *Listening to the Jewish voice.* A conference at the Leo Baeck Institute in New York City. [See No. 42558.]

——— BODEMANN, Y. MICHAL: *In den Wogen der Erinnerung. Jüdische Existenz in Deutschland.* [See No. 42977.]

42911. BODEMANN-OSTOW, NAOMI/VOGEL, DIRK: *Augenblicke. Portraits von Juden in Deutschland.* Berlin: Deutsche Presse, 2003. IX, 156 pp., ports.

42912. BRODER, HENRYK M./DOLLINGER, ROLAND: *Henryk M. Broder über sein Leben in Deutschland und Israel, Antisemitismus in Deutschland, die Beziehung zwischen Deutschen und Juden.* Ein Gespräch mit

Roland Dollinger. [In]: The German Quarterly, Vol. 76, No. 1, Winter, 2003. Pp. 1–10. [H.M.B., b. 1946 in Katowice, journalist, has lived since 1957 in Germany and Israel.]

42913. CHEMNITZ. DIAMANT, ADOLF: *Denkschrift zur Einweihung der Neuen Synagoge und des Gemeindehauses zu Chemnitz am 24. Mai 2002.* [In Zusammenarb. mit dem Chemnitzer Geschichtsverein e.V. 1990]. [Frankfurt am Main, Hansa-Allee 32 b]: A. Diamant, 2003. 49 pp., illus.

42914. *Dachauer Hefte.* [With the issue title] Zwischen Befreiung und Verdrängung. Jg. 19, H. 19, Berlin, Nov. 2003. 299 pp., illus., footnotes. [Cont. 17 contribs. on Dachau, Neuengamme, Moringen, Krakau-Plaszow, Flossenbürg, Bergen-Belsen, Sachsenhausen, Auschwitz; also personal recollections. Selected articles are listed according to subject.]

42915. DRESDEN. DIAMANT, ADOLF: *Denkschrift zur Einweihung der neuen Synagoge und des Gemeindehauses zu Dresden am 9. November 2001.* [Frankfurt am Main, Hansa-Allee 32b]: A. Diamant, 2003. 57 pp., illus.

42916. DRESDEN. GLASER, GERHARD: *Die neue Synagoge zu Dresden am historischen Ort.* [In]: Sächsische Heimatblätter, H. 1, Dresden, 2002. Pp. 19–24, illus.

42917. DÜSSELDORF. JAKOBS, GUIDO/BAYER, KAREN: *Vertriebene jüdische Hochschullehrer—Rückkehr erwünscht?* [In]: Nach der Diktatur. Die Medizinische Akademie Düsseldorf vom Ende des Zweiten Weltkriegs bis in die 1960er Jahre. Hrsg. von Wolfgang Woelk [et al.]. Essen: Klartext, 2003. (Düsseldorfer Schriften zur Neueren Landesgesch. und zur Gesch. Nordrhein-Westfalens, Bd. 66.) Pp. 115–138, footnotes.

42918. FISHBURN, JONATHAN: *'Surviving remnant': Jewish publishing in the immediate aftermath of the Holocaust.* [In]: The Jewish Quarterly, Vol. 50, No. 2, London, Summer 2003. Pp. 25–28, illus. [Discusses the publishing of newspapers and Jewish religious texts in DP camps after the liberation.]

——— FÜRTH. BERTHOLD-HILPERT, MONIKA: *Jüdisches Leben in Franken nach 1945 am Beispiel der Gemeinde Fürth.* [See No. 42340.]

42919. GEIS, JAEL: *"Die Juden essen Schokolade, nur 6 Millionen sind vergast—schade!" Antisemitismus "auf Gummisohlen"? Antisemitismus im unmittelbaren Nachkriegsdeutschland aus jüdischer Perspektive.* [In]: nurinst 2002. Beiträge zur deutschen und jüdischen Geschichte, Bd. 1, Nürnberg, 2002. Pp. 20–37, notes.

42920. GEIS, JAEL: *"Leben danach"—Aspekte jüdischen Lebens in Deutschland nach der Vernichtung der europäischen Juden.* [In]: "Habt den Mut zu menschlichem Tun". Die Jüdin und Demokratin Jeanette Wolff in ihrer Zeit (1888–1976) [see No. 43486]. Pp. 167–184, notes.

42921. GIORDANO, RALPH: *Versöhnend, integrierend, widerborstig.* Die Jüdische Allgemeine war immer offen—für Demokratie. Ein Rück- und Ausblick auf die Wochenzeitung von ihrem dienstältesten Mitarbeiter. [In]: Jüdische Allgemeine, Jg. 58, Nr. 23, Berlin, 6. Nov. 2003. P. 46.

——— *"Habt den Mut zu menschlichem Tun". Die Jüdin und Demokratin Jeanette Wolff in ihrer Zeit (1888–1976).* [See No. 43486.]

42922. HARTEWIG, KARIN/MEINING, STEFAN: *Der "Volksaufstand" vom 17. Juni und die Juden.* [In]: Jüdische Allgemeine, Jg. 58, Nr. 13, Berlin, 19. Juni 2003. P. 3. [Title of K.H.'s contrib.: Auf der anderen Seite der Barrikade; title of St.M.'s contrib.: Ein "faschistischer Umsturzversuch"?.]

42923. *Horch und Guck. Historisch-literarische Zeitschrift des Bürgerkomitees "15. Januar" e.V.* Jg. 12, H. 44, Berlin, 2003. 1 issue, 80 pp., illus., notes. [Issue title: (Nicht-)Auseinandersetzung mit dem Nationalsozialismus in der DDR. Incl. contribs. on anti-Zionism/antisemitism and the Jews (incl. Helmut Eschwege) in the former GDR, also on Jewish cemeteries by Konrad Weiß, Clemens Vollnhals, Thomas Haury, Henryk M. Broder, Peter Maser, Christian Halbrock, Annette Leo, Wolfgang Kraushaar, Werner Kiontke.]

42924. KASSEL. HASS, ESTHER: *'Und sie sollen mir machen ein Heiligtum ...'. Die neue Synagoge zu Kassel.* Kassel: Jüd. Gemeinde, 2002. 40 pp., illus.

42925. KLAUSNER, ABRAHAM J.: *A letter to my children from the edge of the Holocaust.* Introd. by Yehuda Bauer. San Francisco: Holocaust Center of Northern California, 2002. XI, 184 pp., appendixes, notes. [Tells the story of a US army Rabbi who helped to liberate Dachau, and for several years subsequently, as helper and mentor, devoted himself to working with displaced persons, organising lists of survivors, and writing reports to his superiors on conditions in the camps.]

42926. KORN, SALOMON: *Die fragile Grundlage. Auf der Suche nach der deutsch-jüdischen "Normalität".* Mit einem Geleitwort von Joschka Fischer. Berlin: Philo, 2003. 196 pp., notes (163–172). bibl. S.K. (173–194). index. [Incl. previously publ. essays arranged under the sections: Einführung: Versuch, sich der deutsch-jüdischen "Normalität" im Gespräch zu nähern. I. Für Ignatz Bubis. II. Architektur und Judentum. III. Gegenwart der Vergangenheit. IV. Kultur und Judentum. V. Jüdisches Leben in Deutschland.] [Cf.: Der große Bogen (Klaus Hildebrand) [in]: 'FAZ', Nr. 6, Frankfurt am Main, 8. Jan. 2003, p. 8. Was könnte da normal sein? (Richard Herzinger) [in]: Die Zeit, Nr. 5, Hamburg, 22. Jan. 2004, p. 48. Einbrüche auf dünnem Eis (Susanne Urban) [in]: Tribüne, Jg. 42, H. 168, Frankfurt am Main, 2003, pp. 190–194.]

42927. KRAUSS, MARITA: *Exil, Neuordnung und Erneuerung Deutschlands: Jüdische Remigranten im Politischen Leben Nachkriegsdeutschlands.* [In]: "Gegen alle Vergeblichkeit". Jüdischer Widerstand gegen den Nationalsozialismus [see No. 42899]. Pp. 388–406, footnotes. [Also in this vol.: Das Reeducation-Programm der USA (Uta Gerhardt, 407–431, footnotes).]

——— LEIPZIG. *Ernst Blochs Leipziger Jahre.* [See No. 43237.]

42928. LOCHER, LIESELOTTE: *Jewish and German emigration from the former Soviet Union in the 1990s.* Berlin: de-Verlag im Internet, 2002. 129 pp., tabs., diagrs. Zugl.: Bonn, Univ., Diss., 2002.

——— LOWER SAXONY. OBENAUS, HERBERT: *Jüdisches Leben in Niedersachsen nach dem Holocaust.* [See in No. 42365.]

42929. LUDWIGSHAFEN. NEWMAN, HERTA: *On being back: a Ludwigshafen journal.* [In]: Midstream, Vol. 49, No. 7, New York, Nov./Dec. 2003. Pp. 9–12. [A German Jew revisits the city of her birth.]

42930. MANNHEIM. SCHADT, JÖRG: *Zur Erinnerung an den US-Militärarzt Hauptmann Franz S. Steinitz.* [In]: Badische Heimat, Jg. 80, H. 2, Freiburg, 2000. Pp. 225–226, port. [Deals with the role of F.S.St. (1910 Beuthen–1999 Chicago) in the occupation of Mannheim in March 1945.]

42931. MANKOWITZ, ZEEV W.: *Life between memory and hope: the survivors of the Holocaust in occupied Germany.* Cambridge; New York: Cambridge Univ. Press, 2002. 348 pp., illus., notes, bibl., index. [Tells the story of ca. 250,000 Holocaust survivors who converged on the American Zone of occupied Germany between 1945–1948.] [Cf.: Review (Ronald W. Zweig) [in]: English Historical Review, Vol. 119, Issue 480, Harlow, Feb. 2004, pp. 261– 262. Review (Michael Berkowitz) [in]: H-Net Reviews in the Humanities and Social Sciences, April, 27, 2004, www.h-net.org/reviews.]

42932. MASER, PETER: *Juden in der DDR.* [In]: Bilanz und Perspektiven der DDR-Forschung. Hrsg. von Rainer Eppelmann [et al.] im Auftrag der Stiftung zur Aufarbeitung der SED-Diktatur. Paderborn: Schöningh, 2003. Pp. 217–225. [Also, by the same author: Helmut Eschwege. Ein Historiker in der DDR [in]: Horch und Guck, Jg. 12, H. 44, Berlin, 2003. Pp. 21–23, port., notes; followed by: Verketzerung Israels und der Juden in der DDR (Helmut Eschwege, 26–29).]

42933. MUNICH. GANOR, SOLLY: *Der historische Seder in München 15./16. April 1946.* [In]: Dachauer Hefte, Jg. 19, H. 19, Berlin, Nov. 2003. Pp. 281–285. [Author, orig. Sali Genkind, b. 1928 in Heydekrug/Memel, emigr. 1948 to Palestine.]

42934. MUNICH. *9. November 2003. Aus der Vergangenheit für die Zukunft.* Hrsg.: Israelitische Kultusgemeinde München und Oberbayern [et al.]. München: Israel. Kultusgemeinde München und Oberbayern [et al.], [2003]. 60 pp., illus., facsims. [Incl. addresses by Charlotte Knobloch, Harald Strötgen, Anne-Barb Hertkorn on the occasion of laying the foundation stone of the new synagogue in Munich. Incl. also essays: Die ehemalige Hauptsynagoge (Andreas Heusler, 15–30). 9. November

1938 (Anne-Barb Hertkorn, 31–40). Jeder Mensch hat einen Namen. Namenslesung 1998–2003 (Anne-Barb Hertkorn, 41–48).] [Cf.: Die Steine mit Leben zu füllen. Heute setzen wir das Zeichen eines Neubeginns: Jüdisches Leben in München und das Gedächtnis des 9. November (Michael Brenner) [in]: Süddeutsche Zeitung, Nr. 257, München, 8./9. Nov. 2003, p. 13.]

——— NACHAMA, ANDREAS: *Mehr als ein Fragezeichen: Die Zukunft der Juden in Deutschland.* [See in No. 42217.]

42935. NORTH-RHINE-WESTPHALIA. STRATHMANN, DONATE: *Auswandern oder Hierbleiben? Jüdisches Leben in Düsseldorf und Nordrhein 1945–1960.* Essen: Klartext, 2003. 427 pp., illus., footnotes, tabs., bibl. (397–424), gloss. (Düsseldorfer Schriften zur Neueren Landesgeschichte und zur Geschichte Nordrhein-Westfalens, Bd. 63.) Zugl.: Paderborn, Univ., Diss., 2001 u.d.T.: Von der "Liquidationsgemeinde" zum "Zentralpunkt jüdischen Lebens"?

42936. ROGGENKAMP, VIOLA: *Die jüdisch-deutsche Mamme.* [In]: Jüdischer Almanach [2003] des Leo Baeck Instituts, Frankfurt am Main, 2003. Pp. 10–21. [Personal recollections of the author, b. 1948 in Hamburg to a Jewish mother and a non-Jewish father.]

42937. ROHLFES, JOACHIM: *Der Liberale als Kommunist. Victor Klemperers SBZ/DDR-Jahre im Spiegel seiner Tagebücher.* [In]: Geschichte in Wissenschaft und Unterricht, Jg. 54, H. 7/8, Stuttgart, 2003. Pp. 427–439, footnotes.

42938. SCHORSCH, JONATHAN: *Jewish ghosts in Germany.* [In]: Jewish Social Studies, Vol. 9, No. 3, Bloomington,IN, Spring/Summer, 2003. Pp. 139–169, notes. [Deals with present-day Germany.]

42939. SCHULTE, KLAUS: *"Was ist denn das überhaupt, ein Jude?"* Anna Seghers' Einspruch anlässlich der antisemitischen Hetze gegen die Insassen der Berliner Transitlager für 'displaced persons' in der Presse der Vier-Sektoren-Stadt im Jahre 1948: Rekonstruktion, Lektüre, Kommentar. [In]: Jahrbuch für Kommunikationsgeschichte, Bd. 4, Stuttgart, 2003. Pp. 196–231, notes.

42940. SPIEGEL, PAUL: *Was ist koscher? Jüdischer Glaube—jüdisches Leben.* Berlin: Ullstein, 2003. 303 pp. [Aimed at the non-Jewish German reader, the author, president of the Zentralrat der Juden in Deutschland, addresses frequently asked questions; incl.: Wie kann man als Jude in Deutschland leben? (289–303).]

42941. SÜDDEUTSCHE ZEITUNG: *Jüdisches Leben in Deutschland.* [Hrsg.: Hans-Herbert Holzamer, Red.: Ingrid Brunner]. [München: Süddt. Zeitung, 2003]. 90 pp., illus. [Incl.: Staatsvertrag (9–20; incl. the text). Preisverleihung (21–32; presentation of the Berlin Jewish Museum prize to Berthold Beitz). Interview (33–38; with Charlotte Knobloch, Munich). Porträts (39–50; with Paul Spiegel, Dov-Levy Barsilay). Meinungsbeiträge (51–66; contribs. by Avi Primor, Julius H. Schoeps, Hans-Herbert Holzamer). Reportagen (67–80; on Frankfurt am Main, Munich, Berlin).]

42942. *Thema: Jüdisches Leben in Deutschland.* [Issue title of] Das Parlament, Jg. 53, Berlin, 28. Juli/4. Aug. 2003. 29 pp., illus. [Incl. contribs. by/interviews with Annette Rollmann, Micha Guttmann, Hermann Simon, Julius H. Schoeps, Inge Lammel, Paul Spiegel, Meinhard Tenné, Jörg Magenau, Wolfgang Benz, Rafael Seligmann et al.]

42943. TOBIAS, JIM G.: *Das geheime Militärprogramm der 'Hagana' im Nachkriegsdeutschland am Beispiel der Offiziersschulen Wildbad und Hochland.* [In]: nurinst 2002, Beiträge zur deutschen und jüdischen Geschichte, Bd. 1, Nürnberg, 2002. Pp. 53–70, notes.

42944. TOBIAS, JIM G./ZINKE, PETER: *Nakam. Jüdische Rache an NS-Tätern.* Berlin: Aufbau Taschenbuch Verlag, 2003. 179 pp., notes, bibl. [Incl. the search for Adolf Eichmann. First publ. in 2000.]

——— TRIER. *Themen des Judentums—Juden im Trierer Land.* Hrsg. von Vladimir Raskin. [See No. 42437.]

——— VIENNA. BOTZ, GERHARD [et al.], eds.: *Eine zerstörte Kultur. Jüdisches Leben und Antisemitismus in Wien seit dem 19. Jahrhundert.* [See No.42467.]

42945. VIENNA. GOODMAN-THAU, EVELINE: *Eine Rabbinerin in Wien*. Betrachtungen. Wien: Czernin, 2003. 182 pp. [Deals with the author's rabbinate in the liberal "Or Chadasch" congregation in Vienna, from May 2001 to April 2002.] [Cf.: Eine Rabbinerin in Wien (Cécile Cordon) [in]: Zwischenwelt, Jg. 20, Nr. 2, Wien, Sept. 2003.]

42946. ZIELINSKI, ANDREA: *Die anderen Juden: Identitätenbildung von Menschen jüdischer Herkunft im Nachkriegsdeutschland*. Hamburg: LIT, 2002. 326 pp., notes, bibl. (285–326). (Interethnische Beziehungen und Kulturwandel, 42.) Zugl.: Hamburg, Univ., Diss., 1999. [Based on 64 interviews with persons of partly Jewish descent.]

——— KAUDERS, ANTHONY D.: *Vergangenheitsbewältigung am Beispiel Münchens*. [See No. 43549.]

B. **Prosecution of Nazi Crimes. Restitution**

42947. AUSCHWITZ TRIAL. WITTMANN, REBECCA ELIZABETH: *Indicting Auschwitz: the paradox of the Auschwitz trial*. [In]: German History, Vol. 21, No. 4, London, 2003. Pp. 505– 532, footnotes. [Discusses the paradox of the state attorney's office's use of the Nazi penal code for the trial to show that the defendants had acted above and beyond orders from Berlin.]

42948. AUSTRIA. BAILER-GALANDA, BRIGITTE: *Die Entstehung der Rückstellungs- und Entschädigungsgesetzgebung*. Die Republik Österreich und das in der NS-Zeit entzogene Vermögen. Wien: Oldenbourg, 2003. 618 pp., footnotes, bibl. (597–611). (Veröff. der Österreichischen Historikerkommission. Vermögensentzug während der NS-Zeit sowie Rückstellungen und Entschädigungen seit 1945 in Österreich, Bd. 3.)

42949. AUSTRIA. BLIMLINGER, EVA: *"... Das geht sich nie aus, das könnt ihr nicht verlangen, Wahnsinn!". Konzeption und Organisation von Auftragsforschungsprojekten am Beispiel der Historikerkommission*. [In]: Zeitgeschichte, Jg. 30, H. 5, Salzburg, Sept./Okt. 2003. Pp. 281–292, notes. [On the recent development and nature of restitution and indemnification in Austria, also on the public debates.]

42950. AUSTRIA. EMBACHER, HELGA: *Restitutionsverhandlungen mit Österreich aus der Sicht jüdischer Organisationen und der Israelitischen Kultusgemeinde*. Wien: Oldenbourg, 2003. 333 pp., footnotes, bibl. (Veröff. der Österreichischen Historikerkommission. Vermögensentzug während der NS-Zeit sowie Rückstellungen und Entschädigungen seit 1945 in Österreich, Bd. 27.)

42951. AUSTRIA. GRAF, GEORG: *Die österreichische Rückstellungsgesetzgebung*. Eine juristische Analyse. Wien: Oldenbourg, 2003. 559 pp., footnotes, bibl., index. (Veröff. der Österreichischen Historikerkommission. Vermögensentzug während der NS-Zeit sowie Rückstellungen und Entschädigungen seit 1945 in Österreich, Bd. 2.) [Covers the period 1945–1998.]

42952. AUSTRIA. JABLONER, CLEMENS [et al.]: *Schlussbericht der Historikerkommission der Republik Österreich*. Vermögensentzug während der NS-Zeit sowie Rückstellungen und Entschädigungen seit 1945 in Österreich. Zusammenfassungen und Einschätzungen. Wien: Oldenbourg, 2003. 517 pp., footnotes, tabs., bibl. (Veröff. der Österreichischen Historikerkommission 1.) [Section II.2 is entitled: Juden und Jüdinnen ("Arisierungen") (85–155).]

42953. AUSTRIA. PAMMER, MICHAEL: *Die Rückstellungskommission beim Landesgericht für Zivilrechtssachen Wien*. Wien: Oldenbourg, 2002. 114 pp., footnotes, tabs., graphs, bibl. (Veröff. der Österreichischen Historikerkommission. Vermögensentzug während der NS-Zeit sowie Rückstellungen und Entschädigungen seit 1945 in Österreich, Bd. 4/1.)

42954. AUSTRIA. *Revisiting the National Socialist legacy: coming to terms with forced labour, expropriation, compensation and restitution*. Ed. by Oliver Rathkolb. Innsbruck: Studien Verlag, 2002. 480 pp., notes. (Bruno Kreisky International Studies, Bd. 3.) [Expanded versions of contributions to an international conference in October 2001, organised by the Bruno Kreisky Archives Foundation.]

42955. BAZYLER, MICHAEL J.: *Holocaust justice: the battle for restitution in America's courts.* New York: New York Univ. Press, 2003. XIX, 411 pp., illus., notes, bibl. (393–396), index. [Discusses how American courts have been able to order restitution for Holocaust survivors from corporations such as banks and insurance companies.]

42956. BIELEFELD. ROECKNER, KATJA: *Der Konflikt um die Rückerstattung "arisierten" Eigentums am Beispiel der Bielefelder Wäschefabrik Juhl/Winkel.* [In]: 88. Jahresbericht des Historischen Vereins für die Grafschaft Ravensberg, Jg. 2002/2003. Bielefeld, 2003. Pp. 181–192, footnotes.

42957. BROWN, PAUL B.: *The senior leadership cadre of the Geheime Feldpolizei, 1939– 1945.* [In]: Holocaust and Genocide Studies, Vol. 17, No. 2, Oxford, Fall 2003. Pp. 278–304, notes. [Discusses the fact that 45 senior leaders were never prosecuted despite their role in exterminations.]

42958. EIZENSTAT, STUART: *Imperfect justice: looted assets, slave labor, and the unfinished business of World War II.* Foreword by Elie Wiesel. New York: Public affairs, 2003. 401 pp., illus., ports., facsims., notes, bibl., index. [German edn.: Unvollkommene Gerechtigkeit. Der Streit um die Entschädigung der Opfer von Zwangsarbeit und Enteignung. Mit einem Vorwort von Elie Wiesel. München: Bertelsmann, 2003. 477 pp.] [Cf.: Bespr. (Jan Surmann) [in]: Sozial.Geschichte, N.F., Jg. 18, H. 3, Bern, Okt. 2003, pp. 160–162.]

42959. GREENE, JOSHUA: *Justice at Dachau: the trials of an American prosecutor.* New York: Broadway Books, 2003. 385 pp., illus., ports., notes, bibl.(365–373), index. [Discusses the Dachau trial, held by an American military tribunal from 1945 to 1948 and led by Chief Prosecutor Lt. Col. William Dowell Denson.]

42960. HANOVER. SZABÓ, ANIKÓ: *Juristische Wiedergutmachung für die in der NS-Zeit verfolgten Hochschullehrer der TH Hannover nach 1945.* [In]: Hannoversche Geschichtsblätter, Bd. 54, Hannover, 2003. Pp. 41–56, footnotes.

42961. *Im Labyrinth der Schuld. Täter—Opfer—Ankläger.* Hrsg. im Auftrag des Fritz Bauer Instituts von Irmtrud Wojak und Susanne Meinl. Frankfurt am Main; New York: Campus, 2003. 362 pp., illus., notes. (Jahrbuch 2003 zur Geschichte und Wirkung des Holocaust.) [Selected essays (some titles condensed): Einführung (eds., 7–15). Fritz Bauer und die Aufarbeitung der NS-Verbrechen nach 1945 (Irmtrud Wojak, 17–40). Zu den Ermittlungen der "Zentralen Stelle der Landesjustizverwaltungen zur Aufklärung nationalsozialistischer Verbrechen" in Ludwigsburg (Michael Greve, 41–64). Adolf Eichmanns zwiespältige Erinnerungen an sein ungarisches "Meisterstück" (Christian Kolbe, 65–94). Überlebende als Zeugen im Auschwitzprozess—Rudolf Vrba und seine Aussage gegen den Angeklagten Robert Mulka (Dagi Knellessen, 95–132). Die ukrainischen Nationalisten als Zeugen im Auschwitz-Prozess (Franziska Bruder, 133–162). Robert Kempner und Ernst von Weizsäcker im Wilhelmstraßenprozess (Dirk Pöppmann, 163–198). Topf & Söhne—die Ofenbauer für Auschwitz (Annegret Schüle, 199–230). Die Opfer sind unter uns (Marcel Atze, 231–264; on the first reading of Peter Weiss' 'Ermittlung' in the GDR). Autobiographische Texte zum ersten Frankfurter Auschwitz-Prozess (265–332; texts by Heinz Düx, Hermann Langbein, Joachim Kügler, Gerhard Wiese). One further contrib. is listed according to subject.]

42962. KELLENBACH, KATHARINA VON: *Vanishing acts: perpetrators in post-war Germany.* [In]: Holocaust and Genocide Studies, Vol. 17, No. 2, Oxford, Fall 2003. Pp. 305–329, notes. [Essay traces the career, trial and subsequent discontinuation of the trial of one SS officer, the author's uncle. Discusses the family's denial and silence surrounding these issues, as well as the larger context of the West German justice system's failure adequately to convict and punish Nazi perpetrators.]

——— KWIET, KONRAD: *Von Tätern zu Befehlsempfängern. Legendenbildung und Strafverfolgung nach 1945.* [See in No. 42680.]

42963. MÜNSTER. VOLMER, JULIA: *Verwaltete Wiedergutmachung. Entschädigung für nationalsozialistische Verfolgung im Regierungsbezirk Münster.* [In]: Geschichte im Westen, Jg. 17, H. 2, Köln, 2002 [publ. 2003]. Pp. 150–164, footnotes.

42964. NORTH-RHINE WESTPHALIA. ZIEHER, JÜRGEN: *Die Grenzen der Wiedergutmachung auf der lokalen Ebene: Die Beispiele Dortmund, Düsseldorf und Köln.* [In]: Geschichte im Westen, Jg. 17, H. 2, Köln, 2002 [publ. 2003]. Pp. 165–181, footnotes.

42965. *NS-Unrecht vor Kölner Gerichten.* Für die Kölnische Gesellschaft für Christlich-Jüdische Zusammenarbeit hrsg. von Anne Klein und Jürgen Wilhelm. Köln: Greven Verlag, 2003. 288 pp., notes (215–286). [Documents the contribs. to a conference in Cologne, Nov. 2002. Cont. the sections I. Brüche und Kontinuitäten: der Kölner Justizapparat und die Aufarbeitung der NS-Verbrechen nach 1945. II. "Wiedergutmachung"? Die 1950er Jahre. III. Justiz und Öffentlichkeit—Die 1960er Jahre. IV. Der "Fall Lischka": ein Kölner Prozess mit internationaler Dimension—Die 1970er Jahre. Selected essays: Sühne von NS-Unrecht unter deutscher Strafjustiz vor und nach Gründung der Bundesrepublik (Gerhard Pauli, 37–44). Ost- und westdeutsche Prozesse gegen die Verantwortlichen für die Deportation der Juden: Das Beispiel der Kölner Gestapo (Christiaan Frederik Rüter, 45–56). "In der Justiz lebe ich wie im Exil". Zur Rückkehr jüdischer Juristen und Juristinnen (Cordula Lissner, 75–88). Die Rechtsprechung in Entschädigungsverfahren (Katharina von Bebber, 89–99). Restitution: Die Rückerstattung von unberechtigt entzogenen Vermögensgegenständen (Maik Wogersien, 100– 128). Antisemitismus vor Gericht: Die Hakenkreuzschmierereien an der Kölner Synagoge 1959 und andere Übergriffe (Werner Bergmann, 131–149). Kölner Justiz nach 1945: Kritisches Resümee zu einer Tagung (Horst Matzerath, 203–213). Further essays by Raphael Gross, Wolfgang Weber, Peter Liebermann, Heiner Lichtenstein, Beate Klarsfeld, Heinz Faßbender, Bernhard Brunner.]

42966. NUREMBERG TRIALS. BARD, MITCHELL GEOFFREY: *The Nuremberg Trials.* San Diego, CA: Greenhaven Press, 2002. 223 pp., notes, bibl. (212–213), index.

42967. ROSENSAFT, MENACHEM Z./ROSENSAFT, JOANA D.: *A measure of justice: The early history of German-Jewish reparations.* New York; Berlin: Leo Baeck Institute, 2003. 28 pp., notes. (LBI Occasional Paper, No. 4.)

42968. SCHRAFSTETTER, SUSANNA: *The diplomacy of Wiedergutmachung: memory, the Cold War, and the Western European victims of Nazism, 1956–1964.* [In]: Holocaust and Genocide Studies, Vol. 17, No. 3, Oxford, Winter 2003. Pp. 459–479, notes.

42969. SWITZERLAND. STADLER, PETER: *Der Bergier-Bericht.* [In]: Historische Zeitschrift, Bd. 276, München, 2003. Pp. 677–693. [Review of *Veröffentlichungen der Unabhängigen Expertenkommission Schweiz – Zweiter Weltkrieg.* Zurich: Chronos, 2001–2002. 25 vols. in 27 parts.]

C. **Education and Teaching. Memorials and Remembrance**

42970. AK ERINNERUNGSKULTUR IN DER MARBURGER GESCHICHTSWERKSTATT, ed.: *Weiter erinnern? Neu erinnern? Überlegungen zur Gegenwart und Zukunft des Umgangs mit der NS-Zeit.* Münster: Unrast, 2003. 235 pp., footnotes. [Essays, some of them focusing on recent debates about antisemitism and the "politics of the past", by Bernd Boll, Günter Saathoff, Hannes Heer, Gerd Wiegel, Hanno Loewy, Kai Köhler, Sabine Manke, Barbara Distel.]

42971. AUSCHWITZ. BERENBAUM, MICHAEL: *Auschwitz must be preserved.* Excerpts from an address given at Auschwitz, June 24, 2003. [In]: Midstream, Vol. 49, No. 7, New York, Nov./Dec. 2003. Pp. 4–5. [Address given at the Conference for Conservation and Preservation held at Auschwitz-Birkenau, June 23–24, 2003. Also in this issue another address: Auschwitz-Birkenau: a sacred zone of inviolability (Kalman Sultanik, 6–8).]

42972. AUSTRIA. *Memorial sites for concentration camp victims in Upper Austria.* Ed. by Siegfried Haider and Gerhart Marckhgott. Transl. by Barbara Zehetmayr and James Zimmer. [Publ. on behalf of Land Upper Austria]. Linz: Provincial Archives of Upper Austria, 2002. 272 pp., illus., maps. [For German edn. see No. 40260/YB XLVII.]

42973. BAUMGÄRTNER, ULRICH: *"Holocaust education" oder Geschichtsunterricht? Politisch-moralische Herausforderungen des historischen Lernens in der Schule.* [In]: Jüdische Geschichte: Alte Herausforderungen, neue Ansätze [see No. 42230.]. Pp. 178–193, footnotes. [Deals with changes in the perception of "the Holocaust", esp. its transformation from historical phenomenon into moral portent, thus impeding the learning and understanding of history.]

42974. BERLIN. *Netzwerk der Erinnerung.* 10 Jahre Gedenkstättenreferat der Stiftung Topographie des Terrors. [Hrsg.: Reinhard Rürup, Red.: Meinke Bruhns et al.]. Berlin: Stiftung Topographie des Terrors, 2003. 96 pp., illus.

42975. BERLIN, HOLOCAUST MEMORIAL. KIRSCH, JAN-HOLGER: *Nationaler Mythos oder historische Trauer?* Der Streit um ein zentrales "Holocaust-Mahnmal" für die Berliner Republik. Köln: Böhlau, 2003. X, 400 pp., illus., footnotes, chronol., bibl. (339–395), index. (Beiträge zur Geschichtskultur, Bd. 25.) [Cf.: Bespr. (Holger Thünemann) [in]: Geschichte, Politik und ihre Didaktik, Jg. 31, H. 3/4, Paderborn, 2003, pp. 271–272.]

42976. BERLIN, HOLOCAUST MEMORIAL. THÜNEMANN, HOLGER: *Das Denkmal für die ermordeten Juden Europas. Dechiffrierung einer Kontroverse.* Münster: Lit, 2003. 128 pp., footnotes, bibl. (Zeitgeschichte—Zeitverständnis, Bd. 11.) [Cf.: Bespr. (Martin Liepach) [in]: Geschichte, Politik und ihre Didaktik, Jg. 31, H. 3/4, Paderborn, 2003, pp. 270–271.]

42977. BODEMANN, Y. MICHAL: *In den Wogen der Erinnerung. Jüdische Existenz in Deutschland.* München: Deutscher Taschenbuch Verlag, 2002. 218 pp., notes, bibl., index. Orig.-Ausg. [A collection of essays; most deal with Holocaust historiography and commemoration, "Vergangenheitsbewältigung", the Walser-Bubis debate; others deal with Jewish life in contemporary Germany.]

42978. BRÖNING, MICHAEL: *"Jewish monopoly capitalists". Jewish history in East-German schoolbooks (1948–1972).* Berlin: Wiss. Verlag Berlin, 2003. 130 pp., illus., footnotes, bibl., graphs.

42979. *Deutsch-jüdische Geschichte im Unterricht.* Orientierungshilfe für Lehrplan- und Schulbucharbeit sowie Lehrerbildung und Lehrerfortbildung. Hrsg.: LBI-Kommission für die Verbreitung deutsch-jüdischer Geschichte c/o Jüd. Museum der Stadt Frankfurt am Main. Frankfurt am Main: VAS-Verlag, 2003. XX pp. [Incl. a preface by Michael A. Meyer, Georg Heuberger and Joachim Schulz-Hardt.]

42980. ERLER, HANS, ed.: *Erinnern und Verstehen. Der Völkermord an den Juden im politischen Gedächtnis der Deutschen.* Frankfurt am Main; New York: Campus, 2003. 348 pp., footnotes. [Partly based on a conference held by the Akademie der Konrad-Adenauer-Stiftung, Berlin, Feb. 24, 2003. Cont. (some titles abbr.): Einleitung: Erinnern und politisches Gedächtnis in Deutschland (ed., 9–19). Teil 1: Der Kontext—Erinnern jüdisch, heute; cont.: Erinnern und Vergessen (Alphons Silbermann, 23–29). Der Umgang mit der Erinnerung (Ernst Ludwig Ehrlich, 30–37). Die moderne "Entjudung" in Deutschland und ihr Nachher (Emil L. Fackenheim, 38–45). Gedankensplitter eigener Erfahrung (Günter B. Ginzel, 46–50). Grenzen des Darstellbaren. Der Holocaust als Gegenstand von Denkmalkunst (Salomon Korn, 51–54). In jeder Woche ein "Heiliger Abend" (Lea Fleischmann, 56–59). Wie dunkel der Raum des Vergessens (Hanna Rheinz, 60–63). Teil 2: Auf der Grenze; cont.: Zur unsichtbaren Grenze zwischen Juden und Nichtjuden (Erhard Roy Wiehn, 67–74). Zweimal Nachdenken über Martin Walsers "Erfahrungen beim Verfassen einer Sonntagsrede" (Matthias Heyl, 75–99). Von der Täter- zur Opfergesellschaft: Zum Umbau der deutschen Erinnerungskultur (Harald Welzer, 100–106). Teil 3: Wahrnehmung des Völkermords und politisches Gedächtnis; cont.: Gegenwärtige Vergangenheit, Politik und Gedächtnis (Julia Kölsch, 109–115). Erinnern für die Zukunft (Erhard Roy Wiehn, 116–125). Persönliche Erinnerung und kollektives Gedächtnis in Deutschland nach 1945 (Aleida Assmann, 126–138). "Vergangenheitsbewältigungsrituale" und die "Rückkehr der toten Juden" (Richard Chaim Schneider, 139–144). Judentum und Schoah im Denken jüdischer Studenten Europas (Julian Voloj, 145–151). Teil 4; cont.: Das Führungskorps des Reichssicherheitshauptamtes (Michael Wildt, 155–165). Der Beitrag des Erzieherausschusses im Deutschen Koordinierungsrat zur Aufarbeitung der Vergangenheit (Rudolf W. Sirsch, 166–176). Politische Erziehung nach Auschwitz—aber welche? Max Horkheimer oder Theodor W. Adorno (Clemens Albrecht, 177–188). Zur Erforschung eines "blinden Flecks" in der Pädagogik des

Erinnerns (Stephan Marks, 189–201). "Aufarbeitung der Vergangenheit" heute (Matthias Heyl, 202–222). Didaktische Implikationen einer Erziehung nach Auschwitz (Hanns-Fred Rathenow, 223–229). Teil 5: Pädagogische Projekte; cont.: Seminare im Haus der Wannsee-Konferenz (Lore Kleiber, 233–245). Das Projekt: www.lernen-aus-der-geschichte.de (Regina Wyrwoll, 246–250). "DenkT@g" der Konrad-Adenauer-Stiftung e.V. (Ariane Vorhang, 251–258). Ein Jugendprojekt der Alten Synagoge Essen (Peter Schwiderowski, 259–266). DaimlerChrysler AG—Lehren aus der Vergangenheit ziehen (Lothar Ulsamer, 267–272). Zwangsarbeit und Geschichtsbewusstsein im Volkswagenwerk (273–283). Bahn-Azubis gegen Hass und Gewalt (Birgit Gantz-Rathmann, 284–286). Teil 6: Gedenken und Erinnern; cont.: Der didaktische Impetus des Jüdischen Museums Berlin (Cilly Kugelmann, 289–293). Das Denkmal für die ermordeten Juden Europas und der Ort der Information im Kontext der Gedenk- und Erinnerungskultur (Sibylle Quack, 294–304). "Niemand ist tot, solange man über ihn spricht" (Michael Fürst, 305–308). Der Gedenktag 27. Januar—eine Zwischenbilanz (Rita Süssmuth, 309–316). Israel—eine andere Erinnerung, ein anderes Gedenken (Theo Schwedmann, 317–328). Statt eines Nachwortes: "Dieses Volk". Die Erwählung Israels und die zentrale Paradoxie des Judentums (ed., 329–340).]

42981. FUCHS, EDUARD/PINGEL, FALK/RADKAU, VERENA, eds.: *Holocaust und Nationalsozialismus.* Wien: Studienverlag, 2002. 126 pp., bibl. (Konzepte und Kontroversen, Bd. 1.) [Incl.: Einleitung (Falk Pingel/Eduard Fuchs, 8–10). Unterricht über den Holocaust. Eine kritische Bewertung der aktuellen pädagogischen Diskussion (Falk Pingel, 11–23). Holocaust-Unterricht an Schulen und Universitäten in Polen heute (Feliks Tych, 24–25). Shoah—eine Reise der Erinnerung. Ein Lehrbuch zum Holocaust für Oberschüler (Nili Keren, 26–32). Erinnern oder auseinandersetzen? Kritische Anmerkungen zur Gedenkstättenpädagogik (Volkhard Knigge, 33–41). Authentische Orte von KZ-Verbrechen. Chancen und Risiken aus der Sicht der Besucherforschung (Günter Morsch, 42–47). Teilhabe am Trauma? Zeitzeugen in der pädagogischen Annäherung an die Geschichte des Holocaust (Gottfried Kößler, 48–57). "Ich konnte viele Dinge aus eigener Erfahrung nachvollziehen". Das Thema Holocaust im Unterricht in multikulturellen Klassen (Angelika Rieber, 58–73). "... verschollen in Izbica". Eine Spurensuche (Hannelore Lutz, 74–87). Gedenkstättenarbeit und Jugendaustausch bei Volkswagen (Dirko Thomsen, 88–95). Pädagogische Konzeption der Gedenkstätte Buchenwald (Daniel Gaede, 96–99). Vermittlungsarbeit als Erinnerungsarbeit. Museumspädagogik im Jüdischen Museum Hohenems (Bruno Winkler/Helmut Schlatter, 100–105). Zeitgeschichte Museum und KZ-Gedenkstätte Ebensee. Auseinandersetzung mit Vergangenheit im historischen Museum und am authentischen Ort (Bernhard Denkinger/Ulrike Felber/Wolfgang Quatember, 106–113). CD-ROMS zum Nationalsozialismus (Dietmar Sedlaczek, 114–117). Neue Medien zum Thema (Eduard Fuchs, 118–124).]

42982. GHOBEYSHI, SILKE: *Nationalsozialismus und Schoah als landeskundliche Themen im DaF-Unterricht.* Frankfurt am Main; New York: Lang, 2002. IX, 149 pp., graphs. (Werkstattreihe Deutsch als Fremdsprache, Bd. 72.) Zugl.: Bielefeld, Univ., Diss., 2002.

42983. HAMBURG. *Gedenkstätten in Hamburg. Ein Wegweiser zu Stätten der Erinnerung an die Jahre 1933–1945.* Hrsg. im Auftrag der Hamburgischen Bürgerschaft und des Senats von der KZ-Gedenkstätte Neuengamme und der Landeszentrale für politische Bildung Hamburg. Redaktion: Detlef Garbe und Jens Michelsen. Textgrundlage: Ursula Richenberger. Hamburg: KZ-Gedenkstätte Neuengamme, Landeszentrale für politische Bildung, Hamburg, 2003. 89 pp., illus., index.

42984. HAUS DER WANNSEE-KONFERENZ—GEDENKSTÄTTE: *The Wannsee conference and the genocide of the European Jews.* Guide and reader to the permanent exhibit in the House of the Wannsee Conference. 3rd edn. Berlin: Edition Hentrich; Gedenkstätte Haus der Wannsee Konferenz/House of the Wannsee Conference Memorial and Educational Site, 2002. 205 pp., illus., ports., facsims., maps, chronol.

42985. HOBA, KATHARINA/LÖBBECKE, GESA: *Judentum.* Berlin: Cornelsen Verlag Scriptor, 2002. 128 pp., illus. (Pocket Thema.) [General introduction, with special focus on German-Jewish history; present Jewish life in Germany.]

42986. HUYSSEN, ANDREAS: *Review essay.* [In]: The Germanic Review [with the issue title] A Festschrift to Inge Halpert [see No. 43307]. Pp. 86–91. [On 'Erinnerung im globalen Zeitalter: Der Holocaust' by Daniel Levy and Natan Sznaider; see No. 40280/YB 47.]

42987. *Image and remembrance: representation and the Holocaust.* Ed. by Shelley Hornstein and Florence Jacobowitz. Bloomington: Indiana Univ. Press, 2003. VIII, 332 pp., illus., maps, notes, bibl., index. [Examines visual representation of the Holocaust in film, architecture, photography, paintings, memorials.]

42988. KAHLENBERG, FRIEDRICH P.: *Erinnern und Gedenken. Zur aktuellen Relevanz von Erinnerungsorten.* [In]: Das Gedächtnis der Verwaltung und ein Haus der Geschichte. Stadtarchivarbeit im 21. Jahrhundert. Festschrift für Jörg Schadt anlässlich seines 65. Geburtstags. Hrsg. von Ulrich Nieß [et al.]. Heidelberg: Verlag Regionalkultur, 2003. Pp. 57–63.

42989. KAPLAN, BRETT ASHLEY: *"Aesthetic pollution": the paradox of remembering and forgetting in three commemorative sites.* [In]: Journal of Modern Jewish Studies, Vol. 2, No. 1, Abingdon, 2003. Pp. 1–18, notes, illus. [Discusses the problems of Holocaust presentation by analysing the architectural aesthetics of the Holocaust memorials in Berlin, Hamburg-Harburg and Washington DC.]

42990. KIPPENHEIM. MARGIN-PELICH, EVA: *Die Gedenkstätte "Ehemalige Synagoge Kippenheim".* [In]: Aufbau, Vol. 69, No. 20, New York, Oct. 16, 2003. P. 7, illus. [On the "pre-history" of the museum's opening on Sept. 7, 2003.]

42991. KOKKOLA, LYDIA: *Representing the Holocaust in children's literature.* New York: Routledge, 2003. IX, 206 pp., illus., notes, bibl. (189–198), index. (Children's literature and culture, Vol. 26.)

——— KOKEMÜLLER, BIRGITT: *Jüdische Identität nach der Schoah als Thema in ausgewählten Kinder- und Jugendbüchern.* Inhaltliche Analyse und didaktische Untersuchungen auf deren Verwendbarkeit im Katholischen Religionsunterricht der Sekundarstufe I. [See No. 43073.]

42992. LEVI, TRUDE: *Did you ever meet Hitler, Miss?: a Holocaust survivor talks to young people.* London; Portland, OR: Beth Shalom Holocaust Centre in association with Vallentine Mitchell, 2003. XVII, 126 pp., illus., ports., bibl. (115–118), index. [A collection of questions and answers generated by the author when lecturing to young people in schools on her own experiences in the Holocaust.] [T.L., b. in Hungary 1924, deported to Auschwitz and various other camps in 1944, after liberation lived in France, Israel and South Africa before settling in London.]

42993. LÜDERWALDT, MITJA: *Judenverfolgung—Begegnung mit Auschwitz. Ein Unterrichtsprojekt zum Nationalsozialismus—Schwerpunkt der Lernort Gedenkstätte Auschwitz.* Ein Unterrichtsprojekt für Schüler der Jahrgangsstufen 10–13 der Geschichts-AG des Friedrich-Dessauer-Gymnasiums und der Leibnizschule in Frankfurt am Main. [In]: Geschichte, Politik und ihre Didaktik, Jg. 31, H. 3/4, Paderborn, 2003. Pp. 250–263.

42994. MARIENFELD, WOLFGANG: *Jüdische Geschichte im Schulbuch der Gegenwart.* [In]: Geschichte in Wissenschaft und Unterricht, Jg. 54, H. 3, Stuttgart, 2003. Pp. 167–174, footnotes.

42995. MAYER, GABRIELE: *Post-Holocaust religious education for German women.* Münster: LIT Verlag, 2003. 218 pp., footnotes, bibl. (Tübinger Perspektiven zur Pastoraltheologie und Religionspädagogik, Bd. 18.) (zugl.: Claremont School of Theology, CA, Univ., Diss., 2000.).

42996. MUNICH. PFOERTNER, HELGA: *Mahnmale, Gedenkstätten, Erinnerungsorte für die Opfer des Nationalsozialismus in München 1933–1945.* München: Literareon im Herbert Utz Verlag, 2001; 2003. 2 vols., illus., footnotes, bibl. [Bd. 1: A-H. VII, 225 pp.; Bd. 2: I-P. 309 pp.]

42997. PADERBORN. REINKING, LARS: *Das Mahnmal für die ehemalige Synagoge in Paderborn.* Zu den Entscheidungsprozessen um einen Ort des Gedenkens im öffentlichen Raum. [In]: Mitteilungen des Vereins für Geschichte an der Universität Paderborn, Nr. 15, H. 1, 2002. Pp. 4–38, footnotes. [On a memorial by Per Kirkeby, dedicated Nov. 1993.]

42998. RAVENSBRÜCK. JACOBEIT, SIGRID: *KZ-Gedenkstätten als nationale Erinnerungsorte.* Zwischen Ritualisierung und Musealisierung. Berlin: Humboldt-Universität zu Berlin, 2003. 31 pp. [Mainly on Ravensbrück.]

42999. REIF-SPIREK, PETER: *Rechtsextremismus, Geschichtsrevisionismus und Gedenkstättenpädagogik.* [In]: Wolfgang Benz/Peter Reif-Spirek: Geschichtsmythen. Legenden über den Nationalsozialismus. Berlin: Metropol, 2003. Pp. 151–161, footnotes.

43000. STEFFENS, GERD: *Familiengedächtnis, Didaktik und Geschichtspolitik. Zu zwei neuen Studien über den Umgang mit dem Holocaust in Deutschland und den USA.* [In]: Jahrbuch für Pädagogik 2003, Jg. 11, Frankfurt am Main, 2003. Pp. 173–183. [On: Heike Deckert-Peaceman: Holocaust als Thema für Grundschulkinder? and Harald Welzer [et al.]: "Opa war kein Nazi". Nationalsozialismus und Holocaust im Familiengedächtnis, both publ. 2002.]

43001. VAN DEN BERG, KAREN/VAN DEN BERG, JÖRG/MANHART, SEBASTIAN: *Kein Ende. Skulpturenprojekte an jüdischen Landfriedhöfen.* Von Christine Borland, Stefan Kern, Jörg Lenzlinger/Gerda Steiner, Thomas Locher und Richard Serra. Berlin: Kadmos, 2003. 139 pp., illus., notes (Copyrights, Bd. 12.) [Deals with projects of "Echo's Pool", planning sculptures for the Rhineland cemeteries of Winterswick, Hoerstgen, Issum, Alpen, Xanten.]

43002. WERTHEIMER, JÜRGEN: *'Unser Auschwitz'—Tabu und Tabubruch als Marketing-Konzept.* Eine Glosse vom Rande der Philologie. [In]: Aufklärungen: Zur Literaturgeschichte der Moderne. Festschrift für Klaus-Detlef Müller zum 65. Geburtstag. Hrsg. von Werner Frick [et al.]. Tübingen: Niemeyer, 2003. Pp. 455–463.

43003. WETTE, WOLFRAM/HOFFMANN, DETLEV, eds.: *Litauen 1941 und 2001. Auf den Spuren des SS-Massenmörders Karl Jäger.* Erlebnisberichte von Freiburger Schülern und Studenten. Bremen: Donat, 2002. 178 pp., illus., facsims., index.

V. JUDAISM

A. Jewish Learning and Scholars

43004. BAECK, LEO: *Briefe, Reden, Aufsätze.* Hrsg. von Michael A. Meyer. In Zusammenarbeit mit Bärbel Such. Gütersloh: Gütersloher Verlagshaus, 2003. 702 pp., frontis. (facsim.), chronol., index. (Leo Baeck Werke, Bd. 6.). [Final vol. of the 6–vol. edn.]

43005. BERGER, RUTH: *Die Verstoßung der epileptischen Ehefrau. Eine Studie über Geschlechterdifferenz im ashkenazischen Scheidungsrecht des Mittelalters.* [In]: Frankfurter Judaistische Beiträge, Bd. 30, Frankfurt am Main, 2003. Pp. 103–146, footnotes. [On how medieval developments in Jewish matrimonial law failed to improve the lot of women.]

43006. BERGER, RUTH: *Sexualität, Ehe und Familienleben in der jüdischen Moralliteratur (900–1900).* Wiesbaden: Harrassowitz, 2003. VIII, 374 pp., footnotes, bibl. (347–364), index (Jüdische Kultur, Studien zur Geistesgeschichte, Religion und Literatur, Bd. 10.) [Also analyses Ashkenazi texts.] [Cf.: Bespr. (Monika Preuß) [in]: Trumah, Bd. 13, Heidelberg, 2003, pp. 281–282.]

43007. BROCKE, MICHAEL: *Auf den Knien der Zeit ... Traumgestalten, wer von euch ist Jehuda ben Halevy?* [In]: Kalonymos, Jg. 6, H. 1, Duisburg, 1–7. [Compares three translations of a "Havdala" by Jehuda Halevi by Seligmann Heller, Gerhard (Gershom) Scholem and Franz Rosenzweig.]

43008. BUBER, MARTIN. FORMAN-BARZILAI, DAVID: *Agonism in faith: Buber's eternal Thou after the Holocaust.* [In]: Modern Judaism, Vol. 23, No. 2, Oxford, May 2003. Pp. 156–179, notes.

43009. BUBER, MARTIN. GANTNER, BRIGITTA ESZTER: *"Was wir sind, das sind unsere Vorfahren in uns". Der Einfluß Martin Bubers auf die deutsch-jüdische Intelligenz (bis 1914).* [In]: Mnemosyne, H. 28 (2002), Münster, 2003. Pp. 101–118, footnotes.

43010. BUBER, MARTIN. KRAMER, KENNETH PAUL (with MECHTHILD GAWLICK): *Martin Buber's I and thou: practicing living dialogue.* New York; Mahwah, NJ: Paulist Press, 2003. 215 pp., diagrs.

43011. BUBER, MARTIN. ROSS, DENNIS S.: *God in our relationships: spirituality between people from the teachings of Martin Buber.* Woodstock, VT: Jewish Lights Publ., 2003. XXI, 118 pp., notes, bibl. (116–120).

43012. BUBER, MARTIN. SCHOEPS, JULIUS H.: *Wer redet, ist nicht tot. Vor 125 Jahren wurde der jüdische Religionsphilosoph Martin Buber geboren.* [In]: Dialog, H. 20, Potsdam, 2003. Pp. 1 & 4.

43013. BUBER, MARTIN. STÖGER, PETER: *Martin Buber. Eine Einführung in Leben und Werk.* Innsbruck: Verlagsanstalt Tyrolia, 2003. 140 pp., notes, bibl. Orig.-Ausg.

43014. BUBER, MARTIN: *The Martin Buber reader: essential writings.* Ed. by Asher D. Biemann. New York: Palgrave Macmillan, 2002. VI, 303 pp., notes, index.

43015. COHEN, HERMANN. WIEDEBACH, HARTWIG: *Hebräisches "Fühlen". Hermann Cohens Deutung des Schma' Jisra'el/"Höre Israel".* [In]: Kalonymos, Jg. 6, H. 2, Duisburg, 2003. Pp. 1–4, illus., facsims., notes.

43016. COHN-SHERBOK, DAN: *Judaism: history, belief, and practice.* London; New York: Routledge, 2003. XVIII, 590 pp., illus., maps, notes, index. [Incl. chaps. on the Enlightenment, the rise of antisemitism, Reform Judaism, the Nazi period, Jewry after the Holocaust; also on Solomon Ludwig Steinheim, Samson Raphael Hirsch, Heinrich Graetz i.a.]

43017. FORMSTECHER, SALOMON. MEYER, THOMAS: *Salomon Formstechers "Religion des Geistes"—Versuch einer Neulektüre.* [In]: Aschkenas, Jg. 13, H. 2, Tübingen, 2002. Pp. 441–460, footnotes. [On 'Religion des Geistes, eine wissenschaftliche Darstellung des Judenthums nach seinem Charakter, Entwicklungsgange und Berufe in der Menschheit', publ. 1841.]

43018. GOODMAN, MARTIN: *The problems of Jewish studies.* [In]: Zutot 2002, Dordrecht, 2003. Pp. 182–188, footnotes.

43019. HESCHEL, ABRAHAM JOSHUA. EISEN, ROBERT: *A.J. Heschel's rabbinic theology as a response to the Holocaust.* [In]: Modern Judaism, Vol. 23, No. 3, London, Oct. 2003. Pp. 211–225, notes.

43020. HOLDHEIM, SAMUEL. MEYER, MICHAEL A.: *"Most of my brethren find me unacceptable": the controversial career of Rabbi Samuel Holdheim.* [In]: Jewish Social Studies, Vol. 9, No. 3, Bloomington, IN, Spring/Summer 2003. Pp. 1–19, notes. [S.H., 1806 Kempen/Posen–1860 Berlin, exponent of Reform Judaism, rabbi in Frankfurt am Main, Schwerin and Berlin.]

43021. JACOB, BENNO. *Benno Jacob—der Mensch und sein Werk* [issue title of] Trumah, Bd. 13, Heidelberg, 2003. VI, 289 pp., illus., footnotes. [Incl. the section: Jüdische Bibelauslegung: Benno Jacob—der Mensch und sein Werk (1–154; cont. contribs. by Walter Jacob, Almuth Jürgensen, Andreas Schüle, Hanna Liss, Manfred Oeming, Meir Seidler). Second part of this vol. deals with rabbinical literature; one further essay is listed according to subject.] [B.J. Sept. 7, 1862 Frankenstein (Silesia)–Jan. 1945 London, biblical scholar, rabbi in Göttingen (1891–1906), Dortmund (1906–1931), after retirement lived in Hamburg (1931–1939), emigr. to the UK.]

43022. JACOB, WALTER. KNOBEL, PETER S./STAITMAN, MARK N., eds.: *An American rabbinate. A Festschrift for Walter Jacob.* Pittsburgh, PA: Rodef Shalom Press, 2000. XIV, 324 pp., frontis., illus., bibl. W.J. (253–320). [Cont. 14 essays dealing with J.'s rabbinical activities and current Jewish-theological issues. Incl.: Jewish theology as a product of cultural intercourse. A history of Jewish thought in post-Enlightenment Germany (Walter Homolka, 43–72, followed by a response of Debra Pine, 74–76).] [W.J., b. March 13, 1930 in Augsburg, rabbi, president of the Abraham Geiger College, Potsdam, Senior Scholar/Rabbi Emeritus of the Rodef Shalom Congregation, Pittsburgh.]

43023. *Jewish Studies Quarterly.* Vol. 10, No. 3, Tübingen, 2003. 1 issue, footnotes. [All but one contribs. were presented at a workshop on the subject of "Jewish Renaissance" (unfolding in the first decades of the 20th cent.) at Schloss Blankensee (Brandenburg), July 2002. Incl.: Editorial (Paul Mendes-Flohr, 291–295). Introductory remarks (Klaus Reichert, 296–299). Theses on the historical context of the modern Jewish revolution (Benjamin Harshav, 300–319). Jewish Renaissance and 'Tehiyya'—two that are one? (Barbara Schäfer, 320–335; mainly on Shimon Ravidowicz and Martin Buber). Renewing the Jewish Past: Buber on history and truth (Leora Batnitzky, 336–350). The Jewish Renaissance and the plastic arts (Avner Holtzman, 351–359). Ludwig Geiger as the redactor of Jacob Burckhardt's 'Die Cultur der Renaissance in Italien' (Klaus Herrmann, 377–400). One essay is listed according to subject.]

43024. *Jewish studies between the disciplines = Judaistik zwischen den Disziplinen: papers in honor of Peter Schäfer on the occasion of his 60th birthday.* Ed. by Klaus Herrmann [et al.] Leiden; Boston: Brill, 2003. XIII, 502 pp., index of refs., index of modern authors. [Incl. English summaries. Cont.: I. Rabbinic Judaism. II. Early Jewish mysticism and magic; incl.: R. El'azar of Worms' "Stairway to heaven" (Annelies Kuyt, 218–225). III. Medieval and early modern Judaism; incl.: Payyetanim as heroes of medieval folk narrative: the case of R. Shim'on b. Yishaq of Mainz (Lucia Raspe, 354–372). IV. Modern Judaism; incl.: Entkontextualisierung als Programm: Die Bedeutung des göttlichen Namens bei Franz Rosenzweig und die pronominale "Er-Setzung" des Tetragramms (Hanna Liss, 372–403). Zwischen "Krieg und Frieden" und "Im Westen nichts Neues": Zwei Antikriegserzählungen aus dem jüdisch-orthodoxen Frankfurter Ostend (Matthias Morgenstern, 405–420). Jüdische Katechismen in Deutschland am Beispiel eines Katechismus aus der Feder von Samuel Hirsch, 1815–1889 (Bernd Schröder, 456–478).]

—— KONKEL, MICHAEL [et al.], eds.: *Die Konstruktion des Jüdischen in Vergangenheit und Gegenwart.* [See No. 43072.]

43025. KROCHMAL, NACHMAN. AMIR, YEHOYADA: *The perplexity of our time: rabbi Nachman Krochmal and modern Jewish existence.* [In]: The Jewish Journal of Sociology, Vol. 45, Nos. 1–2, London, Chur, 2003. Pp. 264–301, notes. [On the 'Moreh Nevukhei ha-Zeman'/'Guide for the perplexed of the time'] [N.K., 1785 Brody/Galicia–1840 Tarnopol/Galicia, historian, philosopher.]

43026. LAENEN, J.H.: *The twilight between scholarship and mysticism.* [In]: Zutot 2002, Dordrecht, 2003. Pp. 189–199, footnotes. [Mainly on Gershom Scholem.]

43027. LIBRETT, JEFFREY: *Review essay: on the matter of method in modernist German- Jewish studies.* The German Quarterly, Vol. 76, No. 1, Cherry Hill, NJ, Winter 2003. Pp. 86–93, notes.

43028. MAIMON, SALOMON. BRAESE, STEPHAN: *"Redendes Tier" und "gläserner Jude"—Bilder jüdischen Sprachwandels bei Maimon und Hebel.* [In]: Leipziger Beiträge zur jüdischen Geschichte und Kultur, Bd. I, München, 2003. Pp. 169–195, footnotes.

43029. MENDELSSOHN, MOSES. BREUER, EDWARD/SORKIN, DAVID: *Moses Mendelssohn's first Hebrew publication: An annotated translation of the 'Kohelet Mussar'.* [In]: Leo Baeck Institute Year Book 2003, Vol. XLVIII, Oxford; New York, 2003. Pp. 3–23, footnotes. [Orig. publ. anonymously in the 1750s.]

43030. MENDELSSOHN, MOSES. DAUBER, JEREMY: *New thoughts on "night thoughts": Mendelssohn and translation.* [In]: Journal of Modern Jewish Studies, Vol. 2, No. 2, Philadelphia; London, Oct. 2003. Pp. 132–147, notes.

43031. MENDELSSOHN, MOSES. EHRENFREUND, JACQUES: *Moses Mendelssohn: la construction d'un héros juif-allemand sous le second Reich.* [In]: Les cahiers du judaisme, No. 13, Paris, 2003. Pp. 84–95, notes.

43032. MENDELSSOHN, MOSES. *Moses Mendelssohn. Rezensionsartikel in Allgemeine deutsche Bibliothek (1765–1784). Literarische Fragmente. Kommentare.* Bearb. von Eva J. Engel. Mit Beiträgen von Michael Albrecht und Elisabeth Blakert. Stuttgart-Bad Cannstadt: Fromann Holzboog, 2003. XIX, 506 pp., notes (369–486), index. (Moses Mendelssohn, Gesammelte Schriften, Jubiläumsausgabe, Bd. 5,4.)

43033. MENDELSSOHN, MOSES. SCHMID, DORIS: *Moses Mendelssohn. Jüdischer Aufklärer und Bildungsreformer.* Eine Einführung. Doris Schmid: Selbstverlag, 2003. 127 pp., footnotes, chronol., bibl. (Books on Demand, Norderstedt.)

43034. MENDELSSOHN, MOSES. SCHORCH, GRIT: *Zwischen Sakralität und Säkularität—Die 'Hohelied'-Übersetzung Moses Mendelssohns.* [In]: Leipziger Beiträge zur jüdischen Geschichte und Kultur, Bd. I, München, 2003. Pp. 123–144, footnotes.

43035. MENDELSSOHN, MOSES. SIMON, HERMANN: *Moses Mendelssohn.* Gesetzestreuer Jude und deutscher Aufklärer. Berlin: Hentrich & Hentrich; Centrum Judaicum Berlin, 2003. 61 pp., illus., facsims., bibl. (Reihe Jüdische Miniaturen, Bd. 1.)

43036. MUNK, REINIER: *Athens in Jerusalem. On the definition of Jewish philosophy.* [In]: Zutot 2001, Dordrecht, 2002. Pp. 107–111, footnotes.

43037. MYERS, DAVID N.: *Resisting history: historicism and its discontents in German-Jewish thought.* Princeton, NJ: Princeton Univ. Press, 2003. X, 253 pp., illus., ports., notes, bibl., index. (Jews, Christians, and Muslims from the ancient to the modern world.) [Discusses the views on historicism of Isaac Breuer, Hermann Cohen, Franz Rosenzweig, Leo Strauss.]

43038. NORDEN, JOSEPH: *Auge um Auge—Zahn um Zahn.* Eine vielumstrittene Bibelstelle. Neu hrsg. von der "Gesellschaft für Christl.-Jüd. Zusammenarbeit in Wuppertal e.V." und dem "Trägerverein Begegnungsstätte Alte Synagoge Wuppertal e.V." nach dem Original des Philo-Verlags, Berlin 1926. Wuppertal: [privately printed], 2003. 32 pp., frontis., illus. [Incl.: Vorwort (Baruch Rabinowitz, 3).] [J.N., 1870 Hamburg–1943 Theresienstadt, rabbi in Elberfeld; see also No. 42336.]

43039. *The Oxford handbook of Jewish studies.* Ed. by Martin Goodman. Assoc. eds. Jeremy Cohen, David Sorkin. Oxford: Oxford Univ. Press, 2002. XIV, 1037 pp., index. [Cont. 39 chaps. dealing with history and related research/historiography from "Biblical Studies" to "Modern Jewish Society and Sociology", incl. bibl. references; selected contribs.: 1. The nature of Jewish Studies (ed., 1–13). 7. The narratives of medieval Jewish history (Joseph Dan, 141–152). 8. Medieval Jewry in Christendom (Ram Ben-Shalom, 153–192). 10. Rabbinic literature in the middle ages: 1000–1492 (Israel Ta-Shma, 219–240). 14. European Jewry in the early modern period: 1492–1750 (Elisheva Carlebach, 363–375). 15. Western and Central European Jewry in the modern period: 1750–1939 (David Rechter, 376–395). 17. The Holocaust (Saul Friedländer, 412–444). 22. Yiddish Studies (Cecile E. Kuznitz, 541–571). 26. Halacha and law (Bernard Jackson et al., 643–679). 28. Mysticism (Philip A. Alexander, 705–732). 29. Jewish liturgy and Jewish scholarship: method and cosmology (Lawrence A. Hoffman, 733–755). 30. Jewish philosophy and theology (Paul Mendes-Flohr, 756–769). 32. Jewish women's studies (Tal Ilan, 770–798). 32. Demography (Sergio della Pergola, 797–823). 33. Art, architecture, and archaeology (Lee I. Levine, 824–851). 34. Music (Philip V. Bohlman, 852–869). 35. Jewish theatre (Ahuva Belkin/Gad Kaynar, 870–910). 37. Anti-semitism research (Wolfgang Benz, 943–955). 38. Jewish folklore and ethnography (Galit Hasan-Rokem, 956–974). 39. Modern Jewish society and sociology (Harvey E. Goldberg, 975–1002).] [Cf.: Die Welt der "Jüdischen Studien"—von außen betrachtet (Robert Jütte) [in]: Aschkenas, Jg. 13, H. 2, Tübingen, 2003, pp. 513–518, footnotes.]

43040. ROSENZWEIG, FRANZ. AMIR, YEHOYADA: *Judaism despite Christianity—Judaism with Christianity: Reflections on Rosenzweig's concept of the relationships between the two religions.* [In Hebrew.] [In]: Mahanaim, No. 15, Jerusalem, Dec. 2003. Pp. 147–153.

43041. ROSENZWEIG, FRANZ. BIENENSTOCK, MYRIAM: *Recalling the past in Rosenzweig's "Star of Redemption".* [In]: Modern Judaism, Vol. 23, No. 3, London, Oct. 2003. Pp. 226–242, notes.

43042. ROSENZWEIG, FRANZ. GORDON, PETER ELI: *Rosenzweig redux: the reception of German-Jewish thought.* [In]: Jewish Social Studies, Vol. 8, No. 1, Bloomington, IN, Fall 2001. Pp. 1–57, notes.

43043. ROSENZWEIG, FRANZ. GORDON, PETER ELI: *Rosenzweig and Heidegger: between Judaism and German philosophy.* Berkeley: Univ. of California Press, 2003. XXIX, 328 pp., notes, bibl., index. (Weimar and now, 33.)

43044. ROSENZWEIG, FRANZ. SURALL, FRANK: *Juden und Christen—Toleranz in neuer Perspektive.* Der Denkweg Franz Rosenzweigs in seinen Bezügen zu Lessing, Harnack, Baeck und Rosenstock-Huessy. Gütersloh: Chr. Kaiser/Gütersloher Verlagshaus, 2003. 392 pp., footnotes, bibl.

(364–390), index. Zugl.: Bonn, Univ., Diss., 2001. [Incl. the sections: 2. Die Toleranz Lessings im Kontext des Wilhelminischen Deutschland. 3. Die Begrenzung inhaltlicher Toleranz bei Adolf von Harnack und Leo Baeck. 4. Inhaltliche Toleranz im Verhältnis von Judentum und Christentum bei Franz Rosenzweig. 5. Komplementäre Toleranz im Anschluss an Rosenzweig. Systematisch-theologische Reflexionen.]

43045. SCHOLEM, GERSHOM. HUSS, BOAZ: *To ask no questions—Gershom Scholem and the study of contemporary Jewish mysticism.* [In Hebrew]. [In]: Pe'amim, No. 94–95, Jerusalem, 2003. Pp. 57–72.

43046. SCHOLEM, GERSHOM. WEIDNER, DANIEL: *Gershom Scholem. Politisches, esoterisches und historiographisches Schreiben.* München: Fink, 2003. 446 pp., footnotes, bibl. (421–442). indexes. Zugl.: Berlin, Freie Univ., Diss., 2002. [Cf.: Bespr. (Thomas Meyer) [in]: Zeitschrift für Geschichtswissenschaft, Jg. 51, H. 5, Berlin, 2003, p. 457.]

43047. SCHOLEM, GERSHOM: *"Es gibt ein Geheimnis in der Welt". Tradition und Säkularisation.* Ein Vortrag und ein Gespräch. Hrsg. und mit einem Nachwort von Itta Shedletzky. Frankfurt am Main: Jüdischer Verlag im Suhrkamp Verlag, 2002. 127 pp., gloss. [Incl.: Einige Betrachtungen zur jüdischen Theologie in dieser Zeit (7–48; first German and complete edn. of lecture given in English in Sept. 1973 in Santa Barbara). Mit Gershom Scholem. Gespräch im Winter 1973/74 (49–110; first German edn. of a talk with Muki Tsur in winter 1973/1974). Nachwort (ed., 111–120).]

43048. SCHREINER, STEFAN: *Protestant bible study and the Jewish response in the 19th and 20th century.* [In]: Jewish Studies Quarterly, Vol. 10, No. 2, Tübingen, 2003. Pp. 140–171, notes. [Deals with the reception of the Protestant Bible study by Wissenschaft des Judentums, its rejection on the part of (neo)Orthodox Jewish Bible scholarship, and Jewish Bible interpretations as developed in the context of the "Hebrew Renaissance"; incl. Abraham Geiger, Heinrich Graetz, Leopold Zunz.]

43049. SHAVIT, YAACOV: *'Babel und Bibel'—The controversy as a Jewish event.* [In]: Leipziger Beiträge zur jüdischen Geschichte und Kultur, Bd. I, München, 2003. Pp. 263–279, footnotes. [On the involvement of Jewish scholars in the "Babel and Bibel" controversy centred around a series of lectures given in 1902/1903 by the assyriologist Friedrich Delitzsch; on their response to F.D.'s antisemitism in particular and to the challenge of higher biblical criticism in general.]

43050. *Von Enoch bis Kafka.* Festschrift für Karl E. Grözinger zum 60. Geburtstag mit Beiträgen von J. Friedrich Battenberg [et al.]. Hrsg. von Manfred Voigts. Wiesbaden: Harrassowitz, 2002. 456 pp., footnotes. [Selected essays: "Heidentum" und "Judentum" in der jüdischen Religionsphilosophie des 19. Jahrhunderts. Zu Steinheims "Offenbarung nach dem Lehrbegriffe der Synagoge" und Formstechers "Religion des Geistes" (Hans-Michael Haußig, 43–53). Martin Buber über Adam Mickiewicz und die Sendung Israels (Stefan Schreiner, 117–130). Les trois pilliers du monde d'après le Maharal de Prague (Roland Goetschel, 133–144). Karl Anton: Die kurze, aber stürmische akademische Karriere eines Schülers des Jonathan Eibeschütz (Jan Doktór, 145–157; on Mosche Gerson Levi, a convert to Protestantism, Prof. at Helmstedt Univ., re-converted to Judaism). Martin Buber: Zionismus und Chassidismus (Eleonore Lappin, 183–204). Further selected essays are listed according to subject.]

—— WASSERMANN, HENRY: *False start. Jewish studies at German universities during the Weimar Republic.* [See No. 42567.]

—— WILKE, CARSTEN: *"Den Talmud und den Kant". Rabbinerausbildung an der Schwelle zur Moderne.* [See No. 42259.]

—— WISSENSCHAFT DES JUDENTUMS. HESCHEL, SUSANNAH: *Die Revolte der Kolonisierten: Abraham Geigers 'Wissenschaft des Judentums' als Herausforderung christlicher Vormachtstellung in der Akademie.* [See in No. 43180.]

43051. WISSENSCHAFT DES JUDENTUMS. HOLLENDER, ELISABETH: *"Verachtung kann Unwissenheit nicht entschuldigen"—die Verteidigung der Wissenschaft des Judentums gegen die Angriffe Paul de Lagarde's* [sic] *1884–1887.* [In]: Frankfurter Judaistische Beiträge, Jg. 30, Frankfurt am Main, 2003. Pp.

169–205, footnotes. [Documents the debate triggered by an attack against Leopold Zunz and other Jewish scholars by Ludwig Techen, which resulted in 1887 in Lagarde's aggressive antisemitic 'Juden und Indogermanen'; incl. David Kaufmann, Bernhard Ziemlich, Abraham Berliner et al. as defenders of "Wissenschaft des Judentums".]

——— WISSENSCHAFT DES JUDENTUMS. SIMON-NAHUM, PERRINE: *Wissenschaft des Judentums in Germany and the science of Judaism in France in the nineteenth century: tradition and modernity in Jewish scholarship.* [See in No. 42228.]

B. **Perception and Identity**

43052. ADORNO, THEODOR W.. NIEWÖHNER, FRIEDRICH: *Theodor Wiesengrund Adorno. Zwischen Auschwitz und Judentum.* [In]: Dialektik. Zeitschrift für Kulturphilosophie, Jg. 10, H. 2, Hamburg, 2003. Pp. 157–168. [Lecture given at the Jewish Museum in Frankfurt on Main, Sept. 21, 2003. Discusses A.'s relationship to Jews and the "Jewishness" of his work.]

43053. BENBASSA, ESTHER/ATTIAS, JEAN-CHRISTOPHE: *Haben die Juden eine Zukunft?* Ein Gespräch über jüdische Identitäten. Aus dem Französ. übers. von Béatrice Raboud. Zürich: Chronos, 2002. 237 pp.

43054. BORCHARDT, RUDOLF. KAUFFMANN, KAI: *Rudolf Borchardt und der "Untergang der deutschen Nation": Selbstinszenierung und Geschichtskonstruktion im essayistischen Werk.* Tübingen: Niemeyer, 2003. IX, 463 pp. (Studien zur deutschen Literatur, Bd. 169.) Zugl.: Berlin, Techn. Univ., Habil.-Schr., 2001.

43055. CONWAY, DAVID: *'In the midst of many peoples'- some nineteenth-century Jewish composers and their Jewishness.* [In]: European Judaism, Vol. 36, No. 1, London, Spring 2003. Pp. 36–59, illus., notes, bibl. [Incl. Felix Mendelssohn Bartholdy and Giacomo Meyerbeer.]

43056. DRACH, ALBERT. COSGROVE, MARY: *Melancholisches Leiden im Sex-Ghetto: Spuren des Affektiven im autobiographischen Werk von Albert Drach.* [In]: Sentimente, Gefühle, Empfindungen: Zur Geschichte und Literatur des Affektiven von 1770 bis heute. Tagung zum 60. Geburtstag von Hugh Ridley im Juli 2001. Hrsg. von Anne Fuchs [et al.]. Würzburg: Königshausen & Neumann, 2003. Pp. 213–220, footnotes.

43057. FISCHER, JENS MALTE: *Die "Judenfrage" als Trauerspiel und als Komödie. Zwei dramatische Diskussions-Vorschläge um 1900.* [In]: Theater ohne Grenzen. Festschrift für Hans-Peter Bayerdörfer zum 65. Geburtstag. Hrsg. von Katharina Keim [et al.]. München: Herbert Utz Verlag, 2003 (Theaterwissenschaft, Bd. 1.). Pp. 154–160, footnotes. [On Max Nordau's play 'Doktor Kohn' and Ferdinand Bronner's 'Schmelz, der Nibelunge' (1903).]

43058. *Fremdes Begehren. Transkulturelle Beziehungen in Literatur, Kunst und Medien.* Hrsg. von Eva Lezzi [et al.]. Köln: Böhlau, 2003. VIII, 415 pp., footnotes. [Selected essays (some titles abbr.): Gott liebt den Fremden. Das Begehren des Fremden im Talmud und in der jüdischen Philosophie (Christoph Schulte, 159–170). Die erotische Rede von Gott in der mittelalterlichen jüdischen und christlichen Mystik (Helga Völkening, 185–196). Kultur als Travestie: Else Lasker-Schüler und 'Minn, der Sohn des Sultans von Marokko' (Sylke Kirschnick, 222–234). "Als ... Israel sich oft erlustigt." Sehnsucht und kulturelle Aneignung in Heines Lyrik (Jeffrey A. Grossman, 245–255). Tradition oder Akkulturation? Liebeskonflikte in der Ghettoliteratur von Leopold Kompert (Eva Lezzi, 256–268). Paula Bubers jüdische Identität im Zeichen der Konversion (Uta Werner, 269–280).]

43059. FREUD, SIGMUND. SCHÄFER, PETER: *Der Triumph der reinen Geistigkeit. Sigmund Freuds 'Der Mann Moses und die monotheistische Religion'.* Berlin: Philo, 2003. 46 pp., notes. (Schriftenreihe Ha'Atelier Collegium Berlin.) [On F.'s last book, publ. 1939, analysing it from the perspective of his view of Judaism and the Jewish religion; incl. Engl. summary (45–46).]

43060. GILMAN, SANDER L.: *Jewish frontiers: essays on bodies, histories, and identities.* New York; Basingstoke: Palgrave Macmillan, 2003. XI, 243 pp., notes, bibl., index. [Part I deals with representing the

Holocaust in film; incl.: The first comic film about the Shoah: Jurek Becker and cultural opposition within the GDR. Part II deals with Jewish illnesses and questions of identity.]

43061. GORDON, SHARON: *'T'emura' and 'Hamara'—Meanings of conversion in Biblical and modern Hebrew.* [In]: Leipziger Beiträge zur jüdischen Geschichte und Kultur, Bd. I, München, 2003. Pp. 27–46, footnotes. [Analyses the linguistic development of the word "conversion" in Hebrew and its implications for discussing "identity" questions.]

43062. HALL, KATHARINA: *"Bekanntlich sind Dreiecksbeziehungen am kompliziertesten": Turkish, Jewish and German identity in Zafer Senocak's 'Gefährliche Verwandtschaften'.* [In]: German Life and Letters, Vol. 56, No. 1, Oxford, Jan. 2003. Pp. 72–88, footnotes. [Deals with the novel of a Turkish-German writer exploring the similarities between German-Turkish and German-Jewish identity. The protagonist is the child of a Turkish father and German-Jewish mother.]

43063. HAWKINS, BETH D.: *Reluctant theologians: Franz Kafka, Paul Celan, Edmond Jabès.* New York: Fordham Univ. Press, 2003. XXXIV, 265 pp., notes, bibl. (251–261), index. (Studies in religion and literature, No. 4.) [Focuses on the role Judaism plays in the works of the three authors.]

43064. HEYM, STEFAN. FOX, THOMAS C.: *Stefan Heym and the negotiation of Socialist-Jewish identity.* [In]: Stefan Heym: Socialist—dissenter—Jew [see No. 43320]. Pp. 145–160, footnotes.

43065. HONIGMANN, BARBARA. GUILLOT, VIRGINIE: *Identitätsreise als Hauptbegriff in Barbara Honigmanns Werk inbezug auf zwei ihrer Romane: "Soharas Reise" und "Eine Liebe aus nichts".* Poitiers: Univ. de Poitiers, 2003. M.A. Thesis. [Available at the Zentralarchiv zur Erforschung der Gesch. der Juden in Deutschland, Heidelberg.]

——— HUML, ARIANE/RAPPENECKER, MONIKA, eds.: *Jüdische Intellektuelle im 20. Jahrhundert. Literatur- und kulturgeschichtliche Studien.* [See No. 43164.]

43066. *Identität und Gedächtnis in der jüdischen Literatur nach 1945.* Hrsg. von Dieter Lamping. Berlin: Erich Schmidt Verlag, 2003. 229 pp., footnotes. (Allgemeine Literaturwissenschaft—Wuppertaler Schriften, Bd. 5.) [Selected essays dealing with German-speaking authors (some titles abbr.): Einleitung (ed., 7–16). Der Holocaust im literarischen Experiment: Jüdische Schriftsteller im 'Double bind' (Elrud Ebisch, 29–45; incl. Edgar Hilsenrath). Canettis Beitrag zur jüdischen Literatur in deutscher Sprache (Rüdiger Zymner, 46–61). Über Zwang und Unmöglichkeit, Jude zu sein: Jean Amérys Testimonium (Andreas Solbach, 62–89). Identität als Fiktion bei Wolfgang Hildesheimer (Bernhard Spies, 90–103). Wurzelgeträum, blutunterwaschen. Zu einem Motiv im Werk Paul Celans (Vivian Liska, 104–115). Georges-Arthur Goldschmidt: Die Absonderung. Identitätsbildung eines jüdischen Flüchtlingskindes im französischen Exil (Andreas Wittbrodt, 186–202). "Who is Weiskopf?" Representing Jewish identity in 'Ghetto' on East and West German stages (Alan Bern, 217–225; on productions of Joshua Sobol's play (1883) in Essen and Berlin (East) in 1992).]

43067. JESSNER, LEOPOLD. FEINBERG, ANAT: *Leopold Jessner: German theatre and Jewish identity.* [In]: Leo Baeck Institute Year Book 2003, Vol. XLVIII, Oxford, 2003. Pp. 111–133, footnotes, illus. [L.J., 1878 Königsberg–1945 Los Angeles, theatre director in Königsberg, later in Berlin (1919–1933), emigr. to London, worked for two years in Palestine before finally settling in the US in 1937.]

——— *Judentum und Antisemitismus. Studien zur Literatur und Germanistik in Österreich.* [Incl. several essays on "Jewish identity"; see No. 43167.]

43069. KAFKA, FRANZ. GILMAN, SANDER: *A dream of Jewishness on the frontier: Kafka's tumor and "The country doctor".* [In]: Von Enoch bis Kafka. Festschrift für Karl E. Grözinger zum 60. Geburtstag [see No. 43050]. Pp. 393–406, footnotes. [Also in this vol. on Kafka: "Übrigens weiß ich schon aus meiner Naturheilkunde, daß alle Gefahr von der Medicin herkommt ...". Franz Kafka als Medizinkritiker und Naturheilkundiger (Robert Jütte, 421–435, footnotes).]

43070. KAFKA, FRANZ. GRÖZINGER, KARL ERICH: *Kafka und die Kabbala. Das Jüdische im Werk und Denken von Franz Kafka.* Berlin: Philo, 2003. 271 pp., notes (245–271). [New augm. (4th) edn.; first publ. 1992, see No. 29795/YB XXXVIII.]

43071. KAFKA, FRANZ. NEKULA, MAREK: *Franz Kafkas Sprachen.* "... in einem Stockwerk des innern babylonischen Turmes ..." Tübingen: Niemeyer, 2003. XIII, 397 pp., footnotes, bibl. [Analyses the use of German, Czech, Yiddish, Hebrew in Kafka's family, education, and in his own reading and texts; also on his identity.]

43072. KONKEL, MICHAEL [et al.], eds.: *Die Konstruktion des Jüdischen in Vergangenheit und Gegenwart.* Paderborn: Schöningh, 2003. 239 pp., footnotes, bibl. [Cont. (some titles abbr.): Einleitung (eds., 7–14). "Christliche Ethnographien" von Juden und Judentum. Die Konstruktion des Jüdischen in frühneuzeitlichen Texten (Yaacov Deutsch/Maria Diemling, 15–28). Der Verein für Cultur und Wissenschaft der Juden (1819–1824). Zur ersten Konzeption einer "Wissenschaft des Judentums" und ihrer Bedeutung für die Neubestimmung jüdischer Identität (Oliver Bertrams, 29–48). Manuel Joel (1826–1890) über Maimonides (Görge K. Hasselhoff, 49–68). Geschichte Israels und Judentum in der protestantischen Exegese des 19. Jahrhunderts (Michael Konkel, 69–86). Die Orthodoxie erfindet sich neu. Psalmenauslegung bei Samson Raphael Hirsch (Egbert Ballhorn, 87–102). Die evangelische Eschatologie der Moderne und das Judentum (Henning Theißen, 103–118). Die Konstruktion der jüdischen Heimat im Roman—der Jüdische Heimatroman? (Alexandra Pontzen, 119–134). Zur Konstruktion einer 'zionistischen' Ethik in Max Brods Romanen 'Reubeni. Fürst der Juden' und 'Zauberreich der Liebe' (Axel Stähler, 135–154). Typisch jüdisch? Merkwürdige Attribuierungen psychoanalytischer Theorien (Marie-Luise Wünsche, 155–168). "Jüdische Wissenschaft"—zur Rhetorik der/über Psychoanalyse (Céline Kaiser, 169–186). Ein konstruktiver Dialog zwischen Judentum und Christentum. Der Briefwechsel zwischen Eugen Rosenstock-Huessy und Franz Rosenzweig (Ute Freisinger-Hahn, 187–206). "Der überwindende Jude". Geistiger Widerstand als Grundprinzip jüdischer Erwachsenenbildung (Jan Woppowa, 207–222). Jüdischer Gottesdienst im Urteil christlicher Theologen (Peter Ebenbauer, 223–239).]

43073. KOKEMÜLLER, BIRGITT: *Jüdische Identität nach der Schoah als Thema in ausgewählten Kinder- und Jugendbüchern.* Inhaltliche Analyse und didaktische Untersuchungen auf deren Verwendbarkeit im Katholischen Religionsunterricht der Sekundarstufe I. Frankfurt am Main; New York: Lang, 2003. 337 pp., illus., footnotes, bibl. (305–330), index. (Übergänge, Studien zur Ev. und Kath. Theologie/Religionspädagogik, Bd. 4.) Zugl.: Freiburg/Brsg., Päd.HS, Diss., 2001. [Part one deals with Jewish identity as shaped by literary education of children and young people, part two analyses Jewish identity in post-1945 children's literature from Israel and Germany, part three is devoted to pedagogic proposals.]

43074. KRAUS, KARL. REITTER, PAUL: *Karl Kraus and the Jewish self-hatred question.* [In]: Jewish Social Studies, Vol. 10, No. 1, Bloomington, IN, Fall 2003. Pp. 78–116, notes.

43075. KUH, ANTON: *Juden und Deutsche.* Hrsg. und mit einer Einleitung von Andreas B. Kilcher. Wien: Löcker, 2003. 205 pp., frontis., illus. [Incl.: Einleitung: Anton Kuh und sein Essay "Juden und Deutsche" (ed., 7–65). Juden und Deutsche (Anton Kuh, 69–157). Anhang (159–204; cont. reviews and essays on K.'s polemical essay (publ. 1921) by Max Brod, Berthold Viertel, Felix Weltsch, Robert Weltsch, Elias Hurwicz, Max Dienemann, Johannes Urzidil).] [Cf.: Vier tragische Irrtümer (Friedrich Niewöhner) [in]: 'FAZ', Nr. 192, Frankfurt am Main, 20. Aug. 2003, p. N 3. Selbsthass als Befreiung. Anton Kuhs furiose Streitschrift "Juden und Deutsche" (Lothar Müller) [in]: Süddeutsche Zeitung, Nr. 195, München, 26. Aug. 2003, p. 14. "Polemisch mäandrierende Prosa". Zu Anton Kuhs geistiger Signatur aus Anlaß einer Neuausgabe seines Buchs "Juden und Deutsche" (Claudia Albert) [in]: Aschkenas, Jg. 13, H. 2, Tübingen, 2003, pp. 543–547, footnotes.]

——— LEOPOLDI, HERMANN. JACOBS, NEIL G.: *Soirée bei Kohn: Jewish elements in the repertoire of Hermann Leopoldi.* [See No. 42472.]

43076. RATHENAU, FRITZ. SCHÖLZEL, CHRISTIAN: *Fritz Rathenau (1875–1949). On antisemitism, acculturation and slavophobia. An attempted reconstruction.* [In]: Leo Baeck Institute Year Book 2003, Vol. XLVIII, Oxford, 2003. Pp. 135–162, footnotes, illus. [Author focuses on questions of Jewish identity.]

——— WALTER, HANS-ALBERT: *Deutsche Exilliteratur 1933–1950.* Band 1.1: *Die Mentalität der Weimardeutschen/Die "Politisierung" der Intellektuellen.* [See No. 42258.]

43077. WASSERMANN, JAKOB. OCH, GUNNAR: *Zion, Heimat, Golus—Jakob Wassermann zwischen jüdischer Selbstbesinnung, Assimilation und Antisemitismus.* [See in No. 42340.]

43078. WEISS, IRIS: *Jewish Disneyland. Die Enteignung und Aneignung des "Jüdischen".* [In]: nurinst 2002, Beiträge zur deutschen und jüdischen Geschichte, Bd. 1, Nürnberg, 2002. Pp. 8–19, notes.

——— ZIELINSKI, ANDREA: *Die anderen Juden.* Identitätenbildung von Menschen jüdischer Herkunft im Nachkriegsdeutschland. [See No. 42946.]

C. **Jewish Life and Organisations. Genealogy**

43079. *Selbstbildnisse der 20er Jahre. Die Sammlung Feldberg.* Self-portraits from the 1920s. The Feldberg Collection. Berlin: Berlinische Galerie [et al.], 2003. 167 pp., illus., bibl. [Incl.: Die Sammlung Feldberg (Freya Mülhaupt, 10–23). Zur Geschichte der Familie Feldberg (Dietlinde Hamburger, 24–31); all texts also in Engl. On the textile manufacturing family F. in Stettin and Berlin, some members of which emigr. to India and returned to Europe in the 1960s.]

43080. BARKAI, AVRAHAM: *Jiddisch-putkamerisch verpackt. Oscar Wassermanns Grüße zum Neuen Jahr.* [In]: Kalonymos, Jg. 6, H. 3, Duisburg, 2003. Pp. 1–3, illus., facsim. [On a letter written in Berlin, 1908, by the banker O.W.]

43081. BEIDER, ALEXANDER: *Jewish surnames in Russia, Poland, Galicia and Prussia.* [In]: Avotaynu, Vol. 19, No. 3, Bergenfield, NJ, Fall 2003. Pp. 28–32, tabs. [Also in this issue, in the context of Jewish geneal. research: Austro-Hungarian military records (Henry Wellisch, 32–33).]

——— BEYER, BERND-M.: *Der Mann, der den Fußball nach Deutschland brachte.* Das Leben des Walther Bensemann. Ein biographischer Roman. [See No. 43230.]

43082. BLOCHEL-DITTRICH, IRIS: *Fürs verwöhnte Publikum. Von Neujahrsgrüßen und anderen Kostbarkeiten aus Papier.* Hrsg.: Stiftung Jüd. Museum Berlin. Köln: Dumont, 2003. 119 pp., illus., notes. (Zeitzeugnisse aus dem Jüdischen Museum Berlin.) [Deals with greeting cards for the Jewish public and their Jewish motifs.]

43083. DAVIES, MARTIN L.: *Klassische Aufklärung. Überlegungen zur Modernisierung der deutsch-jüdischen Kultur am Beispiel des Exlibris von David Friedländer.* [In]: Zeitschrift für Religions- und Geistesgeschichte, Jg. 55, H. 1. Leiden, 2003. Pp. 40–61, illus., footnotes.

43084. FRANK, WERNER L.: *Legacy: the saga of a German-Jewish family across time and circumstance.* Bergenfield, NJ: Avotaynu Foundation, 2003. 927 pp., illus., ports., facsims., maps, geneal. tabs. 1 CD-ROM. [History of several families of rural Jews from the Kraichgau in Baden (Eppingen, Bretten, Weingarten, Breisach, Hohenems, Biesheim, Göppingen Weil-der-Stadt); covers the period from the Thirty Years' War to the Nazi period. Author's family fled to the US in 1937. The CD-Rom cont. information which the author has collected about more than 30,000 individuals.] [Cf.: My ancestors were Schutzjuden (Werner L. Frank) [in]: Avotaynu, Vol. 19, No. 2, Bergenfield, NJ, Summer 2003, pp. 11–15, facsims; incl. reprint of Schutzbrief.]

43085. GOLD, DAVID L.: *Ever fewer family names are now describable as "typically Jewish".* On some Jewish family names beginning Fitz-, Mac-, Mc-, and O'. [In]: Beiträge zur Namenforschung, Bd. 38, H. 4, Heidelberg, 2003. Pp. 435–438, footnotes. [See also No. 42585.]

43086. GOMPERZ FAMILY. KAUFMANN, DAVID/FREUDENTHAL, MAX: *The Gomperz family.* Transl. from the orig. German by Bernard Standring. London: Tymsder Publ., 2003. 239 pp., illus., ports., notes, index. 1 CD-ROM. [Transl. of the first publication by Kommissionsverlag J. Kauffmann, Frankfurt/Main, 1907. Book traces the genealogy of the Gomperz family from 1600 along the Lower Rhine, to Berlin, Frankfurt, Metz, Vienna, Prague, as well as to Holland, England, and later to the US. The book also deals with Jewish emancipation and the Enlightenment, focusing on Moses Mendelssohn. The CD-ROM documents the Gomperz family from Reb Mordechai Gumpel, born about 1520, up to 1945. Also included is a geneal. bibl.]

43087. HÖDL, KLAUS: *Die deutschsprachige Beschneidungsdebatte im 19. Jahrhundert.* [In]: Aschkenas, Jg. 13, H. 1, Tübingen, 2003. Pp. 189–210, footnotes.

——— JANKRIFT, KAY PETER: *Jüdische Heilkundige im Münchener Medizinalwesen des 14. und 15. Jahrhunderts.* [See No. 42393.]

43088. JUDD, ROBIN: *The politics of beef: animal advocacy and the kosher butchering debates in Germany.* [In]: Jewish Social Studies, Vol. 10, No. 1, Bloomington, IN, Fall 2003. Pp. 117–150, notes. [Discusses debates about banning kosher slaughter practices between 1850–1890.]

43089. KLAPHECK, ELISA: *Regina Jonas: die weltweit erste Rabbinerin.* Teetz: Hentrich und Hentrich, 2003. 61 pp., illus., bibl. (Jüdische Miniaturen, Bd. 4.)

43090. *Maajan—Die Quelle.* Zeitschrift für jüdische Familienforschung. Organ der Schweizerischen Vereinigung für jüdische Genealogie [und der] Hamburger Gesellschaft für jüdische Genealogie e.V. Jg. 17, Zürich, 2003. 4 issues.

43091. MARX, C. THEO: *The Kohnstamm and allied families. A family history.* Wembley, UK: [Privately printed], 2002. 504 pp. [On a family from Lower Franconia. Available at the LBI New York.] [Cf.: Review (Karen S. Franklin) [in]: Stammbaum, Issue 23, New York, 2003, p. 22.]

43092. SCHULZE-MARMELING, DIETRICH, ed.: *Davidstern und Lederball. Die Geschichte der Juden im deutschen und internationalen Fußball.* Mit Beiträgen von Erik Eggers, Werner Skrentny, Michael John [et al.]. Göttingen: Verlag die Werkstatt, 2003. 509 pp., illus., notes. [Index of persons: www.werkstatt-verlag.de.] [Cont. (titles abbr.): Grußwort (Paul Spiegel, 11–12). Einführung (ed., 11–24). Teil I: Deutschland (27–230; 13 contribs. on football in various parts of Germany before and during the Nazi era, also on football played in DP-camps by the ed., Erik Eggers, Jan Buschbom, Werner Skrentny, Bernd-M. Beyer, Georg Röwekamp; incl. essays on Walther Bensemann, Gottfried Fuchs). Teil II: International (231–506; 15 contribs. on football in Austria, Vienna, Budapest, Amsterdam, Paris, and as played in exile in New York and Shanghai, also on Israel by Michael John, Matthias Marschick, Erik Eggers, the ed., W. Ludwig Tegelbeckers, Werner Skrentny, Günter Rohrbacher-List, Albert Lichtblau, Stefan Mayr; incl. essays on Hugo and Willy Meisl, Friedrich Torberg, Béla Guttmann).] [Cf.: Bespr. (Rudolf Oswald) [in]: SportZeiten, Jg. 3. Göttingen, 2003, pp. 112–116.]

43093. SCHWARZ, ISRAEL: *Glaube und Pflicht. Lehrbuch der israelitischen Religion für Schulen.* Dritte, gänzlich umgearbeitete Auflage. Frankfurt am Main: I. Kauffmann, 1877. 239 pp. [Facsim. reprint, ed. by Roland B. Miller, Leipzig, 2003.]

43094. SIMON, HERMANN: *Jüdische Feiertage.* Festtage im jüdischen Kalender. Berlin: Hentrich & Hentrich; Centrum Judaicum Berlin, 2003. 63 pp., frontis., illus. (Jüdische Miniaturen.)

43095. *Stammbaum.* The Journal of German-Jewish Genealogical Research. Publ. by the Leo Baeck Institute. Issues 22 & 23. [Ed.: Paula Zieselman.] New York, 2003. [Incl. biographical essays, reports on archival holdings and reviews relating to German-Jewish family research; selected essays are listed according to subject.]

43096. STEINBERG, MICHAEL, ed.: *Mother's recipes.* San Francisco, CA: The Steinberg Family, 2003. 107 pp., illus., facsims. [Translation of handwritten recipes collected by the editor's mother Alice Steinberg née Gumprich and her mother-in-law Else Steinberg née Steindorf from Lübbecke and Münster in Westphalia. Available at the Bibliothek Germania Judaica, Cologne.]

D. Jewish Art and Music

43097. *Ein Leben für die jüdische Kunst. Gedenkband für Hannelore Künzl.* Hrsg. von Michael Graetz. Heidelberg: Winter, 2003. VI, 236 pp., footnotes. [Incl.: Zum so genannten Bilderverbot (Felicitas Heimann-Jelinek, 21–32). Zwischen Tradition und Innovation. Bedeutende gedruckte Haggadot des 16. und 17. Jahrhunderts (Esther Graf, 117–130). Ephraim Moses Lilien: The working process of an artist (Avinoam Shalem, 141–150). Der Zionismus und die hebräische Literatur und Kunst: die Geschichte einer Wechselbeziehung (Ori und Reuven Kritz, 195–214); further essays are listed according to subject.]

43098. FRÜHAUF, TINA: *Jüdisch-liturgische Musik in Wien. Ein Spiegel kultureller Vielfalt.* [In]: quasi una fantasia. Juden und die Musikstadt Wien [see No. 42476]. Pp. 77–92. [Also in this book: Jüdische Popularmusik in der Öffentlichkeit der Habsburger Metropole (Philip V. Bohlman, 93–106).]

43099. *In einem neuen Geiste/In a new spirit. Synagogen von Alfred Jacoby/Synagogues of Alfred Jacoby.* Frankfurt am Main: Deutsches Architektur Museum—Aktuelle Galerie, 2002. 47 pp., illus. [A.J., b. 1950 in Offenbach/Main, architect, since 2000 director of Inst. of Architecture, Dessau, designed seven synagogues in Germany.]

43100. LUBELL, STEPHEN: *The Hebrew typeface designs of Zvi Narkis.* [In]: Gutenberg-Jahrbuch 2003, Mainz, 2003. Pp. 217–233, illus., footnotes. [Incl. German-born typeface designers.]

43101. METZGER, THÉRÈSE: *Le manuscrit Norsa. Une copie Ashkenaze achevée en 1349 et enluminée du 'Guide des Égarés' de Maimonide.* [In]: Mitteilungen des Kunsthistorischen Institutes in Florenz, Bd. XLVI, H. 1, München, 2002. Pp. 1–73, facsims., notes. [On an illuminated manuscript from Ashkenaz kept since the 16th cent. in the Norsa family in Mantua. Incl. German abstract.]

43102. NEUGEBAUER, ROSAMUNDE: *Du darfst dir ein Bild machen. Heines "Rabbi von Bacherach" in der Illustration deutschsprachig-jüdischer Künstler.* [In]: Imprimatur, N.F. XVII, München, 2002. Pp. 124–153, illus., notes. [Deals with Joseph Budko, Hermann Fechenbach, Ludwig Schwerin, Max Liebermann.]

43103. *Das Recht des Bildes: Jüdische Perspektiven in der modernen Kunst.* Hrsg. von Hans Günter Golinski und Sepp Hiekisch-Picard. Heidelberg: Edition Braus, 2003. 381 pp., plates, illus., facsims., notes, bibl. [Catalogue for exhibition with the same title held in Bochum, Sept. 21, 2003–Jan. 4, 2004; incl.: Die verborgene Spur—Jüdisches Denken in der Kunst nach 1945 (Martin Roman Deppner, 27–44). Zum Stereotyp des biblischen Bilderverbots (Felicitas Heimann-Jelinek, 53–64). Acht Handschriften suchen einen Sinn oder Die Krönung des Buchstabens (Michel Garel, 65–77; on eight medieval Hebrew Bible manuscripts, shown in a special exhibition). Selbstporträts: Zur Frage der jüdischen Identität (Milly Heyd, 86–99). Maler jüdischer Herkunft im 19. Jahrhundert—zur Programmatik ihrer Kunst (Annette Weber, 121–135). Der Koscherstempel: Jüdische Themen im Werk von Max Liebermann (Emily D. Bilski, 136–147). Jüdische Kunst als Theorie und Praxis vom Beginn der Moderne bis 1933 (Inka Bertz, 148–161). Russisch-jüdische Künstler: zwischen nationaler Identität und Universalismus (Marc Scheps, 186–192). Jüdische Künstler und die 'École de Paris' (Sepp Hiekisch-Picard, 193–204). Der jüdische Jesus (Ziva Amishai-Maisels, 223–237). "Man lebt hier wie in der Wüste". Zu jüdischen Exilkünstlern und ihrer Rezeption (Erik Riedel, 238–251). Über "fremde" und "eigene" Zeichen. Die Verneinung des Authentischen nach der Shoah (Kristin Platt, 246–251). Erinnerung und Gedächtnis (Micha Ullman, 253–254). Jüdische Philosophie in der Postmoderne (Micha Brumlik, 311–316). Jüdische Identitäten in der Bundesrepublik Deutschland (Edna Brocke, 317–321). Denn was ist der Mensch ... Ein Erlebnisbericht aus jüdisch-deutschen Kindertagen (Günther B. Ginzel, 322–326; personal recollections, also on a Torah scroll from Zwickau). Künstlerbiographien (338–366).]

43104. SCHILLER, DAVID MICHAEL: *Bloch, Schoenberg, and Bernstein: assimilating Jewish music.* Oxford, New York: Oxford Univ. Press, 2003. VII, 199 pp., scores, notes, bibl. (181–194), index.

43105. SCHRIJVER, EMILE G.L.: *An unknown Passover Haggadah by Joseph ben David of Leipnik in the Library of Blickling Hall.* [In]: Zutot 2002, Dordrecht, 2003. Pp. 170–180, footnotes. [On a Haggadah, combining Ashkenazi and Sephardi rites, copied and illustrated by Joseph Leipnik in Altona, 1739/1740.]

43106. SCHÜTZ, CHANA C.: *Lesser Ury and the Jewish Renaissance.* [In]: Jewish Studies Quarterly, Vol. 10, No. 4, Tübingen, 2003. Pp. 360–376, footnotes, illus. [Deals with Ury's religious/biblical paintings in the context of the Zionists' discussions about Jewish art, among them esp. Martin Buber. See also No. 43023.]

43107. SHALEM, AVINOAM: *Die komplexe Identität jüdischer Kunst.* [In]: Jüdische Geschichte: Alte Herausforderungen, neue Ansätze [see No. 42230.]. Pp. 103–110, footnotes.

43108. WARD, SETH: *The liturgy of Bloch's 'Avodath Ha-Kodesh'.* [In]: Modern Judaism, Vol. 23, No. 3, London, Oct. 2003. Pp. 243–263, tabs., notes. [E.B., July 24, 1880 Geneva–July 15, 1959 Portland, OR, composer of Jewish music, lived from 1916 in the US, composed "The Sacred Service" between 1930–1933 for a Reform Synagogue in San Francisco.]

VI. ZIONISM AND ISRAEL

43109. BARNOUW, DAGMAR: *Fundamentalismus und politischer Zionismus.* Zur historischen Problematik eines jüdischen Staates in Palästina. [In]: Leviathan, Jg. 31, H. 1, Wiesbaden, 2003. Pp. 53–71, footnotes. [Incl. Engl. abstract. Reflects the pre-State Palestinian-Jewish conflicts debated between 1944–1948 and illustrates the current relevance of analyses by i.a. Hannah Arendt and Judah L. Magnes.]

——— BEN-NATAN, ASHER: *Die Chuzpe zu leben.* Stationen meines Lebens. [See No. 43497.]

43110. BLUM, HOWARD: *Ihr Leben in unserer Hand. Die Geschichte der Jüdischen Brigade im Zweiten Weltkrieg.* Aus dem Amerikanischen von Michael Arndt. München: Econ, 2002. 326 pp., illus. [Orig. publ. in 2001 with the title The Brigade. An epic story of vengeance, salvation and World War II.]

43111. BRENNER, MICHAEL: *Die zionistische Utopie begegnet der Realität: Palästina in der deutsch-jüdischen Literatur.* [In]: Utopie und politische Herrschaft im Europa der Zwischenkriegszeit. Hrsg. von Wolfgang Hardtwig [et al.]. München: Oldenbourg, 2003. Pp. 119–131, footnotes. [On Theodor Herzl, Karl Kraus, Max Brod, Arnold Zweig and others.]

——— *Deutschsprachige Zeitungen aus Palästina und Israel/German newspapers from Palestine and Israel.* [See No. 42551.]

43112. DIECKHOFF, ALAIN: *The invention of a nation: Zionist thought and the making of modern Israel.* Transl. from the French by Jonathan Derrick. London: C. Hurst, 2003. X, 297 pp., footnotes, bibl., index. [Incl. the political, socialist beginnings of Zionism with Theodor Herzl as its founder; also on Zionism and Orthodox Jewry.]

——— DISSELNKÖTTER, ANDREAS/ZABEL, HERMANN, eds.: *Deutsch in Israel: Eine Bestandsaufnahme.* [See No. 42552.]

43113. FÖRG, GÜNTHER: *Photographs Bauhaus Tel Aviv—Jerusalem.* [Ed. by Politischer Club Colonia (PCC)] Ostfildern-Ruit: Hatje Cantz, 2002. 207 pp. [Catalogue for exhibition at Schillermuseum, Weimar, Spring 2002 and Tel Aviv Museum of Art, Winter 2002. Cont. mainly photographs; also essays on the Bauhaus architects in Palestine in English, German and Hebrew by Hermann Beil and Rudolf Schmitz.]

43114. GOREN, HAIM: *"Zieht hin und erforscht das Land".* Die deutsche Palästinaforschung im 19. Jahrhundert. Aus dem Hebr. übers. von Antje Clara Naujoks. Mit einem Vorwort von Moshe Zuckermann. Göttingen: Wallstein, 2003. 432 pp., illus., maps, footnotes, bibl. (363–413), index. (Schriftenreihe des Instituts für deutsche Geschichte der Universität Tel Aviv, Bd. 23.) [Also, related to this topic: Christliche Pioniere in Palästina. Der deutsche Beitrag zum Wiederaufbau des Heiligen Landes 1799–1918. Begleitheft zur Ausstellung des "Gottlieb-Schumacher-Instituts zur Erforschung des Christlichen Beitrags zum Wiederaufbau Palästinas im 19. Jahrhundert" und der Universität Haifa und des "Instituts für Jüdische Studien" der Universität Basel in der Württembergischen Landesbibliothek Stuttgart vom 10. Okt. bis 23. Dez. 2003. Künzelsau: Swiridoff, 2003. 19 pp., illus.]

43115. HERZL, THEODOR. FELDSTEIN, ARIEL: *The last will and testament of Theodor Herzl.* [In]: Midstream, Vol. 49, No. 6, New York, Sept./Oct. 2003. Pp. 28–32, notes. [Deals with Herzl's last wish to be buried in Israel.]

43116. HERZL, THEODOR. GUTWEIN, DANIEL: *The reconstruction of Herzl's image in Israeli collective memory: From formative radicalism to an adapting fringe.* [In Hebrew.] [In]: Iyunim Bitkumat Israel, Vol. 12, Ramat Gan, 2002. Pp. 29–73.

43117. HERZL, THEODOR. KAGAN, GENNADI E.: *Der Prophet im Frack. Theodor Herzls russische Mission 1903.* Wien: Böhlau, 2003. 138 pp.

43118. HERZL, THEODOR. LIKIN, MAX: *Rights of man, reasons of state: Emile Zola and Theodor Herzl in historical perspective.* [In]: Jewish Social Studies, Vol. 8, No. 1, Bloomington, IN, Fall 2001. Pp. 126–152, notes.

43119. KATZNELSON, MICHAL: *Meilenstein im Aufbau des Landes.* 70 Jahre Irgun Olej Merkas Europa. [In]: 'MB', Mitteilungsblatt des Irgun Olei Merkas Europa, Jg. 71, Nr. 183, Tel Aviv, Juni-Juli 2003. Pp. 1–3. [Transl from the Hebrew by Oded Baumann.]

43120. KIRCHHOFF, MARKUS: *Konvergierende Topographien—Protestantische Palästinakunde, Wissenschaft des Judentums und Zionismus um 1900.* [In]: Leipziger Beiträge zur jüdischen Geschichte und Kultur, Bd. I, München, 2003. Pp. 217–238, footnotes.

43121. KROBB, FLORIAN: *Gefühlszionismus und Zionsgefühle: Zum Palästina-Diskurs bei Schnitzler, Herzl, Salten und Lasker-Schüler.* [In]: Sentimente, Gefühle, Empfindungen. Zur Geschichte und Literatur des Affektiven von 1770 bis heute. Tagung zum 60. Geburtstag von Hugh Ridley im Juli 2001 hrsg. von Anne Fuchs [et al.]. Würzburg: Königshausen & Neumann, 2003. Pp. 149–164, footnotes.

43122. MAASS, ENZO: *Forgotten prophet? William Henry Hechler and the rise of political Zionism.* [In]: Nordisk Judaistik, Vol. 23, No. 2, Lund, 2002. Pp. 157–192, notes. [On the relationship between Reverend W.H. Hechler and Theodor Herzl and the emerging Zionist movement, focusing on his role in transforming Herzl's political message into a semi-political or religious one.]

43123. PONTZEN, ALEXANDRA/STÄHLER, AXEL, eds.: *Das gelobte Land. Erez Israel von der Antike bis zur Gegenwart.* Quellen und Darstellungen. Reinbek: Rowohlt Taschenbuch Verlag, 2003. 383 pp., notes, maps, bibl. (337–362), indexes. (Rowohlts Enzyklopädie.) Orig.-ausgabe. [Selected essays: Religion, Territorium und Genealogie: Exklusions- und Inklusionsargumente von Christen und Juden im Streit um die Judenemanzipation (1781–1823) (Oliver Bertrams, 132–164). Das "Land der Väter" im politischen Zionismus Theodor Herzls (Alexandra Pontzen, 165–190). Palästina als Einwanderungsland (Astrid Mehmel, 191–204). Das Land als Aufgabe. Felix Weltsch, Max Brod und die "exemplarische Tat" (Axel Stähler, 205–221). Zwischen Chaluz und Talmid Chacham. Zur Bedeutung des Zionismus in Fragen jüdischer Erziehung (Jan Woppowa, 222–242; deals with Ernst Simon). Schwellenangst. Die Wüste in 'Nenn die Nacht nicht Nacht' von Amos Oz (Karen Grumberg, 269–283). 'Himmel' anstelle von 'Erde'? Das 'Land der Verheißung' aus der Sicht der katholischen Systematik (Bernhard Wunder, 284–299). Der 'Staat Israel' im Spannungsfeld von Politik und Religion. Theologische Wahrnehmungsübungen bei Karl Barth und Friedrich-Wilhelm Marquardt (Stefan Kläs, 300–328).]

——— PORAT, DAN A.: *One historian, two histories: Jacob Katz and the formation of a national Israeli identity.* [See No. 43345.]

43124. PORAT, ORNA: *Wie das israelische Kinder- und Jugendtheater entstand.* [In]: Jüdischer Almanach [2003] des Leo Baeck Instituts, Frankfurt am Main, 2003. Pp. 148–154. [Author emigr. in 1947 from Germany to Palestine, in 1970 founded the Israel Children's Theatre.]

43125. RATSABI, SHALOM: *Between Zionism and Judaism: the radical circle in Brith Shalom, 1925–1933.* Leiden; Boston: Brill, 2002. XVII, 455 pp., footnotes, bibl. (433– 445), index. (Brill's series in Jewish studies, Vol. 23.) [On Brith Shalom, founded in 1925 in Jerusalem to foster Arab-Jewish friendship, advocating a binational state; had many German-Jewish supporters and members: Ahad Ha'am, Hugo Bergmann, Ernst Simon, Gershom Scholem, Robert Weltsch.]

43126. *"Rettet die Kinder!" Die Jugend-Aliyah 1933 bis 2003.* Einwanderung und Jugendarbeit in Israel. Frankfurt am Main: Jüd. Museum Frankfurt am Main, 2003. 112 pp., frontis., illus., bibl. [Exhibition catalogue; cont. addresses by Eli Amir, Shimon Stein, Georg Heuberger (5–7); contribs. by Susanne Urban, Gudrun Maierhof, Juliane Wetzel, Rachel Heuberger.]

43127. SCHOEPS, JULIUS H.: *Theodor Herzl (1860–1904). Die Utopie des Judenstaates.* Berlin: Hentrich & Hentrich/Centrum Judaicum Berlin, 2003. 61 pp., frontis., illus. (Jüdische Miniaturen.)

——— SCHÄFER, BARBARA: *Berliner Zionistenkreise. Eine vereinsgeschichtliche Studie.* [See No. 42297.]

43128. SCHLÖR, JOACHIM: *Endlich im Gelobten Land? Deutsche Juden unterwegs in eine neue Heimat.* Berlin: Aufbau, 2003. 223 pp., frontis., illus., facsims. [Cont. the sections: Abschied. Passage. Ankunft. Nachwirkungen. Incl. numerous personal photographs, letters, written and oral recollections collected by the author.] [Cf.: Vom Vaterland ins Land der Väter (Carsten Hueck) [in]: Jüdische Literatur [Beilage von] Jüdische Allgemeine, Jg. 58, Nr. 26, Berlin, Winter, 2003, p. 22. Bespr. (Hanni Mittelmann) [in]: 'MB', Jg. 72, Nr. 191, Tel Aviv, Mai 2004, p. 13.]

43129. SELA-SHEFTY, RAKEFET: *The Jekkes in the legal field and bourgeois culture in pre-Israel British Palestine.* [In Hebrew]. [In]: Iyunim Bitkumat Israel, Vol. 13, Beer Sheva, 2003. Pp. 295–322.

43130. UNGAR, JACQUES: *"Man kann auch von Israel aus die Welt erobern". Industriekapitän Stef Wertheimer.* [In]: tachles, Jg. 3, Nr. 33, Zürich, 15. Aug. 2003. Pp. 14–17, illus.

——— WIESEMANN, FALK: *Die nationaljüdische Antwort: 'Das Jüdische Echo. Bayerische Blätter für die jüdischen Angelegenheiten' (1913–1933).* [See No. 42396.]

43131. WITTBRODT, ANDREAS: *'Hebräisch im Deutschen'. Das deutschsprachige Werk von Elazar Benyoetz.* [In]: Zeitschrift für Deutsche Philologie, Bd. 121, Berlin, 2002. Pp. 584–606, footnotes.

——— *Zwischen Pruth und Jordan.* Lebenserinnerungen Czernowitzer Juden. [See No. 42489.]

VII. PARTICIPATION IN CULTURAL AND PUBLIC LIFE

A. General

43132. ARNOLD, WERNER: *Bürgertum und mäzenatische Entwicklung im 19. und frühen 20. Jahrhundert in Deutschland.* [In]: Zeitschrift für Bibliothekswesen und Bibliographie, Jg. 49, H. 1, Frankfurt am Main, 2002. Pp. 18–25, notes. [Also on Jewish philanthropists in general, on Rudolf Mosse, Aby Warburg in particular.]

43133. BRANDL, HELLFRIED: *Begegnungen. Gespräche mit Zeitzeugen.* Wien: Böhlau, 2003. 182 pp. [Cont. 14 interviews; incl. Leon Harari, Bruno Bettelheim, Günther Anders, Erwin Chargaff, Victor Weiskopf, Tuvia Rübner, Doron Rabinovici.]

43134. *Dem Ideal der Freiheit dienen—ihrer Vorkämpfer gedenken.* Festgabe für Wolfgang Michalka. Hrsg. vom Förderverein Erinnerungsstätte für die Freiheitsbewegungen in der Deutschen Geschichte. [Red.: Christof Müller-Wirth et al.]. Rastatt: Förderverein Erinnerungsstätte für die Freiheitsbeweg. in der Dt. Gesch., [2003]. 227 pp., illus. [Incl.: Freiheitliche Kunstpolitik und reaktionäre Künstler. Die Berliner Akademie der Künste unter Max Liebermanns Präsidentschaft 1920–1932 (Norbert Kampe, 95–101). Gustav Mayer und sein unerfüllter Traum von Freiheit (Gottfried Niedhart,

129–133). Walther Rathenau: Preuße—Deutscher—Europäer? (Martin Sabrow, 179–186). Eduard Lasker und die 48er Revolution (Martin Vogt, 201–205).]

43135. *Dennoch leben sie. Verfemte Bücher, verfolgte Autorinnen und Autoren. Zu den Auswirkungen nationalsozialistischer Literaturpolitik.* Hrsg. von Reiner Wild [et al.]. München: ed. text + kritik, 2003. 454 pp., notes. [Deals with 43 books burnt and forbidden after 1933, and with the fate of their authors; incl.: (titles condensed): Julius Bab (Hajo Kurzenberger, 15–24). Joseph Breitbach (Rolf Paulus, 69–76), Veza Canetti (Alexander Kosenina, 77–86). Alfred Döblin (Matthias Luserke-Jaqui, 87–94). Sigmund Freud (Manfred Engel, 113–124). Heinrich Eduard Jacob (Eckhard Faul, 145–154). Gina Kaus (Marie-Louise Roth, 167–174). Alfred Kerr (Sandra Kerschbaumer, 175–182). Alfred Kleinberg, Uwe-K. Ketelsen, 193–200). Georg Lukács (Silvio Vietta, 239–250). Joseph Roth (Gerhard vom Hofe, 333–342). Arthur Schnitzler (Karl Richter, 353–366). Anna Seghers (Gudrun Loster-Schneider, 377–386). Kurt Tucholsky (Sabina Becker, 395–406). Jakob Wassermann (Stéphane Michaud, 419–424). Arnold Zweig (Sascha Kiefer, 433–440). Stefan Zweig (Dirk Baldes, 441–448).]

43136. *Deutsche Geschichte des 20. Jahrhunderts im Spiegel der deutschsprachigen Literatur.* Hrsg. von Moshe Zuckermann. Göttingen: Wallstein Verlag, 2003. 203 pp., footnotes. [Selected essays: Einführung (ed., 7–12). Envisioning the 20th century: Heinrich Heine's historical prognoses (Zvi Tauber, 13–26). History and memory in exile literary writing: the case of Lion Feuchtwanger (Sandra Goldstein, 51–62). Die Geschichte als literarisches Palimpsest: Über die Verarbeitung der Shoah in der Belletristik (Alexandre Métraux, 63–86). The Fassbinder affair: the missing link in West German historical discourse (Yitzhak Laor, 138–147). Literatur der Gefühle: Die Widerspiegelung der Waldheim-Affäre in der österreichischen Literatur (Helga Embacher, 148–165).]

43137. DUNKER, AXEL: *Die anwesende Abwesenheit.* Literatur im Schatten von Auschwitz. München: Fink, 2003. 333 pp., footnotes, bibl. (299–333). [Deals with individual and collective traumatisation; incl. Paul Celan, Peter Weiss.]

43138. *StadtLandFluß.* Urbanität und Regionalität in der Moderne. Festschrift für Gertrude Cepl-Kaufmann zum sechzigsten Geburtstag. Hrsg. von Antje Johanning [et al.]. Neuss, Ahasver Verlag, 2002. 727 pp., illus, notes. [Incl. the section 'Die Erfahrung der Stadt in der Moderne'; selected contribs.: Bilder der Erinnerung. Walter Benjamins 'Berliner Kindheit' (Bernd Witte, 265–276). Alfred Döblins Anschauung vom 'Nutzen der Musik für die Literatur' (1930) und die musikalischen Strukturelemente im Roman 'Berlin Alexanderplatz' (1929) (Klaus Wolfgang Niemöller, 277–288). "Die Stadt in meinem Schoße"- Zu Gertrud Kolmars Gedicht 'Wappen von Berlin' aus dem Zyklus 'Das Preussische Wappenbuch' (Vera Viehöver, 289–304). Further selected essays are listed according to subject.]

43139. EXILE. ASPER, HELMUT G.: *Neuerscheinungen zum Filmexil.* [In]: Archiv für Sozialgeschichte, Bd. 43, Bonn, 2003. Pp. 518–528. [Review essay.]

43140. EXILE. *Drehbuchautoren im Exil* [issue title of] Filmexil 18, München, Okt. 2003. 64 pp. [Incl. contribs. by and on Willy Haas by Günter Agde, Christoph von Ungern-Sternberg (4–47); also: Frauenarbeit in der "Kunstfabrik mit Regeln". Drehbuchautorinnen im Exil in Hollywood (Nicole Brunnhuber, 48–63; incl. Vicki Baum, Salka Viertel, Gina Kaus, Victoria Wolff).]

43141. EXILE. *Film und Filmografie* [issue title of] Exilforschung. Ein Internationales Jahrbuch, Bd. 21. Hrsg. im Auftrag der Gesellschaft für Exilforschung von Claus-Dieter Krohn [et al.]. München: edition text + kritik, 2003. 296 pp., illus., notes. [Selected contribs. (some titles abbr.): Ungeliebte Gäste: Filmemigranten in Paris 1933–1940. Mit einer Filmografie von Jean-Christopher Horak: Exilfilme in Frankreich 1933–1950 (40–61). Filmarbeit deutscher Emigranten in Moskau und die Produktionsfirma Meshrabpom (Günter Agde, 62–84). Flucht oder Alija. Filmemigranten in Palästina (Ronny Loewy, 85–94). Exiltheater in Los Angeles: Max Reinhardt, Leopold Jessner, Bertolt Brecht und Walter Wicclair (Ehrhardt Bahr, 95–111). Kurt Gerron als Filmregisseur, Schauspieler und Cabaretier in den Niederlanden (Katja B. Zaich, 112–128). Martin Miller in London, 1939–1945 (Charmian Brinson/Richard Dove, 129–140). Fotografen im Exil (Klaus Honnef, 170–182). Die Geschichte der österreichischen Exilfotografie (Anna Auer, 183–206). Die Hamburger Fotografen Emil Bieber, Max Halberstadt, Erich Kastan und Kurt Schallenberg

(Wilfried Weinke, 225–253). Gespräch mit Wolfgang Suschitzky, Fotograf und Kameramann, geführt in seiner Wohnung in Maida Vale, London (Julia Winckler, 254–279). One contrib. is listed according to subject.]

43142. EXILE. *Exil. Forschung, Erkenntnisse, Ergebnisse.* Hrsg. von Edita Koch und Frithjof Trapp. Jg. 23, Nr. 1, Frankfurt am Main, 2003. 108 pp., notes, index. [Selected contribs.: Bleiben oder gehen? Zu Leben und Werk des Malers und Kunstpädagogen Hermann Henry Gowa (Barbara Müller-Wesemann, 27–35). Hans Sahl und Hermann Broch: Ein Briefwechsel im Exil 1941–1950 (Andrea Reiter, 36–49). "Melde gehorsamst: Renegat Sahl mit Pauken und Trompeten zur Stelle". Drei Briefe Hans Sahls an Willi Schlamm (Reinhard Müller, 50–61; incl. letters written in 1937). Drei Schwestern—Die Schauspielerinnen Maria Solveg, Katta Sterna und Johanna Hofer (Burcu Dogramaci, 62–77; née Stern).] [Hermann Henry Gowa, May 25, 1902 Hamburg–May 23, 1990 Munich, artist, teacher, in 1933 fled to France, joined the resistance in Southern France, survived in hiding, remigr. in the 1950s.]

43143. EXILE. FEINBERG, ANAT: *"Die Schauspieler haben es wohl in der Emigration am schwersten". Anmerkungen zu einem Standardwerk über Verfolgung und Exil deutschsprachiger Theaterkünstler.* [In]: Aschkenas, Jg. 13, H, 2, Tübingen, 2003. Pp. 535–541, footnotes. [Review essay of Handbuch des deutschsprachigen Exiltheaters 1933–1945. Hrsg. von Frithjof Trapp [et al.]. München: Saur, 1999. 2 vols.; see No. 37451/YB 45.]

43144. EXILE. *Intellectual migration and cultural transformation: refugees from National Socialism in the English-speaking world.* Ed. by Edward Timms and Jon Hughes. Wien; New York: Springer, 2003. VI, 267 pp., notes, bibl. (Veröff. des Instituts Wiener Kreis, Bd. 12.) [Cont.: Introd. (1–6). 1. Some issues in intellectual method and approach (Jennifer Platt, 7–19). 2. The role of refugee help organizations in the placement of German and Austrian scholars abroad (Christian Fleck, 21–36). 3. Mapping the trade routes of the mind: the Warburg Institute (Dorothea McEwan, 37–50). 4. The significance of Austrian émigré art historians for English art scholarship (Johannes Feichtinger, 51–69). 5. Refugees and émigré architects in Britain, 1933–39 (Charlotte Benton, 71–86). 6. Designs for the future: Gaby Schreiber as an exponent of Bauhaus principles in Britain (Ulrike Walton-Jordan, 87–108). 7. Franz Borkenau, Sebastian Haffner and George Orwell: depoliticisation and cultural exchange (Nick Hubble, 109– 127). 8. Siegfried Kracauer's extraterritorial critique (Nick Warr, 129– 138). 9. From Berlin to Hollywood: German-speaking refugees in the American film industry (Feiwel Kupferberg, 139–154). 10. The 'Wiener Kreis' in Great Britain: emigration and interaction in the philosophy of science (Friedrich Stadler, 155–179). 11. The persistence of Austrian motifs in Wittgenstein's later writings (Roland Graf, 181–194). 12. Self-knowledge and sociology: Nina Rubinstein's studies in exile (David Kettler, 195–206). 13. Gender and migration: a feminist approach to German-Jewish women refugees and their texts (Andrea Hammel, 207–218). 14. New approaches to child psychology: from red Vienna to the Hampstead nursery (Edward Timms, 219–239). 15. Forced migration or scientific change after 1933: steps towards a new overview (Mitchell Ash, 241–263).]

43145. EXILE. *Kabarett im Exil.* [Issue title of] Zwischenwelt, Jg. 20, Nr. 1, Wien, Mai 2003. 1 issue, 92 pp., illus., facsims. [Incl.: Kabarett im Exil. Hrsg. und zusammengestellt von Marcus G. Patka und Regina Thumser (17–79; contribs./texts by the eds. and Leo Askin, Friedrich Torberg, Horst Schumacher, Martin Miller, Rudolf Spitz, Robert Gilbert, Erich Juhn/Victor Schlesinger, Katja B. Zaich, Birgit Lang, Monika Kiegler-Griensteidl, Beppo Beyerl, Fritz Kalmar).]

43146. EXILE. NEUGEBAUER, ROSMAMUNDE: *Zeichnen im Exil—Zeichen des Exils? Handzeichnung und Druckgraphik deutschsprachiger Emigranten ab 1933.* Weimar: VDG, 2003. 527 pp., illus., plates, notes (327–434), bibl. (479–490), index. (Schriften der Guernica-Gesellschaft, Bd. 14.) [Incl. a chap. entitled Jüdische Kunst? (31–33); also bio-bibliographic data of the artists (435–479).]

43147. EXILE. *Quellen zur Geschichte emigrierter Musiker/Sources relating to the history of émigré musicians 1933–1950.* I. Kalifornien/California. Hrsg. von/ed. by Horst Weber, Manuela Schwartz. München: Saur, 2003. LII, 364 pp., docs., indexes. (Quellen zur Geschichte emigrierter Musiker.)

43148. EXILE. STEFAN APPELIUS, ed.: *"Der Teufel hole Hitler". Briefe der sozialdemokratischen Emigration.* Essen: Klartext Verlag, 2003. 406 pp., illus., footnotes. [Incl. Jewish émigrés.]

43149. EXILE LITERATURE. BAUER, MARKUS: *Exil und Holocaust in Rumänien. Am Beispiel von Edgar Hilsenrath (und F.Th. Csokor).* [In]: Deutsche Regionalliteratur im Banat und in Siebenbürgen im Vielvölkerraum. Klausenburg/Cluj-Napoca, 2002. Pp. 179–186, footnotes.

43150. EXILE LITERATURE. *Buchgestaltung im Exil 1933–1950.* Eine Ausstellung des Deutschen Exilarchivs 1933–1945 Der Deutschen Bibliothek. Wiesbaden: Harrassowitz, 2003. 217 pp., illus., facsims., notes. [Cont.: Vorwort (Elisabeth Niggemann, 7–8). Buchgestaltung im Exil 1933–1950. Annäherungen an ein Thema (Ernst Fischer, 11–135). Buchgestalter, Typografen und Buchillustratoren aus Deutschland und Österreich im Exil 1933–1950. Eine Biobibliografie. Zusammengestellt von Ernst Fischer, Brita Eckert und Mechthild Hahner (139–217; cont. 110 illustrators, most of whom were Jews or of Jewish descent).]

43151. EXILE LITERATURE. *Dorothea Sella.* [Issue title of] Mnemosyne, H. 28 (2002). Hrsg.: Armin A. Wallas, Andrea M. Lauritsch. Münster, 2003. 194 pp., notes. [Incl. four autobiographical texts by Dorothea Sella (7–36); also in this issue stories/memoirs by Ernst Eisenmayer, Wolfgang Klaghofer, Herbert Kuhner, Arthur Horowitz and Robert G. Weigel (on Soma Morgenstern's 'Die Blutsäule'); reports and reviews. One essay is listed according to subject.] [D.S., b. in Czernowitz, German language author, in 1964 emigr. from Bucharest to Israel.]

43152. EXILE LITERATURE. KOMFORT-HEIN, SUSANNE: *"Inzwischenzeit"—Erzählen im Exil.* Anna Seghers' 'Der Ausflug der toten Mädchen' und Peter Weiss' 'Der Schatten des Körpers des Kutschers'. [In]: Aufklärungen. Zur Literaturgeschichte der Moderne. Festschrift für Klaus-Detlef Müller zum 65. Geburtstag. Hrsg. von Werner Frick [et al.]. Tübingen: Niemeyer, 2003. Pp. 343–356, footnotes.

43153. EXILE LITERATURE. MÜLLER, KARL: *"Österreichische Schriftstellerinen und Schriftsteller des Exils seit 1933. Texte und Kontexte".* Online-Projekt. [In]: Zwischenwelt, Jg. 19, Nr. 4, Wien, Feb. 2003. Pp. 56–58. [Describes the internet platform www.literaturepochen.at/exil made available in July 2002, with its two sections entitled "Literatur in der Wiener Moderne" and "Österreichische Literatur im Exil".]

43154. EXILE LITERATURE. *Placeless topographies: Jewish perspectives on the literature of exile.* Ed. by Bernhard Greiner. Tübingen: Niemeyer Verlag, 2003. VI, 232 pp., notes, index of names. [Cont.: Vorwort: Exil und Exilliteratur im jüdischen Horizont (Ed., 1–19). From the exile experience to exile studies (Guy Stern, 21–37). When exiles return: Jerusalem as topos of the mind and soil (Sidra DeKoven Ezrahi, 39– 52). Heinrich Heine's Reisebilder as images of exile (Jakob Hessing, 53–59). Erde/Papier. Kafka, Literatur und Landnahme (Philipp Theisohn, 61–87). Yishuv as Teshuvah: Gershom Scholem's settlement in Jerusalem as return from assimilation (Pierre Bouretz, 89–101). Stefan Zweig's conceptions of exile (Mark H. Gelber, 103–113). Deus sive natura. The transformation of the Jewish apocalyptic version of history into a natural history in Jizchak Fritz Baer's treatise of "Galut" (exile) (Christoph Schmidt, 115–125). Exile, trauma and the modern Jewish experience: the example of Else Lasker-Schüler (Doerte Bischoff, 127–148). German exiles in the 'Orient'. The German-language weekly Orient (Haifa, 1942–1943) between German exile and Zionist aliya (Adi Gordon, 149–159). Re-Präsentation: Exil als Zeichenpraxis bei Anna Seghers (Bernhard Greiner, 161–174). The homecoming of a word: mystical language philosophy in Celan's "Mit allen Gedanken" (Rochelle Tobias, 175–185). "The land of others". Geographies of exile in Hélène Cixous's writings (Carola Hilfrich, 187–201). The two-way ticket to Hollywood and the master-images of 20th century modernism (Frank Stern, 203– 215). Nach Jerusalem (Philipp Theisohn, 217–221).]

43155. EXILE LITERATURE. SAUTERMEISTER, GERT/BARON, FRANK, eds.: *Goethe im Exil.* Deutsch-amerikanische Perspektiven. Bielefeld: Aisthesis, 2002. 297 pp., footnotes. [Deals mainly with the reception of Goethe by émigré authors. Selected essays (some titles abbr.): Heimat und Fremde, Exil und innere Emigration (Gert Sautermeister, 19–70). Ernst Toller und Goethe (Leonie Marx, 71–84). Brochs Verhältnis zu Goethe (Hartmut Steinecke, 85–100). Goethe as a figure in exile literature (Guy Stern, 185–198). Goethe in Moscow: Georg Lukács's 'anti-fascist' readings 1933–1945 (Nicholas Vazsonyi, 199–216). Die Rezeption von Kurt R. Eisslers Buch 'Goethe—a psychological study 1775–1786' in den USA (1963) und nach Erscheinen der deutschen Übersetzung (1983) (Monika Moyrer, 217–244).]

43156. EXILE LITERATURE. SCHÖLL, JULIA, ed.: *Gender—Exil—Schreiben.* Mit einem Vorwort von Guy Stern. Würzburg: Königshausen & Neumann, 2002. 199 pp., notes. [Incl. (some titles abbr.): Visiting the place that was home (Susan Groag Bell, 21–40). Die Schriftstellerin Maria Gleit (1908–1981) im Exil (Anke Heimberg, 41–66; M. G., orig. Hertha Gleitsmann, and on her husband, the journalist Werner Voigt, orig. Walther Victor). Texte und Zeugnisse aus dem Exil der "Künstler" (Brigitte Bruns, 69–89; incl. Ludwig and Else Meidner). Das politische Exilwerk Ruth Landshoff-Yorcks (Christine Pendl, 91–105). Geschlechterbilder in Exilromanen von Ödön von Horváth, Maria Leitner, Anna Gmeyner und Irmgard Keun (Anja C. Schmidt-Ott, 109–126). Junge "Girl"-Autorinnen im Exil (Barbara Drescher, 129–146; on Irmgard Keun, Dinah Nelken, Ruth Landshoff-Yorck). Groteske Körperdarstellungen im Exilwerk Alfred Döblins (Meike Mattick, 185–195). Two further contribs. on Heinrich and Thomas Mann.]

43157. EXILE LITERATURE. STERN, GUY: *Exil und literarisches Schaffen.* [In]: Auswanderung, Flucht, Vertreibung, Exil im 19. und 20. Jahrhundert [see No. 42513]. Pp. 171–182.

43158. EXILE LITERATURE. STRELKA, JOSEPH P.: *Exil, Gegenexil und Pseudoexil in der Literatur.* Tübingen: Francke, 2003. IX, 172 pp., footnotes. [Incl. essays on the works of Jacob Klein-Haparash, Afred W. Kneucker, Robert Pick, Soma Morgenstern, Ernst Lothar, Ernst Schönwiese, Ernst Weiß, Hermann Broch, Ernst Glaeser and authors from Czernowitz.]

43159. EXILE LITERATURE. THURNER, CHRISTINA: *Der andere Ort des Erzählens.* Exil und Utopie in der Literatur deutscher Emigrantinnen und Emigranten 1933–1945. Köln: Böhlau, 2003. VIII, 309 pp., footnotes, bibl. (283–304), index. Zugl.: Basel, Univ., Diss., 2002. [Incl. chaps. on Anna Seghers, Alice Rühle-Gerstel, Lion Feuchtwanger.]

43160. FÄHNDERS, WALTER/KARRENBROCK, HELGA, eds.: *Autorinnen der Weimarer Republik.* Bielefeld: Aisthesis, 2003. 297 pp., footnotes, bibl. (Aisthesis Studienbuch, Bd. 5.) [Selected essays (titles abbr.): Über Gertrud Kolmar (Marion Brandt, 59–78). Zur Genese der Autorschaft von Anna Seghers (Sonja Hilzinger, 79–96). Vicki Baum und der Berliner Ullstein-Verlag (Julia Bertschik, 119–136). Zum Status von Reporterinnen in der Weimarer Republik—das Beispiel Gabriele Tergit (Erhard Schütz, 215–238). Die 'Neue Frau' im nationalsozialistischen Deutschland und im Exil (Sabine Rohlf, 257–277).]

43161. GANGL, MANFRED, ed.: *Linke Juristen in der Weimarer Republik.* Frankfurt am Main; New York: Lang, 2003. 332 pp., footnotes. (Schriften zur politischen Kultur der Weimarer Republik, Bd. 7.) [Incl.: Verfassung, Demokratie und Pluralismus in den Weimarer Schriften von Ernst Fraenkel (Hubertus Buchstein, 246–275). Otto Kirchheimer: Linkssozialistische Analysen der Weimarer Republik (Frank Schale, 276–290). Aufstieg und Niedergang. Otto Kirchheimers politische Interpretation der Weimarer Reichsverfassung (Alfons Söllner, 291–327).]

43162. GUMBRECHT, HANS ULRICH: *Vom Leben und Sterben der großen Romanisten.* Karl Vossler, Ernst Robert Curtius, Leo Spitzer, Erich Auerbach, Werner Krauss. München: Hanser, 2002. 232 pp., notes (209–230).

43163. HEUER, RENATE, ed.: *Verborgene Lesarten. Neue Interpretationen jüdisch-deutscher Texte von Heine bis Rosenzweig.* In memoriam Norbert Altenhofer. Frankfurt am Main; New York: Campus, 2003. 243 pp., footnotes. [Selected contribs.: Kein Rabbi in Bacharach. Zur Geschichte des "Heiligen" Werner von Oberwesel (Winfried Frey, 11–32). Jüdisch-deutsche und deutsche Rhein- und Nationalromantik zwischen 1824/25 und 1840/41 (Ernst Erich Metzner, 33–58). Shylock im Osten. Shylock-Interpretationen bei Nathan Samuely, Karl Emil Franzos und Alexander Granach (Maria Klanska, 73–97). In der Spur des ewigen Juden. Heinrich Heine und das Ahasver-Motiv (Gunnar Och, 98–119). Metaphern des Unbewussten. Die Literatur und die Religion bei Sigmund Freud (Frank Kind, 120–134). Theologie der Blicke. Über Franz Rosenzweigs 'Stern der Erlösung' (Lorenz Jäger, 135–140). Adolph Donath im Berlin seiner Zeit (Doris Bensimon, 141–150). Heinrich Heine in der zionistischen Rezeption (Hanni Mittelmann, 173–186). "Eine Menschheit über allen Völkern"—Auguste Hauschner, Schriftstellerin zwischen Prag und Berlin (Birgit Seemann, 187–203). "Dieser erstaunliche Jude": Abraham Nochem Stenzels Berliner Jahre (Heather Valencia, 204–229; incl. Abraham Nochem Stenzel: Fischerdorf). Ludwig Börnes Freundinnen: Henriette Herz aus Berlin, Jeanette Wohl aus Frankfurt (Renate Heuer, 230–241).]

43164. HUML, ARIANE/RAPPENECKER, MONIKA, eds.: *Jüdische Intellektuelle im 20. Jahrhundert.* Literatur- und kulturgeschichtliche Studien. Würzburg: Königshausen & Neumann, 2003. 296 pp., footnotes. [Cont. the sections I. Kultur: Malerei, Musik, Theologie und Gesellschaft (17–76; cont. (most titles abbr.).: Charlotte Salomon, Mark Rothko, Alberto Burri (Christiane Esche-Ramshorn, 17–33). Komponieren nach Auschwitz (Lydia Jeschke, 35–42). Die Herausforderung der Literatur für eine Theologie im Gedenken an die Shoah (Christian Wiese, 43–62). Der Name als Zeichen—Jüdische Namen und jüdische Identität im Wandel (Elisabeth Beck-Gernsheim, 63–76; on Jewish name-giving reflecting assimilation and antisemitism). II.a. Judentum zwischen Kaiserreich und NS-Diktatur (77–132; cont.: Theodor Lessing (Barbara Beßlich, 77–98). Karl Kraus (Joachim W. Storck, 99–118). Selma Stern (Hiltrud Häntzschel, 119–131). II.b. Emigration und Exil (133–180; cont.: Hannah Arendt und Susan Taubes (Sigrid Weigel, 133–149). Käthe and Werner Vordtriede (Beate Schmeichel-Falkenberg, 151–165). Jenny Rosenbaum (Hartmut Steinecke, 167–179). II.c.: Auf dem Weg ins 21. Jahrhundert (181–296; cont.: Aharon Appelfeld (Hannah Liron, 181–190). Jean Améry (Manuela Günter, 191–206). Ilse Aichinger (Ursula Renner, 207–222). Hilde Domin (Ulrike Böhmel Fichera, 223–236). Ruth Klüger (Claudia Liebrand, 237–248). Hedda Zinner, Monika Maron, Barbara Honigmann (Uta Klaedtke/Martina Ölke, 249–274). Vom "Eigenleben" jüdischer Erinnerungsarchive (Mona Körte, 275–296).]

43165. *Hundert Jahre Kabarett.* Zur Inszenierung gesellschaftlicher Identität zwischen Protest und Propaganda. Hrsg. von Joanne McNally und Peter Sprengel. Würzburg: Königshausen & Neumann, 2003. 218 pp., illus., footnotes. [Selected essays: Karl Kraus, die Wiener Moderne und das Wiener Kabarett nach der Jahrhundertwende (Hans Veigl, 39–50). 'In eigener Sache?'—Jüdische Stimmen im deutschen und österreichischen Kabarett der Zwischenkriegszeit: Fritz Grünbaum—Fritz Löhner—Walter Mehring (Hans-Peter Bayerdörfer, 64–86).]

43166. JOCHNOWITZ, GEORGE: *Jewish performers and composers.* [In]: Midstream, Vol. 49, No. 2, New York, Feb./March 2003. Pp. 34– 35, notes. [Incl. Gustav Mahler, Felix Mendelssohn, Giacomo Meyerbeer, Jacques Offenbach.]

43167. *Judentum und Antisemitismus. Studien zur Literatur und Germanistik in Österreich.* Hrsg. von Anne Betten und Konstanze Fliedl [et al.]. Berlin: Erich Schmidt Verl., 2003. 253 pp., footnotes. (Philologische Studien und Quellen, H. 176.) [Incl. the sections: I. Literatur vor 1945; cont. (some titles abbr.): Das jüdische Selbstverständnis jüdischer Autoren im 'Fin de siècle' (Egon Schwarz, 21–31). Carl Schmitt, Theodor Herzl, Joseph Roth (Wolfgang Müller-Funk, 32–47). Is Freud's art of memory Jewish? (Abigail Gillman (48–61). Zur Thematisierung 'jüdischer' Identität in Franz Werfels Erzählung 'Pogrom' (Hildegard Kernmayer, 62–83). Völkische Literatur und Antisemitismus in der Zwischenkriegszeit (Johann Sonnleitner, 84–92). Österreichische Literatur im Exil (Johann Holzner, 93–108). II. Literatur nach 1945; cont.: Fred Wanders 'Der siebente Brunnen' im Kontext der Literatur über die Shoah (Hans Höller, 109–119). Authentischer Bericht oder Roman? Einige Überlegungen zur Typologie von Holocaust-Texten (Andrea Reiter, 120–131). Renaissance des 'jüdischen' Romans nach 1986 (Günther Scheidl, 132–150). III. Literaturwissenschaft; cont.: Zu Judentum und Antisemitismus bei Wilhelm Scherer und Erich Schmidt (Werner Michler, 151–166). Literatur und Kultur des Judentum in der Zweiten Republik (Karl Müller, 167–188). IV. Interviewprojekte; cont.: Edith Rosenstrauch-Königsberg (Beatrix Müller-Kampel, 189–198). Auswertung von Interviews mit SchriftstellerInnen österreichischer Herkunft (Bernadette Rieder, 199–211). Sprachwechsel und Identitätsproblematik jüdischer Emigranten aus Wien (Ingrid Hudabiunigg, 212–229). Funktionen von Humor in biographischen Interviews mit deutschsprachigen Emigranten in Israel (Monika Dannerer, 230–248).]

43168. KAISER, CÉLINE/WÜNSCHE, MARIE-LUISE, eds.: *Die "Nervosität der Juden" und andere Leiden an der Zivilisation. Konstruktionen des Kollektiven und Konzepte individueller Krankheit im psychiatrischen Diskurs um 1900.* Unter Mitarbeit von Christine Schaffrath. Paderborn: Schöningh, 2003. 258 pp., bibl., footnotes (Studien zu Judentum und Christentum.) [Selected essays: Ernst Simmel und Viktor von Weizsäcker: Zwei Pioniere der psychosomatischen Medizin des 20. Jahrhunderts im wissenschaftshistorischen Vergleich (Ulrich Schultz-Venrath, 133–157). Ernst Simmels Konzept der Zivilisationskrankheit im Kontext psychoanalytischer Rhetorik (Marie-Luise Wünsche, 159–179). Felix Deutsch und die Entwicklung der psychosomatischen Medizin (Gerrit Hohendorf, 207–226).]

——— MACK, MICHAEL: *German idealism and the Jew: the inner anti-Semitism of philosophy and German-Jewish responses.* [See No. 43658.]

43169. MAURER, TRUDE: *Der Krieg als Chance? Frauen im Streben nach Gleichberechtigung an deutschen Universitäten 1914–1918.* [In]: Jahrbuch für Universitätsgeschichte, Bd. 6, Stuttgart, 2003. Pp. 107–138, footnotes. [Deals also with Jewish women students.]

43170. *Mélanges d'histoire de la médecine hébraique.* Études choisies de la 'Revue d'histoire de la médecine Hébraique' (1948–1985). Réunies par Gad Freudenthal et Samuel Kottek. Leiden; Boston: Brill, 2003. XIV, 591 pp., footnotes. (Études sur le Judaisme Médiéval, Tome XXIV.) [Incl.: L'enseignement médicale et les juifs à l'université de Halle au XVIIIe siècle & Qui fut le premier professeur juif ayant enseigné la médecine en Allemagne à titre officiel (Wolfram Kaiser, 347–370; 371–375; on Markus Hertz). La vie et l'oeuvre de Gumpertz Levison, savant juif du XVIIIe siècle (Hans-Joachim Schoeps, 377–387). Le grand botaniste et bactériologiste Ferdinand Cohn (1828–1898) (Jacob Seide, 389–416). Moritz Benedikt (1835–1929) (Henri F. Ellenberger, 417–434; a Viennese doctor, not to be confused with the ed. of 'Neue Freie Presse').]

——— *Metzler Lexikon jüdischer Philosophen.* [See No. 42581.]

43171. MÖLLERS, GEORG: *Jüdische Tierärzte im Deutschen Reich in der Zeit von 1918 bis 1945.* Berlin: Tenea, 2002. 337 pp., illus., chron., bibl., index. Zugl.: Hannover, Tierärztl. Hochschule Hannover, Diss., 2002. [Incl. summaries in German and Engl., a chap. on antisemitism, short biographies of all Jewish veterinarians (108–283).]

43172. MÜLLER-FUNK, WOLFGANG [et al.], eds.: *Kakanien revisited. Das Eigene und das Fremde (in) der österreichisch-ungarischen Monarchie.* Tübingen: A. Francke Verlag, 2002. 362 pp., footnotes, index. (Kultur—Herrschaft—Differenz, Bd. 1.) [Incl. contribs. on Karl Emil Franzos (Gesa von Essen, 222–238), Joseph Roth (Telse Hartmann, 239–253).]

43173. OBERHÄNSLI-WIDMER, GABRIELLE: *Hiob in jüdischer Antike und Moderne. Die Wirkungsgeschichte Hiobs in der jüdischen Literatur.* Neukirchen-Vluyn: Neukirchener Verlag, 2003. X, 356 pp., footnotes, bibl. [Incl. Joseph Roth, Margarete Susman, German-Jewish poetry and theology.]

43174. *Politische Theorien des 19. Jahrhunderts. Konservatismus, Liberalismus, Sozialismus.* Zweite, völlig neu bearb. Aufl. Hrsg. von Bernd Heidenreich. Berlin: Akademie Verlag, 2002. 666 pp., footnotes. [Incl. contribs. on Friedrich Julius Stahl (Wilhelm Füßl, 179–192), Karl Marx (Theo Stammen, 447–486), Ferdinand Lassalle (Thilo Ramm, 487–506), Eduard Bernstein (Wilfried Rudloff, 507–536).]

43175. *Der Potsdamer Forte-Kreis.* Eine utopische Intellektuellenassoziation zur europäischen Friedenssicherung. Hrsg. von Richard Faber und Christine Holste. Würzburg: Königshausen & Neumann, 2001. 242 pp., frontis., notes. [Cont. 14 papers delivered at a conference in 1997, organised by the Moses Mendelssohn Zentrum in Potsdam; incl.: "Menschen von Potsdam—der Forte-Kreis (1910–1915) (Christine Holste, 11–30; also on one of the two founders of the Forte-Kreis, Erich Gutkind). "Parallelaktion"—Satire der Kulturkritik. Robert Musil über Walther Rathenau (Werner Graf, 85–100). Martin Buber oder: Entscheidung und Gemeinschaft (Manfred Voigts, 101–122). Vom "Gemeingeist". Über Gustav Landauers Räteutopie (Ulrich Linse, 123–144). Franz Oppenheimers Utopie des "liberalen Sozialismus" (Bernhard Vogt, 145–156). "Es werden keine esoterischen Gemeinden die Führung ergreifen". Walther Rathenau und der Forte-Kreis (Dieter Heimböckel, 163–184).]

43176. RÜSING, HANS-PETER: *Die nationalistischen Geheimbünde in der Literatur der Weimarer Republik. Joseph Roth, Vicki Baum, Ödön von Horváth, Peter Martin Lampel.* Frankfurt am Main; New York: Lang, 2003. 315 pp., notes (235–296), bibl. (Historisch-Kritische Arbeiten zur Deutschen Literatur, Bd. 33.) Zugl.: Münster (Westfalen), Univ., Diss., 2002. [First half deals with Joseph Roth's 'Spinnennetz' and Vicki Baum's 'Feme' against the background of right-wing organisations and their terrorist activities during the Weimar years.]

43177. SCHLOSSER, HORST D., ed.: *Das Deutsche Reich ist eine Republik.* Beiträge zur Kommunikation und Sprache der Weimarer Zeit. Frankfurt am Main: Lang, 2003. 226 pp., footnotes. (Frankfurter

Forschungen zur Kultur- und Sprachwissenschaft, Bd. 8.) [Incl.: "Fort mit dem Erzberger!"—"Knallt ab den Walther Rathenau!". Zwei politische Morde im Spiegel der Presse (Andreas Krämer, 79–90). Tucholskys Waffe. Thematische und sprachliche Beobachtungen an den Sprachglossen von Kurt Tucholsky (Susanne Barth/Tim Zühlke, 191–200). "Sie! sag'n Sie mal: Kann ick Ihr Mitleid pachten?" Beobachtungen zu Form und Sprache in Friedrich Hollaenders Chansonzyklus "Lieder eines armen Mädchens" (Elke Heidl, 201–212).]

43178. SCHNEIDER, HEINZ-JÜRGEN/SCHWARZ, ERIKA/SCHWARZ, JOSEF: *Die Rechtsanwälte der Roten Hilfe Deutschlands. Politische Strafverteidiger in der Weimarer Republik.* Geschichte und Biographien. Bonn: Pahl-Rugenstein, 2002. 364 pp., facsims. [Incl. the biographies of about 300 lawyers (68–305), among them many Jews.] [Cf.: Bespr. (Werner Schubert) [in]: Das Historisch-Politische Buch, Jahrgang 2003, H. 3, Göttingen, 2003, pp. 316–317.]

43179. SEBALD, WINFRIED GEORG: *On the natural history of destruction: with essays on Alfred Andersch, Jean Améry and Peter Weiss.* Transl. from the German by Anthea Bell. London: Hamish Hamilton, 2003. X, 205 pp., illus., ports., bibl. [German edn. in 1999.]

43180. STERN, FRANK/GIERLINGER, MARIA, eds.: *Die deutsch-jüdische Erfahrung. Beiträge zum kulturellen Dialog.* Berlin: Aufbau, 2003. 334 pp., notes. [Most papers were delivered at an int. conference at Ben-Gurion Univ. in June 1998, with the title "Jewish voices—German words. The impact of the German-Jewish experience on Western culture". Cont. (all essays transl. from English into German): Vorwort: Der deutsch-jüdische Kontext: Eine interdisziplinäre Perspektive (Frank Stern, 7–12). Einleitung: Gestalter der Kultur: Nebenfiguren aus allen Bereichen (Guy Stern, 13–40). 1. Wissenschaft und Vision; cont.: Die Revolte der Kolonisierten: Abraham Geigers 'Wissenschaft des Judentums' als Herausforderung christlicher Vormachtstellung in der Akademie (Susannah Heschel, 41–58). Von Glogau nach Paris: Deutsch-jüdische Gelehrte in der französischen Kultur (Dominique Bourel, 59–68). 2. Eine Kultur der Andersdenker: Literatur von Fin de Siécle zu Fin de Siècle; cont.: Internationalismus in der deutsch-jüdischen Literatur: Glückel von Hameln, Georg Hermann, Julius Bab und das "Yale-Handbuch" (Mark H. Gelber, 69–84; "Yale-Handbuch": The Yale companion to Jewish writing and thought in German culture, ed. by Sander Gilman and Jack Zipes, 1997). Zwischen Dialog und Konflikt: Deutsch-hebräische kulturelle Beziehungen (Na'ama Sheffi, 85–102). Sehstörungen der Wiener Moderne (Andreas Huyssen, 103–126; on Hugo von Hofmannsthal, Arthur Schnitzler and Robert Musil). Blumen der Geschichte, Blumen der Erinnerung: Paul Celan und der postmoderne Diskurs (Amir Eshel, 129–146). Sofies Engel. Die Gruppe 47 und Ilse Aichingers Poetik der Widerstands (Vivian Liska, 147–164). "Am Rande einer Wüste, einem Punkt des Zufalls"—Die Erfahrung Wolfgang Hildesheimers und die "neue" deutsche Literatur (Stephan Braese, 165–176). Jüdische Geschichte und Geschichten: Barbara Honigmann und ihr Roman "Soharas Reise" (Jeffrey M. Peck, 177– 196). 3. Visuelle Kultur: Das Bildergebot; cont.: Universalismus und Film. Von Fritz Lang bis Jean-Luc Godard (Frank Stern, 197–214). Von Theben zur Ufa: Reinhold Schünzels Filmsatire "Amphytrion" (1935) und ihre Ursprünge in der westlichen Kulturgeschichte (Gabriela Hermer, 215–236). "Ich werde den Film—wie er heut zwischen Europa und Hollywood lebt—auf neue Beine stellen." Alfred Kerrs Hoffnungen im Exil (Deborah Vietor-Engländer, 237–257). 4. Kultur und Politik: Das deutsch-amerikanisch-israelische Dreieck; cont.: Heimatversionen: Deutsch-jüdische Flüchtlingspapiere aus dem Schrank in die Archive (Atina Grossmann, 259–292; deals with the author's family, esp. with her grandfather Heinrich Busse in Berlin). Das Deutschland von heute und die amerikanischen Juden: Notwendigkeit und Unmöglichkeit einer 'Normalisierung' (Alvin H. Rosenfeld, 293–308). Annäherung, Widerstreben und Ablehnung. Das Dreiecksverhältnis zwischen Deutschland, Israel und dem amerikanischen Judentum (Lily Gardner Feldman, 309–330).]

43181. STEVENS, LEWIS: *Composers of classical music of Jewish descent.* Foreword by Rabbi Julia Neuberger. London; Portland, OR: Vallentine Mitchell, 2003. XXIII, 384 pp., illus., ports., facsims., maps, tabs., glossary, appendix, notes, bibl., index. [Incl. many German-Jewish composers: Hanns Eisler, Felix Mendelssohn, Giacomo Meyerbeer, Jacques Offenbach, Kurt Weill et al.; also on antisemitism and Jewish identity, incl. the Nazi period. Appendix cont. the Nazi publication from 1940: Lexikon der Juden in der Musik (Theophil Stengel and Herbert Gerigk).]

43182. SUCHY, BARBARA: *"Wir halten treu und fest zu Republik und Verfassung". Deutsche Juden und die Verteidigung der Weimarer Republik.* [In]: "Gegen alle Vergeblichkeit". Jüdischer Widerstand gegen den Nationalsozialismus [see No. 42899]. Pp. 68–100, footnotes. [Deals with 13 personalities from politics and the senior civil service.]

43183. VÖLTER, BETTINA: *Judentum und Kommunismus. Deutsche Familiengeschichten in drei Generationen.* Opladen: Leske + Budrich, 2003. 336 pp., footnotes, bibl. [Abbr. and revised doctoral diss., Techn. Univ., Berlin; on families, some of whom emigr. to the Soviet Union, some to "Western" countries, and after 1945 went to East Germany (GDR); with pseudonyms.]

——— WALTER, HANS-ALBERT: *Deutsche Exilliteratur 1933–1950. Band 1.1: Die Mentalität der Weimardeutschen/Die "Politisierung" der Intellektuellen.* [See No. 42258.]

43184. WASZKIS, HELMUT/WASZKIS, PETER MARC: *The story of metal trading: metal trading, metal traders, ore and metal merchants from early times to today.* London: Metal Bulletin Books, 2003. 284 pp. [Incl. material on Jews in the German metal trade, focusing on traders incl. the Philipp brothers, the Rothschilds, Zacharias Hochschild, Moritz Hochschild.]

43185. WEINKE, WILFRIED: *Verdrängt, vertrieben, aber nicht vergessen. Die Fotografen Emil Bieber, Max Halberstadt, Erich Kastan, Kurt Schallenberg.* Weingarten: Weingarten, 2003. 303 pp., illus., facsims., bibl. [Incl. addresses by Paul Spiegel and Rolf Sachsse (7–8); biographies of the four photographers from Hamburg.]

43186. *Zeitgenössische jüdische Autobiographie.* Hrsg. von Christoph Miething. Tübingen: Niemeyer, 2003. XI, 199 pp., footnotes. (Romania Judaica, Bd. 7.) [Cont. 14 essays, mostly in French, some in English, some in German; incl.: Gibt es jüdische Autobiographien? (ed., 43–74). In den Körper verbrachte Erinnerung. Autobiographische Texte von deutsch-jüdischen Autorinnen der zweiten Generation (Eva Lezzi, 147–178; on Lea Fleischmann, Laura Waco, Esther Dischereit, Barbara Honigmann).]

B. **Individual**

43187. ADLER, FRIEDRICH. ALTHAUS, HERMANN: *Friedrich Adler, ein jüdischer Künstler in der Zeit des Jugendstils 1878–1942.* [In]: Badische Heimat, Jg. 80, H. 2, Freiburg, 2000. Pp. 254–258, illus., notes. [F.A., 1878 Laupheim–1942 Auschwitz, designer, for further data see No. 32131/YB XL.]

43188. ADLER, PAUL. HOFFMANN, DANIEL: *"Eine Vision jüdischer Art". Paul Adlers Roman 'Die Zauberflöte' von 1916.* [In]: Trumah, Jg. 13, Heidelberg, 2003. Pp. 209–226, footnotes. [P.A., April 4, 1878 Prague–June 8, 1946 Zbraslav nr. Prague, jurist, author.]

43189. ADORNO, THEODOR W.. *Adorno 100.* [Section title of] Neue Gesellschaft/Frankfurter Hefte, Jg. 49, H. 9, Frankfurt am Main, 2003. Pp. 50–66. [Incl. essays by Til Schulz, Kurt Lenk, Michael Schmidt, Martin Hielscher, Harro Zimmermann. Also, in this issue, review essay on books about Adorno (Roman Kuckscheiter, 74–76).]

43190. ADORNO, THEODOR W.. *Adorno in Frankfurt.* Ein Kaleidoskop mit Texten und Bildern. Hrsg. von Wolfram Schütte. Frankfurt am Main: Suhrkamp, 2003. 423 pp., illus., facsims.

43191. ADORNO, THEODOR W.. *Adorno. Eine Bildmonographie.* Hrsg. vom Theodor W. Adorno Archiv. [Bearb. von Gabriele Ewenz, Christoph Gödde, Henri Lonitz und Michael Schwarz.] Frankfurt am Main: Suhrkamp, 2003. 309 pp., illus., facsims., chronol., index.

43192. ADORNO, THEODOR W.. CLAUSSEN, DETLEV: *Theodor W. Adorno. Ein letztes Genie.* Frankfurt am Main: S. Fischer, 2003. 479 pp., illus., notes (431–470).

43193. ADORNO, THEODOR W.. HASGALL, ALEXANDER: *Adorno Tagung: Höhepunkt im Jubiläumsjahr.* [In]: tachles, Jg. 3, Nr. 50, Zürich, Dec. 12, 2003. Pp. 32–33. [On a conference in Jerusalem.]

43194. ADORNO, THEODOR W.. JÄGER, LORENZ: *Adorno.* Eine politische Biographie. München: Deutsche Verlags-Anstalt, 2003. 319 pp., notes (302–313). [Cf.: "Ein Intellektueller in der

Bravissimo-Version" (Hermann Glaser) [in]: Das Parlament, Jg. 53, Nr. 40/41, Berlin, 29. Sept./6. Okt. 2003, p. 12; also on Detlev Claussen's biography.]

43195. ADORNO, THEODOR W.. KAUBE, JÜRGEN: *So gut wie nichts macht alles wieder gut.* Das Bedürfnis im Denken will, daß gedacht werde: Theodor W. Adorno zum einhundertsten Geburtstag. [In]: 'FAZ', Nr. 207, Frankfurt am Main, 6. Sept. 2003. P. 38, port.

43196. ADORNO, THEODOR W.. MÜLLER-DOOHM, STEFAN: *Adorno.* Eine Biographie. Frankfurt am Main: Suhrkamp, 2003. 1032 [24] pp., illus., geneal., chronol., notes (744–920), indexes (persons; works, 1001–1032). [Incl. the sections: Erster Teil. Ursprünge: Familie, Kindheit und Jugend. Die Schul- und Studienjahre in der Stadt am Main. Zweiter Teil. Ortswechsel: Zwischen Frankfurt, Wien, Berlin. Vielfalt geistiger Interessen. Dritter Teil. Emigrationsjahre: Eine intellektuelle Existenz im Fremden. Vierter Teil. Das unbedingte Denken und das bedingte Ertragen.] [Cf.: Adorno als Adorno. Biografische Versuche im Jahr des hundertsten Geburtstags (Uwe Justus Wenzel) [in]: 'NZZ', Nr. 194, Zürich, 23./24. Aug. 2003, p. 37.]

43197. ADORNO, THEODOR W.. NOVAC, NANA: *Das Adorno-Jahr in Frankfurt/Main.* Die Kulturindustrie feiert ihren vehementesten Kritiker. [In]: Tribüne, Jg. 42, H. 168, Frankfurt am Main, 2003. Pp. 86–90.

43198. ADORNO, THEODOR W.. REEMTSMA, JAN PHILIPP: *Der Traum von der Ich-Ferne. Adornos literarische Aufsätze.* [In]: Mittelweg 36, Jg. 12, Nr. 6, Hamburg, Dez. 2003/Jan. 2004. Pp. 3–40, footnotes.

43199. ADORNO, THEODOR W.. SÖLLNER, ALFONS: *Adornos Amerika.* [In]: Mittelweg 36, Jg. 12, H. 4, Hamburg, Aug./Sept. 2003. Pp. 3–45, footnotes. [On A.'s experiences during exile years in the US.]

43200. ADORNO, THEODOR W.. WOLF, SIEGBERT: *Philosoph, Jude, Emigrant, Remigrant.* Zum 100. Geburtstag Theodor W. Adornos (1903–1969). [In]: Tribüne, Jg. 42, H. 167, Frankfurt am Main, 2003. Pp. 102–118, footnotes.

43201. ADORNO, THEODOR W.: *Can one live after Auschwitz?: a philosophical reader.* Ed. by Rolf Tiedemann. Transl. by Rodney Livingstone and others. Stanford, CA: Stanford Univ. Press, 2003. XXVII, 525 pp., notes, bibl.(473–517), index. (Cultural memory in the present.) [For orig. German edn. 1997 see No. 35466/YB XLIII.]

43202. AGNON, SHMUEL YOSEF. ASCHKENASY, NEHAMA: *Agnon's Dickensian moment: "Baya'ar uva'ir".* [In]: Journal of Modern Jewish Studies, Vol. 2, No. 2, Philadelphia, London, Oct. 2003. Pp. 174–190, notes.

43203. ALTMAIER, JAKOB. MOSS, CHRISTOPH: *Jakob Altmaier. Ein jüdischer Sozialdemokrat in Deutschland (1889–1963).* Köln: Böhlau, 2003. VIII, 310 pp., illus., footnotes, bibl., index. [J.A., Nov. 23, 1889 Flörsheim–Feb. 8, 1963 Bonn, Social Democrat, journalist, politician, fled in 1933 to France, worked as a journalist in France, Yugoslavia, North Africa, remigrated to Germany in 1949, member of the Federal Parliament from 1949 until his death as a representative of Jewish and Israeli interests, instrumental in the restitution negotiations between Israel and the FRG.]

43204. AMÉRY, JEAN. HEIDELBERGER-LEONARD, IRENE: *Jean Améry im Dialog mit der zeitgenössischen Literatur.* Essays. Hrsg. von Hans Höller. Stuttgart: Akad. Verlag Hans-Dieter Heinz, 2002. 178 pp. (Stuttgarter Arbeiten zur Germanistik, Nr. 402: Unterreihe Salzburger Beiträge, Nr. 42.) [Cf.: Irene Heidelberger-Leonards Essays über Jean Améry (Konstantin Kaiser) [in]: Zwischenwelt, Jg. 20, Nr. 3, Wien, Dez. 2003, p. 75.]

43205. AMÉRY, JEAN. *Jean Améry.* [Issue title of] Zwischenwelt, Jg. 20, Nr. 3, Wien, Dez. 2003. 1 issue. [Incl. contribs. by and on J.A. by Irene Heidelberger-Leonard, Gerhard Scheit, Doron Rabinovici, Hans Höller (43–68).]

43206. AMÉRY, JEAN. SCHLEMM, SONJA: *Aufbegehren als Lebenskonzept.* Zum 25. Todestag von Jean Améry. [In]: Tribüne, Jg. 42, H. 168, Frankfurt am Main, 2003. Pp. 90–94.

43207. APPELFELD, AHARON. *Encounter with Aharon Appelfeld.* Ed. by Michael Brown and Sara R. Horowitz. Oakville, ONT: Mosaic Press, 2003. 115 pp., ports., notes, bibl. [Incl. interviews with, and contributions by, A.A.]

43208. ARENDT, HANNAH. GRUNENBERG, ANTONIA: *Arendt.* Freiburg: Herder, 2003. 160 pp., bibl., index. (Herder Spektrum, Bd. 4954.) Orig.-Ausg. [Biography and introduction to A.'s work.]

43209. ARENDT, HANNAH. LEIBOVICI, MARTINE: *Hannah Arendt et la tradition juive: le judaisme à l'épreuve de la sécularisation.* Genève: Labor et Fides, 2003. 92 pp. (Religions en perspective, No. 14.) [Lecture given at the Faculty of Theology, University of Lausanne, May 2002.]

43210. ARENDT, HANNAH. MEINTS, WALTRAUD: *Globalisierung und Menschenrechte. Zur Aktualität der Krisendiagnose von Hannah Arendt.* [In]: Mittelweg 36, Jg. 12, Nr. 5, Hamburg, Okt./Nov. 2003. Pp. 53–68, footnotes.

43211. ARENDT, HANNAH. STUCHTEY, BENEDIKT: *Herrschen und Verwalten. Hannah Arendt über den Imperialismus.* [In]: Saeculum, Bd. 54, Halbbd. 2, Köln, 2003. Pp. 301–328 footnotes.

43212. ARENDT, HANNAH & ADORNO, THEODOR W.. *Arendt und Adorno.* Hrsg. von Dirk Auer, Lars Rensmann und Julia Schulze Wessel. Frankfurt am Main: Suhrkamp, 2003. 313 pp., footnotes. (Suhrkamp Taschenbuch Wissenschaft.) Orig.-Ausg. [Incl.: Einleitung: Affinität und Aversion. Zum theoretischen Dialog zwischen Arendt und Adorno (eds., 7–31). I. Intellektuelle im Exil; cont.: Paria wider Willen. Adornos und Arendts Reflexionen auf den Ort des Intellektuellen (Dirk Auer, 35–56). Die amerikanische Erfahrung. Adorno, Arendt und das Exil in den USA (Joanna Vecchiarelli Scott, 57–73). Verborgene Tradition und messianisches Licht. Arendt, Adorno und ihr Judentum (Micha Brumlik, 74–93). II. Totale Herrschaft und Nachkriegsdeutschland; incl.: Radikalisierung und "Verschwinden" der Judenfeindschaft? Arendts und Adornos Theorien zum modernen Antisemitismus (Julia Schulze Wessel/Lars Rensmann, 97–129). Also essays by Alexander Garcia Düttmann and Lars Rensmann (130–195). III. Politisches Denken und philosophische Kategorienbildung (199–310; essays by Samir Gandesha, Jörn Ahrens, Alex Demirovic, Thorsten Bonacker).]

43213. ARENDT, HANNAH & JONAS, HANS. HARMS, KLAUS: *Hannah Arendt und Hans Jonas: Grundlagen einer philosophischen Theologie der Weltverantwortung.* Berlin: WiKu-Verlag, 2003. 532 pp. Zugl.: Freiburg (Breisgau), Univ., Diss., 2003.

43214. ARENDT, HANNAH: *Responsibility and judgment.* Ed. and with an introd. by Jerome Kohn. New York: Schocken Books, 2003. 295 pp., illus. [Previously unpubl. writings from the last ten years of H.A.'s life dealing with "Eichmann in Jerusalem".]

43215. ARENDT, HANNAH: *The portable Hannah Arendt.* Ed. with an introd. by Peter Baehr. New York: Penguin Books, 2003. 575 pp. [Cont. excerpts from "The origins of totalitarianism", "The human condition", "Eichmann in Jerusalem", as well as other essays and some correspondence.]

43216. ARNHOLD, EDUARD. DORRMANN, MICHAEL: *Eduard Arnhold (1849–1925). Eine biographische Studie zu Unternehmer- und Mäzenatentum im Deutschen Kaiserreich.* Berlin: Akademie, 2002. 414 pp., illus., tabs., notes (256–344), bibl. (360–403), index. [Abbr. Ph.D. thesis, Berlin, Humboldt Univ., 2001/2002.] [Cf.: [E.A., 1849 Dessau–1925 Neuhaus/Schliersee, entrepreneur, owner of Fa. Caesar Wollheim, one of the biggest coal wholesale businesses, philanthropist, art collector, founder of the Villa Massimo in Rome.] [Cf.: Bespr. (Christof Biggeleben) [in]: Zeitschrift für Unternehmensforschung, Jg. 48, H. 2, München, 2003, pp. 245–246. Bespr. (Dieter Hertz-Eichenrode) [in]: Jahrbuch für die Geschichte Mittel- und Ostdeutschlands, Bd. 49, München, 2004, pp. 381–382.]

43217. AUERBACH, BERTHOLD. SCHUDER, ROSEMARIE: *Deutsches Stiefmutterland. Wege zu Berthold Auerbach.* Mit einem Nachwort von Thomas Scheuffelen. Teetz: Hentrich & Henrich, 2003. 492 pp., illus., chronol., bibl., index. (Jüdische Memoiren, Bd. 9.) [Incl.: Wie ein gegenläufiger Zugvogel. Ein Gang durch das Berthold-Auerbach-Museum im Schloß Nordstetten bei Horb (Thomas Scheuffelen, 418–423).]

43218. AUSLÄNDER, ROSE. *Rose Ausländer. De la Bucovine à l'après-Shoah.* Études réunies par Claire de Oliveira et Jean-Marie Valentin. [Issue title of] Études Germaniques, Année 58, No. 2, Paris, 2003. 377 pp., illus., footnotes. [Incl. 14 essays (147–378), some in French, some in German, by Florence Heymann, Marc Sagnol, Leslie Morris, Mireille Tabah, Stéphane Mosès, Laurent Cassagnau, Klaus Werner, Harald Vogel, Claire de Oliveira, Maria Behre, Michel Lemercier, Jacques Lajarrige, Rémy Colombat, Andrei Corbea-Hoisie.]

43219. BAER, REINHOLD. GRUENBERG, K.W.: *Reinhold Baer.* [In]: Illinois Journal of Mathematics, Vol. 47, No. 1/2, Chicago, Ill., Spring/Summer 2003. Pp. 1–30, notes, bibl. R.B. [Deals with B.'s life and scientific work.] [R.B., July 22, 1902 Berlin–Oct. 22, 1978 Zurich, prof. of mathematics, expelled from Halle Univ. in 1933, thereafter worked at Manchester Univ. and from 1935 until his return to Germany at various universities in the US. From 1956 until his retirement in 1967, prof. at Frankfurt Univ.]

43220. BALLIN, ALBERT. WIBORG, SUSANNE: *Momente der Entscheidung, 19: Mit Volldampf seiner Zeit voraus.* Der geniale Außenseiter Albert Ballin machte aus der verschlafenen Reederei Hapag den größten Schiffahrtskonzern der Welt. [In]: Die Zeit, Nr. 30, Hamburg, 17. Juli 2003.

43221. BARON, ERICH. GRAHN, GERLINDE: *Erich Baron—eine biographische Studie (1881–1933).* [In]: JahrBuch für Forschungen zur Geschichte der Arbeiterbewegung 2002/II, Berlin, 2002. Pp. 127–140, notes. [E.B., July 20, 1881 Berlin–April 29, 1933 Berlin (suicide in prison after torture), journalist, Communist functionary, secretary general of the Gesellschaft der Freunde des neuen Rußland.]

43222. BARON, HANS. BRADY, THOMAS A., JR.: *German Imperial cities, Reformation, and Republicanism—the legacy of Hans Baron.* [In]: Historische Anstöße. Festschrift für Wolfgang Reinhard zum 65. Geburtstag am 10. April 2002. Hrsg. von Peter Burschel [et al.]. Berlin: Akademie, 2002. 40–54, footnotes. [H.B., 1900 Berlin–1988 Champaign, Ill; for further data see No. 36779/YB XLIV.]

43223. BECKER, JUREK. GILMAN, SANDER L.: *Jurek Becker: a life in five worlds.* Chicago: Univ. of Chicago Press, 2003. XIII, 282 pp., illus., notes, bibl., index.

43224. BECKER, JUREK. GILMAN, SANDER L.: *Jurek Becker. Die Biographie.* Aus dem Amerik. von Michael Schmidt. München: Ullstein, 2002. 336 pp., illus., notes (296–336). Dt. Orig.-Ausg.

43225. BEHR, ISASCHAR FALKENSOHN: *Gedichte von einem polnischen Juden.* Mit einem Nachwort hrsg. von Andreas Wittbrodt. Göttingen: Wallstein, 2003. 102 pp., frontis. [Incl.: Nachwort: Die Bikulturalität der 'Gedichte von einem pohlnischen Juden' (ed., 65–102, notes).]

43226. BEHR, ISASCHAR FALKENSOHN: *Gedichte von einem pohlnischen Juden.* Mit Behrs Lobgedicht auf Katharina II. und Goethes Rezension der "Gedichte" hrsg. von Gerhard Lauer. St. Ingbert: Röhrig, 2002. 113 pp. [Incl.: Nachwort (ed., 91–113).] [I.F.B., 1746 Salantin (Lithuania)–1817 Kamenez-Podolsk, physician, lived from 1768 to 1775 in Königsberg, Berlin and Halle, 1781 conversion to Russian Orthodoxy.]

43227. BENJAMIN, WALTER. KRAMER, SVEN: *Walter Benjamin zur Einführung.* Hamburg: Junius, 2003. 162 pp., notes (139–152), bibl., chronol.

43228. BENJAMIN, WALTER. SCHOLEM, GERSHOM: *Walter Benjamin: the story of a friendship.* Transl. from the German by Harry Zohn. Introd. by Lee Siegel. New York: New York Review Books, 2003. xvii, 302 pp., illus., ports., facsims., index. (New York Review Books Classics.) [For orig. German edn. see No. 12980/YB XXI. For first English edn. see No. 19334/YB XXVIII.]

43229. BENJAMIN, WALTER & BERNFELD, SIEGFRIED. DUDEK, PETER: *Fetisch Jugend. Walter Benjamin und Siegfried Bernfeld—Jugendprotest am Vorabend des Ersten Weltkrieges.* Bad Heilbrunn: Klinkhardt, 2002. 268 pp., illus., footnotes, bibl.

43230. BENSEMANN, WALTHER. BEYER, BERND-M.: *Der Mann, der den Fußball nach Deutschland brachte.* Das Leben des Walther Bensemann. Ein biografischer Roman. Göttingen: Verlag Die Werkstatt, 2003. 542 pp., illus. [16 pp.], notes, bibl. [W.B., Jan. 13, 1873 Berlin–Nov. 12, 1934

Montreux, Switzerland, pioneer of the German football movement, founder of numerous football clubs, founder of 'Der Kicker' (1920).]

43231. BERGMAN, SHMUEL HUGO. PELEG, EREZ: *The meaning of "Judaism" in Shmuel Hugo Bergman's youth and early thoughts.* [In Hebrew.] Jerusalem: LBI Jerusalem, 2003. 21 pp. (Chiduschim becheker toledot Yehudei Germania Series of pamphlets, No. 4.)

43232. BERGMANN, PETER GABRIEL. GOLDBERG, JOSHUA N./SCHUCKING, ENGELBERT L.: *Peter Gabriel Bergmann.* [In]: Physics Today, Vo. 56, No. 8, Aug. 2003. Pp. 64–66, port. [Obit.] [P.G.B., March 24, 1915 Berlin–Oct. 19, 2002 Seattle, Prof. of Theoretical Physics at various US universities, emigr. via Prague to the US, research assistant to Einstein in Princeton, 1936–1941.]

43233. BERGMANN, PETER GABRIEL. SCHMUTZER, ERNST: *Obituary: Peter Gabriel Bergmann—outstanding scientist and good friend.* [In]: Annalen der Physik, Jg. 12, Nr. 7–8, Leipzig, 2003. Pp. 411–414, port. [For data see No. 43232.]

43234. BERNFELD, SIEGFRIED. WEISS, EDGAR: *Verdrängung in der Erinnerung?—Das Beispiel Siegfried Bernfeld.* [In]: Jahrbuch für Pädagogik 2003, Jg. 11, Frankfurt am Main, 2003. Pp. 105–124. [S.B., psychoanalyst, data see No. 30972/YB XXXIX.]

43235. BLAU, MARIETTA. ROSNER, ROBERT/STROHMAIER, BRIGITTE, eds.: *Marietta Blau—Sterne der Zertrümmerung. Biographie einer Wegbereiterin der modernen Teilchenphysik.* Wien: Böhlau, 2003. 229 pp., illus., notes. (Beiträge zur Wissenschaftsgeschichte und Wissenschaftsforschung, 3.) [Incl.: Geleitwort (Walter Kutschera, 9–11). First part of book deals with B.'s biography, second part with her scientific work.] [M.B., data see No. 35494/YB XLIII.]

43236. BLAU, PETER M.. MÜLLER, HANS-PETER: *Nachruf auf Peter M. Blau.* [In]: Berliner Journal für Soziologie, Jg. , H. 3, Opladen, 2002. Pp. 405–406. [P.M.B., Feb. 7, 1918 Vienna–March 12, 2002 USA, sociologist, after the Anschluss fled via France to the US.]

43237. BLOCH, ERNST. *Ernst Blochs Leipziger Jahre.* Beiträge des Fünften Walter-Markov-Kolloquiums. Hrsg. von Manfred Neuhaus und Helmut Seidel. Leipzig: Rosa-Luxemburg-Stiftung Sachsen, 2001. 145 pp., footnotes.

43238. BLOCH, ERNST. MÜNSTER, ARNO: *Ernst Blochs Religionsphilosophie im Spannungsfeld von jüdischem Messianismus, ketzerischem Christentum und materialistischem Atheismus,* [In]: VorSchein. Jahrbuch der Ernst-Bloch-Assoziation, Nr. 22/23, Berlin, 2002. Pp. 48–64.

43239. BÖRNE, LUDWIG. JASPER, WILLI: *Ludwig Börne. Keinem Vaterland geboren.* Eine Biographie. Berlin: Aufbau Taschenbuch Verlag, 2003. 331 pp., illus., facsims., notes, chronol., bibl., index. [Revised new edn., orig. publ. 1989.]

43240. BÖRNE, LUDWIG. STERN, FRANK/GIERLINGER, MARIA, eds.: *Ludwig Börne. Deutscher, Jude, Demokrat.* Berlin: Aufbau, 2003. 272 pp., frontis., notes. [Incl.: Deutsch-jüdisch par excellence (Frank Stern, 9–18). The four sections are entitled: Annäherungen an ein deutsch-jüdisches Phänomen (with essays by Liliane Weissberg, Willi Jasper, Deborah Hertz, Dieter Lamping). Paris: Das Jerusalem des Westens (with essays by Dominique Bourel, Mark M. Anderson, Norbert Waszek). Über Komödianten und andere Politiker (with essays by Mark H. Gelber, Bernhard Greiner, Ruth Eitan). Ludwig Börne und Heinrich Heine: Ein literarisches Duell? (with essays by Zvi Tauber and Klaus Briegleb).] [Cf.: Löw, Lion, Louis, Ludwig (Jonathan Scheiner) [in]: Jüdische Literatur [Beilage von] Jüdische Allgemeine, Jg. 58, Nr. 26, Berlin, Winter 2003, p. 32.]

43241. BONDY, FRANÇOIS. ALTWEGG, JÜRG: *Zum Glück folgte er seinem Gebot nicht selbst.* Ein brillanter Vermittler zwischen den getrennten Welten: Zum Tod von François Bondy. [In]: 'FAZ', Nr. 124, Frankfurt am Main, 30. Mai 2003. P. 35. [F.B., Jan. 1, 1915 Berlin–May 27, 2003 Zurich, essayist, journalist, literary critic, author.]

43242. BRAUER, RICHARD. CURTIS, CHARLES W.: *Richard Brauer: Sketches from his life and work.* [In]: The American Mathematical Monthly, Vol. 110, Oct. 2003, Menasha, Wisconsin. Pp. 665–678, port., footnotes, bibl. [R.B. 1903 Berlin–1977 Cambridge, MA, mathematician, expelled from the Univ. of Königsberg in 1933, with the help of the Emergency Committee for Displaced German Scholars resumed his career in Lexington and Princeton, from 1935 at the Universities of Toronto, Michigan and Harvard.]

43243. BREITBACH, JOSEPH. MEYER, JOCHEN: *Joseph Breitbach oder Die Höflichkeit des Erzählers.* Hrsg.: Ulrich Ott. Marbach am Neckar: Dt. Schillergesellschaft, 2003. 110 pp., frontis., illus., notes. (Marbacher Magazin, 102.) [J.B., Sept. 20, 1903 Ehrenbreitstein/Koblenz–May 9, 1980 Munich, journalist, author, fled in 1933 via Greece to France, worked for the French intelligence service in Switzerland and Southern France until 1945, lived in Munich from 1961.]

43244. BROCH, HERMANN. *Hermann Broch, visionary in exile: the 2001 Yale symposium.* Ed. by Paul Michael Lützeler [et al.]. Rochester, NY: Camden House, 2003. XIV, 266 pp., bibl., notes, index. (Studies in German literature, linguistics, and culture.) [Papers presented at an international symposium held April 27–29, 2001 at Yale Univ., New Haven.]

43246. BROCH, HERMANN. *Hermann Broch.* Etudes réunies par Christine Mondon. Rouen: Centre d'Etudes et de Recherches Autrichiennes, 2002. 209 pp. (Austriaca, No. 55.) [Cont. partly German, partly French essays.]

43247. BROCH, HERMANN. LÜTZELER, PAUL MICHAEL: *Hermann Brochs Kosmopolitismus: Europarecht, Menschenrechte, Universität.* Mit einem Vorwort von Hubert Christian Ehalt und Manfried Welan. Wien: Picus, 2002. 54 pp. (Wiener Vorlesungen im Rathaus, Bd. 91.)

43248. BROCH, HERMANN. LÜTZELER, PAUL MICHAEL: *Hermes redivivus: 'Aus der Luft gegriffen'. Hermann Brochs zynische Komödie der Globalisierung.* [In]: Theater ohne Grenzen. Festschrift für Hans-Peter Bayerdörfer zum 65. Geburtstag. Hrsg. von Katharina Keim [et al.]. München: Herbert Utz Verlag, 2003 (Theaterwissenschaft, Bd. 1.). Pp. 337–349, footnotes. [On B.s comedy written in 1934.]

43249. BROCH, HERMANN. STEINECKE, HARTMUT: *Broch und Goethe; oder: Goethe im österreichischen Exil.* [In]: Jahrbuch des Wiener Goethe-Vereins, Bd. 102/103—1998/1999, Wien, 2003 [sic]. Pp. 145–156, footnotes.

43250. BRON, WALTER ERNEST. MILLS, DOUGLAS L./MARADUDIN, ALEXEI A.: *Walter Ernest Bron.* [Obit.] [In]: Physics Today, Vol. 56, No. 7, July 2003. [W.E.B., Jan. 17, 1930 Berlin–Nov. 16, 2002 Irvine, CA, physicist, emigr. via Netherlands to the US, Prof. at the Univ. of California in Irvine from 1986.]

43251. BRUCH, HILDE. TAPKEN, HERMANN: *Von der Ratinger Kinderärztin zur prominenten amerikanischen Wissenschaftlerin—Hilde Bruch, ein jüdisches Schicksal.* [In]: Ratinger Forum, H. 8, Ratingen, 2003. Pp. 170–215, illus., footnotes. [The paediatrician and psychiatrist H.B. (1904–1984) lived and worked in Ratingen 1932/1933; article deals also with her family from Dülken (today part of Viersen). For biography of H.B. see No. 34428/YB XLII.]

43252. BUCHDAHL, GERD. JARDINE, NICHOLAS: *Obituary: Gerd Buchdahl (1914–2001): Founding editor.* [In]: Studies in History of Philosophy and Science, Vol. 32, No. 3, Oxford, 2001. Pp. 401–405, footnotes. [G.B., Aug. 12, 1914 Mainz–May 17, 2001 Cambridge, UK, engineer, historian of philosophy, Kant scholar, emigr. to the UK, in 1940 deported on the 'Dunera' to Australia, 1957 went to Cambridge Univ. as Lecturer, later Head of the Department and Reader in Philosophy of Science, founding fellow of Darwin College, together with Larry Laudan, founder of Studies in History of Philosophy and Science.]

43253. CANETTI, ELIAS. MICHAELIS, KRISTINA: *Dimensionen einer europäischen Identität.* Studien zu Elias Canetti. Frankfurt am Main; New York: Lang, 2003. 368 pp., footnotes, bibl. (339–368). (Europ. Hochschulschriften, Reihe I: Deutsche Sprache und Literatur, Bd. 1862.) Zugl.: Münster (Westf.), Univ., Diss., 2002.

——— CANETTI, ELIAS. SOKEL, WALTER H.: *The love affair with the mother tongue: on the relation between autobiography and novel in Elias Canetti.* [See in No. 43307.]

43254. CARMEL, ALEX. HAUMANN, HEIKO: *Palästina—anders gesehen. Zum Tode von Alex Carmel.* [In]: Kirche und Israel. Neukirchener Theologische Zeitschrift, Jg. 18, H. 1, Neukirchen-Vluyn, 2003. Pp. 74–76. [A.C., orig. Alexander Buchman, 1931 Berlin–Dec. 19, 2002 Haifa, historian, emigr. to Palestine with his parents in 1938.].

43255. CASSIRER, BRUNO & PAUL. FEILCHENFELDT, RAHEL F./BRANDIS, MARKUS: *Paul Cassirer Verlag Berlin 1890–1933.* Eine kommentierte Bibliographie. Bruno und Paul Cassirer Verlag 1898–1901, Paul Cassirer Verlag 1908–1933. München: Saur, 2003. 615 pp., frontis., footnotes. [Incl. short chap. on the history of the two publishing houses.]

43256. CASSIRER, ERNST. *Cassirer und Goethe. Neue Aspekte einer philosophisch-literarischen Wahlverwandtschaft.* Hrsg. von Barbara Naumann und Birgit Recki. Berlin: Akademie Verl., 2002. XX, 225 pp., footnotes, index. [Selected essays: Cassirer's Goethe-Lektüre im Kontext der deutsch-jüdischen Goethe-Rezeption (Gert Mattenklott, 57–74). Prometheus und die "Tragödie der Kultur": Goethe—Simmel—Cassirer (Günter Peters, 113–136). Further essays by Barbara Naumann, Roger H. Stephenson, Ernst Wolfgang Roth, Karl Robert Mandelkow, Hans Günter Dosch, Enno Rudolph, John Michael Krois, Massimo Ferrari, Birgit Recki.]

43257. CASSIRER, ERNST. FERRARI, MASSIMO: *Stationen einer philosophischen Biographie.* Von der Marburger Schule zur Kulturphilosophie. Aus dem Ital. übers. von Marion Lauschke. Hamburg: Meiner, 2003. XVI, 366 pp., footnotes, bibl. (327–358), index. (Cassirer-Forschungen, Bd. 11.) [Incl.: Vorwort zur deutschen Ausgabe (M.F., VII-XVI).]

43258. CASSIRER, ERNST. *Kultur und Symbol.* Ein Handbuch zur Philosophie Ernst Cassirers. In Zusammenarbeit mit Silja Freudenberger, Barend van Heusden, Arend Klaas Jagersma, Martin Plümacher und Wolfgang Wildgen hrsg. von Hans Jörg Sandkühler und Detlev Pätzold. Stuttgart: Metzler, 2003. 336 pp., footnotes, bibl. (309–326), indexes.

43259. CELAN, PAUL. BOHM, ARND: *Landscapes of exile: Celan's "Gespräch im Gebirg".* [In]: The Germanic Review, Vol. 78, No. 2, Washington, Spring 2003. Pp. 99–111, notes.

43260. CELAN, PAUL. *Celan-Jahrbuch 8 (2001/02).* Hrsg. von Hans-Michael Speier. Heidelberg: Winter, 2003. 440 pp., footnotes, bibl. [Selected contribs.: "Aufrechte Worte". Paul Celan—Margarete Susman: eine "Cor-Respondenz" (Lydia Koelle, 7–32; 33–62; followed by the previously unpubl. correspondence 1963–1965). Übersetztes Gedächtnis: Celans Beitrag zu 'Nacht und Nebel' (Ewout van der Knaap, 259–278). Kommentar zu Paul Celans Lesung in Bonn, 17. November 1958 (Jean Firges, 331–334). Paul Celan in Berlin im Dezember 1967 (Marlies Janz, 335–346). Erinnerungen an Paul Celan und Gisèle Celan-Lestrange (Edith Aron, 347–352).]

43261. CELAN, PAUL. HAINZ, MARTIN A.: *'Trojanisches Pferd', negativ, oder: Günther Anders als 'falscher Feind' Paul Celans.* [in]: Arcadia, Int. Zeitschrift für Literaturwissenschaft, Bd. 38, H. 1, Berlin; New York, 2003. Pp. 66–76, footnotes.

43262. CELAN, PAUL. *"Im Geheimnis der Begegnung".* Ingeborg Bachmann und Paul Celan. Hrsg. von Dieter Burdorf. Iserlohn: Institut für Kirche und Gesellschaft, 2003. 100 pp., footnotes. (Tagungsprotokolle—Inst. für Kirche u. Ges.) [Cont. five papers by Dieter Burdorf, Barbara Wiedemann, Lydia Koelle, Andrea Krauß, Luigi Reitani, delivered at a conference in May 2002.]

43263. CELAN, PAUL. WILLIAMS, SCOTT G.: *The Deukalion and Pyrrha myth in Paul Celan and Christoph Ransmayr.* [In]: German Life and Letters, Vol. 56, No. 2, Oxford, 2003. Pp. 142–155, footnotes.

43264. COHEN, HERMANN. ALBERTINI, FRANCESCA: *Das Verständnis des Seins bei Herrmann Cohen.* Vom Neukantianismus zu einer jüdischen Religionsphilosophie. Würzburg: Königshausen & Neumann, 2003. 212 pp., footnotes, bibl., index. (Epistemata: Würzburger wissenschaftliche Schriften, Reihe Philosophie, Bd. 335.) Zugl.: Freiburg (Breisgau), Univ., Diss., 2001.

43265. COHEN, HERMANN. MITTLEMAN, ALAN: *"The Jew in Christian culture" by Hermann Cohen.* An introd. and transl. [In]: Modern Judaism, Vol. 23, No. 1, Oxford, Feb. 2003. Pp. 51–73, notes. [Transl. of Cohen's essay, publ. in 1917.]

43266. COHEN, HERMANN. SIEG, ULRICH: *Der frühe Hermann Cohen und die Völkerpsychologie.* [In]: Aschkenas, Jg. 13, H. 2, Tübingen, 2003. Pp. 461–483, footnotes.

43267. COHEN, HERMANN & CASSIRER, ERNST. DEUSER, HERMANN/MOXTER, MICHAEL, eds.: *Rationalität der Religion und Kritik der Kultur: Hermann Cohen und Ernst Cassirer.* Würzburg: Echter, 2002. 214 pp., footnotes. (Religion der Moderne, Bd. 9.) [Cont. contribs. to a conference in Frankfurt am Main, June 1999; incl.: Vernunft in der Religion—Religion in der Kultur. Hermann Cohens kritische Kulturphilosophie aus den Quellen des Judentums (Helmut Holzhey, 21–38). Also essays by Hans-Ludwig Ollig, Michael Zank, Ze'ev Levy, Micha Brumlik, Oswald Schwemmer, Matthias Jung, Thomas H. Stark, Michael Bongardt, Heinz Paetzold, Eveline Goodman-Thau, Reinhard Margreiter.]

43268. COHEN, HERMANN & CASSIRER, ERNST. MOYNAHAN, GREGORY B.: *Hermann Cohen's 'Das Prinzip der Infinitesimalmethode', Ernst Cassirer, and the politics of science in Wilhelmine Germany.* [In]: Perspectives on Science, Vol. 11, No. 1, Cambridge, MA, 2003. Pp. 55–75, footnotes. [Examines the political relevance of Cohen's philosophy of science in the Wilhelmine era and its changing reception as reflected in the philosophy of Cohen's closest disciple, Ernst Cassirer.]

43269. COHN-BENDIT, DANIEL. STAMER, SABINE: *Cohn-Bendit.* Die Biografie. Hamburg: Europa Verlag, 2001. 288 pp., illus. [D.C.-B., b. April 4, 1945 in Montauban/France to German-Jewish parents from Berlin, politician (Greens), has lived since 1958 in Frankfurt, M.E.P.]

43270. DÖBLIN, ALFRED. *Internationales Alfred-Döblin-Kolloquium Berlin 2001.* Hrsg. von Hartmut Eggert und Gabriele Prauß. Bern; New York: Lang, 2003. 320 pp., footnotes. (Jahrbuch für Internationale Germanistik, Reihe A: Kongressberichte, Bd. 69.) [Cont. 20 essays and a Döblin bibl.]

43271. DÖBLIN, ALFRED. JOOS, HEINZ-DIETER: *Endstation einer Schicksalreise: Alfred Döblins Grab in Housseras.* [In]: Badische Heimat, Jg. 81, H. 1, Freiburg, 2001. Pp. 152–153, illus. [Housseras: nr. Rambervilliers, Département Vosges.]

43272. DÖBLIN, ALFRED. KOEPKE, WULF: *The critical reception of Alfred Döblin's major novels.* Rochester, NY: Camden House, 2003. XII, 249 pp., bibl. (223– 236), notes, index. (Studies in German literature, linguistics and culture.)

——— DOMIN, HILDE. *50 Jahre Woche der Brüderlichkeit.* Eröffnungsveranstaltung der Kölnischen Gesellschaft für Christlich-Jüdische Zusammenarbeit e.V. am 14. April 2002 im Stiftersaal des Wallraf-Richartz-Museums. [See No. 43543.]

43273. DOMIN, HILDE. SCHELLER, WOLF: *Das Wort, das Wirklichkeit sucht. Zum 90. Geburtstag von Hilde Domin.* [In]: Die Politische Meinung, Jg. 48, H. 392. Berlin, 2002. Pp. 94–95.

43274. DRACH, ALBERT. SCHOBEL, EVA: *Albert Drach: Ein wütender Weiser.* Salzburg: Residenz, 2002. 559 pp., illus., facsims., notes (499–526), bibl., index. [A.D., Dec. 17, 1902 Vienna–March 27, 1995 Vienna, for further data see No. 33333/YB XLI.]

43275. EDINGER, TILLY. KOHRING, ROLF/KREFT, GERALD, eds.: *Tilly Edinger. Leben und Werk einer jüdischen Wissenschaftlerin.* Stuttgart: E. Schweizerbart'sche Verlagsbuchhandlung, 2003. 637 pp., frontis., illus., footnotes, bibl., bibl. T.E., indexes. (Senckenberg-Buch Nr. 76.) [Incl.: Tilly Edinger—Stationen ihres Lebens (Rolf Kohring, 21–298). Tilly Edinger: Scientific legacy (Emily Buchholtz, 299–358). Tilly Edinger's deafness (Harry Lang, 359–372). Teaching interlude: Tilly Edinger at Wellesley College (Emily Buchholtz, 373–384). Tilly Edinger im Kontext ihrer deutsch-jüdischen Familiengeschichte (Gerald Kreft, 385–608).] [T.E., Nov. 13, 1897 Frankfurt am Main–May 27, 1967 Cambridge, MA, daughter of the neurologist Ludwig E., founder of paleoneurology, 1921–1938 honorary anatomist at the Senckenberg Museum, 1931–1933 assistant at the Neurologisches Institut, emigr. 1938 via England to the US (Cambridge/MA), co-founder of the Society of Vertebrate Paleontology, long-time editor of its 'News Bulletin'.]

43276. EICHNER, HANS: *Against the grain: selected essays = Gegen den Strich: ausgewählte Aufsätze.* Ed. by Rodney Symington. Bern: Lang, 2003. 411 pp. (Kanadische Studien zur deutschen Sprache und

Literatur/Canadian studies in German language and literature, Bd. 47.) [Previously published essays covering more than 50 years. For data see No. 39566/YB XLVI.]

43277. EINSTEIN, ALBERT. GREEN, JIM, ed.: *Albert Einstein: rebel lives.* Melbourne: Ocean Press, 2003. 88 pp. (Rebel lives series.) [Book concentrates on Einstein's pacifism, anti-nuclear activity and his support for socialism.]

43278. EINSTEIN, ALBERT. HOWARD, DON/STACHEL, JOHN, eds.: *Einstein: The formative years, 1879–1909.* Basel: Birkhäuser, 2000. XIV, 258 pp., illus., index. (Einstein Studies, 8.)

43279. EINSTEIN, ALBERT. JEROME, FRED: *The Einstein file: J. Edgar Hoover's secret war against the world's most famous scientist.* New York: St. Martin's Press, 2002. XXII, 358 pp., illus., notes, bibl., index. [Deals with the FBI's interest in Einstein because of his anti-war activities and socialist leanings.]

43280. EINSTEIN, ALBERT. LEVENSON, THOMAS: *Einstein in Berlin.* New York; London: Bantam, 2003. 486 pp., illus., notes (433–460), bibl., index. [Cf.: An uneasy fit (Cecilia Rothschild) [in]: Aufbau, Vol. 69, No. 13, New York, July 10, 2003, p. 16.]

43281. EINSTEIN, ALBERT. PARKER, BARRY: *Einstein: the passions of a scientist.* New York: Prometheus Books, 2003. 297 pp., illus., gloss., notes, bibl., index. [Deals also with his personal life, his love of music and his anti-war activities.]

43282. EINSTEIN, ALBERT. ROSENKRANZ, ZE'EV: *The Einstein scrapbook.* Baltimore, London: Johns Hopkins Univ. Press, 2002. 199 pp., illus., ports., facsims.

43283. EINSTEIN, ALBERT & MILEVA. ILIC, MIRJANA/KLEINERT, ANDREAS: *"Herzallerliebstes Helenchen". Mileva Einsteins Briefe an Helen Savic.* [In]: Internationale Zeitschrift für Geschichte und Ethik der Naturwissenschaften, Technik und Medizin, Bd. 11, Basel, 2003. Pp. 29–33, notes. [Discusses Milan Popovic: Eine Freundschaft. Briefe von Mileva und Albert Einstein an Helene Savic, 1998 (in Russian, title transl.).]

43284. EINSTEIN, CARL. WURM, CARSTEN: *Carl Einstein: 1885–1940.* Bearb. von Carsten Wurm. Berlin: Stiftung Archiv der Akad. der Künste, 2002. 105 pp., frontis., chronol., bibl. (Findbuch-Editionen.) [Herstellung: Books on Demand, Norderstedt.]

43285. ELIAS, NORBERT: *Engagement und Distanzierung.* Hrsg. und übers. von Michael Schröter. Einleitung übers. von Detlef Bremecke. Frankfurt am Main: Suhrkamp, 2003. 386 pp., notes, bibl., index. (Norbert Elias. Gesammelte Schriften, Bd. 8.) [Incl.: Editorischer Bericht (Johan Heilbron, 372–373). Orig. title: 'Involvement and detachment', publ. 1987.]

43286. ELSAS, JOHN: *Meine Bilder werden immer wilder.* 33 Blätter mit Versen und Zeichnungen. Hrsg. von Marion Herzog-Hoinkis unter Mitarb. von G.H. Herzog. Frankfurt am Main: Insel, 2003. 64 pp., illus., facsims. [Incl.: Nachwort (ed., 39–59).] [J.E., orig. Jonas Mayer E., July 6, 1851 Frankfurt am Main–June 5, 1935 Frankfurt am Main, banker, stockbroker, began a painting career in his seventies; in 1999 his collection was given to the Stiftung für schweizerische naive Kunst und art brut St. Gallen, Museum im Lagerhaus.]

43287. FABIAN, WALTER. OPPERMANN, DETLEF: *Walter Fabian (1902–1992). Journalist—Pädagoge—Gewerkschafter.* [In]: Gewerkschaftliche Monatshefte, Jg. 54, H. 7, Düsseldorf, 2003. Pp. 409–420, footnotes. [W.F., Aug. 24, 1902 Berlin–Feb. 1992 Cologne, Social Democrat (SAPD), fled 1933 to Switzerland, later via Prague to France, 1942 escaped illegally to Switzerland, from 1961 settled permanently in Germany, 1957–1917 editor-in-chief of 'Gewerkschaftliche Monatshefte'.]

43288. FACKENHEIM, EMIL. KRELL, MARC A.: *Post-Holocaust vs. postmodern: Emil Fackenheim's evolving dialogue with Christianity.* [In]: The Journal of Jewish Thought and Philosophy, Vol. 12, No. 1, London, April 2003. Pp. 69–96, notes.

43289. FECHENBACH-FEY, IRMA. SCHÄFER, INGRID: *Jüdin—Sozialistin—Emigrantin 1895–1973.* Lemgo: Inst. für Lippische Landeskunde, 2003. 432 pp., illus., notes, chronol. (Lippische Studien,

Bd. 19.) [I.F.-F. née Epstein, Oct. 16, 1895 Augsburg–Dec. 1973 Dietikon, Switzerland, nurse, Social Democrat, co-founder of Reichsarbeitsgemeinschaft der Kinderfreunde, wife of Felix Fechenbach (shot in 1933), in 1933 fled from Detmold to Switzerland, emigr. 1946 to the US, 1956 returned to Switzerland.]

43290. FEDERN, ERNST & HILDE. KUSCHEY, BERNHARD: *Die Ausnahme des Überlebens. Ernst und Hilde Federn.* Eine biographische Studie und eine Analyse der Binnenstruktur des Konzentrationslagers. Gießen: Psychosozial Verlag, 2003. 2 vols., 1082 pp., illus., facsims., footnotes, docs., bibl. (1040–1064), index. (edition psychosozial.) [Vol. 1 deals with the family background of Ernst Federn and of Hilde, his wife, daughter of a Jewish mother and a non-Jewish father; with their illegal political campaign as members of a Trotskyite group in Vienna 1934–1938; with the imprisonment of E.F. in Dachau and Buchenwald. Vol. 2 deals with Buchenwald in general, and E.F.'s personal recollections.] [E.F., b. Aug. 26, 1914 in Vienna, Social Democrat, historian of psychoanalysis, founder and teacher of psychoanalytical social work, imprisoned between March 1937 and Sept. 1938 in Dachau, thereafter until April 1945 in Buchenwald, after liberation went to Brussels, emigr. 1948 to the US, remigr. to Vienna 1972.]

43291. FEUCHTWANGER, LUDWIG: *Gesammelte Aufsätze zur jüdischen Geschichte.* Hrsg. und mit einem Nachwort versehen von Rolf Rieß. Berlin: Duncker & Humblot, 2003. 249 pp., frontis., illus., footnotes, bibl. L.F. (166–189), bibl. (226–242), indexes. [Incl.: Geleitwort (Michael Brenner, 5–6). Nachwort des Herausgebers (190–225; on life and work of L.F.; incl. numerous letters addressed to his brother Lion F.). Essays are arranged under the sections: I. Moses Mendelssohn. II. Jüdische Geschichte und Rechtsgeschichte in Bayern, Österreich und England. III. Zeitfragen im Angesicht des Nationalsozialismus.] [Cf.: Im Schatten des Bruders. Eine Aufsatzsammlung bewahrt Ludwig Feuchtwanger vor dem Vergessen (Irene Preisinger) [in]: Tribüne, Jg. 42, H. 167, Frankfurt am Main, 2003, pp. 66–71.] [L.F., Nov. 28, 1885 Munich–July 17, 1947 Winchester, England, jurist, historian, 1914–1933 director of the publishing house Duncker & Humblot, 1933–1938 editor of the Bayerisches Israelitisches Gemeindeblatt, emigr. in 1939 to the UK.]

43292. FRANKL, VIKTOR. PYTELL, T.E.: *Redeeming the unredeemable: Auschwitz and 'Man's search for meaning.'* [In]: Holocaust and Genocide Studies, Vol. 17, No. 1, Oxford, Spring 2003. Pp. 89–112, notes. [Deals with Viktor Frankl and his 1967 book "Man's search for meaning" (1967).] [V.F., data see No. 36992/YB XLIV.]

43293. FREUD, SIGMUND. BERNSTEIN, RICHARD J.: *Freud und das Vermächtnis des Moses.* Aus dem Engl. von Dirk Westerkamp. Berlin: Philo, 2003. 244 pp., notes (191–224), bibl., indexes. [Chap. 3 is entitled: Antisemitismus, Christentum und Judentum (123–144). For orig. edn. see No. 38104/YB XLV.]

43294. FREUD, SIGMUND. LIPPMAN, ROBERT L.: *Freud, the law, and Michelangelo's Moses.* [In]: Midstream, Vol. 49, No. 1, New York, Jan. 2003. Pp. 32– 35, notes. [Discusses Freud's visit to Rome and the impact of Michelangelo's statue on his view of Moses and Jewish law.]

43295. FREUD, SIGMUND. SAID, EDWARD: *Freud and the non-European.* With an introd. by Christopher Bollas and a response by Jacqueline Rose. Publ. in assoc. with the Freud Museum, London. London: Verso, 2003. 84 pp., port., notes. [Based on a talk given at the Freud Museum, incl. Freud's relationship to Judaism and his interest in other cultures.]

43296. FRIEDMANN, FRIEDRICH GEORG. GÄSSLER, SUSANNE: *Die Entdeckung der menschlichen Würde. Jüdische Lebenswelt und humanistische Lebensgestaltung bei Friedrich Georg Friedmann.* Münster: Lit Verl., 2002. 214 pp., footnotes, bibl. (Forum Christen und Juden, Bd. 2.) Zugl.: Augsburg, Univ., Diss., 2002. [F.G.F., data see No. 40697/YB XLVII.]

43297. GERNSHEIM, FRIEDRICH. BROCKE, MICHAEL: *Nach rückwärts und vorwärts Freiheit bewahren. Der Komponist Friedrich Gernsheim.* [In]: Kalonymos, Jg. 6, H. 4, Duisburg, 2003. Pp. 5–12, illus. [F.G., July 17, 1839 Worms–Sept. 1916 Berlin, composer, conductor.]

43298. GIORDANO, RALPH. MERTEN, JOLA: *Ein Citoyen und radikaler Moralist.* Ralph Giordano erhielt den Leo-Baeck-Preis des Zentralrats. [In]: Jüdische Allgemeine, Jg. 58, Nr. 20, Berlin, 25. Sept.

2003. P. 2. [Also, in this issue, excerpts from speeches made on the occasion by Paul Spiegel, Charlotte Knobloch, and R.G.]

43299. GIORDANO, RALPH. ROMBERG, OTTO R.: *Beharrlichkeit und Friedenswillen.* Der Leo-Baeck-Preis 2003 ging an Ralph Giordano. [In]: Tribüne, Jg. 42, H. 168, Frankfurt am Main, 2003. Pp. 18–27.

43300. GIORDANO, RALPH: *Ralph Giordano zum 80. Geburtstag.* [Issue title of] Europäische Ideen, H. 127, Berlin [Sterckmannweg 23, c/o D. Gissler], 2003. 32 pp., frontis. [Incl. several texts by R.G.; for bibl. of his works, compiled by Martin Rooney, see No. 128 (14–16). Also, by R.G.: Essay zum 9. November. "Warum ich in Deutschland geblieben bin" [in]: tachles, Jg. 3, Nr. 45, Zürich, 7. Nov. 2003. Pp. 28–30 (address given on the occasion of the award of the "Leo-Baeck-Preis" in Berlin, Sept. 17, 2003).]

43301. GLÜCKEL VON HAMELN. DAVIS, NATALIE ZEMON: *Mit Gott rechten: Das Leben der Glikl bas Judah Leib, genannt Glückel von Hameln.* Aus dem Amerik. von Wolfgang Kaiser. Berlin: Wagenbach, 2003. 175 pp., illus. (Wagenbach Taschenbuch, 485.) [Orig. publ. as part of 'Women on the margins: three seventeenth-century lives', 1995; see No. 33365/YB XLI.]

43302. GOITEIN, SHLOMO DOV (FRITZ). ORMSBY, ERIC: *The "born Schulmeister".* [In]: The New Criterion, Vol. 22, No. 1, New York, Sept. 2003. Pp. 30–36. [S.D.G., April 3, 1900 Burgkundstadt–Feb. 6, 1985 Princeton, islamicist, biblical scholar, palaeographer, ethnologist, Hebrew poet and playwright, prof. at the Hebrew Univ., later at the Univ. of Pennsylvania and the Inst. for Advanced Study at Princeton, in 1923 emigr., together with Gershom Scholem, to Palestine, in 1957 emigr. to the US.]

43303. GOLDSTEIN, MORITZ. UBBENS, IRMTRAUD: *Aus meiner Sprache verbannt: Moritz Goldstein, ein deutsch-jüdischer Journalist und Schriftsteller im Exil.* München: Saur, 2002. 284 pp., chronol., notes (264–273), bibl., illus. (X-XXVI). (Dortmunder Beiträge zur Zeitungsforschung, Bd. 59.) [Incl. about 50 articles by M.G. in exile publications, written between 1939 and 1952.]

43304. GRAB, WALTER. KESSLER, MARIO: *Jakobinismus, Demokratie und Arbeiterbewegung: Der Historiker Walter Grab.* [In]: Jahrbuch für Forschungen/Beiträge zur Geschichte der Arbeiterbewegung, Berlin, Jan. 2002. Pp. 55–68. [About the name of the periodical see No. 43460.]

43305. GRAETZ, HEINRICH. REUVEN, MICHAEL: *Hirsch (Heinrich) Graetz: The historian of the Jewish people.* [In Hebrew.] Jerusalem: Mossad Bialik; LBI Jerusalem, 2003. 218 pp., index.

43306. GUMBEL, EMIL JULIUS. VOGT, ANNETTE: *Emil Julius Gumbel im Interview.* Berlin: Max-Planck-Institut für Wissenschaftsgeschichte, 2002. 12, 3 pp., port., footnotes. [First publ. of an interview with E.J. G. broadcast in Spring 1959 by Radio Bremen.]

——— HALLGARTEN, CHARLES. LUSTIGER, ARNO, ed.: *Charles Hallgarten.* Leben und Wirken des Frankfurter Sozialreformers und Philanthropen. Mit Beiträgen von Jens Friedemann [et al.] und einem Vorwort von Klaus Töpfer. [See No. 42343.]

43307. HALPERT, INGE. *The Germanic Review.* Vol. 78, No. 1 [with the issue title] *A Festschrift to Inge Halpert*, Washington, DC, Winter 2003. Editor: Mark M. Anderson. Pp. 3–92, notes. [Selected essays: Introduction (ed., 3–6). A personal tribute (Ellin Feld, 7). The way we were: reminiscences of Columbia's German Department (Guy Stern, 13–19). The silent generation? Jewish refugee students, "Germanistik", and Columbia University (ed., 20–38). The love affair with the mother tongue: on the relation between autobiography and novel in Elias Canetti (Walter H. Sokel, 39–48). A musical drama as cultural catalyst: the byways of Kurt Weill's 'Der Weg der Verheißung' (Guy Stern, 49–54). Further essays are listed according to subject.] [I.H., b. in Berlin to a Jewish mother and a non-Jewish father, emigr. 1941 to the US via Austria, France and Spain, prof. of German at Columbia Univ., editor of 'The Germanic Review' from 1984 until 1996.]

43308. HAMBURGER, KÄTE. *Käte Hamburger. Zur Aktualität einer Klassikerin.* Hrsg. von Johanna Bossinade und Angelika Schaser. Göttingen: Wallstein, 2003. 220 pp., ports., footnotes. (Querelles, Jahrbuch für Frauen- und Geschlechterforschung 2003/Bd. 8.) [Cont. 11 essays, eight children's tales by K.H. and bio-bibl. of K.H. (209–214); selected essays: Remigration und Wissenschaftspolitik (Christa Kersting, 50–71). Käte Hamburger im Kontext ihrer jüdischen Verhältnisse (Gert Mattenklott, 72–82).] [K.H., Sept. 21, 1896 Hamburg–April 8, 1992 Stuttgart, philosopher, literary scholar, lived and worked as a private scholar in Hamburg and Berlin until 1933, 1934–1956 in Göteborg, remigr. to Stuttgart, lecturer and prof. at the TH Stuttgart 1957–1976.]

43309. HARDEN, MAXIMILIAN. NEUMANN, HELGA: *Maximilian Harden (1861–1927): Ein unerschrockener deutsch-jüdischer Kritiker und Publizist.* Würzburg: Königshausen und Neumann, 2003. 214 pp., frontis., illus., footnotes, bibl. [Incl. a chap. entitled 'Die Judenfrage'.] [M.H., orig. Felix Ernst Witkowski, 1861 Berlin–1927 Berlin, publicist, editor of 'Die Zukunft'.]

43310. HEIDENHEIM, MORITZ. FRANZ-KLAUSER, OLIVIA: *Moritz Heidenheim—Ein vergessener Gelehrter.* [In]: Kirche und Israel. Neukirchener Theologische Zeitschrift, Jg. 18, H. 1, Neukirchen-Vluyn, 2003. Pp. 31–34, notes. [M.H., Oct. 23, 1824 Worms–Oct. 12 1898 Zurich, lecturer in Rabbinic Theology and Literature at Zurich Univ., lived from 1864 in London becoming an Anglican chaplain.]

43311. HEINE, HEINRICH. FÜLLNER, KARIN: *"Ja, Zuckererbsen für Jedermann". Kulinarische Metaphorik in Heines Texten.* [In]: StadtLandFluß. Urbanität und Regionalität in der Moderne. Festschrift für Gertrude Cepl-Kaufmann zum sechzigsten Geburtstag [see No. 43138]. Pp. 631–641, notes.

43312. HEINE, HEINRICH. HAUSCHILD, JAN-CHRISTOPH/WERNER, MICHAEL: *Heinrich Heine.* München: Deutscher Taschenbuch Verlag, 2002. 159 pp., frontis., illus., chronol., bibl., index. Orig.-ausgabe (dtv portrait.) [Biography.]

43313. HEINE, HEINRICH. *Heine-Jahrbuch 2003.* Jg. 42. Hrsg. von Joseph A. Kruse, Heinrich-Heine-Institut der Landeshauptstadt Düsseldorf. Stuttgart: Metzler, 2003. 292 pp., illus., notes. [Incl. essays, speeches, reviews and reports; also a bibl. of recent publs. on H.H. (259–278); selected essays: Exil auf Erden. Facetten einer Zumutung in Heines Spätwerk (Olaf Briese, 14–36). Vergessenheit und Instrumentalisierung. Die deutsche Heine-Rezeption im ersten Nachkriegsjahrzehnt (Jörg Bernig, 105–123). "Schickt einen Philosophen nach London; bey Leibe keinen Poeten!" Heinrich Heine und Georg Christoph Lichtenberg (Sikander Singh, 140–149). Das verleugnete Heine-Porträt. Eine Dokumentation (Gerhart Söhn, 158–163; on a portrait by Isidor Popper of 1843, bought in 1969 by the author's art gallery in Oxford, now in the Heine-Institut).]

43314. HEINE, HEINRICH. KISS, ENDRE/LICHTMANN, TAMÁS, eds.: *Heine (1797–1856).* Debrecen: Kossuth Egyetemi K., 2002. 334 pp. (Német filológiai tanulmányok, 26.) [Cont. contribs. to a conference held in 1997 in Hungary.]

43315. HEINE, HEINRICH. KORTLÄNDER, BERND: *Heinrich Heine.* Stuttgart: Philipp Reclam jun., 2003. 367 pp., illus., bibl. [On H.s life and work.]

43316. HEINE, HEINRICH. *Rezensionen und Notizen zu Heines Werken aus den Jahren 1846 bis 1848.* Hrsg. und eingel. von Sikander Singh. Stuttgart: Metzler, 2003. XXXVII, 747 pp., illus. (Heinrich Heines Werk im Urteil seiner Zeitgenossen, Bd. 9; Heine-Studien.)

43317. HERZ, HENRIETTE. GOOZÉ, MARJANNE E.: *Posing for posterity: the representations and portrayals of Henriette Herz as "beautiful Jewess".* [In]: Amsterdamer Beiträge zur neueren Germanistik, Bd. 55, Amsterdam; New York, 2003. Pp. 67–95, ports., footnotes.

43318. HESSEL, FRANZ. NIERADKA, MAGALI LAURE: *Der Meister der leisen Töne. Biographie des Dichters Franz Hessel.* Oldenburg: Igel, 2003. 231 pp., footnotes, bibl. (211–231). (Literatur- und Medienwissenschaft, Bd. 91.) [Incl. an interview with Stéphane Hessel.] [F.H., 1880–1941, for further data see No. 40534/YB XLVII.]

43319. HEYM, STEFAN. HAHN, REGINA U.: *The democratic dream: Stefan Heym in America.* Bern; New York: Lang, 2003. 148 pp., bibl. (133–146). (Exile studies, Vol. 10.)

43320. HEYM, STEFAN. HUTCHINSON, PETER/ZACHAU, REINHARD K., eds.: *Stefan Heym: Socialist—dissenter—Jew/Stefan Heym: Sozialist—Dissident—Jude.* Oxford; New York: Lang, 2003. 220 pp., footnotes. [Incl. contribs. on various aspects of St.H.'s biography and work, his exile years in the US; also on the reception of his writings in West Germany, by the eds., Martin Kane, Herbert Krämer, Meg Tait, Gregory L. Ketcham, Marc Temme, Thomas C. Fox, Christine Cosentino, Claude D. Conter, Hans-Peter Ecker.]

43321. HEYM, STEFAN: *Offene Worte in eigener Sache.* Gespräche, Reden, Essays 1989–2001. Ausgew. und hrsg. von Inge Heym [et al.]. München: btb/Goldmann, 2003. 258 pp.

43322. HIRSCHBERGER, FRITZ. FEINSTEIN, STEPHEN C., ed.: *Fritz Hirschberger: the sur-rational Holocaust paintings.* Minneapolis: Univ. of Minnesota, Center for Holocaust Studies, 2002. 73 pp., illus., bibl. [Catalogue of an exhibition first shown at the Univ. of Minnesota in 2002, and from Nov. 2003–Feb. 2004 at the Florida Holocaust Museum, St.Petersburg, comprising 40 paintings representing Holocaust themes.] [F.H., b. 1912 in Dresden, deported to Poland in 1938, joined the Polish Army in 1939, later the Free Polish Army, went to the US in 1947, lives in San Francisco.]

43323. HIRSCHFELD, MAGNUS. WEINTHAL, BENJAMIN: *The legacy of Magnus Hirschfeld.* [In]: Aufbau, Vol. 64, No. 11, New York, June 5, 2003. P. 6, port.

43324. HOCHWÄLDER, FRITZ: *Holocaust: a court for the dead.* Transl. from the German by Henry and Ruth W. Gerlach. Riverside, CA: Ariadne Press, 2003. 118 pp. [Orig. title of the three-act play: Holokaust (Totengericht); first publ. in 1998 (Graz: Styria, with an epilogue by Martin Esslin). Based on historical facts, deals with the dilemma of Jewish leaders involved in selecting fellow Jews for deportation in Budapest, 1944.] [F.H. 1911, Vienna–1986, Zurich, playwright.] [Cf.: Fritz Hochwälder's Holokaust: a choice of evils (Judith Beniston) [in]: Austrian Studies, Vol. 11, No. 1, London, Sept. 2003, pp. 65–84, notes.]

43325. HOLLAENDER, FRIEDRICH. *Literatur zum Gebrauch: Hollaender und andere.* Beiträge zu einer Kulturgeschichte der Weimarer Republik. Hrsg. von Walter Delabar und Carsten Würmann. Berlin: Weidler, 2002. 289 pp., illus. (Juni, Magazin für Literatur und Politik, 2002.) [Incl. contribs. on F.H. by the eds. and Gregor Ackermann, Viktor Rotthaler, Christiane Hackl, Bruno Franceschini, Tillmann Rammstedt, Astrid Freyeisen et al.; also texts by F.H.]

43326. HORKHEIMER, MAX. SEEMANN, BIRGIT: *"... die Hoffnung auf Gerechtigkeit".* Zum 30. Todestag von Max Horkheimer (1895–1973). [In]: Tribüne, Jg. 42, H. 166, Frankfurt am Main, 133–142, bibl.

43327. HUSSERL, EDMUND. WELTON, DON, ed.: *The new Husserl: a critical reader.* Bloomington, Indiana Univ. Press, 2003. XXV, 334 pp., illus., notes, bibl., index. [E.H., 1858 Prossnitz, Moravia–1938 Freiburg/Brsg., philosopher (baptised).]

43328. JACOB, MATHILDE. LUBAN, OTTOKAR: *Mathilde Jacob: Mehr als Rosa Luxemburgs Sekretärin. Mit dem Text von M. Jacobs einziger öffentlicher Rede (19.12.1820).* [In]: JahrBuch für Forschungen zur Geschichte der Arbeiterbewegung III, Berlin, Sept. 2002. Pp. 110–128, notes.

43329. JANOWITZ FAMILY. SCHARTNER, IRMGARD: *Heute vergessen: Otto, Hans und Franz Janowitz und ihre Verbundenheit mit Karl Kraus.* [In]: Zwischenwelt, Jg. 20, Nr. 2, Wien, Sept. 2003. Pp. 46–54, illus., notes. [On members of a German-speaking family from Podebrad nr. Prague.]

43330. JONAS, HANS. *Hans Jonas: 1903–1933–2003.* [Issue title of] Synthesis Philosophica, Vol. 18, No. 1–2, Zagreb, 2003. 415 pp., footnotes. [Incl. 15 contribs. (3–340; in German) on Hans Jonas and his philosophy by Hrvoje Juric, Vittorio Hösle, Franz Josef Wetz, Christian Wiese, Jens Peter Brune, Frank Vogelsang, Hans Lenk, Karen Joisten, Mirko Wischke, Dietrich Böhler, Horst Gronke, Micha H. Werner.]

43331. JONAS, HANS. MÜLLER, ERICH WOLFGANG, ed.: *Hans Jonas—Von der Gnosisforschung zur Verantwortungsethik.* Mit Beiträgen von Wilhelm Büttemeyer [et al.]. Stuttgart: Kohlhammer, 2003.

243 pp., notes. (Judentum und Christentum, Bd. 10.) [Cont.: Vom Schüler Heideggers und Bultmanns zum Verantwortungsethiker (ed., 9–24). 14 essays on different aspects of H.J.'s philosophy, based on lectures at Oldenburg Univ., 2001/2002.]

43332. JONAS, HANS. WIESE, CHRISTIAN: *Hans Jonas. "Zusammen Philosoph und Jude".* Essay. Frankfurt am Main: Jüdischer Verlag, 2003. 183 pp., notes (167–183). [Deals with the Jewish dimension in the biography and philosophy of H.J. Incl. the friendship and discussions with Gershom Scholem, Hannah Arendt and the Eichmann debate.]

43334. KAFKA, FRANZ. BINDER, HARTMUT: *"nachdem der Handschlag auf die deutsche Gesinnung geleistet worden ...". Kafka in der "Lese- und Redehalle".* [In]: Else Lasker-Schüler-Jahrbuch zur Klassischen Moderne, Bd. 2, Trier, 2003. Pp. 160–207, footnotes.

43335. KAFKA, FRANZ. DIAMANT, KATHI: *Kafka's last love: the mystery of Dora Diamant.* London: Secker & Warburg, 2003. XIV, 402 pp., illus., ports., notes, bibl. (387–393), index. [D.D., 1902 Poland–1952 Great Britain, actress, met Kafka in Berlin in 1923 and was his companion until his death.]

43336. KAFKA, FRANZ. *"Erst im Chor mag eine gewisse Wahrheit liegen ...". Zur Konstruktion von Vielfalt und Fremde im Werk von Franz Kafka.* Hrsg. von Rüdiger Sareika. Iserlohn: Inst. für Kirche und Gesellschaft Iserlohn, 2003. 137 pp., footnotes. (Tagungsprotokolle—Inst. für Kirche und Gesellschaft.) [Incl. eight essays, one on Martin Buber.]

43337. KAFKA, FRANZ. *Kafka and the theater.* [Issue title of] The Germanic Review, Vol. 78, No. 3, Washington DC, Summer 2003. 1 issue. [Guest editor: Martin Puchner. Cont. the sections: Introduction (Martin Puchner, 163–166). I. Kafka and the theater (167–193; contribs. by Mark M. Anderson, Martin Puchner). II. The theater in Kafka (194–249; contribs. by Wolf Kittler (in German), Klaus Mladek). III. Kafka on the New York stage.]

443339. KAFKA, FRANZ. *Kafkas Fabriken.* [Issue title of] Marbacher Magazin, No. 100. Bearb. von Hans-Gerd Koch und Klaus Wagenbach unter Mitarbeit von Klaus Hermsdorf, Peter Ulrich Lehner und Benno Wagner. Marbach: Deutsche Schillergesellschaft, 2002. 162 pp., frontis., illus., facsims., plan. [Catalogue of exhibition in Marbach with the same title, Nov. 2002–Feb. 2003. Deals with Kafka's work as a clerk with the "Arbeiter-Unfall-Versicherungs-Anstalt" and social conditions in Bohemian factories.]

43340. KAFKA, FRANZ. NEKULA, MAREK: *Franz Kafkas tschechische Lektüre im Kontext.* [In]: Bohemia, Bd. 43, H. 2, 2002, München, 2003. Pp. 350–384, footnotes. [Deals with K.'s good knowledge of Czech and Czech literature. Incl. Engl. summary.]

43341. KAFKA, FRANZ. ZISCHLER, HANNS: *Kafka goes to the movies.* Transl. by Susan H. Gillespie. Chicago: Univ. of Chicago Press, 2003. 143 pp., illus., filmography, bibl., index. [For orig. German edn. see No. 34462/YB XLII.]

43342. KALEKO, MASCHA. NOLTE, ANDREAS: *"Mir ist zuweilen so als ob das Herz in mir zerbrach".* Leben und Werk Mascha Kalékos im Spiegel ihrer sprichwörtlichen Dichtung. Bern; New York: Lang, 2003. 327 pp., illus., footnotes, bibl., index. (Sprichwörterforschung, Bd. 23.) [M.K. née Golda Malka Aufen, June 7, 1907 Schidlow, Galicia–Jan. 21, 1975 Zurich, poet, lived from 1917 in Germany, mostly in Berlin, 1928 married the Russian-Jewish philologist Saul K., 1938 the musician Chemjo Vinaver, emigr. 1938 to New York, lived from 1966 in Jerusalem.]

43343. KALISCH, ARNOLD. BORRIES, MARIA VON:... *einer der aktivsten deutschen Pazifisten. Arnold Kalisch.* Eine Dokumentation. Bramsche: Rasch Verl., 2003. 212 pp., illus., facsims., docs., footnotes. [A.K., Jan. 22, 1882 Berlin–Oct. 29, 1957 Copenhagen, jurist, 1933 fled to Denmark, imprisoned by Gestapo Feb. 1943, freed by the Danish resistance and brought to safety in Sweden, Oct. 1943, after the war returned to Copenhagen.]

43344. KATZ, JACOB. *The pride of Jacob: essays on Jacob Katz and his work.* Ed. by Jay M. Harris. Cambridge, MA: Harvard Univ. Press, 2002. 180 pp., footnotes. [Cont.: Preface (Jay M. Harris,

7–8). Rebel in Frankfurt: the scholarly origins of Jacob Katz (David N. Myers, 9–27). Jacob Katz on Halakhah and Kabbalah (Israel Ta-Shma, 29–39). Jacob Katz on Jews and Christians in the Middle Ages (David Berger, 41–63). Early modern Ashkenaz in the writings of Jacob Katz (Elisheva Carlebach, 65–83). Jacob Katz as social historian (Paula E. Hyman, 85–96). Jacob Katz on the origins and dimensions of Jewish modernity: the centrality of the German experience (David Ellenson, 97–123). How central was anti-semitism to the historical writing of Jacob Katz (Richard I. Cohen, 125–140). A Hungarian rhapsody in blue: Jacob Katz's tardy surrender to Hagar's allure (Michael K. Silber, 141–161). Jacob Katz on Halakhah, Orthodoxy, and history (Moshe Halbertal, 163–172). Jacob Katz as a dissertation advisor (Immanuel Etkes, 173–180).]

43345. KATZ, JACOB. PORAT, DAN A.: *One historian, two histories: Jacob Katz and the formation of a national Israeli identity.* [In]: Jewish Social Studies, Vol. 9, No. 3, Bloomington, IN, Spring/Summer, 2003. Pp. 56–75, notes.

43346. KAUFMANN, HANS. FUHRMANN, MANFRED: *Aus der Bahn geworfen. Stationen des jüdischen Theatermannes Dr. Hans Kaufmann.* Mit einem Geleitwort von Martin Walser. Bielefeld: Aisthesis, 2003. 132 pp., illus. (Sonderveröff. des Naturwissenschaftlichen und Historischen Vereins für das Land Lippe, Bd. 70.) [H.K. 1876 Charlottenburg–1957 Detmold, theatre director, survived the Second World War in the Detmold area, helped by the author's parents.]

43347. KLEINOVA, ELISKA. AMBROS, PETER: *Leben vom Blatt gespielt. Eine dramatische Lebenspartitur.* Dresden: Thelem, 2003. (Lesecher ... Judentum in Mitteleuropa, Bd. 2.) [Based on tapes recorded in 1994, author describes the life of Eliska Kleinová, 1912 Prerau/Moravia as Elisabeth Klein–1999 Prague, piano teacher, author of 'Die Klavierschule des Blattspiels', sister of composer and pianist Gideon Klein, in Theresienstadt married and divorced the composer Hans Krása, after liberation from a satellite camp of Auschwitz returned to Prague.]

43348. KLEMPERER, VICTOR. LANDT, SÖNKE: *Faschismuskritik aus dem Geist des Nationalismus. Victor Klemperers antifaschistische Sprachkritik.* Bremen: Asta Univ. Bremen, 2002. 30 pp., footnotes, bibl. (Schriftenreihe zu Bildung & Wissenschaft des Asta Uni Bremen, Bd. 5.)

43349. KLEMPERER, VICTOR. WATT, RODERICK H.: *'Ich triumphiere sozusagen': the publication history of Victor Klemperer's 'Zion-Kapitel' in LTI (1947–1957).* [In]: German Life and Letters, Vol. 56, No. 2, Oxford, April 2003. Pp. 132–141, footnotes. [Deals with K.'s post-war reinstatement in East Germany and the accommodations he had to make with the regime, as illustrated in the chap. on Zionism in his book LTI: Notizbuch eines Philologen, first publ. in the former GDR.]

43350. KNEPLER, GEORG. GÖLLNER, RENATE/SCHEIT, GERHARD: *"... bestünde Lieb' und Bruderbund"—Georg Knepler zum Gedächtnis.* Ein Nachruf. [In]: Zwischenwelt, Jg. 19, Nr. 4, Wien, Feb. 2003. Pp. 27–28, port. [Obit. is followed by: "Also Raunzen können die Engländer überhaupt nicht". Aus einem Interview mit Georg Knepler über Widerstand, Antisemitismus und Exil (28–35, facsims.; interview with Gerhard Scheit, May 1992 in Berlin); also an excerpt from Knepler's book on Mozart, publ. 1991 (36–38).] [G.K., Dec. 21, 1906 Vienna–Jan. 14, 2003 Berlin, conductor, musicologist, Communist, emigr. in the 1930s to the UK, remigr. 1946 to Vienna, 1949 went to Berlin (East).]

43351. KOERNER, HENRY. BALAS, EDITH: *The early work of Henry Koerner.* Exhibition at the Frick Art and Historical Center, Sept. 13–Nov. 9, 2003 in Pittsburgh. Pittsburgh: Frick Art and Historical Center, 2003. 85 pp., illus., port. [H.K., 1915 Vienna–1991 Pittsburgh, painter, graphic designer, emigr. via Italy to the US in 1938, returned to Germany in 1945 with the US army, commissioned to sketch Nazi war criminals at the Nuremberg trials; settled in Pittsburgh 1953.]

43352. KOHN, HEDWIG. WINNEWISSER, BRENDA P.: *Hedwig Kohn—eine Physikerin des zwanzigsten Jahrhunderts.* Von den Nazis vertrieben, emigrierte die dritte habilitierte Physikerin von Breslau in die USA. [In]: Physik Journal, Jg. 2, Nr. 11, Weinheim, 2003. Pp. 51–55, illus., notes. [Also, by same author: The emigration of Hedwig Kohn, physicist, 1940 [in]: Mitteilungen, Österreichische Ges. für Wissenschaftsgesch., Jg. 18, Wien, 1998. Pp. 41–58, footnotes.] [H.K., April 5, 1887 Breslau–1964 Durham, NC, Prof. of Physics at Wellesley College and Duke Univ., emigr. in 1940 to the US.]

43353. KOLMAR, GERTRUD. Struck, Hanna: *"Ich liebe dich, mein Volk".* Vor 60 Jahren wurde Gertrud Kolmar in Auschwitz ermordet. [In]: Tribüne, Jg. 42, H. 165, Frankfurt am Main, 2003. Pp. 69–72.

43354. KOMPERT, LEOPOLD. Wittemann, M. Theresia: *"Dem deutschen Volke schrieb ich zu Dank ...". Die späte Wiederentdeckung des böhmisch-jüdischen Autors Leopold Kompert (1822–1886).* [In]: Stifter-Jahrbuch, N.F., Jg. 16, München, 2002. Pp. 66–94.

43355. KRACAUER, SIEGFRIED. Reil, Harald: *Siegfried Kracauers Jacques Offenbach: Biographie, Geschichte, Zeitgeschichte.* New York; Frankfurt am Main: Lang, 2003. VI, 159 pp., bibl. (Exil-Studien, Vol. 5.) [On 'Jacques Offenbach und das Paris seiner Zeit', first publ. in Amsterdam, 1937; American edn.: Jacques Offenbach and the Paris of his time. Transl. by Gwenda David and Eric Mosbacher. Foreword by Gertrud Koch. New York: Zone Books, 2002. 418 pp., illus.]

43357. KRACAUER, SIEGFRIED. Stalder, Helmut: *Siegfried Kracauer. Das journalistische Werk in der 'Frankfurter Zeitung' 1921–1933.* Würzburg: Königshausen & Neumann, 2003. VIII, 302 pp., footnotes, bibl. (Epistemata, Würzburger wissenschaftliche Schriften, Bd. 348.)

43358. KRAUS, HERTHA. Schirrmacher, Gerd: *Hertha Kraus—zwischen den Welten. Biographie einer Sozialwissenschaftlerin und Quäkerin (1897–1968).* Frankfurt am Main; New York: Lang, 2003. 665 pp., illus., footnotes, bibl. (621–656), index. [H.K., Sept. 11, 1897 Prague–May 16, 1968 Haverford, PA, conversion to Protestantism in 1914, later member of the Quakers, director of the Social Welfare Dept. in Cologne 1923–1933, emigr. in 1933 to the US, Prof. of Social Sciences at Bryn Mawr College, PA.]

43359. KRAUS, KARL. Rothe, Friedrich: *Karl Kraus. Die Biographie.* Mit 49 Abbildungen. München: Piper, 2003. 423 pp., frontis., notes (391–410), index. [Incl. a chap. entitled: Ein "jüdischer Antisemit"? (121–170).] [Cf.: Karl Kraus und die Folgen. Friedrich Rothe schreibt ein spannendes Zeitbild der "Fackel" (Willi Jasper) [in]: Zeitliteratur [Beilage von] Die Zeit, Jg. 58, Nr. 42, Hamburg, Okt. 2003, p. 28. Neue Lockerungen (Hans-Christian Kosler) [in]: 'NZZ', Nr. 35, Zürich, 12. Feb. 2004, p. 35, port. Wie der Menschenfresser zum Oberlehrer wurde (Burkhard Müller) [in]: Süddeutsche Zeitung, Nr. 198, München, 29. Aug. 2003, p. 16.]

43360. KRAUS, KARL. Scheichl, Sigurd Paul: *Karl Kraus und der Halsmann-Prozeß.* [In]: Zeitgeschichte, Jg. 30, H. 2, Salzburg, März/April, 2003. Pp. 106–111. [On the Halsmann case see No. 41079/YB XLVIII.]

43361. Kuh, Anton: *Der unsterbliche Österreicher.* Hrsg. und mit einem Vorwort von Ulrich N. Schulenburg. Wien: Löcker, 2001. 384 pp. [An anthology of contribs. to newspapers and periodicals publ. between 1916 and 1940.]

43362. LASERSTEIN, LOTTE. Krausse, Anna-Carola: *Lotte Laserstein—my only reality—meine einzige Wirklichkeit.* [Eine Ausstellung des Vereins Das Verborgene Museum in Zusammenarbeit mit der Stiftung Stadtmuseum Berlin im Museum Ephraim-Palais]. Dresden: Philo Fine Arts, 2003. 367 pp., illus., bibl., index. 1 CD-ROM. [All texts also in Engl.] [L.L., Nov. 28, 1898 Preussisch-Holland, East Prussia–Jan. 21, 1993 Kalmar, Sweden, painter, lived from 1912 in Berlin, in 1937 emigr. to Sweden.] [Cf.: Kühle Bereitschaft. Die Malerin Lotte Laserstein im Berliner Ephraim-Palais (Camilla Blechen) [in]: 'FAZ', Nr. 3, Frankfurt am Main, 5. Jan. 2004, p. 28.]

43363. LASKER, EMANUEL. *Emanuel Lasker. Homo ludens—homo politicus.* Beiträge über sein Leben und Werk. Hrsg. von Elke-Vera Kotowski [et al.]. Potsdam: Verl. für Berlin-Brandenburg, 2003. 256 pp., illus., facsims., notes. (Schriftenreihe des Wilhelm-Fraenger Instituts Potsdam, Bd. 5.) [Cont. contribs. to an int. conference held in Potsdam, Jan. 2001; incl.: Meine Liebe zu Lasker—Intentionen einer Tagung (Paul Werner Wagner, 15–18). Emanuel Lasker als homo politicus. Politisches Denken und Handeln im Zeitalter des Totalitarismus (Michael Dreyer, 19–38). Ein selbstbewußter Querdenker?—Emanuel Lasker als Philosoph (Ulrich Sieg, 39–54). Lasker und die Philosophie der Gegenwart (Bernd Gräfrath, 55–68). Wildwechsel von Ideen—Über Wilhelm Steinitz und Emanuel Lasker (Hans Holländer, 95–116). Gedächtnis und Phantasie. Emanuel

Laskers kulturalistische Sicht der Verhältnisse von Judentum und Schachspiel und ihre Grenzen (Michael Ehn/Ernst Strouhal, 161–172). Lasker in Holland (Henriette Reerink, 173–186). Lasker in Rußland (Juri Awerbach, 187–194). Laskers Moskauer Exil (Isaak Linder, 195–204). Lasker und der Beginn meiner Sammlung (Lothar Schmid, 203–206). Lasker in Thyrow & Irrtümer und Fehler in der Lasker-Literatur (Siegfried Augustat, 211–220; 221–224). Family business—Kleine Erinnerungen an meine erste Begegnung mit Lasker (Ernst Strouhal, 237–240). Also contribs. on L.'s chess playing by Oliver Lembcke, Tim Hagemann, Egbert Meissenburg, Helmut Pfleger, Wolfgang Unzicker, Robert Hübner, Kazimierz Hoffmann, Hans-Christian Wohlfahrt.] [E.L., 1868 Potsdam–1941 New York, further data see No. 40576/YB XLVII.]

43364. LASKER-SCHÜLER, ELSE. *Else Lasker-Schüler-Jahrbuch zur Klassischen Moderne.* Hrsg. von Lothar Bluhm und Andreas Meier. Trier: WVT Wissenschaftlicher Verlag Trier, 2003. 233 pp., footnotes, index. [Incl. contribs. on E.L.-Sch. by Eberhard Sauermann, Herbert Uerlings, Theresia Birkenhauer, Thomas Höfert, Lothar Bluhm, Dierk Hoffmann/Angela Rheinthal, Andreas Meier (also on Ernst Toller). One further contrib. is listed according to subject.]

43365. LASKER-SCHÜLER, ELSE. FALKENBERG, BETTY: *Else Lasker-Schüler: a life.* Jefferson, NC; London: McFarland, 2003. 238 pp., illus., ports., facsims., notes, bibl. (223–229).

43366. LASKO, PETER. HESLOP, T.A.: *Obituary: Professor Peter Lasko: Energetic director of the Courtauld Institute.* [In]: The Independent, London, May 28, 2003. [P.E.L., March 5, 1924 Berlin–May 18, 2003 London, art historian, emigr. to UK in the 1930s; Assistant Keeper, British Museum, 1950–1965; Prof. of Visual Arts, Univ. of East Anglia, 1965–1973; Prof. of the History of Art and Director, Courtauld Institute, London Univ. 1974–1985.]

43367. LAZARUS, MORITZ: *Grundzüge der Völkerpsychologie und Kulturwissenschaft.* Hrsg., mit einer Einleitung und Anmerkungen versehen von Klaus Christian Köhnke. Hamburg: Meiner, 2003. XLII, 290 pp., notes (243–274), bibl., indexes. [Incl.: Einleitung (ed., IX-XLII, footnotes; on the author's life and work).]

43368. LEICHTER, KÄTHE. BROESSLER, AGNES, ed.: *"Man ist ja schon zufrieden, wenn man arbeiten kann". Käthe Leichter und ihre politische Aktualität.* Hrsg. vom Institut für Gewerkschafts- und AK-Geschichte. Wien: Mandelbaum, 2003. 171 pp., illus., bibl. [Cf.: "... und viele Pussi von Deinem Heinz". Neue Käthe Leichter-Dokumente gefunden (Agnes Broessler) [in]: Zwischenwelt, Jg. 20, Nr. 3, Wien, Dez. 2003. Pp. 12–14, facsims., notes. See also No. 42768.]

43369. LESSING, THEODOR. CAPKOVÁ, KATERINA: *Theodor Lessing—vom Außenseiter zum Symbol der antinazistischen Opposition.* [In]: Theresienstädter Studien und Dokumente 2003, Prag, 2003. Pp. 11–32, footnotes. [On the the reaction of the Slovakian public to the assassination of L. in Marienbad, Aug. 1933; also on his somewhat dubious contacts with Czech and German right-wing representatives in Czechoslovakia. Also in this vol.: Über die Familie Ehrmann und die Kraft der menschlichen Solidarität (Alena Hajková, 33–70; on the fate of friends of Th.L., who helped refugees from Germany, Austria and the Sudetenland).]

43370. LESSING, THEODOR. WITTHOEFT, MAREN: *"Zum Lose der Kassandra bestimmt". Zum 70. Todestag des Philosophen und Publizisten Theodor Lessing.* [In]: Zeitschrift für Geschichtswissenschaft, Jg. 51, H. 9, Berlin, 2003. Pp. 832–843.

43371. LIEBERMANN, MAX. BRÖHAN, NICOLE: *Max Liebermann.* Berlin: Jaron, 2002. 176 pp., illus., bibl. (Berliner Köpfe.) [Biography.]

43372. LIEBERMANN, RICHARD. TEMME, MICHAL: *Spurensuche: Richard Liebermann 1900–1966. Lebenslinien eines gehörlosen, jüdischen Künstlers.* [Also on title page: Edwin-Scharff-Museum, Neu-Ulm 9. Nov. 2001 bis 3. Feb. 2002]. [Neu-Ulm]: [Edwin Scharff Museum und Städtische Sammlungen Neu-Ulm], [2001]. 40 pp., illus., facsims. [Incl. contribs. by Helga Gutbrod and Gernot Römer.] [R.L., Oct. 21, 1900 Neu-Ulm–Dec. 10, 1966 St. Rambert, artist, 1923 conversion to Catholicism, 1936–1939 art teacher at the Landschulheim Herrlingen, 1940 deported to Gurs, later survival in hiding in France.]

43373. LISSAUER, ERNST. BRÄNDLE, RAINER: *Am wilden Zeitenpaß: Motive und Themen im Werk des deutsch-jüdischen Dichters Ernst Lissauer.* Mit einem Vorwort von Guy Stern. Frankfurt am Main; New York: Lang, 2002. 286 pp., footnotes, bibl. (Analysen und Dokumente, Bd. 46.) Zugl.: Frankfurt am Main, Univ., Diss., 2000.

43374. LITTEN, HANS. SCHÜLER-SPRINGORUM, STEFANIE: *Hans Litten 1903–2003: The public use of a biography.* [In]: Leo Baeck Institute Year Book 2003, Vol. XLVIII, Oxford, 2003. Pp. 205–219, illus., footnotes. [On the reception of L.s biography in West Germany and in the GDR from the early post-1945 years up to the present; also on L.'s role in the youth group Schwarzer Haufen in Königsberg. Also, by same author: Hans Litten 1903–2003. Oder: Vom öffentlichen Gebrauch einer Biographie [in]: Die Mahnung, Jg. 50, Nr. 8/9, Berlin, 1. Aug./Sept. 2003. Pp. 3–5.] [H.L., 1903 Halle–1938 Dachau, left-wing lawyer, imprisoned after the Reichstag fire.]

43375. LÖHNER-BEDA, FRITZ. DENSCHER, BARBARA: *Kein Land des Lächelns: Fritz Löhner-Beda. 1883–1942.* Salzburg: Residenz-Verl., 2002. 218 pp., illus., bibl. [Biography.]

43376. LÖWENSTEIN, OTTO. LINDNER, ERIK: *Otto Löwenstein. Carl Heymanns Verlag und sein Verleger im Kaiserreich.* Köln: Carl Heymanns Verlag, 2003. VII, 99 pp., frontis., illus., facsims. [Incl.: Geleitwort (Bertram Gallus, V-VI).] [O.L., July 30, 1841 Berlin–Oct. 29, 1896 Berlin, publisher, grandson of Carl Heymann.]

43377. LOEWY, ERNST. BENZ, WOLFGANG: *Ernst Loewy: Vom Buchhandelslehrling in Tel Aviv zum Pionier der Exilforschung.* [In]: Exilforschung, Bd. 21, München, 2003. Pp. 16–23. [Obituary.] [Cf.: In memoriam Ernst Loewy (Eugen Gerritz) [in]: Die Heimat. Krefelder Jahrbuch, Jg. 74, Krefeld, 2003. Pp. 16–17. Die schwierige Heimat stets im Kopf. Zum Tode von Ernst Loewy (Hans Jörgen Gerlach) [in]: Zwischenwelt, Jg. 19, Nr. 4, Wien, Feb. 2003. Pp. 13–15, illus., bibl.] [E.L., April 4, 1920 Krefeld–Sept. 17, 2002 Frankfurt am Main, author, emigr. 1936 to Palestine, remigr. 1956, director of the Judaica Dept. of the Univ. Library, Frankfurt am Main, 1964–1983, co-founder and chairman of the Gesellschaft für Exilforschung.]

43378. LUBITSCH, ERNST. HANISCH, MICHAEL: *Ernst Lubitsch (1892–1947).* Von der Berliner Schönhauser Allee nach Hollywood. Berlin: Hentrich & Hentrich; Centrum Judaicum Berlin, 2003. 63 pp., frontis., illus., bibl. (Reihe Jüdische Miniaturen, Bd. 5.) [E.L., 1892 Berlin–1947 Hollywood, actor, film director, lived from 1921 in Hollywood.]

43379. LUXEMBURG, ROSA. *Rosa Luxemburg und die Arbeiterbewegung: Neuere Ansätze in Rezeption und Forschung.* [Issue title of] Mitteilungsblatt des Instituts für Soziale Bewegungen, Nr. 29, Essen, 2003. 99 pp., footnotes. [Cont.: Vorwort des Herausgebers (Klaus Tenfelde, 5–6). Rosa Luxemburg zwischen Ost und West: Instrumentalisierung im Kalten Krieg bis 1990 (Hermann Weber, 7–18). Die revolutionäre Ungeduld: Rosa Luxemburg und ihre Verbindungen zu den Massen (August 1914 bis Januar 1919) (Ottokar Luban, 19–30). Der Zukunftsmacher: Das Bild des Arbeiters bei Rosa Luxemburg und Karl Kautsky (Till Schelz-Brandenburg, 31–42). Rosa Luxemburgs Auftritte im Ruhrgebiet und ihre Teilnahme an der Wahlrechtsdemonstration der SPD vom 10. April 1910 in Kamen (Horst Hensel, 59–67). Rosa Luxemburg, Clara Zetkin und die Frauen (Tânia Puschnerat, 69–74). Rosa Luxemburg als Mythos? Zur Bedeutung der historischen Rosa Luxemburg für die heutige Sozialdemokratie (Bernd Faulenbach, 75–88). Bericht über die Internationale Rosa-Luxemburg-Konferenz 2002 (Dimitrij Owetschkin, 89–96).]

43380. MADOL, HANS ROGER. POLLAK, OLIVER B.: *The biography of a biographer: Hans Roger Madol (1903–1956).* [In]: The Germanic Review [with the issue title] A Festschrift to Inge Halpert [see No. 43307]. Pp. 74–85, notes. [H.R.M., orig. Gerhard Salomon, 1903 Berlin–1956 New York, journalist, biographer, book collector, diarist, diplomat, converted to Christian Science, lived in several European countries and the US.]

43381. MAHLER, GUSTAV. FISCHER, JENS MALTE: *Gustav Mahler. Der fremde Vertraute.* Biographie. Wien: Zsolnay, 2003. 992 pp., illus., chronol., bibl., notes (945–974), bibl. G.M., index. [Cf.: Bespr. (Daniel Jütte) [in]: 'MB', Jg. 72, Nr. 191, Tel Aviv, Mai 2004.]

43382. MAHLER, GUSTAV. *Gustav Mahler: Briefe und Musikautographen aus den Moldenhauer-Archiven in der Bayerischen Staatsbibliothek.* [Hrsg.: Kulturstiftung der Länder/Bayerische Staatsbibliothek] [Berlin: Kulturstiftung der Länder, 2003]. 248 pp., frontis., illus., facsims., notes. (Patrimonia, 157.) [Incl.: Prefaces (Hans Zehetmair, Hermann Leskien, 6–9). Gustav Mahlers Beziehungen zu München (Günther Weiß, 11–34). Gustav Mahlers Briefe (Sigrid von Moisy (35–68).]

——— MAHLER, GUSTAV. HILMES, OLIVER: *Im Fadenkreuz: politische Gustav-Mahler-Rezeption 1919–1945. Eine Studie über den Zusammenhang von Antisemitismus und Kritik an der Moderne.* [See No. 43600.]

43383. MAHLER, GUSTAV. MITCHELL, DONALD: *Gustav Mahler: the early years.* Woodbridge, Suffolk: Boydell & Brewer; Rochester, NY: Univ. of Rochester Press, 2003. XVIII, 275 pp., illus., ports., facsims., scores. [Revised paperback edn.; first publ. in 1958, rev. edn. 1980.]

43384. MAHLER, GUSTAV. MITCHELL, DONALD: *Gustav Mahler: the Wunderhorn years.* Woodbridge, Suffolk: Boydell & Brewer; Rochester, NY: Univ. of Rochester Press, 2003. 461 pp., illus., ports., facsims., scores. [Revised paperback edn.; first publ. in 1975, rev. edn. 1980.]

43385. MAHLER, GUSTAV. SCHEIT, GERHARD/SVOBODA, WILHELM: *Feindbild Gustav Mahler.* Zur antisemitischen Abwehr der Moderne in Österreich. Wien: Sonderzahl, 2002. 336 pp. [Cf.: Von antisemitischer Feindseligkeit zur globalisierten Akzeptanz. Mahlers Nachleben in der Republik Österreich 1918–1988 (Herta Blaukopf) [in]: Zwischenwelt, Jg. 20, Nr. 1, Wien, Mai 2003, pp. 15–16.]

43386. MAIMON, SALOMON. WOLFF, SABATTIA JOSEPH: *Maimoniana oder Rhapsodien zur Charakteristik Salomon Maimons.* Hrsg. von Martin L. Davies und Christoph Schulte. Berlin: Parerga, 2003. 153 pp., footnotes. (Jüdische Geistesgeschichte, Bd. 4.) [Biography of S.M. written by his friend, the physician S.J.W., publ. in Berlin, 1813; incl.: Vorwort (Christoph Schulte, 7–12). Nachwort (Martin L. Davies, 139–153).]

43387. MANN, KATIA. JENS, INGE & WALTER: *Frau Thomas Mann. Das Leben der Katharina Pringsheim.* Reinbek: Rowohlt, 2003. 352 pp., illus., chronol., bibl., index. [Cf.: Wer wäre frei mit beschwerter Seele? Ein kompliziertes Leben in einem komplizierten Jahrhundert an der Seite eines komplizierten Mannes: Zwei Biographien Katia Manns (Ernst Osterkamp) [in]: 'FAZ', Nr. 63, Frankfurt am Main, 15. März 2003, p. 46.]

43388. MANN, KATIA. JÜNGLING, KIRSTEN/ROSSBECK, BRIGITTE: *Katia Mann. Die Frau des Zauberers.* Biografie. München: Propyläen, 2003. 416 pp., illus., notes (341–396), bibl., index. [K.M., née Pringsheim, July 24, 1883 Munich–April 25, 1980 Kilchberg nr. Zurich.]

43389. MARX, KARL. IORIO, MARCO: *Karl Marx—Geschichte, Gesellschaft, Politik.* Eine Ein- und Weiterführung. Berlin; New York: de Gruyter, 2003. XII, 370 pp., notes (325–348), bibl., indexes.

43390. MARX, KARL. KAISER, VOLKER: *Karl Marx: Darstellung und Kritik als Versprechen zur Moderne.* [In]: 1848 und das Versprechen der Moderne. Hrsg. von Jürgen Fohrmann [et al.]. Würzburg: Königshausen & Neumann, 2003. Pp. 65–84, footnotes.

43391. MARX, KARL. MARLOWE, CHRISTOPHER: *Der Jude von Malta.* Deutsch von Erich Fried. Mit Essays von Karl Marx und Stephen Greenblatt. Hrsg. und mit einem Nachwort von Friedmar Apel. Neuausgabe. Berlin: Wagenbach, 2003. 164 pp. [First publ. 1991. Cont.: Der Jude von Malta in der Übersetzung von Erich Fried (Christopher Marlowe, 9–92). Zur Judenfrage (Karl Marx, 93–124). Marlowe, Marx und Antisemitismus (Stephen Greenblatt, 125–152; on the controversial history of the reception of Marlowe's play and K.M.'s essay). Zwei Provokationsagenten: Christopher Marlowe und sein Jude (ed., 153–164).]

43392. MAYER, HANS. WERTHEIMER, JÜRGEN: *Hans Mayer—Ansichten eines komparatistischen Außenseiters.* [In]: Arcadia, Int. Zeitschrift für Literaturwissenschaft, Bd. 38, H. 2, Berlin; New York, 2003. Pp. 375–378.

43393. MENDELSSOHN FAMILY. *Die Mendelssohns in Italien.* Ausstellung des Mendelssohn-Archivs der Staatsbibliothek zu Berlin—Preußischer Kulturbesitz. 6. Dez. 2002 bis 18. Jan. 2003. [Ausstellung und Katalog: Hans-Günter Klein]. Wiesbaden: Reichert, 2002. 116 pp., illus., notes, bibl., index. (Ausstellungskataloge, N.F., 46.)

43394. MENDELSSOHN, FELIX. TODD, LARRY R.: *Mendelssohn: a life in music.* Oxford; New York: Oxford Univ. Press, 2003. XXIX, 683 pp., illus., map, scores, notes, bibl. (629–644), indexes.

43395. MENDERSHAUSEN, HORST. NAUMANN, MICHAEL: *Der Tod eines Emigranten.* Eine deutsche Geschichte. [In]: Die Zeit, Nr. 34, Hamburg, 14. Aug. 2003. P. 47, illus. [Obituary.] [H.M., 1911 Köthen–2003 California, economist, political scientist, emigr. 1937 to Sweden (where he became a friend of Willi Brandt), 1939 to the US, as an assistant to General Lucius Clay, returned to Germany 1945–1948, later settled in Santa Monica as member of the Rand-Think-Tank.]

43396. MEYSEL, INGE. STAMER, SABINE: *Inge Meysel. Ihr Leben.* Hamburg: Europa Verl., 2003. 285 pp., illus. (6 pp.). [I.M., May 30, Berlin–July 10, 2004 Hamburg, Germany's most popular actress, banned from her profession 1935–1945 because of her Jewish father, after the war met and later married her partner, John Olden (1918–1965), a Viennese Jew, British officer and later theatre and film director.]

43397. MISES, RICHARD VON. SIEGMUND-SCHULTZE, REINHARD: *"Deutsches Denken" in "kulturfeindlicher Wiener Luft". Ein Brief Georg Hamels aus dem Jahre 1908 an seinen Assistenten Richard von Mises.* [In]: Mitteilungen der deutschen Mathematikervereinigung (DMV), H. 3, Berlin, 2003. Pp. 8–17, illus., facsims., footnotes, bibl. [Incl. a reprint of a letter recently found in the Richard von Mises collection in the Harvard Univ. archives. Also, by the same author, on R.v.M.'s biography: Richard von Mises—ein früher Emigrant in Distanz und Nähe zur österreichischen Mathematik, Literatur und Philosophie [in]: Internationale Mathematische Nachrichten, Vol. 55, No. 187, Wien, 2001. Pp. 21–32, illus., port., footnotes. Richard von Mises [in]: C.C. Heyde et al.: Statisticians of the centuries. New York: Springer, 2001. Pp. 352–357, bibl.] [R.v.M., April 19, 1883 Lemberg–July 14, 1953 Boston, Prof. of Aerodynamics and Applied Mathematics, brother of the economist Ludwig M., 1920–1933 Prof. at Berlin Univ., converted to Catholicism before World War I, 1933 emigr. to Turkey, 1939 to the US, 1939–1953 Prof. at Harvard Univ.]

——— MOSSE, WERNER EUGEN. PULZER, PETER: *Obituary: Professor Werner Eugen Mosse, 1918–2001.* [In]: Toward normality. Acculturation and modern German Jewry. [See No. 42255.]

43398. MOSSE, GEORGE: *Nazi culture: intellectual, cultural and social life in the Third Reich.* Transl. by Salvator Attanasio and others. Madison: Univ. of Wisconsin Press, 2003. XLI, 386 pp., illus., ports., notes, bibl. [Orig. publ.: New York: Grosset & Dunlap, 1966.]

43399. MOSZKOWICZ, IMO. *Oberbayerischer Kulturpreis: Verleihung an Imo Moszkowicz, Regisseur* [et al.] *in Miesbach, 27. Sept. 2003.* Hrsg.: Bezirk Oberbayern, Pressestelle. 80535 München: Bezirk Oberbayern, 2003. 24 pp., illus. [Incl. a eulogy by Hans Clarin; see also No. 42590.] [I.M., b. 1925 in Ahlen, Westphalia, actor, theatre and film director, 1942 deported to Auschwitz, after liberation in Reichenberg returned to Westphalia, actor in Warendorf and Gütersloh, assistant to Gustav Gründgens and Fritz Kortner, from 1959 film and television film director.]

43400. MÜHSAM, ERICH. *Das Tagebuch im 20. Jahrhundert—Erich Mühsam und andere.* Dreizehnte Erich-Mühsam-Tagung in der Gustav-Heinemann-Bildungsstätte in Malente, 10.–12. Mai 2002. [Lübeck: Erich-Mühsam-Gesellschaft, 2003]. 109 pp., frontis., illus., footnotes. (Schriften der Erich-Mühsam-Gesellschaft, H. 22.) [Incl.: Aus den Tagebüchern Erich Mühsams (7–27). Selbsterziehung eines Anarchisten (Chris Harte, 43–52). Die Moritat von Finny Morstedt. Erich Mühsams Notizen vom Rande der Boheme (Bärbel Reetz, 53–69).]

43401. MÜHSAM, ERICH: *Wir geben nicht auf! Texte und Gedichte.* Hrsg. von Günther Gerstenberg. München: Allitera Verlag, 2003. 215 pp., illus., notes, chronol., index. (edition monacensia.) [Incl.: Erich Mühsam in acht Schlaglichtern (ed., 11–70, footnotes).]

43402. MÜHSAM, ERICH: *Sich fügen heißt lügen*. Hrsg. von Marlies Fritzen. Göttingen: Steidl, 2003. 2 vols., 271, 168 pp., frontis., illus., facsims., chronol., notes. [Vol. 1, 'Ein Lesebuch', cont. autobiographical texts and poetry; Vol. 2, 'Leben und Werk in Texten und Bildern' incl. numerous illus., facsims. and docs.]

43403. MUELLER, LEO. SCHEIT, GERHARD: *Leben mit dem Vorbehalt des Exils. Leo Mueller 19.9.1906–16.9.2003*. [In]: Zwischenwelt, Jg. 20, Nr. 3, Wien, Dez. 2003. Pp. 34–36, ports., notes. [L.M., 1906 Vienna–2003 Vienna, conductor, emigr. in the 1930s to the US, lived from the 1970s in Vienna.]

43404. MULLER, ROBERT. MÜLLER-WESEMANN, BARBARA: *Auf der Suche nach der gestohlenen Jugend. Zu Leben und Werk des Hamburger Schriftsteller Robert Muller (1925–1998)*. [In]: Zeitschrift des Vereins für Hamburgische Geschichte, Bd. 88, Hamburg, 2002. Pp. 235–253, illus., ports., footnotes. [R.M., Sept. 1, 1925 Hamburg–May 27, 1998 London, novelist, dramatist, screenwriter, 1938 went on a Kindertransport to the UK, as a "non-Aryan" helped by the Quakers.]

43405. NUSSBAUM, FELIX: *Fragezeichen an jeder Straßenecke. Zwölf Briefe von Felix Nussbaum*. Bearbeitet und mit Anmerkungen versehen von Peter Junk und Wendelin Zimmer. Hrsg. vom Felix Nussbaum-Haus Osnabrück [et al.]. Bramsche: Rasch Verlag, 2003. [48] pp., frontis., illus., facsims., plan. [Incl. letters to Ludwig Meidner, Margret and Dolf Ledel, the Klein family, Paul and Erna Blum.]

43406. OPPLER, EDWIN. ROHDE, SASKIA: *Im Zeichen der Hannoverschen Architekturschule: Der Architekt Edwin Oppler (1831–1880) und seine schlesischen Bauten*. [In]: Hannoversche Geschichtsblätter, Bd. 54, Hannover, 2003. Pp. 67–86, illus., facsims., footnotes. [Incl. some of O.'s synagogues.]

43407. PAUCKER, ARNOLD: *Deutsche Juden im Kampf um Recht und Freiheit*. Studien zu Abwehr, Selbstbehauptung und Widerstand der deutschen Juden seit dem Ende des 19. Jahrhunderts. Bearb. von Barbara Suchy. Mit einer Einführung von Reinhard Rürup. Teetz: Hentrich & Hentrich, 2003. XII, 403 pp., frontis., notes, illus., facsims., index. (Veröffentlichung des Leo Baeck Instituts.) [Cont. the sections: Arnold Paucker—Historiker und Zeitzeuge der deutsch-jüdischen Geschichte. Eine Einführung (Reinhard Rürup, IX-XII). I. Jüdischer Abwehrkampf (3–180). II. Selbstbehauptung und Widerstand (183–289). III. Berlin-London: Historiographie und Exilerfahrung (293–386; incl.: Dimensions of biography. A personal comment (329–338). Speaking English with an accent (339–354). Erfahrungen und Erinnerungen. Ein Rückblick (355–386; first publ. of the author's personal memoirs). IV. Anhang (389–403; incl. bibl. A.P., 389–395). Further essays (orig. publ. between 1968 and 2003) are listed according to subject.] [Cf.: Chronist des Widerstands. Der Historiker Arnold Paucker hat das Klischee von den passiven Juden in der NS-Zeit widerlegt (Ludger Heid) [in]: Jüdische Allgemeine, Jg. 59, Berlin, 22. Jan. 2004. Abwehr, Selbstbehauptung und Widerstand. Die politische Lektion der deutschen Juden (1893–1945) (Claude Weber) [in]: d'Letzebuerger Land, Luxemburg, 7. Nov. 2003, pp. 15. Bespr. (hl) [in]: Kalonymos, Jg. 7, H. 1, Duisburg, 2004, p. 11.]

43408. PAPPENHEIM, BERTHA: *Gebete*. Mit einem Nachwort von Margarete Susman. Prayers. Transl. into English by Estelle Forchheimer. Hrsg. von Elisa Klapheck und Lara Dämmig. Teetz: Hentrich & Hentrich, 2003. 70 pp., frontis., illus., facsims., gloss., footnotes. [Incl.: Bat Kol—Die Stimme der Bertha Pappenheim (eds., 7–21; text also in Engl.). Gebete (26–57). Nachwort (Margarete Susman, 58–61; written in 1936). Vorwort/Preface (Stephanie Forchheimer, 62–63; written in 1946). Die Seminar- und Gedenkstätte Bertha Pappenheim in Neu-Isenburg (Noemi Staszewski, 64–68).]

43409. PERLS, KÄTE & HUGO. *Kunstsammlungen Chemnitz: Edvard Munch—Käte und Hugo Perls, 1913*. [Hrsg.: Kulturstiftung der Länder in Verbindung mit den Kunstsammlungen Chemnitz. Autoren: Kerstin Drechsel et al.]. [Berlin: Kulturstiftung der Länder, 2003]. 107 pp., illus., facsims., bibl. (Patrimonia, 229.) [Selected contribs.: Vorwort und Dank (Ingrid Mössinger, 4–5). "Sie fährt nach Norwegen, er nach Italien." Edvard Munch porträtiert Käte und Hugo Perls (Hans Dieter Haber, 7–40, notes; followed by letters, short biographies of K. & H.P. and bibl. H.P. (42–48).] [H.P., 1886 Rybnik–1977 New York, jurist, art dealer, author, owner of the Perls Galleries, New York; K.P. née Kolker, 1889 Breslau–1945 New York, art dealer.]

43410. PERUTZ, LEO. FORSTER, BRIGITTE/MÜLLER, HANS-HARALD, eds.: *Leo Perutz. Unruhige Träume—Abgründige Konstruktionen.* Dimensionen des Werks, Stationen der Wirkung. Wien: Sonderzahl, 2002. 260 pp., notes. [Papers delivered at the first Int. Perutz symposium in Paris, March 1991; cont. 14 essays and two texts by L.P.]

43411. POLLARD, SIDNEY. RENTON, DAVID: *Sidney Pollard: the refugee historian.* [In]: Representing the Holocaust: essays in memory of Bryan Burns [see No. 12, repres .] Pp. 184–200, notes. [S.P., orig. Siegfried Pollak, 1925 Vienna–1998 Sheffield, prof. of economic history, 1938 emigr. to UK on a Kindertransport, from 1950 at Univ. of Sheffield, from 1980 at Univ. of Bielefeld.]

43412. POPPER, KARL. MORSCHER, EDGAR, ed.: *Was wir Karl R. Popper und seiner Philosophie verdanken.* Zu seinem 100. Geburtstag. Sankt Augustin: Academia Verlag, 2002. 501 pp., facsims., notes, bibl., index. (ProPhil, Projekte zur Philosophie, Bd. 4.) [Incl. a section entitled Persönliche Erinnerungen und Briefe (465–494).]

43413. PREUSS, HUGO. LEHNERT, DETLEF/MÜLLER, CHRISTOPH, eds.: *Vom Untertanenverband zur Bürgergenossenschaft.* Symposion zum 75. Todestag von Hugo Preuß am 9. Oktober 2002. Baden-Baden: Nomos, 2003. 280 pp., footnotes, index. [Incl.: Zur Einführung: Perspektiven und Probleme einer Wiederentdeckung von Hugo Preuß (eds., 11–48); contribs. by Hans Mommsen, Lothar Albertin, Dian Schefold, Karsten Malowitz, Christoph Schönberger, Manfred Friedrich, Marcus Llanque and the eds.]

43414. RAPPAPORT, MAURYCY. HECKER, HANS: *Nach Galizien.* [In]: StadtLandFluß. Urbanität und Regionalität in der Moderne. Festschrift für Gertrude Cepl-Kaufmann zum sechzigsten Geburtstag [see No. 43138]. Pp. 535–541, notes. [On the Polish-Jewish poet Maurycy Rappaport, who wrote in German.]

43415. RATHENAU, WALTHER. *Leitbild oder Erinnerungsort? Neue Beiträge zu Walther Rathenau.* Hsrg. von Karl-Heinz Hense und Martin Sabrow. Berlin: BWV, 2003. 134 pp., footnotes. [Incl.: Grußwort (Heinz Dürr, 9–14). Essays by Jürgen Frölich, Martin Sabrow, Ernst Schulin, Wolfgang Michalka, Hans Dieter Hellige, Dieter Heimböckel and Gangolf Hübinger on aspects of R.'s work, his political life and his changing image.]

43416. RATHENAU, WALTHER. SCHÖLZEL, CHRISTIAN: *Walther Rathenau.* Industrieller, Schriftsteller, Politiker. Berlin: Hentrich & Hentrich; Centrum Judaicum Berlin, 2003. 63 pp., illus., bibl. (Reihe Jüdische Miniaturen, Bd. 2.)

43417. RATHENAU, WALTHER: *Das Wiesbadener Abkommen. Rede am 9. November 1921.* Mit einem einführenden Kommentar von Ursula Mader. Leipzig: Akad. Verlagsanstalt, 2003. 51 pp. (Freienwalder Hefte, Bd. 6.). [First complete publ. of the speech; incl.: Das "Wiesbadener Abkommen" (Ursula Mader, 8–20, footnotes).]

43418. REUTER, JULIUS. ZÖTTL, INES: *Momente der Entscheidung, 12: Er wollte immer der Erste sein. Julius Reuter schuf das früheste Informationsimperium der Welt.* Sein Erfolgsrezept: Schneller sein als alle anderen. [In]: Die Zeit, Nr. 21, Hamburg, 15. Mai 2003. P. 26, illus. [Paul Julius R., Freiherr von, 1816 Kassel–1899 Nice, founder of the international news agency Reuters Ltd., London, ennobled in 1871.]

43419. RIESSER, GABRIEL. KAUFMANN, URI R.: *Ein jüdischer Deutscher: Der Kampf des jungen Gabriel Riesser für die Gleichberechtigung der Juden.* [In]: Aschkenas, Jg. 13, H. 1, Tübingen, 2003. Pp. 211–236, footnotes.

43420. ROSENBERG, ARTHUR. KESSLER, MARIO: *Arthur Rosenberg* Ein Historiker im Zeitalter der Katastrophen (1889–1943). Köln: Böhlau, 2003. 335 pp., footnotes, chronol., docs., bibl., index. [Cont. the sections: Vorwort (Theodor Bergmann (9–12). Der Althistoriker im kaiserlichen Berlin (1889–1918). Der kommunistische Publizist (1918–1923). Der kommunistische Politiker (1923–1927). Der Kritiker revolutionärer Illusionen (1927–1933). Der Zeithistoriker im Exil (1933–1943). Incl. English summary.] [A.R., data see No. 38198/YB 45.]

43421. ROSENBERG, LUDWIG. AHLAND, FRANK: *Ludwig Rosenberg. Jugend, beruflicher Anfang und Emigration (1903–1946).* [In]: Gewerkschaftliche Monatshefte, Jg. 54, H. 7, Düsseldorf, 2003. Pp. 394–401. [In the same issue: Jugendtraum: Vorsitzender. Der DGB-Vorsitzende Ludwig Rosenberg (Hans Dieter Baroth, 402–408).] [L.R., June 29, 1903 Charlottenburg–Oct. 23, 1977 Düsseldorf, Social Democrat, trade unionist, 1933 fled to the UK, 1946 returned to Germany, 1962–1969 Chairman of the DGB (Deutscher Gewerkschaftsbund).]

43422. ROSENKRANZ, MOSES. HONOLD, ALEXANDER: *Die Blutfuge. Chronist eines Jahrhunderts der Auslöschungen: Zum Tod des Dichters Moses Rosenkranz.* [In]: 'FAZ'. Nr. 118, Frankfurt am Main, 22. Mai 2003. P. 36. [Cf.: Der letzte Große der bukowinischen Dichtung. Moses Rosenkranz nachgerufen (Hans Jörgen Gerlach) [in]: Zwischenwelt, Jg. 20, Nr. 2, Wien, Sept. 2003. Pp. 16–18, port.] [M.R., 1904 Berhomet/Bukowina–May 19, 2003 Lenzkirch/Black Forest, poet; further data see No. 40716/YB 47.]

43423. ROSENTHAL, FRANZ. VOLLAND, VIOLA: *Ein Leben der Forschung gewidmet. Zum Tod des Orientalisten Franz Rosenthal.* [In]: Aufbau, Vol. 69, No. 9, New York, May, 1, 2003. P. 21, port. [F.R., Aug. 31, 1914 Berlin–April 8, 2003 Branford, CO., Orientalist, Arabist, emigr. 1938 via Sweden and England to the US, from 1967 Sterling Professor at Yale Univ.]

43424. ROSENZWEIG, FRANZ. FRICKE, MARTIN: *Franz Rosenzweigs Philosophie der Offenbarung: eine Interpretation des Sterns der Erlösung.* Würzburg: Königshausen und Neumann, 2003. 295 pp. (Epistemata, Reihe Philosophie, Bd. 348.) Zugl.: Heidelberg, Univ., Diss., 2002.

43425. ROSENZWEIG, FRANZ. SCHWARTZ, MICHAL: *Metapher und Offenbarung.* Zur Sprache von Franz Rosenzweigs 'Stern der Erlösung'. Mit einem Vorwort von Stéphane Mosès. Berlin: Philo, 2003. 226 pp., notes, index.

43426. ROSENZWEIG, FRANZ. ZANK, MICHAEL: *The Rosenzweig-Rosenstock triangle, or, what we can learn from 'Letters to Gritli': a review essay.* [In]: Modern Judaism, Vol. 23, No. 1, Oxford, Feb. 2003. Pp. 74–98, notes. [On the edn. of Franz Rosenzweig's "Gritli"-Briefe. Briefe an Margrit Rosenstock-Huessy, publ. 2002; see No. 42052/YB XLVIII.]

43428. ROSENZWEIG, FRANZ: *"Innerlich bleibt die Welt eine". Ausgewählte Texte zum Islam.* Hrsg., eingel. und mit einem Nachwort von Gesine Palmer und Yossef Schwartz. Berlin: Philo, 2003. 151 pp., footnotes. [Title on book cover: Ausgewählte Schriften zum Islam.]

43429. ROTH, JOSEPH. BLAHUTKOVÁ, DANIELA: *'Österreicher par excellence' ... Joseph Roths Beamte und Offiziere.* [In]: Brücken, N.F. 9–10, Prag, 2003. Pp. 315–328, footnotes.

43430. ROTHFELS, HANS. ROTH, KARL HEINZ: *"Richtung halten": Hans Rothfels und die neo-konservative Geschichtsschreibung diesseits und jenseits des Atlantik.* [In]: Sozial.Geschichte, Zeitschrift für Sozialgeschichte des 20. und 21. Jahrhunderts, N.F., Jg. 18, H. 1, Bern, 2003. Pp. 41–71, footnotes. [Incl. German and Engl. abstract, p. 163; 'Sozial.Geschichte': new name for '1999'.]

43431. ROTHSCHILD FAMILY. FERGUSON, NIALL: *Die Geschichte der Rothschilds. Propheten des Geldes.* Aus dem Engl. von Irmela Arnsperger und Boike Rehbein. Stuttgart: Deutsche Verlags-Anstalt, 2002. 2 vols., 709 pp., illus., graphs., tabs., geneal., notes (581–709); 830 pp., illus., tabs., notes (607–720), bibl. (721–751), indexes (persons; subjects, 753–830). [For orig. Engl. edn. publ. 1998 with the title 'The world's banker' see No. 36762/YB XLIV.]

43432. ROTHSCHILD FAMILY. WEINTRAUB, STANLEY: *Charlotte and Lionel: a Rothschild love story.* New York: Free Press, 2003. XVIII, 316 pp., illus., notes, bibl. (295–306), index. [Charlotte de Rothschild, 1819–1884, Naples branch of family; Lionel Nathan de Rothschild, Baron, 1808–1879, son of Nathan Mayer R., founder of the London banking branch.]

43433. ROTH, JOSEPH: *Die Filiale der Hölle. Schriften aus der Emigration.* Hrsg. und mit einem Vorwort von Helmut Peschina. Köln: Kiepenheuer & Witsch, 2003. 187 pp. [A collection of political articles and letters testifying to R.'s struggle against Nazism 1933–1939. Incl.: Vorwort (ed., 9–22).]

43434. ROTH, JOSEPH: *What I saw: reports from Berlin, 1920–1933.* Transl. with an introd. by Michael Hofmann. German selection by Michael Bienert. London: Granta; New York: Norton. 227 pp., frontis., illus., map, bibl., index. [Cont.: Introduction (Michael Hofmann, 11–20). Newspaper articles; incl. the Jewish Quarter, Walther Rathenau.] [Cf.: This is Germany calling: Joseph Roth captures the bizarre vitality of Weimar Berlin (David Jays) [in]: The Observer Review, London, Feb. 2, 2003, p. 15. A tribute to a city of lost souls (Paul Bailey) [in]: The Sunday Times, London, Feb. 23, 2003, p. 43. Rough guide (Ritchie Robertson) [in]: TLS, London, Feb. 28, 2003, p. 6.]

43435. SALOMON BARTHOLDY, JAKOB . TALLNER, KATJA: *Jakob Salomon Bartholdy. Untersuchungen zu einem Porträtgemälde von Carl Joseph Begas.* [In]: Heimatkalender des Kreises Heinsberg 2004. Heinsberg, 2003. Pp. 140–146, port., illus., notes. [On a portrait of the diplomat J.S.B., orig. Levin Salomon (1779–1825).]

43436. SALOMON, RICHARD. NICOLAYSEN, RAINER: *"vitae, nicht vita". Über Vertreibung und Exil des Osteuropa-Historikers Richard Salomon (1884–1966).* [In]: Lebendige Sozialgeschichte. Gedenkschrift für Peter Borowsky [see No. 43599]. Pp. 633–658, footnotes. [R. Georg S., April 22, 1884 Berlin–Feb. 3, 1966 Mount Vernon, Ohio, Prof. of East European History and Medieval Church History, Prof. at Hamburg Univ. 1916–1933, emigr. 1937 to the US.]

43437. SCHAPIRO, BERNHARD. BORGWARDT, GÖTZ: *Bernhard Schapiro—Ein orthodoxer Jude als früher Androloge im 20. Jahrhundert.* [In]: Sudhoffs Archiv. Bd. 86, H. 2. Wiesbaden, 2002. Pp. 181–197, ports., illus., footnotes. [Incl. Engl. abstract.] [B.Sch., 1888 Dünaburg/Dvinsk/Latvia–1966 Jerusalem, dermatologist, andrologist, studied and worked in Berlin, Breslau and Zurich, 1922–1933 at the Berlin Institut für Sexualwissenschaften, emigr. in 1940 from Zurich to the US, in 1951 to Israel.]

43438. SCHLOSS, KARL: *Die Blumen werden in Rauch aufgehn.* Ausgewählte Gedichte und Briefe. Ein Gedenkbuch. Hrsg. von Wulf Kirsten und Annelore Schlösser im Auftrag der Stadt Alzey. Frankfurt am Main: Brandes & Apsel, 2003. 238 pp., illus. [Incl. a biographical essay by Annelore Schlösser on K. Sch. and his family, incl. his daughter, the actress Sybille Sch.] [K.Sch., Jan. 6, 1876 Framersheim nr. Alzey–Jan. 1944 Auschwitz, author, lyricist, emigr. to the Netherlands.]

43439. SCHNITZLER, ARTHUR. LE RIDER, JACQUES: *Juifs et antisémites dans le théatre d'Arthur Schnitzler.* [In]: Les cahiers du judaisme, No. 14, Paris, 2003. Pp. 72–84, illus., notes.

43440. SCHNITZLER, ARTHUR. LINDGREN, IRÈNE: *"Seh'n Sie, das Berühmtwerden ist doch nicht so leicht!"* Arthur Schnitzler über sein literarisches Schaffen. Ausgewählt, kommentiert und mit einem Vor- und Nachwort versehen von Irène Lindgren. Frankfurt am Main; New York, 2003. X, frontis., footnotes, chronol., bibl., indexes.

43441. SCHNITZLER, ARTHUR. LORENZ, DAGMAR C.G., ed.: *A companion to the works of Arthur Schnitzler.* Rochester, NY: Camden House, 2003. VII, 427 pp., bibl., notes, index.(Studies in German literature, linguistics, and culture.)

43442. SCHNITZLER, ARTHUR. PONTZEN, ALEXANDRA: *"... mehr als manchem geschmackvoll, notwendig und gerecht erscheinen dürfte". Zur Darstellung des Judentums im Werk Arthur Schnitzlers.* [In]: Convivium, Germanistisches Jahrbuch Polen 2002, Bonn, 2002. Pp. 203–229, footnotes, bibl. [Incl. Polish, German and English abstracts.]

43443. SCHOCKEN, SALMAN. DAVID, ANTHONY: *The patron. A life of Salman Schocken, 1877–1959.* New York: Metropolitan Books, 2003. 451 pp., illus., bibl. (415–435), index. [The lost tycoon. Ha'aretz is his monument (Steven E. Aschheim) [in]: 'TLS', London, Feb. 27, 2004, p. 6, port.] [S.Sch., Oct. 30. 1877 Margonin/Posen–Aug. 6, 1959 Pontresina/Switzerland (on vacation), owner of department stores, publisher, Zionist activist, 1933 emigr. to Palestine, in 1940 went to the US.]

43444. SCHÖNBERG, ARNOLD. AUNER, JOSEPH: *A Schoenberg reader: documents of a life.* New Haven, CT: Yale Univ. Press, 2003. XXVI, 428 pp., illus., notes, bibl. (353–409), index.

43445. SCHÖNBERG, ARNOLD. *Die Visionen des Arnold Schönberg: Jahre der Malerei/The visions of Arnold Schönberg: The painting years.* Hrsg./ed. by Max Hollein [et al.]. Mit Beiträgen von/with contribs. by Otto Breicha [et al.]. Ostfildern-Ruit: Hatje Cantz, 2002. 231 pp., illus., chronol., index, bibl. [Catalogue publ. for the exhibition with the same title at Schirn Kunsthalle, Frankfurt am Main, Spring 2002; all texts in English and German.]

43446. SCHOLEM, GERSHOM & ARENDT, HANNAH. EDDON, RALUCA MUNTEANU: *Gershom Scholem, Hannah Arendt and the paradox of "non- nationalist" nationalism.* [In]: The Journal of Jewish Thought and Philosophy, Vol. 12, No. 1, London, April 2003. Pp. 55–68, notes.

43447. SCHOTTLAENDER, RUDOLF. ALY, GÖTZ: *"Von den tragenden Volkskräften isoliert." Zum 100. Geburtstag von Rudolf Schottlaender.* [In]: Jahrbuch für Universitätsgeschichte, Bd. 6, Stuttgart, 2003. Pp. 197–204, footnotes. [R.Sch., Aug. 5, 1900 Berlin–Jan. 4, 1988 Berlin (East), teacher, philosopher, survived the Nazi period in a "mixed marriage", after the war Prof. of Philosophy at Dresden Techn. Univ., dismissed in 1949, High School Teacher in Berlin (West), dismissed in 1960, Prof. of Philosophy at the Humboldt Univ. in Berlin (East).]

43448. SCHOTTLAENDER, RUDOLF. ALY, GÖTZ: *Von den tragenden Volkskräften isoliert. Rudolf Schottlaender oder die Verbreitung von Licht.* [In]: Rasse und Klasse [see No. 42593]. Pp. 216–229. [On R.Sch. as reflected in the Stasi's telephone tapping of the author's telephone conversations with him.]

43449. SCHUR, ISSAI. STAMMBACH, URS: *Die Zürcher Vorlesung von Schur über Darstellungstheorie.* [In]: Mathematische Semesterberichte 50, Heidelberg, 2003. Pp. 131–142, footnotes. [Discusses, in its historical context, Sch.'s lecture in Zurich immediately after his dismissal from Berlin Univ. in 1936.]

43450. SEBASTIAN, ANNA: *Das Monster.* Roman. Aus dem Engl. übers. von Christel Wiemken. Mit einem Nachwort von Susanne Ovadia. Hrsg. von Thomas B. Schumann. Hürth bei Köln: Edition Memoria, 2003. 328 pp., frontis. [First German edn. of a novel orig. publ. 1944 in London. Incl. a postscript by the author's sister.] [A.S., orig. Friedl Benedikt, 1916 Vienna–1953 Paris; author, daughter of the publisher Ernst Martin Benedikt (Neue Freie Presse), followed Elias Canetti to London in 1939 to become one of his lovers.]

43451. SEGHERS, ANNA. GUTZMANN, GERTRAUD: *Von der Unzerstörbarkeit des Ich in Anna Seghers' Roman 'Transit'.* [In]: Lebendige Sozialgeschichte. Gedenkschrift für Peter Borowsky [see No. 43599]. Pp. 748–759, footnotes.

43452. SEGHERS, ANNA. ZEHL ROMERO, CHRISTIANE: *Anna Seghers.* Eine Biographie 1947–1983. Berlin: Aufbau, 2003. 479 pp., illus., notes (331–422), indexes, bibl. (436–476). [For first vol. see No. 39373/YB XLVI.]

43453. SEGHERS, ANNA: *Aufstand der Fischer St. Barbara.* Bandbearbeitung: Helen Fehervary. Mitarbeit: Jennifer William. Berlin: Aufbau, 2003. 171 pp. (Anna Seghers Werkausgabe.) [Incl.: Kommentar (97–171; on the reception of the book before and after 1933.]

43454. SERKIN, RUDOLF. LEHMANN, STEPHEN/FABER, MARION: *Rudolf Serkin: a life.* London; New York: Oxford Univ. Press, 2003. X, 344 pp., frontis., illus., notes (315–328), bibl., index. [Incl. a discography (Paul Farber, 273–314) and a CD-ROM. Cf.: He changed the study of music in America. A new biography of Rudolf Serkin (Styra Avins) [in]: Aufbau, Vol. 69, No. 7, New York, April 3, 2003, p. 17.] [R.S., March 28, 1903 Eger/Bohemia–May 8, 1991 Guildford/Vermont, pianist.]

43455. SIMMEL, GEORG. *Georg Simmels 'Philosophie des Geldes'. Aufsätze und Materialien.* Hrsg. von Otthein Rammstedt unter Mitwirkung von Christian Papilloud [et al.]. Frankfurt am Main: Suhrkamp, 2003. 345 pp., footnotes, bibl. (Suhrkamp Taschenbuch Wissenschaft, Bd. 1584.) [Incl.: Die Juden und das Geld nach Georg Simmel (Freddy Raphael, 45–57). 'Die Absicht, dem historischen Materialismus ein Stockwerk unterzubauen': Zur Beziehung von Simmel zu Marx (Gregor Fitzi, 215–244).]

43456. SPERBER, MANES. ISLER, RUDOLF: *Manès Sperber—Zeuge des Jahrhunderts: eine Lebensgeschichte.* Aarau: Bildung Sauerländer, 2003. 199 pp., illus., bibl.

43457. SPERBER, MANES. STANCIC, MIRJANA: *Manès Sperber. Leben und Werk.* Frankfurt am Main: Stroemfeld/Nexus, 2003. 687 pp., illus., facsims., footnotes, bibl. (647–668), index.

43458. SPIEGEL, FRITZ. ANDERSON, MARTIN: *Fritz Spiegel: Liverpool's Renaissance man.* [In]: The Independent, March 31, London, 2003. P. 20 [Obituary.] [Fritz Spiegel, Jan. 27, 1926 Zürndorf/Austria–March 23, 2003 Liverpool, flautist, impresario, writer, broadcaster.]

43459. STEIN, EDITH. *Edith Stein.* Themen—Bezüge—Dokumente. Hrsg. von Beate Beckmann und Hanna-Barbara Gerl-Falkovitz. Würzburg: Königshausen & Neumann, 2003. 318 pp., footnotes, bibl., index. (Orbis Phaenomenologicus.) [Incl. 14 essays, some related to biographical aspects.]

43460. STEINER, HERBERT. KONRAD, HELMUT: *Über Herbert Steiner (1922–2001). Gedenkrede am 13.09.2001 in Linz.* [In]: Jahrbuch für Beiträge/Forschungen zur Geschichte der Arbeiterbewegung, Berlin, Jan. 2002. Pp. 69–73. [On inside title page: Beiträge; name of periodical had to be changed: Forschungen replaced Beiträge.] [H.St., 1922 Vienna–2001 Vienna, Communist, Socialist, historian of social history, labour movement and resistance, university lecturer, founder of Dokumentationsarchiv des österreichischen Widerstands (DÖW), emigr. after the Anschluss to the UK, after the war remigr. to Vienna.]

43461. STEINER, KURT. WELZIG, ELISABETH/KILIAN, ERNST: *Zwischen den Welten. Kurt Steiner: Ein Wiener beim Tokioter Kriegsverbrecherprozess.* Wien: Mandelbaum, 2002. 172 pp., illus., notes. [Biography, based on interviews in 1998 and 1999.] [K.St., b. 1912 in Vienna, jurist, emigr. 1938 to the US, one of the US prosecuting counsel in the Tokyo War Tribunal 1946–1948, Prof. of Political Sciences at Stanford Univ. 1955–1977.] [Cf.: Kurt Steiner und der Tokyoter Kriegsverbrecherprozeß (Konstantin Kaiser) [in]: Zwischenwelt, Jg. 19, Nr. 4, Wien, Feb. 2003, pp. 69–70.]

43462. STEINITZ, WILHELM. *The Steinitz papers: letters and documents of the first world chess champion.* Ed. by Kurt Landsberger. Jefferson, NC: McFarland, 2002.VIII, 325 pp., illus., ports., facsims., tabs., index. [W.St., 1836 Prague–1900 New York, lived in Vienna, London and New York, world chess champion 1886–1894.]

43463. STONBOROUGH-WITTGENSTEIN, MARGARET. PROKOP, URSULA: *Margaret Stonborough-Wittgenstein. Bauherrin, Intellektuelle, Mäzenin.* Wien: Böhlau, 2003. 283 pp., illus., footnotes, geneal., index. [Cf.: Schöpferisch ohne ein Werk zu hinterlassen (Sonja Asal) [in]: Süddeutsche Zeitung, Nr. 173, München, 30. Juli 2003, p. 14.] [M.St., née Wittgenstein, Sept. 19, 1882 Neuwaldegg–Sept. 27, 1958 Vienna, sister of Ludwig W.]

43464. STRAUSS, LEO. MÜLLER, RUTH: *"Noch ein Strauss".* [In]: Zwischenwelt, Jg. 20. Nr. 1, Wien, Mai, 2003. Pp. 11–14, ports. [On Leo Strauss, son of the composer Oscar St.] [L.St., Jan. 21 1897 Teplitz–Oct. 28, 1944 Auschwitz, jurist, theatre director, author of poems and chansons in the Theresienstadt ghetto.]

43465. STRAUSS, LEO. SORENSEN, KIM: *Revelation and reason in Leo Strauss.* [In]: The Review of Politics, Vol. 65, No. 3, Notre Dame, IND, Summer 2003. Pp. 383–408, footnotes. [Refers also to St.'s philosophical-theistic devotion to Judaism.]

43466. STRAUSS, LUDWIG. HORCH, HANS OTTO: *Das Gedicht 'Hochmünster zu Aachen' (1932) von Ludwig Strauß im Licht des jüdischen Messianismus.* [In]: Zeitschrift des Aachener Geschichtsvereins. Jg. 2002/2003, Bd. 104/105. Aachen 2003. Pp. 735–744, footnotes.

43467. TABORI, GEORGE. FEINBERG, ANAT: *George Tabori.* München: Deutscher Taschenbuch Verlag, 2003. 189 pp., illus., chronol., bibl., index. Orig.-Ausg. (Dtv-Portrait.) [Biography.] [G.T., b. May 24, 1914 in Budapest, film and theatre director, author, lived in the 1930s and 1940s in Germany, England, Hungary, Turkey, Palestine, emigr. in 1947 to the US, returned to Europe in 1971, since then has been working mainly in Germany and Austria.]

43468. TABORI, GEORGE. STEDRON, PETR: *Tabori im Kontext der deutschen Erinnerungskultur.* [In]: Brücken, N.F. 9–10, Prag, 2003. Pp. 329–360, footnotes.

43469. TANZER, FRANCISCO. KAUKOREIT, VOLKER: *"Man muß sich erinnern, damit man vergessen kann". Ein Gespräch mit dem Autor Francisco Tanzer.* [In]: Zwischenwelt, Jg. 20, Nr. 3, Wien, Dez. 2003. Pp. 20–26, port., notes. [F.T., Sept. 12, 1921 Vienna–Oct. 25, 2003 Düsseldorf, author, fled via Czechoslovakia to France, later via Spain, Portugal to the US, 1954 remigr. to Germany, lived in Düsseldorf.]

43470. TUCHOLSKY, KURT. HAMMERSCHMIDT, JÖRG: *Literarische Justizkritik in der Weimarer Republik: Der Beitrag der Schriftsteller in der Auseinandersetzung mit der Justizwirklichkeit unter besonderer Berücksichtigung des Werkes von Kurt Tucholsky.* Göttingen: Cuvillier Verl., 2002. 167 pp., footnotes, bibl. Zugl.: Kiel, Univ., Diss., 2002.

43471. ULLSTEIN FAMILY. NADOLNY, STEN: *Ullsteinroman.* Roman. München: Ullstein, 2003. 495 pp., family trees, index. [Tells the factually authentic story of the publishing family from the early 19th cent. up to 1933.] [Cf.: Sten Nadolny erzählt die aufregende, verwirrende Geschichte der Verlegerfamilie (Petra Kipphoff) [in]: Zeitliteratur [Beilage von] Die Zeit, Jg. 58, Nr. 42, Hamburg, Okt. 2003, p. 38–39.]

43472. UNGAR, HERMANN: *Sämtliche Werke in drei Bänden.* Hrsg. von Dieter Sudhoff. Paderborn: Igel, 2001–2002. 3 vols. [Bd. 1: Romane (352 pp., chronol.); incl. Nachwort (ed., 338–352). Bd. 2: Erzählungen (266 pp.); incl. Nachwort (ed., 249–266). Bd. 3: Gedichte, Dramen, Feuilletons, Briefe (471 pp., bibl., index); incl. Nachwort (ed., 388–391).] [H.U., April 20, 1893 Boskowitz (Moravia)–Oct. 28, 1929 Prague, jurist, author, diplomat, after the First World War lived in Prague and Berlin.]

43473. UTITZ, EMIL. MEHRING, REINHARD: *Das Konzentrationslager als ethische Erfahrung.* Zur Charakterologie von Emil Utitz. [In]: Deutsche Zeitschrift für Philosophie, Jg. 51, H. 5, Berlin, 2003. Pp. 761–775, footnotes. [Deals with U.'s 'Charakterologie' (1925) and 'Psychologie des Lebens im Konzentrationslager Theresienstadt' (publ. 1948 in Vienna).] [E.U., 1883 Prague–1956 Jena (on a lecture tour), prof. of history of philosophy, emigr. 1933 from Halle to Prague, in July 1942 deported to Theresienstadt, after liberation returned to Prague.]

43474. VARNHAGEN, RAHEL. BECKER, SABINA, ed.: *Rahel Levin Varnhagen.* Studien zu ihrem Werk im zeitgenössischen Kontext. St. Ingbert: Röhrig Univers.-verl., 2001. 286 pp., notes. [Incl.: (some titles abbr.): Einleitung & Rahel Varnhagen und die frühromantische Gesprächs- und Geselligkeitskultur (ed., 9–52). Die Ordnung des Werks in Rahel Levin Varnhagens Schriften (Ulrike Landfester, 53–80). Rahel Varnhagen und die deutsch-jüdische Identität um 1800 (Dagmar Barnouw, 81–118). Zur Pathologie des Salons (Liliane Weissberg, 119–162). Rahel Varnhagen und Heinrich Heine (Joseph A. Kruse, 163–200). Rahel Varnhagen und das junge Deutschland (Jürgen Eder, 201–230). Rahel Varnhagens Goethe-Rezeption in der Interpretation von Käte Hamburger (Claudia Schulze, 231–258). Rahel-Varnhagen-Philologie im Zeichen der Nachlaß-Edition aus dem Krakauer Depot (Konrad Feilchenfeldt, 259–286).]

43475. VARNHAGEN, RAHEL & WIESEL, PAULINE. CALLEJÓN CALLEJÓN, LUISA: *Briefliche Momentbilder: Lektüren zur Korrespondenz zwischen Rahel Levin Varnhagen und Pauline Wiesel.* Berlin: Saint-Albin-Verl., 2002. 234 pp., footnotes, chronol., bibl. (Berliner Beiträge zur Germanistik.) Zugl.: Berlin, Freie Univ., veränd. Diss., 2000.

43476. WAMBACH, LINDA. ORNITZKI, WALBURGA: *Von der Ontologie zur Önologie. Das vergessene Frühwerk der Linda Wambach.* Mit einem Beitrag von Hans Wohlgemuth und einem Nachwort von Denise Leclerk. Bütschwil: Meyer & Mühlstein, 2003. 267 pp., port., illus. [Incl.: Situationsspezifische Aspekte im essentialistischen Differenzfeminismus der frühen Jahre (Hans Wohlgemuth, 181–255; incl. excerpts from L.W.'s memoirs and essays). "… wer lange lebt, hat viel erfahren …" Identität und Retraditionalisierung. Ein Nachwort: (Denise Leclerk, 257–267).] [L.W., orig. Sieglinde Henriette Ledermann, 1907 Oberwambach (Westerwald) – 1997 Ascona, teacher, philosopher, anthroposophist, viniculture expert, emigr. in the 1930s to

South Africa, founder of "Orthobiotikum & Vinetum", a guest farm and college located near Cape Town.]

43477. WANDER, FRED. MÜLLER, KARL: *Laudatio für Fred Wander.* Theodor Kramer Preis für Schreiben im Widerstand und im Exil 2003. [In]: Zwischenwelt, Jg. 20, Nr. 2, Wien, Sept. 2003. Pp. 23–26, illus. [Eulogy followed by F.W.'s speech: Worte zum Theodor Kramer Preis (27).] [F.W., data see No. 28987/YB XXXVII.]

43478. WARBURG, ABY M.. RAULFF, ULRICH: *Wilde Energien. Vier Versuche zu Aby Warburg.* Göttingen: Wallstein, 2003. 151 pp., frontis. [One essay is entitled: Der Teufelsmut der Juden. Warburg und Nietzsche in der Transformatorenhalle (117–150).]

43479. WASSERMANN, JAKOB. STRUCK, HANNA: *Wider die "Trägheit des Herzens".* Vor siebzig Jahren starb Jakob Wassermann. [In]: Tribüne, Jg. 42, H. 168, Frankfurt am Main, 2003. Pp. 95–98.

43480. WEIGEL, HELENE. HÄNTZSCHEL, HILTRUD: *Brechts Frauen.* Reinbek b. Hamburg: Rowohlt, 2002. 317 pp., illus., notes, bibl., index. [Incl. chap. on Helene Weigel (97–146); also on this topic: Sabine Kebir: Ein akzeptabler Mann? Brecht und die Frauen. Berlin: Aufbau Taschenbuch Verlag, 2003. 232 pp., illus., bibl.]

43481. WEILL, KURT. HIRSCH, FOSTER: *Kurt Weill on stage: from Berlin to Broadway.* New York: Knopf, 2002. VI, 403 pp., illus., bibl. [Biography.]

——— WEILL, KURT. STERN, GUY: *A musical drama as cultural catalyst; the byways of Kurt Weill's 'Der Weg der Verheißung'.* [See No. 43307.]

43482. WEININGER, OTTO. SCHMIDINGER, THOMAS: *Angst vor dem Anteil "W".* Zum hundertsten Todestag von Otto Weininger. [In]: Aufbau, Vol. 69, No. 21, New York, Oct. 20, 2003. P. 14.

43483. WEISS, PETER. BERWALD, OLAF: *An introduction to the works of Peter Weiss.* Rochester, NY: Camden House, 2003. VII, 170 pp., bibl. (131– 160), index. (Studies in German literature, linguistics, and culture.)

43484. WEISSKOPF, VICTOR. GOTTFRIED, KURT/JACKSON, J. DAVID: *Mozart and Quantum mechanics. An appreciation of Victor Weisskopf.* [In]: Physics Today, Vol. 56, No. 2, Washington, Feb. 2003. Pp. 43–47, illus., notes. [V.W., data see No. 28839/YB XXXVII.]

43485. WOLF, FRIEDRICH. HORN, MAREN: *"Früchte vom Baum des Lebens der Weltliteratur". Friedrich Wolf und seine Bibliothek.* [In]: Marginalien, H. 170, Wiesbaden, 2003. Pp. 43–59, illus., notes. [On F.W.'s library in Lehnitz.]

43486. WOLFF, JEANETTE. *"Habt den Mut zu menschlichem Tun". Die Jüdin und Demokratin Jeanette Wolff in ihrer Zeit (1888–1976).* Hrsg.: Bernd Faulenbach unter Mitarb. von Anja Wißmann. Essen: Klartext, 2002. 232 pp., illus., facsims., notes. [Book is based on a symposium held at Bocholt in Spring 2000; incl. addresses by Wolfgang Clement, Paul Spiegel, Klaus Ehling (9–15). Contribs. relating to J.W. (some titles abbr.): Dimensionen einer deutsch-jüdischen Biographie im 20. Jahrhundert (Bernd Faulenbach, 17–24). Jeanette Wolffs biographisch-politische Entwicklung bis 1933 (Birgit Seemann, 43–60). Die Generation Jeanette Wolffs in der Sozialdemokratie der Weimarer Republik (Christiane Eifert, 61–74). Widerstand und Leiden Jeanette Wolffs in der NS-Zeit (Christoph Moß, 85–100). Sadismus und Wahnsinn (1947) (J.W., 101–136). Die soziale Demokratin Jeanette Wolff in der deutschen Politik 1945–1975 (Ludger Heid, 137–166). Jeanette Wolffs gesellschaftspolitische Anliegen im Nachkriegsdeutschland (Anja Wißmann, 185–214). Jeanette Wolffs Arbeit in der Jüdischen Gemeinde zu Berlin und im Zentralrat der Juden in Deutschland (Andreas Nachama, 215–224). Jeanette Wolff in der Erinnerungskultur. Nachwort (225–228); further essays are listed according to subject.] [J.W., 1888 Bocholt–1976 Berlin, Social Democratic politician; further data see No. 39413/YB XLVI.]

43487. ZADEK, PETER. DERMUTZ, KLAUS: *Die Außenseiter-Welten des Peter Zadek.* Mitarbeit: Karin Meßlinger. Salzburg: Residenz Verlag, 2001. 239 pp., illus., chronol. (Edition Burgtheater, Bd. 1.)

[On Z.'s theatre productions; incl.: Peter Zadek im Gespräch: "Ich fühle mich nirgend ansässig, außer auf meinen Koffern" (180–203). Peter Zadek ist wie ein alter Rabbiner (Luc Bondy, 217–224). Incl. list of his theatre productions.]

43488. ZWEIG, STEFAN. *Stefan Zweig im Zeitgeschehen des 20. Jahrhunderts.* Im Auftrag des Auslandsgesellschaft NRW, der Internationalen Stefan Zweig Gesellschaft und der Gesellschaft für österreichische Literatur und Kultur hrsg. von Thomas Eicher. Oberhausen: Athena, 2003. 316 pp., footnotes. (Übergänge—Grenzfälle, Österreichische Literatur in Kontexten, Bd. 8.) [Papers presented at the 3rd Int. Stefan Zweig Conference, Dortmund, Sept. 2002. Cont.: (some titles abbr.): Vorwort (ed., 7–12). Stefan Zweigs Haltung zum Zeitgeschehen (Knut Beck, 13–42). Vom Erasmus-Buch zur Schachnovelle (Hans-Albrecht Koch, 43–58). Der Festspieldichter Stefan Zweig (Gert Kerschbaumer, 59–76). Anmerkungen zum Verhältnis Zwischen Richard Strauss und Stefan Zweig (Rüdiger Görner, 77–91). Wandlungen in Stefan Zweigs Verhältnis zum Zionismus (Mark H. Gelber, 93–108). Stefan Zweig und der italienische Faschismus (Gabriella Rovagnati, 109–128). Stefan Zweigs ungeschriebenes Buch: 'Getúlio Vargas' (Ingrid Schwamborn, 129–158). Erasmus, Luther und Calvin bei Stefan Zweig und Thomas Mann (Bernd Hamacher, 159–178). Der Kriegsheimkehrer als Verbrecher (Thomas Eicher, 179–208; also on Hugo Bettauer). Stefan Zweigs 'Sternstunden' (Fritz Hackert, 209–224). Stefan Zweigs Humanitätsgedanke während des Ersten Weltkrieges (Matjaz Birk, 225–242). Zu Stefan Zweigs 'Joseph Fouché' (Gerhard Rademacher, 243–258). Stefan Zweig im Spiegel der Wiener Presse der dreißiger Jahre (Leopold Decloedt, 259–280). Stefan Zweigs historische Biographien und die Gegner der 'bürgerlichen Literatur' (Michel Reffet, 281–292). Zur Rezeption Stefan Zweigs im Wandel der politischen Verhältnisse in Rumänien (Mariana-Virginia Lazarescu (293–304). Der doppelte Bruch (Vladimir Vertlib, 305–312; autobiographical essay).]

VIII. AUTOBIOGRAPHIES, MEMOIRS, LETTERS

43489. ADORNO, THEODOR W.: *Kindheit in Amorbach.* Bilder und Erinnerungen. Mit einer biographischen Recherche hrsg. von Reinhard Pabst. Frankfurt am Main: Insel, 2003. 228 pp., illus., facsims., bibl. [Incl. A.'s short recollections about childhood days in Amorbach (15–24), first publ. 1966; Adornos Wiesengrund. Eine biographische Recherche (Reinhard Pabst, 27–215).]

43490. ADORNO, THEODOR W.: *"So müßte ich ein Engel und kein Autor sein". Adorno und seine Frankfurter Verleger.* Der Briefwechsel mit Peter Suhrkamp und Siegfried Unseld. Hrsg. von Wolfgang Schopf. Frankfurt am Main: Suhrkamp, 2003. 767 pp., bibl., indexes. [Incl. also a letter from Peter Suhrkamp to Carl Zuckmayer and a speech by Siegfried Unseld on the occasion of Th.A.'s 60th birthday (693–702). Nachwort (703–718).]

43491. ADORNO, THEODOR W.: *Briefe an die Eltern 1939–1951.* Hrsg. von Christoph Gödde und Henri Lonitz. Frankfurt: Suhrkamp, 2003. 569 pp., frontis., illus., index. (Theodor W. Adorno, Briefe und Briefwechsel, Bd. 5.) [Cf.: Atempausen und Schlupflöcher. Theodor Adornos Briefe an die Eltern (Christian Schneider) [in]: Mittelweg 36, Jg. 12, Nr. 6, Hamburg, Dez./Jan. 2004, pp. 41–56.]

43492. ADORNO, THEODOR W./HORKHEIMER, MAX: *Briefwechsel 1927–1969. Bd. I: 1927–1937.* Hrsg. von Christoph Gödde und Henri Lonitz. Frankfurt am Main: Suhrkamp, 2003. 608 pp., notes, index. (Theodor W. Adorno. Briefe und Briefwechsel, Bd. 4.) [Incl.: Briefe Adornos an Dritte (519–545). Gutachten (546–559). Berichte (560–580). Editorische Nachbemerkung (581–585).] [Cf.: Knurrender Rottweiler, schreiender Hirsch. Eine Rezension zum 100. Geburtstag von Theodor W. Adorno (Gerhard Scheit) [in]: Zwischenwelt, Jg. 20, Nr. 2, Wien, Sept. 2003, pp. 30–32.]

43493. ARENDT, HANNAH: *Denktagebuch: 1950 bis 1973.* Hrsg. von Ursula Ludz und Ingeborg Nordmann. In Zusammenarbeit mit dem Hannah-Arendt-Institut, Dresden. München: Piper, 2003. 2 vols., VIII, 614 pp., frontis., illus., facsims.; VIII, 617–1232, illus., notes (905–1170), bibl. (1181–1192), indexes (1193–1231, persons; subjects). [Incl.: Nachwort (eds., 825–862).] [Cf.: Hannah Arendts "Denktagebuch" ist eine Entdeckung (Andreas Platthaus) [in]: 'FAZ', Nr. 257, Frankfurt am Main, 5. Nov. 2002, p. L 14.]

43494. BARTMANN, SYLKE/BLÖMER, URSULA/GARZ, DETLEF, eds.: *"Wir waren die Staatsjugend, aber der Staat war schwach"*. Jüdische Kindheit und Jugend in Deutschland und Österreich zwischen Kriegsende und nationalsozialistischer Herrschaft. Oldenburg: Bis, 2003. 440 pp., frontis., ports., illus., facsims., bibl. (423–439). (Oldenburgische Beiträge zu Jüdischen Studien, Bd. 14.) [Selected memoirs written in 1939 for the competition "Mein Leben in Deutschland vor und nach dem 30. Jan. 1933", organised at Harvard Univ. by G.W. Allport et al. Cont.: "Eingegliedert und erfüllt von der neuen Freiheit"—Jüdische Kindheit in der Weimarer Republik (Friedrich Wißmann, 11–19). 15 texts (61–227). Part III cont. historical essays; incl.: Der Antisemitismus in der Weimarer Republik (Ilse Ernst, 293–336). Die jüdische Gemeinde in Wien (Sylke Bartmann, 375–384). See also No. 42693.]

43495. BAUMANN, SABINE: *Berlin—Montevideo—Frankfurt/Main.* J. Hellmut Freund: Erinnerungen an Vertreibung und Exil. [In]: Tribüne, Jg. 42, H. 168, Frankfurt am Main, 2003. Pp. 170–181. [Memoirs, based on interviews with the author.] [J.H.F., b. Sept. 12, 1919 in Berlin, journalist, editor, emigr. in 1939 to Uruguay, remigr. in 1960 to Germany, worked for S. Fischer Verlag in Frankfurt am Main from 1960.]

43496. BEN-CHORIN, SCHALOM: *Ich lebe in Jerusalem. Ein Bekenntnis zu Geschichte und Gegenwart.* Hrsg. und eingel. von Verena Lenzen unter Mitwirkung von Avital Ben-Chorin. Gütersloh: Gütersloher Verlagshaus, 2003. XII, 193 pp., footnotes, index. (Schalom Ben-Chorin Werke, Bd. 2.) [First publ. in 1972. Incl.: Einleitung (eds., IX-XII).]

43497. BEN-NATAN, ASHER: *Die Chuzpe zu leben.* Stationen meines Lebens. Düsseldorf: Droste, 2003. 328 pp., gloss., index. (Eine Veröffentlichung der Konrad-Adenauer-Stiftung e.V.) [Incl. Vorwort (Shimon Peres, 11–12).] [A.B.-N., b. Feb. 15, 1921 in Vienna, Israeli senior civil servant, diplomat, first ambassador to Germany (1965–1969), president of the Deutsch-Israelische Gesellschaft, 1938 emigr. to Palestine.]

43499. BERGGRUEN, HEINZ: *Spielverderber, nicht alle.* Betrachtungen. Berlin: Wagenbach, 2003. 75 pp., illus. [Autobiographical sketches, some of them first publ. in Frankf. Allg. Ztg. Also, by the same author: Ein Berliner kehrt heim: Reden von 1996 bis 2000. Fotogr. von Barbara Klemm. Erw. Neuaufl. Berlin: Bücherbogen, 2002. 101 pp.]

43500. BERGMANN, GRETEL: *"Ich war die grosse jüdische Hoffnung". Erinnerungen einer außergewöhnlichen Sportlerin.* Aus dem Amerik. von Irmgard Hölscher. Karlsruhe: G. Braun Buchverl., 2003. XV, 245 pp. (Südwestdeutsche Persönlichkeiten.) [Covers the author's life to 1947. Incl. a preface by Anna-Ruth Löwenbrück (XI-XV).] [Margaret Lambert-Bergmann, orig. Gretel B., b. April 12, 1914 in Laupheim, emigr. 1933 to the UK, returned to Germany for the Olympic Games, excluded from participation, emigr. 1939 via UK to US.]

43501. BERNSTEIN, EDUARD: *Eduard Bernsteins Briefwechsel mit Karl Kautsky (1895–1905).* Eingel. und hrsg. von Till Schelz-Brandenburg unter Mitarbeit von Susanne Thurn. Frankfurt am Main; New York: Campus, 2003. LIV, 1159 pp., footnotes, indexes (1079–1159). (Quellen und Studien zur Sozialgeschichte, Bd. 19.) [Incl.: Einleitung (ed., VII-LIV).]

43502. BEER, FRITZ: *Kaddisch für meinen Vater.* Essays, Erzählungen, Erinnerungen. Mit einem Nachwort von Christoph Haacker. Wuppertal: Arco, 2002. 390 pp., illus. (Bibliothek der böhmischen Länder.) [Cf.: Würdevoller Untergang: Fritz Beers unverwüstlicher Idealismus (Jakob Hessing) [in]: 'FAZ', Nr. 253, Frankfurt am Main, 30. Okt. 2003, p. 34. "Kaddisch für meinen Vater" (Konstantin Kaiser) [in]: Zwischenwelt, Jg. 20, Nr. 3, Wien, Dez. 2003, p. 72.] [F.B., data see No. 29870/YB 38.]

43503. BOCK, RUDOLF H.: *Gratefully looking back: a doctor's special journey.* Riverside, CA: Ariadne Press, 2002. 125 pp., illus., ports., facsims. (Studies in Austrian literature, culture, and thought. Biography, autobiography, memoirs series.) [R.H.B., b. in Vienna 1915, ophthalmologist, escaped 1938 via Zagreb, Tokyo to Beijing, where he finished his medical studies in 1941. Also lived in Shanghai; returned to Europe in 1947, went to US in 1951; now lives in Woodside, CA.]

43504. BORCHARDT, RUDOLF: *Anabasis.* Aufzeichnungen—Dokumente—Erinnerungen 1943–1945. Hrsg. von Cornelius Borchardt in Verbindung mit dem Rudolf Borchardt Archiv. München: Edition Tenschert bei Hanser, 2003. 424 pp., frontis., illus., facsims., notes (379–408), bibl. R.B., index. [Incl.: Vorwort (7–16). Anabasis (1944) (R.B., 17–96). Tagebuchaufzeichnungen aus Florenz (Corona Borchardt, 97–206). Erinnerungen an 1944/45 (1999) (Cornelius Borchardt, 207–254). Chronik der Ereignisse (Gerhard Schuster, 255–373).] [Cf.: Rudolf Borchardts "Anabasis" in exzellenter Edition (Martin Mosebach) [in] Süddeutsche Zeitung, Nr. 229, München, 6. Okt. 2003, p. 20.]

43505. BRILL, MARTE: *Der Schmelztigel.* Mit einem Nachwort von Reinhard Andress. Frankfurt am Main: Büchergilde Gutenberg, 2002. 351 pp. [First publ. of autobiographical novel depicting life in Hamburg, flight to Majorca and Brazil. Incl.: Nachwort (Reinhard Andress, 337–351). See also No. 42518.] [M.B., née Leider, Sept. 5, 1894 Cologne–Oct. 27, 1969 Sao Paulo, journalist, writer, 1933 spent several months in Alcudia/Majorca, researched the history of the Marannos of Majorca, emigr. 1934 to Brasil.]

43506. CANETTI, ELIAS: *Party im Blitz. Die englischen Jahre.* [Aus dem Nachlaß hrsg. von Kristian Wachinger. Mit einem Nachwort von Jeremy Adler.] München: Hanser, 2003. 246 pp., illus., notes, index. [Incl.: Nachwort (Jeremy Adler, 211–228).] [Cf.: Ende der Maskerade. In "Party im Blitz" zeigt sich Elias Canetti von unbekannter Seite (Andreas Platthaus) [in]: 'FAZ', Nr. 236, Frankfurt am Main, 11. Okt. 2003, p. 46. Nebenan der Krieg. Die nachgelassenen Erinnerungen von Elias Canetti zeigen das Prinzchen im Autor (Susanne Mayer) [in]: ZeitLiteratur [Beilage von] Die Zeit, Jg. 58, Nr. 40, Hamburg, Sept. 2003, p. 38.]

43507. DRACH, ALBERT: *"Z.Z." das ist die Zwischenzeit.* Ein Protokoll. Hrsg. und mit einem Nachwort von Wendelin Schmidt-Dengler unter Mitarb. von Eva Schobel. Red.: Bernhard Fetz. Wien: Zsolnay, 2002. 446 pp., notes (397–422), bibl. (Albert Drach Werke in 10 Bänden, Bd. 2.) [Memoirs, covering the years 1935–1938; incl.: Nachwort (385–398).]

43508. EBERSTADT, WALTER ALBERT: *Whence we came, where we went: from the Rhine to the Main to the Elbe, from the Thames to the Hudson.* Edison, NJ: W.A.E. Books, Whitehurst & Clark, 2002. XV, 472 pp., illus., index. [Autobiography.] [W.A.E., journalist, investment banker, emigr. to the UK, served in the British Army 1940–1946, returned to Hamburg as a military control officer, later settled in New York.] [Bespr. (Hans-Ulrich Wagner) [in]: Rundfunk und Geschichte, Jg. 29, Nr. 1/2, Frankfurt am Main, pp. 80.]

43509. ELBOGEN, PAUL: *Der Flug auf dem Fleckerlteppich. Wien—Berlin—Hollywood.* Hrsg. von Günter Rinke mit einem Nachwort von Günter Rinke und Hans-Harald Müller. Wien: Picus, 2002. 200 pp., index. [Autobiographical stories; 'Nachwort' deals with P.E.'s biography and work.] [P.E., 1894 Vienna–1987 Canada (car accident), author, editor of numerous popular anthologies, emigr. via various countries to the US, lived in California.]

43510. FREUD, SIGMUND: *Unser Herz zeigt nach dem Süden. Reisebriefe 1895–1923.* Hrsg. von Christfried Tögel unter Mitarbeit von Michael Molnar. Berlin: Aufbau, 2002. 422 pp., illus., bibl., index.

43511. FREY, ERNST: *Vietnam, mon amour. Ein Wiener Jude im Dienst von Ho Chi Minh.* Hrsg. von Doris Sottoppietra. Wien: Czernin, 2001. 320 pp., illus., maps. [Memoirs of the author's childhood and youth in Vienna incl. his flight as a Communist, from Austria in 1938 via various countries to Vietnam, where he lived until 1951. Incl. epilogue by his children Irma Schwartz and Silvia Machto-Frey (313–315).] [Cf.: Zum Leben verdammt. Als Oberst von Ho Chi Minh führte Jude und Kommunist Ernst Frey die vietnamesische Armee gegen die Franzosen an (Sibylle Fritsch) [in]: Illus. Neue Welt, Nr. 4/5, Wien, April/Mai, 2001, p. 16. Bespr. (Heinz Schütte) [in]: Comparativ, Jg. 13, H. 2, Leipzig, 2003, pp. 165–167.]

43512. FRIEDLAENDER, SALOMO/MYNONA: *Ich (1871–1936). Autobiographische Skizzen.* Aus dem Nachlaß hrsg. von Hartmut Geerken. Mit einem einführenden Essay von Hartmut Geerken und Detlef Thiel. Bielefeld: Aisthesis, 2003. 151 pp., chronol., index. [First complete edn. of F.s memoirs written in

Paris in 1936. Incl.: heliozentrisch/vulgivaginal (Hartmut Geerken, 99–118). Autoheliobiogravur. Das Kindlein Salomo Friedlaender/Mynona auf dem Weg zu sich (Detlef Thiel, 119–136).]

43513. GOLDSCHMIDT, GEORGES-ARTHUR: *In Gegenwart des abwesenden Gottes.* Zürich: Ammann, 2003. 95 pp. [Incl. three autobiographical essays; orig. title: En présence du Dieu absent. Paris: Bayard Édition, 2001.]

43514. GRANACH, ALEXANDER: *Da geht ein Mensch.* Autobiographischer Roman. Ungekürzte, vollständig überarbeitete Neuausgabe. Mit einem Vorwort von Rachel Salamander. Augsburg: Ölbaum Verlag, 2003. 363 pp., (plus 11 pp. of illus.), gloss. [Incl.: Das Schauspielergenie aus dem Schtetl (Rachel Salamander, 7–11). The text of this edn. is identical with the first edn. publ. 1945 in Stockholm.] [A.G., April 18, 1890 Werbowitz/Galicia–March 14, 1945 New York, actor, 1933 fled to Switzerland, 1934–1937 lived in Poland and the Soviet Union, after release from imprisonment in Moscow escaped in 1938 via Switzerland to the US.] [Cf.: Yehudi Menuhins schweres Erbe (Gad Granach) [in]: Jüdischer Almanach [2003] des Leo Baeck Instituts, Frankfurt am Main, 2003. Pp. 43–45; author, the son of A.G. recalls how, in 1924 in Berlin, his father made him play the violin.]

43515. HEYM, STEFAN: *Immer sind die Männer schuld.* Erzählungen. Mit Illustrationen von Horst Hussel. München: Bertelsmann, 2002. 223 pp. [Autobiographical stories.]

43516. HOBSBAWM, ERIC: *Gefährliche Zeiten.* Ein Leben im 20. Jahrhundert. Aus dem Engl. von Udo Rennert. München: Hanser, 2003. 499 pp., illus., notes, index. [Incl. a preface to the German edn. by the author (14–16). For Engl. orig. edn. and data see No. 42042/YB XLVIII.]

43517. HOFMANNSTHAL, HUGO VON: *Brief-Chronik.* Regest-Ausgabe. Band I: 1874–1911, Band II: 1912–1929, Band III: Register. Hrsg. von Martin E. Schmid. Unter Mitarbeit von Regula Hauser und Severin Perrig. Red.: Jilline Bornand. Heidelberg: Winter, 2003. 3 vols., XVII, 1438; 1443–2869 cols., ports.; 128 pp. [Incl. extracts from his letters.]

43518. JONAS, HANS: *Erinnerungen: nach Gesprächen mit Rachel Salamander.* Vorwort von Rachel Salamander. Geleitwort von Lore Jonas. Hrsg. und mit einem Nachwort versehen von Christian Wiese. Frankfurt am Main: Insel, 2003. 503 [24] pp., illus., notes (427–497), chronol., bibl. H.J. (480–490), bibl., index. [Cont.: Geleitwort (Lore Jonas, 7–9). Vorwort (Rachel Salamander, 11–21). I. Erlebnisse und Begegnungen. II. Philosophie und Geschichte. Anhang: "Aber die Welt ist für mich niemals ein feindlicher Ort gewesen". Nachwort (Christian Wiese, 387–425).] [Cf.: Bespr. (Joachim H. Knoll) [in]: Zeitschrift für Religions- und Geistesgeschichte. Jg. 55, H. 4, Leiden, 2003, pp. 373–375. Die Aktualität der "Erinnerungen" von Hans Jonas (Christian Hacke) [in]: Das Parlament, Jg. 54, Nr. 14, Berlin, 29. März 2004, p. 15. Die postumen Lebenserinnerungen von Hans Jonas als faszinierende Bilanz einer Verlustrechnung (Christian Geyer) [in]: 'FAZ', Nr. 65, Frankfurt am Main, 18. März 2003, p. L 15. Vom Überleben mit einem menschenfernen Gott. Zum hundertsten Geburtstag des Philosophen Hans Jonas (Wolf Scheller) [in]: Jüdische Allgemeine, Jg. 58, Nr. 10, Berlin, 8. Mai 2003, p. 8.]

43519. KELLEN, KONRAD: *Katzenellenbogen.* Erinnerungen an Deutschland. Wien: edition selene, 2003. 246 pp., illus. [Personal memoirs about growing up in Berlin as a millionaire's son, intertwined with temperamental reflections on the past and present. Incl.: "Aber was könnte ich Ihnen denn erzählen? Begegnungen mit Konrad Kellen (Michael Lentz, 243–246).] [K.E., orig. Katzenellenbogen, b. 1913 in Berlin into a baptised family, emigr. 1935 via France and Yugoslavia to the US.]

43520. KLEMPERER, VICTOR: *The lesser evil: diaries 1945–1959.* Abbr. and transl. by Martin Chalmers. London: Weidenfeld & Nicholson, 2003. XVII, 637 pp., illus., ports., facsims., chron., notes. [Vol. 3 of the Engl. edn. For earlier vols. see Nos. 37001/YB XLIV and 38276/YB XLV.] [Cf.: In lingua veritas (Stevie Davies) [in]: The Guardian, Jan. 10, 2004.]

43521. KRAUS, KARL/WALDEN, HERWARTH: *Feinde in Scharen. Ein wahres Vergnügen dabeizusein. Karl Kraus—Herwarth Walden: Briefwechsel 1909–1912.* Hrsg. von George C. Avery. Göttingen: Wallstein, 2002. 676 pp., illus., facsims., notes (421–572), bibl., index. (Veröff. der Deutschen Akademie für Sprache und Dichtung, 79.) [Incl. Nachwort (ed., 615–632); facsim. reprint of a brochure entitled "Ein Protest in Sachen Herwarth Walden", 1909, attached to book cover.]

43522. KUHN, ANNETTE: *Ich trug einen goldenen Stern. Ein Frauenleben in Deutschland.* Berlin: Aufbau, 2003. 232 pp., illus. [A.K., b. May 22, 1934 in Berlin to a Jewish mother and a "half-Jewish" father, Prof. emer. of History and Historical Women's Studies at Bonn Univ., emigr. 1937 via UK to the US, returned to Germany with her family 1948.]

43523. LASKER-SCHÜLER, ELSE: *Briefe 1893–1913.* Bearb. von Ulrike Marquardt. Frankfurt am Main: Jüdischer Verlag im Suhrkamp Verlag, 2003. 837 pp., notes (390–750), indexes. (Else Lasker-Schüler, Werke und Briefe, Kritische Ausgabe, Bd. 6.)

43524. LERNER, GERDA: *Fireweed: a political autobiography.* Philadelphia: Temple Univ. Press, 2002. XIII, 377 pp., illus., ports., notes. (Critical perspectives on the past.) [Memoirs end in 1958, when the author's academic career began.] [G.L., née Kronstein, b. 1920 in Vienna, historian, political activist, champion of women's history, Prof. emer. of History at Univ. of Wisconsin, emigr. 1938 via Liechtenstein to the US.] [Cf.: Review (Bryant Simon) [in]: Reviews in American History, Vol. 31, No. 3, Baltimore, Sept. 2003, pp. 479–483.]

43525. LÖWENTHAL, LEO/KRACAUER, SIEGFRIED: *In steter Freundschaft: Leo Löwenthal—Siegfried Kracauer. Briefwechsel 1921–1966.* Hrsg. von Peter-Erwin Jansen und Christian Schmidt. Mit einer Einleitung von Martin Jay. Aus dem Engl. von Bob Detobel und Susanne H. Löwenthal. Aus dem Franz. von Bob Detobel. Lüneburg: zu Klampen, 2003. 292 pp., footnotes. [Cf.: Freddies oder vielmehr Teddies Lehrjahre. Der junge Adorno in Briefen Siegfried Kracauers an Leo Löwenthal (Lorenz Jäger) [in] 'FAZ', Nr. 98, Frankfurt am Main, April 28, 2003, p. 46.]

43526. MEYERHOF, WALTER E.: *In the shadow of love: stories from my life.* Santa Barbara, CA: Fithian Press, 2002. 106 pp. [A collection of autobiographical essays.] [W.E.M., b. in Kiel 1922 to a Nobel-Prize-winner in physiology, physicist, emigr. to France, rescued by Varian Fry from internment, later joined his parents in Philadelphia, Prof. emer. of Physics at Stanford University, co-director of the Varian Fry Foundation.]

43527. MOSSE, GEORGE L.: *Aus großem Hause. Erinnerungen eines deutsch-jüdischen Historikers.* Aus dem Amerik. von Karl-Heinz Silber. Mit einem Nachwort von Elisabeth Kraus. München: Ullstein, 2003. 397 pp., illus. [For orig. edn. see No. 39440/YB 46. Incl. bibl. G.L.M. (382–387). Nachwort (Elisabeth Kraus, 388–398).] [Cf.: Der doppelte Außenseiter. Bewegend und unkonventionell: Die Autobiografie des Historikers George Mosse (Julius H. Schoeps) [in]: Zeitliteratur [Beilage von] Die Zeit, Jg. 58, Nr. 47, Hamburg, Nov. 2003, p. 31.]

43528. MÜHSAM, ERICH: *Unpolitische Erinnerungen.* Mit einem Nachwort von Hubert van den Berg. Berlin: Aufbau Taschenbuch Verlag, 2003. 223 pp., illus. [New edn., first publ. 1949 in the GDR.]

43529. NOETHER, EMMY. TOBIES, RENATE: *Briefe Emmy Noethers an P.S. Alexandroff.* [In]: 'NTM', Int. Zeitschrift für Gesch. und Ethik der Naturwiss., Technik und Medizin, Jg. 11, Basel, 2003. Pp. 100–115, notes. [Letters provide an insight into E.N.'s life in Göttingen and the US after 1933.]

43530. PANOFSKY, ERWIN: *Korrespondenz 1937 bis 1949.* Hrsg. von Dieter Wuttke. Wiesbaden: Harrassowitz, 2003. XXVIII, 1363 pp., frontis., illus., facsims., footnotes, index (names, subjects, 1281–1363). (Erwin Panofsky Korrespondenz 1910 bis 1968, Bd. II.) [For vol. I see No. 40710/YB XLVII.] [Cf.: Exil, Krieg und Nachkrieg in den Briefen des Kunsthistorikers Erwin Panofsky (Horst Bredekamp) [in]: Süddeutsche Zeitung, Nr. 37, München, 14./15. Feb. 2004, p. 14. Mit der Bescheidenheit des praktizierenden Humanisten: Der Kunsthistoriker Erwin Panofsky in seinen politischen und privaten Ansichten (Willibald Sauerländer) [in]: 'FAZ', Nr. 106, Frankfurt am Main, 7. Mai 2004, p. 37.]

——— PAUCKER, ARNOLD: *Erfahrungen und Erinnerungen. Ein Rückblick.* [See in No. 43407.]

43531. REICH-RANICKI, TEOFILA/REICH-RANICKI, MARCEL: *Wir sitzen alle im gleichen Zug.* Bilder und Texte. Ausgew. von Hans-Joachim Simm. Frankfurt am Main: Insel, 2003. 124 pp. [Autobiographical texts by M.R.-R., with illus. by his wife.]

43532. ROSENFELD, JAKOB: *Ich kannte sie alle: das Tagebuch des chinesischen Generals Jakob Rosenfeld.* Aufgefunden und ausgew. von Ann Margaret Frija-Rosenfeld. Hrsg.: Gerd Kaminski. Wien: Löcker, 2002. 230 pp., illus. [Diary covering the years 1941–1949.] [J.R., data see No. 40042/YB 47.]

43533. SCHOEPS, JULIUS H.: *Mein Weg als deutscher Jude.* Autobiographische Notizen. Zürich: Pendo, 2003. 319 pp., illus. [Cf.: Klärung und Klarheit (Joachim H. Knoll) [in]: Tribüne, Jg. 42, H. 166, Frankfurt am Main, 2003, pp. 159–160.] [J.H.Sch., b. June 1, 1942 in Djursholm (Sweden), historian, further data see No. 41991/YB 48.]

43534. WAGNER, EFRAIM FRANZ: *Prélude und Fügung. Lebensmosaik eines früheren Frankfurters.* Scheidegg: Via Verbis Verl., 2003. 532 pp., illus. [Memoirs.] [E.F.W., b. 1919 in Breslau, grew up in Frankfurt, emigr. 1939 to Palestine, lives in Jerusalem.]

43535. *Die Welt ist eine schmale Brücke: Yaakov Zur—ein Israeli aus Rostock. Erinnerungen und Begegnungen.* Hrsg. von Christine Gundlach. Schwerin: Helms Verlag, 2003. 256 pp., illus. (Schriften aus dem Max-Samuel-Haus, 3.) [Memoirs deal with the Zuckermann family in Rostock, school years in Frankfurt am Main, life in Palestine/Israel, visits to Rostock from 1987, lectures at Rostock Univ., and encounters at the Max-Samuel-Haus.] [Cf.: Von der Jugendaliyah gerettet (Helga Krohn) [in]: Tribüne, Jg. 42, H. 168, Frankfurt am Main, 2003, pp. 195–198.] [Y.Z., orig. Alfred Jacques Zuckermann, b. 1924 in Rostock, educator, historian, emigr. in 1939 to Palestine, in 1946 joined the religious Kibbutz En Hanaziv.]

43536. WOLFF, CHARLOTTE: *Augenblicke verändern uns mehr als die Zeit.* Autobiographie. Aus dem Engl. von Michaela Huber. Pfungstadt: Kranichsteiner Literaturverl., 2003. 319 pp., illus. [Orig. publ. in London 1980, with the title 'Hindsight'. Incl. a preface by Christa Wolf.] [Ch.W., Sept. 30, 1897 Riesenburg (West Prussia)–Sept. 12, 1986 London, psychiatrist, sexologist, emigr. 1933 to France, 1936 to the UK, from 1952 private psych. practice in London. See also No. 43678.]

43537. WYLAND-HERZFELDE, GEORGE: *Glück gehabt. Erinnerungen 1925–1949.* München: Deutscher Taschenbuch Verlag, 2003. 299 pp., frontis., illus. Orig.-Ausg. [G.W.-H., b. Oct. 14, 1925 in Berlin, son of the publisher Wieland Herzfelde, 1933 emigr. to Prague, 1938 to the US and Canada, lives since 1968 in Switzerland.]

43538. ZUCKMAYER, CARL: *Carl Zuckmayer—Annemarie Seidel. Briefwechsel.* Hrsg. von Gunther Nickel. Göttingen: Wallstein, 2003. 327 pp., frontis., notes (223–312), bibl., index. (Zuckmayer-Schriften.) [Incl.: Einleitung (ed., 7–39). Cont. the correspondence between A.S., an actress and later wife of Peter Suhrkamp and C.Z. between 1922 and 1958.]

IX. GERMAN-JEWISH RELATIONS

A. General

43539. *Annäherungen. 50 Jahre christlich-jüdische Zusammenarbeit in Hamburg.* Hrsg. vom Vorstand der Ges. für christl-jüd. Zus.-arb. in Hamburg. [Hamburg]: [Ges. für christl.-jüd. Zus.-arb. e.V. in Hamburg], 2002. 172 pp., illus., ports., bibl. [Incl. contribs. by Wilm Sanders, Ursula Büttner, Siegfried von Kortzfleisch et al.]

43540. *Austrian Studies* [with the issue title] 'Hitler's first victim?': memory and representation in post-war Austria. Vol. 11, Issue 1, London, Sept. 2003. 1 issue, notes. [Cont.: Introd.: Hitler's first victim? (Judith Beniston, 1–13). The myth of Austria as Nazi victim, the emigrants and the discipline of exile studies (S. Niederacher, 14–32). Maria Frischauf's Der graue Mann: National Socialism and the Austrian novel (A. Barker, 33–44). A memoir of the years 1938–1945 (B. Stillfried, 45–64). Fritz Hochwälder's Holokaust: a choice of evils (Judith Beniston, 65–84). Casual brutalities: Hans Lebert's Die Wolfshaut, Gerhard Fritsch's Fasching and Austrian collective memory (Jonathan James Long, 85–101). Architecture of memory: Rachel Whiteread's memorial to the 65,000 murdered Austrian Jews (N.C. Pages, 102–121). Erich Hackl's Abschied von Sidonie: breaking the silence (Elin N. Vestli, 122– 137). Repossessing the past? Property, memory and Austrian

Jewish narrative histories (Lisa Silverman, 138–153). Post-Shoah positions of displacement in the films of Ruth Beckermann (Dagmar C.G. Lorenz, 154–170). The Iberian dimension of the German-Jewish discourse: Robert Menasse's Die Vertreibung aus der Hölle (Florian Krobb, 171–184); incl. also review articles on related subjects.]

43541. BRIEGLEB, KLAUS: *Missachtung und Tabu. Eine Streitschrift zur Frage: "Wie antisemitisch war die Gruppe 47?"* Berlin: Philo, 2003. 413 pp., footnotes, notes. [Discusses antisemitism after the Second World War and how the authors of "Gruppe 47" dealt with these phenomena; also on their attitude towards exiled authors.] [Cf.: Wider den Antisemitismus, aber auch wider die Literatur: Klaus Brieglebs neue Studie zur Gruppe 47 (Christoph Bartmann) [in]: Süddeutsche Zeitung, Nr. 15, München, 20. Januar 2003, p. 16. Ein Bärendienst (Dorothea Dieckmann) [in]: Die Zeit, Nr. 2, Hamburg, 2. Jan. 2003, p. 40. Mythos Neuanfang (Renate Göllner) [in]: Zwischenwelt, Jg. 20, Nr. 1, Wien, Mai 2003, pp. 3–4.]

43542. *Freiburger Rundbrief.* Zeitschrift für christlich-jüdische Begegnung. Neue Folge. Hrsg.: Freiburger Rundbrief e.V. Hauptschriftleiter: Clemens Thoma. Geschäftsführende Schriftleiterin: Elisabeth Weidinger. Freiburg, 2003. 4 issues. [Incl. essays and book reviews pertaining to theological and historical aspects of Christian-Jewish relations. Selected articles and reviews are listed according to subject.]

43543. *50 Jahre Woche der Brüderlichkeit.* Eröffnungsveranstaltung der Kölnischen Gesellschaft für Christlich-Jüdische Zusammenarbeit e.V. am 14. April 2002 im Stiftersaal des Wallraf-Richartz-Museums. Köln: Kölnische Gesellschaft für Christlich-Jüdische Zusammenarbeit e.V., 2003. 34, 7 pp., illus. [Cover title: "Abel steh auf, damit es anders anfängt zwischen uns allen" (Hilde Domin). Cont.: Vorwort (Christa Pfarr, 5–7). Begrüßungsrede (Jürgen Wilhelm, 9–14). Dichtung als Brücke—Zur deutsch-jüdischen Lyrik (Walter Hinck, 15–22; on Hilde Domin). 12 poems (Hilde Domin, 23–34).]

43544. GILMAN, SANDER L.: *"We're not Jews": imaging Jewish history and Jewish bodies in contemporary multicultural literature.* [In]: Modern Judaism, Vol. 23, No. 2, Oxford, May 2003. Pp. 126–155, notes. [Incl. the novels by Zafer Senocak, and by Thomas Meinecke which include Jewish themes.]

43545. HAASIS, HELLMUT G.: *"Jud Süß"—Joseph Süß Oppenheimer.* Rezeption und Verdrängung eines Justizmordes. [In]: Tribüne, Jg. 42, H. 167, Frankfurt am Main, 2003. Pp. 178–184.

43546. HALHUBER, MAX-JOSEPH [et al.], eds.: *Fünf Fragen an drei Generationen. Der Antisemitismus und wir heute.* Wien: Czernin, 2002. 142 pp., notes, bibl. [Incl. three essays dealing with the relationship of non-Jewish Germans and Austrians with Judaism, the Jews and antisemitism; incl.: Vorwort (eds., 7–12). Einleitung (Christina Kleiser, 13–22). Bekenntnishafte Überlegungen eines so genannten Zeitzeugen (Max-Joseph Halhuber, 23–52; Nicht "die Judenfrage"—der Antisemitismus ist das Problem (Anton Pelinka, 53–90). Die zweite Nachkriegsgeneration—Auf der Suche nach einer eigen-ständigen Deutung (Daniela Ingruber, 91–132).]

43547. HELL, JULIA: *Eyes wide shut: German post-Holocaust authorship.* [In]: New German Critique, No. 88, Ithaca, NY, Winter 2003. Pp. 9–36, footnotes. [Discusses how leading German post-war writers (Jewish and non-Jewish) have dealt with the Nazi past. Incl. Paul Celan, Durs Grünbein, Wolfgang Hilbig, Uwe Johnson, W.G. Sebald, Martin Walser.]

43548. KAMMERER, GABRIELE: *Wie hältst du's mit dem Judentum? Christliche Suchbewegungen im Gespräch.* 50 Jahre Evangelischer Arbeitskreis Kirche und Israel in Hessen und Nassau. Heppenheim: Ev. AK Kirche und Israel in Hessen und Nassau, 2003. 184 pp., illus., index, docs. (Schriftenreihe des Ev. AK Kirche und Israel in Hessen und Nassau, Nr. 19/2003.) [Also on relations with Israel.]

43549. KAUDERS, ANTHONY D.: *Vergangenheitsbewältigung am Beispiel Münchens.* [In]: Jüdische Geschichte: Alte Herausforderungen, neue Ansätze [see No. 42230]. Pp. 167–177, footnotes. [Discusses manifestations of antisemitism in post-war Germany, gradual changes in political and theological language up to the early 1960s; also examines the usefulness of terms such as "suppression" and "philosemitism" in the context of "Vergangenheitsbewältigung".]

43550. KAUDERS, ANTHONY D.: *"Repression" and "Philo-Semitism" in post-war Germany.* [In]: History and Memory, Vol. 15, No. 1, Bloomington, IN, Spring/Summer 2003. Pp. 97–123, notes. [Author contends that the inflationary use of terms such as "repression" and "philosemitism" does not do justice to the complexities of "Vergangenheitsbewältigung" in post-war Germany.]

——— KONKEL, MICHAEL [et al.], eds.: *Die Konstruktion des Jüdischen in Vergangenheit und Gegenwart.* [See No. 43072.]

43551. KONZETT, MATTHIAS, ed.: *A companion to the works of Thomas Bernhard.* Rochester, NY: Camden House, 2002. VI, 251 pp., bibl. (229– 242), index.(Studies in German literature, linguistics, and culture.) [Incl. discussions about how B. relates to the legacy of Austrian-Jewish culture.]

43552. KORN, SALOMON: *Das unbewältigte Erbe. Sechzig Jahre Wannsee Konferenz.* [In]: Tribüne, Jg. 42, H. 165, Frankfurt am Main, 2003. Pp. 84–90, footnotes. [Speech, made at the Westend synagogue, Frankfurt am Main, Nov. 9, 2002, dealing mainly with how the Germans live with the burden of the past.]

43553. KREBS, WOLFGANG: *"Lettre sur les Juifs" (1783). Ein bemerkenswertes Buch von Jean-Baptiste (Anacharsis) Cloots.* [In]: Kalender für das Klever Land, Jg. 2004. Kleve, 2003. Pp. 179–183, port., facsim.

43554. LAMB-FAFFELBERGER, MARGARETE: *Beyond 'The sound of music': the quest for cultural identity in modern Austria.* [In]: The German Quarterly, Vol. 76, No. 3, Cherry Hill, NJ, Summer 2003. Pp. 189–299, notes. [Deals with Austria's coming to terms with its Nazi past, the Holocaust, the Waldheim affair.]

43555. MILETTO, GIANFRANCO/VELTRI, GIUSEPPE: *Die Hebraistik in Wittenberg (1502–1813): von der "Lingua Sancta" zur Semitistik.* [In]: Henoch, Vol. XXV, No. 1, Turin, April 2003. Pp. 93–112, footnotes. [Incl. Italian summary.]

43556. QUANDT, SIEGFRIED: *Geschichtskultur in Deutschland.* Die Aschaffenburger Gespräche. München: Econ, 2003. 223 pp. [On 25 years of "Aschaffenburger Gespräche"; incl.: 1980: Deutsche und Juden. Wunden, Wirklichkeit, Wege (43–52). 1996: Hitlers willige Helfer? Die Deutschen und der Holocaust (173–180).]

43557. ROTHSCHILD, MARY: *The curse of intolerance.* [In]: Jewish Frontier, Vol. 69, No. 2, New York, Spring 2003. Pp. 9–19; 32–33. [Author, child of survivors, describes her experiences to a meeting of "second-generation Germans" held at Wannsee.]

43558. *Toleranz. Drei Lesarten zu Lessings Märchen vom Ring im Jahre 2003.* Von Angelika Overrath, Navid Kermani, Robert Schindel. Göttingen: Wallstein, 2003. 56 pp. (Göttinger Sudelblätter.) [Essays, presented at Herzog August Bibliothek, Wolfenbüttel. May 9, 2003.]

43559. WEISSBERG, LILIANE: *Eduard Fuchs und die Ökonomie der Karikatur.* [In]: Babylon, H. 20, Frankfurt am Main, 2002. Pp. 113–128, notes. [On F.'s very successful book 'Die Juden in der Karikatur' and on Werner Sombart's equally successful 'Die Juden und das Wirtschaftsleben'.]

B. **German-Israeli Relations**

43560. BARZEL, RAINER: *Nicht nur Holocaust, auch Dankbarkeit. Anmerkungen zum deutsch-israelischen Verhältnis.* [In]: Die Politische Meinung, Jg. 47, H. 392. Berlin, 2002. Pp. 51–56.

43561. JÄGER, SIEGFRIED/JÄGER, MARGARETE: *Medienbild Israel. Zwischen Solidarität und Antisemitismus.* Unter Mitarbeit von Gabriele Cleve [et al.]. Münster: LIT Verlag, 2003. 368 pp., graphs, bibl., footnotes (Medien. Forschung und Wissenschaft, Bd. 3.).

43562. SCHOENFELD, GABRIEL: *Israel and the anti-Semites.* [In]: Commentary, Vol. 113, No. 6, New York, June 2002. Pp. 13–20. [Incl. German antisemitism disguised as opposition to Israel.]

43563. SIETZ, HENNING: *Attentat auf Adenauer. Die geheime Geschichte eines politischen Anschlags.* Berlin: Siedler, 2003. 335 pp., illus., notes (285–312), gloss., bibl., index. [Deals with the attempt by a group of former Irgun activists/Cheruth members to assassinate Adenauer with a parcel bomb in March 1952 thus sabotaging German-Israeli restitution negotiations.]

43564. *"Wagner im Kontext". Aus Anlass eines Symposiums des Instituts für deutsche Geschichte, November 2001.* [Section title of] Tel Aviver Jahrbuch für deutsche Geschichte, Jg. 13. Göttingen: Wallstein, 2003. Pp. 361–410, footnotes. [Cont.: "Der Ring der Mythen"—Wagner und die Israelis (Na'ama Sheffi, 361–371). Das Gesamtkunstwerk und sein Widerhall bei Hanoch Levin und anderen (Gad Kaynar, 372–384). Der Ring schließt sich—Wahnhaftes Wähnen über Musik und Geschichte (Bazon Brock, 401–410).]

C. **Church and Synagogue**

43565. ARIEL, YAAKOV S.: *Philosemites or antisemites?: evangelical Christian attitudes towards Jews, Judaism, and the State of Israel.* Jerusalem: Vidal Sassoon International Center for the Study of Antisemitism, 2002. 49 pp., bibl. (Analysis of current trends in antisemitism, No. 20.)

43566. BACHMANN, MICHAEL: *Jesus mit dem Judenhut. Ikonographische Notizen.* [In]: Zeitschrift für Theologie und Kirche, Jg. 100, 2003, H. 3. Tübingen, 2003. Pp. 378–398, footnotes. [Incl. Engl. summary.]

43567. BROCKE, EDNA: *Dreißig Jahre in Folge. Erfahrungen einer Jüdin bei Kirchentagen.* [In]: Kirche und Israel, Neukirchener Theologische Zeitschrift. Jg. 17, H. 1, Neukirchen-Vluyn, 2002. Pp. 86–100, notes.

43568. DOKTÓR, JAN: *Talmud und Disputationen. Zum christlich-jüdischen Diskurs im 18. Jahrhundert.* [In]: Leipziger Beiträge zur jüdischen Geschichte und Kultur, Bd. I, München, 2003. Pp. 105–119, footnotes. [Focuses on the role of the Sabbatians and the Frankists in these debates.]

43569. FREY, WINFRIED: *Ein geborner Jud von Jerusalem. Überlegungen zur Entstehung der Ahasver-Figur.* [In]: Von Enoch bis Kafka. Festschrift für Karl E. Grözinger zum 60. Geburtstag [see No. 43050]. Pp. 207–217, footnotes.

43570. HERZIG, ARNO: *Die Juden als Argument in den konfessionellen Auseinandersetzungen der Frühen Neuzeit.* [In]: Von Enoch bis Kafka. Festschrift für Karl E. Grözinger zum 60. Geburtstag [see No. 43050]. Pp. 83–91, footnotes. [Demonstrates how traditional anti-Judaism was fomented in the confessional controversies of the Reformation Era.]

43571. *Das jüdische Leben Jesu 'Toldot Jeschu'.* Die älteste lateinische Übersetzung in den 'Falsitates Judaeorum' von Thomas Ebendorfer. Kritisch hrsg., eingel., übers. und mit Anmerkungen versehen von Brigitta Callsen, Fritz Peter Knapp, Manuela Niesner und Martin Przybilski. München: Oldenbourg, 2003. 107 pp., footnotes. (Veröff. des Instituts für Österreichische Geschichtsforschung, Bd. 39.) [On a 15th cent. transl. of 'Toledot Jeschu', instrumental in the late medieval anti-Jewish agitation.]

43572. KINZIG, WOLFRAM: *Closeness and distance: towards a new description of Jewish- Christian relations.* [In]: Jewish Studies Quarterly, Vol. 10, No. 3, Tübingen, 2003. Pp. 274–290, footnotes. [Deals also with both Christian antisemitism and philosemitism throughout history.]

43573. RAISIG, CHRISTOPH: *Wege der Erneuerung. Christen und Juden: Der Rheinische Synodalbeschluss von 1980.* Potsdam: Verlag für Berlin-Brandenburg, 2002. 312 pp., docs. (Schriften des Steinheim-Instituts, Bd. 2.)

43574. SCHUBERT, KURT: *Christentum und Judentum im Wandel der Zeiten.* Wien: Böhlau, 2003. 229 pp., notes. [Sections I–V deal with early Christian-Jewish relations, subsequent sections are: VI. Die mittelalterlichen Beschuldigungen gegen die Juden und die Abwehr in der jüdischen Apologetik. VII. Konfrontation nach Symbiose im mittelalterlichen Spanien. VIII. An der Schwelle der

Neuzeit. IX. Barock und Aufklärung. X. Aufklärung—Emanzipation/Assimilation—Antisemitismus. XI. Vom Rassenhass zum Völkermord. XII. Der christlich-jüdische Dialog als Antwort auf die Herausforderung des Nationalsozialismus.]

43575. WEBER, ANNETTE: *Glaube und Wissen—Ecclesia et Synagoga.* [In]: Wissenspopularisierung. Konzepte der Wissensverbreitung im Wandel. Hrsg. von Carsten Kretschmann. Berlin: Akademie Verlag, 2003. (Wissenskultur und gesellschaftlicher Wandel, Bd. 4.) Pp. 89–126, illus., footnotes.

D. **Antisemitism**

43576. *Antisemitismus—Erscheinungsformen der Judenfeindschaft gestern und heute.* Tagung der Gesellschaft für Christlich-Jüdische Zusammenarbeit Görlitz und der Friedrich-Ebert-Stiftung (Büro Dresden) am 7. Oktober 2002 in Dresden. Frankfurt am Main: GEP, Gemeinschaftswerk der Evangelischen Publizistik, 2003. 78 pp. (epd Dokumentation, 2003, Nr. 10.) [Incl. contribs. on Christian antisemitism, manifestations of antisemitism in the former GDR and in the present day by Rudolf W. Sirsch, Peter von der Osten, Christoph Münz, Christian Wiese, Marten Marquardt, Peter Philipp, Lothar Mertens, Friedrich-Wilhelm Marquardt, Rolf Rendtorff, Martin Stöhr.]

43577. AUSTRIA. WASSERMANN, HEINZ P., ed.: *Antisemitismus in Österreich nach 1945.* Ergebnisse, Positionen und Perspektiven der Forschung. Innsbruck: Studien Verl., 2002. 296 pp. (Schriften des David-Herzog-Centrums für jüdische Studien, 3.)

43578. BAJOHR, FRANK: *"Unser Hotel ist judenfrei". Bäder-Antisemitismus im 19. und 20. Jahrhundert.* Frankfurt am Main: Fischer Taschenbuch Verlag, 2003. 233 pp., illus., notes (198–219), bibl., indexes. [Incl. a chap. on the Nazi era.]

43579. BERGMANN, WERNER: *Survey-Fragen als Indikatoren für den Wandel in der Wahrnehmung politischer Probleme: Antisemitismus in der Bundesrepublik Deutschland 1949–1998.* [In]: Jahrbuch für Antisemitismusforschung 12, Berlin, 2003. Pp. 231–255, footnotes.

——— *Der Berliner Antisemitismusstreit" 1879–1881.* Eine Kontroverse um die Zugehörigkeit der deutschen Juden zur Nation. Kommentierte Quellenedition. [See No. 42209.]

——— BOTZ, GERHARD [et al.], eds.: *Eine zerstörte Kultur. Jüdisches Leben und Antisemitismus in Wien seit dem 19. Jahrhundert.* [See No. 42467.]

43581. BRAUN, STEFAN/WURSTER, JOACHIM: *Antisemitismus und Antizionismus.* Alles in Ordnung? [In]: Tribüne, Jg. 42, H. 168, Frankfurt am Main, 2003. Pp. 130–140, footnotes,

43582. BRUSTEIN, WILLIAM: *Roots of hate: anti-semitism in Europe before the Holocaust.* Cambridge; New York: Cambridge Univ. Press, 2003. XV, 384 pp., illus., tabs., diagr., footnotes, bibl. (361–376), index. [Deals with religious, racial, economic and political roots of antisemitism and extensively covers Germany.]

43583. BUTTARONI, SUSANNA/MUSIAL, STANISLAW, eds.: *Ritualmord. Legenden in der europäischen Geschichte.* Wien: Böhlau, 2003. 289 pp., illus., facsims., notes, bibl., indexes. [Incl. Engl. abstracts. Selected essays: Die Ritualmordlegende: Von den Anfängen bis ins 20. Jahrhundert (Rainer Erb, 11–20). Zur Frage der Historizität des Andreas von Rinn (Georg R. Schroubek, 173–196). Die Instrumentalisierung von Ritualmordbeschuldigungen zur Rechtfertigung spätmittelalterlicher Judenverfolgungen (Markus J. Wenninger, 197–212). Other contribs. deal with Simon of Trent, the Vatican, theological aspects, blood libel accusations in Lithuania.]

43584. CHESLER, PHYLLIS: *The new anti-semitism: the current crisis and what we must do about it.* San Francisco: L. Jossey-Bass, 2003. IX, 307 pp., notes, bibl., index. [Incl. contemporary German antisemitism; also chap.: Is anti-Zionism the new anti-Semitism? (161–194).]

43585. DAHL, JOSÉ DAVID LEBOVITCH: *The role of the Roman Catholic church in the formation of modern antisemitism: La civiltá catholica, 1850–1879.* [In]: Modern Judaism, Vol. 23, No. 2, Oxford, May 2003. Pp. 180–197, notes. [Discusses the influence this Jesuit journal had on fomenting antisemitism.]

43586. DEFENCE. GYSSLING, WALTER: *Mein Leben in Deutschland vor und nach 1933 und Der Anti-Nazi: Handbuch im Kampf gegen die NSDAP.* Hrsg. und eingeleitet von Leonidas E. Hill. Mit einem Vorwort von Arnold Paucker. Bremen: Donat, 2003. 504 pp., notes, bibl. [Cont.: Vorwort (Arnold Paucker, 7–10; also on the involvement of the London Leo Baeck Institute in collecting testimonies about the defense work of the C.V.). Walter Gyßling (1903–1980)—Ein deutscher Demokrat und Gegner des Nationalsozialismus (ed., 11–60). Mein Leben in Deutschland vor und nach 1933 (W.G., 61–226; memoirs of the former (non-Jewish) archivist of the "Büro Wilhelmstraße" about the defense and propaganda activities against the Nazis). Der Anti-Nazi—Handbuch im Kampf gegen die NSDAP (W.G., 227–478; annotated reprint of the 1932 edn.).] [Cf.: Bespr. (Christiane Hoss) [in]: Mitgliederrundbrief Nr. 50, Verein aktives Museum, Berlin, Dez. 2003, pp. 36–39. "Pillen gegen Erdbeben"—Antisemitismusabwehr des Centralvereins deutscher Staatsbürger jüdischen Glaubens vor 1933 (Jürgen Matthäus) [in]: Jahrbuch für Antisemitismusforschung 12, Berlin, 2003, pp. 281–304; also on Avraham Barkai's book, see No. 40836/YB XLVIII.]

43587. *"Die Deutschen werden den Juden Auschwitz nie verzeihen". Antisemitismus in Deutschland.* Materialien zum Rechtsextremismus, Bd. 5. Düsseldorf: IDA-NRW, Informations- und Dokumentationsstelle gegen Gewalt, Rechtsextremismus und Ausländerfeindlichkeit in Nordrhein-Westfalen, 2002. 58 pp., tabs., notes, bibl. (Materialien zum Rechtsextremismus, Bd. 5.) [Red.: Gisbert Schürig, Anne Broden. Incl. contribs. by Wolfgang Benz, Werner Bergmann, Alfred Schobert, Cornelia Schmitz-Berning, Harald Welzer, Sabine Moller, Karoline Tschuggnall, Henryk M. Broder, Oskar Niedermayer, Elmar Brähler, Hajo Funke, Lars Rensmann, Uri Avnery, Netanel Schwarz, Erich Fried, Isaac Deutscher, Elisabeth Beck-Gernsheim, Klaus Ganser.]

43588. *Eingriffe: Antisemitismus und Universität Potsdam.* sigaa_up. Studentische Initiative gegen Antisemitismus und Antizionismus an der Universität Potsdam. Potsdam: SigAA_UP, 2003. 71 pp., notes, illus. (Beiträge zur Aufklärung und Kritik.) [Also on "anti-Israelism" and philosemitism.]

43589. ENDEMANN, MARTIN: *Sie bauen U-Bahnen nach Auschwitz. Antisemitismus im deutschen Fußball.* [In]: Gerd Dembowski/Jürgen Scheidle, eds.: Tatort Stadion. Rassismus, Antisemitismus und Sexismus im Fußball. Köln: PapyRossa Verl., 2002. Pp. 80–89.

43590. *Entwicklungen im Rechtsextremismus: Die Bedeutung des Antisemitismus im aktuellen deutschen Rechtsextremismus.* Köln: Bundesamt für Verfassungsschutz, Presse- und Öffentlichkeitsarbeit, 2002. 41 pp., facsims., tabs., footnotes. [Text: Claudia Dillmann.]

43591. *Gegen-Bewegung der Moderne. Verbindung von Antifeminismus, Antisemitismus und Emanzipation um 1900.* [Issue title of] Ariadne, H. 43, Kassel, 2003. 80 pp., illus., notes. [Selected articles (some titles abbr.): Die proletarisch-sozialistische Frauenbewegung im Kaiserreich und der Antisemitismus (Stephanie Brauckmann, 6–13). Frauenbewegte Jüdinnen zwischen Antisemitismus und Antifeminismus im Wien der Jahrhundertwende (Michaela Raggam-Blesch, 14–21). Vom Antifeminismus zum Antisemitismus. Kontroversen um Hans Blüher in der Frauen- und Jugendbewegung (Claudia Bruns, 46–51). Einige Bemerkungen zum Thema Antisemitismus und Antifeminismus (Angelika Schaser, 66–71).]

43592. GRAETZ, MICHAEL: *Vom Text zum Bild: die antisemitische Karikatur.* [In]: Ein Leben für die jüdische Kunst. Gedenkband für Hannelore Künzl. Hrsg. v. Michael Graetz, Heidelberg, Winter, 2003. Pp. 163–180.

43593. HALBRAINER, HEIMO, ed.: *"Feindbild Jude". Zur Geschichte des Antisemitismus.* Graz: Clio, 2003. 116 pp., illus., bibl. (Historische und gesellschaftspolitische Schriften des Vereins Clio, 1.)

43594. HASTINGS, DEREK: *How "Catholic" was the early Nazi movement? Religion, race, and culture in Munich, 1919–1924.* [In]: Central European History, Vol. 36, No. 3, Boston; Leiden, 2003. Pp. 383–433, footnotes. [Incl. Catholic antisemitism.]

43595. *Heinrich Mann-Jahrbuch.* Jg. 21, Lübeck, 2003. 1 vol. [Incl.: Judentum und Antisemitismus zwischen 1870 und 1890 in Lübeck (Ingaburgh Klatt, 9–26). Judentum und Antisemitismus im wilhelminischen Berlin (Karsten Krieger, 27–47).]

43596. HEINEMANN, MIRKO/SCHOBERT, ALFRED/WAHJUDI, CLAUDIA: *Handbuch Antirassismus. Projekte und Initiativen gegen Rassismus und Antisemitismus in Deutschland.* Essen: Kokerei Zollverein, 2002. 225 pp., index.

43597. HELLIG, JOCELYN: *The Holocaust and antisemitism: a short history.* Oxford: Oneworld Publications, 2003. XII, 354 pp., notes, bibl. (325–336), index. [Cont. sections: I. The Holocaust and antisemitism: theoretical issues. II. Pre-Christian antisemitism. III. Inter-religious rivalry and antisemitism. IV. The secularisation of antisemitism. Epilogue (deals with contemporary antisemitism and Holocaust deniers).]

43598. HERING, RAINER: *Konstruierte Nation. Der Alldeutsche Verband 1890–1939.* Hamburg: Christians, 2003. 560 pp., illus., footnotes, bibl. (507–582), indexes. (Hamburger Beiträge zur Sozial- und Zeitgeschichte, 40.) [Deals passim with antisemitism; incl. the chap.: Alldeutsche und Antisemitismus (187–219); also a section focusing on Hamburg (221–318).] [Cf.: Eliten des Hasses. Wegbereiter Hitlers: Rainer Hering zeigt, welche verhängnisvolle Rolle der Alldeutsche Verband in der Vorgeschichte des "Dritten Reiches" spielte (Volker Ullrich) [in]: Die Zeit, Nr. 7, Hamburg, 5. Feb. 2004, p. 44.]

43599. HERING, RAINER/NICOLAYSEN, RAINER, eds.: *Lebendige Sozialgeschichte.* Gedenkschrift für Peter Borowsky. Opladen: Westdeutscher Verlag, 2003. 827 pp., footnotes, index. [Incl.: Die "metaphysische Pathologie" des Juden. Erkenntnistheoretische Dimensionen eines religiösen Rassismus um 1920 (Claudia Bruns, 278–295; on Hans Blüher). Antijüdische Aktionen der Neuen Linken 1969/70 und jüdische Reaktionen. Anmerkungen zu einem belasteten Verhältnis (Knud Andresen, 464–486). Further selected essays are listed according to subject.]

43600. HILMES, OLIVER: *Im Fadenkreuz: politische Gustav-Mahler-Rezeption 1919–1945: eine Studie über den Zusammenhang von Antisemitismus und Kritik an der Moderne.* Frankfurt am Main; New York: Lang, 2003. 259 pp. (Europäische Hochschulschriften: Reihe 3, Geschichte und ihre Hilfswissenschaften, Bd. 958.) Zugl.: Potsdam, Univ., Diss., 2002.

43601. HIMMELSTEIN, KLAUS: *Die Juden müssen "aufhören, Juden sein zu wollen"—Antisemitismus bei Pädagogen vor 1933.* [In]: Jahrbuch für Pädagogik 2003, Jg. 11, Frankfurt am Main, 2003. Pp. 81–103, notes, bibl.

43602. JAHR, CHRISTOPH: *Ahlwardt on trial: reactions to the antisemitic agitation of the 1890s in Germany.* [In]: Leo Baeck Institute Year Book 2003, Vol. XLVIII, Oxford; New York, 2003. Pp. 67–85, illus., footnotes.

——— *Judenemanzipation und Antisemitismus in Deutschland im 19. und 20. Jahrhundert.* Ein Tagungsband. Hrsg. von Wolfgang Michalka und Martin Vogt. [See No. 42229.]

43603. LEGGE, JEROME S.: *Jews, Turks, and other strangers: the roots of prejudice in modern Germany.* Madison: Univ. of Wisconsin Press, 2003. XVI, 205 pp., illus., notes, bibl. (189–197), index. [Incl. present-day antisemitism.]

43604. LEY, MICHAEL: *Kleine Geschichte des Antisemitismus.* München: Fink, 2003. 164 pp., footnotes, bibl.

43605. LOOSE, INGO: *"In der Seele ein Gefühl des 16. Jahrhunderts". Der Ritualmordprozess gegen Mendel' Bejlis in Kiev 1913.* [In]: Jahrbuch für Antisemitismusforschung 12, Berlin, 2003. Pp. 281–304, footnotes. [Also on its repercussions in Germany.]

43606. MALINOWSKI, STEPHAN: *Vom blauen zum reinen Blut. Antisemitische Adelskritik und adliger Antisemitismus 1871–1944.* [In]: Jahrbuch für Antisemitismusforschung 12, Berlin, 2003. Pp. 147–168, footnotes. [Deals with the "Deutsche Adelsgenossenschaft".]

——— MACK, MICHAEL: *German idealism and the Jew: the inner anti-Semitism of philosophy and German-Jewish responses.* [See No. 43658.]

43607. McNUTT, JAMES E.: *Adolf Schlatter and the Jews.* [In]: German Studies Review, Vol. 26, No. 2, Tempe, AZ, May 2003. Pp. 353–370, notes. [Deals with the antisemitic writings of the Swiss Protestant theologian during the Nazi period; refers also to the fact that, without reference to his antisemitism, his theological writings have a new following in several countries.]

43608. MEYER ZU UPTRUP, WOLFRAM: *Kampf gegen die "jüdische Weltverschwörung": Propaganda und Antisemitismus der Nationalsozialisten 1919 bis 1945.* Berlin: Metropol, 2003. 560 pp., illus. (242–271), footnotes, bibl. (494–547), index. (Dokumente, Materialien, Texte, Bd. 46.)

——— MICHLER, WERNER: *Lessings "Evangelium der Toleranz". Zu Judentum und Antisemitismus bei Wilhelm Scherer und Erich Schmidt.* [See in No. 43167.]

43609. MORGENSTERN, CHRISTINE: *Rassismus—Konturen einer Ideologie.* Einwanderung im politischen Diskurs der Bundesrepublik Deutschland. Hamburg: Argument Verlag, 2002. 496 pp., footnotes, bibl. (480–495). (Argument Sonderband, N.F. AS 292.) [Incl. a section on racism and antisemitism (173–224).]

43610. MÜLLER, HANS PETER: *Antisemitismus im Königreich Württemberg zwischen 1871 und 1914.* [In]: Württembergisch Franken, Bd. 86, Schwäbisch Hall, 2002. Festschrift für Gerhard Taddey. Pp. 547–583, footnotes.

43611. NIVEN, BILL: *Martin Walser's Tod eines Kritikers and the issue of anti-Semitism.* [In]: German Life and Letters, Vol. 56, No. 3, Oxford, July 2003. Pp. 299–311, footnotes.

43612. OWZAR, ARMIN: *Die "größten Schurken" zuerst vernichten! Zur Kommunikation zwischen Sozialdemokraten und Antisemiten im wilhelminischen Deutschland.* [In]: Politische Gewalt in der Moderne. Festschrift für Hans-Ulrich Thamer. Hrsg. von Frank Becker [et al.]. Münster: Aschendorff, 2003. Pp. 110–132, footnotes.

43613. PELINKA, ANTON/WODAK, RUTH, eds.: *"Dreck am Stecken". Politik der Ausgrenzung.* Wien: Czernin Verlag, 2003. 279 pp., notes (incl. bibl., 244–276). [Incl. several experts' reports from the trial of Jörg Haider following his attacks on Ariel Muzicant, the president of the Israelitische Kultusgemeinde Österreichs in 2001. Cont. (titles abbr.): Der Skandal heisst nicht nur "Haider" (eds., 7–10). Jörg Haider, die FPÖ und der Antisemitismus (Heribert Schiedel/Wolfgang Neugebauer, 11–31). Struktur und Funktion der "Aschermittwochrede" Jörg Haiders (Anton Pelinka, 61–74). Zum Vor- und Umfeld von Jörg Haiders "Aschermittwochrede" 2001 (Sieglinde Katharina Rosenberger/Christian Stöger, 75–92). Jörg Haider und die Rhetorik antijüdischer Vorurteile (Richard Mitten, 93–133). Ein linguistisches Gutachten zur politischen Funktionalisierung antisemitischer Ressentiments in Österreich (Ruth Wodak/Martin Reisigl, 134–172). Gutachten über den antisemitischen Charakter einer namenpolemischen Passage aus der Rede Jörg Haiders vom 28. Februar 2001 (Dietz Bering, 173–186). Über Analogien zwischen den Äußerungen Haiders gegenüber Muzicant und NS-antisemitischer Argumentation (Alexander Pollak/Nina Eger, 187–210). Zur Entwicklung, Klassifizierung und Beurteilung antisemitischer und antijüdischer Äußerungen in der Bundesrepublik Deutschland (Frank Stern, 211–222). Eine kommunikativ-pragmatische Analyse der Äußerungen Jörg Haiders zu Ariel Muzicant (Konrad Ehlich, 223–225). Anhang: Aschermittwoch-Treffen in Ried, 28. Februar 2001, Rede von Jörg Haider. Ehrenerklärung aus dem Vergleich Jörg Haider—Ariel Muzicant. Presseerklärung (228–243).]

43614. PERRY, MARVIN/SCHWEITZER, FREDERICK M.: *Antisemitism: myth and hate from antiquity to the present.* New York: Palgrave, 2002. X, 309 pp., notes, bibl., index. [Incl. German antisemitism, blood libel, Holocaust denial.]

43615. PETZOLD, LEANDER: *Religion zwischen Sentiment und Protest.* Zur Sistierung des Kultes um "Andreas von Rinn" in Tirol. [In]: Leander Petzold: Tradition im Wandel. Studien zur Volkskultur und Volksdichtung. Frankfurt am Main; New York: Lang, 2002. Pp. 303–326, illus., notes (359–360). [First publ. 1987.]

43616. PRIESTER, KARIN: *Rassismus.* Eine Sozialgeschichte. Leipzig: Reclam, 2003. 320 pp., notes (294–308), bibl., index. [Refers passim to antisemitism.]

43617. *Rechtsextreme Ideologien in Geschichte und Gegenwart.* Hrsg. von Uwe Backes. Köln: Böhlau, 2003. 400 pp., footnotes, bibl. (341–386), index. (Schriften des Hannah-Arendt-Instituts für Totalitarismusforschung, Bd. 23.) [Cont. papers delivered at the international conference in Dresden, June 2002, organised by the Hannah-Arendt-Institut. Selected essays: Der "Totale Krieg" gegen den "jüdischen Bolschewismus"—Weltanschauliche und propagandistische Einlassungen der NS-Elite und deren Interpretation durch Carl Schmitt (Norbert Kapferer, 159–192). Freimaurer und Juden, Kapitalisten und Kommunisten als Feindbilder rechtsextremistischer Verschwörungsideologien vom Kaiserreich bis zur Gegenwart (Armin Pfahl-Traughber, 193–234). Ideologische Anleihen, Geschichtsbilder und Symbole rechtsextremer Jugendgruppen—"Neonazis" und "Skinheads" (Rainer Erb, 289–310).]

43618. ROGALLA VON BIEBERSTEIN, JOHANNES: *"Jüdischer Bolschewismus". Mythos und Realität.* Mit einem Vorwort von Ernst Nolte. Dresden: Edition Antaios, 2002. 311 pp., notes, index. [Incl. passim references to German-speaking Jews and German antisemitism.]

43619. ROSENMAN, STANLEY: *The blood libel: A study in dehumanization, torture, and immolation.* [In]: Journal of Psychohistory, Vol. 30, No. 1, New York, 2002. Pp. 67–85, notes.

43620. RUBENSTEIN, RICHARD L./ROTH, JOHN K.: *Approaches to Auschwitz: the Holocaust legacy.* 2nd rev. edn. Louisville, KY: Westminster John Knox Press, 2003. XI, 499 pp., notes, bibl. (457–459), index. [Orig. edn. in 1987. Incl. the history of antisemitism, especially Christian antisemitism.]

43621. SABROW, MARTIN: *Der Mord an Walther Rathenau und die Zerstörung der Weimarer Republik.* [In]: "Gegen alle Vergeblichkeit". Jüdischer Widerstand gegen den Nationalsozialismus [see No. 42899]. Pp. 55–67, footnotes.

43622. SCHELLER, WOLF: *Das hohe Ross der Moral. Der neue Antisemitismus in Europa.* [In]: Gewerkschaftliche Monatshefte, Jg. 54, H. 12, Düsseldorf, 2003. Pp. 679–682.

43623. SIEG, ULRICH: *Auf dem Weg zur "dichten Beschreibung". Neuere Literatur zur Geschichte des Antisemitismus im Kaiserreich.* [In]: Jahrbuch für Antisemitismusforschung 12, Berlin, 2003. Pp. 329–342, footnotes. [Review essay.]

43624. SIGNORI, GABRIELA: *Kultwerbung—Endzeitängste—Judenhaß: Wunder und Buchdruck an der Schwelle zur Neuzeit.* [In]: Mirakel im Mittelalter. Konzeptionen, Erscheinungsformen, Deutungen. Hrsg. von Martin Heinzelmann [et al.]. Stuttgart: Steiner, 2002. (Beiträge zur Hagiographie, Bd. 3.) Pp. 433–472, footnotes. [Deals also with anti-Jewish miracle books of the late 15th and early 16th cent.]

—— SONNLEITNER, JOHANN: *Völkische Literatur und Antisemitismus in der Zwischenkriegszeit.* [See in No. 43167.]

43625. VICTOR, GEORGE: *Scapegoating—a rite of purification.* [In]: Journal of Psychohistory, Vol. 31, No. 3, New York, 2003. Pp. 273–288, notes, bibl. [Incl. Jews as traditional scapegoats throughout German history.]

43626. WAHL, KLAUS, ed.: *Fremdenfeindlichkeit, Antisemitismus, Rechtsextremismus.* Drei Studien zu Tatverdächtigen und Tätern. Berlin: [Bundesministerium des Innern, Referat IS 3], 2001. 347 pp., footnotes, tabs., bibl.

43627. WALDENEGG, GEORG CHRISTOPH BERGER: *Antisemitismus: "Eine gefährliche Vokabel?"* Diagnose eines Wortes. Wien: Böhlau, 2003. 219 pp., notes (139–185), bibl., index. [On the history of the term "antisemitism". Discusses also recent controversies about antisemitic events in Germany (Nachwort, 119–138).] [Cf.: Bespr. (Christoph Jahr) [in]: Zeitschrift für Geschichtswissenschaft, Jg. 51, H. 12, Berlin, 2003, p. 1135.]

43628. WASSERMANN, HENRY: *On the construction of anti-semitism.* [In]: Aschkenas, Jg. 13, H. 1, Tübingen, 2003. Pp. 237–255, footnotes. [Examines, against the background of the Goldhagen debate, the work of some younger German scholars in the field of antisemitism and Nazism, analysing their tendency to magnify the continuity, intensity, depth and omnipresence of antisemitism throughout German history; also, in this context, on Johann Gottlieb Fichte. A response to this essay: Henry Wassermann, die deutsche Kollektivschuld und das Ausbleiben des Messias (Stefan Rohrbacher) [in]: Aschkenas, Jg. 13, H. 2, Tübingen, 2003, pp. 509–512.]

43629. WEBER, THOMAS: *Antisemitism and philosemitism among British and German elites: Oxford and Heidelberg before the First World War.* [In]: English Historical Review, Vol. 118, Issue 475, Oxford, Feb. 2003. Pp. 89–119, notes.

43630. WEIKART, RICHARD: *Progress through racial extermination: social Darwinism, eugenics, and pacifism in Germany, 1860–1918.* [In]: German Studies Review, Vol. 26, No. 2, Tempe, AZ, May 2003. Pp. 273–294, notes. [Describes how eugenics and other racial theories were used by antisemites of the period and later by the Nazis for their "extermination" policy.]

43631. WEISS, JOHN: *The politics of hate: anti-Semitism, history, and the Holocaust in modern Europe.* Chicago: Ivan R. Dee, 2003. IX, 245 pp., notes, bibl. (226–232), index. [On the history of antisemitism from the late 19th cent. to the Holocaust; incl. sections on Austria and Germany.]

43632. WISSE, RUTH R.: *On ignoring anti-Semitism.* [In]: Commentary, Vol. 114, No. 3, New York, Oct. 2002. Pp. 26– 33. [Compares Nazi antisemitism to Arab anti-Zionism.]

43633. WULF, PETER: *"Jüdische Weltherrschaftspläne". Antisemitismus in bürgerlichen und bäuerlichen Parteien und Verbänden in Schleswig-Holstein zu Beginn der Weimarer Republik.* [In]: Zeitschrift der Gesellschaft für Schleswig-Holsteinische Geschichte. Bd. 128, Neumünster, 2003. Pp. 149–183.

43634. ZIEGE, EVA-MARIA: *Angekommen bei einer Theorie des Antisemitismus?* [Review essay.] [In]: Zeitschrift für Religion und Geistesgeschichte, Jg. 55, H. 4. Leiden, 2003. Pp. 364–373, footnotes.

43635. ZUMBINI, MASSIMO FERRARI: *Die Wurzeln des Bösen. Gründerjahre des Antisemitismus: Von der Bismarckzeit zu Hitler.* Frankfurt am Main: Klostermann, 2003. 774 pp., illus., footnotes, tabs., bibl. (683–749), index. [Revised edn. of 'Le radici del male. L'antisemitismo in Germania: da Bismarck a Hitler', 2001. Incl. chaps. on the Jews in Imperial Germany and Eastern Jews.]

E. Noted Germans and Jews

43636. ARNDT, ERNST MORITZ. HERZIG, ARNO: *Ernst Moritz Arndt und der Diskurs um die Emanzipation der Juden.* [In]: Hefte der Ernst-Moritz-Arndt-Gesellschaft, H. 8 [with the issue title] Ernst Moritz Arndt weiterhin im Widerstreit der Meinungen. Neue Materialien zu einer alten Diskussion, Groß-Schoritz/Rügen, 2003. Pp. 86–99, footnotes. [Also on a related topic in an earlier issue: Ernst Moritz Arndts Judenbilder. Ein unbekanntes Kapitel (Jens Rybak) [in]: Hefte der Ernst-Moritz-Arndt-Gesellschaft, Jg. 6, H. 5, 1997.]

43637. ARNIM, ACHIM VON. ROBERTSON, RITCHIE: *Antisemitismus und Ambivalenz. Zu Achim von Arnims Erzählung "Die Majoratsherren".* [In]: Romantische Identitätskonstruktionen: Nation, Geschichte und (Auto-)Biographie. Glasgower Kolloquium der Int. Arnim-Gesellschaft. Hrsg. von Sheila Dickson und Walter Pape. Tübingen: Niemeyer, 2003. Pp. 51–63, footnotes.

43638. BAHR, HERMANN. DAVIAU, DONALD G.: *Understanding Hermann Bahr.* St.Ingbert: Röhrig Universitätsverlag, 2002. 473 pp., footnotes, bibl. H.B., index. (Österreichische und internationale Literaturprozesse, Bd. 14.) [Incl. the chaps.: Hermann Bahr and anti-Semitism, Zionism and the Jewish Question (235–255). Hermann Bahr and Arthur Schnitzler (265–314). Hermann Bahr and Karl Kraus (315–339).]

43639. BAUMGARTEN, SIEGMUND JACOB. SORKIN, DAVID: *Reclaiming theology for the enlightenment: the case of Siegmund Jacob Baumgarten (1706–1757).* [In]: Central European History, Vol. 36, No. 4, Boston; Leiden, 2003. Pp. 503–530, footnotes. [Deals also with B.s attitude towards the Jews' status and plight marked by sympathy and tolerance.]

43640. BRUMLIK, MICHA: *Deutscher Geist und Judenhaß. Das Verhältnis des philosophischen Idealismus zum Judentum.* München: Luchterhand, 2002. 351 pp., frontis., notes (321–346), index. [Incl. essays on Immanuel Kant, Johann Gottlieb Fichte, Friedrich Schleiermacher, Friedrich Wilhelm Hegel, Friedrich Wilhelm Schelling, Karl Marx.]

—— BURCKHARDT, JACOB. HERMANN, KLAUS: *Ludwig Geiger as the redactor of Jacob Burckhardt's 'Die Cultur der Renaissance in Italien'.* [See in No. 43023.]

43641. BURCKHARDT, JACOB. MATTIOLI, ARAM: *"Jacob Burckhardt und die Grenzen der Humanität".* Essay. München: Bibliothek der Provinz, 2001. 79 pp., notes. (Edition München.) [Argues that B.'s antisemitic tirades should be taken more seriously in the context of his work.]

—— DELITZSCH, FRIEDRICH. SHAVIT, YAACOV: *'Babel und Bibel'—The controversy as a Jewish event.* [See No. 43049.]

43642. DROSTE-HÜLSHOFF, ANNETTE. GRAY, RICHARD T.: *Red herrings and blue smocks: ecological destruction, commercialism, and anti-Semitism in Annette von Droste- Hülshoff's 'Die Judenbuche'.* [In]: German Studies Review, Vol. 26, No. 3, Tempe, AZ, Oct. 2003. Pp. 515–542, notes.

43643. FICHTE, JOHANN GOTTLIEB. BECKER, HANS-JOACHIM: *Fichtes Idee der Nation und das Judentum.* Den vergessenen Generationen der jüdischen Fichte-Rezeption. Amsterdam; Atlanta, GA: Rodopie, 2002. 417 pp., footnotes, bibl., index. (Fichte-Studien-Supplementa, Bd. 14.) [Incl. chaps. on antisemitism, Haskalah; deals mainly with the "affinity" of many Jewish contemporaries of Fichte to his philosophy; also on the later reception of Fichte by numerous Jewish Liberals, Socialists and Zionists. See also No. 43628.]

43644. FICHTE, JOHANN GOTTLIEB. VOIGTS, MANFRED: *Wir sollen alle kleine Fichtes werden! Johann Gottlieb Fichte als Prophet der Kultur-Zionisten.* Berlin; Wien, Philo-Verlag, 2003. 230 pp., footnotes, index. [On the reception of Fichte by antisemites and Zionists.]

43645. FONTANE, THEODOR. "Erschrecken Sie nicht, ich bin es selbst". Erinnerungen an Theodor Fontane. Hrsg. von Wolfgang Rasch und Christine Hehle. Berlin: Aufbau, 2003. 318 pp., index. [Incl. reminiscences of several Jewish friends and authors.]

43646. FONTANE, THEODOR. KOLBE, JOCELYNE: *Historisches Vorbild und künstlerische Alchemie. Heine, Wagner und Antisemitismus in Fontanes 'L'Adultera'.* [In]: Lebendige Sozialgeschichte. Gedenkschrift für Peter Borowsky [see No. 43599]. Pp. 721–734, footnotes.

43647. FRENSSEN, GUSTAV. CRYSTALL, ANDREAS: *Gustav Frenssen. Sein Weg vom Kulturprotestantismus zum Nationalsozialismus.* Gütersloh: Kaiser, Gütersloher Verlagshaus, 2002. 519 pp., footnotes, bibl. (Religiöse Kulturen der Moderne, Bd. 10.) Zugl.: Kiel, Univ., Diss., 2000. [Incl. the chap.: Entwicklung zum Antisemiten (397–418).]

43648. GRIMMELSHAUSEN, HANS JACOB CHRISTOFFEL. HORCH, HANS OTTO: *Die Neugier des Satirikers. Zum Judenbild des Hans Christoffel von Grimmelshausen.* [In]: Von Enoch bis Kafka. Festschrift für Karl E. Grözinger zum 60. Geburtstag [see No. 43050]. Pp. 345–361, footnotes.

43649. HAUFF, WILHELM. LANDWEHR, JÜRGEN: *'Jud Süß'—Hauffs Novelle als literarische Legitimation eines Justizmords und als Symptom und (Mit-)Erfindung eines kollektiven Wahns.* [In]: Ulrich Kittstein, ed.: Wilhelm Hauff. Aufsätze zu seinem poetischen Werk. Mit einer Bibliographie der Forschungsliteratur. St. Ingbert: Röhrig, 2002. (Mannheimer Studien zur Literatur- und Kulturwissenschaft, Bd. 28) Pp. 113–146, footnotes.

—— HEBEL, JOHANN PETER. BRAESE, STEPHAN: *"Redendes Tier" und "gläserner Jude"—Bilder jüdischen Sprachwandels bei Maimon und Hebel.* [See No. 43028.]

43650. JUNG, CARL GUSTAV. MAIDENBAUM, ARYEH, ed.: *Jung and the shadow of anti-semitism: collected essays.* York Beach, ME: Nicolas-Hays, 2003. 384 pp. [First publ. in 1991 under the title Lingering

Shadows; essays are based on papers given at a conference in New York, and in workshops at the Int. Assoc. for Analytical Psychology conference in Paris in 1989.]

43651. LESSING, GOTTHOLD EPHRAIM. GOETSCHEL, WILLI: *Lessing's "Jewish" questions.* [In]: The Germanic Review [with the issue title] Festschrift to Inge Halpert [see No. 43307]. Pp. 62–73, notes.

43652. LESSING, GOTTHOLD EPHRAIM. LIBRETT, JEFFREY S.: *Destabilizing typologies: Jewish works, Christian faith, and the passage from Orient to Occident in G.E. Lessing's Ernst und Falk: Gespräche für Freimäurer.* [In]: The Germanic Review, Vol. 78, No. 4, Washington, Fall, 2003. Pp. 301–318, notes.

43653. LUTHER, MARTIN. *Ebernburg-Hefte.* Jg. 36, Speyer, 2002. 1 issue, footnotes. [Incl.: Josel von Rosheim, "Fürsprecher" der deutschen Juden, und seine Kontaktaufnahme zu Martin Luther (Hans-Joachim Bechtoldt, 13–30). Martin Luther und die Juden (Michael Tilly, 31–40).]

43654. LUTHER, MARTIN. OSTEN-SACKEN, PETER VON DER: *Martin Luther und die Juden. Neu untersucht anhand von Anton Margarithas "Der gantz Jüdisch glaub" (1530/31).* Stuttgart: Kohlhammer, 2002. 351 pp., footnotes, bibl., index.

43655. MANN, THOMAS. DARMAUN, JACQUES: *Thomas Mann, Deutschland und die Juden.* Aus dem Franz. von Jacques Darmaun. Tübingen: Niemeyer, 2003. IX, 319 pp., footnotes, bibl., index. (Conditio Judaica, 40.) [For French orig. edn. (1995) see No. 33604/YB XLI.]

43656. MANN, THOMAS. ELSAGHE, YAHYA: *Die "Judennase" in Thomas Manns Erzählwerk.* [In]: Journal of English and Germanic Philology, Vol. 102, No. 1, Jan. 2003. Champaign, IL. Pp. 88–104, footnotes.

43657. MANN, THOMAS/MUSIL, ROBERT. MARQUARDT, FRANKA: *Erzählte Juden: Untersuchungen zu Thomas Manns "Joseph und seine Brüder" und Robert Musils "Mann ohne Eigenschaften.* Münster: Lit, 2003. LXII, 400 pp., footnotes, bibl. (369–400). (Literatur—Kultur—Medien, Bd. 4.) Zugl.: Köln, Univ., Diss., 2003. [Maintains that Mann's biblical novel is imbued to a greater extent with traditional antisemitism than is usually assumed.]

43658. MACK, MICHAEL: *German idealism and the Jew: the inner anti-Semitism of philosophy and German Jewish responses.* Chicago: Univ. of Chicago Press, 2003. VII, 229 pp., notes, bibl. (179–220), index. [In the first part of the book the author demonstrates the "antisemitic core" in the philosophy of Immanuel Kant, Georg Friedrich Hegel, Anselm Feuerbach; also on Richard Wagner, Heinrich von Treitschke. The second part deals with Jewish "responses"; incl. Moses Mendelssohns, Heinrich Heine, Abraham Geiger, Heinrich Graetz, Otto Weininger, Hermann Cohen, Franz Rosenzweig, Sigmund Freud, Walter Benjamin, Elias Canetti, Franz Baermann Steiner.]

43659. MEHRING, FRANZ. FISCHER, LARS: *"Es ist überall derselbe Faden, an dem ich spinne". Annäherungen an Franz Mehrings Haltung zu Antisemitismus und Judentum.* [In]: Dem freien Geiste freien Flug. Beiträge zur deutschen Literatur für Thomas Höhle. Hrsg. von Dieter Bähtz [et al.]. Leipzig: Leipziger Universitätsverlag, 2003. (Schriften der Ernst-Ortlepp-Gesellschaft, Nr. 2.) Pp. 129–132, notes.

43660. MERKER, PAUL. MENDES, PHILIP: *German, communist, and philosemitic: the remarkable case of Paul Merker.* [In]: Midstream, Vol. 49, No. 4, New York, May/June 2003. Pp. 16–18, notes. [Deals also with Jewish Communists in the GDR; P.M., data see No. 31898/YB XL.]

43661. NIENHAUS, STEFAN: *Geschichte der deutschen Tischgesellschaft.* Tübingen: Niemeyer, 2003. VII, 405 pp., footnotes, bibl. (377–405). (Untersuchungen zur deutschen Literaturgeschichte, Bd. 115.) [Incl. the chaps: Exkurs: Die Debatte über die Emanzipation der Juden in Preußen. Antisemitische Tendenzen vor der deutschen Tischgesellschaft. Zote und Groteske: Arnims Abhandlung 'Ueber die Kennzeichnung des Judenthums'. Der Judenhaß und seine Folgen: Tischreden von Beuth, Beckedorff und Arnims Rechtfertigungsreferat zum Itzig-Skandal.

Wirkungen und Nachwirkungen des Itzig-Skandals (182–271). Neuere Untersuchungen zum Antisemitismus der deutschen Tischgesellschaft (324–330).]

43662. ORTLEPP, ERNST. ZIEMANN, RÜDIGER: *Den ihr der Hölle wähnt verfallen. Ernst Ortlepps "Rede des ewigen Juden"*. [In]: Dem Freien Geiste freien Flug. Beiträge zur deutschen Literatur für Thomas Höhle. Hrsg. von Dieter Bähtz [et al.]. Leipzig: Leipziger Universitätsverlag, 2003. (Schriften der Ernst-Ortlepp-Gesellschaft, Nr. 2.) Pp. 7–13. [On an epic poem publ. 1836 in Leipzig.]

43663. SCHMITT, CARL: *Tagebücher: Oktober 1912 bis Februar 1915.* Hrsg. von Ernst Hüsmert. Berlin: Akademie Verlag, 2003. XI, 432 pp., frontis., illus., footnotes, bibl., index. [Cf.: "Ob das nicht mit meinem jüdischen Komplex zusammenhängt?"—In ihrer Leidenschaftlichkeit geben Carl Schmitts Tagebücher aus den Jahren 1912–1915 auch Aufschluss über seine spätere Begeisterung für die Nürnberger Gesetze (Raphael Gross) [in]: Frankfurter Rundschau, Frankfurt am Main, 4. Mai, 2004, p. 19.]

43664. STEINER, RUDOLF. SONNENBERG, RALF: *"Keine Berechtigung innerhalb des modernen Völkerlebens". Judentum, Zionismus und Antisemitismus aus der Sicht Rudolf Steiners.* [In]: Jahrbuch für Antisemitismusforschung 12, Berlin, 2003. Pp. 185–209, footnotes.

43665. TREITSCKE, HEINRICH VON. WYRWA, ULRICH: *Heinrich von Treitschke. Geschichtsschreibung und öffentliche Meinung im Deutschland des 19. Jahrhunderts.* [In]: Zeitschrift für Geschichtswissenschaft, Jg. 51, H. 9, Berlin, 2003. Pp. 781–792, footnotes. [Analyses how T.'s dictum "Die Juden sind unser Unglück" (1879) could exert such influence.]

43666. VARNHAGEN, KARL AUGUST. ROSENSTRAUCH, HAZEL: *Karl August Varnhagen und die Kunst des geselligen Lebens. Eine Jugend um 1800.* Biographisches Essay. Berlin: Das Arsenal, 2003. 224 pp., frontis., notes (203–224).

—— WAGENSEIL, JOHANN CHRISTOPH. BOBZIN, HARTMUT: *Judenfeind oder Judenfreund? Der Altdorfer Gelehrte Johann Christoph Wagenseil.* [See in No. 42340.]

X. FICTION AND POETRY

43667. APPELFELD, AHARON: *Alles, was ich liebte.* Roman. Aus dem Hebr. von Anne Birkenhauer. Berlin: Alexander Fest Verl., 2002. 287 pp. [Autobiographical novel about childhood years in Czernowitz and surroundings; orig. publ. in Jerusalem, 1999.] [Cf.: Von Czernowitz nach Jerusalem. Eine Begegnung mit dem Schriftsteller Aharon Appelfeld (Naomi Bubis) [in]: 'NZZ', Nr. 157, Zürich, 10. Juli 2003, p. 35.]

43668. GOLDBERG, LEA: *Briefe von einer imaginären Reise.* Aus dem Hebr. von Lydia Böhmer. Frankfurt am Main: Jüdischer Verlag im Suhrkamp Verlag, 2003. 111 pp. [Orig. publ. in Tel Aviv 1936/1937; the story of a young woman and her unfulfilled love, set in 1930s Nazi Berlin and other cities.] [L.G., 1911 Königsberg–1970 Jerusalem, author, translator, emigr. 1935 to Palestine.]

43669. HACKER, KATHARINA: *Eine Art Liebe.* Roman. Frankfurt am Main: Suhrkamp, 2003. 267 pp. [Love story, based on Saul Friedländer's survival story in France, see No. 28813/YB 37.] [Cf.: Abel lebt, doch Kain muß sterben. Ein Roman als Übertragung: Katharina Hackers jüdische Lebensgeschichte (Jörg Magenau) [in]: 'FAZ', Nr. 232, Frankfurt am Main, 7. Okt. 2003, p. L 10.]

43670. HONIGMANN, BARBARA: *A love made out of nothing; Zohara's journey: two novels.* Transl. from the German by John Barrett. Boston: Godine, 2003. 167 pp. (Verba mundi: international literature series.)

43671. LASKER-SCHÜLER, ELSE: *Mein Herz.* Ein Liebes-Roman mit Bildern und wirklich lebenden Menschen. Hrsg. von Ricarda Dick. Frankfurt am Main: Jüdischer Verlag im Suhrkamp Verlag, 2003. 213 pp., frontis., illus., notes (132–180), gloss. [Reprint of the first edn. (1912) with the author's illustrations. Incl.: Nachwort (ed., 200–213; on L.Sch.'s life in Berlin in 1912, the brief relationship with her husband Herwarth Walden, and on other personalities of the pre-war Berlin Bohème visiting the 'Café des Westens'.]

43672. Levit, Leon: *Ein Mercedes im Sand.* Frankfurt am Main: Edition Büchergilde, 2003. 456 pp. [Autobiographical novel written in the 1960s in German, depicting the life of a Berlin Jew who emigr. in 1932 to Palestine; incl.: Mein Vater (Daphna Levit, 447–456; on the background to the book.] [L.L., 1906 Berlin–1974 Tel Aviv, economist, travel agent, Israeli diplomat, emigr. 1932 to Palestine.]

——— Nadolny, Sten: *Ullsteinroman.* Roman. [See No. 43471.]

43673. Pressler, Mirjam: *Die Zeit der schlafenden Hunde.* Roman. Weinheim: Beltz & Gelberg, 2003. 270 pp. [1990s German-Israeli love story for young persons; uses as a backdrop "aryanisation" and suppression of its Nazi past in the German protagonist's family.]

43674. Raphael, Lev: *The German money: a novel.* Wellfleet, MA: Leapfrog Press: Distrib. by Consortium Book Sales, St. Paul, MN, 2003. 200 pp. [Deals with a "second generation survivor" and his family's past, especially with the mother's legacy as a Holocaust survivor and recipient of German restitution money.]

43675. Ringer-Nenner, Brigitte: *The angel of poetry: a poetic perspective on living through the Holocaust.* Jerusalem: Mazo Publishers, 2003. 95 pp., illus. [B.R.-N., b. 1922 in Berlin, escaped in 1938 to the Netherlands, survived Bergen-Belsen, settled in Israel in 1966. Book is her poetic eyewitness account of the November Pogrom; poems are in German, Dutch and English.]

——— Schloss, Karl: *Die Blumen werden in Rauch aufgehn.* Ausgewählte Gedichte und Briefe. Ein Gedenkbuch. [See No. 43438.]

43676. Silbermann, Edith: *Rose Ausländer. Die Sappho der östlichen Landschaft.* Eine Anthologie. Aachen: Rimbaud, 2003. 80 pp., frontis. [Incl. annot. poems; also personal recollections of E.S., b. 1921 in Czernowitz.]

43677. Stern, Gerson: *Auf drei Dingen steht die Welt.* Erzählung. Zus. mit dem "Heimat- und Geschichtsverein Holzminden e.V." hrsg. mit einem Nachwort und einem Glossar von Friedrich Voit. Siegen: Böschen, 2003. 206 pp., illus. (Gerson Stern, Werkausgabe in Einzelbänden.) [First book edn. of story orig. publ. in 'Jüdische Rundschau', 1935; depicts conflicts of adolescence and Jewish identity in a Jewish family ca. 1900.] [G.St, 1874–1956, data see No. 38399/YB XLV.]

43678. Wolff, Charlotte: *Späte Liebe.* Roman. Aus dem Engl. von Gerline Kowitzke. München: Frauenoffensive, 2003. 221 pp. [New German edn. of the autobiographical novel 'An older love', first publ. 1976, in German with the title 'Flickwerk' (publ. 1977). Deals with the lesbian love between Jewish refugee women and their English friends; see also No. 43536.]

Index to Bibliography

List of Contributors

BAUERKÄMPER, Arnd, Ph.D., b. 1958 in Detmold, Germany. Managing Director of the Zentrum für Vergleichende Geschichte Europas, Berlin. Author of *Ländliche Gesellschaft in der kommunistischen Diktatur. Zwangsmodernisierung und Tradition in Brandenburg 1945–1963* (2002); *"Junkerland in Bauernhand"? Durchführung, Auswirkungen und Stellenwert der Bodenreform in der Sowjetischen Besatzungszone* (1996); *Die "radikale Rechte" in Großbritannien. Nationalistische, antisemitische und faschistische Bewegungen vom späten 19. Jahrhundert bis 1945* (1991). Editor of *Die Praxis der Zivilgesellschaft. Akteure, Handeln und Strukturen im internationalen Vergleich* (2003); *Britain and the GDR. Relations and Perceptions in a Divided World* (2002).

BERG, Nicolas, Ph.D., b. 1967 in Berlin, Germany. Research Fellow at the Simon Dubnow Institute, University of Leipzig. Author of *Der Holocaust und die westdeutschen Historiker—Erforschung und Erinnerung* (2004); 'Formen der Verdrängung: Zur intellektuellen Marginalisierung des Holocaust in Deutschland nach 1945', in *Transversal* (2004); 'Intellektuelle Distanzen. Versuch über Gottfried Benn, Peter de Mendelsohn und die Frage nach dem Gegenteil von Gedächtnis', in *Freiburger Literaturpsychologische Gespräche* (2003). Co-editor with Bernd Stiegler and Jess Jochimsen of *Shoah. Formen der Erinnerung. Geschichte, Philosophie, Literatur, Kunst* (1996).

HACKESCHMIDT, Jörg, Ph.D., b. 1961 in Munich, Germany. Currently working as a senior consultant in a public relations agency. Author of *Von Kurt Blumenfeld zu Norbert Elias. Die Erfindung einer jüdischen Nation* (1997); '"Die Kulturkraft des Kreises". Norbert Elias als Vordenker der zionistischen Jugendbewegung. Zwei unbekannte Briefe aus den Jahren 1920 und 1921', in *Berliner Journal für Soziologie* (1997).

KOSSERT, Andreas, Ph.D., b. 1970 in Münden, Germany. Research Fellow, German Historical Institute, Warsaw. Author of *Masuren Ostpreußens vergessener Süden* (2001); *Preußen, Deutsche oder Polen? Die Masuren im Spannungsfeld des ethnischen Nationalismus, 1870–1956* (2001); '"Grenzlandpolitik" und Ostforschung an der Peripherie des Reiches 1919–1945. Eine Regionalstudie im ostpreußischen Masuren', in *Vierteljahrshefte für Zeitgeschichte* (2003).

KRAUSS, Marita, Ph.D., b. 1956 in Zurich, Switzerland, teaches Social and Economic History at the University of Bremen. Author of *Die Frau der Zukunft. Dr. Hope Bridges Adams Lehmann (1855–1916), Ärztin und Reformerin* (2002); *Heimkehr in ein fremdes Land. Geschichte der Remigration nach 1945* (2001); *Nachkriegskultur in München. Münchner städtische Kulturpolitik 1945–1954* (1985). Co-editor with Holger Sonnabend, *Frauen und Migration* (2001); with Andreas Gestrich, *Migration und Grenze* (1999).

MCEWAN, Dorothea, Ph.D., b. 1941 in Eisenstadt, Austria. Archivist, Warburg Institute, London; at present cataloguing the Aby Warburg correspondence comprising 32,000 letters. Author of *Wanderstrassen der Kultur. Die Aby Warburg—Fritz Saxl Korrespondenz von 1920 bis 1929* (2004); *Das Ausreiten der Ecken. Die Aby Warburg—Fritz Saxl-Korrespondenz 1910–1919* (1998) and of numerous articles on Aby Warburg, Fritz Saxl and The Warburg Institute.

MENDEL, Meron, b. 1976 in Tel Aviv, Israel. Ph.D. candidate, Haifa University.

MOTZKIN, Gabriel, Ph.D., b. 1945 in Jerusalem, Israel. Dean of the Humanities and Associate Professor of History, Philosophy and German, Hebrew University, Jerusalem. Author of *Time and Transcendence: Secular History, the Catholic Reaction and the Rediscovery of the Future* (1992); 'Science, Secularization and Desecularization at the Turn of the Last Century' in *Science in Context* (2002); 'Cassirer's *Philosophy of Symbolic Forms*: A Foundational Reading' in Jeffrey Barash, (ed.), *Cassirer: Symbol, Science, and Culture* (2003).

PELLI, Moshe, Ph.D., b. 1936 in Israel. Professor and Director of Judaic Studies, University of Central Florida, Orlando. Author of *The Me'asefim Generation at the Dawn of Haskalah. The Literary Contribution of the Writers of Hame'asef, the First Hebrew Periodical 1783-1811* (2001) (Hebrew); *The Gate to Haskalah: An Annotated Index to Hame'asef, the First Hebrew Journal* (2000) (Hebrew); *Kinds of Genres in Haskalah Literature: Types and Topic* (1999) (Hebrew). Contributor to Year Books XIX, XXI, XXVI, XLIII.

RENSMANN, Lars, Ph.D., b. 1970 in Bochum, Germany. Visiting Fellow, Yale Center for International and Area Studies, Yale University; Lecturer in Political Science, Department of Political and Social Sciences, Free University of Berlin. Author of *Demokratie und Judenbild: Antisemitismus in der politischen Kultur der Bundesrepublik Deutschland* (2004); 'Collective Guilt, National Identity, and Political Processes in Contemporary Germany', in Nyla Branscombe and Bertjan Doosje, eds., *Collective Guilt: International Perspectives* (2004); 'The New Politics of Prejudice: Comparative Perspectives on Extreme Right Parties in Contemporary European Democracies' in *German Politics and Society* (2003).

WINSTEL, Tobias, M.A., b. 1972 in Munich, Germany. Research Assistant for the research project *The Fiscal Administration and the Persecution of Jews in Bavaria* of the University of Munich and the Bavarian Ministry of Finance in co-operation with the State Archives of Bavaria. Author of 'Über die Bedeutung der Wiedergutmachung im Leben der jüdischen NS-Verfolgten. Erfahrungsgeschichtliche Annäherungen', in Hans Günter Hockerts and Christiane Kuller (eds.), *Nach der Verfolgung. Wiedergutmachung nationalsozialistischen Unrechts in Deutschland?* (2003); 'Verordnete "Ehrenpflicht"—Wiedergutmachung für jüdische NS-Opfer', in Angelika Baumann and Andreas Heusler (eds.), *München arisiert—Entrechtung und Enteignung der Juden während des Nationalsozialismus* (2004).

WISTRICH, Robert S., Ph.D., b. 1945 in Kazakstan. Erich and Foga Neuberger Professor of Modern European History and Director of the Vidal Sassoon International Centre for the Study of Antisemitism, Hebrew University, Jerusalem. Author of *Muslim Antisemitism: A Clear and Present Danger* (2002); *Hitler and the Holocaust* (2001). Co-editor with Jacob Golomb, *Nietzsche: Godfather of Fascism?* (2002). Contributor to Year Books XX, XXI, XXV, XXXII, XXXVI.

WIESE, Christian, Ph.D., b. 1961 in Bonn, Germany. Assistant Professor of Jewish Studies, University of Erfurt. Author of *Challenging Colonial Discourse: Jewish Studies and Protestant Theology in Wilhelmian Germany, 1890–1914* (2004); *Hans Jonas—Zusammen Philosoph und Jude. Essay* (2003); *Wissenschaft des Judentums und Protestantische Theologie im Wilhelminischen Deutschland—ein "Schrei ins Leere"?* (1999).

General Index to Year Book XLIX of the Leo Baeck Institute